S0-EKZ-478

Handbook of Public Management Practice and Reform

PUBLIC ADMINISTRATION AND PUBLIC POLICY

A Comprehensive Publication Program

Executive Editor

JACK RABIN
Professor of Public Administration and Public Policy
School of Public Affairs
The Capital College
The Pennsylvania State University—Harrisburg
Middletown, Pennsylvania

1. *Public Administration as a Developing Discipline* (in two parts), Robert T. Golembiewski
2. *Comparative National Policies on Health Care*, Milton I. Roemer, M.D.
3. *Exclusionary Injustice: The Problem of Illegally Obtained Evidence*, Steven R. Schlesinger
4. *Personnel Management in Government: Politics and Process*, Jay M. Shafritz, Walter L. Balk, Albert C. Hyde, and David H. Rosenbloom
5. *Organization Development in Public Administration* (in two parts), edited by Robert T. Golembiewski and William B. Eddy
6. *Public Administration: A Comparative Perspective, Second Edition, Revised and Expanded*, Ferrel Heady
7. *Approaches to Planned Change* (in two parts), Robert T. Golembiewski
8. *Program Evaluation at HEW* (in three parts), edited by James G. Abert
9. *The States and the Metropolis*, Patricia S. Florestano and Vincent L. Marando
10. *Personnel Management in Government: Politics and Process, Second Edition, Revised and Expanded*, Jay M. Shafritz, Albert C. Hyde, and David H. Rosenbloom
11. *Changing Bureaucracies: Understanding the Organization Before Selecting the Approach*, William A. Medina
12. *Handbook on Public Budgeting and Financial Management*, edited by Jack Rabin and Thomas D. Lynch
13. *Encyclopedia of Policy Studies*, edited by Stuart S. Nagel
14. *Public Administration and Law: Bench v. Bureau in the United States*, David H. Rosenbloom
15. *Handbook on Public Personnel Administration and Labor Relations*, edited by Jack Rabin, Thomas Vocino, W. Bartley Hildreth, and Gerald J. Miller
16. *Public Budgeting and Finance: Behavioral, Theoretical, and Technical Perspectives, Third Edition*, edited by Robert T. Golembiewski and Jack Rabin
17. *Organizational Behavior and Public Management*, Debra W. Stewart and G. David Garson
18. *The Politics of Terrorism: Second Edition, Revised and Expanded,* edited by Michael Stohl

19. *Handbook of Organization Management*, edited by William B. Eddy
20. *Organization Theory and Management*, edited by Thomas D. Lynch
21. *Labor Relations in the Public Sector*, Richard C. Kearney
22. *Politics and Administration: Woodrow Wilson and American Public Administration*, edited by Jack Rabin and James S. Bowman
23. *Making and Managing Policy: Formulation, Analysis, Evaluation*, edited by G. Ronald Gilbert
24. *Public Administration: A Comparative Perspective, Third Edition, Revised*, Ferrel Heady
25. *Decision Making in the Public Sector*, edited by Lloyd G. Nigro
26. *Managing Administration*, edited by Jack Rabin, Samuel Humes, and Brian S. Morgan
27. *Public Personnel Update*, edited by Michael Cohen and Robert T. Golembiewski
28. *State and Local Government Administration*, edited by Jack Rabin and Don Dodd
29. *Public Administration: A Bibliographic Guide to the Literature*, Howard E. McCurdy
30. *Personnel Management in Government: Politics and Process, Third Edition, Revised and Expanded*, Jay M. Shafritz, Albert C. Hyde, and David H. Rosenbloom
31. *Handbook of Information Resource Management*, edited by Jack Rabin and Edward M. Jackowski
32. *Public Administration in Developed Democracies: A Comparative Study*, edited by Donald C. Rowat
33. *The Politics of Terrorism: Third Edition, Revised and Expanded*, edited by Michael Stohl
34. *Handbook on Human Services Administration*, edited by Jack Rabin and Marcia B. Steinhauer
35. *Handbook of Public Administration*, edited by Jack Rabin, W. Bartley Hildreth, and Gerald J. Miller
36. *Ethics for Bureaucrats: An Essay on Law and Values, Second Edition, Revised and Expanded*, John A. Rohr
37. *The Guide to the Foundations of Public Administration*, Daniel W. Martin
38. *Handbook of Strategic Management*, edited by Jack Rabin, Gerald J. Miller, and W. Bartley Hildreth
39. *Terrorism and Emergency Management: Policy and Administration,* William L. Waugh, Jr.
40. *Organizational Behavior and Public Management: Second Edition, Revised and Expanded*, Michael L. Vasu, Debra W. Stewart, and G. David Garson
41. *Handbook of Comparative and Development Public Administration*, edited by Ali Farazmand
42. *Public Administration: A Comparative Perspective, Fourth Edition*, Ferrel Heady
43. *Government Financial Management Theory*, Gerald J. Miller
44. *Personnel Management in Government: Politics and Process, Fourth Edition, Revised and Expanded*, Jay M. Shafritz, Norma M. Riccucci, David H. Rosenbloom, and Albert C. Hyde
45. *Public Productivity Handbook*, edited by Marc Holzer
46. *Handbook of Public Budgeting*, edited by Jack Rabin
47. *Labor Relations in the Public Sector: Second Edition, Revised and Expanded*, Richard C. Kearney

48. *Handbook of Organizational Consultation*, edited by Robert T. Golembiewski
49. *Handbook of Court Administration and Management*, edited by Steven W. Hays and Cole Blease Graham, Jr.
50. *Handbook of Comparative Public Budgeting and Financial Management*, edited by Thomas D. Lynch and Lawrence L. Martin
51. *Handbook of Organizational Behavior*, edited by Robert T. Golembiewski
52. *Handbook of Administrative Ethics,* edited by Terry L. Cooper
53. *Encyclopedia of Policy Studies: Second Edition, Revised and Expanded,* edited by Stuart S. Nagel
54. *Handbook of Regulation and Administrative Law,* edited by David H. Rosenbloom and Richard D. Schwartz
55. *Handbook of Bureaucracy,* edited by Ali Farazmand
56. *Handbook of Public Sector Labor Relations*, edited by Jack Rabin, Thomas Vocino, W. Bartley Hildreth, and Gerald J. Miller
57. *Practical Public Management*, Robert T. Golembiewski
58. *Handbook of Public Personnel Administration*, edited by Jack Rabin, Thomas Vocino, W. Bartley Hildreth, and Gerald J. Miller
59. *Public Administration: A Comparative Perspective, Fifth Edition*, Ferrel Heady
60. *Handbook of Debt Management*, edited by Gerald J. Miller
61. *Public Administration and Law: Second Edition*, David H. Rosenbloom and Rosemary O'Leary
62. *Handbook of Local Government Administration*, edited by John J. Gargan
63. *Handbook of Administrative Communication*, edited by James L. Garnett and Alexander Kouzmin
64. *Public Budgeting and Finance: Fourth Edition, Revised and Expanded*, edited by Robert T. Golembiewski and Jack Rabin
65. *Handbook of Public Administration: Second Edition*, edited by Jack Rabin, W. Bartley Hildreth, and Gerald J. Miller
66. *Handbook of Organization Theory and Management: The Philosophical Approach*, edited by Thomas D. Lynch and Todd J. Dicker
67. *Handbook of Public Finance*, edited by Fred Thompson and Mark T. Green
68. *Organizational Behavior and Public Management: Third Edition, Revised and Expanded*, Michael L. Vasu, Debra W. Stewart, and G. David Garson
69. *Handbook of Economic Development*, edited by Kuotsai Tom Liou
70. *Handbook of Health Administration and Policy*, edited by Anne Osborne Kilpatrick and James A. Johnson
71. *Handbook of Research Methods in Public Administration*, edited by Gerald J. Miller and Marcia L. Whicker
72. *Handbook on Taxation*, edited by W. Bartley Hildreth and James A. Richardson
73. *Handbook of Comparative Public Administration in the Asia-Pacific Basin*, edited by Hoi-kwok Wong and Hon S. Chan
74. *Handbook of Global Environmental Policy and Administration,* edited by Dennis L. Soden and Brent S. Steel
75. *Handbook of State Government Administration,* edited by John J. Gargan
76. *Handbook of Global Legal Policy,* edited by Stuart S. Nagel
77. *Handbook of Public Information Systems,* edited by G. David Garson
78. *Handbook of Global Economic Policy,* edited by Stuart S. Nagel
79. *Handbook of Strategic Management: Second Edition, Revised and Expanded,* edited by Jack Rabin, Gerald J. Miller, and W. Bartley Hildreth
80. *Handbook of Global International Policy,* edited by Stuart S. Nagel

81. *Handbook of Organizational Consultation: Second Edition, Revised and Expanded,* edited by Robert T. Golembiewski
82. *Handbook of Global Political Policy,* edited by Stuart S. Nagel
83. *Handbook of Global Technology Policy,* edited by Stuart S. Nagel
84. *Handbook of Criminal Justice Administration*, edited by Toni DuPont-Morales, Michael K. Hooper, and Judy H. Schmidt
85. *Labor Relations in the Public Sector: Third Edition*, edited by Richard C. Kearney
86. *Handbook of Administrative Ethics: Second Edition, Revised and Expanded,* edited by Terry L. Cooper
87. *Handbook of Organizational Behavior: Second Edition, Revised and Expanded*, edited by Robert T. Golembiewski
88. *Handbook of Global Social Policy,* edited by Stuart S. Nagel and Amy Robb
89. *Public Administration: A Comparative Perspective, Sixth Edition,* Ferrel Heady
90. *Handbook of Public Quality Management*, edited by Ronald J. Stupak and Peter M. Leitner
91. *Handbook of Public Management Practice and Reform*, edited by Kuotsai Tom Liou

Additional Volumes in Preparation

Handbook of Crisis and Emergency Management, edited by Ali Farazmand

Handbook of Comparative and Development Public Administration: Second Edition, Revised and Expanded, edited by Ali Farazmand

Personnel Management in Government: Politics and Process, Fifth Edition, Jay M. Shafritz, Norma M. Riccucci, David H. Rosenbloom, Katherine C. Naff, and Albert C. Hyde

Online at www.netLibrary.com

Principles and Practices of Public Administration, edited by Jack Rabin, Robert F. Munzenrider, and Sherrie M. Bartell

Annals of Public Administration

1. *Public Administration: History and Theory in Contemporary Perspective*, edited by Joseph A. Uveges, Jr.
2. *Public Administration Education in Transition*, edited by Thomas Vocino and Richard Heimovics
3. *Centenary Issues of the Pendleton Act of 1883*, edited by David H. Rosenbloom with the assistance of Mark A. Emmert
4. *Intergovernmental Relations in the 1980s*, edited by Richard H. Leach
5. *Criminal Justice Administration: Linking Practice and Research*, edited by William A. Jones, Jr.

Handbook of Public Management Practice and Reform

edited by

Kuotsai Tom Liou
University of Central Florida
Orlando, Florida

MARCEL DEKKER, INC.   NEW YORK • BASEL

ISBN: 0-8247-0429-0

This book is printed on acid-free paper.

Headquarters
Marcel Dekker, Inc.
270 Madison Avenue, New York, NY 10016
tel: 212-696-9000; fax: 212-685-4540

Eastern Hemisphere Distribution
Marcel Dekker AG
Hutgasse 4, Postfach 812, CH-4001 Basel, Switzerland
tel: 41-61-261-8482; fax: 41-61-261-8896

World Wide Web
http://www.dekker.com

The publisher offers discounts on this book when ordered in bulk quantities. For more information, write to Special Sales/Professional Marketing at the headquarters address above.

Current printing (last digit):
10 9 8 7 6 5 4 3 2 1

PRINTED IN THE UNITED STATES OF AMERICA

To my father,
Jiunn-Jin Liou
and
in memory of my mother,
Der-Jy Wann

Preface

Public management reform is one of the most popular topics in the field of public administration. Both academics and practitioners have been actively involved in studying it. Researchers have published numerous articles and books examining the background, motives, concepts, strategies, implementation, effectiveness, and lessons of many reform policies and programs. Practitioners are interested in learning new managerial ideas and reform policies to advance their knowledge and skills so that they can improve their management of public organizations and provide better service to their communities.

Over the past several decades, many reform ideas, policies, and programs have been recommended and implemented in major areas of public administration. In budgeting and financial management, for example, recent reform efforts introduced new policies to improve performance, increase productivity, promote accountability, cut expenditures, and reduce the size of government. Similar reform efforts have been recommended in the human resource management area. Latest reform efforts emphasize the importance of accountability, flexibility, decentralization, privatization, and deregulation in civil service systems at all levels of government.

My interest in public management reform has to do with three aspects of my academic research at both micro- and macro-levels. First, I was interested in the topic of public budgeting reform and focused not only on the concept and techniques of various budgeting systems but also on the politics and challenges involved in the reform process. Then, I addressed this topic from the organizational development and policy implementation approaches and concentrated on such issues as organizational environment, leadership, culture, communication, and strategies that are important to the success of any reform policies and organizational changes. Finally, I emphasized the importance of public management reform in my recent studies of economic development in many developing and economic-transition countries. The issues of interest are broader and include the role of government in economic development, decentralization and deregulation, institutional arrangement and support, and corruption and bureaucratic dysfunctions in the transition process, as well as cooperation among public, private, and nonprofit organizations.

To edit a big book on public management reform and practice is not an easy task. It has taken more than four years to develop and prepare this volume. I first proposed to develop a book related to the ideas, changes, and challenges in recent public management reforms. Based on comments and recommendations from Dr. Jack Rabin and Mr. Marcel Dekker, I expanded the scope by incorporating many changes and challenges in the environment of public administration, the practices and functions of public management, the experience and issues of recent reform efforts, and the new ideas and directions in public administration, as well as the development and contribution of public administration education, research, and professional associations.

The process of editing this book has been a pleasant experience for me. I have had opportunities to work with many outstanding scholars who were interested in this project. I thank Dr. Jack Rabin, the editor of the Public Administration and Public Policy series, for his acceptance of my original proposal and suggestions on the content of the book. All the contributors have been wonderful as they worked hard to finish their chapters according to my general guidelines, and they were patient with the review and revision process. I am also grateful for the assistance of my outstanding staff, John Mullen and Michelle Morales at the University of Central Florida, during the research and communication stage of this project. I especially appreciate the professional dedication of staff members at Marcel Dekker, Inc. Their dedication and skills were important to the final production of this book. Finally, strong support from my family has been critical in finishing this book. My wife, Susan, has spent a lot of time taking care of our three children (Alan, Anna, and Alex) and other family business, which allowed me to concentrate on my research. I owe all to their love and encouragement.

Kuotsai Tom Liou

Contents

Part II. Changes in Budgeting and Financial Management

Part III. Changes in Human Resource Management

Part IV. Issues in Organizational and General Management

Contributors

Mohamad Alkadry Division of Public Administration, West Virginia University, Morgantown, West Virginia

Lisa M. Arndt Public Administration Program, University of South Florida, Tampa, Florida

John R. Bartle Department of Public Administration, University of Nebraska at Omaha, Omaha, Nebraska

Frances Stokes Berry Askew School of Public Administration and Policy, Florida State University, Tallahassee, Florida

Michael A. Brintnall National Association of Schools of Public Affairs and Administration, Washington, D.C.

Kathe Callahan Graduate Department of Public Administration, Rutgers University, Newark, New Jersey

N. Joseph Cayer School of Public Affairs, Arizona State University, Tempe, Arizona

James L. Chan Department of Accounting, University of Illinois at Chicago, Chicago, Illinois

Kenneth E. Cox Department of Public and International Affairs, George Mason University, Fairfax, Virginia

Dennis M. Daley Department of Political Science and Public Administration, North Carolina State University, Raleigh, North Carolina

John Donohue School of Public Administration, Florida Atlantic University, Fort Lauderdale, Florida

Robert F. Durant School of Public Affairs, University of Baltimore, Baltimore, Maryland

Richard C. Feiock Askew School of Public Administration and Policy, Florida State University, Tallahassee, Florida

Mary Ann Feldheim Department of Public Administration, University of Central Florida, Cocoa, Florida

Jerry A. Gianakis Department of Public Administration, University of Central Florida, Orlando, Florida

Mary R. Hamilton American Society for Public Administration, Washington, D.C.

Steven W. Hays Department of Government and International Studies, University of South Carolina, Columbia, South Carolina

Keith M. Henderson Department of Political Science, State University College–Buffalo, Buffalo, New York

John Hindera Department of Political Science, Texas Tech University, Lubbock, Texas

Marc Holzer Graduate Department of Public Administration, Rutgers University, Newark, New Jersey

Patricia W. Ingraham Department of Public Administration, Syracuse University, Syracuse, New York

Van R. Johnston Department of Management, University of Denver, Denver, Colorado

Daniel J. Jorgensen Department of Social Sciences, Texas A & M University Corpus Christi, Corpus Christi, Texas

Jamil E. Jreisat Public Administration Program, University of South Florida, Tampa, Florida

Richard C. Kearney Department of Political Science, East Carolina University, Greenville, North Carolina

Cheryl Simrell King Graduate Program in Public Administration, The Evergreen State College, Olympia, Washington

W. Earl Klay Askew School of Public Administration and Policy, Florida State University, Tallahassee, Florida

Kuotsai Tom Liou Department of Public Administration, University of Central Florida, Orlando, Florida

Donald C. Menzel Division of Public Administration, Northern Illinois University, DeKalb, Illinois

Hugh T. Miller School of Public Administration, Florida Atlantic University, Fort Lauderdale, Florida

Donald P. Moynihan Department of Public Administration, Syracuse University, Syracuse, New York

Stuart S. Nagel Political Science Department, University of Illinois, Urbana, Illinois

Kathryn E. Newcomer Department of Public Administration, George Washington University, Washington, D.C.

Sandra J. Parkes Department of Political Science, University of Utah, Salt Lake City, Utah

A. Premchand National Institute of Public Finance, New Delhi, India

Joan E. Pynes Public Administration Program, University of South Florida, Tampa, Florida

Danielle Roth-Johnson Department of Political Science, Texas Tech University, Lubbock, Texas

A. Carol Rusaw Department of Communications, University of Southwestern Louisiana, Lafayette, Louisiana

Paul Seidenstat Department of Economics, Temple University, Philadelphia, Pennsylvania

Camilla Stivers Maxine Goodman Levin College of Urban Affairs, Cleveland State University, Cleveland, Ohio

Henry B. Thomas Department of Political Science and Public Administration, University of North Florida, Jacksonville, Florida

John P. Tuman Department of Political Science, Texas Tech University, Lubbock, Texas

Susan J. Tolchin Department of Public and International Affairs, George Mason University, Fairfax, Virginia

Montgomery Van Wart Department of Political Science, Texas Tech University, Lubbock, Texas

Thomas Vocino Department of Political Science and Public Administration, Auburn University at Montgomery, Montgomery, Alabama

Charles W. Washington School of Public Administration, Florida Atlantic University, Fort Lauderdale, Florida

Jay D. White College of Public Affairs and Community Service, University of Nebraska at Omaha, Omaha, Nebraska

Linda C. Wilson Department of Political Science and Public Administration, Auburn University at Montgomery, Montgomery, Alabama

Introduction

Public management reform has been one of the major policy and research issues in the field of public administration for many decades. The interest in reforming the management of public organizations results from the emergence of new ideas and issues related to many changes and challenges in the political, social, economic, and technical environments of the public sector. After being examined in the political process, these new reform ideas and issues will be implemented as official public policies and programs that gradually become major components of public management practices. Researchers of public administration and policy have been actively involved in providing new concepts and ideas of public management to policymakers, debating about the values of reform proposals during the policy formulation stage, examining the effectiveness of official policies during the implementation and evaluation stages, and discussing the final experience and lessons (good and bad) of the reform policies. The field of public administration in many ways represents a continuous cycle and process of ideas, reforms,

---

I recognize that there may be conceptual problems associated with many terms used in this book. For example, public management reform has also been related to other similar terms, such as administrative reform, administrative improvement and modernization, and administrative change and innovation. I use the term public management reform because it represents the latest effort in improving the management of government business. The contributors to this book may select other terms as result of different backgrounds and interests in their research.

practives, feedback, and new ideas that are influenced by changes and challenges in the environment.

For policymakers, the interest in reforming government bureaucracies is not a new policy issue in the United States. In the 20th century, we have experienced a series of new ideas and policies attempting to improve the federal government (Moe, 1992). These reform efforts include many official commissions or commitees on reforms, including 1) The Keep Commission (1905–1909, under President T. Roosevelt), 2) The President's Commission on Economy and Efficiency (1910–1913, under President Taft), 3) The Joint Committee on Reorganization (1921–1924, under President Harding), 4) The President's Committee on Administrative Management (1936–1937, under President F. D. Roosevelt), 5) The First Hoover Commission (1947–1949, under President Truman), 6) The Second Hoover Commission (1953–1955, under President Eisenhower), 7) The Study Commissions on Executive Reorganization (1953–1968, under Presidents Eisenhower, Kennedy, and Johnson), 8) The Ash Council (1969–1971), under President Nixon), 9) The Carter Reorganization Effort (1977–1979), 10) The Grace Commission (1982–1984, under President Reagan), and 11) Gore's National Performance Review (since 1993, under President Clinton).

The motives behind these reform efforts have to do with policy changes that are related to specific political needs and vision, emerging social values and attitudes, and new managerial principles and strategies. Based on different considerations, these reform commissions and committees had recommended many policy and managerial changes in the size of federal government and on the power of the Executive Office of the President and its control over administration agencies, regarding the management of human resources, budgeting and finance, organizational structures, and agency operation and procedure.

For example, the recent National Performance Review (NPR) represents one of the latest efforts to improve the management of U.S. government. Affected by Osborne and Gaebler's Reinventing Government work (1992), the NPR works to identify many root problems of the federal government and attempts to change governmental agencies to entrepreneurial organizations (Gore, 1993). The problems of federal government include out-of-date bureaucratic rules and procedures, hierarchical organization designs and structures, and political interest and influence of distrust in public employees. The NPR's suggestions for creating entrepreneurial organizations are based on such principles as: 1) cutting red tape and asking employees to be accountable for achieving results, 2) putting customers first and insisting on customer satisfaction, 3) empowering employees (through labor–management cooperation, training, and assistance) to get results, and 4) cutting back to basics by re-examining programs and procedures and re-engineering how employees do their work to make government work better and cost less. These reform suggestions have been emphasized and implemented in many functional areas of public management, such as human resource management, budgeting, and financial management, at all levels of government.

Similar reform ideas and policies for improving the management of government have been emphasized in many developed and developing countries. One of the recent reforms that received worldwide attention is the New Zealand model, which is based on theoretical concepts of public choice theory, principal-agent theory, transaction-cost theory, and the new public management ideas of privatization, decentralization, deregulations, taxation reduction, performance-oriented management, and the streamlining of public business. The policy components of the New Zealand model consist of reform of government commercial enterprises (to corporatize these public enterprises), reform of the core departments (to emphasize the contract relationship between the government and bureaucrats by addressing accountability, performance, delegation, incentives and punishments, value of money, and customer service), and economic policy reforms (to address the government's overall economic policy in the Reserve Bank Act and the Fiscal Responsibility Act) (Bale and Dale, 1998; Boston et al., 1991)

These reform ideas and policies have quickly attracted attention in developing countries. For developing countries, the interests in public management reform are based not only on the desire to introduce modern management systems (ideas, techniques, or processes) to make the administration more efficient and effective in the delivery of services to the public, but also on the need for an administrative apparatus adequate for performing the important roles of government in managing the economy (United Nations, 1983; Liou, 1998). To promote economic growth and social development, many international development and aid organizations have stressed the importance of public management reform in their financial assistance plans. For example, the International Monetary Fund, the United Nations development organizations, and the World Bank have always demanded some type of public management reform in developing countries, including the privatization of many government organizations and activities, the reorganization and adjustment of government structures, and the overhaul of banking and financial systems. Government reform is one of the key factors and challenges for these countries to promote economic development (Liou, 2000).

Recognizing the importance of reform policies, public administration researchers have been actively involved in the study of reform experience and lessons. For example, researchers generally agree that reform policies are popular, but the records of the reform policies have been disappointing (Caiden, 1991). There are many environmental, organizational, and personality obstacles to the reform policies (Caiden, 1999, 1991, 1969; Rosenbloom, 1998). The environmental obstacles refer to many factors related to geography, history, technology, polity, culture, and society. The organizational obstacles consist of common managerial problems such as resources, planning, schedules, strategies, implementation, monitoring, and evaluation. The personality obstacles have to do with problems of the reformer, including the reform's ideologies and responses to the difficulties and failures, and the limitations of the reform's ideas, knowledge, data base, analyses, and recommendations. To overcome these problems, many researchers (Caiden, 1991; Peters and Savoe, 1994; Rosenbloom, 1998) have emphasized a diagnostic reform model, which promotes the importance of a pragmatic approach, specific strategies and treatments for different situations, and a gradual and long-term commitment to the reform (Liou, 1999).

The purpose of this book is to offer the latest and most comprehensive information on changes and issues related to public management reform, practice, education, and professional development. The book emphasizes the link between public management practice and reform ideas and experience. It also identifies several new challenges and potential markets in public management. The book especially recognizes the important contribution of public administration education to professional development and examines many issues related to changes in public management education, research, and professional associations.

The organization of this book consists of eight parts and 35 chapters. Part I (Chapters 1 to 4) provides background information about environmental changes and their impact on public management. Part II (Chapters 5 to 8) focuses on changes in the area of public budgeting and financial management. Part III (Chapters 9 to 12) covers major changes in public human resource management. Part IV (Chapters 13 to 16) identifies important issues and changes that related to organizational and general public management. Part V (Chapters 17 to 20) includes several selected policy issues and their impact on public management. Part VI (Chapters 21 to 25) examines past reform experiences and critical issues in public management reform. Part VII (Chapters 26 to 30) addresses new ideas, challenges, and emerging markets in public management. Part VIII (Chapters 31 to 35) reviews challenges to public administration education and changes in professional associations.

Finally, in each chapter, all the authors have tried to explain the importance of their topic issue, provide a background review of theoretic or policy development of the topic, examine major concepts and critical issues that are related to the topic, and discuss the impact, implication, and future development of the topic issue.

REFERENCES

Bale, M. and T. Dale (1998). Public Sector Reform in New Zealand and Its Relevance to Developing Countries, *The World Bank Research Observer* 13(1):103–121.

Boston, J., J. Martin, J. Pallor, and P. Walsh (eds.) (1991). *Reshaping the State: New Zealand's Bureaucratic Revolution*, Auckland: Oxford University Press.

Caiden, G. E. (1969). *Administrative Reform*, Chicago: Aldine Publishing Company.

Caiden, G. E. (1991). *Administrative Reform Comes of Age*, Berlin: Walter De Gruyter.
Caiden, G. E. (1999). "Administrative Reform—Proceed with Caution," *International Journal of Public Administration* 22(6):815–832.
Gore, A. (1993). *Creating a Government that Works Better and Costs Less: Report of the National Performance Review*, Washington, D.C.: U.S. Government Printing Office.
Liou, K. T. (1998). *Managing Economic Reforms in Post-Mao China*, Westport, CT: Praeger.
Liou, K. T. (1999). "Strategies and Lessons of China's Post-Mao Economic Development," *Policy Studies Review* 16(1):183–208.
Liou, K. T. (ed.) (2000). *Administrative Reform and National Economic Development*, Aldershot, England: Ashgate Publishing Ltd.
Moe, R. C. *Reorganizing the Executive Branch in the Twentieth Century: Landmark Commission*, Report 92-293 GOV, Washington, D.C.: Congressional Research Service, Library of Congress, March 19, 1992
Osborne, D. and T. Gaebler (1992). *Reinventing Government*, Reading, MA: Addison-Wesley.
Peters, B. G. and D. J. Savoie. (1994). "Civil Service Reform: Misdiagnosing the Patient," *Public Administration Review* 54(5):99–106.
Rosenbloom, D. H. (1998). "Observations on American Administrative Reform," *International Journal of Public Administration* 21(10):1393–1421.
United Nations. (1983). *Enhancing Capabilities for Administrative Reform in Developing Countries*, New York: The Author.

1

Politics, Paradox, and the "Ecology" of Public Administration: Challenges, Choices, and Opportunities for a New Century

Robert F. Durant
School of Public Affairs, University of Baltimore, Baltimore, Maryland

In his classic *Reflections on Public Administration* (1947), John Gaus wrote perceptively of the "ecology" of public administration and its relationship to the rise of the administrative state (Waldo, 1948). Specifically, he recounted how crises and changes in people, place, physical technology, social technology, and philosophy during the first half of the 20th century led citizens repeatedly to look to government for relief from the negative externalities accompanying them. Politicians, in turn, created or expanded the powers of public agencies to "help craft new institutional bases . . . [to] . . . enable the individual to find development . . . satisfaction . . . and some sense of purpose."

Implicit in Gaus's work was how the "administrative orthodoxy" of the Progressive reform movement informed society's response to these transformations (Knott and Miller, 1987). A central linchpin of this orthodoxy was the unique ability of public agencies to pursue the public interest if organized on Weberian principles, if run like businesses by strong executives, if staffed by nonpartisan professional experts, and if focused on procedural fairness. Central as well for realizing the public interest was a vibrant economic regulatory regime animated by two overriding purposes: to protect the public from market failures in various industries (mostly from monopolies) and to promote the growth and prosperity of those same industries (e.g., the financial securities, transportation, and energy sectors of the economy). As time passed a final, albeit implicit, linchpin of the administrative orthodoxy became the superiority of national solutions to society's ills. The federal government was the only institution with sufficient authority, will, and capacity to offset concentrations of economic power; to ameliorate the problems that accompanied otherwise positive societal changes; and to build a floor of security below which no citizen should fall.

Gaus's depiction of an expanding administrative state as the answer to modernity's problems held true for nearly a quarter-century after *Reflections*. For example, as racism, chronic unemployment, and inadequate housing plagued minorities, and as health care maintenance problems soared among the impoverished elderly, the Great Society was launched in the 1960s. Indeed, so ingrained and apparently irreversible was this predisposition that the early 1970s saw President Nixon expand the administrative state even further by adding what scholars called the "new social regulation" (e.g., environmental protection, employee health and safety, and consumer protection) to the earlier economic mix (Lilly and Miller, 1977). With the new social regulation, of course, came agencies to implement these rights-based statutes (e.g., the Environmental Protection Agency, the Occupational Safety and Health Administration, the Consumer Product Safety Commission, and the Equal Employment Opportunity Commission).

Since the mid-1970s the United States has continued to undergo social, economic, and technological transformations not unlike those described by Gaus, and at a decidedly more rapid pace. Known widely as the "Third Wave" shift from an industrial to an information-based economy (Toffler, 1980), these transformations caused unprecedented gains alongside protean pains of social, economic, and political adjustment. Curiously, however, the Third Wave has evoked a decidedly different response to the challenges, choices, and opportunities it affords. Philosophically, the administrative state is now portrayed as the problem to which markets are the solution, rather than vice versa.

Regnant as a new millennium begins is a "downsizing, defunding, and devolution" (D^3) agenda that turns the Progressive reform vision on its head (Durant, 1998). Decidedly "neoliberal" in philosophy (Peters, 1996), the D^3 agenda values

- "busting" bureaucracies, not building them
- devolving policy and program responsibilities to states, localities, nonprofit agencies, and private contractors, not centralizing them in Washington or within organizations
- devolving administrative authority to, and within, agencies, not concentrating it in central administrative units or hierarchies

deregulating business and financial capital to let markets flourish in a global economy, not regulating them
exposing public agencies to market and quasi-market competition, not insulating them
focusing on results, not on procedures
politicizing whatever public bureaucracy remains, not depoliticizing it

What caused this epochal change in zeitgeist from the one that Gaus depicted for the first half of the 20th century? The reasons are multiple, complex, and entangled. Some see in it the result of overreaching by the administrative state. Supporters of the Great Society portray it as an effort to complete Roosevelt's unfinished New Deal agenda of expanding "political rights" to include the protection of equal *opportunity*. Critics say that much of it violated citizens' sense of fairness by creating "entitlements" without obligations and promoting equality of *outcome* rather than opportunity (Milkis, 1993; Etzioni, 1994; Galston, 1999).

Similarly, others argue that the new social regulation went too far beyond "old-style" economic regulation, thus planting the seeds of its own political destruction (Wilson, 1990; Whitman, 1999). The latter *promoted* as well as regulated industry, whereas the former eschewed promoting industry interests. Moreover, whereas old-style regulation proceeded on an industry-by-industry basis, social regulation cut across *all* industries and imposed high compliance costs upon them. Thus, as Arab oil embargoes, economic slowdowns, and international competition strained corporate profits, a formidable cross-industry coalition existed to demonize all regulation.

Still others elaborate and extend the first two arguments. They either view the administrative state itself as an aberration of the values that Lipset (1996) associates with American exceptionalism (Galston, 1999) or claim that proponents of the D^3 agenda were more adroit in "selling" their agenda politically by grounding it in these values (Durant, 1998). Most notable among these are liberty, egalitarianism (predicated on equality of opportunity), individualism, populism, laissez-faire market orientation, optimism, pragmatism, and affinity toward local rather than national political institutions (Lipset, 1996). As such, the expansion of the administrative state from the New Deal through the Cold War reflected a pragmatic response to difficult circumstances. However, it was premised on values so incongruent with American exceptionalism that it could not last once circumstances changed (Galston, 1999).

Plausible as well are explanations that the administrative state *is* ineffective and inefficient, although this argument is more of a caricature than an apt generalization. Serious scholars, political appointees from both parties, and impartial observers have marshaled a great deal of empirical evidence to the contrary (e.g., Goodsell, 1994; Rainey, 1996; Holzer and Callahan, 1998). Moreover, citizens typically rank three programs administered *directly* by the federal government as exemplary (Social Security, Medicare, and the national parks). Still, even a cursory reading of administrative law texts, of the bureaucratic politics and public management literatures, or of policy implementation studies affords enough scholarly support to make the case against bureaucracy compelling in many instances. Whether the fault lies in a "bureaucracy problem" or a "governance problem" is debatable (Meier, 1997).

At the same time the realpolitik of administrative reform in the United States is also partially responsible for the ascendancy of the neoliberal agenda. As Rosenbloom and Ross (1994) argue, the dominance of administrative theories has historically had less to do with their validity than with the power of a dominant political coalition to offer and sustain them. In this instance, and premised on very different values, New Democrats trying to protect a positive state agenda and vying with Republicans for the Perot vote after the 1992 presidential election combined with minimalist state proponents to enact and preserve the D^3 agenda. Each could claim that the federal government was shrinking, "doing more with less," and attacking federal budget deficits.

Still, others in the realpolitik school note that cross-party alliances on U.S. trade policy have coalesced around the neoliberal agenda because of the benefits they and their corporate constituents derive from the rise of global capitalism, the information and telecommunications revolution, and vast improvements in global transportation systems. These trends are used to buttress arguments that the administrative state is an obstacle to prosperity, must be redesigned to make it more "market friendly," and can be effectively reconfigured by following the D^3 agenda (Korten, 1996). The global economy, this coalition argues, requires nations to prune the size of their public sector welfare and regulatory regimes. Doing so will stimulate their economies, attract and maintain international business and investor capital, and position them better to compete globally on the basis of comparative advantage. To be sure, some see no mischief afoot in the ascendancy of this cross-party alliance (e.g., Friedman, 1999; Whitman, 1999). Yet others see the coalition driven by the increasing reliance of the Republican *and* Democratic parties on campaign contributions from transnational corporations and the securities industry (e.g., Greider, 1997).

Finally, others maintain that the ascendancy of the D^3 agenda (and most especially its "reinventing government" components) depends less on the merits of neoliberal arguments than on the multimillion-dollar consulting industry that markets its precepts globally (Saint-Martin, 1998). Students of economic reforms in former Communist and totalitarian nations would add another, more nefarious reason: the illicit financial gains that accrue to some political leaders and their friends when they privatize state-owned enterprises (Chari, 1998; Rosenberg, 1999). Not all from the political economy perspective agree, however. Some looking at privatization and contracting in France, Great Britain, and the United States see more noble, yet nevertheless controversial, reasons for the privatizing and contracting components of the D^3 agenda. Specifically, they are efforts to reduce budget deficits both to stimulate the economy and to reinvigorate industries especially hard hit by recession or global competition (Zahariadis, 1995; Whitman, 1999).

Whatever its fundamental causes, the D^3 agenda is said by some to produce a "hollow state" in its wake (Milward and Provan, 1993; Milward, 1994). Left are downsized federal agencies trying to catalyze and monitor nonhierarchical implementation structures of cross-sectoral (public, private, and nonprofit) partnerships with a scale, level of complexity, and opaqueness that are unprecedented in the United States. Moreover, what remains of the administrative state too often lacks the capacity to do effectively what reformers say is necessary (e.g., set priorities, focus on results, and monitor partners for accountability). This is the case because of inadequate financial management, capital investment, human resource, and information management systems (The Government Performance Project, 1999). This would not be as worrisome if the condition of these systems were better in the states, but wide and disturbing disparities in capabilities exist among these as well (ibid.).

If Paul Light's (1999) estimates are taken as a point of departure, a vast chasm now exists between the political rhetoric and reality of downsizing the administrative state in Washington to 1.8 million employees. Counting the number of jobs involving contractors, grants-in-aid to state and local governments, and nonprofit agencies now delivering devolved federal responsibilities, a "shadow state" of nearly 17 million employees exists and is growing. The Pentagon, for example, expects to outsource another 230,000 jobs to the private sector by 2005, and the Federal Activities Inventory Reform Act (FAIR) of 1998 requires federal agencies to submit to the Office of Management and Budget (OMB) a list of all positions that can be outsourced to private firms in the future. Thus, the United States is not so much shrinking the administrative state as it is altering its metes and bounds. Created in the process is a "neoadministrative state" in which combinations (or "partnerships") of public, private, and nonprofit actors are given the authority to act on behalf of the state.

How likely are these trends to continue in the United States? Although no one can say for sure, examining the potential durability of the political economy that presently supports the rise of the neoadministrative state offers important clues. Arguably, no better approach exists for doing this than applying the "ecology" of public administration framework Gaus used to chronicle the rise of the administrative state in America. Taking this approach, the remainder of this chapter (a) identifies the major trends that have led to the rise of the neoadministrative state, (b) assesses how likely they are to endure, and (c) enumerates some of the major challenges, choices, and opportunities that they create for public administration practice, research, and theory. From this analysis, I conclude that political debates framed in terms of markets versus bureaucracy misstate the quintessential issues posed by the emergence of the neoadministrative state in the United States.

The real questions it poses as this nation enters the 21st century are which bureaucracy, operated in whose interests, with what capacity, and held accountable to democratic values in what ways? Moreover, how public administrationists engage and respond to these questions will either advance or marginalize the field well into the new millennium.

THE ECOLOGY OF PUBLIC ADMINISTRATION: PRINCIPLES, PRACTICES, AND PARADOXES IN A GLOBAL ERA

How likely is it that the D^3 political agenda will continue to drive administrative theory in the United States in the 21st century?[1] Arguably, this "one-size-fits-all" agenda has staying power. To be sure, crises may develop that are directly linked to the reforms or the forces driving them. Absent these, however, several global trends affecting the ecology of public administration appear so enduring that downward pressures on the size, scope, and responsibilities of the administrative state as Gaus knew it will continue indefinitely.

In the process, the "fundamentals" driving the neoadministrative state bring in their wake three major paradoxes that will challenge the acumen and creativity of public administrationists for the foreseeable future. First, the same forces in the ecology that produce negative externalities for societies to address can also reduce the capacities of government alone to respond to them. Second, although these global forces can democratize nations and invigorate their economies, they simultaneously can reduce some of the political and economic choices open to them. Finally, the technological advances underpinning globalization that can produce economic growth, democratization, and the acceptance of diversity and inclusivity can simultaneously threaten these values.

Dwight Waldo (1980) alerted us two decades ago to a dialectical "happening" between democracy and bureaucracy in the administrative state that was a result of their disparate values. In revisiting Waldo's argument, Gawthrop (1997: 205) recently referred to this "happening" as a "hell of a train wreck." Yet the neoadministrative state that globalization has advanced should give us even greater pause. If engineered on the basis of ideology rather than pragmatism, the neoadministrative state might engender a far more chilling metaphor: a "train hijacking" of both bureaucracy *and* democracy in the 21st century.

Changes in People

As Gaus notes, changes in the sociodemographic characteristics of nations are critical components of the ecology of public administration. One of the most significant aspects of today's ecology is the continuation of a global "age wave" that

---

[1]With additions and further explications, the following discussion borrows very heavily from Durant, 2000b.

Peterson (1999) calls "the Gray Dawn." This wave, of course, has direct implications for managers working in the health and pension fields; aging entails more costly medical care and the maturation of pension liabilities. It also has indirect implications, however, for public managers generally because of its potential to divert resources from the pursuit of other public purposes.

Over the next several decades, demographers project that countries in the *developed* world will experience an unprecedented growth in the number of their elderly and an unprecedented decline in the number of their youth. This will put tremendous pressures on retirement and medical systems as the "Floridazation" of nations continues apace. By 2003, 20 percent of Italy's population will be over age 65; Japan hits that mark in 2005 and Germany in 2006. They are followed by France and Britain in 2016, and the United States and Canada in 2021 and 2023, respectively.

As a consequence, developed nations will have to pay anywhere from 9 to 16 percent of their gross domestic product (GDP) over the next quarter-century to meet their existing old-age-pension promises. Presently, they have $35 trillion in unfunded pension liability. Clearly the potential impacts of this debt burden for the world economy, as well as for intergenerational conflict within nations, are enormous. Japan, for example, has been funding sizable portions of the United States's budget deficits for over a decade. What happens when Japan's own "pension deficits" explode and they are less able to fund U.S. debt? Moreover, unless the situation is handled adroitly, dysfunctional fault lines could easily develop between young and old around the world.

In contrast, many nations in the *developing* world will experience precisely the opposite trend: a youth boom that could be destabilizing for civil servants in the U.S. defense, national security, and international aid fields. Fertility rates in the Gaza Strip, for instance, are nearly three times as high as those in Israel (Peterson, 1999). Today, Pentagon planners routinely refer to "youth bulges" in the world's urban centers, and they expect that high unemployment, poverty, and institutional instability in these centers will produce outbreaks of regional conflict worldwide. Demography is not destiny, but these trends are real and worrisome, and they are constraints on public administrators that they ignore at their peril.

To be sure a projected $4-trillion budget surplus, by 2010 could commence a long-avoided debate over dealing with the Gray Dawn in America. Still unclear, though, is whether surpluses of this magnitude will materialize. If conventional 5-year budget projections are notorious for their inaccuracy, what confidence should 10-year projections inspire? To materialize, surpluses of this magnitude require future congresses to make tough and politically difficult decisions regarding service delivery. Alternatively, they can hope that the economy can perform at historically unprecedented levels of growth, a potential that technology breakthroughs make a distinct possibility. Yet with the slow growth policy adopted by the Federal Reserve Board so successful since 1992 in reducing inflation during 8 years of economic expansion, it is unlikely that the nation will soon opt for higher levels of growth.

Even were congressional commitments kept and economic growth targets met or exceeded, three significant pension problems remain to challenge public administrationists. First, President Clinton's plan still closes only about half of the gap between Social Security obligations and projected revenues. Moreover, his plan shifts general revenues into both Social Security and Medicare, thus reducing the amount of revenue available for other programs. And with discretionary funds the source of agency operating budgets and intergovernmental grant transfers, a variety of programs outside the limited number of priorities pursued could be especially hard hit. Nor, as the Gray Dawn proceeds, can an equity question already plaguing the United States be ignored: The Congressional Budget Office reports that whereas children are twice as likely as the elderly to live in poverty, the federal government spends seven times as much per capita on seniors as it does on young people (Peterson, 1999).

Changes in Technology Leading to Changes in Global Finance

Changes in physical and social technologies also are likely to continue to place growing demands on politicians for redress, while they erode the ability of the administrative state to respond effectively. Indeed, as the remainder of this section will chronicle, the information and telecommunications revolutions have—for better and worse—helped propel the D^3 agenda. They do this by placing downward pressures on public taxing and spending while ginning up additional demands for government redress.

What follows is not meant as a screed against evil corporations, greedy financiers, or inept central bankers conspiring to privatize the benefits of technological innovations for themselves, while socializing the costs of the negative externalities produced. Rather it is a cautionary tale of rational actors responding in the short term to revamped incentives driven by relentless technology-driven changes. Determinative among these have been the confluence of periodic economic slowdowns (during the late 1970s, early 1980s, and early 1990s), product and market volatility, sharpened international competition, diminished government scrutiny during the Reagan years, and rising scrutiny by institutional and other investors bent on maximizing profit dividends (Friedman, 1999; Whitman, 1999).

Nor is this meant as a Luddite attack on "technology as Satan." Arguably, the democratizing and economic development effects of the global economy in developing nations such as Indonesia, Malaysia, and Thailand are quite positive. As Friedman (1999) argues, however, as these technology-driven changes expand democratic and economic opportunities, they simultaneously contract the political and economic choices open to nations. The "closed-loop" logic of this paradox is straightforward. Nations need investments in physical and social infrastructure to grow their economies; with governments under pressure worldwide to balance budgets, the largest source of "excess" capital exists in financial markets; and the price exacted by the financial markets from nations wishing this capital is further fiscal austerity. As such, public administrationists should understand the trends that are likely to continue to push political leaders to "take their nations public" in an era of investor capitalism (Friedman, 1999).

Financial Market Deregulation

First and foremost, changes in information and telecommunications technology have made possible the deregulation of financial markets, as well as their subsequent global integration (Sassen, 1999). In turn, these developments have special implications for public managers dealing with labor, economic development, and equity issues because of the power asymmetries that concentrations of financial capital are spawning (Sassen, 1999). Mergers among the top 10 of the 50 largest financial services firms roughly doubled from 1992 to 1997. Megagroups are rapidly developing among such firms as Merrill Lynch, Morgan Stanley Dean Witter, and Goldman Sachs.

These, in turn, are helping to spark the multiple mergers occurring worldwide among firms that support or track the transactions of this infrastructure: accounting firms, law practices, stock exchanges, and insurance brokers. The New York Stock Exchange, for example, is considering partnering with exchanges in Canada and Latin America and is already talking with the Paris Bourse. Similar discussions are under way between The National Association of Securities Dealers Automated Quotations' (NASDAQ's) parent company and counterparts in Frankfort and London. Neither can one ignore the "global bonding" of supranational alliances—e.g., among semiconductor companies in London, New York, and Tokyo—as costs and risks of research and development (R&D) spiral. These alliances put competitors for market share into "strategic collaboration" alliances with each other, a development that the emerging "Eurozone" will likely accelerate.

Thus, precisely as governments worldwide are deregulating the international flow of financial capital, market concentration is growing within that industry, a pattern reminiscent of trends witnessed a century ago. What is more, with breakthroughs in telecommunications, the low-inflation, slower-growth agenda of these financiers races electronically around the globe, 24 hours a day, to inform policy judgments. For business and government, a major side effect of that agenda is pressure to keep real interest rates high enough to attract international capital for debt service and investment. Yet this also makes the costs of doing business more expensive for corporations everywhere, in turn pressuring them to cut costs and resize their work forces downward (Whitman, 1999).

For governments, this also means that the social costs of resizing corporate structures have fallen largely to them. Yet precisely as these responsibilities have increased, shrinking and reconfiguring the public sector to reduce budget deficits or to enter international trade agreements have become high priorities worldwide (discussed later). As such, cash-strapped governments must turn to the partnering networks of the neoadministrative state to leverage their resources to meet these needs.

Meanwhile, a subtle but detectable shift in power is generated by these trends, one that is likely to continue unless steps are taken by governments to alter its course. As Friedman (1999) notes, nations worldwide have an unprecedented opportunity to capitalize on the economic, social, and cultural opportunities that international financial markets can give them. But to do so they must first convince international investors that they are prepared to put on a "golden straitjacket." Specifically, they must agree to privatize state-owned enterprises, cut subsidies to those that remain, lower trade barriers, remove restrictions on foreign direct investment (FDI), and balance their budgets. All this, in turn, shifts power to the financial market sector. With funds for government investment limited by the straitjacket, borrowers grow more dependent for success on pleasing capital markets.

Deflationary Pressures

A second technologically driven trend that is occurring worldwide and that shows no signs of abating is deflationary pressure on prices. In essence, the bounties of technological prowess also have produced a tendency toward oversupplying goods relative to worldwide demand. In fact, a downward spiral in prices was partially responsible for disruptive economic, social, and political readjustments (some say, "upheavals") during the 1990s in such geographically dispersed nations as Brazil, Chile, Japan, Mexico, South Korea, and Thailand. These, in turn, have drawn criticism in some circles of the United States–dominated International Monetary Fund (the IMF) and the World Bank. They are accused of imposing economically counterproductive, politically incendiary, and natural resource–depleting "austerity" policies on developing countries worldwide.

Meanwhile, within the United States deflationary threats in other parts of the world have placed further downward pressure on the capacity of the administrative state to survive and grow according to Gaus's historical patterns. The nation, serving as the world's "buyer of last resort," experienced a balance of trade deficit that spiraled during the 1980s and 1990s. To finance it (as well as its national debt), the United States has relied on other nations (especially Japan) to use their trade surpluses to buy Treasury bonds. This, again, has meant further pressure on the United States to keep real interest rates at high enough levels to attract foreign investment and to keep inflation low lest the Federal Reserve raise interest rates to counteract it. Meanwhile, outside the United States, nations seeking regional economic integration in supranational bodies such as the European Union are feeling similar downward pressures on public spending as preconditions for membership.

Winner-Take-All Markets

A third trend occasioned by technological change that shows no signs of abating is "winner-take-all" markets (Madrick, 1995). This occurs wherever information technology and global transportation systems produce specialty markets dominated by one or two top firms that are "best in class." Is there turnover in these "winners"? Most assuredly. Yet market dominance still exists because of the amount of capital needed to enter and remain in the game. What is more, this problem may be growing larger in some industries. In computer technology, spiraling R&D costs are pushing giants of the industry into the "global bonding" of supranational alliances mentioned earlier.

Again, all this will continue to put downward pressures on corporate profit margins, making them focus on efficiency as the sole value pursued. Diminished in the process, according to the economist and former General Motors vice president Marina Whitman (1999), are many of the commitments to communities that corporations who dominated markets in the past pursued. Significantly, given the neoadministrative state's emphasis on volunteerism and corporate giving, these cuts occur largely in the area of philanthropy—and precisely at a time when geographic and employee loyalty wanes. What is more, those civic contributions that corporations *do* make tend largely to be product related, leaving gaps in the civic "social safety net" that D^3 proponents see business as helping to create. As in the past, governments and public managers will be left to fill the gaps left by corporate disengagement.

Changes in Place

As noted, population movements tended to occupy most of Gaus's attention in terms of changes in place that had occurred during the first half of the 20th century. As the following illustrates, similar and important changes in place will continue to confront public administrationists in the new millennium. But for the foreseeable future, equally salient for them will be the continuation of paradoxical changes related to workplace composition, business location, and tax mobility.

Population Migration

As the 21st century dawns, population migration remains a major source of demands upon government for action. We see it within the United States (e.g., into the Sunbelt), into the United States (e.g., from Mexico and Southeast Asia), and among or within other nations (e.g., into France, Germany, and England). But wherever it occurs, migration continues to pose service delivery, regulatory, and income redistributive challenges, choices, and opportunities for public administrators in the United States and abroad.

As in Gaus's day, the ethnic diversity that results from immigration affords in the long run the kinds of new skills, talents, work ethic, and cultures that have always leavened and advanced U.S. economic and national security interests. In the short run, however, migration places unaccustomed tax, service delivery, and regulatory burdens on society that can help topple governments (local, state, or national) should citizens either tire of them or conclude they are ineffective (e.g., the defeat of Helmut Kohl in Germany and the election of Lionel Jospin in France). They also can stoke xenophobic, antisocial, and right-wing political reactions among citizens who feel they are threatened economically by newcomers (e.g., Jean-Marie Le Pen's National Front in France and Pauline Hanson's One Nation movement in Australia).

Less chilling though nonetheless significant for public administrationists, the political consequences of population migration into the Sunbelt are felt everywhere in the United States. Not only has this migration enhanced the electoral and policy clout of politicians from that region in presidential and congressional politics, but it also has joined with the demands of the global economy (discussed later) to catapult a more socially conservative and economically neoliberal philosophy to national and subnational prominence. Neither do these trends promise soon to reverse themselves in any way, thus buttressing the movement to expand the neoadministrative state at the expense of the old administrative state.

Not since the election of John Kennedy in 1960, for instance, have voters elected a president from outside the Sunbelt. Moreover, at all levels of government the decade of the 1990s was a horrible one for the Democratic party, known historically for holding a distinctly more positive view than Republicans about expanding the administrative state. In 1992 the Democrats held majorities of over 100 seats in the U.S. House of Representatives and 14 seats in the U.S. Senate. They also outnumbered Republican governors by a 30-to-20 margin and held an aggregate 1537-member majority in state legislatures. As the year 2000 approached, they were in the minority by 12 members in the House and by 10 members in the Senate. Moreover, they held only 17 governorships, and they were reduced to a 359-member majority in state legislatures nationwide (Faux, 1999).

At the same time, however, migration from Mexico has gradually begun to alter the message that prominent Republican governors are beginning to carry to the electorate in states with high numbers of Hispanics. Electoral success by Republicans in key states like Florida and Texas (by Jeb Bush and George W. Bush, respectively), and defeat in California (of Dan Lundgren) have depended on political appeals or policy slights to culturally and economically conservative Hispanic voters. And partially because each of these states holds huge numbers of electoral votes, leading presidential aspirants in both parties during the 2000 presidential campaign designed themes to attract these voters (e.g., family and responsibility).

The need to package political appeals in these terms was further reinforced, ironically, by a "migratory" success story that the administrative state helped foster: the migration of minorities into the suburbs (or "ethnoburbs") (Booth, 1999). They joined with their neighbors in what demographers term the *suburbanization* of America. For public administrationists, this is a trend that produces much more than soccer moms; it engenders a political philosophy that public opinion pollsters find is more centrist in orientation than that which propelled the rise of the administrative state. Moreover, it is a philosophy that politicians of both parties are finding they can ill afford to ignore given the political activism of suburbanites relative to inner-city voters.

Meanwhile, as corporate workplaces, state legislatures, and government agencies have begun to reflect this diversity in their own leadership positions and membership, management issues related to differences in ethnicity, gender, sexual preference, and physical challenges have grown more salient. These include ensuring a harassment-free work environment, upward mobility, and pay comparability for women, minorities, gays, and the physically challenged. And were these traditional challenges not difficult enough for public managers to cope with, "time" in place is already adding a new dimension to their concerns.

As worldwide competition increases the urgency of raising productivity while cutting labor costs, businesses have turned to employing part-time (or temporary) workers in the "24-hour workday" that a global economy often mandates (Epstein, 1999). Although quite rational for business, this trend produces serious social consequences: These jobs typically do not carry health or pension benefits. Some argue that women—who compose the largest segment of this temporary work force—stand to benefit by having more "face time" with their families. Others worry, however, that the face time that professional women (or men) lose in the workplace with colleagues may limit their upward mobility (Epstein, 1999). Not only does networking play a role in professional advancement, but many employers question whether part-time workers are sufficiently career-oriented to merit promotion or pay increases.

Given these trends, one sees in population migration several contributing factors to the paradoxical effects of globalization on public administration. Politics becomes more homogenized, while diversity in communities, workplaces, cultures, and life-styles becomes more heterogeneous. Economic policy choices get narrowed, while democratization expands. And the capacities of the administrative state to respond to negative externalities decrease, while these externalities increase.

Tax Migration

A second trend related to paradoxes caused by changes in place involves the location of where transnational corporations pay their taxes. This, in turn, is linked to the globalization of business product lines that, itself, is made possible by computer networks (discussed later). The latter make possible "real-time" monitoring of product lines, wherever in the world they are located. Indeed, the consensus among economists is that approximately one-third of the United States world trade deficit is now composed of *intrafirm* sales made to subsidiaries in foreign countries (Friedman, 1999).

Certainly, the globalization of product lines has produced very positive effects for many developing countries (e.g., employment opportunities otherwise unavailable and an improvement in the social status of women). At the same time, however, it also has afforded opportunities for corporations to engage in "income shifting." Through "creative accounting," corporations can claim deductions for costly production expenditures that they incur against the taxes they owe to countries with higher corporate tax rates. Conversely, corporations can assign high profits to production facilities in other nations that have lower corporate tax rates (Greider, 1997). A 1997 study of 200 American corporations found that the average multinational used income shifting to reduce its taxes by over 50 percent, a tremendous amount of revenue that might otherwise have been used for public purposes. But actual income shifting need not take place to affect public sector revenues; merely the potential for corporations to do so will continue to put downward pressures on corporate tax rates worldwide.

Job Migration

Another continuing trend related to changes in place is "labor market" arbitrage. This involves the shifting of jobs to other nations to take advantage of lower wage rates than in the United States. Nor will arbitrage be limited to manufacturing jobs; even high-technology jobs are increasingly fair game in the global economy. A reversal in the collective bargaining power of unions worldwide might help attenuate this trend somewhat, but underlying political and economic fundamentals are not encouraging. After two decades of neoliberalism, the United States has labor laws that make it "the most difficult place to organize workers in the advanced world" (Faux, 1999: 72). As the nation enters a new millennium, only 14.1 percent of the U.S. labor force is unionized. Consequently, corporations will continue (implicitly or explicitly) either to threaten or actually to move operations or parts of business lines to other nations or to jurisdictions within nations with lower labor costs. In the process, they will continue to pit regions, states, localities, and nation states against each other to gain tax subsidies, tax preferences, and infrastructure commitments.

Another serious driver of job migration, which attracts much less attention than wage differentials, is the "offset" agreements that corporations must often sign to do business in other nations. More precisely, when United States–based multinationals sign sales contracts with developing nations such as China, Indonesia, or Zaire, they have to agree to offset part of the sales price by sharing a portion of the production process with companies in these countries. These arrangements effectively trade U.S. manufacturing and technology jobs for market access that will create more net jobs in the United States. This will occur, the theory goes, as the purchasing power in foreign countries rises and U.S. exports expand to meet this new demand (Greider, 1997; Whitman, 1999).

To be sure, consumers benefit from lower prices when producers save on labor costs. Moreover, a net increase in jobs *has* occurred as a result of export-led economic growth in the United States. The rub, of course, is that the new workers hired are not necessarily the same workers displaced. The economic, social, and psychological costs to these dislocated workers are profound and typically left to government to ameliorate or offset. Thus, with corporate downsizing "democratizing" the pains of dislocation to both the laboring and professional classes (albeit with greater ferocity still on the former), 25 percent of all workers displaced during the 1990s remained unemployed for at least 1 year. Moreover, those displaced in 1991 were still earning at least 10 percent less on average in 1997 than when they lost their job (*Economic Report of the President,* 1997, as cited in Whitman, 1999). Fifteen percent of those reemployed were still without the health insurance they had lost (ibid.).

The Internationalization of Lines of Business

Another important trend that is related to changes in place is the globalization of "lines of business." As noted earlier, corporations are organizing for sales of product lines worldwide and are moving away from their traditional country-by-country approach to production. Nor is this happening exclusively in markets for domestic products; we are seeing it as well in the national security area. As such and in addition to the tax shifting noted earlier, three components of this trend are noteworthy for public administrationists and likely to remain a part of the ecology they face.

Privatizing National Security? In the aftermath of the Cold War, defense intellectuals talk routinely about the advent of "world weaponry." By this they mean that different parts of the same weapons are contracted out for production to companies in different nations (Markusen, 1999). Lockheed Martin, for example, is seeking European partners to build weapons components, and transatlantic buyouts of smaller firms are becoming common in the United States. Meanwhile, British, French, and German industrialists and their governments are trying to form the European Aerospace and Defense Company to produce common weaponry for them.

Driving this phenomenon in the United States is the shakeout of dozens of defense firms worldwide. Today, for example, four major weapons producers dominate the U.S. market: Boeing, Lockheed Martin, Northrop Grumman, and Raytheon. This shakeout, in turn, is spawned by repeated and sizable cuts in U.S. military spending and by a nearly 40 percent decrease in defense budgets worldwide. With competition for weapons contracts keen in a shrinking market, the pressure to buy weapons from a nation's own domestic suppliers is strong throughout the world. Thus, access to lucrative foreign weapons markets is easier for American contractors if they partner with foreign companies. In return, the Pentagon is redrafting its regulations to make it easier for foreign buyers to acquire American firms. In effect, the defense equivalent of an "offset plan" is now in place.

The ultimate consequences of global weaponry are unclear. Some observers argue that an increasing international orientation by defense firms could portend a shift in the balance of defense thinking from governments and toward business (Markusen, 1999). Others argue that global weaponry, at its best, will produce economies of scale, promote international collaboration, and reduce the chances of war among cooperating nations. Indeed, some impishly claim that market globalization and line-of-business production more broadly could replace mutually assured destruction (MAD) as a preventive to global warfare in the post–Cold War era (Friedman, 1999). But all agree that knowledge sharing among firms from different countries affords national security challenges, as the opportunities for espionage spiral accordingly. Thus, for public administrationists, issues regarding knowledge sharing, market coordination, and joint procurement and oversight will become priority items.

Toward "DOS Kapital"? Domestically, the internationalization of business product lines will continue to have major implications for public administrationists working on human and physical capital needs at local, state, and regional levels of government. As noted, globalization renders competitive advantages to those that provide higher qualities of life, as well as necessary human and physical infrastructures. Put concisely by Kanter (1997), success for companies in the global economy depends on concepts (ideas), competence (an educated and trained work force), and connections (the integration of financial, telecommunications, and transportation services). They press these investment demands on governments, however, as they simultaneously pit states, localities, and regions against each other for tax breaks and subsidies that might otherwise help pay for them. Reconciling these contradictory trends could become leverage for savvy managers to exploit for new capital investment from otherwise reluctant politicians. Conversely, the failure to reconcile them could become a prescription for relative economic stagnation or decline. But in either event, the neoadministrative state will have to find the wherewithal to help citizens build assets (e.g., better education, health care, and retirement protections) that buffer them from Third Wave paradoxes like these.

Same Highway, Different Ramps, Varying Speeds? A final and related implication of global lines of business is the unevenness of globalization. Some nations, regions, or jurisdictions will continue to lack either the will or the capacity to participate in it or will try different paths toward it. As such, this trend has special implications for public administrationists working in or studying international aid, economic development, and foreign service bureaucracies (Ottaway, 1999). Meanwhile, public administrationists more generally will face on their agendas the continuing prospect of pronounced and perhaps politically destabilizing income gaps. These will occur both within nations and between the developed and developing worlds. And those expecting that globalization and the economic growth it brings will automatically lead to democracy in these nations will be disappointed.

Nations in Africa, for example, have a long way to go to make these economic and political transitions (Ottaway, 1999). As such, they remain on the periphery of world trade, with scant hopes of joining it soon. Presently, sub-Saharan Africa accounts for only about 1.5 percent of world trade, although it holds just over 13 percent of the world's population. It also receives less than 0.006 percent of foreign direct investment (FDI). Even South Africa, which receives nearly 45 percent of FDI in sub-Saharan Africa, is still heavily dependent on export of minerals (particularly gold). What is more, its industries are highly protected and its agriculture remains highly subsidized, characteristics that will make global capital difficult to come by until reformed.

At the same time other nations will lack the will to reform on the terms articulated by the international investment community. As Friedman (1999) again notes, the "globalution" that neoliberalism is exacting from participants can be politically liberating as it overthrows tyrants in many countries whose families have profited enormously and inequitably from "crony capitalism" and corrupt bureaucracies. But a backlash is also afoot because of the toll exacted on the lower classes by the austerity measures imposed by the golden straitjacket, as well as the corruption that privatization can create (discussed earlier). Further fanning these reactions in more strident ways is globalization's clash with traditional social and economic values (also see, for example, Ohmae, 1995; Barber, 1996; Gonzalez, 1999; Speth, 1999).

Consider, for example, the experiences of some of the admittedly most difficult reform cases in Africa, Eastern Europe, and Latin America. As Rosenberg (1999) summarizes, the most progress in global neoliberal reform has occurred in former Communist nations that have had experience with democratic institutions in their past: Poland (one in four Poles was a member of Solidarity), Hungary (the most liberal Communist state, with no political prisoners held since 1973), and the Czech Republic (with a democracy between World Wars I and II, high levels of education, and a significant business class). In many of the others, Communists have retaken control under different party banners emphasizing nationalism or ethnic identity, rather than markets. This is especially true in nations like Azerbaijan and Kazakhstan with despotic histories in Central Asia and the Caucasus.

Similarly disadvantaged are those without the regulatory (especially banking and environmental standards) and judicial "rule of law" necessary to make markets work effectively, without corruption, and absent wanton waste of natural resources. In Africa and Latin America, respectively, Angola and Colombia—sites previously pawns in Cold War politics—have been returned, respectively, to strongmen bent on either power or wealth from drug sales. Moreover, even where neoliberal reforms have successfully lifted economic performance after austerity measures, the rising tide has left behind a residue of class disparities that either can spark or already is sparking class conflict (e.g., in Mexico).

Reprise. All is not lost, of course, for public administrationists. The globalization of business lines has combined with offset policies and with global pressures to restructure economic and political systems in useful ways for peace, growth, and democracy. Moreover, the potential arises for politicians to see government reform and investments in administrative capacity as central to economic advancement, competitive advantage, and direct foreign investment. Governments, after all, provide the rules of law without which commerce cannot confidently and profitably occur. As such, and in their own self-interest, even "government bashers" worldwide may come to see the advantages of a vibrant and competent public sector and bureaucracy. Still, for the indefinite future, challenges regarding the unequal distribution of the burdens and benefits of the globalization of business lines promise to confront—and propel—the neoadministrative state in the United States as the world's major superpower.

Changes in Philosophy

Major shifts in philosophy from those described by Gaus also promise to continue challenging public administrationists in the 21st century. Of these, five are especially noteworthy. These are philosophical shifts related to the "Washington Consensus" on global integration, the privatization of regulation, the democratic deficit, the return of civism, and the internationalization of human rights policy.

The Washington Consensus

As the preceding suggests, it is difficult to exaggerate the importance to public administrationists of the nation's embrace of the "Washington Consensus" by a Baptist-bootlegger, cross-party coalition of neoliberal and conservative U.S. politicians. As noted, this philosophy ostensibly embraces a consumer-driven, laissez-faire free market model of global economic development. In reality, of course, it still has elements of a managed economy, as the over 1000 rules and regulations setting the terms of trade in the North American Free Trade Agreement (NAFTA) attest.

Another reality is that this model of capitalism is not unchallenged in the world. It has two primary competitors that contrast sharply with it: the Asian or producer-dominated "development" model of capitalism and the "social market" mixed-economy model of capitalism endorsed by the Europeans (Whitman, 1999). The former focuses on the state's protecting new or threatened markets, identifying product winners and channeling investments to them, facilitating industrywide cooperation, and stimulating an export-led economy (but see Wilson, 1990). The latter focuses on the state's creating high-paying jobs and making it difficult by law to close or downsize plants without sufficient warning. Concomitantly, the European model affords generous welfare benefits to those unemployed, codevelops policy with peak associations, and protects certain domestic markets with trade barriers (Wilson, 1990).

Each model has its relative advantages and disadvantages. For example, the Washington Consensus comes up shorter than the others on protecting against, and buffering citizens from, the negative social externalities of global markets. Indeed, the IMF, U.S. Treasury, and advocates of "shock therapy" like the Harvard economist Jeffrey Sachs have admitted mistakes in handling some of the Eastern European and Southeast Asian financial crises (Smadja, 1998–1999). The IMF, in fact, has since allowed several of these nations to run modest deficits and to lower interest rates. Similarly, the World Bank is now finding a constructive role for government: It has urged nations like Kenya and Argentina to increase funding for health and education. Meanwhile, the IMF has withheld loans to Cambodia and Kenya until government corruption is reduced (Rosenberg, 1999).

Closer to home, the Washington Consensus is touted by Democrats and Republicans alike as producing an incredibly robust and durable economic recovery during the 1990s. Although impressive, however, it is actually about average as rates of economic recovery go after recessions, as the Federal Reserve Board has deliberately pursued a slow-growth policy (Madrick, 1995; Faux, 1999). Moreover, although lasting longer than earlier recoveries, the latter were typically interrupted by the Federal Reserve Board's reacting abruptly and harshly to inflation caused by war or energy price shocks. At the same time, cross-national comparisons of per capita growth in gross domestic product (GDP) reveal that the United States actually grew more slowly between 1990 and 1997 than either Germany or Japan, and at about the same level as Great Britain. Finally, the United States Business Conference Board estimates that the average rate of productivity in Belgium, France, the Netherlands, and Western Germany (an important qualification given German reunification with East Germany) has caught up with the U.S. rate (Faux, 1999).

Each of the other models of capitalism, however, has fallen short in particular and comparatively more serious ways. A lack of transparency in the Asian model renders it vulnerable to crony capitalism and accountability problems. Thus, ironically in an information age led by these nations, "disinformation" reduces prudent choices by investors and regulators. This occurs as the opaqueness of partnerships combines with "creative accounting" to hide or exaggerate profits or conceal mismanagement. When this happens (as in Thailand), governments rush in to bail out investors and cope with the social unrest that austerity measures cause. This, of course, is not peculiar to the Asian model, as the stunning savings and loan bailout in the United States attests. Nor is the masking of the true social costs of economic growth peculiar to any model of capitalism; almost all national accounting systems fail to incorporate the depreciation of human capital (e.g., sweatshop and child labor, drugs, and corruption) and natural resources that development can bring (Van Dieren, 1995).

Finally, the European model has serious shortfalls of its own. Whereas the U.S. economy added nearly 18 million jobs during the 1990s, there was a net loss of approximately 8 million jobs in Europe. Average rates of income and productivity (although important computations as Europe attempts economic integration) mask vast cross-national variations, especially when Great Britain is included. For instance, the income of the average British citizen is 20 percent less than that of the average Frenchman or German, and Great Britain's average productivity rate is 40 percent and 20 percent lower than those in the United States and Germany, respectively (Faux, 1999).

Given the performance of the U.S. economy during the 1990s, the Washington Consensus (albeit with slight modifications) is likely to remain ascendant into the 21st century in the United States. Whether or not it eventually becomes the dominant model worldwide, however, remains in doubt. What is certain is that the negative externalities spawned by each model will continue to rest on the doorstep of this nation's public administrationists for years to come. Ensuring this are the continuing interdependence of global markets, the power of investor capitalism, and the dominant position of the United States as the world's sole remaining superpower.

Privatizing Regulation?

Likely to continue as well is the consensus among government and business elites on the need to standardize technological and environmental regulations for global markets to function effectively. Multinational corporations want the standardization of mass production lines that common standards permit. For cash-strapped governments, standardization can ease the enforcement and compliance costs of regulation.

Not only does this philosophical trend have special implications for public managers who are regulators, but it raises serious issues of public accountability because of who is setting these standards. Typically, world commercial standards are developed by international associations that comprise unelected representatives of business, government, and (less prominently) nongovernmental organizations (NGOs). Witness, for example, the International Standardization Organization (ISO) promulgation of product quality and environmental protection standards (viz., ISO 9000 and 14000 standards, respectively).

This development has both advantages and disadvantages. On the one hand, international standards may really be useful in breaking down protectionist barriers to trade. Moreover, they may ultimately have a leavening effect on lax product and environmental standards in both developed and developing countries. ISO certifications of compliance, in fact, could become marketing advantages for products, making regulatory compliance a business advantage. If these advantages do not pan out, however, the neoadministrative state will have to address any negative externalities that arise. Most prominent among these downside risks are the following: (a) a lack of regulatory vigilance (e.g., increased health costs from pollution), (b) a tendency to compromise standards to the lowest common denominator of quality or safety, and (c) a strategy to drive smaller competitors out of business by setting standards that are too costly for them to meet.

Certainly, nations could still raise standards above these minimums, but they risk "regulatory arbitrage" if they do so. But questions of success aside, shifting regulatory responsibilities to supranational bodies also raises the specter of a loss of democratic accountability and state sovereignty to firms and international bureaucratic elites (Dahl, 1999). As such, the proverbial question of "who guards the guardians" arises in a new venue and sets off questions for public administrationists about whether the fox is guarding the chicken coop.

The Democratic Deficit

During the 1990s a variety of civic commissions, academic associations, and private foundations tried to ascertain the reasons for, and what could be done about, the decline they perceived in civic trust, civic engagement, and civic identification with government in the United States.[2] These include the National Commission on Civic Renewal, the American Political Science Association's Task Force on Civic Education for the Next Century, the Bradley Foundation's National Commission on Philanthropy and Civic Renewal, the Pew Charitable Trusts, the National Civic League, and the Alliance for National Renewal. What are stunning and paradoxical about these, however, are how little attention they pay to the role that public agencies can play in this regard, how negative the perception of their role is when they do talk about public agencies, and how uninformed these perceptions are by recent empirical research (adapted from Durant, 1999a; for a more robust discussion of the image of public administration generally, see Thompson, 1999).

The Marginalizing of Public Agencies. Whenever panel members mention public agencies, they tend mostly to take a pejorative view, linking the nationalization of the administrative state (with its trained experts and professionals) to a failed attempt at building national community (see, for example, Schambra, 1997). Others talk of how the "credentialing" of elites has harmed civic engagement by making professional "credentialism" a precondition of becoming engaged in social or community services (Woodson, 1997). Even among those few who explicitly defend public agencies from these charges, most do so only indirectly by talking of the *state's* role in nurturing volunteer associations and other forms of social capital (Sirianni, 1997; Skocpol, 1997). Others among them concede that the "bigness" of the nation state (i.e., of the administrative state) inevitably produces diseconomies and inefficiencies of scale that also discourage citizen engagement (Nunn, 1997).

---

[2]This section borrows heavily from Durant, 2000b.

Thus, by design or inadvertence these task forces, commissions, and opinion leaders tend overwhelmingly to convey the impression that public agencies and the professionals who work within them are (a) unimportant to developing a policy savvy, politically astute, and engaged citizenry (hereafter referred to as developing "civic capital"), (b) decidedly less important than other sociocultural factors in producing it, (c) tangential to the work of governance as volunteer associations spring up to take their places, or (d) (and much less frequently) a primary reason for declines in the trust of government (Brehm and Rahn, 1997; Carter and Elshtain, 1997; Barr, 1998; Broder, 1998; Thompson, 1999).

To be sure, critiques of what size, credentialism, and expertise-based models of service delivery have done to disengage citizens from civic activities are valid in many respects and beg reform. What is puzzling to public administrationists, however, is this: How can the role of public agencies—for better or for worse—be either so marginalized or caricatured in today's public debates over building civic capital? Citizens, after all, have their primary interactions with government when they deal with street-level bureaucrats (from either the public, private, or nonprofit sector) (Lipsky, 1980). Public agencies also have long been excoriated for not taking their responsibility seriously enough to build civic capital (Frederickson, 1980, 1997; Gawthrop, 1984). On the other hand, bureaucracies at the local level of government across the United States—as well as many agencies at the federal level—have been engaged over the past decade in major efforts at collaborative policymaking and partnering within their communities (e.g., the Environmental Protection Agency, the Forest Service, and the Bureau of Land Management).

There also exists an insightful and growing research literature on involving citizen volunteers in public service delivery (Brudney, 1990). Many public agencies go beyond traditional citizen participation models and toward a true coproduction service ethic geared toward building civic capital (see, for example, Berry et al., 1993; John, 1994; Sirianni and Friedland, 1997; Farazmand, 1998; Harwood and Williams, 1998; Peters, 1998). Finally, recent research finds that higher levels of citizen influence over policy or trust in government exist in cities where public managers encourage high levels of citizen participation (Streib, 1990; Watson et al., 1991; Berman, 1997).

Thus, as elites in the United States look for ways to rebuild civic capital, they largely ignore the role that public agencies can, and increasingly do, play in this effort. This oversight seems likely to continue unabated, despite the efforts of some to induce the print and electronic media to pay attention to agency successes (e.g., Holzer and Callahan, 1998). Media indifference to positive news, as well as the perverse market incentives within the industry to focus on controversy and scandal, do not bode well for change (see, for example, Pearce, 1995).

A Dispirited Citizenry. Perhaps the best way to appreciate how far public confidence in the federal government fell over the last half of the 20th century is to examine trends in polling data between 1933 and 1999. Belief that too much power is concentrated in Washington has risen in public opinion polls from one-third agreeing with the statement to two-thirds routinely agreeing (Penn, 1999). Spiraling as well during this era was rhetorical support for minimalist government. Approximately 60 percent of respondents in a recent survey agreed that "the best government is that which governs least," compared to only 32 percent in 1973 (Penn, 1999). Since then, trust in the federal government "to do the right thing" had dropped by half. Significantly, there is also a generational divide that has implications for the future of the administrative state; younger Americans (18 to 29 years) are decidedly less trusting of elected officials than those over age 65. The former are also significantly less likely than their cohort of a generation earlier (26 percent to 58 percent) to feel that keeping up with public affairs is important (Galston, 1999).

The Rise of Interest Group Conservativism. Another noteworthy trend in philosophy that public opinion polls continue to show is a dramatic jump in the number of respondents who feel that government is run on behalf of special interests and is not interested in their thoughts and everyday problems (Penn, 1999). Although no doubt underestimating their own contributions as "special interests," citizens may partially be reflecting their interpretation of trends that promise to continue. Prominent in this regard are three developments: the dramatic growth of interest groups in Washington since 1970 (Berry, 1984), the increasing effort of corporations to influence public policy (and especially their large role in promoting the Washington Consensus), and the relative diminution of the power (both political and intellectual) of progressive NGOs as greater numbers of conservative NGOs are created (Faux, 1999). Again, this is not to suggest either conspiracy or untrammeled success by conservative actors. It is to say, however, that these trends do not bode well for a reframing of policy debates geared toward a return to the administrative state.

A Return to Exceptionalist Values?

The preceding changes in philosophy should not be interpreted as citizens rejecting the idea that government can play a positive role in their lives. Recall, for instance, how in 1996 and 1998 President Clinton's and the Democratic Congress's electoral successes hinged on portraying Republicans and their policies on education, welfare, and the environment as draconian. Instead, evidence abounds in surveys that citizens wish to *reframe* government's role in meeting society's needs, not end it (Penn, 1999). Neither are younger Americans satisfied with the condition of civic life in America, and those of all ages would like to see government promote more of it.

Respondents tend also and overwhelmingly to be unconvinced that business or volunteerism (individually or in cooperation) is capable by itself of meeting society's needs (Galston, 1999; Penn, 1999). Instead, nearly three-quarters of respondents agree that social problems facing Americans can best be handled by closer cooperation between government and voluntary associations (be they secular or faith-based). In turn, surveys tend to reveal that citizens are uncomfortable with prior nostrums touting either personal responsibility *or* societal responsibility for the fate of individuals (Penn, 1999). Thus, in place of either rights-based entitlements (the philosophy most associated with the positive state) or responsibility-based obligations (the philosophy of the minimal state), polls indicate increasing interest in a public philosophy stressing *fairness through reciprocity.* Equally attractive is replacing a "problem-centered" approach to human services with an "asset-centered" approach. Operationalized broadly, this reciprocity ethic stresses the following: Those who contribute to building civic society and capital are rewarded for it and those who benefit from it must give something back.

Most illustrative of this philosophy is the "welfare-to-work" component of today's welfare reform. Polls indicate that citizens are now increasingly favorable toward spending tax dollars on training welfare recipients now that a commitment to work and asset building is required and that time limits on benefits are in place. On the reward side of the "reciprocity" philosophy, programs using "time dollars" are illustrative. In return for civic engagement (e.g., helping others to read, counseling junior offenders, or helping senior citizens), participants can earn other types of assistance for themselves and their families or they can get discounts in stores (Cahn, 1999).

In effect, these data portray a pronounced proclivity toward and preference for what the neoadministrative state at its best can provide if done smartly: networks of individuals in communities where the dynamism of markets, the passion of volunteers, and the public service ethic of public managers are harnessed for public purposes. At its worst, however, the neoadministrative state is also capable of its own versions of crony capitalism, not the least of which can transpire in the awarding and inadequate performance monitoring of contracts. It also can cause volunteers and their civil service cohorts to be dispirited by handling their needs and insecurities insensitively or maladroitly (Brudney, 1990). Too, the neoadministrative state can further demoralize what remains of the civil service if the devolution of personnel decisions to agencies and front-line supervisors fails to protect merit principles in the process (West and Durant, 2000). Equally demoralizing for them would be a failure by the neoadministrative state to replace the employer-employee covenant it shreds (lower pay in exchange for job security) with a new covenant based on "employability" (Hammer, 1996). In the latter, civil servants would provide their commitment to public purposes in exchange for commitments from their government to invest in training that would make them more employable should their jobs be eliminated or outsourced (Durant, 1998).

The Revolt of the Judges?

The final change in philosophy is an emergent one with a highly uncertain future. Nonetheless, its implications for politicians and public administrationists are already noticeable worldwide and could flourish in the post–Cold War era. Put most simply, judges are beginning to apply the standards of international law to what were previously considered purely domestic concerns beyond their jurisdiction. Consider, for example, the recent extradition proceedings in Great Britain against the former Chilean dictator Augusto Pinochet. Some also see a "revolt of the judges" in the notable corruption trials of government officials in France, Italy, and Spain (Lagos and Munoz, 1999); still others see a global judicial network dedicated to these ends (Slaughter, 1999). Importantly, these trends could stretch beyond human rights violations toward international speculation and other forms of corruption by public managers as borders tumble and as interdependence spirals. Thus, at a time when public administrators in defense and other policy areas find themselves partnering domestically and internationally in the neoadministrative state, they may find not only their own but their partners' behavior the subject of international courts. As such, a major issue that will need sorting out in both the domestic and international legal arenas is the liability public managers hold for the actions of their partners. Whatever is decided, there is already empirical evidence to suggest that they will certainly be held liable in the "court" of public opinion when their partners fall short on their commitments (see, for example, Romzek and Dubnick, 1987; Vaughan, 1996; Durant, 1998; Durant, 1999b).

CONCLUSION

Applying John Gaus's analytical framework to assess the ecology of public administration as the 21st century dawns has revealed formidable choices, challenges, and opportunities for practice, research, and theory. Most notably, the three paradoxes related to capacity building, policy choice, and democratic accountability suggest that debates framed in terms of markets versus governments misstate the quintessential issues posed by the neoadministrative state. More apropos for the United States as it enters the 21st century are four questions: which bureaucracy, operated in whose interests, with what capacity, and held accountable to democratic values in what ways?

As such, public administrationists have three major tasks confronting them. First, and most notably, they must determine when and how best to link the dynamism of markets, the passion and commitment of volunteers and nonprofits, and the public service ethos of a deregulated and more flexible public service. Second, they must do this while ensuring that the values shared in a democracy (e.g., efficiency, effectiveness, due process, and accountability) are not lost in the process. Finally, they have an obligation and opportunity to commence a larger intellectual project to identify a normative theory of public administration, one that is more consonant with the values associated with American exceptionalism than public administrationists have marshaled in the past.

Gaining Synergies Smartly

This essay's review of trends and paradoxes suggests that learning how to attain the synergies that the neoadministrative state requires while protecting and advancing the values treasured in a democracy will not be easy. However, they also suggest that we have no choice but to try. Others, of course, might argue that public administrationists should merely wait for what they see as an untenable, illegitimate, and dangerous D^3 agenda or global economic order to fall of its own weight. They could be right. Yet anyone so inclined should recall that it took decades of perceived and actual failures, an information and telecommunications revolution, and the end of the Cold War to create forces strong enough to challenge the administrative state.

The trends recounted in this essay suggest that the D^3 agenda and the neoadministrative state appear resilient as the United States enters the 21st century. They have strong social and economic forces to buoy them (in this instance, the Third Wave), as well as powerful beneficiaries that will be loath to give them up easily (e.g., transnational corporations, corporate investors, and contractors). They also have successes to point to (e.g., welfare reform and economic resurgence in the United States and many developing countries), as well as secular electoral trends to enhance their chances of survival (e.g., Sunbelt migration patterns and the decline of Democratic party fortunes at all levels of government). Finally, they are premised on values consonant with those of American exceptionalism, a consistency that eludes existing competitors. Consequently, it appears that public administrationists need to engage the D^3 agenda and the neoadministrative state constructively, or else risk irrelevancy.

Fortunately, public administration has a storied and expanding wealth of knowledge that it can contribute to this enterprise. Space does not permit a full review of the lessons afforded by the trends reviewed in this essay. Neither does it permit a detailed review of what prior research already tells us about the conditions under which administrative reforms are more or less likely to succeed (for recent summaries, see Durant, 2000a, 2000b; Rainey and Steinbauer, 1999). Stated broadly, however, these efforts suggest that success in "constructive engagement" will go to those practitioners, researchers, and educators who can integrate both in persuasive ways. They will have to think

- about global opportunities, demands, and constraints and how public administration (PA) practice and research can address them
- about the intergenerational responsibilities and implications of PA practice
- cross-functionally, interorganizationally, and cross-nationally about the costs and benefits of PA practice
- "virtually" and technologically about how to practice PA more effectively for results and by unconventional means
- about the importance, strategies, and conditions best suited for reconnecting agencies with citizens

about how best to reengage limited capital, labor, and information resources for resetting and realizing priorities
about understanding, harnessing, and reframing for public purposes the disparate motivational factors driving the behavior of actors operating in different sectors
about maintaining transparency and public accountability in cross-sectoral networks and partnerships that grow increasingly more dense and opaque
about developing a new covenant with civil servants that is premised on training for "employability," "mobility," and "merit protection" rather than tenure and security
about the conditions under which various types of reforms are more or less likely to work as advertised and consistently with constitutional values
ethically, legally, and morally about the agency and personal liability or responsibility of public administrators operating in the neoadministrative state
that their actions and recommendations are no longer protected from international scrutiny
about the protean implications for democracy when governing responsibilities are shifted to *supranational* and *subnational* bodies
about how best to design, implement, and promote policies and programs in ways consonant with the values associated with American exceptionalism

Toward Reframing the Capacity Debate?

Railing against the rise of the neoadministrative state, lamenting the forces driving it, or pining for a return to business as usual in the administrative state might feel good. Unfortunately, this has done—and will continue to do—little to make calls for additional capacity building in public agencies compelling to most citizens or elected officials. Public administrationists will always find this a "hard sell" in a political culture shaped by the United States' "peculiar stateless origins" (Stillman, 1990), one steeped in antistatist sentiments and jaded by sometimes shattered expectations. More prudent perhaps would be an approach stressing the infinitely more critical role and contributions that vibrant public agencies *must* make if the neoadministrative state is to work effectively for Americans in the 21st century.

Reframing calls for capacity building on the basis of self-interest of network partners, citizens, and political officials is an appeal that is not unprecedented. But the tentacular metes and bounds of the neoadministrative state give them an unprecedented urgency and potential appeal. As implementation scholars have long known, chances of policy and program success decrease whenever the complexity of joint action increases (i.e., the greater the number of actors involved) (Pressman and Wildavsky, 1973). Equally debilitating to success is the tendency toward social entropy: Never design policies or programs that depend on extraordinary people to do heroic things over long periods (Bardach, 1977). The logic of the political process, of course, means that advice of this kind may be wise, but mostly beside the point. Rewards go to those who pass legislation first and worry about capacity later.

Yet the neoadministrative state seems especially prone to complexity and vulnerable to social entropy. Indeed, one need only review how difficult it has been to make partnership arrangements work and endure in the private sector to appreciate these points (Kanter, 1997). *Cross-sector* partnerships like those evolving for the neoadministrative state can only magnify these problems. Thus, not unlike in the private sector, neoadministrative prescriptions will only be as good as the weakest link in their implementation structures, with failures or embarrassments in service delivery redounding to no one's benefit in the network. Consequently, both corporate partners and elected officials may find that increasing the capacity of public agencies to deliver on their commitments is a decidedly more attractive option than it has been in the past. So too may they (and public unions) be more willing than in the past to recast the employment covenant in terms of employability. In the neoadministrative state, training may no longer work solely to the advantage of given public agencies; employees are likely to move back and forth among sectors during their careers.

At the same time, public administrationists have a strong and growing knowledge base from which to draw, one that other parts of the neoadministrative state need but lack. For example, if prominent business scholars like Kanter (1997) and Hammer (1996) are correct, private companies and nonprofits will need to learn to become more like public agencies in an era of investor capitalism and customer service (also see Whitman, 1999). Similarly, the generic models of management still dominant in business school curricula will prove too simplistic for private sector partners. Indeed, they will ignore public-private differences in the "ecology" of administration at their legal, political, and managerial peril. Employees working for private contractors still often fail to understand that their activities must comport with the written and unwritten standards that workers must adhere to in the public sector. And contracts have been lost in the process (O'Leary et al., 1999).

Toward a Normative Theory of Public Administration?

Opportunities to reframe debates about improving the capacity of public agencies and making the neoadministrative state work more effectively in democratically accountable ways are not the only ones that public administrationists can seize. The rise of the neoadministrative state also affords an opportunity for them to create a normative theory of public administration that is more consonant with America's exceptionalist values than those attempted previously to justify the administrative state. What is more, if framed adroitly, this normative theory might raise appreciably the chances of matching the structures and capacity of the public sector with the changing responsibilities heaped upon it.

Historically, public administrationists have attempted to legitimate the administrative state by treating it, successively, as an extension of the socioeconomic elite, of political parties, of professional expertise, and of the chief executive (Ingraham and Rosenbloom, 1990). Indeed, the founding fathers of the field were unabashed admirers of parliamentary systems, with their concentration of legislative and executive power in prime ministers and their parties (Rohr, 1986). With a few notable exceptions since then (e.g., Ostrom, 1989), public administration has been decidedly more prone to Hamiltonian than Madisonian justifications for the legitimacy of the administrative state.

The merits or demerits of this quest aside, a normative theory of public administration that passes muster with citizens and elected officials has proved elusive. Playing no small part in this failure to persuade, I would argue, has been the tendency to impose Hamiltonian visions on a Madisonian system informed by America's exceptionalist values. In contrast, public administration's critical role in a neoadministrative state seems decidedly more consonant with Madisonian and American exceptionalist values.

Certainly, public administration's role as catalyst for, and arranger and monitor of, the provision of goods, services, and opportunities to citizens is consistent with the virtues of community, decentralization, and self-help that American exceptionalism espouses. Moreover, when it catalyzes, arranges, and monitors programs premised on an ethic of reciprocity and asset building, public administration's role and efforts fit nicely with the American creed that Lipset (1996) identifies and that seems acutely on the minds of survey respondents today. Such a role or ethic, of course, will not always be the most suitable one for addressing citizen needs. But a public administration that empirically informs the conditions under which various service delivery and regulatory options are more likely to be effective and constitutionally grounded is also consistent with American pragmatism. As such, if a normative theory premised on these tenets of American exceptionalism is developed, public administration, in the 21st century, may yet regain the stature in statesmen's eyes that it enjoyed in the halcyon days of the New Deal as President Roosevelt laid the foundations for the administrative state.

REFERENCES

Barber, Benjamin R. (1996). *Jihad vs. McWorld: How Globalism and Tribalism Are Reshaping the World.* Ballantine Books, New York.

Bardach, Eugene (1977). *The Implementation Game: What Happens After a Bill Becomes a Law.* MIT Press, Cambridge, Mass.

Barr, Stephen. (1998). Vote of support for employees: Civil servants favored over politicians, 67 percent to 16 percent. *The Washington Post.* March 10, A15.

Berman, Evan M. (1997). Dealing with cynical citizens. *Public Administration Review.* *57*(2): 105–112.

Berry, Jeffrey M. (1984). *The Interest Group Society.* Little, Brown, Boston.

Berry, Jeffrey M., Portney, Kent E., and Thomson, Ken (1993). *The Rebirth of Urban Democracy.* The Brookings Institution, Washington, D.C.

Booth, William (1999). The battle for California: With a new script, the action's in the middle. *The Washington Post.* June 27, A01.

Brehm, John, and Rahn, Wendy, (1997). Individual-level evidence for the causes and consequences of social capital. *American Journal of Political Science. 41*(3): 999–1023.

Broder, David S. (1998). Trust in government edges up: state of nation, attitude toward leaders are key, survey finds. *The Washington Post.* March 10, A15.

Brudney, Jeffrey L. (1990). *Fostering Volunteer Programs in the Public Sector: Planning, Initiating, and Managing Voluntary Activities.* Jossey-Bass, San Francisco.

Cahn, Edgar S. (1999). Time dollars at work. *Blueprint. 3*(Spring): 62–65.

Carter, Lief H., and Elshtain Jean B. (1997). Task force on civic education statement of purpose. *PS: Political Science and Politics. XXX*(4): 745.

Chari, Raj S. (1998). Spanish socialists, privatising the right way? *West European Politics. 21*(4): 163–179.

Dahl, Robert A. (1999). *On democracy.* Yale University Press, New Haven, Conn.

Durant, Robert F. (1998). Agenda setting, the "Third Wave," and the administrative state. *Administration & Society. 30*(3): 211–247.

Durant, Robert F. (1999a). Missing links? Civic trust, civic capital, and public administration. *Journal of Public Affairs Education. 5*(2): 135–144.

Durant, Robert F. (1999b). The political economy of results-oriented management in the 'Neoadministrative State': Lessons learned from the MCDHHS experience. *American Review of Public Administration.* 29(4): 1–16.

Durant, Robert F. (2000a). A way out of no way? Strategy, structure, and the "New Governance." In *Handbook of Organizational Behavior* (Robert T. Golembiewski ed.), 2nd ed. Marcel Dekker, New York.

Durant, Robert F. (2000b). Whither the neoadministrative state: Toward a polity-centered theory of administrative reform. *Journal of Public Administration Research and Theory.* 10(1): 79–109.

Epstein, Cynthia F. (1999). The part-time solution and the part-time problem. *Dissent.* Spring: 96–98.

Etzioni, Amitai (1994). *The Spirit of Community: The Reinvention of American Society.* Touchstone Books, New York.

Farazmand, A. (1998). Building a community-based administrative state. Paper presented at the *Annual Meeting of the American Political Science Association.* Boston, September.

Faux, Jeff (1999). Lost on the Third Way. *Dissent.* Spring: 67–76.

Frederickson, H. George (1980). *The New Public Administration.* University of Alabama Press, Tuscaloosa.

Frederickson, H. George (1997). Facing the community. *The Kettering Review.* December: 28–37.

Friedman, Thomas L. (1999). *The Lexus and the Olive Tree.* Farrar, Straus & Giroux, New York.

Galston, William A. (1999). Where we stand. *Blueprint. 3* (Spring): 6–13.

Gaus, John (1947). *Reflections on Public Administration.* University of Alabama Press, Birmingham.

Gawthrop, Louis C. (1984). Civis, civitas and civilitas: A new focus for the year 2000. *Public Administration Review. 44:* 101–107.

Gawthrop, Louis C. (1997). Democracy, bureaucracy, and hypocrisy redux: A search for sympathy and compassion. *Public Administration Review. 57*(3): 205–210.

González, Felipe (1999). European union and globalization. *Foreign Policy.* Summer (115): 28–43.

Goodsell, Charles T. (1994). *The Case for Bureaucracy: A Public Administration Polemic.* Chatham House Publishers, Chatham, N. J.

The Government Performance Project (1999). *Government Executive.* February [http://www.govexec.com/gpp].

Greider, William (1997). *One World, Ready or Not: The Manic Logic of Global Capitalism.* Simon & Schuster, New York.

Hammer, Michael (1996). *Beyond Reengineering.* HarperBusiness, New York.

Harwood, P., and Williams, D. (1998). Collaborative planning in BLM. A different view of communities and the BLM. *Natural Resources & Environmental Administration. 19*(2): 5–7.

Holzer, Marc, and Callahan, Kathe (1998). *Government at Work: Best Practices and Model Programs.* Sage Publications, Thousand Oaks, Calif.

Ingraham, Patricia W., and Rosenbloom, David H. (1990). Political foundations of the American federal service: Rebuilding a crumbling base. *Public Administration Review. 50*(2): 210–219.

John, Dewitt (1994). *Civic Environmentalism: Alternatives to Regulation in States and Communities.* CQ Press, Washington, D.C.

Kanter, Rosabeth Moss (1997). *On the Frontiers of Management.* Harvard Business School Press, Boston.

Knott, Jack H., and Miller, Gary J. 1987. *Reforming Bureaucracy: The Politics of Institutional Choice.* Prentice-Hall, Englewood Cliffs, N.J.

Korten, David C. (1996). *When Corporations Rule the World.* West Hartford, Conn., Kumarian Press and Berret-Koehler Publishers, San Francisco.

Lagos, Ricardo, and Muñoz, Heraldo (1999). The Pinochet dilemma. *Foreign Policy.* Spring(114): 26–39.

Light, Paul C. (1999). *The True Size of Government.* The Brookings Institution, Washington, D.C.

Lilly, William, and Miller, James C. (1977). The new social regulation. *The Public Interest. 47*(Spring): 28–36.

Lipset, S. M. (1996). *American Exceptionalism: A Double-Edged Sword.* W. W. Norton, New York.

Lipsky, Michael (1980). *Street-Level Bureaucracy.* Russell Sage Foundation, New York.

Madrick, Jeffrey (1995). *The End of Affluence: The Causes and Consequences of America's Economic Dilemma.* Random House, New York.

Markusen, Ann (1999). The rise of world weapons. *Foreign Policy.* Spring(114): 40–51.

Meier, Kenneth J. (1997). Bureaucracy and democracy: The case for more bureaucracy and less democracy. *Public Administration Review. 57*(3): 193–199.

Milkis, Sidney M. (1993). *The President and the Parties: The Transformation of the American Party System Since the New Deal.* Oxford University Press, New York.

Milward, H. Brinton (1994). Implications of contracting out: New roles for the hollow state. In *New Paradigms for Government* (Patricia W. Ingraham, Barbara S. Romzek, and Associates). Jossey-Bass, San Francisco.

Milward, H. Brinton and Provan, Kenneth, G. (1993). The hollow state: Private provision of public services. In *Public Policy for Democracy,* (Helen M. Ingram and Steven R. Smith, eds). The Brookings Institution, Washington, D.C.

Nunn, S. (1997). Comments: National community and civil society. *National Commission on Civic Renewal.* January 4 [http://www.cpn.org/sections/new_citizenship/nccr-jan4.html].

Ohmae, Kenneth (1995). *The End of the Nation State: The Rise of Regional Economies.* Free Press, New York.

O'Leary, Rosemary, Durant, Robert F., Fiorino, Daniel J., and Weiland, Paul S. (1999). *Managing for the Environment: Understanding the Legal, Organizational, and Policy Challenges.* Jossey-Bass, San Francisco.

Ostrom, Vincent (1989). *The Intellectual Crisis in American Public Administration.* University of Alabama Press, Birmingham.

Ottaway, Marina (1999). Think again Africa. *Foreign Policy.* Spring(114): 13–25.

Pearce, D. D. (1995). *Wary Partners: Diplomats and the Media.* Congressional Quarterly, Washington, D.C.

Penn, Mark J. (1999). The community consensus. *Blueprint. 3*(Spring): 44–56.

Peters, B. Guy (1996). *Governing: Four Emerging Models.* University Press of Kansas, Lawrence.

Peters, B. Guy (1998). Community-based administrative state: A comparative perspective. Paper presented at the *Annual Meeting of the American Political Science Association.* Boston, September.

Peterson, Peter G. (1999). Gray dawn: The global aging crisis. *Foreign Affairs.* January/February: 42–55.

Pressman, Jeffrey L., and Wildavsky, Aaron B. (1973). *Implementation.* University of California Press, Berkeley.

Rainey, Hal G. (1996). *Understanding and Managing Public Organizations,* 2nd ed. Jossey-Bass, San Francisco.

Rainey, Hal G., and Steinbauer, Paula (1999). Galloping elephants: Developing elements of a theory of effective government organizations. *Journal of Public Administration Research and Theory. 9*(1): 1–32.

Rohr, J. B. (1986). *To Run a Constitution: The Legitimacy of the Administrative State.* University Press of Kansas, Lawrence.

Romzek, Barbara S., and Dubnick, Melvin J. (1987). Accountability in the public sector: Lessons from the Challenger tragedy. *Public Administration Review. 47*(3): 227–238.

Rosenberg, Tina (1999). The unfinished revolution of 1989. *Foreign Policy.* Summer(115): 91–105.

Rosenbloom, David H., and Ross, Bernard (1994). Administrative theory, political power, and government reform. In *New Paradigms for Government: Issues for the Changing Public Service* (Patricia Ingraham and Barbara S. Romzek, eds.). Jossey-Bass, San Francisco.

Saint-Martin, Denis (1998). How the reinventing government movement in public administration was exported from the US to other countries. Paper presented at the *Annual Meeting of the American Political Science Association.* Boston, September.

Sassen, Saskia (1999). Global financial centers. *Foreign Affairs.* January/February: 75–87.

Schambra, W. A. (1997). Comments: National community and civil society. *National Commission on Civic Renewal.* January 4 [http://www.cpn.org/sections/new_citizenship/nccr-jan4.html].

Sirianni, C. (1997). Comments from senior advisory council. *National Commission on Civic Renewal.* January 5 [http://www.cpn.org/sections/new_citizenship/nccr-jan5.html].

Sirianni, C., and Friedland, L. (1997). Civic innovation and American democracy. *Change Magazine. 29*(1), as reprinted at [http://www.cpn.org/sections/new_citizenship/change.html].

Skocpol, Theda (1997). Comments: National community and civil society. *National Commission on Civic Renewal.* January 4 [http://www.cpn.org/sections/new_citizenship/nccr-jan4.html].

Slaughter, Anne-Marie (1999). The long arm of the law. Pages 34–35 in Lagus, Ricardo, and Mañor, Heraldo (1999). The Pinochet dilemma. *Foreign Policy.* Spring (114): 26–39.

Smadja, Claude (1998–1999). The end of complacency. *Foreign Policy.* Winter(113): 67–71.

Speth, James Gustave (1999). The plight of the poor. *Foreign Affairs. 78*(3): 13–17.

Stillman, Richard J. (1990). *Preface to Public Administration: A Search for Themes and Direction.* St. Martins Press, New York.

Streib, G. (1990). Dusting off a forgotten management tool: The citizen survey. *Public Management. 72:* 17–19.

Thompson, Frank J. (ed.) (1999). Symposium on the advancement of public administration: Introduction. *Journal on Public Affairs Education. 5*(2).

Toffler, Alvin (1980). *The Third Wave.* Bantam Books, New York.

Van Dieren, Wouter (ed.) (1995). *Taking Nature into Account: A Report to the Club of Rome.* Copernicus, New York.

Vaughan, Diane (1996). *The Challenger Launch Decision: Risky Technology, Culture, and Deviance at NASA.* The University of Chicago Press, Chicago.

Wade, Robert (1998–1999). The coming fight over capital flows. *Foreign Policy.* Winter(113): 41–54.

Waldo, Dwight (1948). *The Administrative State: A Study of the Political Theory of American Public Administration.* Ronald Press, New York.

Waldo, Dwight (1980). *The Enterprise of Public Administration.* Chandler & Sharp, Novato, Calif.

Watson, D. J., Juster, R. J., and Johnson, G. W. (1991). Institutionalized use of citizen surveys in the budgetary and policy-making processes: A small city case study. *Public Administration Review. 51*(3): 232–239.

West, William F., and Durant, Robert F. (2000). Merit, management, and neutral competence: Lessons from the U.S. Merit Systems Protection Board, FY 1988-FY 1997. *Public Administration Review.* 60(2): 111–122.

Whitman, Marina v.N. (1999). *New World, New Rules: The Changing Role of the American Corporation.* Harvard Business School Press, Boston.

Wilson, Graham K. (1990). *Business and Politics: A Comparative Introduction.* Chatham House Publishers, Chatham, N.J.

Woodson, R. (1997). Comments: Social trust and civic engagement. *National Commission on Civic Renewal.* January 2 [http://www.cpn.org/sections/new_citizenship/nccr-jan2.html].

Zahariadis, Nikolaos (1995). *Markets, States, and Public Policy: Privatization in Britain and France.* University of Michigan Press, Ann Arbor.

2

Global Economic Changes and Public Management

Susan J. Tolchin and Kenneth E. Cox
School of Public Policy, George Mason University, Fairfax, Virginia

The purpose of this chapter will be to provide an appreciation of the nature of global economic change and suggest roles for public managers in this critical area of public policy.

A number of issues highlight the urgent need for revising the role of U.S. public managers to heighten their impact on issues affecting international competitiveness in the era of globalization. They involve clarifying roles to prevent duplication, eliminating entities that do not work, removing barriers that inhibit business development, and widening opportunities wherever possible to enhance technology. However, in the euphoria of globalization, one issue remains paramount and must be kept in perspective: maintaining our national security.

This chapter will briefly review the impact of global economic change in its various guises, discuss the current forces behind them, and cite some specific cases in which governance has been beneficial or lacking. The final section will discuss the impacts and implications to the profession and present some suggestions to integrate the United States into the emerging world economy better, while protecting that security.

THE COX REPORT AND GLOBALIZATION

As the 20th century drew to a close, the startling Congressional Select Committee report *U.S. National Security and Military/Commercial Concerns with the People's Republic of China* (the "Cox Report") revealed that the People's Republic of China had spirited away vital U.S. technology critical to the nation's present and future military security.[1] Americans, comfortably cosseted in an environment of unprecedented growth and political stability, virtually ignored the Cox Report, whose limited impact belied its crucial warning.

It was the "worst scandal in terms of transfer of deadly technology to a potential enemy of the United States since the Rosenbergs transferred the atomic bomb secret to Josef Stalin back in the 1940s," according to Rep. Dana Rohrabacher (Republican, California). (National Security Council, 1999: 1), and "Aldrich Ames [another spy] sold us out for a mess of pottage" (de Graffenreid, 1999: foreword).

The report was issued in the wake of a massive body of evidence indicating that critical technologies, owned and developed in the United States, found their way to China via routes with more twists than the old Silk Road: old-fashioned spying, lax export licensing procedures, and perfectly straightforward, legal Chinese investment in U.S. high-tech companies. One company was actually purchased by a Chinese general's daughter, who was savvy enough to contribute to the first Clinton presidential campaign.

But in contrast to the dangers that beset the caravans of old, modern adventurers pirated American technology with a relatively free hand. "American lapses and even American policies have [actually] helped the [People's Republic of China] PRC leaders pursue their strategy" (de Graffenreid, 1999: introduction).

What actually happened? How did heretofore arcane U.S. trade policy affect national security? And why should Americans care? Ironically U.S. taxpayers financed the purloined technology, much of it classified, which ended up off limits to those citizens who bankrolled it in the first place.

Other charges in the Cox Report included the following disclosures:

The People's Republic of China had stolen designs of the United States's most advanced thermonuclear weapons: This meant that classified information was stolen from the national laboratories, allowing the PRC to "design, develop, and successfully test . . . strategic nuclear weapons sooner than would otherwise have been possible." These thefts allegedly began in the late 1970s and continued until the mid-1990s (de Graffenreid, 1999: 2).

The PRC also stole "classified information for neutron bomb warheads": This information came from the Lawrence Livermore Laboratory, although other national labs (Sandia, Los Alamos, and Oak Ridge) have also suffered from lax security (de Graffenreid, 1999: 3–4).

"The stolen nuclear secrets give the PRC design information on thermonuclear weapons on a par with our own": The committee estimated that this would give the PRC the ability to build the next generation of mobile intercontinental ballistic missiles (ICBMs), which would be used to transport small nuclear warheads (Cox, 1999: 5, 6).

The Cox Report was not the last word on the issue of the Chinese's acquiring nuclear secrets. In its wake, additional investigations are being pursued by federal agents into evidence of espionage and a search for alternative explanations to ascertain the who, what, and when of the purported leaks (Risen and Johnson, 1999: A1).

Of greatest concern to members of Congress as well as the Executive Branch were the geopolitical questions raised by the Cox Report. Is China an enemy or a friendly trading partner? When Clinton renewed China's status as a most-favored nation in 1998, this politically explosive issue seemed resolved: China was to be officially regarded as a benign trading partner, with all the potential benefits that only 1 billion consumers can confer. American companies looked forward to long and fruitful relationships; Loral and the Hughes companies openly traded technology, including ballistic missile technology, to their later distress as the environment boomeranged between China as friend and foe.

In other words, if China was receiving the treatment of a friendly trading partner, why did she violate the Comprehensive Test Ban Treaty in order to accelerate her nuclear capability? Are Chinese consumers buying Coca-Cola or warheads, and what is the difference? And why did the PRC engage in this "aggressive espionage campaign" in the first place—especially since so much technology was so easily accessible on the open marketplace, thanks to lax security at the national labs, unevenly applied and ill-conceived export controls, and for all practical purposes, no serious limits on foreign direct investment even for national security purposes (Tolchin and Tolchin, 1992; Milhollin and Richie, 1999).

Nipping at the heels of the adamant White House policy are also the nagging issues of human rights. Memories of troops firing on the students in Tiananmen Square remain fresh in the minds of Americans, thanks to congressional critics and interest groups like Amnesty International; dissidents are jailed regularly by Chinese leaders; and promises of enhanced democracy through enhanced trade appear hollow.

GOVERNANCE AND THE PUBLIC SECTOR

The relationship between trade and national security assumes a different dimension when examined from the perspective of the public sector. Despite the academic and media hoopla, "globalization" has become a meaningless mantra, whose rhetoric has twisted reality. Indeed, the appealing concepts of "free trade," "free markets," and "open borders" have overtaken the issues of governance that provide the critical balance to some of globalization's unfortunate consequences—in this case the hemorrhage of nuclear technology to an unfriendly power.

Who cannot support the concepts of "free trade" and "free markets"? They are especially appealing to Americans, whose national identity embraces notions of an expanding frontier, unlimited economic opportunity, and democratic ideology that rests on the word *freedom*.

In a global context, where does government fit in? Money crosses borders with the speed of light; international transactions dwarf the economies of most countries; mergers and acquisitions wield far more influence on national economies than elections or laws; and multinational corporations wield far more power than the vast majority of the world's governments. If political leaders find themselves irrelevant, where do public managers fit into this buccaneer global environment?

On July 16, 1999, for example, the Microsoft stock holdings of Bill Gates, the company's founder and CEO, exceeded $100 billion, making him richer than most nations, ninth, in fact, ahead of Spain, whose gross national product was slightly more than half of Gates's portfolio (Harmon, 1999: B1).

Is government as we know it becoming irrelevant? If not, what are the new roles for public managers in this rapidly changing environment? Most important: Is there a U.S. national interest worth protecting, and what role should public managers play in preserving those interests?

A number of issues confront U.S. public managers and analysts as they struggle to resolve this basic dilemma: how to merge globalization and governance so that they do not conflict. And on a positive note: how to elevate government's role to enhance national competitiveness in an era of rapidly evolving global change.

Leaders in the United States have functioned for too long on the assumption that because internationalization is incompatible with national interests, those interests must be sacrificed in the name of progress. This is why international agreements like North American Free Trade Agreement (NAFTA) and the General Agreement on Tariffs and Trade (GATT) virtually ignore the role of government agencies, trusting instead to the mysterious forces of the marketplace. Members of

Congress were given 48 hours to read and ratify the GATT treaty, a 1000-page document (with 20,000 pages of supporting material). Similarly, few members of Congress either read or understood the consequences of their votes for the World Trade Organization (WTO), which divided power equally among all signatories, giving America the same vote as Costa Rica. Democratic, to be sure; but why wasn't the structure of the world's major trading organization modeled after the United Nations, which vests the lion's share of power with the major powers in the Security Council?

Why did Congress vote unquestioningly for the abdication of its own power, fraught as it was with so much uncertainty for government agencies, U.S. national sovereignty, and industrial competitiveness? Most likely because members bought the theory that government doesn't matter in the new world order, and that market forces will take on a life of their own that will obviate the need for public management.

As the Cox Report and many incidents before and since have shown, current laissez-faire policies do not address national needs, particularly when military security is at stake. Only the public sector can bridge that gap. There is today an urgent need not for more investigations, but for public managers to revise their role from passive observers to active and practical participants. In that spirit, they must fight

- To clarify their own and their agencies' roles to prevent duplication
- To remove barriers that unnecessarily inhibit business development and technological advancement
- To enforce existing laws vigorously to protect military security
- To trust but verify the forces of the international marketplace

ACADEMIC CONTRIBUTIONS TO GLOBALIZATION POLICY

On a theoretical level, analysts of globalization have made significant contributions to understanding this phenomenon, mostly from an economic perspective. A great deal of opportunity remains for political scientists to add the governance perspective to the current body of literature.

The most common terms—*globalization, interdependence, interconnectedness,* and *transgovernmentism*—relate to global economic change and the structures that govern it.

Briefly, globalization involves a dynamic ongoing process involving the integration of markets, nation states, and technologies to a degree never witnessed before. At its best, this process enables individuals, corporations, and governments to extend their reach around the world more rapidly and cheaply than ever before (Friedman, 1999: 7). The cross-border movement of capital—in the form of finance, technology, and information—changes the competitive environment and triggers supranational governance, as witness the creation of the WTO and regional agreements like NAFTA (Sanholtz and Sanholtz, 1998).

Another popular concept, interdependence, is also characterized in terms of economic exchanges, specifically, "situations . . . [involving] reciprocal effects among countries or among actors in different countries" (Keohane and Nye, 1989: 8). These "effects" flow from international transactions, such as flows of money, goods, technology, and people across international boundaries. The gradual disappearance of boundaries among the European nations, for example, significantly increases these flows, which in turn boost the commerce of the region.

Current literature retains the distinctions among interdependence, interconnectedness, and globalization. Interdependence occurs when there are reciprocal effects among transactions, Japan's dependence on a continual flow of oil from the Middle East, for example. This term also denotes a quantitative trend that means closer macroeconomic cooperation among sovereign states. Interconnectedness, on the other hand, involves luxury goods, which are dispensable. To complicate matters further, globalization involves microeconomic cooperation that represents a qualitative change in the international system (Reinicke, 1997).

The term *transgovernmentalism* has also gained prominence in the discussion about the fast-moving global environment. This is basically a process by which subnational governmental units, such as courts, regulatory agencies, and legislatures, work closely with their counterparts in other countries. Many government institutions have formed networks of their own, such as the Balse Committee of Central Bankers, or informal ties among law enforcement agencies, which can then work on mutual problem solving as well as international cooperation.

The important point to remember is that globalization is not new; in fact, many scholars today date the birth of globalization more than 500 years back in time. The explosion of science and technology during the Renaissance, coupled with the invention of modern banking, set in motion a process that is accelerating today more rapidly than ever before. The explorations that began in the 15th century brought the Americas and the far side of Asia into the then-global market that centered on Europe and the eastern Mediterranean (Joffe, 1999).

As stock markets tumbled around the world in 1875, Baron Carl Mayer von Rothschild declared, "The world is a city." Indeed, from a historical perspective, globalization may be older than nationalism (Kristof, 1998: 5).

The resurgence of globalism at the turn of the new century was jump-started primarily by the end of the Cold War and the advent of the digital revolution. The elimination of the confrontation between the Soviet Union and the United States freed both nations of their political burdens and allowed them—not to mention the rest of the world—to pursue their economic goals.

Advances in computer and telecommunications technology have also been powerful engines of change. Widely accessible and affordable technology has broken government monopolies on the collection and management of information and deprived them of the deference they enjoyed only because of their monopolistic control. Seven years ago, a 10-minute telephone call to the United States from Germany cost over $50, thanks to the government monopoly of telecommunications. Today, that same call costs a fraction of that amount. Multiply that by tens of millions and the savings for corporations—not to mention their trade and investment opportunities—are incalculable. In every sphere of activity, instantaneous access to information and the ability to put it to use multiply the number of players who matter and reduce the number who can dominate decisions (Matthews, 1997).

The academic discussion on globalization still focuses on the exchange of goods across borders and gives short shrift to governance structures that negotiate those transactions. In fact, the advent of the information age has eroded the power of individuals, nations, and old hierarchies (Wriston, 1997). Conversely, organizations such as the United Nations cannot function effectively without the support of the major powers; nor will those nations cede their power and sovereignty to an international institution (Slaughter, 1997).

The driving force behind globalization remains free-market capitalism, with its implicit faith in the rule of the market, an open economy, and the forces of international competition (Friedman, 1999: 8). If all these factors are allowed to flourish unencumbered—a process that often involves deregulating and privatizing government industries—then the economy of a nation will operate at optimal efficiency.

The field remains wide open for scholars to bridge the gap between globalism and governance. Too many problems have arisen from these theoretical deficiencies; how else can the Cox Report be explained?

TRADE POLICY AND U.S. NATIONAL SECURITY

The Redistribution of Power

National governments around the world suddenly find themselves sharing power with states, businesses, international organizations, and nongovernmental citizens' organizations, known as NGOs (Matthews, 1997). Nigerian women doctors, for example, banded together to force their government to honor the commitments on women's health that their delegates agreed to at United Nations conferences from Mexico City to Copenhagen. Farmers in the parched Sudan bitterly complain about the privatization of water and other policies they regard as unduly harsh imposed by the International Monetary Fund (IMF) and the World Bank.

The trend persists in the industrialized world as well, albeit in different forms. Job-seeking state governments in America have set up offices around the world, mostly in Tokyo, Seoul, and Europe, to attract foreign investment and promote domestic exports. They neither sought nor wanted permission from Washington and were grateful for the freedom from regulatory constraint.

The absence of a national presence also meant no coordinating mechanism existed to evaluate whether Komatsu's investment of a U.S. branch of its earthmoving equipment company in Tennessee hurt the Caterpillar and John Deere companies in the Midwest. No matter: The international environment bypassed Washington, elevating state and local governments over national government in many areas of trade policy.

Criticism of this development arose from two sources. Governors of many states banded together to try to induce the federal government to slow down the bidding war that pitted them against each other as foreign investors waited them out. On the state and local levels, budget watchdogs objected to the high costs of these bidding wars (Tolchin and Tolchin, 1988). Does the attraction of investment through state "incentives" (i.e., new roads, special education programs, tax breaks) rob the taxpayer, as Kentucky was accused of doing when it spent $125 million attracting Toyota to the town of Georgetown? The governor, then Martha Layne Collins, responded that she would rather subsidize development than welfare.

Globalization also tends to dominate relationships among advanced industrial countries. The increased focus on financial regulations and health, environmental, and safety standards in the European Community (EC) is a good example of this process, although the EC is unique among the world's regions in its concern for health and welfare.

Interdependence remains the rule for industrializing countries. Although the artifacts of "external sovereignty"—such as collecting tariffs, altering exchange rates, and maintaining territorial interests—remain important in determining foreign policy, the state is hardly withering away (Reinicke, 1997). In fact, the role of the state in Europe has grown in the areas of regulation and expenditures (Joffe, 1999).

Preserving Critical Industries

The Cox Report raised the curtain once again in 1999 on the perennial issue of preserving information critical to the nation's security and industrial base. Not a new problem by any means, preserving the nation's technological edge remains a major area of U.S. policy still subject to considerable abuse. In the 1990s alone, the United States experienced a serious crisis in its efforts to guard industries vital to the nation's military security and international competitiveness. Dozens of studies, emanating from government agencies that sought to address these problems, documented the erosion of the nation's technological dominance, which spelled future problems for industries that relied on those technologies to maintain their competitive edge. The Commerce Department, for example, reported in 1990 that the United States was losing ground to Japan, in all but 3 of 12 key technologies

(U.S. Dept of Commerce: 1990); other agencies followed suit with similar warnings about semiconductors, aerospace, robotics, and a host of other industries and technologies. Their findings were buttressed by private blue-ribbon groups representing industry, such as the Council on Competitiveness. The price of ignoring these reports was high in terms of lost jobs, lost national income, lost market share, a lower standard of living, and an increase in the annual trade deficit and national debt.[2]

Accompanying these technological losses were data showing the shrinking industrial base, again documented extensively by government agencies but largely ignored by the White House throughout recent Republican and Democrat administrations. Once the world's leader in the manufacture of machine tools and industrial machinery, for example, the United States watched its worldwide market steadily decline in favor of German and Japanese companies. Similar patterns tracked autos, semiconductors, aerospace, and photolithography. The semiconductor industry alone, for example, saw its market share fall from 57 to 35 percent in the decade of the 1980s.[3] In the late 1990s, the machine tool industry showed signs of reviving.

Another agency, the Department of Defense (DoD), entered the critical industry debate with two riveting reports (U.S. Dept. of Defense, 1988a, 1988b), both issued during the waning months of the Reagan administration. These reports sharply diverged from official White House policy in their criticism of escalating foreign acquisition of vital U.S. assets, and both recommended substantial changes in U.S. trade, technology, and investment policies to preserve the assets in the interest of national security. *Bolstering Economic Competitiveness,* the more controversial of the two DoD studies, ventured bravely into an area that has since become mainstream thinking: the close link between military and economic security (U.S. Dept. of Defense, 1988a)—or military and trade policy. Supported by the prestigious Center for Strategic and International Studies, high-ranking Pentagon officials specializing in acquisition reform argued strongly for halting the steady erosion of the nation's defense industrial base (Center for Strategic and International Studies, 1989: 5).

Thanks to the vigorous activities of federal agencies, the public's awareness rose to new heights, and economic competitiveness became an important part of the national agenda. It was all the more remarkable that these agencies were able to defend their view as strongly as they did, because they faced the heated opposition of the administrations of Ronald Reagan and George Bush, both equally committed to laissez-faire trade policies. "In my view there is no difference between [industries representing] computer chips and potato chips," said a Bush appointee, in a remark that soon became widely reported. Whether the statement was apocryphal or not—no one has ever documented who said it or when, but neither did the White House ever deny it—it accurately represented the prevailing philosophy that the marketplace could select critical industries more accurately than government bureaucrats. Contrary to popular impression, the private sector was sharply divided on this issue, with some companies' putting more faith in government than the marketplace. Immediately after the computer chips/potato chips episode, Andrew Grove, president of Intel, one of the nation's leading semiconductor manufacturers, sent a gift-wrapped violin to the Office of Management and Budget director, Richard Darman, an allusion to Nero and the burning of Rome.[4]

The Iron Triangle Strategy

Failing to get the attention of the White House, several key agencies traveled to familiar corners of the iron triangle for support. Backed by interest groups representing the semiconductor, defense, and electronics manufacturers, the Pentagon, along with the Department of Energy and other agencies (including several major government labs), received substantial backing from Capitol Hill. One of their earliest and most vocal supporters was Senator Jeff Bingaman, Democrat from New Mexico, who sponsored legislation requiring DoD to identify critical industries and report on their status every year. Setting the stage for a national debate on what government should do about protecting its critical industries, Bingaman asked: "If semiconductors are [a critical industry], should we be disturbed when Monsanto sells the only silicon-wafer production plant in the U.S. to a German firm? . . . [or what] about the Hitachi-Texas Instruments joint venture on sixteen-megabit D-RAMS?" (Tolchin and Tolchin, 1992: 28).

Bingaman's efforts were buttressed by the Office of Technology Assessment, which reported that U.S. "technological superiority . . . is not crumbling, but over the last decade had weathered considerably . . . with foreign companies (making) deep inroads into high technology markets" (U.S. Congress, Office of Technology Assessment, 1990). Unfortunately, although Congress could mandate reports, it could not implement them: For 4 years, both Energy and the Pentagon issued studies ordered by Congress documenting America's eroding technological base, including in their data rankings of where U.S. technologies stood in relation to the major industrial nations. The reports emerged with great fanfare but soon faded into obscurity, continuing to gather dust in the very places they were shelved.

It was natural that the Pentagon found itself in the first line of defense in the competitiveness wars because in the natural course of implementing its programs it was bound to confront shortages traced directly to technological losses. The Gulf War, for example, revealed the true cost of what DoD officials termed "dangerous dependence": specifically, when defense officials reported being put in the embarrassing position of beseeching the French and Japanese embassies to speed components for military equipment in the Gulf War (Auerbach, 1991: A1). For the first time since Pearl Harbor, the United States found its military readiness seriously compromised by equipment shortages: Parts for display terminals used to analyze intelligence data, video panels, as well as vital components for search and rescue radios and navigational systems represented just a few of the items missing from the arsenal of democracy. There was also no question that recent budget pressures had contributed to defense dependence in two respects: (a) by discouraging the Pentagon from maintaining the kind of stockpiles necessary in wartime and (b) by promoting the purchase of foreign supplies and equipment, particularly if they were cheaper than American products (General Accounting Office, 1991).

Throughout the decade of the 1980s and the early 1990s, the debate continued over what role government should have in balancing trade and military needs. Policymakers belatedly recognized the need to strengthen their own roles, if only to compete with foreign governments, who typically backed their companies with large doses of subsidies, tax breaks, low-cost loans, government grants, money for research and development, and protection against overseas competitors. None of America's major trade competitors wasted any time dithering over "industrial policy" with such high stakes at risk. The focus sharpened in 1992, when two U.S. multinationals, Lockheed and Martin Marietta, were outbid by a French government–owned company, Thomson CSF, in the attempted purchase of the missile and aerospace division of LTV. The public outcry about a foreign-owned company's purchasing technology supported by the U.S. taxpayer eventually led Thomson to withdraw its offer, but not without considerable cost to U.S.-French relations. Perhaps influenced by this experience, Lockheed and Martin Marietta merged several years later into a new company, Lockheed Martin, leaving both companies better prepared in terms of size to meet their global competition. Many other companies also merged throughout the 1990s, triggered by a lax antitrust environment, competition from the *keiretsu* and other *keiretsu*-sized conglomerates in other parts of the world, and the knowledge that government would remain committed to laissez-faire trade policies and neither help nor hurt them.

The Message of the FSX Venture

The Thomson case should not have surprised anyone, since a similar crisis had erupted over the FSX joint aircraft venture between the United States and Japan 4 years before. Both imbroglios stemmed from the uncertainty of where agencies stood vis-à-vis the curious mix of trade, investment, and technology policies. Thomson was initially decided in the unlikely venue of a New York City bankruptcy court, which rendered its verdict in Thomson's favor—on the basis of protecting shareholders' assets. The FSX, on the other hand, dealt with federal involvement from the beginning, although the outcome was just as dissatisfying in terms of the relevant agencies' inability to meet the challenges of protecting U.S. interests in a global environment. The FSX dispute highlighted how agencies were forced to render critical decisions with outmoded, ad hoc, and fragmented structures. The pattern became all too familiar, involving public conflict, battles among the agencies over turf, and congressional intervention. In the final analysis, the United States became embroiled in an intense international conflict with a valued ally, sacrificed trade in favor of foreign policy interests, and compromised the global competitiveness of precious technologies—some of them developed with the help of U.S. taxpayers—in the process. All these problems stemmed from the lack of readiness of the agencies involved, all of whom suffered to some extent from mixed mandates, confusion over trade and technology policy, and multiplicity of actors.

The FSX began in the early 1980s as a routine joint production and development agreement between defense officials in Japan and in the United States to build the next generation of advanced fighter planes. Bilateral agreements of this kind, called *Memoranda of Understanding,* are common, and no one foresaw any problems, especially since previous generations of U.S. fighter aircraft had all been built with foreign components (Tolchin and Tolchin, 1992: 71–114). Almost without warning, the FSX exploded in the United States as a trade and competitiveness issue, flagged by a number of groups who saw the agreement as yet another Japanese trade victory, threatening the aerospace industry—which at that time boasted a healthy export surplus—with the same fate (invented here, produced abroad) as videocassette recorders (VCRs) and semiconductors. The mounting trade deficit with Japan, which by 1989 had risen to well over $50 billion a year and increased thereafter, only exacerbated the issue. (By 1999, the trade deficit with Japan was just as bad, even though the Japanese economy was plagued with slow growth and unemployment.)

The most interesting question for public managers involved the divergent role of U.S. agencies in their futile attempts to manage this crisis. What emerged was a curious picture of U.S. technological superiority, on the one hand, set off against a decidedly inadequate government bureaucratic response on the other.

Perhaps more than any other crisis of the last decade, the FSX showed that competitiveness was a governance issue at least as much as it was an economic one. Unquestionably, the Japanese government demonstrated that its agencies were far better able to defend and promote local industries because top priority was accorded to technological advancement, economic growth, and continuing growth of international markets. Japanese bureaucrats also broadened participation by including representatives from trade and the budget ministries in defense negotiations and, despite their internal struggles, went to the bargaining table with a united front. Ironically, Japan won the trade battle but lost the economic war. Many blamed the very bureaucrats who had so effectively fought industrial battles for their rigidity in moving with the flows of the world economy in the late 1990s.

In contrast to the Japanese, Pentagon negotiators from the Defense Security Assistance Agency (DSAA) negotiated the agreement in a total vacuum, acting solely on the basis of military criteria; no other agencies were consulted except the Department of State, which routinely supported the Pentagon's efforts. Why, asked DSAA officials, should they consult other agencies? DSAA holds primary responsibility for negotiating international agreements, and nothing in DSAA's mandate, enabling legislation, or instruction from their leaders indicated any reason for changing the agency's normal pattern of doing business. Initially approached by Japanese officials on instructions from the White House, DSAA representatives proceeded to negotiate as they had in the past, without input from Commerce, the U.S. Trade Representative, or any other agencies. They insisted they got the best deal possible and charged they were blind-sided by "trade hawks" (their term) from the Commerce Department.

The trade hawks were energized by their own agency's studies documenting Japan's extensive economic victories over the United States. They felt they should have been included at the bargaining table when defense issues affecting trade were being discussed; after all, officials from the Japanese Ministry of International Trade and Industry (MITI) were present from the very beginning of the FSX negotiations in Japan. Commerce's request for FSX information was answered by a flat no from DSAA, an easy response from a first-tier agency (Defense) with far greater prestige and power than Commerce.

Ignored by Defense, Commerce then recruited its own allies in Congress and the media. Stung by ensuing outcry, newly elected President Bush temporarily withdrew the agreement. While he regrouped his forces, widely publicized hearings were held in the House and the Senate during which an acrimonious trade dispute erupted between the United States and Japan (U.S. Congress, House of Representatives, *Congressional Record,* 1989; U.S. Congress, Senate, *Congressional Record,* 1989). The deal eventually was consummated with slightly better terms for the United States—namely, a greater share of production and development—but at a considerable cost in international prestige. The venture has been plagued with problems ever since.

Ironically, the qualities that fostered technical innovation in the United States worked against it in individual trade disputes. Instead of cooperating to facilitate industrial development, agencies squared off against each other with little direction from the White House. Defense and State publicly battled Commerce, the General Accounting Office (GAO), and a host of other agencies as well as Congress, with an assortment of actors all airing their differences while they vied for turf. In one of the most interesting sidelights of this issue, it appeared that Defense Department officials had never even met their counterparts in Commerce; in fact, their enduring relationships with bureaucrats from the Japan Defense Agency and retired Japanese military officials appeared much stronger than any other linkages with managers from any other U.S. agencies. One Defense official even blamed the problems with the FSX on the fact that Commerce had never developed alliances with MITI to parallel their own connections with the Japanese military.

There is also no doubt that the United States was hurt by the inadequacy of its technical assessment capability. For years, Senator Bingaman had tried to establish such an office in Tokyo for the purpose of averting such "technology surprises," as well as improving the sharing of information between U.S. industry and government. The funds were there, but at the time of the FSX dispute, no such information gathering capability existed.

When Congress entered the struggle, it fanned the flames of controversy but was unable to override the president's objections. As the most visible targets, the agencies were blamed, but unfairly so; consider how they were forced to act in a swiftly changing international environment with tools that were grossly inadequate.

The FSX served as a prototype for similar trade disputes, revealing various public sector inadequacies.

Mixed Mandates

Commerce and Defense both felt responsible for addressing the nation's concerns but relied on very different and unconnected mandates: economic promotion for Commerce, military alliances and arms sales for Defense. Neither Congress nor the president had seen fit to change these mandates, either formally or informally, forcing the agencies to expose their differing perspectives before a global audience. Today, despite all the rhetoric linking military and economic security, the turf battles continue—although now they have somewhat abated—and the mandates remain unchanged with everything still riding on White House involvement and philosophy.

Confusing Boundaries

Hazy boundary lines between trade and technology also cloud the nation's governance structures. How can the United States react in a timely fashion to a global environment with agencies best suited to an isolationist era? Is avionics considered technology or trade? The answer is both, of course, but what does that mean for agencies like Defense, whose mandate clearly calls for supporting the *defense* industrial base? (Many products share both military and civilian uses; in fact, companies were encouraged by the Clinton administration's emphasis on "dual use" policy to reduce their Defense dependency, in favor of products that can also sell in commercial markets.) In this light, it is easy to see what happened to the agencies in the FSX crisis: The Pentagon saw the FSX as defense related, whereas Commerce viewed the joint venture not only as a trade issue, but also as a serious problem of technology transfer. The Commerce argument held sway with those who made a convincing case that Japan planned to use FSX avionics technology to start its own military aircraft industry, while some argued that Japanese industries intended to transpose the technology to build airbuses or other civilian products.

Multiplicity of Actors

Over 25 people from at least four key agencies had key responsibilities for the FSX venture, some with fairly low-level status within their agencies, and others with absolutely no relationship to each other. What was the U.S. Trade Representative throughout the FSX debate? Treasury? The cabinet secretaries? They all eventually weighed in late in the game, but only after the issue had exploded into a full-fledged crisis.

Exon-Florio and the CFUIS Challenge

Finally, in the wake of the FSX, an agency emerged with new tools that promised to address the knotty issues that combined trade, economic competitiveness, technology, and military security. Through passage of the Exon-Florio Amendment to the 1988 Omnibus Trade and Competitiveness Act, Congress vested the president with the authority to prevent foreign acquisitions of critical technologies that imperiled national security, without having to resort to the drastic measures involved in declaring a national emergency.[5] If Exon-Florio were truly operative, perhaps the events leading to the Cox Report would never have occurred.

Acting under the misguided presumption that the president would follow the legislative mandate, members of Congress vested the implementation power in an interagency committee housed in the Treasury Department, the Committee on Foreign Investment in the United States (CFIUS). Created in 1975 to respond to concerns that foreign investors from the Middle East were purchasing too many U.S. companies, the new and improved CFIUS was beefed up to respond to its increased responsibilities under Exon-Florio; it included in its ranks representatives from Defense, Treasury, Commerce, the Central Intelligence Agency, and assorted other agencies, depending on which issue was under consideration (Tolchin and Tolchin, 1992: 45–70).

Unfortunately, CFIUS soon revealed itself to be incapable of fulfilling its mandate, for the simple reason that Treasury's unspoken mandate—to defray the deficit by selling off part of the debt to private foreign investors and foreign governments—directly opposed the intent of Exon-Florio, to preserve defense-related assets. In such a contest, Treasury always wins. Any hint that the U.S. government screened foreign acquisitions, even for national security reasons, generated threats from foreign ministers to stop purchasing T-bills. Treasury officials responded swiftly; there was no way the White House, via the Treasury Department, was going to allow a rogue agency to stop the vital money flow.

In the meantime, from 1988 to 1998 CFIUS received over 1000 notices of transactions and conducted 13 investigations. Not surprisingly, only one transaction was blocked and it was insignificant from both a technological and a security point of view. Sailing through the process unimpeded by scrutiny were acquisitions by foreign investors of companies involved in the manufacture of nuclear triggers, gas cabinets for semiconductors, space technology, advanced ceramics, and silicon wafers. Many of the corporations were involved directly in military work; several were the last remaining manufacturers in the United States of critical products—such as the sale of the last American-produced 8-inch silicon wafer to Montsanto-Huels, a German multinational. One acquisition was halted by direct order from President George Bush to CFIUS: the sale of MAMCO, a Seattle-based company manufacturing metal parts for aircraft, to CATIC, a company owned by the Chinese government (Auerbach, 1990: 1). Given the low level of technology involved, no real security threat existed; CFIUS's action was regarded as a political act by the president, who wished to send a message to the government of China after their attack on protesters at Tiananmen Square.

CFIUS's existence held out the false hope that the nation's technological interests were protected by the government. But the agency was never given the power to support its mandate: protecting the nation's defense-industrial base and preserving its economic and national security. Exon-Florio and CFIUS were creatures of Capitol Hill and wholly sustained by congressional interest. This means very little if the president is not interested, or, as has been the case since its inception, is downright hostile. Congressional intent also does not matter much if the issue involves foreign trade and technology, conflicts that are still relatively remote to the general public and carefully guarded as the prerogative of the executive branch. Even the most dramatic acquisitions under the CFIUS rubric, such as those involving nuclear power, attracted scant public attention.

Déjà Vu—the Cox Report

The May 1999 issuance of the unclassified version of the Cox Report provided a glaring example of the inadequacies of America's security apparatus and the failure of government to cope with those inadequacies. The details of the Cox Report relating to the theft of design information on the United States's most advanced thermonuclear weapons and the illegal acquisition of missile and space technology by the PRC were riveting. The PRC has allegedly used a wide variety of means including but not limited to illegally transferring U.S. military technology from third countries, applying pressure to U.S. commercial companies to transfer licensable technology in joint transfers, exploiting dual-use products for military advantage in unforeseen ways, illegally diverting licensable dual-use technology to military purposes, using front companies to acquire technology illegally, using commercial enterprises and other organizations as cover for technology acquisition, acquiring interests in U.S. technology companies, and covertly conducting espionage by personnel from government ministries, commissions, institutes, and military industries independent of the PRC intelligence services (de Graffenreid, 1999: 54).

The Cox Report's recommendation number 34 and the Clinton administration's response are particularly illuminating. The Select Committee recommended that appropriate congressional committees report legislation amending the Defense Production Act of 1950 to require notice to CFIUS by all U.S. companies that conduct national security–related business of any planned mergers, acquisition, or takeover of a company by a foreign entity or by a U.S. entity controlled by a foreign entity. The amendment also should require executive departments and agencies to notify CFIUS of their knowledge of any such merger, acquisition, or takeover (de Graffenreid, 1999: 358).

The administration's response, as reported by the National Security Council Press Office (1999: 25–26), was that its "concern with mandatory notification was that it could chill legitimate foreign investment that is strongly in our nation's interest, while not making a meaningful contribution to enhanced national security." The administration proposed to undertake comprehensive consultations with the relevant congressional committees to discuss details of the current CF1US process: how that process responds to the concerns in the report, how the CFIUS procedures protect the national security, and whether any changes are required. In their view, CFIUS already exercised sufficient authority to meet the nation's security needs. They argued that although Exon-Florio notices are voluntary, any of the 11 CFIUS participating agencies can notify and review any transaction that they believe worthy of attention since these agencies are involved in government contracting, industry analysis, and export licensing, and many maintain industry contacts through cooperative government-industry export promotion and/or research and development channels. In addition, foreign acquisitions that are not reviewed by CFIUS remain potentially subject to presidential action for an indefinite period. In implementing the Exon-Florio provision, the administration maintained that CFIUS sought to protect national security in the context of an U.S. open investment policy, which creates new capital for investment, technologies, and management techniques; and, very importantly, it helps offset the trade deficit and adds jobs to the economy.[6]

Other Nations' Governments

America's major competitors in the industrial world see no need for an Exon-Florio Amendment; nor do issues like the FSX, Thomson, or the Cox Report ever erupt into full-blown crises. Unlike in the United States, critical technologies and assets are not only nurtured but protected as a matter of national policy in Japan, France, Germany, and even Great Britain, although no one ever talks about it. These nations may fly the flags of free trade, but in practice they often move in the opposite direction.

CONCLUSION

Findings

The depth of the global market renders economic theory based on national markets suspect. Information technology has also produced a new source of wealth that is not material: information and knowledge applied to work to create value.

Walter B. Wriston, the former chairman and chief executive officer of Citicorp/Citibank (1997: 176), noted: "When we apply knowledge to ongoing tasks, we increase productivity. When we apply it to new tasks, we create innovation. The pursuit of wealth is now largely the pursuit of information and its application to the means of production. The *rules, customs, skills,* and *talents* necessary to uncover, capture, produce, preserve, and exploit information are now humankind's most important [emphasis added]."

In the new global economy, commercial entities are increasingly forced to shift from multinational to transnational roles. The traditional multinational firm is a national company with foreign subsidiaries that are clones of the parent company. In a transnational company, there is only one economic unit. Selling, servicing, public relations, and legal affairs are conducted locally. Parts, machines, planning, research and development, finance, marketing, and management are conducted in contemplation of the world market. Successful transnational companies see themselves as separate, nonnational entities. In many developed countries, businesses integrated transnationally now account for one-third to one-half of their industry's output (Drucker, 1997).

International trade theory takes for granted that investment follows trade. But, according to Peter Drucker (1997), increasingly today, trade follows investment. International movement of capital rather than international movement of goods has become the engine of the world economy. Although trade in goods has grown faster since World War II than in any period of history, trade in services has been growing faster, whether it be financial services, management consulting, accounting, insurance, retailing. Today services constitute a quarter of U.S. exports, with the producers of sizable American export surpluses following few, in any, of the rules of traditional international trade.

The real challenge for public sector managers is how to take advantage of the benefits of the global economy without sacrificing the public goods that they have worked so hard to achieve in the last 100 years. Participation in the global economy should not mean wholesale capitulation on issues that will determine the nation's national security and economic health. A nation can only globalize after strengthening its economic base at home (Tolchin and Tolchin, 1992: 322).

Public managers are perfectly positioned to capitalize on the communications revolution. According to Keohane and Nye, "The future lies neither with the state nor with transnational relations: geographically based states will continue to structure politics in the information age, but they will rely less on material resources and more on their ability to remain credible to a public with increasingly diverse sources of information" (Keohane and Nye, 1998: 94). In an economy that consists largely of information products, the government's power to tax and regulate erodes rapidly, with many laws and systems of measurement rendered artifacts of another age (Wriston, 1997).

New realities in trade and investment require different economic theories and different international economic policies. The international economic policies likely to emerge over the next generation will be neither free-trade nor protectionist, but focused on investment rather than trade (Drucker, 1997). The greatest challenge for U.S. leaders is to reconcile the national interest with the global economy—to prepare for a world with blurring borders and rapid change, while still preserving the nation's jobs, technologies, and profits (Tolchin and Tolchin, 1992: 294).

Suggestions

The real choice for the public administration profession lies not with fighting globalization, but managing it. This will require creative policies both at home and abroad. With certain exceptions, government agencies are generally working better and more cooperatively today in many areas of trade and technology. But much of their activity still depends on the interest and involvement of the Executive Branch. In too many cases, problems still are addressed in an ad hoc fashion by a plethora of agencies or are not addressed at all. In fact, the evidence suggests that public managers need to downplay their contributions, if only to preempt the critics. Indeed, although the FSX and other issues point to the need for more sophisticated government involvement, America retains a historical distrust of government that inhibits agencies from moving proactively to meet challenges from abroad.

A more positive approach asserts that government can make a substantial contribution to the new world order. Several potential policies balance an international perspective with recognition of national interests:

1. Eliminating agencies that do not work. CFIUS, the interagency Committee on Foreign Investment in the United States, located in the Treasury Department, is one example; there are others as well. Why, for example, do we need two agencies (in Justice as well as the Federal Trade Commission) to deal with antitrust issues?
2. In fact, jettison interagency committees altogether. They do not work well with complex international issues, in which government needs a united front, as well as a more carefully defined role.
3. Clarify agencies' roles to preempt the next FSX crisis and the next Cox Report, preserve technologies, and prevent creating an impression of chaos.
4. Remove the barriers between military and commercial technologies and formally change the Pentagon's mandate to include the support of selected technologies. This also means continuing to restructure defense procurement, which is an ongoing process.

5. Define the turf that divides Treasury, Commerce, Energy, the U.S. Trade Representative, and the Pentagon on international responsibilities.

Implications

In effect, reinventing government takes on new meaning, since competing on the global stage without adequate backup is like playing tennis at Wimbledon with a wooden racket. Until a global policy exists to mediate differences—increasingly unlikely in this rapidly balkanizing world—nation states and agencies that represent them still matter. In failing to recognize this, we risk becoming "the globalist from nowhere" (Tolchin, 1992: 7) while the rest of the world competes very effectively from home bases in the nation state. A nation can only globalize from a position of strength: the strength of its democratic institutions and the governing agencies that support them.

NOTES

1. The "Cox Report" (Report 015-851 of the House of Representatives 105th Congress, 2nd Session) is contained in the book of the same name edited by Kenneth de Graffenreid (1999); it is hereinafter referred to in the text as "the Cox Report," but specific pages of the report in the text are cited as de Graffenreid.
2. Additional major studies that formed the core of the movement to reverse declining U.S. competitiveness included reports from the Carnegie Commission, the U.S. General Accounting Office, the Council on Competitiveness, and, eventually, the White House.
3. Some of the material for this chapter was drawn from Tolchin and Tolchin (1992).
4. Under pressure, President George Bush finally spoke up on behalf of linking economic and technological competitiveness (in a speech on November 13, 1990) but at the same time threatened to veto a strong bipartisan effort to improve U.S. competitiveness, the American Technology Preeminence Act, largely because it would have provided government loans to selected companies, in effect exercising industrial policy by picking winners and losers.

   An extensive literature on international competitiveness has arisen in the last decade, most of it focusing on economic and historical issues. Up until 1990, the "industrial policy" debate occupied many scholars, with no definitive answer emerging about whether the nation would be better or worse off if government took a more proactive role. The best of the literature posed the critical questions; an outstanding example is Otis Graham's *Losing Time—The Industrial Policy Debate* (1992). Robert Kuttner's *The End of Laissez-Faire* (1991) broke new ground, discussing in depth not whether government ought to have a role but what that role should be in export controls and a variety of other policies critical to enhancing U.S. global competitiveness. The significance of Roger Porter's *The Competitive Advantage of Nations* (1990) cannot be underestimated, since Porter represented a new wave of economists who admitted that government determines a nation's competitive advantage—a marked reversal of the traditional view that a "hidden hand," or market forces, was the deciding factor. It was significant that they replaced the more common term *comparative advantage* with *competitive advantage.* Scholars representing the perspectives of public administration and political science were still relatively absent from the debate.

Opponents of industrial policy debate point out that despite their nation's industrial policy, the Japanese lost out in the race for high-definition television. Japan invested heavily in analog technology while U.S. researchers developed the superior digital version. The fallacies in this argument are clear from a competitiveness point of view: Since the United States no longer manufactures television sets, the "invented-here" technology will inevitably be licensed to Japan, whose manufacturers (in Japan and throughout Asia) will harvest at least 90 percent of the profits.

5. The Exon-Florio bill originated as an amendment to the Omnibus Trade Act of 1988, where it was specifically designated as an amendment to the Defense Production Act, which is subject to annual renewal. On the basis of guarantees under the Defense Production Act, CFIUS could continue to work in secrecy, claiming an exemption from the Freedom of Information Act (FOI)(as it did when it refused an FOI request from one of the authors of this chapter).
6. In the review of the circumstances surrounding the Cox Report, an article in *The Economist,* "The Theft That Nobody Saw," labeled the report "disturbing," for (a) what it suggested about China's military capability, (b) its timing, and (c) what it revealed about America's failure to safeguard nuclear secrets, a problem the article editorialized became considerably worse during the Clinton administration.

REFERENCES

Anchordoguy, Marie (1989). *Computers Inc: Japan's Challenge to IBM.* Harvard Council on East Asian Studies, Cambridge, Mass.

Auerbach, Stuart (1990). President tells China to sell Seattle firm. *Washington Post.* February 3, 1.

Auerbach, Stuart (1991). US relied on foreign-made parts for weapons. *Washington Post.* March 25, A1, A17.

Center for Strategic and International Studies (1989). *Deterrence in Decay: The Future of the U.S. Defense Industrial Base.* May, Washington, D.C.

de Graffenreid, Kenneth (ed.) (1999). *The Cox Report.* Regnery. Washington; D.C.

Drucker, Peter F. (1997). The global economy and the nation-state. *Foreign Affairs. 76*(5): 159–171.

Friedman, Thomas L. (1999). *The Lexus and the olive tree.* Farrar, Straus, Giroux, New York.

Graham, Otis, (1992). *Losing Time—the Industrial Policy Debate* Harvard University Press, Cambridge, Mass.

Harmon, Amy. (1999). Gates Hits $100 Billion Mark, More or Less. *The New York Times,* July 17, C-1.

Joffe, Josef (1999). One dollar, one vote. *The New York Times Book Review.* April 25, 14.

Keohane, Robert O., and Nye, Joseph S. (eds.) (1972). *Transnational Relations and World Politics.* Harvard University Press, Cambridge, Mass.

Keohane, Robert O. and Nye, Joseph S. (eds.) (1989). *Power and Independence,* 2nd ed. Scott, Foreman, Glenview, Ill.

Keohane, Robert O., and Nye, Joseph S. (1998). Power and interdependence in the information age. *Foreign Affairs. 77*(5): 81–94.

Kristof, Nicholas D. (1999). A better system in the 19th century: At this rate, we'll be global in another hundred years. *The New York Times.* May 23, WK 5.

Kuttner, Robert. (1991). *The End of Laissez-Faire.* Alfred A. Knopf, New York.

Markoff, John (1994). A declaration of chip independence. *The New York Times.* October 6, D1, D14.

Matthews, Jessica T. (1997). Power shift. *Foreign Affairs. 76*(7): 50–66.

Milhollin, Gary, and Richie, Jordan (1999). What China didn't need to steal. *The New York Times.* May 5, A31.

National Security Council, Press Office Release (1999). Recommendations re Cox Committee Report. February 2.

Porter, Roger. (1990). *The Competitive Advantage of Nations.* Free Press, New York.

Reinicke, Wolfgang (1997). Global public policy. *Foreign Affairs. 76*(7): 172–182.

Risen, James, and Johnson, David (1999). U.S. will broaden investigation of China nuclear secrets case. *The New York Times.* September 22, p. A1.

Sandholtz, Wayne, and Sweet, Alec Stone (eds.) (1998). *European Integration and Supranational Governance.* Oxford Press, New York.

Slaugher, Anne-Marie (1997). The real new world order. *Foreign Affairs. 76*(5): 183–197.

The theft that nobody saw. (1999). *The Economist.* (May 29): 23–24.

Tolchin, Martin, and Tolchin, Susan J. (1992). *Selling Our Security: The Erosion of America's Assets.* Alfred A. Knopf, New York.

Tolchin, Martin, and Tolchin, Susan J. (1988) Buying Into America: How Foreign Money is Changing the Face of Our Nation. Times Books/Random House, New York.

Tolchin, Susan J. (1996). The Globalist from Nowhere: Making Governance Competitive in the International Environment, Public Administration Review; 56(1): 1–8.

U.S. Department of Commerce. International Trade Association. *The Competitive Status of the U.S. Electronics Sector from Materials to Systems.* April 1990.

U.S. Congress. Office of Technology Assessment. *Arming Our Allies: Cooperation and Competition in Defense Technology.* May 1990.

U.S. Department of Defense. Report to the Under Secretary of Defense (Acquisitions). *Bolstering Defense Industrial Competitiveness.* July 1988.

U.S. Department of Defense. Defense Science Board. *Of the Defense Industrial and Technology Base.* October 1988.

U.S. General Accounting Office. International Trade. *U.S. Business Access to Certain Foreign State-of-the-Art Technology.* September 1991.

U.S. House of Representatives. Congressional Record. 101st Congress. Statement by Representative Marge Roukema, June 7, 1989, p. H 2391.

U.S. Senate. Congressional Record. 101st Congress. Statement by Senator John Danforth. May 16, 1989, p. S 5346.

Wriston, Walter B. (1997). Bits, bytes, and diplomacy. *Foreign Affairs. 76*(5): 172–182.

3

Society's Values and Public Management

Montgomery Van Wart
Department of Political Science,
Texas Tech University, Lubbock, Texas

The values of every society change over time (Rokeach, 1973). As values change, changes in political and public administration systems are also inevitable (Mosher, 1982). Some of the most relevant questions are, What are the types of social values and over what time frame do changes generally occur in each type? How do these types of social values affect the management and reform of public administration? And what are the current ramifications of changes in social values? These are the questions that this chapter seeks to answer.

HOW SOCIETY'S VALUES OPERATE AND CHANGE OVER TIME

The types of values that a society emphasizes constitute its primary culture (Schein, 1985; Keesing, 1974). Some of the values are very broad and change slowly. Others are very narrow, affect daily actions, and change rapidly. Ultimately, however, no matter how broad or narrow, or slow or rapid to change, these different types of values are interrelated. Four types of values are identified here: basic assumptions, beliefs, value patterns, and concrete values (Ott, 1989; Van Wart, 1998).

The *basic assumptions* level is the most conceptual and least visible aspect of culture (Goodenough, 1971; Geertz, 1973). Basic assumptions tend to shape the broadest and most profound systems of values. The basic assumptions level deals with those aspects of culture that are so commonly accepted that members of the group take such assumptions for granted or are largely or wholly unconscious of their existence during times of relative stability. Only in times of great change, such as war or famine, do basic assumptions tend to become more explicit, as pressure to adapt to a significantly changed environment causes fundamental questioning of society's structure. Basic assumptions include the implicit understanding of how the society as a whole operates and thus constitute a worldview. Examples of basic assumptions include ideas about the nature of the universe, about human nature, and about political and economic organization.

Basic assumptions normally take hundreds of years to change, although in highly stable societies basic assumptions may not change for thousands of years. For example, many of the original American colonies were set up as theocratic states in which religion played a direct role in the governance and laws of the polity. By the time of the American Revolution this basic assumption had shifted, particularly because of the enormous influence of the 18th-century Enlightenment, resulting in a Constitution that institutionalized a nontheocratic state, a basic assumption that has since remained quite stable. An example of a basic assumption that has been constant since colonial times has been the notion of a state's being organized by explicit political contract. The American colonies were virtually all set up with contracts: religious covenants, business syndicate rules of order, and/or deeds of ownership that spelled out rights and responsibilities of various parties (Fischer, 1989). This basic assumption was expanded in the Articles of Confederation and the Constitution and since has become a basic assumption for most countries in the world.

The *beliefs* level includes the explicit values about how particular social systems do and should operate. It includes expressed principles and rationales, justifications, and codes. Because beliefs are conceptual in nature, they organize the general reference for action, rather than being narrow or detailed enough to direct specific actions. Although explicit, beliefs are often unquestioned in the short term, in times of stability, and when general conditions contribute to consensual decision making. However, because beliefs are explicit, they are sometimes debated, as when difficult or evolving times cause rethinking and when common concerns no longer have a shared alignment.

Beliefs often change after two or three generations. That is, a discernible change in beliefs is often evident every 60 to 100 years. For example, many political, economic, and administrative beliefs were (re)constituted during the Great Depression. The role of the activist state was formulated and articulated, in a shift from the noninterventionist conception of the state of the preceding period. Franklin Delano Roosevelt's assertion that doing anything was better than doing nothing was a marked change in belief. Today, the global economy is causing a rethinking of activist government in both the social welfare and economic spheres.

Similarly, the New Deal emphasis on due process was important for the proper working of the increasingly large, unelected bureaucracies that typified government. Due process concerns were themselves integrated into the mass production systems that were common. Today, because of the perceptions of the excesses of due process (e.g., procedural red tape, litigation, and complexity) and the demand for more customized process for clients and employees, strict due process protocols are increasingly being challenged in favor of broader guidelines (e.g., streamlining) or nonlegalistic means (e.g., alternate dispute resolution). Even such a widely and deeply held belief as the propriety of maintaining a civil service structure, a notion introduced in the 19th century and disseminated broadly in the first half of the 20th, is under substantial attack as states diminish or abolish civil service systems and organizations rein in members' tenure systems, widely perceived as unduly inefficient and self-serving. Although the current transformation is unlikely to be as great as that from the patronage system to the civil service system, the modifications are still likely to produce a substantially different belief system about public employment.

The next two levels (the third and fourth) are the tangible levels that deal with the most physical, visible, and immediate aspects of culture (Malinowski, 1944; Radcliffe-Brown, 1952; Harris, 1979). The tangible levels generally can be seen and heard, and actions resulting from these values can generally be easily counted. The third level comprises *value patterns,* which include the norms, rules, celebrations, and rites of a culture. What are the patterns of behavior and how do people learn them? Examples of public administration culture from this level include rigorous procedural safeguards, equity of service, standardization of pay; requirements for open examinations and competitive bidding and injunctions against nepotism; observance of anniversary dates of employment and awards for attendance; training, mentoring, and coaching programs for indoctrinating new members into the culture; and official indications of success, numbers of cases processed, an accuracy rate, and ability to interact with powerful members of the organization that lead to notice and promotions.

Although some patterns of action can be nearly as stable as beliefs, and in rare cases fossilized patterns can outlive the beliefs that initiated them, generally they are more amenable to adaptation or change. For example, the civil service belief in selecting from among the top candidates has seen a value pattern shift in common usage from the "rule of three" to more flexible options to select from the top five or seven or even all qualified candidates.[1] An example at the policy level would be the tendency of Congress in recent decades to delegate more rule-making authority to agencies in an age of complexity in which legislators are generalists. This pattern has been upheld by the Supreme Court, which has affirmed that Congress cannot do its job absent an ability to delegate power under broad general directives.

The final level is that of *concrete values,* in which the specific values are directly and immediately connected to specific actions, objects, or other observables. The specific actions include the millions of discrete decisions that administrators make daily. Yet concrete values are also lodged in physical trappings as well. To catalog them, one asks, What are the material aspects (such as structures, consumables, and clothing)? The technology? The art and symbols? The language, including jargon? Examples of public administration cultures from this level would include buildings, stationery, and uniforms; fire trucks, police cars, and special sirens; badges, insignia, and flags; and specialized language and nomenclature stemming from both authorizing legislation ("That's a Title 1" or "That's a Section 6") and the professional nomenclature (such as biological terms for "natural resource agencies").

Although the concrete value level is stabilized by the general continuity of patterns of values and action, close inspection always shows variation: exceptions and accepted deviations, ranges of allowable behavior or action, and outright violations of accepted norms. Of course, when exceptions become the rule, new patterns are established, in practice if not always in formal guidelines. Examples of the typical actions that generate ordinary concrete values include the routine rulings on welfare cases, zoning requests, restaurant inspections, or water pollution standards, and they might include the assessment of fees at a park or museum or for a fishing license. Values of those implementing these actions involve subordination to legal authority, consistency with agency implementation standards (equity), and a general sense of fulfilling the public interest. Yet concrete values include the exceptions and violations of customary practice as well. A public administrator may use her authorized discretion to exempt one person from a regulation, but not another, because of the unique circumstances involved. Such an administrator is still subordinate to legal authority and mindful of the public interest; however, rather than using a strict equity standard as the primary concrete value, the administrator emphasizes the values of fairness and need. Or, more ominously, a public administrator may inappropriately use government property for personal use, misuse confidential information, distort data to aggrandize his position, or take a bribe (i.e., place the concrete value of personal need over authorized compliance).

To use a legal analogy to explain the four levels of values, the values espoused in the Constitution tend to be basic assumptions, the laws of legislatures tend to be beliefs, the rules and implementation guidelines tend to be patterns, and the enforcement and service actions of individuals tend to be concrete values. See Table 1 for a review of the four levels of values and the general time lines of change.

This section has set out the basic definitions of social values that constitute the culture of an entire society.[2] The next section examines these four levels relative to management practice and reform in more detail.

TABLE 1 Levels of Values in Society

Types of values	Characteristics of value level	General time frame for change or evolution of value level
Basic assumptions	The most fundamental views about the organization of society; generally unconscious or assumed and highly abstract; an implicit worldview shared throughout society over long periods	Hundreds, sometimes thousands, of years
Beliefs	Broad views about how major social systems should operate; generally conscious but abstract; an explicit social view shared throughout much of society over generations	Two or more generations (frequently 60–100 years in public administration)
Patterns of values	General views about the operations of specific systems; generally conscious and narrow; explicit views about operational principles agreed upon by a majority	Years, decades
Concrete values	Specific views about concrete situations; generally conscious and distinct; views about the application of values to concrete cases as interpreted by individuals	Constant, years

HOW SOCIETY'S FUNDAMENTAL VALUES (BASIC ASSUMPTIONS) OPERATE RELATIVE TO MANAGEMENT PRACTICE AND REFORM

Some of society's values operate through basic assumptions about the selection and organization of major social systems.[3] These values include the view that society should be organized as a relatively pure form of capitalism, a representative democracy, and a federal style of government that uses checks and balances of power at each level (Van Wart, 1998). What sorts of basic administrative assumptions flow from these political assumptions? A primary set of assumptions is the subordination of public administration to the political system, the law, elected officials and legislative intent, and the courts. In contrast, administrative entities in authoritarian states frequently have law-making jurisdiction, rather than the far narrower rule-making authority allowed in most democracies. Flowing from the political assumption of a democratic system is the notion of an open administrative process so that power cannot operate in secret. Emanating from the idea of checks and balances on power, due process is another cardinal value. Finally, because of the basic assumption that administrative systems serve the public good, rather than their own well-being, they are constrained to be efficient and effective for public goals. Basic assumptions are, by definition, remarkably stable over time and change little in principle. However, although basic assumptions are highly stable, they are reinterpreted every few generations, and that reinterpretation significantly changes the belief structure. The U.S. Social Security system will provide a good example of the permanence of basic assumptions juxtaposed against the evolution of beliefs structures.

The U.S. Social Security system, for all of its importance in the late 20th century and its seeming stability for decades, is certainly not a basic assumption for society. Not only is Social Security too new, it is simply no longer an assumption of the younger generations. Typically, middle-aged people are unsure of the long-term health of the system, and those in their 20s fundamentally doubt the system's long-term viability. This is significant because young people are the most idealistic and the least attentive to retirement issues. Increasingly, serious proposals to privatize Social Security partially (as well as radical calls to privatize Social Security completely) further illustrate the point. As one commentator states, "The sheer size of the system and the economic pressures facing it raise the possibility for failure of the safety net" (Roberts, 1998:2082). Yet even though the system is not itself a basic assumption, as an administrative entity in the public sector it must operate under such basic assumptions as openness, due process, and efficiency. The rules and workings of the system are widely reported and easily tracked, claimants have numerous opportunities for administrative review and/or legal proceedings, and the organization is required to send out its 35 million plus checks each month without delays or substantial administrative expense.

Social Security is a part of the American belief system today and, as such, is characteristic of the New Deal era that spawned it. Social Security is long term and it fits the paradigm of a large, stable state with a strong social posture supporting "safety net" regulation. The benefits are highly stable and the administration is quite hierarchical. Yet like all New Deal beliefs, it is being fundamentally questioned. Even though Medicare will be solvent at least until 2015 and Social Security until 2035 as currently constituted according to current analysts, eligibility and contribution requirements are likely to be adjusted significantly in the next few years. An even more fundamental change would be the investment of some Social Security Funds in the stock market, a notion that would have been considered too farfetched to consider only a decade ago. Further, the evolution of the system in the last few decades seems to be a change from a widespread belief that Social Security should function as a relatively comprehensive retirement system, to the emerging/returning idea that it may best be considered a "safety net" for the poorest sectors of a wealthy society.

As beliefs change, they affect the patterns of actions in two ways. As changes occur in legislation (which are authoritative beliefs), public administrators in the agency modify the eligibility, contribution, or benefits accordingly. Yet people also change their actions, such as planning for Social Security to be a smaller part of their total retirement income. If the belief that Social Security be partially privatized were acted on, requiring people to be responsible for some of its investment, it would change patterns of action from a legal, rationalistic, rule-oriented, and expert-driven system to one emphasizing actions that demonstrated democratic anarchy (individualism), a market mentality, and individual determination.

At the level of individual actions, currently individuals do little (such as make quarterly payments in the case of the self-employed) or nothing (in the case of those whose contributions are automatically made for them) because of the paternalistic nature of the system. It is only in the options for payout that individual determination pays a significant factor. Should an individual retire early at 62, at the standard age of 65, or should he or she allow the benefits to increase by not receiving them until they are 70? Specific actions would shift dramatically, however, with privatization. Although individuals would still be required to invest and therefore contribute to their own retirement, they would be given a far greater latitude to determine the nature of the investment and would be liable for the associated risks. For their part, the public administrators delivering Social Security perform based on a blend of their personal beliefs and commitments with the powerful effects of basic assumptions, beliefs, and patterns of action authoritatively determined by society. These basic assumptions, beliefs, and patterns largely govern the determination of benefits, the dissemination of information, the provision of services, the ethic of stewardship of resources, and the use of regulation.

The changes in Social Security also provide a good example of the dynamics and speed with which social values affect management practice and reform.

Although the provision of a comprehensive retirement system is not a basic assumption, fulfillment of a political contract certainly is. Therefore, changes are rarely retroactive, and in the case of entitlement systems, they often exempt those currently covered so that they do not experience a significant change of expectations as a result of government reductions. Further, it is a basic assumption that changes will be discussed in political forums rather than through administrative decrees. At the beliefs level, the New Deal conception of a comprehensive, hierarchically managed, paternalistic retirement system will take decades to reconfigure through expert opinion, extensive social discourse, political debate, and legislative action. However, the new system will likely—following postmodern trends—be less comprehensive (reduced benefits); be more self-managed, allowing participants a greater say in investment decisions; and require more "personal responsibility" so that program participants are liable for greater risks as well as greater benefit opportunities. As authoritative changes in the system reflect the new belief structure, patterns of actions by administrators will shift (immediately) and the patterns of savings and spending by program enrollees will shift (albeit more slowly), and just as surely individuals will reevaluate their concrete values in situations leading to specific actions.

HOW SOCIETY'S CHANGING BELIEFS ARE FUNDAMENTALLY CHANGING PUBLIC ADMINISTRATION

Major changes in the beliefs about the role of public administration are certainly nothing new; nor are the shifts in the values emphasized (Mosher, 1982). In fact, they seem to occur at fairly regular intervals of 50 years or so. For example, Federalist administrators emphasized virtue in a genteel era (perhaps 1789 to the 1830s). Jacksonian era administrators (1830s through the 1880s) are known for emphasizing political responsiveness, and thus public opinion, but are probably more important for their shift to a democratization of public service. In the 1880s the civil service reform movement began the Progressive era (1883 to 1932) in earnest although it took many decades for most public employees to be covered. The 1930s ushered in the New Deal or "modern" era (1932–1992) with activist government, which was by definition larger and more technically oriented. The second half of this era, the Great Society period, only reinforced this tendency for a technocratically designed society. The current era, characterized by terms such as *postmodern, new public management, and reinventing government,* was most visibly launched by the publication of *Reinventing Government* (Osborn and Gaebler, 1992) and the creation of the National Performance Review (Gore, 1992) and the Winter Commission on state and local government service (1993). This era seems to emphasize the limits of government at the policy level, and the reinvigorization of administration through increased entrepreneurialism, customer focus, and flexibility (Peters, 1994).

Today, then, the dominant modern paradigm of public administration is systematically being challenged at all levels of government in thousands and thousands of discrete actions by both policy makers and administrators (Barzelay, 1992; Kravchuk, 1992; Ingraham and Romzek, 1994). Before the emerging paradigm can be understood, it is necessary to understand the traditional paradigm. There are at least seven key features of the dominant paradigm. First, politically, the dominant paradigm has emphasized a relatively strict chain of democratic authority, from voters to elected officials to appointed officials and finally to civil servants. Civil servants are not to take their cues directly from citizens or the private sector, in this model, because they are considered biased or inappropriate sources for substantive change, unless directed to do so through executive order or legislative mandate. This conception of policy-making has been called top-down democracy (Redford, 1969) and it places the whole of administration in a neutral, technical role. It emphasizes detailed control by legislative and elected executive masters, even though this control would sometimes have to be delegated because of the highly technical aspects of some policies (or sometimes willfully delegated to avoid political conundrums).

This pattern inexorably leads to a highly hierarchical effect on administration itself. If administration is to be highly controlled from "above," then a relatively steep form of hierarchy is required. Further, if society demands a fairly high level of services from government and thus relatively large organizations, then these hierarchies are naturally going to have many layers so that rules can be monitored and managed and unplanned variation (deviation or innovation) can be discouraged. Managers in this paradigm rarely create genuinely new rules themselves, but they frequently articulate existing laws, sometimes appropriately fleshing them out, but sometimes encrusting them with layers of redundant protections and prohibitions against rare problems that could be handled better by common sense (Howard, 1993).

In this paradigm the role of experts is enhanced, as it is in any true bureaucracy (Mintzberg, 1979). Experts, primarily those serving in staff rather than line functions, help policymakers design the laws and rules proposed in the first place. They are thought to have the best understanding of and be best able to fashion policies that will balance substantive issues. The experts later design the administrative rules for the implementing agencies. Although decision making is reduced to the lowest possible level for line workers and supervisors, their interpretive function is emphasized as they apply technical rules to highly complex cases that frequently defy easy categorization. Thus line workers are encouraged to become narrow technical specialists as well, who see the source of wisdom (and power) as derived through encyclopedic mastery of rules that may be both massive and byzantine.

Fourth, highly structured hierarchy and technocratically designed missions require a great deal of planning that should be highly logical, rational, and long term. Therefore, planning should be conceived and detailed from beginning to end by staff experts at the direction of executives, so that everyone knows exactly what is expected of him or her at all times. Extreme caution is used in all planning activities since small mistakes are punished, and adaptation is discouraged in this centralized model because it leads to inconsistency and inequality. This model can be thought of as "blueprinting" after the planning model used by engineers in large construction projects.

Since society wants a great quantity of services at relatively low cost, a mass production model is also preferred. Customization is expensive and raises concerns about consistency and equity. On the regulatory side, absolute conformity is preferred to reduce legal liability while allowing a standard implementation protocol to be applied to a broad array of cases, largely denying or ignoring cases with exceptional circumstances. Traditional hierarchical bureaucracies are generally efficient mass producers as long as the rules are clear, the exceptions few, and the quality standards limited to a narrow range of technical concerns.

Sixth, market forces and issues are exclusively interpreted by policymakers who get their primary cues from voters through the electoral process. Since special interests are more critical of nonsupportive policymakers than is the general public, there is a tendency to interpret market forces casually, disconnecting the market from the costs of specific public services. This tendency to disconnect market forces from public agencies is exacerbated by the emphasis on the control of inputs (rather than outputs) in hierarchical bureaucracies, such as the use of line item budgets and full-time equivalency counts (FTEs), which is largely untied to concrete productivity measures.

Finally, this paradigm leads to administrative agencies with "closed" systems. Systems attempt to become as self-contained as possible so that integration and control of the elements can be maintained. This means that input from clients, attention to private sector trends, and collaboration with other organizations (private or public) all diminish the ability of the organization to turn out large quantities of service/product with as few hitches, interruptions, or stoppages as possible. Furthermore, traditional hierarchical bureaucracies that become "open" (without modifying their structure and mission) generally become inefficient, and their personnel become confused by competing demands for large production quotas on one hand and expectations of personalized attention on the other. These general trends concerning the traditional (modern) paradigm are illustrated in Fig. 1.

The emerging paradigm challenges all of these beliefs. First, there is a looser chain of authority in the postmodern conception. The traditional loop of power—from voters to elected official to administrators to citizens—continues to function but without the exclusive command of authority it once embraced in most instances. For example, direct citizen input to administrators is more emphasized through customer satisfaction data, more responsive public hearings, and greater attention to complaints. The collection of customer satisfaction data at the federal level is not only recommended, it is legally authorized. Furthermore, the input of

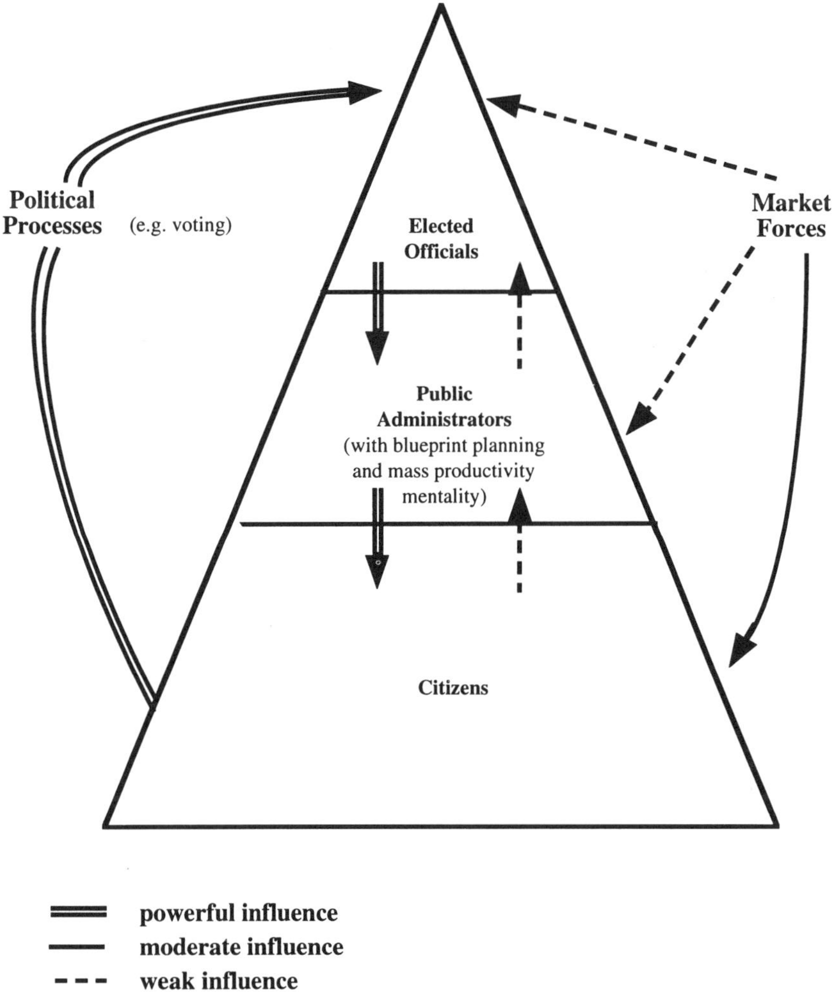

FIG. 1 The traditional "loop" administration paradigm.
Note: Primary power is centralized in a single, unidirectional loop.

administrators to elected officials, although not new by any means, is far more acknowledged. For example, entrepreneurial government requires administrators to come up with ideas and be willing to take more of the blame. The hugely popular continuous improvement philosophies infusing government today assume that public servants will make countless small changes without statutory, and often without even executive, authority. Reengineering strategies—deeper organizational changes—do the same with cursory statutory oversight but strong executive leadership. Although administrators are in no way expected or allowed to usurp the role of voters and elected officials in the democratic process, the "new public management" philosophy does dramatically invigorate the administrative role.

Because there is less control through statute and rules, public organizations can be flatter (Kamensky, 1996). This also provides an opportunity to cut expensive management overhead expenses to "rightsize" government. Following the private sector lead, public agencies have stabilized or decreased management ranks at all levels of government. Simultaneously, there has been a movement to enhance professional development career tracks, so that employees do not feel stifled by a lack of career opportunities.

Third, since executives and managers are encouraged to have significantly larger spans of control, more of the planning and decision making is encouraged at the front line and first level of supervision. Problem solving is more frequently done by cross-functional or line teams rather than by managers acting unilaterally.

The type of planning changes dramatically in the new paradigm as well. No longer is planning engineered by experts who mastermind detailed activities far into the future. Much social planning is done with a greater reliance on pilot projects, mass involvement, and evolutionary chains of events (Kiel, 1994). Large-scale projects stress adaptation of the original pilot, rather than fidelity of implementation. The new federal reliance on block grants and the use of waivers for experimentation is a prime example. Organizational learning is emphasized over expert forecast (Senge, 1990).

Clients and customers are not expected to accept monopolistic, one-size-fits-all production strategies as often. Instead, more use is made of customized production methods that allow recipients alternatives to reflect differences in taste and quality (Berman, 1998). One creative example is that in many cities the increased number of driving under the influence of alcohol (DUI) incarcerations has led some of them to allow clients to purchase far better jail accommodations (essentially converted motels). This keeps middle- and upper-class customers more satisfied, without increasing taxpayer expense.

Sixth, market forces are expected to play a far more direct role in the process of governance at the administrative level. This is largely done by using competitive mechanisms and comparative tools whenever possible, rather than relying primarily on control of budgetary, personnel, and capital improvement inputs (Savas, 1987; Ammons, 1996; Keehley et al., 1997). Competitive bids for services (e.g., waste disposal, maintenance, repair, social rehabilitation, prison management, construction, utilities, and public safety) have become commonplace and continue to expand in use (Morley, 1999). The use of vouchers in schools and public housing is a mechanism that allows competition for individual services. High-quality comparative data are more commonplace, and more often a powerful tool for policy decisions regarding administrative reform. For example, 1999 state "report cards" in six different areas sent a ripple through the state houses and affected state agencies as they found themselves competently graded in a widely read, government trade magazine (Barrett and Greene, 1999).

Finally, administrative systems are encouraged to be more "open" (Chrislip and Larson, 1994). This may mean more collaboration with other public agencies, partnering with private companies, or simply more awareness and proactivity regarding current trends outside the organization. For example, public agencies may attempt to share expensive or unusual services more than in the past. Training, dispatch services, building space, and laboratory facilities are the types of services that are once again being pooled with greater frequency. The increased use of outsourcing has necessarily meant more open systems, with a need for both better contract administration and cooperative mechanisms as well. These general trends concerning the emerging (postmodern) paradigm are illustrated in Fig. 2.

Of course each of these paradigms has variants. One prominent variant for the traditional conception is called a *strong administration paradigm* because the independent institutional authority of public organizations is enhanced, and public organizations are more frequently envisioned as the repositories of the "state" than are political institutions (Wamsley and Wolf, 1996). France and Japan would be examples of countries whose administrative structures are much closer to this conceptualized role of administration. This view encourages career public admin-

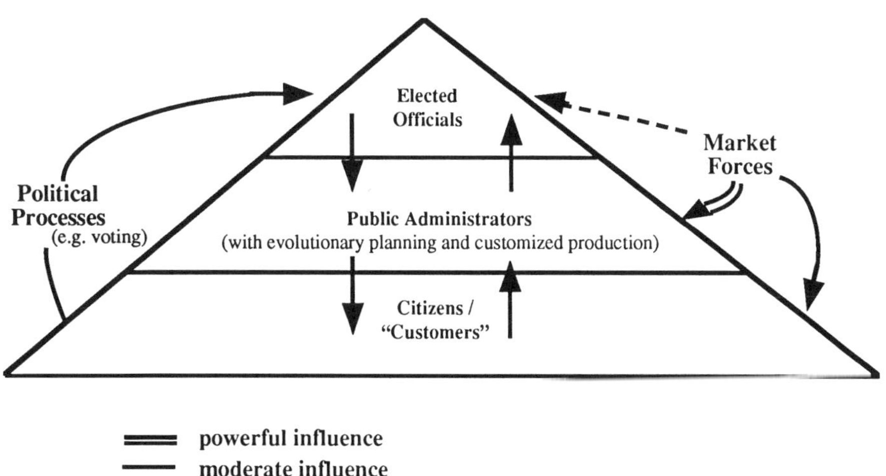

FIG. 2 The public choice administrative paradigm.
Note: Power is more dispersed than in the traditional paradigm and public administrators pay attention to more signals.

istrators to advise elected officials (confidently but strongly) about policy decisions and allows them relatively wide berth in implementation according to their professional dictates after legislative authorization. This paradigm idealizes the (extensively acculturated) "philosopher" administrators who dedicate themselves to a lifetime of career public service. It typically casts the citizen as client (whose lay input should be considered but who is expected to defer to professional wisdom). It emphasizes the values of administrative virtue and character, professional calling to the public service as one's discipline, professional bureaucracy in which professionals receive substantial deference and power, considerable administrative decision-making authority, and an administrative legitimacy equal to that of political branches. Although this paradigm does not currently enjoy popular favor in the United States, it is promoted within the American academic tradition by John Rohr and others, and it is a quietly held belief of many public administrators themselves.

A variant of the emerging entrepreneurial paradigm is one encouraged by both the communitarian school of thought as well as zealous postmodernists (Fox and Miller, 1995).[4] Of all the contemporary versions, it makes the role of citizens the most robust. It tends to encourage government structures to be as decentralized and open as possible, not so that market forces can have a greater hand in creating fiscal accountability, but so that citizens can more easily and directly engage in community discussions, constructive debates, and social oversight. In this conceptualization, one of the prime beliefs about administration is its responsibility to encourage vigorous discourse and local control wherever possible. Although conceptually attractive in idealist terms, it raises a number of technically difficult issues. Because people are busier in a world more reliant on two-person incomes and because issues are more complex, it is difficult for people to find the time to increase civic contribution, which is an underlying assumption of this belief structure. Also, how do you know when you have "authentic discourse" and who determines the community's exact will after ambiguous debates about convoluted local matters? Yet new technologies such as the Internet make direct forms of cyberdemocracy more accessible, and large segments of the population interested in new civic activism and increased personal/family responsibility indicate that this variant could nonetheless have a powerful effect on the evolution of beliefs about the proper role of administration—at least at the local level.

CONCLUSION

Values do change over time. However, not all levels of value change occur at all times. Four levels of value change are discussed in this chapter. Concrete values are related to the unique circumstances of specific decisions and actions. They vary constantly as individual decision makers in administrative roles interpret their response to rules, personal dictates, professional norms, organizational requirements, and notions of the public good. Yet fairly stable patterns of values emerge at the next level. Averaging out the many actions that occur of a similar type, there emerges a constancy revolving around select social value priorities. These patterns shift over the years and decades. At the more macrosocial level, beliefs are those values that shape patterns of actions over multiple generations. They are necessarily broader and relatively conceptual in nature. Change is termed evolutionary here because of the regularity of change at this value level in the nation's history. In the modern or traditional belief system, public administration was dominated by a strict democratic chain of authority, steep hierarchies, strong roles for managers and experts, rigid planning models, mass production techniques, insulation from market forces, and closed administrative systems. The emerging model (for better and worse) tends to emphasize a looser chain of democratic accountability, flatter hierarchy, increased input by the market and citizens, more flexible and porous planning models, and open systems of administration.

Yet even though this change of belief may feel revolutionary to those experiencing it, revolutionary change generally only results from major societal crises that threaten survival over the long term or social circumstances that are dramatically altered. Such a revolutionary shift occurred from the time of the colonial founding of the country to the time of the American Revolution. By the conclusion of the revolution the country was ready to recast the administrative structure of the nation fundamentally because the circumstances of the country had changed so dramatically. Unlike colonial existence, which was harsh and dangerous and in which religion and royal power were exceedingly prominent in most instances, that in postcolonial America was economically stable, self-sufficient, and religiously and economically diverse. The fundamental recasting of the American state in terms of a robust representative democracy (in line with the radical "liberal" thought of its day) led to a fundamental recasting of the civil administration as well. Loyalty to the crown and individuals gave way to legal subordination and a refined sense of the public good. Widespread prerogatives of administrative privacy and ownership gave way to basic assumptions about openness and stewardship in administration. Civil service reform and New Deal expansion of the administrative state felt revolutionary in their times, but even now the tides of reform are curbing the "excesses" of these past eras. For good or ill, just as the American people hold tenaciously to bedrock *basic assumptions* about representative democracy with its federal system and checks and balances in a capitalistic economic system, they also pragmatically insist on reinterpreting their *beliefs* to fit the functional aspects of the times through changes in parties, legislation, Supreme Court interpretations, and new economic policies. The fundamental beliefs about American public administration inexorably follow these large social trends over time. We are now in one of those interesting eras of evolutionary change, in which society's beliefs shifted in the 1980s and 1990s and in which the administrative state seems to be rushing to catch up.[5]

NOTES

1. Of course, public safety is an area in which the opposite trend occurred. There, frequently only the candidate with the top score can be selected, especially in promotional situations.
2. Such a conceptualization can be fruitfully applied to organizational or systemic cultures as well. When used in this context, as is common, the characteristics generally must be adjusted. For example, the time frame becomes far more compressed when speaking of most organizations.
3. Other basic assumptions of society include views about the nature of the universe and the nature of humankind.
4. I say this even though Fox and Miller deny any similarity. Nonetheless, proponents with many similarities often argue most vehemently among themselves.
5. Of course, the administrative elements of society should be some of the last to change and to reflect social shifts rather than to lead in a healthy society in which the private sector, rather than the public sector, is responsible for the majority of social dynamism.

REFERENCES

Ammons, D. N. (1996). *Municipal Benchmarks.* Sage, Thousand Oaks, Calif.

Barrett, K., and Greene, R. (1999). Grading the states: a management report card. *Governing.* (February):17.

Barzelay, M. (1992). *Breaking Through Bureaucracy: A New Vision for Managing Government.* University of California Press, Berkeley.

Berman, E. M. (1998). *Productivity in Public and Nonprofit Organizations: Strategies and Techniques.* Sage, Thousand Oaks, Calif.

Chrislip, D. D., and Larson, C. E. (1994). *Collaborative Leadership.* Jossey-Bass, San Francisco.

Fischer, D. H. (1989). *Albion's Seed; Four British Folkways in America.* Oxford University Press, New York.

Fox, C. J., and Miller, H. T. (1995). *Postmodern Public Administration: Toward Discourse.* Sage, Thousand Oaks Calif.

Geertz, C. (1973). *The Interpretation of Cultures.* Basic Books, New York.

Goodenough, W. (1971). *Culture, Language and Society.* Addison-Wesley. Reading, Mass.

Gore, A. (1992). *Creating a Government That Works Better and Costs Less: The Report of the National Performance Review.* Plume, New York.

Harris, M. (1979). *Cultural Materialism: The Struggle for a Science of Culture.* Random House, New York.

Howard, P. K. (1993). *The Death of Common Sense: How Law Is Suffocating America.* Random House, New York.

Ingraham, P. W. and Romzek, B. S. (eds.) (1994). *New Paradigms for Government: Issues for Changing Public Service.* Jossey-Bass, San Francisco.

Kamensky, J. M. (1996). Role of the "reinventing government" movement in federal management reform. *Public Administration Review. 56*(3): 247–255.

Keehley, P., Medlin, S., MacBride, S., and Lonmire, L. (1997). *Benchmarking for Best Practices in the Public Sector.* Jossey-Bass, San Francisco.

Keesing, R. (1974). Theories of culture. *Annual Review of Anthropology. 3*: 73–79.

Kiel, L. D. (1994). *Managing Chaos and Complexity in Government: A New Paradigm for Managing Change, Innovation, and Organizational Renewal.* Jossey-Bass, San Francisco.

Kravchuk, R. S. (1992). Liberalism and the American administrative state. *Public Administration Review. 52*(4): 374–379.

Levin, M. A., and M. B. Sanger, (1994). *Making Government Work: How Entrepreneurial Executives Turn Bright Ideas into Real Results.* Jossey-Bass, San Francisco.

Osborne, D., and Gaebler, T. (1992). *Reinventing Government: How the Entrepreneurial Spirit Is Transforming the Public Sector.* Addison-Wesley, Reading, Mass.

Ott, J. S. (1989). *The Organizational Culture Perspective.* Chicago: Dorsey Press.

Malinowski, B. (1944). *A Scientific Theory of Culture and Other Essays.* Galaxy Books, New York.

Mintzberg, H. (1979). *The Structuring of Organizations.* Prentice-Hall, Englewood Cliffs, N.J.

Morley, E. (1999). Local government use of alternative service delivery approaches. In *The 1999 Municipal Year Book.* International City/County Manager Association, Washington, D.C.

Mosher, F. C. (1982). *Democracy and the Public Service.* Oxford University Press, New York.

Peters, B. G. (1994). New visions of government and the public service. In *New Paradigms for Government: Issues for the Changing Public Service* (P. Ingraham and B. Romzek, eds.) Jossey-Bass, San Francisco.

Radcliffe-Brown, A. R. (1952). *Structure and Function in Primitive Society.* Harvard University Press, Cambridge, Mass.

Redford, E. S. (1969). *Democracy in the Administrative State.* Oxford University Press, New York.

Roberts, R. (1998). Social security systems. In *The International Encyclopedia of Public Policy and Administration* (J. M Shafritz, ed.). Westview Press, Boulder, Colo.

Rokeach, M. (1973). *The Nature of Human Values.* Free Press, New York.

Savas, E. (1987). *Privatization: The Key to Better Government.* Chatham House, Chatham, N.J.

Schein, E. (1985). *Organizational Culture and Leadership.* Jossey-Bass, San Francisco.

Senge, P. M. (1990). *The Fifth Discipline: The Art and Practice of the Learning Organization.* Doubleday, New York.

Van Wart, M. (1998). *Changing Public Sector Values.* Garland, New York.

Wamsley, G. L. and Wolf, J. F. (eds.) (1996). *Refounding Democratic Public Administration: Modern Paradoxes, Postmodern Challenges.* Sage, Thousand Oaks, Calif.

Winter Commission (1993). *Hard Truths/Tough Choices: An Agenda for State and Local Reform.* The Nelson A. Rockefeller Institute of Government, Albany, N.Y.

4

Technology and Public Administration

Daniel J. Jorgensen
Department of Social Sciences,
Texas A & M University Corpus Christi,
Corpus Christi, Texas

W. Earle Klay
Askew School of Public Administration
and Policy, Florida State University,
Tallahassee, Florida

Over the past half century, a fundamental transition has begun in society. Information is becoming a transformative force, bringing about pervasive paradigmatic change. The futurist Alvin Toffler (1980) called this transition the "Third Wave," arguing that it will ultimately be as significant as previous transitions from hunter-gatherer to agricultural societies and then to industrial ones. Others have sought to describe this societal transition as "postindustrial" and "postmodern." These labels seek to describe a dramatic confluence of technological and social conditions. One product of the confluence is a dynamic, global, technology-driven capitalist economy. This new economy is replete with opportunities, but it is also giving rise to many problems that will not be solved by an unfettered marketplace. Governments will be called upon to address those problems. But the role of government, and therefore of public administration, in the coming century is uncertain. It is essential, therefore, that public administration theorists and practitioners develop an understanding of technology-driven change.

This chapter begins with a look at government's vital role in the "information era." Government initiative played a pivotal role in developing the defining technology of our age. Yet, amazingly, the literature of public administration has almost completely ignored that historic role. Continued ignorance of our history could weaken claims for a proactive role for government in the creation of knowledge. The second section looks at how technology impacts management. In this section, four perspectives on the effects of technology on organizational management are discussed. In the third section, we use a theory of societal change first laid out by the pioneer sociologist William Fielding Ogburn to look at the implications of technological change for the ecology of public administration. Here we discuss trends and paradoxes that affect the present and future environments of public organizations. In the final section of the chapter, we propose a normative framework for public administrators to use in guiding the development and application of technology. The framework is based in democratic communitarian theory, which asserts the importance of responsible citizenship to bolster traditional democratic values and personal liberties.

GOVERNMENT'S PIVOTAL ROLE IN THE DEVELOPMENT OF TECHNOLOGY

Few practitioners or scholars are aware of the vital role that public administration has played in creating the defining technologies of the emergent information society. That role has been expressed primarily in two ways—through initiation of research and development projects and through establishment of government as a potential customer for new technologies when no private market existed. To illustrate the indispensable role of government in the development of many of the defining technologies of our time, we need only to look at four key technological developments—machine tabulation, electronic computers, microprocessors, and the Internet.

Government involvement in the invention of computers began with Charles Babbage's early-19th-century quest to design a machine that would produce error-free computations (LaMorte and Lilly, 1994). With the financial support of the British government, and in conjunction with Augusta Ada King, countess of Lovelace, Babbage worked to develop an "analytical engine." Though never built and primitive by today's standards, the analytical engine provided the theoretical foundation of today's computers. Later in the 19th century, Herman Hollerith, an employee of the U.S. Census Bureau, invented new technology to help with the mounting task of completing the census. It took 7 years to tabulate the 1880 census and it was predicted that more than 12 years would be needed to calculate the 1890 census. Hollerith's electrically powered tabulation machine, using punch card technology that was employed well into the late 1970s, completed the census in only 12 months. Hollerith left the Census Bureau to form his own company, which through mergers and acquisitions came to be known in 1924 as the International Business Machines (IBM) Corporation.

The onset of World War II spurred the next milestone in computing, the first generation of true electronic computers. Military personnel needed accurate ballistic charts. The Navy and War Departments responded by partnering, and contracting, with universities to develop completely new inventions. The Harvard-IBM Automatic Sequence Controlled Calculator, or Mark I, was delivered to the Navy in 1944. The computer was enormous, 8 feet high, 55 feet long, and it contained 500 miles of wiring. Though it could perform complex equations, it was slow, often taking 3 to 5 seconds to perform a calculation. A similar partnership between the federal government and the University of Pennsylvania produced an electronic computer called the Electronic Numerical Integrator and Computer (ENIAC). It consumed so much electrical energy it literally dimmed the lights of an entire section of Philadelphia when in use. The computer was, however, able to compute 1000 times faster than the Mark I.

Under governmental sponsorship, the University of Pennsylvania team continued to develop computer designs and initiated such concepts as "stored memory" and "conditional control transfer" that remain central to computer design. Both technologies were incorporated into the central processing unit architecture of the Remington Rand Corporation's Universal Automatic Computer (UNIVACI), the first commercially available computer. The company was encouraged to develop UNIVAC by a promise from the U.S. Census Bureau to become one of its first customers. UNIVAC I became famous when it was used to predict the winner of the 1952 presidential election.

Government regulation of the telephone industry gave the AT&T corporation financial stability to support its Bell Laboratories, which produced the transistor. That invention made possible the creation of a second generation of smaller, faster, more reliable, and more energy-efficient computers. By the mid-1960s many government agencies and large businesses routinely used second-generation computers to process financial information. Second-generation computers, though, filled entire rooms; they were too big to take into space. As a consequence, it was public administrators who drove the demand for microprocessing, the third generation in computing technology

In 1961, President Kennedy called for a lunar landing by the end of the decade. Unknown to many is that the National Aeronautics and Space Administration (NASA) was already planning a lunar landing (Lambright, 1976). NASA's management needed computers that would be energy efficient and small enough to be carried aboard small spacecraft. Jack Kilby, an engineer at Texas Instruments, was developing the integrated circuit (IC), which appeared to fit the bill. The United States government, through NASA, funded the development of IC technology for use in space flight. Further refinement of that technology, developed mostly with public funds, resulted in the microprocessor. The microprocessor is a single chip that can be programmed to meet any number of demands. Today the microprocessor is ubiquitous; it is used in such everyday items as microwave ovens, television sets, air conditioners, traffic signals, automobiles, and, most importantly, personal computers.

As computers became more widespread, public administrators dreamed of new ways to harness their potential. In the late 1960s and early 1970s, the U.S. Defense Department's Advanced Research Projects Agency (DARPA) pioneered a research program to link disparate computers at multiple sites throughout the world. Initially, the developers envisioned a set of communication protocols that would allow computers to communicate readily across networks, sharing memory space, software, and information; the researchers called it the Internetting Project (Cref, 1993).

Interest developed in this new project and protocols became standardized. The National Science Foundation (NSF) became a major contributor to the backbone communication service for what was called the NSFNET. NASA and the U.S. Department of Energy also contributed significant resources to create, and link, computer networks, called the NSINET and ESNET. By 1986 the Internet had become a major part of the U.S. research infrastructure, linking federal and state governments with educational institutions. During the late 1980s the population of Internet users and network constituents expanded internationally and began to include commercial sites. In 1992 Vice President Al Gore promised to make the development of this growing "information superhighway" an administrative priority. The Internet grew to the point where Mediamark Research Inc. estimated that more than 40 percent of U.S. adults had Internet access by the late 1990s.

This short history of the development of computer technology has hit only a few high points and, for the most part, focuses on the United States. Public administration elsewhere has contributed to the emergence of the information society. The World Wide Web, for example, is the product of an Englishman working at a Swiss research laboratory sponsored by the European Union. Currently, governments in the United States, Europe, and Japan are spearheading the Human Genome Project. This project to discover the information codes of human life is likely to yield information that could literally revolutionize medicine in the 21st century. It might also revolutionize education. An enhanced understanding of the human brain's genetic codes could lead to a world in which there are no slow learners.

Each of the early innovations in computing began with efforts by public administrators to encourage investments in knowledge development to enable their organizations to do new things that were not previously possible. The investments in knowledge development that were made would not have been made by the private sector alone. They either were too large or did not promise profitable returns for businesses within a decade or less. If left to private initiative alone, those investments might never have been made.

It would be a mistake to think that government investments in new knowledge are solely made by national governments. State governments invest heavily in knowledge development through their staffing of large research universities. A hallmark of the technological breakthroughs is the cooperation between public administrators and university- and laboratory-based researchers. When it comes to basic research, there are almost no "private" universities. Most basic research and much of applied research at such institutions as Stanford and the Massachusetts Institute of Technology are government sponsored. Those institutions are best described as privately governed, publicly sponsored organizations. Even industrial research such as that performed on microprocessing at the Intel Corporation is often spurred and sponsored by public agencies.

Public administrators do not always anticipate the ramifications of the new technologies. The National Science Foundation does expect far ranging impacts from the genome project, but the hard-pressed Navy and War Departments did not worry much about the future of computers. If public administrators do play such a central role in the development of new transformational technologies, though, are they not morally obligated to think well about their possible future uses? That question was asked when the Manhattan Project produced the atomic bomb in World War II. Surprisingly, it is not a question that has often been asked by public administration theorists. Technology assessment remains peripheral to much of our theory. It is even peripheral to much of our writing about ethics. Why? We believe it is because practitioners and scholars of public administration have largely ignored the crucial role played by public administrators in the creation and application of new technology.

Lacking an understanding of our crucial role, we fail to argue strongly the importance of public administration–initiated investments in the development of new technology. The notion that government is an albatross around the neck of private business is a historically inaccurate myth. That myth might help some politicians get elected and some antigovernment intellectuals to curry favor among businesspersons who want to hear it. The fact is that public sector initiatives have spurred the development of the central technologies of the new global information-intensive economy!

THE THEORETICAL NEXUS OF TECHNOLOGY AND ORGANIZATION

For the first six or seven decades of the 20th century, the technology of the office place was remarkably stable. Office workers in 1910 used typewriters, filing cabinets, printing devices, and even telephones. The huge computers of the 1950s–1970s were located outside offices, with access limited to a few gatekeepers. Office work was facilitated by new inventions such as copiers and fax machines but they did not revolutionize that work. The personal computer, the invention with the potential to do that, did not begin to appear in offices until the early 1980s.

Technological change has long been assumed to be an important variable in the study of factories, but theory development for public administration has been mostly office centered. Much of our theory, therefore, was developed in a context that assumed relatively stable technology in the workplace. Consequently, we have neglected technological change in our theory building. That neglect should not continue. Empirical research has already shown that public administrators can use computing technology as a tool for radically changing staffing patterns in a public agency (Klay, 1988).

Even though public administration theory has neglected technology itself, technology has affected our theory. Information technology began to affect organizational theory when computing technology was first invented in the mid-20th century. Since that time, the concept of "information" has played a major role in theory development. In the first half of the century, the "ideal" organization was a well-coordinated hierarchical structure. The emphasis was on effectiveness achieved through command. In the second half of the century, pyramidal structures began to be castigated as impediments to the free flow of information. The new emphasis was on effectiveness achieved through communication.

In the same decade that saw the birth of the electronic computer, pioneering social scientists at the National Training Laboratories began the invention of organization development to transform organizations by overcoming both structural and interpersonal impediments to the effective transmission and use of information. Scholars like Henry Mintzberg began to study the information needs of managers, giving rise to the concepts of management information systems and decision support systems. "Information" has taken its place alongside "human" and "financial" as the three essential resources of management. Today, ideal structures are more likely to be seen as fluid learning-oriented networks. Causation is difficult to prove in history, but the parallel development of information technology and the focus on "information" in organizational theory seem more than coincidental.

Considering information as a key resource is well accepted in public administration theory. Additionally, we certainly seem to prescribe networking much more than new pyramids. Nevertheless, after decades of theorizing in a relatively stable technological environment, we now neglect the full implications of new technologies. The rapid expansion of information generating technology gives cause for public managers to question old assumptions. Peter Drucker (1998) is one who believes that scholars and managers "are preaching, teaching and practicing policies that are increasingly at odds with reality and therefore counterproductive." In their preface to Zuboff's *In the Age of the Smart Machine,* Shafritz and Ott (1996: 540) state: "The evolution from technical systems (in modern organizations) to information technology (in postmodern organizations), is more than an evolutionary step. The texture of relationships between individuals, their work, and their organization is changed irreversibly."

An old assumption that has become outdated is the notion that centralization and decentralization are mutually exclusive. It was once assumed that giving greater discretion to street level bureaucrats necessarily meant that senior administrators had to lose some measure of control because they would be unaware of what was being done in the field. Information technology now allows simultaneous empowerment of both street level employees and senior officials. Those in the field can be empowered with greater discretion, bolstered by access to plentiful information to guide their decisions. Senior officials can readily monitor what is happening in the field and adjust policy guidance accordingly without managing individual cases. The term *reengineering* might have limited staying power, but efforts to reconceive organizational processes fundamentally in the context of what is achievable with new technology are likely to remain.

Public administrators can fashion better policies for the information age if we seek to understand technology. Four emerging theoretical streams from the organization literature that take into account technology and change are the technological imperative, the strategic choice approach, technology as trigger, and structuration (Orlikowski, 1992; DeSanctis and Poole, 1994; Roberts and Grabowski, 1996; Thatcher and Brower, 1998).

The technological imperative model reflects some of the earliest work on the effects of new technology on organizations and management. The model envisions a direct causal relationship between technological change and organizational change (see Fig. 1).

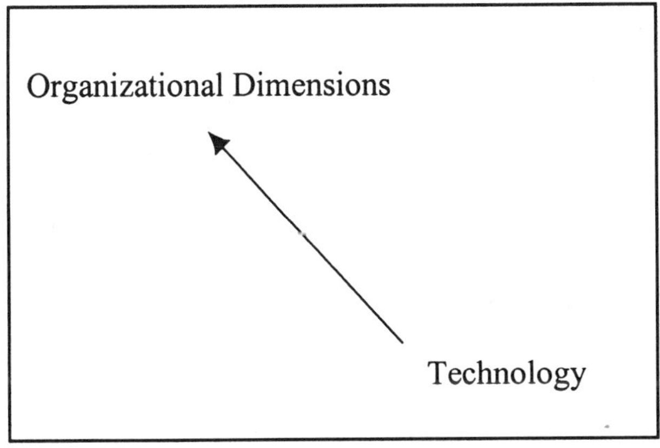

Fig. 1 Technological imperative model. (From Orlikowski, 1992: 400.)

This theory is grounded in the positivist epistemology of the rationalist orthodox approach to management. It begins with the premise that technology and organizational variables can be measured and predicted. The theory suggests that the introduction of technology has hard-line deterministic impacts on organizational properties such as structure, size, performance, and centralization/decentralization.

Technology is looked upon as an objective, external force. New technologies (e.g., new hardware or software) act as independent variables and cause change within the organization. Empirical research employing this model has provided insight about important impacts of technology. The research that is based on this model, however, focuses on technology engineering and mostly ignores the human element in the development and application of technology.

The strategic choice model relaxes the deterministic premise of the previous model. This theory integrates an interpretive epistemology with positivism and examines how organizational context and management strategy can affect technology. Here technology is a dependent variable that is neither a given nor immutable (see Fig. 2).

Empirical research has shown that managerial philosophy and strategy, as well as organizational context, are salient factors in determining how technology impacts an organization (Orlikowski, 1992; Thatcher and Brower, 1998). For example, the introduction of a new client server system in one organization may further management's efforts to control employees by "automating" their tasks. In another organization, a similar client server system could be used to implement a strategy of "informating" (see Zuboff, 1988) in which management seeks to empower employees. "Strategic choice" theory recognizes human discretion, but it is closely tied to orthodox theory in its focus on management choice. It tends to

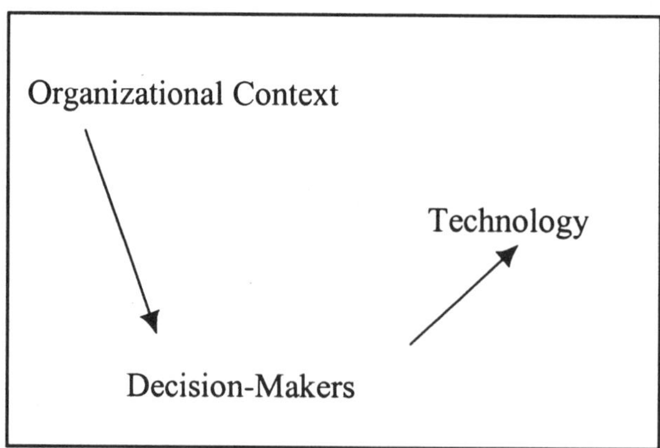

FIG. 2 Strategic choice model. (From Orlikowski, 1992: 401.)

ignore end-users whose thoughts and actions can affect how technology is actually put to use.

The "technology as trigger" approach is a third alternative. It suggests that the consequences of technological change are unpredictable. Consequences emerge over time from the interaction between technology, employees, and other social system influences (Thatcher and Brower, 1998) (see Fig. 3).

Technology as trigger theory posits "a role for technology, not as material cause, but as a material trigger, occasioning certain social dynamics that lead to anticipated and unanticipated structuring consequences" (Orlikowski, 1992). It was influenced by Barley's (1986) studies of computed tomography (CT) technology in hospitals. CT technology has relatively fixed and standardized functions and features, but Barley found no consistent pattern of organizational changes among hospitals employing it. Barley concluded that the differences in organizational changes were attributable to site-specific, socially constructed utilizations of the new technology. It is difficult, therefore, to generalize about the likely effects of technology on an organization. Technology as trigger theory recognizes the importance of social interaction, but the model tends to be time-bound and static. It does not consider that both technology and its organizational context can be modified during use (Orlikowski, 1992).

"Structuration theory" is more dynamic and longitudinal. According to this model, organizational actors engage one another as new technology is put to use. In doing so, they reconstruct technology as it becomes implemented in the workplace. Structuration theory is recursive; technology is both a dependent and an independent variable. Employees and management both contribute to the definition process as they interact, perceive, and use technology in creative and unpre-

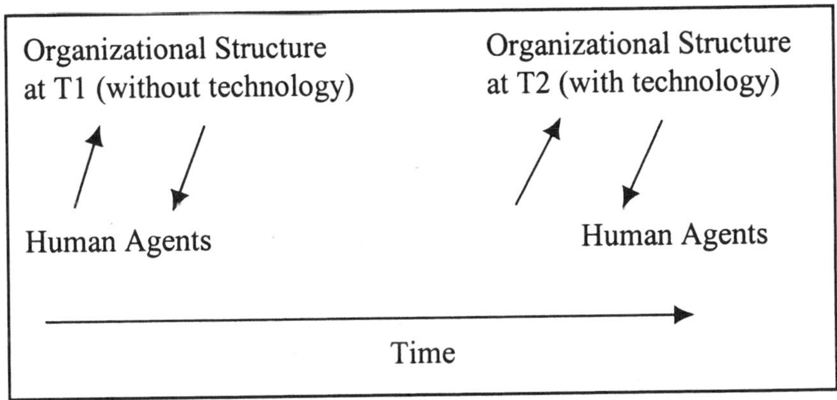

FIG. 3 Technology as trigger. (From Orlikowski, 1992: 402.)

dictable ways (Thatcher and Brower, 1998). The structuration model poses four distinct premises:

1. Technology is a product of human design and development.
2. Technology is a medium of human action.
3. Technology is affected by the institutional conditions of interaction.
4. Technology acts upon institutional properties of an organization (Orlikowski, 1992).

Structuration theory asserts that technology is an artifact, created and maintained by social actors who exist both beyond, and within, the organization. As social actors, people interpret and act upon technology. They modify the functions and meaning of technology as they implement it. They do so in the context of their own circumstances and their knowledge of their organization and its organizational field. Their patterns of interactions eventually become established as standardized practices—such as the use of personal computers to communicate via e-mail. Over time, such practices eventually become institutionalized habits, forming the "deep structure" of organizations (DeSanctis and Poole, 1994). Organizational members then draw upon these institutional properties (institutionalized behavior patterns) in their ongoing interactions in the organization. Subsequent stresses and innovations can either reinforce institutional properties or challenge their continued existence if left unmodified (see Fig. 4).

The structuration model emphasizes an institutional context. Thatcher and Brower (1998) caution, though, that structuration theory may be inattentive to the public sector as a whole. In public administration, technology and its impacts must be studied from many perspectives. Technology affects, and is affected by, gov-

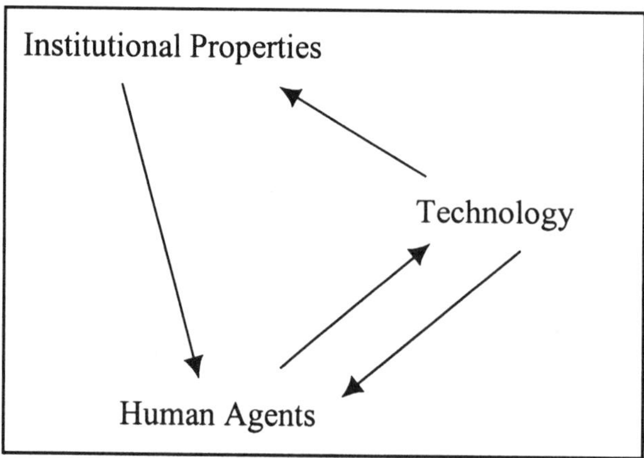

FIG. 4 Structuration model of technology. (From Orlikowski, 1992: 410.)

ernments, industries, communities, and even families. Together these entities constitute a complex context of human ecosystems. Important trends can emerge from numerous points within the complex ecology of public administration, trends that can pose both opportunities and threats to the future. In the next section, we look at some of the promises and threats that seem to accompany technological advancement.

TECHNOLOGY AND EMERGENT TRENDS IN SOCIETY

Technological changes in the 19th century gave rise to industrial society. The emergence of that society created numerous problems that could not be resolved by the marketplace. New forms of government were fashioned to cope with those problems. The study of public administration emerged as an outgrowth of those new forms of government. The history of public administration, therefore, cannot be understood without understanding how technology changed the society within which it operated. Nor can the future of public administration be contemplated without understanding how new technologies might be transforming society and creating new problems in its wake—problems that will have to be addressed by government.

Early in the 20th century, a pioneer sociologist, William Fielding Ogburn (1936, 1964), sought to develop a theoretical perspective that could explain how technology changes societies. He is perhaps best remembered for his concept of *cultural lag,* which posited that new technologies introduced more change in some parts of a society than in other parts. The dissonance that emerges is a major problem for societal adjustment. Ogburn was especially concerned with how the technology of the industrial era affected the family, the most basic institution of society. He concluded that industrial technology changed traditional family life in ways that induced the emergence of modern forms of government.

In agricultural societies, the extended family provided education, employment, social assistance, medical care, and protection from intruders. Industrialization ended village life and family structure evolved. Extended families yielded to nuclear ones in urban settings. The new nuclear families were more vulnerable. They could not provide for themselves as extended families had, so government appropriate to an industrial era was invented to perform many of the tasks once accomplished by extended families. Industrial era government also became an engine of change, especially when its investments in education and new knowledge spawned new technologies.

New information technology could reshape society as profoundly as earlier industrial technology had. Though causation is complicated and unclear, the nuclear family has undergone a profound weakening in most of the industrial nations during the same decades in which information-intensive technology has emerged. The confluence of technological and normative changes associated with the weakening of the nuclear family in most industrial nations has been called the "great disruption" (Fukuyama, 1999). Changes in institutions like the family now challenge us to redefine public administration for the 21st century, just as the industrial revolution of the 19th century challenged our predecessors to create our field as we know it today.

Ogburn's theory directs the public administrator to go beyond addressing parochial concerns in order to recognize the opportunities and threats of technological advancement within the full scope of society. Although some aspects of recent technological change are well known, such as the explosion in telecommunications technology and a concomitant restructuring of financial institutions, much of the future remains uncertain. The ecology of public administration is replete with trends and paradoxes resulting from the recursive relationships among technology, the natural environment, industry, community and family, government, and social philosophy (see Fig. 5). There are many trends and conditions associated with technology that deserve the attention of public administrators. Here we focus on four categories of trends of profound importance—demographic trends, natural environmental trends, the emergence of technology-driven global capitalism, and the rapidity with which information technology itself is expanding.

Demographic Trends

Demography and technology intertwine in many ways. Technology transforms economies and thus alters population dynamics dramatically. Introducing

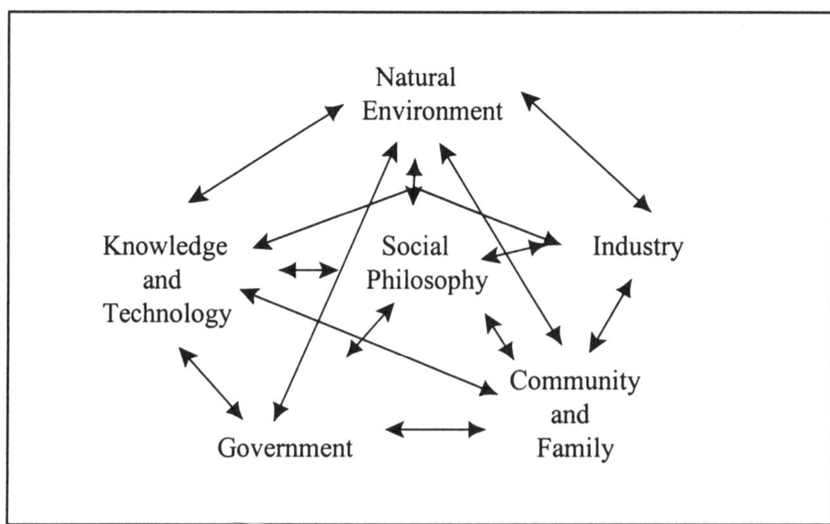

FIG. 5 Some forces underlying societal change. (From Klay, 1998: 136.)

improved sanitation and medical care, industrial technology significantly reduced mortality rates across the globe. Fertility rates, though, remain high in many places and rapid population growth prevails in much of the world, threatening resources and ecosystems. Most residents of industrial nations employ birth control technology to keep their population growth near or below replacement level, but each new child in advanced countries places a considerable load on the natural environment. Within the United States, a profound demographic change is taking place.

As of the 1990s, Americans of European ancestry reached zero replacement levels. The numbers projected for the mid-21st century are nearly the same (slightly more than 190 million) as are living today. For the most part, middle-class Americans of African, Hispanic, and Asian ancestry are also reproducing themselves at a zero growth rate. America is also rapidly aging. As the majority white "baby boomers" age, there might not be an adequate work force to support them. About 34 million Americans are 65 and over, yet it is projected that there will be about 69 million in 2030. If, as projected, the number of new young workers in the labor force (aged 20 to 24) remains close to the current level (18 million), there could be significant pressure to increase immigration—assuming, that is, that new technologies do not enhance the productivity of the existing work force to a point that increased numbers of immigrant workers would not be needed.

The future of the United States is almost certainly one of far greater diversity in ethnic origins. (As this manuscript was being written, high-tech companies were lobbying in Washington to admit more immigrants, especially from East and South Asia, with advanced skills and knowledge.) Public administrators will be challenged to help construct the social glue that is needed to hold a diverse society together. But the degree of diversity to come is uncertain. Some of that uncertainty is due to uncertainties about the future effects of technology within the United States and in foreign economies. If future technologies greatly enhance the productivity of American workers, we will be less worried about the ratio of retirees to active workers. If productivity lags, a worsening "dependency ratio" will become a driving force in the shaping of policies toward such phenomena as immigration and social security. In the past the *dependency ratio* was defined as the ratio of children and retirees to active workers. Will the future dependency ratio be the number of children and retirees relative to the number of active workers and smart machines?

Natural Environment

The spread of industrial technology poses significant threats to the natural environment. Malthus was wrong in his original predictions of human misery because he underestimated the potential of humans to use technology to expand their productive capacity. Some scholars, pointing to decades of improvement in indicators such as life spans and per capita income, argue that new technology will continue to allow humans to develop solutions to environmental problems (Simon, 1995). Other scholars, however, point to conditions such as the depletion of the ozone layer and the increase of greenhouse gases and fear that environmental crisis is looming (Flavin, 1996). Some even fear that ecological "overshoot" (a population passes its sustainable limits and subsequently collapses precipitously) might occur among humans and prove Malthus to be correct after all. Few political leaders have addressed the environmental debate. One who has is Vice President Al Gore, who believes that the 21st century could be defined as much by global environmental threat as the 20th century was defined by global warfare (Gore, 1992).

Gore says that the magnitude of environmental threat is uncertain, but the prudent thing to do is to take appropriate steps to avert it by taking economic advantage of it. He proposed a massive public-private partnership to develop and market environmentally-friendly technology on a global scale. His vision is one in which American government, researchers, and industry combine forces to lead the world in creating and marketing such technology. The industries created would provide high-tech jobs in the future. If global environmental threat in the 21st century creates demands for new technologies, then public administration will play a central role—very similar to its role in the creation and marketing of information technologies in the 20th century.

Technology-Driven Capitalism

With the fall of the Soviet Union, capitalism is the only remaining theoretical framework for economic development. The new global technology-oriented economy is aggressively capitalistic. It would be equally correct to assert that we have "technology-driven capitalism" or that we have "capitalist-driven technology." By themselves, capitalism and new technology are powerful forces for social change. Each now feeds upon the other and reinforces the tendency of the other to produce change.

There is growing inequity in the distribution of income and wealth—both within and among nations. The United Nations (1998) reports that in the 1960s the ratio of income of people in the most affluent one-fifth of nations was approximately 30 times greater than that in countries where the poorest fifth live. By 1998, this gap had widened to 82 times greater. A similar trend is occurring within many industrial nations. U.S. Census Bureau statistics show that in 1973, the income of the top 20 percent of American families was 7.5 times that of the bottom 20 percent. By 1996, it was 13 times. For much of the past three decades, real purchasing power declined for those Americans at the bottom of the economic pecking order (Karoly, 1996). That these people are among the least educated, and therefore least prepared to cope with an information-intensive economy, is not a coincidence. Income disparity, associated with educational differences, has increased within all three of the United States's largest ethnic groups (European, African, and Hispanic ancestries) (U.S. Census Bureau, 1999). Technology in the context of a highly competitive capitalism simultaneously creates and destroys opportunity. If sufficient opportunity fails to reach large segments of society, social order and democratic processes could be threatened.

Technological change has enabled and pushed women to alter their roles in society. Various inventions have eliminated some of the time-consuming drudgery of housekeeping. Contraceptive technology has uncoupled sex from procreation. Other technology-related changes have made it difficult for many males to be sole breadwinners. Some men would like to be sole breadwinners, but their chances of doing so are nil if their skills are limited to the performance of routine tasks, whether physical or mental, no matter how strong their work ethic. The growth of the service sector is one result of female entry to the labor force. Much service sector employment is dedicated to performing tasks once performed by women in the home—food preparation, cleaning, child care, elder care, and so on. Ironically, those tasks are highly resistant to labor-saving technological breakthroughs. Obstacles to informatizing the service sector raise doubts about the future potential of technology to enhance overall labor productivity (and thereby help to cope with the demographic changes just mentioned).

Unique Characteristics of Information Technology

Information technology utilizes information, a resource that is radically different from the traditional resources of economic theory—land (natural resources), labor, and capital. Traditional resources are finite. When a traditional resource changes hands in an economic transaction, as when someone sells a lump of coal, the buyer gains the coal and it is no longer available to the seller. But when information is purchased (or merely shared at no cost) it is available thereafter to both the provider and the recipient. Each transaction expands the supply of the resource. With such geometric expansion of the resource, information technology itself becomes transformed at increasingly rapid rates. Ultimately, nearly all known information could eventually be made accessible to nearly everyone on the planet.

The unique characteristics of information were first described by the British theorist Colin Cherry (1985). George Orwell, reacting to the totalitarian dictatorships of the mid-20th century, once feared that information would be monopolized by "Big Brother" to dominate every aspect of people's lives. Orwell, however, assumed that sources of information would remain limited. Goebbels could dominate the few newspapers, movie houses, and radio stations of 1930s Germany to assure that only the propaganda of the Third Reich reached most of the people. Information sources, however, are proliferating to the point of becoming ubiquitous. Whether the effect of this proliferation will be an extension of democratic processes, or be anarchic, or have both effects is unknown.

Information technology is producing a cacophany of voices, but with that a proliferation of choices. With that proliferation of choices basic social structures could be altered. This possibility has been well summarized by Fukuyama (1999:1):

> A society built around information tends to produce more of the two things people value most in a modern democracy—freedom and equality. Freedom of choice has exploded, in everything from cable channels to low-cost shopping outlets to friends met on the Internet. Hierarchies of all sorts, political and corporate, have come under pressure to crumble.

Some futurists such as Alvin Toffler (1970) believe that information technology opens new opportunities for direct democracy. Some are predicting that the cost of running for political office will drop as candidates will no longer have to buy expensive television time on a few network channels. Children in remote villages can now be taught via advanced instructional technology (given enough political will to do so). New technologies such as radios, and even pencil-sized video cameras, which can be worn on their uniforms, make police feel more secure when getting out of their squad cars to mingle with people in neighborhoods. If advanced information technology has the potential to alter, and democratize, such phenomena as educational and electoral processes and is an enabling factor in such innovations as community policing, should it not become more central to the framing of public administration theory?

Information technology is a powerful force for change. One of its distinguishing characteristics is its extraordinary malleability. The very same microchip can be used in Big Brother fashion to intrude upon an individual's privacy or to empower a poor person by giving him or her access to an information-rich world. When public administrators act to develop or apply new technologies, the impacts can be felt by people within organizations and in the broader society. That is why public administration theory must encompass both the intraorganizational and societal implications of technology. Structuration theory is useful in understanding the intraorganizational effects. To understand societal impacts, public administration scholars need to look to the body of scholarly work begun by people like Ogburn (some of the earliest contributions to it are very relevant today). But seeking knowledge about technology and its implications is not sufficient. Public administrators are active participants in deciding how highly malleable technology is developed and put to use. We need, therefore, to seek normative guidance.

SOCIAL PHILOSOPHY, PUBLIC ADMINISTRATION, AND TECHNOLOGICAL ADVANCEMENT

Public administration theorists encounter a perplexing world when they turn to social philosophy for normative frameworks to guide officials' decisions. Ironically, much of the confusion in contemporary social philosophy is linked to advances in technology and basic science. Knowledge in the natural sciences exploded in the 19th century as new technology allowed increasingly sophisticated research. Some philosophers became concerned that positivism, the epistemological foundation for nearly all natural science research, was becoming so dominant that it might render philosophy an adjunct of science. Husserl, one of those philosophers, set about creating phenomenology, a perspective that reasserts the importance of individuals (and thereby of philosophy) in interpreting all "phenomena" including those observed in a laboratory (Natanson, 1973). Enabled to do so by modern steamships and armed with positivist methods, anthropologists traveled the world to discover amazing variation in human cultures. From these developments, moral relativism emerged. If all phenomena were ultimately subjective, who was to say which moral frameworks were "better"?

Natural science furthered philosophical confusion when Heidegger theorized, and empirical research repeatedly confirmed, that physicists could not identify all properties of an electron simultaneously—to know some of its properties precluded knowing other properties. When physicists had seemingly encountered inescapable uncertainty, philosophers responded by doubting that certainty could exist in other arenas of knowledge. Numerous authors and other artists were deeply affected by these perspectives. The notion that the individual is primary but that he or she lives in an inherently confused world shaped much of the art and literature of the 20th century. Horrible applications of new technology by governments at war with one another (both hot and cold) throughout the past century of global ideological conflict raised both scholarly and popular doubt that new technology can be shaped to improve the quality of life.

At the end of the 20th century, some natural and social scientists criticized the atomistic tendencies of some aspects of social philosophy. New developments in physics suggest that the physical world might be more knowable than Heidegger surmised. "String theory," which posits that subatomic particles, such as quarks, themselves comprise "strings" of pure energy, is emerging. The theory is mind bending because it proposes that those strings exist in more than three physical dimensions, but it promises to "unify" much of Einstinian theory on a macroscale with the minute world of quantum physics. What was once confusion among physicists might have been ignorance, not an end state of knowledge. Natural scientists such as E. O. Wilson (1998) criticize much social philosophy for neglecting the growing connectivity or "consilience" of scientific knowledge. Wilson argues that, although it might never be possible to know everything, we stand a good chance of learning how to know what we need to know. The greatest challenge, it seems, is learning to ask the right questions—What is it that we need to know?

Some theorists, including Amitai Etzioni (1993) and Philip Selznick (1992), believe that we do, in fact, know much of what we need to know to strengthen the processes of democracy. What we need to know begins with understanding the social underpinnings of democratic society. These include social norms that perpetuate a respect for fellow members of society as individuals whose very existence entitles them to "unalienable rights." From that respect comes acceptance of individual liberty, the right to be different: to speak different things, to vote differently, to worship differently or not at all, and so on. Perpetuating norms of respect for one another, it seems, is the best assurance of one's own liberties. Consequently, actions that strengthen the social fabric within which democratic norms are exercised help to perpetuate liberty itself.

Societies in which citizens possess a basic respect for one another are societies in which "trust" is relatively high. Such societies, says Fukuyama (1999), tend to be the most successful in forming businesses in the modern economy. Trust is an important part of "social capital." Where trust prevails, people are more capable of creating the flexible and creative interpersonal relationships that constitute "networking." Full utilization of modern information technology seems to require that people create flexible networks of problem-solving relationships. Businesses that cannot do this seem more vulnerable in a high-tech world. The United States, Fukuyama concluded, is a high-trust society, and that cultural characteristic is a prime factor in its economic prominence in the emergent global economy.

At the beginning of the 21st century, it seems that a possible convergence is emerging among information theory (the study of information technology and its effects), business/economic theory, and public administration theory. This convergence lies in the common ground that undergirds such concepts as social capital, community, and networking. Information theory emphasizes the importance of interpersonal networking to utilize fully the capacities of new information technology. People who live in societies in which norms of mutual respect and trust are higher seem to be able to recognize and exploit economic opportunities better. Possessing a capacity for "spontaneous sociability," they are better at networking. Those societies also seem to be the ones in which democratic processes function better and in which individual liberties are most secure.

Add to the convergence of theoretical perspectives the notion that information is an infinitely expandable resource. What might be the impact of an infinitely expandable resource if it becomes increasingly shared within and among networks of people who fundamentally respect one another? Could entire learning societies emerge in which few, if any, people are information poor? Such an outcome is certainly desirable but is by no means a certainty. To enhance the likelihood that technology will enhance both democracy and economic opportunity in the future, public administrators need to clarify their own responsibilities in the creation and application of new technologies.

TECHNOLOGY AND THE RESPONSIBILITIES OF PUBLIC ADMINISTRATORS

Technology is highly malleable; it can do good or harm. Where, then, should public administrators turn for normative guidance in the development and use of technology? We recommend that sound guidance can be found in the context of understanding public administrators' unique responsibilities to their fellow citizens. Democratic communitarian theory as expounded by scholars like Etzioni, Selznick, and Fukuyama emphasizes that citizens have responsibilities toward one another and that both democratic processes and personal liberties are best protected when citizens embrace a sense of personal responsibility for their actions. The words of the communitarian theorist Henry Tam are suggestive of the sense of ethical responsibility for the actions of public administrators that emerged from the Nuremberg trials: Apart from genuine ignorance when there is no indication that a person should or could have found out about the unforeseen harm of his or her actions, and involuntary behavior arising from the physical force of others or the psychological disruptions within a person, there are no grounds for denying that each individual is responsible for his or her behavior and its effects on others (Tam, 1998: 121).

Communitarian theory links responsibilities to "rights." Each right, or entitlement, carries commensurate responsibilities. A citizen's right to vote is accompanied by commensurate responsibilities to serve on juries. A welfare recipient's entitlement to financial support is accompanied by a responsibility to prepare for employment if possible. A farmer's right to price support payments is accompanied by a responsibility to practice judicious crop planning to prevent unnecessary claims. An operator's right to drive is accompanied by a responsibility to do so safely. The right to own private property is accompanied by a responsibility not to use it in ways that cause undue harm to one's neighbors, and so on. The more these responsibilities are accepted by citizens, the less likely government is to have to monitor their actions and invade their privacy to protect others. The more the norm of responsibility is accepted by citizens, the better democratic processes function.

In the context of communitarian theory, public administrators are citizens who are entrusted by their fellow citizens with an extraordinary "right," the authority to exercise the power of the state. At a minimum, the commensurate responsibility of public administrators is to exercise that authority within legally prescribed parameters. But public administrators have a moral responsibility that extends far beyond minimum legal responsibilities. Ours is a stewardship responsibility to serve our fellow citizens well.

How that stewardship might be exercised in the context of the development and application of new technologies can be illustrated in the context of criminal justice technology. The demise of the Cold War left many companies unable to sell their research to the Department of Defense. The result has been a rapid growth in the numbers of researchers seeking to apply their talents to criminal justice. A rapid expansion of criminal justice technology has followed. Unlike the defense marketplace, in which a single national buyer ultimately decides which technologies will be funded, the criminal justice marketplace is one of thousands of potential buyers. The Department of Defense has long been aware that its procurement decisions shape the direction of new technology. Individual police chiefs and prison wardens, on the other hand, rarely think about the impact of their procurement decisions upon the development of new technology. Nevertheless, their collective decisions about new technologies create the economic demand for them, thereby determining what the marketplace produces.

Based in communitarian theory, a concept called *responsible use* has been proposed to guide the decisions of criminal justice executives as they decide which technologies to purchase and how to apply them (Klay and Sewell, 1996). Police and corrections officers are citizens who have been entrusted with an extraordinary "right"—the authority to investigate, apprehend, and restrain their fellow citizens. Consequently, officers are citizens of the community who bear an extraordinary responsibility toward their fellow citizens. New technologies can increase officers' capacity to accomplish investigation, apprehension, and restraint. Stewardship requires public officials to employ new technology if it creates greater value for taxpayers. If officers do not act with a sense of extraordinary responsibility toward their fellow citizens, however, some new technologies could endanger individual liberties.

No central nationwide "technology board" determines which criminal justice technologies will be encouraged by the marketplace, nor how they will be used. Those decisions will be made in thousands of disparate places. Courts can restrain some applications of technology, but who is to assure that the courts, major users of new technologies themselves. will not misuse technology? Clearly, protecting citizens' liberties while employing new technologies will depend upon the acceptance of a norm of extraordinary responsibility by police, corrections, and court officials.

Responsible use calls for the application of technologies in ways that empower fellow citizens and do the least amount of harm possible, whether physical or sociopsychological. There are four major categories of criminal justice technologies—(a) investigation/surveillance, (b) apprehension/restraint, (c) weaponry, and (d) communication. Responsible use applies to each category. New surveillance technologies include pencil-sized video cameras that can be placed on telephone poles and in officers' uniform pockets. Misuse of those devices could raise the spectre of Big Brother. Responsible use calls for officers to seek neighborhood input to determine how such cameras should be used locally, if at all. New apprehension and restraint technologies include electronic disablers of fleeing vehicles to avert high-speed chases. Foams and fly-paper-like devices are available to restrain unruly inmates. Responsible use calls for organizations to encourage the rapid development of such devices that do less harm to people.

Nonlethal weaponry is one of the most exciting arenas of technology development. Responsible use calls for criminal justice organizations to do what they can to speed the development and application of weapons that can provide officers with adequate protection without doing unnecessary harm to fellow citizens. Advances in nonlethal weaponry could cause a major shift in public opinion about the meaning of the Second Amendment in the coming century. If nonlethal weaponry is perfected to the point that it could give the average citizen effective protection against a perpetrator at a distance of 10 or more yards without blowing away some of that person's flesh, would most citizens support a right to carry lethal weaponry?

Communications technologies are enabling criminal justice organizations to communicate better, not only with each other, but with citizens as well. Radios attached to officers' uniforms give officers a greater sense of security when leaving their squad cars behind. New technologies such as web pages and voice mail are being used to enable neighborhood residents to keep in touch with their community-based police officers. Communication is at the heart of community-based initiatives to avert crime and lessen criminal tendencies. Modern technologies are proving useful in accomplishing such community building efforts.

CONCLUSION

This chapter began with a review of the ways in which public administrators influenced the creation of some of the defining technologies of our time. The example of criminal justice illustrates that we continue to do so. Will we encourage the development and application of new technologies in ways that strengthen individual liberties and enhance democratic processes? That will depend upon the normative framework employed by public administrators today and in the future. The most critical aspect of the relationships between public administration and technology are the norms that guide our development and applications of it. Technology is malleable. We must look carefully at ourselves to anticipate its future effects.

REFERENCES

Barley, S. (1986). Technology as an occasion for structuring: Evidence from observation of CT scanners and the social order of radiology departments. *Administrative Science Quarterly. 31:* 78–108.

Cherry, Colin (1985). *The Age of Access: Information Technology and Social Revolution.* Croom Helm, Dover, N.H.

Cref, V. (1993). "How the Internet Came to Be." *The Online User's Encyclopedia.* [http://www.bell-labs.com/user/zhwang/vcref.html].

DeSanctis, G., and Poole, M. S. (1994). Capturing the complexity in advanced technology use: Adaptive structuration theory. *Organization Science.* 5(3): 121–147.

Drucker, P. F. (1998). Management's New Paradigms. *Forbes* (online). [http://www.forbes.com/forbes/98/1005].

Etzioni, Amitai (1993). *The Spirit of Community: Rights, Responsibilities, and the Communitarian Agenda.* Crown Publishers, New York.

Flavin, C. (1996). Facing up to the risks of climate change. In *State of the World* (L. R. Brown and Colleagues, eds.). W. W. Norton, New York.

Fukuyama, F. (1999). The great disruption: Human nature and the reconstitution of social order. *The Atlantic Monthly* (on-line). [http://www3.theatlantic.com/issues/99may/9905fukuyama.htm].

Gore, Al (1992). *Earth in the Balance.* Penguin Books, New York.

Karoly, Lynn A. (1996). Anatomy of the U.S. income distribution: Two decades of change. *Oxford Review of Economic History. 12*(1) (Spring): 76–95.

Klay, W. E. (1988). Constitutional and administrative implications of computers. *Public Productivity Review 12*(2) (Winter): 193–203.

Klay, W. E. (1998). Trends and paradoxes affecting the present and future environments of public organizations. *Public Administration Quarterly.* (Summer): 133–160.

Klay, W. E., and Sewell, J. D. (1996). Communitarianism and professionalism: A values oriented approach to criminal justice technology. *Technological Forecasting and Social Change. 51.*

Lambright, W. H. (1976). *Governing Science and Technology.* Oxford University Press, New York.

Mediamark Research, New York.

Natanson, Maurice (1973). *Phenomenology and the Social Sciences.* Northwestern University Press, Evanston, Ill.

Ogburn, W. F. (1936, 1964). Technology and government change. *Journal of Business of the University of Chicago. 9* (January). Reprinted in W. F. Ogburn (1964) *On Culture and Social Change: Selected Papers Edited with an Introduction by Otis Dudley Duncan.* University of Chicago Press, Chicago.

Orlikowski, W. J. (1992). The duality of technology: Rethinking the concept of technology in organizations. *Organization Science. 3*(3): 398–427.

Roberts, K. H. and Grabowski, M. (1996). Organizations, technology and structuring, In *Handbook of Organization Studies* (S. R. Clegg, C. Hardy, and W. R. Nord eds.). Sage, Thousand Oaks, Calif.

Selznick, Philip (1992) *The Moral Commonwealth.* University of California Press, Berkeley.

Shafritz, J. M. and Ott, J. S. (eds.) (1996). *Classics of Organization Theory, 4th* ed. Wadsworth, Belmont, Calif.

Simon, J. L. (1995). *The State of Humanity.* Blackwell, Cambridge, Mass.

Tam, H. B. (1998). *Communitarianism.* New York University Press, New York.

Thatcher, J. B. and Brower, R. S. (1998). Modeling the effects of information technology on public organizations: Extending the structuration model. Presented to the *Public and Nonprofit Division, Academy of Management Annual Meeting.* San Deigo, CA.

Toffler, Alvin (1970). *Future Shock.* Random House, New York.

Toffler, Alvin (1980). *The Third Wave.* Bantam Books, New York.

Ulrich, D. and Lake, D. (1990). *Organizational Capability: Competing from the Inside Out.* John Wiley & Sons, New York.

United Nations Development Programme (1998). *Human Development Report 1998.* Oxford University Press, New York.

U.S. Census Bureau (1999). Available on line [http://www.census.gov/population/www/projections].

Wilson, Edward O. (1998) *Consilience: The Unity of Knowledge.* Knopf, New York.

Zuboff, S. 1988. In the age of the smart machine: The limits of hierarchy in an informated organization. In *Classics of Organization Theory,* 4th ed. (J. M. Shafritz, and J. S. Ott eds.). Wadsworth, Belmont, Calif.

5

Reforming American Government Accounting in the 20th Century

James L. Chan
Department of Accounting, University of Illinois at Chicago, Chicago, Illinois

Government accounting and public management in the United States have an ambivalent relationship. Public managers are responsible for their organizations' accounting and financial reporting, yet they have little control over the rules that tell them how to account for and report to the public. During the 20th century, these rules evolved from a few precepts to voluminous codifications that only skilled professionals could decipher. The need for public managers to understand these rules has never been greater regardless of whether they work in federal, state, or local governments. They are required by the accounting standard-setting bodies to provide a "management's discussion and analysis" in their financial reports. Furthermore, they will have to evaluate, present, and justify ever more costly requests to modernize financial management systems. The ability to discharge these responsibilities depends on an understanding of the reforms aimed at improving accounting and financial reporting standards.

As a consequence of the federal system, the United States has two separate institutional structures and bodies of accounting standards for the federal government and for state and local governments. In this chapter, accounting standards for state and local governments refer not to the laws and regulations of each jurisdiction, but to professionally sanctioned rules for nationwide application. These are discussed in Sec. I. The evolution of federal accounting standards are described in Sec. II. Each section identifies and evaluates the changes and explains the who, why, and how of the reforms. Sec. III summarizes the similarities and differences of these institutional structures, processes, and bodies of standards.

STATE AND LOCAL GOVERNMENT ACCOUNTING STANDARDS

During the 20th century, there were three major waves of reform aimed at transforming how state and local governments keep their books and report to the public. The first wave was part of the municipal government reform during the Progressive era at the turn of the 20th century. The reformers saw better financial record keeping as a way to fight corruption and make governments efficient. During the second wave, covering the 1930s through the mid-1970s, public finance professionals developed accounting principles to facilitate financial management and legal compliance. We are now in the third wave. Stimulated by a series of municipal fiscal crises in the 1970s, the call for public accountability led to major institutional and conceptual changes in government accounting. The significant features of these three waves of reform are discussed in the sections that follow.

First Wave of Reform: Fighting Corruption

During the Progressive era (1890s to 1920), America was transformed from a rural to an urban society. Advances in transportation and communication created large industrial corporations and financial institutions with great demand for labor. Immigrants flocked to cities, and municipal governments were hard pressed to provide the necessary public services. The existing institutions proved inadequate and official corruption was widespread. James Bryce observed in 1891, "The government of cities is one of the conspicuous failures of the United States" (quoted in Matika, 1988: 17). Book titles such as *The Shame of the Cities* (Steffens, 1904) and *Theft of the City* (Gardiner and Olson, 1974) reflect the sorry state of civic life. The morally upright and the economic elite demanded an end to official corruption, greater popular control, and the expansion of government functions to cope with the rising demands of urban residents. Businessmen feared that without reform higher taxes would simply feed the bureaucracy run by the patronage system. Their trade associations began a campaign for efficiency and economy in government. On the basis of their experience, business leaders realized that sound business practices and good accounting were essential and recruited members of the young accounting profession to join the crusade (Matika, 1988: 17–33).

In Chicago, a merchants' group hired the certified public accounting (CPA) firm Haskins & Sells to study the city's finances. The firm found many financial and accounting problems and recommended changes. The city council promptly engaged them for the job. In Philadelphia, another CPA, William M. Lybrand, suggested comprehensive annual reports. On the basis of his experience focusing on Minneapolis, H. W. Wilmot (1906; quoted in Davidson et al., 1977: 5) reported to the accounting profession that

> it is generally admitted by students of municipal finance that the accounting methods of most cities of the United States are deplorably behind the times, and that similar methods could not be tolerated for a day in any successful commercial corporation. These methods may possibly have met the local requirements when the cities were smaller, but as municipal affairs have become more complex the multiplication of matters to be recorded has rendered these antiquated accounting systems entirely inadequate.

Perhaps the most concerted and influential efforts were made in New York City, where a businessman, Herman Metz, was elected comptroller in 1906. Metz introduced business practices and accounting procedures and later funded the New York Bureau of Municipal Research. Under the leadership of Frederick A. Cleveland, the bureau staff conducted field studies to document current practices and made constructive recommendations. The results were published in a series of Metz Fund Handbooks of City Business Methods, including one on municipal accounting. Their goal was to create an accounting system to supply "complete, accurate, and prompt information about business transactions and results" (Bureau of Municipal Research, 1913: ix).

Cleveland was in a good position to synthesize the best practices of the time. He and Messrs. Haskins and Sells were all members of the Committee on Uniform Accounting Methods set up by the National Municipal League around 1900 to improve municipal accounting practices. As its name implies, the committee stressed uniformity in accounting, e.g., the proper classification of revenues and expenses, to facilitate statistical comparisons. In addition, it advocated independent audits and recommended a prototype for reporting financial data. Through the energetic efforts of a Boston CPA named Harvey Chase, 11 states and 80 cities soon adopted the committee's model (Fleischman, 1987: 297–298). These were the first examples of government adoption of professionally developed accounting standards.

The Metz Fund researchers basically proposed a business accounting model adapted to take into account the public budget as the key instrument of financial control. They stressed the need to gauge government's ability to operate as going concerns. The result was an emphasis on the government's balance sheet. Year-end balance sheets (or statements of financial position) would provide a continuous series of measures of the assets and liabilities (and residual capital) carried over from one period to the next. This way of looking at municipal finances contrasted sharply with discrete annual budgets, each focusing only on one period's money inflows and outflows. The implementation of the multiperiod continuous accounting model required the accrual basis of accounting and the double-entry system of bookkeeping, both of which were (and still are) standard business practices. Under the accrual system, careful distinctions were drawn between revenues and cash receipts and between expenses and disbursements. Similarly, capital assets would be clearly separated from financial resources on the balance sheet, along with long-term bonded debts and short-term payables. In addition to financial accounting, cost accounting was recommended to give city officials data to achieve economy and efficiency.

The Metz Fund model of government accounting, though remarkably modern, was not unique. As early as 1901, a Canadian accountant, F. H. MacPherson (1901: 3), cited the following assertion by an unnamed eminent author:

> The object of all good book-keeping is the exhibition of the growth or decline and present value of capital, and of each of the parts of which capital is made up. A perfect balance sheet shows all this in the clearest and most concise manner. A perfect balance sheet should not only give the *present value* of each of the component parts of capital, but should also indicate its growth and decline since the last statement. The one object of the skilled book-keeper is, therefore, to be able to produce, when necessary, a clear and correct balance sheet. (Emphasis added)

Apparently, the theory was far ahead of practice. MacPherson (1901: 3) went on to observe:

> In very few instances can be found any system of municipal accounts which within itself exhibits the true condition of the affairs of the municipality. Financial reports, as ordinarily presented, may exhibit a correct statement of the receipts and expenditures, but rarely, if ever, is the statement of assets and liabilities anything more than an approximation of the position of the corporation. Why this is so one need not be altogether at a loss to understand, when one stops for a moment to consider the circumstances which usually surround the appointment of the officials charged with the responsibility of preparation of such a statement. The requirements of a perfect balance sheet cannot be satisfactorily met, unless the system of accounts provides for the application of the principle of double entry to all transactions into which money or money values enter.

Since the idealized business firm was their frame of reference, it was natural for the municipal accounting reformers to adopt the business accounting model uncritically. Cleveland, for example, saw no need for a separate set of municipal government accounting principles. At the same time, however, he clearly understood that the business accounting model had to be enhanced by formal financial control devices in government. The recommended system consequently had the added features of fund accounting and budgetary accounting. The funds included current funds and capital funds, as well as sinking and trust funds. To facilitate timely assessment of financial performance, it was recommended that estimated revenues and appropriations be formally recorded in the accounts. Obligations and encumbrances chargeable to the appropriations would be duly recorded also. The accounting function was clearly meant to monitor budget execution (Bureau of Municipal Research, 1913).

In summary, political reformers and their business and professional allies saw the value of good accounting to honest and efficient government. Their political agenda to some extent has overshadowed their intellectual legacy. During the first decade of the 20th century, American city governments were already urged to adopt businesslike accounting augmented by fund and budgetary accounting. The governments' financial and accounting advisers, being practical men of affairs, spent more time on devising forms and procedures than on constructing accounting theories. As a result, though the outline of a framework for municipal accounting was visible, the articulation of formal standards was to be the agenda of the next wave of reform.

Second Wave of Reform: Supporting Financial Management

After municipal bond defaults during the Great Depression in the early 1930s, municipal accounting standards again received the attention of government groups. Institutional sponsorship for standard setting shifted from the National Municipal League to the financial specialists. The newly created Municipal Finance Officers Association (MFOA) in 1934 established the National Committee on Municipal Accounting (NCMA). The committee, consisting of representatives of nine organizations concerned with government and finance, subsequently issued a set of 10 Principles of Municipal Accounting in 1934 and other bulletins until 1941. In the late 1930s the MFOA formally endorsed these as Standard Practices in Municipal Accounting and Financial Procedure (Remis, 1981).

The NCMA principles codified many of the ideas of the first wave of reform. The NCMA urged that a single finance officer be put in charge of accounting and financial reporting. It advocated close links between accounting and budgeting systems by means of consistent terminology and a common account structure. The committee endorsed the use of budgetary accounts and the recording of encumbrances. It affirmed the use of the double-entry system and the general ledger supported by subsidiary records. The committee specified the following funds for organizing the municipal accounts: general, special revenue, working capital, special assessment, bond, sinking, trust and agency, and utility funds. It also required the use of the accrual basis of accounting but exempted general fixed assets from depreciation calculation except for finding the cost of services. Standard classifications were recommended for assets and liabilities, revenues and expenditures. Finally the committee stressed the consistent flow of information throughout the budget, the accounts, and eventually the financial statements.

The NCMA principles lacked the moral fervor evident in Cleveland's writings (e.g., Cleveland, 1909). The authors, as professional men, valued the systematic nature of accounting. Accounting, after all, was termed "the art of recording, classifying, measuring and communicating in a significant manner and in terms of money, transactions and events which are, in part at least, of a financial character, and interpreting the results thereof" (AICPA, 1953: 3). The task of elaborating the principles and explaining the supporting procedures fell on textbook authors (e.g., Morey and Diehl, 1942).

After fulfilling its mission of codifying the principles, the National Committee on Municipal Accounting was dissolved in 1941. After the pause due to World War II, the MFOA in 1948 reactivated the NCMA and renamed it the National Committee on *Governmental* Accounting to reflect the participation of state governments. The new committee revised NCMA publications and worked on auditing procedures as well. A period of inactivity ensued from 1951 to 1966. After that the committee was again activated to consolidate all previous work in a comprehensive volume. The resulting MFOA (1968) publication, *Governmental Accounting, Auditing, and Financial Reporting* (GAAFR), popularly known as the "Blue Book," became the Bible for government accountants, auditors, and other finance professionals alike. For the first time, there was a common thread running through accounting, financial reporting, and auditing.

The National Committee on Governmental Accounting might as well have added budgeting to the GAAFR title to complete the entire financial management cycle. It did more than recognize the importance of the government budget; the 1968 GAAFR explicitly called for the adoption of an annual budget by every governmental unit, "whether required by law or not" (5). Furthermore, the committee required the accounting system to "provide budgetary control over general governmental revenues and expenditures" (5). This was about as far as an *accounting* professional group went in pushing governments to do financial planning as a matter of sound management practice. This willingness to exceed the legal requirement was, however, an exception to the general tenor of the document.

The 1968 GAAFR (3–4) required a governmental accounting system to make it possible for a government to "show that all applicable legal provisions have been complied with." The system should be capable of determining "fairly and with full disclosure the financial position and results of financial operations." The committee apparently assumed that its principles would provide the basis for judging government's fair presentation and full disclosure.

Most principles of the 1930s were retained. For example, governmental accounting systems would continue to be organized and operated on a fund basis. The committee defined a *fund* as "an independent fiscal and accounting entity with a self-balancing set of accounts recording cash and/or other resources together with all related liabilities, obligations, reserves, and equities which are segregated for the purpose of carrying on specific activities or attaining certain objectives in accordance with special regulations, restrictions, or limitations" (6–7). The fund structure was modified: Bond funds were renamed *capital project funds;* sinking funds became *debt service funds;* utility funds were generalized to *enterprise funds;* working capital funds were dropped; and intragovernmental service funds were added (7–8).

However, the 1968 GAAFR modified the accrual basis. The *modified accrual basis* of accounting was defined as "that method of accounting in which expenditures other than accrued interest on general long-term debt are recorded at the time liabilities are incurred and revenues are recorded when received in cash, except for material or available revenues which should be accrued to reflect properly the taxes levied and the revenues earned" (11). Specifically, the accrual basis of accounting is recommended for enterprise, trust, capital projects, special assessments, and intragovernmental service funds. For the general, special revenue, and debt service funds, the modified accrual basis of accounting is recommended (11). The ambiguity and confusion evident in the definition and exceptions would last for the next 30 years!

The modification of the accrual basis reflected a fundamental problem with basing an accounting system on "funds." The way government accountants used the term *fund* was inconsistent with the common usage of funds as money available for ready use. The committee seemed to think that some funds (as fiscal entities) held liquid financial resources and should be accounted for on a modified accrual basis. Other funds that held economic resources (including capital assets) would use the accrual basis as in business accounting. Unfortunately, the modification could be minor or drastic, making the modified accrual basis an ambiguous concept (Chan, 1998).

The liquidity focus of the general fund also led the committee to exclude fixed assets and long-term liabilities belonging to the government as a whole (but not to specific funds) from the general fund. The committee invented two "account groups" to record these items outside the funds. Couched in terms that only specialists in fund accounting could understand, these accounting artifacts hampered public understanding of government financial reports. The gap between government accounting specialists and laypersons grew wider as a new nomenclature emerged.

Conflict would also arise between local laws and the national standards in GAAFR. On this point, the 1968 GAAFR was rather conciliatory: "If there is a conflict between legal provisions and generally accepted accounting principles applicable to governmental units," it conceded, "legal provisions must take precedence" (4). At the same time, however, governments should install accounting systems that would "make possible the full disclosure and fair presentation of financial position and operating results in accordance with generally accepted principles of accounting applicable to governmental units" (4).

For the first time, "generally accepted accounting principles applicable to governmental units" was invoked, and in doing so the National Committee on Governmental Accounting apparently assumed itself to be their promulgator. At that time, generally accepted accounting principles for business enterprises were set by the Accounting Principles Board (APB) of the American Institute of Certified Public Accountants (AICPA). Since the APB lacked the legal standing or the interest in setting accounting principles for governments, no jurisdictional disputes arose. However, as more municipal governments contracted for independent audits performed by CPAs, the AICPA set up the Committee on Governmental Accounting and Auditing to provide technical guidance. The 1974 "industry audit guide" on state and local governmental units on the whole endorsed the 1968 GAAFR principles.

In summary, the main achievement of the second wave of governmental accounting reform was the formalization of generally accepted accounting principles sanctioned by government finance officers and the accounting (i.e., CPA) profession. These principles emphasized compliance with legal requirements and provision of support to public financial management through fund accounting and budgetary accounting. Even conceding the primacy of legal requirements, a body of generally accepted accounting principles began to emerge independently of individual governments' practices. In the process of developing precepts into principles, however, a number of jurisdictional and conceptual issues emerged. These became the agenda for the third wave of reform starting the mid-1970s.

Third Wave of Reform: Promoting Accountability

The third wave of reform began in the mid-1970s and reached a crescendo in 1999 when a new reporting model was definitively proposed and required. In contrast to the earlier period's emphasis on legal compliance and financial management, government accountability to stakeholders—investors, citizens, and their representatives—was the guiding spirit. This goal was promoted by the National Council on Governmental Accounting (NCGA) from 1974 to the early 1980s, and by the Governmental Accounting Standards Board (GASB) from 1984.

NCGA Phase (1974 to 1983)

Shortly after publishing the 1968 GAAFR, the GFOA in 1974 elevated the National Committee on Government Accounting to the National *Council* on Governmental Accounting by broadening its membership. The 21 part-time members of the NCGA represented state and local governments, the accounting profession, the financial community, the federal government, and academe. The AICPA's audit guide for state and local government created the need to reexamine the 1968

GAAFR requirements in order to reconcile conflicting positions. There was some practical urgency as well. The closing of the capital market to New York City in 1975 exposed the weaknesses of its accounting practices. Similar crises, though less severe, in other cities such as Chicago and Cleveland created a broader sense of uneasiness about the cities' financial and accounting practices, and the underlying principles as well. Alternatives were proposed, such as the call for full accrual and consolidated reporting (Davidson et al., 1977).

In this anxious atmosphere the newly reconstituted NCGA adopted a short-term and a long-term program. The short-term program was to reexamine expeditiously and revise the 1968 GAAFR principles. The long-term program was to seek resources to conduct fundamental research leading to a sound conceptual framework for governmental accounting (Greathouse, 1985).

The reexamination of the GAAFR, led by Professor Robert J. Freeman, resulted in NCGA Statement 1, "Governmental Accounting and Financial Reporting Principles" (NCGA, 1979). Statement 1 made a number of significant changes in tone and substance to the 1968 GAAFR principles. First, it tipped the balance in favor of GAAP in case they came into conflict with legal provisions. Acknowledging the importance of legal compliance, the NCGA called for the reduction of conflicts between GAAP and legal compliance. It advised using the legal compliance basis for accounting during the year and doing a GAAP conversion at year-end for producing external reports. Second, it required the preparation of interim financial reports and the issuance of "general purpose financial statements" that would be lifted and issued separately from the CAFR. These statements, prepared at the level of fund types, would present an overview of the entity's financial picture. The financial statements in a comprehensive annual financial report would resemble a pyramid with successive levels of summarization of financial data. Third, the NCGA classified the fund types into three major groups: governmental, proprietary, and fiduciary. Along another dimension, funds were classified as expendable funds and nonexpendable funds. The expendable funds (i.e., governmental and some fiduciary funds) would use the modified accrual basis of accounting; the nonexpendable funds (i.e., proprietary and certain fiduciary funds) would use the accrual basis of accounting. Fourth, the NCGA explicitly called for reporting of budgetary comparisons in financial reports.

For the implementation of the long-term project, the NCGA received a major grant from a federal agency. The grant enabled the NCGA to hire three academic researchers, including the author, to work on a conceptual framework for government accounting. A broad range of actual or potential users of government financial information, based on the criteria of the need or right to know a government's financial affairs, were identified. The researchers recommended that the objectives of state and local government accounting and financial reporting were to provide "(1) financial information useful for making economic, political and social decisions, and demonstrating accountability and stewardship, and (2) information useful for evaluating managerial and organizational performance" (Drebin et al., 1981: 107). The research report formed the basis of NCGA Concepts Statement 1 and influenced GASB's Concepts Statement 1, both on the objectives of accounting and financial reporting.

The NCGA went on to deliberate and issue several other standards on topics such as pensions and leases. However, its attention was distracted by the protracted negotiations on the possible formation of a Governmental Accounting Standards Board (GASB) to succeed it (Chan, 1985). Eventually, the board was established under the auspices of the Financial Accounting Foundation, the sponsor of the Financial Accounting Standards Board, which succeeded the APB to set GAAP for businesses.

The GASB Period (from 1984 to the Present)

The GASB inherited much unfinished business from the NCGA. In order to ensure continuity, it required the continued enforcement of existing NCGA standards (Antonio, 1985). The board undertook its own research project on user needs in order to arrive independently at a set of objectives emphasizing accountability and decision-making usefulness (Patton, 1992). In 1986 it was recognized by the AICPA as the promulgator of generally accepted accounting principles for state and local governments. The GASB explored the possibility of incorporating nonfinancial measures of service efforts and accomplishments in financial reports but retreated after encountering resistance and difficulties (Brown and Pyers, 1998). In the next 15 years, the GASB adopted a total of 34 standards of varying breadth and depth on diverse topics (GASB, 1998, 1999). The most significant standards were Statement 11, which attempted to change the measurement method, and Statement 34, to recast the reporting model.

In order to appreciate the significance of GASB Statement 11, it is necessary to recall how general governmental activities were accounted. These activities were typically financed by governmental funds, i.e., general, special revenue, capital projects, and debt service funds. The balance sheets of these funds reported current financial resources and current liabilities, i.e., cash and short-term claims to/by others. As a result of this narrow measurement focus, capital assets and long-term debt (capital as well as operating, such as pension and other retirement benefits) were relegated to the account groups shown far away from the governmental fund balance sheets. Their revenues, mostly taxes and grants, would be recognized on a modified accrual basis, i.e., when they were available to finance current operations. The extent of modification could be so much that it could approximate the cash basis (Chan, 1998). Consequently, "significant unpaid expenditures that result from current-period transactions and events" would not be reflected in the operating statement. Furthermore, "long-term debt issued to finance current operating expenditures could be reported as operating inflows rather than as a fund liability," observed the chairman, James Antonio, and the vice-chairman, Martin Ives (GASB, 1993). These flaws had to be addressed.

The GASB from the outset recognized these problems and made concentrated efforts to solve them over a 6-year period. The result was Statement 11, issued in May 1990 to be effective 3 years later. The long waiting period was set to give the GASB time to complete the remainder of the reporting model, as Statement 11 was confined to dealing with the operating statement of the governmental funds. A complete reporting model would encompass at least the balance sheet and the operating statement; besides it would have to deal with the degree of aggregation of funds.

An operating statement reports on an entity's financial performance as measured by revenues and expenditures (or expense) for a period. The GASB decided that the flow of financial resources was the proper measurement focus for the governmental funds' operating statements. Furthermore, an accrual basis would be used. The board reasoned that this combination of measurement focus and basis of accounting would better promote accountability by enabling users to judge whether current-year revenues were sufficient to pay for that year's services. The board termed this criterion *interperiod equity* (GASB, 1990).

Instead of using cash receipt as a criterion for recognizing revenue, the board was concerned with whether the underlying transaction had concurred and the government had demanded payment (in the case of taxes) or had a legally enforceable claim (in the case of fines, licenses, and permits). Expenditures would be recognized to the extent of claims against the government's financial resources. Furthermore, expenditures were to be categorized as capital expenditures (i.e., those giving rise to capital assets) or operating expenditures.

These changes might seem relatively minor as the board had only dropped the adjective *current* for *financial resources.* This action, however, would have enabled governments to pick up longer-term receivables (for revenues) but longer-term liabilities (for expenditures) as well. The standard was adopted by unanimous vote. Subsequently, as its impacts were assessed when government began considering its implementation, opposition emerged. Eventually, after a change of membership, a 3-to-2 majority of the board voted in favor of postponing the effective date of Statement 11, thus effectively killing it (GASB, 1993).

In a sense Statement 11 was only a conservative change of the status quo by reducing the extent to which accrual was modified. The status quo amounted to a strong modification of the accrual basis, whereas the position of Statement 11 was for a weak modification, i.e., allowing more accrual. The mildness of the change from a theoretical point of view belied the potential financial consequences of changing the measurement rule. Under Statement 11, revenue recognition would have been advanced, while postponing payment for current services would not reduce expenditures. The net effect would depend on the balance of the changes.

The requirement for separately identifying operating expenditures seemed innocuous. But analysts were able to anticipate the potential impact of Statement 11 on the balance sheet, even though the board excluded the balance sheet from the scope of Statement 11. The accumulation of unpaid operating expenditures would give rise to greater long-term liabilities. If these liabilities were to move from the general long-term debt account group to the responsible fund, the absence of corresponding assets would result in a reduction in net assets or fund equity. This would signal a worsened financial position.

After decade-long research and deliberations, the GASB released a definite new reporting model in Statement 34, "Basic Financial Statements—and Management's Discussion and Analysis—for State and Local Governments," in June 1999. Governments will be required to include both fund financial statements and *governmentwide* financial statements in a package of basic financial statements. In addition, a management's discussion and analysis is required to give an overview of the government's financial activities. Interested readers are encouraged to refer to the GASB document for a full description and justification of the model.

Briefly, the governmentwide, i.e., consolidated, financial statements resemble the business and nonprofit financial statements required by the FASB. They consist of a statement of net assets (formerly the balance sheet or statement of financial position) and a statement of activities (formerly the operating statement). Governmental and business activities are to be distinguished, whereas fiduciary activities are excluded. The financial statements will adopt economic resources as their measurement focus and use the (full) accrual basis of accounting. This means that capital assets, including infrastructure assets, will be included and report their historical costs. These assets are to be depreciated. Depreciation expense is reported in the statement of activities, and net book value in the statement of net assets. Depreciation is exempted for infrastructure, that is part of a network (e.g., a highway system), if certain requirements to ensure its maintenance are met.

To report additional information, GASB has required the presentation of fund financial statements for governmental and proprietary funds. Large funds are to be presented individually, and the others are grouped together. The measurement methodology would remain the same: modified accrual for governmental funds and full accrual for proprietary funds. The differences between the governmentwide and fund financial statements are reconciled and reported.

It is likely that the merit of the new reporting model will be debated for the foreseeable future. Several issues are involved. First, the addition of another set of financial statements would increase information overload and compliance costs. Second, collecting information about infrastructure is costly, and the historical costs and depreciation expense derived therefrom are of dubious value. Third, the link between the reports and enhanced accountability and better decision making is tenuous and has not been empirically demonstrated. Fourth, accruals would lead to greater divergence between accounting and budgeting, raising contentious issues especially on the funding of long-term liabilities. For these and other reasons, the implementation of GASB Statement 34 will present great challenges to state and local governments and the GASB.

As we complete this review of efforts to improve state and local government accounting, it is worth recalling that the "perfect balance sheet" was the quest of government accountants 100 years ago. Financial integrity, legal compliance, sound financial management, and public accountability guided reforms in the 20th century. Their values may well last into the 21st century.

FEDERAL GOVERNMENT ACCOUNTING

Federal accounting reform has always been conceived as part of improving federal financial management (Comptroller General, 1985; Bowsher, 1987; Hildreth, 1993; Jones and McCaffery, 1992, 1993; Jones, 1993; Chan, 1995). Discussions over the decades have revolved around two separate but related issues: who should determine federal accounting principles and what those principles should be. This section examines these institutional and conceptual issues.

Institutional Issues

Which branch of government—executive or legislative—should set accounting standards for the federal government and its agencies? Specifically, should it be the Treasury Department, the Office of Management and Budget, or the General Accounting Office? This question has been debated at least since the 1930s and was resolved only in the early 1990s. A brief historical review helps put the matter in perspective.

The Constitution of the United States requires the Congress to make appropriations before the Treasury can spend money. It also requires the secretary of the Treasury to produce periodic financial reports. The 1789 Treasury Act established an auditor and comptroller in the Treasury Department and required the department to submit an annual report to the Congress. The Dockery Act of 1894 further required the Treasury Department to submit to Congress annual combined statements of receipts and expenditures. The Treasury Department fulfills its reporting obligation by issuing an Annual Report as the official financial reports of the U.S. government.

Two other players arrived on the scene when the 1921 Budget and Accounting Act created the Bureau of the Budget and the General Accounting Office (GAO) in the Treasury Department. To ensure the GAO's independence of the executive departments, the comptroller general would enjoy a 15-year term. The 1921 act required the comptroller general to "prescribe the forms, systems, and procedures for administrative appropriation and fund accounting in the several departments and establishments, and for the administrative examination of the fiscal officers' accounts and claims against the United States" (Trask, 1996: 563–564). This combination of the accounting and auditing functions in one office became a contentious issue over the next 70 years.

There were two contending schools of thought. The executive perspective was articulated by the President's Committee on Administrative Management (the Brownlow Committee) during the Roosevelt administration and reiterated by the Hoover Commissions in the next two decades. The Brownlow Committee (1937) called for strengthening the Bureau of the Budget "as the right arm of the president for central fiscal management." But it recognized that effective fiscal management required that the budget be reinforced by the accounting system to direct and control expenditures. Since the committee believed that expenditure control was "essentially an executive function"—a part of the president's constitutional duty to execute the law faithfully—it followed that accounting was also an executive prerogative. The committee recommended that the control and audit functions be separated. Specifically, "the authority to prescribe and supervise accounting systems, forms and procedures in the Federal establishments should be transferred to and vested in the Secretary of the Treasury." This would enable the GAO to focus on the postaudit function and not be involved in approving financial transactions.

The congressional perspective has been quite different. Even before the Budget and Accounting Act in 1921, the Dockery-Cockrell Commission in the 1890s had "reaffirmed congressional preeminence with regard to the modes of federal financial management" (Mosher, 1979: 29; quoted in Trask, 1996: 2). Thus the Brownlow Committee's assertion of accounting as an executive function would not be acceptable to Congress and the GAO. In their view, setting accounting policies and procedure was an extension of the congressional budget function and an expression of legislative oversight. Insistence over institutional prerogatives led to numerous clashes over a 50-year period.

It was futile for the executive and the legislative branches to claim exclusive jurisdiction over accounting standard setting, because accounting is inseparable from budgeting and auditing. A good accounting system supports budget execution; it also provides facts for the audit function. Being situated between budgeting and auditing in the integrated financial management cycle (Comptroller General, 1985), accounting is subject to the tug-of-war between the administration and the auditor.

The turf war was detrimental to improvement of financial management in the federal government. In 1947 the comptroller general, the Treasury secretary, and the budget director agreed to cooperate in a joint program to improve federal accounting. The GAO agreed to limit its role to developing standards and guidance and providing expert assistance, leaving the operation of accounting systems to the agencies. After its decline during the tenure of his predecessor, Comptroller General Elmer B. Staats in the 1960s reinvigorated the program and broadened its scope to financial management. This Joint Financial Management Improvement

Program (JFMIP) in 1991 was chosen as the institutional umbrella for cosponsoring the Federal Accounting Standards Advisory Board (Bramlett, 1991).

It would be simplistic to view the interagency conflict only as a bureaucratic rivalry. The constitutional principle of separation of powers was involved. Both sides of the issue recognized the importance of accounting as a tool for managing and controlling the financial operations of the federal government. They were also concerned with the how the financial picture of the government would be portrayed, as will be clear in the next section.

Conceptual Issues

The main conceptual issue facing the U.S. government was whether to adopt the accrual basis of accounting and to present consolidated financial statements. As generally accepted accounting principles (GAAP) have required these methods for business firms, the debate was sometimes couched in terms of whether the federal government should adhere to GAAP. Clearly the federal government was not (and is not) subject to FASB and GASB pronouncements. GAAP was used as a shorthand for business accounting principles.

The first Hoover Commission in 1949 and the second Hoover Commission in 1956 both recommended that the federal government use accrual accounting. Indeed accrual accounting was required by legislation passed in 1956, but the law was not effectively implemented (Rita and Eisenhart, 1992). Contemporary debate on this issue resumed in the mid-1970s, when Arthur Andersen & Co., a major accounting firm, acting on its own initiative, studied the accounting practices of the U.S. government and published the first consolidated financial statements of federal government based on its interpretations of the accrual basis of accounting. Next year, Secretary of the Treasury William E. Simon was sufficiently persuaded to name an advisory committee to follow up on Arthur Andersen's recommendations. The committee developed a guide, and the Treasury Department for the next two decades annually refined and published unaudited *prototype* consolidated financial statements, while continuing to publish its Annual Report as the official report of the U.S. government.

In 1986, Arthur Andersen & Co. reiterated its case. First, the budget deficit measured on the cash basis did not reflect the financial condition and the real cost of government programs. The lack of an appropriate definition of "balanced budget" and budget deficit hindered public debate on how to reduce federal deficits, which had been escalating since the late 1960s. Second, the U.S. government exempted itself from generally accepted accounting principles while requiring publicly held corporations and state and local governments to follow GAAP. Accrual accounting was required by law based on the second Hoover Commission's recommendation and by GAO accounting guidance to federal agencies.

Third, the cash basis hid the cost of current programs and could lead to misallocation of national resources. Disclosure of unfunded liabilities for federal employee retirement pensions and for social security benefits and other entitlement programs was inadequate.

These observations led Arthur Andersen & Co. again to urge the U.S. government to regard consolidated financial statements prepared on the accrual basis as the official financial statements of the U.S. government and subject them to independent audit by the U.S. General Accounting Office. The federal government should improve its accounting system and should concentrate central financial reporting in a single agency. Perhaps the most controversial recommendation was that the federal government should prepare the annual budget in accordance with generally accepted accounting principles.

Arthur Andersen & Co. believed that these recommendations would improve elected officials' accountability, lead to more informed decision making, prevent financial crisis, and facilitate improvement of performance measures. Raising the stakes even higher, it declared, "It is not simply a matter of dollars, but of whether a nation of 240 million free people can govern themselves effectively" (Arthur Andersen & Co., 1986: 1).

At about the same time as the Arthur Andersen update, Comptroller General Charles A. Bowsher issued a major document, *Managing the Cost of Government: Building an Effective Financial Management Structure* (Comptroller General, 1985). The document catalogued a long list of problem areas: poor quality of financial management information; poor linkages between the phases of the financial management process; inadequate attention paid to monitoring and comparing budgeted activities with actual results; primary emphasis on fund control; inadequate disclosure of assets, costs, and liabilities; antiquated and fragmented financial management systems. To address these problems, the comptroller general proposed a structure to integrate planning and programming, budgeting, budget execution and accounting, and audit and evaluation. Specifically, he recommended the following:

Make resource allocation decisions within a unified budget.
Budget and account on the same basis.
Use accounting principles that match the delivery of services with the cost of services.
Encourage financial accountability through management reports that match accomplishments with costs.
Measure outputs as well as inputs.
Prepare consolidated reports.

Similarly to that in the Arthur Andersen proposal, the accrual basis and consolidated financial reporting were the conceptual foundation of the GAO system. The

GAO buttressed its case by linking consolidated financial reporting to the unified budget, which had been the cornerstone of the federal budget since 1968. "Consolidation of annually audited financial statements provided an overall picture of the federal government's financial condition," argued the GAO. The GAO also pointed out that by focusing on the balance sheet, "(d)isclosure of the cumulative financial effects of past decisions aids the public and policy formulators in analysis of resources and commitments" (Comptroller General, 1985: 4).

With regard to measurement, the "same basis" the GAO had in mind for integrating the budgets and accounts was the accrual basis. "Accrual principles," the GAO argued, "provide policymakers and managers with consistent information to compare program/service costs between period or agencies. Interperiod distortions are minimized, and better informed cost/benefit evaluations become possible" (Comptroller General, 1985: 4).

A year earlier, the GAO had already revised its accounting rules—Title 2 of *GAO Policy and Procedure Manual for Guidance of Federal Agencies*—to require the preparation of agencywide (consolidated) financial statements using the accrual basis of accounting. To demonstrate the superiority and feasibility of the proposed accounting rules and reporting model, the GAO conducted a Federal Government Reporting Study with the Office of the Auditor General of Canada (OAG and GAO, 1986). The study cited results from surveys of actual and potential users in support of consolidated financial statements prepared on the accrual basis. Clearly considerable momentum had been generated for a new kind of federal accounting and financial reporting.

According to Rita and Eisenhart (1992: 3–15), it was the *reporting* requirement of Title 2 that upset the executive branch most. Noncompliance with the reporting requirement would be more visible and easily verifiable than noncompliance with the *accounting* requirement. In addition to the jurisdictional issues mentioned earlier, there were genuine conceptual problems with the proposal, especially concerning the accrual basis.

The first and foremost issue is that the federal government is unique. Not only is it a sovereign with the power to print money, it is not accustomed to thinking about its financial condition in terms of the balance sheet. The federal government has many unique assets, among them federal land and weapon systems. Rarely is it feasible or meaningful to talk about the historical costs or market value of these assets. The scope and definition of the federal government's liabilities are particularly problematic. Whenever Congress passes and the president signs a law creating certain rights, their future costs in a sense become a federal liability. If so, federal liabilities include the future costs of promoting general welfare. The bottom line for the federal government is often not financial in nature; even economic considerations are sometimes overridden by political and social concerns. It is therefore doubtful that a body of principles developed to account for commercial transactions could accommodate the unique character of the federal government.

The federal budget community in general had reservations about the assertiveness of the accountant. The first OMB director, Roy Ash, called accrual accounting a "bottomless pit." David Stockman, OMB director under President Reagan, ridiculed corporate accounting for the federal government as "Alice in Wonderland nonsense, not remotely possible or useful" (Chan, 1995: 34). From their perspective, federal accounting should complement the federal budget by playing a supportive role. Over time and especially since the 1968 *Report of the President's Commission on Budget Concepts,* a body of federal budgeting rules or norms has evolved. The idea that accounting rules could or should challenge them struck the federal budget community as presumptuous (Cuny, 1995). First of all, generally accepted accounting principles have been developed primarily for business enterprises, whose objectives and operations are quite different from those of the federal government (Mautz, 1991). Furthermore, the accounting rules in GAO's Title 2 had not been accepted by the other central finance agencies or the line agencies.

Although the accrual basis drew most attack, the usefulness of consolidated financial reporting was also doubted. Consolidated financial reporting would call for the preparation of financial reports on the basis of organizational units (e.g., the Department of Commerce or the General Service Administration) and ultimately of the United States government as a whole. The latter is the accounting counterpart to the unified budget and could be justified on similar grounds. However, budget accounts are what really matter in the federal budget process. Congress appropriates funds to the budget accounts, and these accounts become the accounting entities to track. Furthermore, the federal budget is structured in terms of programs and functions, whereas accountants tend to focus on organizational units.

In summary, the GAO and Arthur Andersen proposals were so different from the established budget practices that they engendered strong negative reaction from the federal budget agencies. The conceptual issues became connected with the jurisdictional issues, making it virtually impossible to have rational discussions at the technical level. Fortunately by the late 1980s, the leaders of the central finance agencies concluded that the prolonged stalemate would have dysfunctional consequences. After considerable negotiations, they reached an agreement to cosponsor a body to work on these issues.

Resolution of the Issues

The jurisdictional issue discussed earlier was resolved by means of the Joint Financial Management Improvement Program (JFMIP). The JFMIP principals—the secretary of the Treasury, the director of the OMB, and the comptroller general—agreed to establish jointly an advisory body—the Federal Accounting Standards Advisory Board (FASAB). FASAB would conduct the necessary research and deliberations in order to recommend accounting standards applicable to the federal government. The assumption was that the JFMIP principals would have sufficient confidence in their own creation that they would require compliance by federal agencies (Bramlett, 1991; Bramlett and Rexford, 1992).

The Chief Financial Officers Act required federal agencies to furnish "complete, reliable, timely and consistent financial information for use by the executive branch of Government and the Congress in the financing, management, and evaluation of Federal programs" (CFO Act, Sec. 102[b][3]). The CFO act also gave OMB the authority to specify the "form and content" of financial statements. Therefore the OMB representative at FASAB for a period argued that FASAB should set accounting—as opposed to financial reporting—standards only. To complicate the matter further, Congress was, however, reluctant to delegate accounting-standard-setting authority completely. For example, the CFO act required congressional approval of accounting standards on capital, including human capital.

Under the watchful eyes of Congress, its sponsors, and the federal agencies, the FASAB thus became a forum for discussing federal accounting issues. The membership of the board was carefully specified to ensure that the perspectives of these stakeholders would be reflected. The agreement creating the FASAB specifies that the Treasury Department, OMB, and GAO, along with the Congressional Budget Office, each have a representative on the board. Two other federal members represent civilian and defense agencies, respectively. There are three public members as well.

The technical issues were so numerous and complex that the board simultaneously adopted a comprehensive and an incremental approach. On the basis of staff research on users and their needs, the board adopted a broad set of objectives for federal financial reporting and specified a reporting model. The FASAB believes that federal financial reports should help users evaluate the government's budgetary integrity, operating performance, stewardship over the government's impact on the nation, and adequacy of systems and control. FASAB has provided an inclusive definition of federal entities and requires their preparation of management discussion and analysis and a half-dozen statements on financial position and changes thereof, net costs, custodial activities, budgetary resources, and program performance measures. Other relevant information is to be provided in supplementary reports.

These concepts statements provided a framework for addressing specific technical issues in almost a dozen documents (FASAB, 1997). FASAB statements give guidance on the measurement and reporting of specific elements of the financial statements. In contrast to the budget, the financial reporting model stresses the reporting of financial position as much as periodic results of operations. The statements attempted to identify the myriad federal assets and liabilities. The assets range from cash and other financial resources to inventories and fixed assets.

Given their diversity and the inconclusiveness of debates over measurement bases, the FASAB has largely allowed the existing practices to continue. The federal government's liabilities are equally numerous and huge in amounts. Besides the familiar national debt, there are other legal and contractual obligations, such as pension and retirement benefits for federal employees. The FASAB soon found itself entering the gray area of commitments and obligations that strain the traditional definition of liabilities. In view of the potential legal and political consequences of defining something (e.g., future benefits under entitlement programs) as a liability, the FASAB prudently refrained from assuming too broad a conception of liability and settled for their reporting off the balance sheet in supplemental disclosures. In one particular area, credit reform legislation called for the use of present value to measure the cost of federal subsidies for loans and loan guarantees. The FASAB accepted this requirement and has developed consistent accounting and reporting requirements. In general then, the FASAB embraced the philosophy of accrual accounting and, subject to measurement technology, provided for a meaningful balance sheet.

The FASAB readily endorsed the recognition of revenues from sales of government services when the services have been rendered. Influenced by current budget practices that regard such revenues as offsetting collections and receipts to reduce expenses, the FASAB coined the concept of *net cost* to reflect share of cost of services (expenses) borne by taxpayers. Costs of services are calculated on the full-accrual basis; that means that even the cost of using equipment and noncash expenses (e.g., future pension benefits of employees) are included.

With regard to revenues, the FASAB believed that in principle revenues from so-called nonexchanged transactions (e.g., taxation) should be recognized when the government has established a legally enforceable claim. Practical considerations arising mainly from the government's inability to have timely information push the recognition to the point near cash collection. Accurate measures of the government's taxes receivable remain a major administrative challenge to the government.

In view of the significant differences between budget and accounting concepts (Cuny, 1995), the FASAB called for their reconciliation and disclosure in the financial statements. This compromise approach acknowledges the budget's power and the division of labor between accountants and budget makers.

It was not realistic to expect to resolve all the complex accounting issues in the federal government. After establishing the basic standards, it has entered the refining phase as agencies encounter difficulties in implementing the standards.

On the whole, the current wave of reform in federal accounting has some positive attributes. Accounting has assumed a strategic position of supporting financial management reform legislation, making it possible to recruit political allies. Both the GAO and the OMB have refrained from insisting on their constitutional prerogatives and have found common grounds. There is team work: Central finance agencies work with line agencies and the central finance agencies cooperate among themselves. The FASAB has adopted a top-down approach. Starting with the U.S. government as a whole, the reporting model views agencies and programs as component units. This ensures consistency and prevents capture by the peculiarities of the existing funds and budget accounts. The board has benefited from multidisciplinary staff research support. Budget experts, many of whom are economists, joined the research process early and made substantial contributions. As a result, professional respect and camaraderie facilitated consensus building. Finally, the board has struck a delicate balance between the ideal content of financial reports and the reality of imperfect accounting systems. FASAB members and staff spent considerable time hearing out the agency representatives on their current practices and unique problems. On the whole, however, it has leaned toward pursuing its mandate for meaningful reports, while being mindful of the need to improve the system producing them.

The FASAB principles have been in use for several years now to guide the preparation of two governmentwide financial reports and scores of agency financial reports. After settling on the major conceptual issues, technical issues are resolved through the refinement and interpretation of existing standards. It will be many years before the federal government will need another major overhaul of its accounting standards.

CONCLUSION

The federal system in the United States has resulted in two separate paths of reforming government accounting standards at the federal and state/local levels. State and local governments have a history of almost seven decades of reforming government accounting standards (Johnson and Langsam, 1991). For the federal government, which has a long history of *budget* reform, contemporary accounting standard setting began in earnest only in the early 1990s. However, in a relatively short period, the federal government made a more clear-cut break from tradition. The similarities and differences between accounting reforms at these two levels of American government are summarized in Table 1.

After several decades of reform, government accounting standards for the federal government and for state and local government have finally achieved a conceptual convergence. Both are requiring governmentwide consolidated reporting using the accrual basis. Such an accounting system is significantly at odds with the public budget systems organized around budget accounts to keep track of the flow of financial resources. This chapter has explained this conceptual convergence as a reflection of the combined effects of several influences. The first is the shift of the objective of accounting from primarily a management tool of budget execution to the government's demonstration of accountability to resource providers. The second is the influence of private-sector accounting where consol-

Table 1 Differences and Similarities

<table>
<tr><th>State and local governments</th><th>Federal government</th></tr>
<tr><td>• GASB standards that cover external reporting exclusively</td><td>• FASAB standards that cover management and cost accounting</td></tr>
<tr><td>• Creditors and investors among primary users</td><td>• Congress and managers among primary users</td></tr>
<tr><td>• Discrete presentation of major funds</td><td>• Separation of financial reports by agency</td></tr>
<tr><td>• GASB an extragovernmental body</td><td>• FASAB an interbranch cooperative mechanism</td></tr>
<tr><td>• Indirect government oversight through public interest groups</td><td>• Direct government oversight</td></tr>
<tr><td>• GASB standards enforced through CPA audits and rating agency requirement</td><td>• FASAB standards enforced through legislative and administrative requirements</td></tr>
<tr><td colspan="2">• Long-term goal of integrating financial and performance measures to promote accountability
• Emphasis on external reporting with a user orientation
• Addition of management discussion and analysis (MDA) to enhance user understanding of financial statements
• Adoption of complete financial reporting model with a balance sheet
• Commitment to accrual, with concessions in implementation
• Commitment to governmentwide reporting
• Requirement for actual and budgetary comparison
• Extensive due process and openness in standard setting</td></tr>
</table>

idation and accrual are the norm. But this influence probably would not have succeeded if it were not for the public demand that government be run more as businesses are. The third influence is the tradition of independent accounting standard setting and external auditing. This has enabled public finance professionals and the CPA profession to become a major and continuous force in championing changes when individual governments and officials lack the incentive and power to make them. These influences led the German scholar Klaus Luder (1989) to conclude that the social, political, and administrative factors in the United States were favorable to the adoption of major conceptual changes in government accounting. These changes have at long last fulfilled Thomas Jefferson's dream in 1802:

> I think it an object of great importance . . . to simplify our system of finance, and to bring it within the comprehension of every member of Congress . . . the whole system [has been] involved in impenetrable fog. [T]here is a point . . . on which I should wish to keep my eye . . . a sim-

plification of the form of accounts . . . so as to bring everything to a single center[;] we might hope to see the finances of the Union as clear and intelligible as a merchant's books, so that every member of Congress, and every man of any mind in the Union, should be able to comprehend them to investigate abuses, and consequently to control them.

ACKNOWLEDGMENT

I thank Robert Bramlett, Richard Brown and Sheldon Langsam for supplying useful reference materials. Jessamine Chan provided able editorial assistance. I am solely responsible for the content.

REFERENCES

American Institute of Certified Public Accountants, Committee on Terminology (1953). *Accounting Terminology Bulletin,* No. 1. AICPA, New York.

Antonio, J.F. (1985). Role and future of the Governmental Accounting Standards Board. *Public Budgeting & Finance. 5*(2): 30–38.

Arthur Andersen & Co. (1986). *Sound Financial Reporting in the U.S. Government.* Arthur Anderson & Co., Chicago.

Bowsher, C.A. (1985). Governmental financial management at the crossroads. *Public Budgeting & Finance. 5*(2): 9–22.

Bowsher, C.A. (1987). Federal financial management: Evolution, challenges and the role of the accounting profession. *Journal of Accountancy* (May): 280–294.

Bramlett, R. (1991). The Federal Accounting Standards Advisory Board: An introduction to non-accountants. *Public Budgeting & Finance. 11*(4): 11–19.

Bramlett, R., and Rexford, F. (1992). The Federal Accounting Standards Advisory Board: A View of its role one year later. *Public Budgeting & Finance. 12*(4): 87–101.

Brown, R.E., and Pyers, J. (1998). Service efforts and accomplishments reporting: Has its time really come? *Public Budgeting & Finance. 18*(4): 101–113.

Bureau of Municipal Research (1913). *[Metz Fund] Handbook of Municipal Accounting.* D. Appleton, New York.

Chan, J.L. (1985). "The birth of the Governmental Accounting Standards Board: How? Why? What Next?" *Research in Governmental and Nonprofit Accounting. 1:* 3–32.

Chan, J.L. (1995). Accounting and financial management reform in the United States: An application of Professor Luder's contingency model. In *Perspectives on Performance Measurement and Public Sector Accounting* (E. Buscher and K. Scheduler ed.). Paul Haupt Publishers, Berne.

Chan, J.L. (1998). The basis of accounting for budgeting and financial reporting. In *Handbook of Public Budgeting* (Roy T. Meyers ed.). Jossey-Bass, San Francisco.

Cleveland, F.A. (1909). *Chapters on Municipal Administration Accounting.* Longmans, Green, New York.

Comptroller General of the United States (1985). *Managing the Cost of Government: Building an Effective Financial Management Structure.* U.S. General Accounting Office, Washington, D.C.

Cuny, T.J. (1995). The pending revolution in federal accounting standards. *Public Budgeting & Finance. 15*(3): 22–34.

Davidson, S., et al. (1977). *Financial Reporting by State and Local Government Units.* The Center for Management of Public and Nonprofit Enterprises, Graduate School of Business, University of Chicago, Chicago.

Drebin, A.R., et. al. (1981). *Objectives of Accounting and Financial Reporting for Governmental Units: A Research Study.* National Council on Governmental Accounting, Chicago.

Federal Accounting Standards Advisory Board (1997). *Statements of Federal Financial Accounting Concepts and Standards.* GAO/AIMD, Washington, D.C.

Fleischman, R.K. (1987). Foundation of the National Municipal League. *Journal of Accountancy* (May): 297–298.

Gardiner, J.A. and Olson, D.J., eds. (1974). *Theft of the City.* Indiana University Press, Bloomington, Indiana.

GASB (1990). Measurement focus and basis of accounting—governmental fund operating statement, *Statement 11.* GASB, Norwalk, Conn.

GASB (1993). Measurement focus and basis of accounting—governmental fund operating statements: amendment of the effective dates of GASB Statement No. 11 and related statements. GASB, Norwalk, Conn.

GASB (1998). *Codification of Governmental Accounting and Financial Reporting Standards.* GASB, Norwalk, Conn.

GASB (1999). Basic financial statements—and management's discussion and analysis—for state and local governments, *Statement 34.* GASB, Conn., Norwalk.

Greathouse, F.L. (1985). The history and evolution of the National Council on Governmental Accounting. *Public Budgeting & Finance. 5*(2): 23–29.

Hildreth, W.B. (1993). Federal financial management control systems: An integrative framework. *Public Budgeting & Finance. 13*(1): 77–86.

Johnson, G.G., and Langsam, S.A. (1991). Historical sources and current status of GAAP for state and local governments. *Government Accountants Journal* (Summer): 54–64.

Jones, L.R. (1993). Counterpoint essay: Nine reasons why the CFO Act may not achieve its objectives. *Public Budgeting & Finance. 13*(1): 87–94.

Jones, L.R., and McCaffery, J.L. (1992). Federal financial management reform and the Chief Financial Officers Act. *Public Budgeting & Finance. 12*(4): 75–86.

Jones, L.R. and McCaffery, J.L. (1993). Implementing the Chief Financial Officers Act and the Government Performance and Results Act in the federal government. *Public Budgeting & Finance. 17*(1): 35–55.

Jones, L.R. and McCaffery, J.L. (1997). Implementing the Federal Chief Financial

Luder, K.G. (1989). *Comparative Government Accounting Study—Interim Summary Report.* rev. ed., Research Report (76). Postgraduate School of Administrative Studies, Speyer, Germany.

Luder, K.G. (1989). *Comparative Government Accounting Study—Interim Summary Report.* rev. ed., Research Report (76). Speyer.

MacPherson, F.H. (1901). *Municipal Accounting.* The Book-Keeper Publishing Company, Detroit.

Matika, L.A. (1988). The contributions of Frederick Albert Cleveland to the development of a system of municipal accounting in the progressive era. Unpublished dissertation, Kent State University.

Mautz, R.K. (1991). Generally accepted accounting principles and federal government financial reporting. *Public Budgeting & Finance.* 11(4): 3–10.

Morey, L., and Diehl, O.W. (1942). *Municipal Accounting: Principles and Procedures.* John Wiley & Sons, New York.

Mosher, F.C. (1979). *The GAO: The Quest for Accountability in American Government.* Westview Press, Boulder, Colorado.

Municipal Finance Officers Association (1968). *Governmental Accounting, Auditing, and Financial Reporting.* MFOA, Chicago.

National Committee on Municipal Accounting (1936). *Bulletin No. 6: Municipal Accounting Statements.* NCMA, Chicago.

National Committee on Municipal Accounting (1968). *Governmental Accounting, Auditing and Financial Reporting.* Municipal Finance Officers Association, Chicago.

National Council on Governmental Accounting (1979). Governmental accounting and financial reporting standards, *Statement 1.* NCGA, Chicago.

Office of the Auditor General of Canada and U.S. General Accounting Office (1986). *Federal Government Reporting Study.* OAG, Ottawa; GAO, Washington, D.C.

Patton, J.M. (1992). Accountability and governmental financial reporting. *Financial Accountability and Management. 8*(3): 165–180.

Remis, J.S. (1981). Governmental accounting standards—a historical perspective. In *Objectives of Accounting and Financial Reporting for Governmental Units: A Research Study* (A.R. Drebin, J.L. Chan and L.C. Ferguson eds.). NCGA, Chicago.

Rita, W.J. and Eisenhart, L.J. (1992). Federal government accounting principles and practices. In *Handbook of Governmental Accounting and Finance* (N.G. Apostolou and D.L. Crumbley, eds.). John Wiley & Sons, New York.

Steffens, L. (1904; 1957). *The Shame of the Cities.* Sagamore Press, New York.

Trask, Roger R. (1996). *Defender of the Public Interest: The General Accounting Office, 1921–1966.* U.S. General Accounting Office, Washington, D.C.

U.S. President's Committee on Administrative Management (The Brownlow Committee) (1937). *Report of the President's Committee on Administrative Management.* Excerpts reprinted in *Public Budgeting & Finance. 1*(1): 85–92.

6

Unfinished Agenda in Public Financial Management

A. Premchand
National Institute of Public Finance,
New Delhi, India

> "How long have you been hearing confessions?"
> "About fifteen years"
> "What has confession taught you about men?"
> "Oh, confession teaches nothing, you know, because when a priest goes into the confessional, he becomes another person—grace and all that. And yet . . . first of all, people are much more unhappy than one thinks . . . and then. . . ."
> He raised his brawny lumberman's arms in the starlit night; "And then, the fundamental fact is that there is no such thing as a grown-up person."
>
> —Andre Malraux, *Anti-Memoirs,* 1968

The title of the chapter may give the impression that there has been an agreed agenda and that some parts have been implemented and a few remain to be implemented. It is therefore appropriate to state the objective and coverage of this chapter at the very outset. The basic premise is to point out that there has been no agreed agenda largely because of differences of opinions among academics and professional practitioners about the identity of financial management, although recently there has been greater convergence in the views on the nature and content of financial management and the broad identity is much clearer than before. It is further intended to point out that notwithstanding a series of efforts aimed at improving financial management in developing countries (which include those countries that have moved away from comprehensive state ownership and centralized planning), a good deal remains to be done. The issue no longer is, Why reform the financial management processes in these countries?, but, How is it to be undertaken and what should be the points of departure from the present practices? Although there are substantial differences in the systems of financial management now in practice, there are also several common features, which permit us to make generalizations that have common applicability albeit with some differences in degree.

NEED FOR CONSIDERATION

The need for stocktaking and consideration of the areas where improvements are needed is inherent in the current situation. First, the fiscal turbulence in the 1980s and 1990s has left the financial management machinery severely tested and battered. There has been a growing recognition that the processes dealing with policy formulation and implementation have not been adequate and that, in general, there has been and continues to be a long lag between the identification of a problem and the formulation of a response to that problem. Experience of many countries, particularly in the developing world, shows that there were no strategies to deal with sudden reversals in economic situations and that the responses of governments have been more often tactical, often contributing to contrary results. Within the financial management machinery, the approach has been to place a disproportionate emphasis on process controls, e.g., payments by governments, in turn contributing to unprecedented accumulation in the payment arrears. Apart from the need to strengthen the financial management machinery so that the objectives of macroeconomic stability could be pursued with greater vigor, the growing globalization of financial transactions is putting new pressures on governments. They are called upon to deal with situations in which their information on the motives and actions of global agents is often limited, but where slowness in policy reactions could have far reaching adverse reactions on the economy.

Second, there is a general view that financial management has not been very effective in ensuring congruence between budgetary intent and outcome. The reasons for a different outcome could have their origins in overoptimistic assumptions about revenues and conservative estimates about expenditures, or difficulties in anticipating critical situations and developments in the local economy. Partly, it could also be due to the pervasive prevalence of soft constraints and perverse incentives in the system, which permit imprudent fiscal behavior in the spending agencies.

Third, there is a perception among the people of both industrial and developing countries that there is considerable wastage in the process of resource utilization by public bodies, and that this wastage continues unabated despite the introduction of innovations including performance oriented budget systems. The legislatures, where active, have been growing skeptical about the capacities of the executive. Although the built-in adversarial relationship between the legislature and the executive is partly responsible for this skepticism, there is some justification for the views of the former.

Fourth, there are meanwhile growing pressures on financial management systems to assume additional tasks. Financial management is now expected to reconcile the needs of macroeconomic stability with efficiency in the provision of services to the community, while being transparent in its actions and fully accountable for its actions. Accountability is no longer viewed in narrow terms, of being responsible for moneys spent but not for results and effectiveness in achieving program objectives. The issue arises as to how the systems that have not hitherto been successful in these efforts can now be expected to be effective. As Shakespeare wrote in *Julius Caesar,* "And men are flesh and blood, and apprehensive." Now the apprehension is a widespread phenomenon.

WHAT TOOK PLACE AND WHY?

Financial management went through major changes during the 19th and 20th centuries. The issues sought to be addressed during the 19th century, for the most part, concentrated on developing systems and structures that would facilitate the exercise of legislative control over the actions of the executive and providing for avenues that would make the executive more accountable to the legislature. Although this aspect continues to be refined, it would appear that because of the changes in the sphere of economic and financial decision making there was a gradual shift of power from the legislature to the executive during the 20th century. The second issue to be addressed related to the pursuit of economy and efficiency in the conduct of financial operations. It was recognized that the annual budget represented only a first step in this pursuit and much would have to be done during the budget implementation phase. But this was a phase, in which much was dependent on the initiative taken by the executive. The legislature could exhort, as it usually did with considerable enthusiasm, but the results were more in the province of the executive. The legislatures therefore decided on an extensive review of the fiscal operations at the end of the fiscal year, thus confirming their right to secure financial accountability. Subsequent experience, particularly during the second half of the 20th century, shows that legislators were more interested in securing budget allocations than in following up on what actually was implemented during a year.

During the third decade of the 20th century, particularly after the First World War, attention shifted to the principles and practice relating to the allocation of resources in the public bodies. The main question that political scientists from Key to Wildavsky sought to answer was how to determine the role of politics in the various phases of financial management. In the course of time, with the emergence of the welfare state and the wide ranging functions assumed by the state, attention also shifted to the provision of resources and the effective performance of the fiscal machinery in this task. This approach was supplemented by the quest for participatory decision making and bridging of the gulf between the community (clients) and the policymakers.

Even as progress was being made to answer the preceding questions, new issues loomed large on the horizon. These related to the burgeoning budget deficits during the sixties and the seventies, and the role of financial management in containing the size of the deficits. The importance of financial management in enhancing implementation of fiscal policy came to be recognized. Such a recognition went beyond the allocation issue that was the main theme during the preceding decades, to the containment of fiscal slippages during the budget implementation stage. In fact, the distinctions between budget formulation and implementation, which hitherto sustained an avoidable distinction in the tasks of economists and accountants, were ignored and the whole process of financial management came to be viewed as continuous.

As a result of these developments, the currents of financial management came to be influenced by the concerns of (a) legislative control, (b) allocation of resources, (c) effective performance, and (d) macroeconomic stability. Each of these contributed to a type of paradigm that in turn had significant and durable influence on the course of financial management. The paradigms and their features are shown in Table 1 (Premchand, 1998a, 1998b). The cumulative impact of the paradigms is that any consideration of the system of financial management should explicitly recognize three features. First, the coherence and stability of a system depend on the image it fosters in the minds of the public and the practitioners. Viewed in segments, it creates a segmented and incomplete picture. Although homogeneity may be difficult to achieve, some degree of reconciliation among the heterogeneous elements should be attained. Second, the consideration should also include the changing public philosophy and the demands that it makes on the financial management machinery. From this point of view, the intellectual tradition elaborated by Weber should be considered not sacrosanct, but as appropriate for revision to reflect the due process, rule of law, an acceptable degree of transparency, and an effective framework of accountability; and third, the consideration should include the application of fruits of rational scientific knowledge to the administrative process of governments and, more specifically, to the area of financial management.

TABLE 1 Changing Paradigms in Financial Management

Paradigm	Features
Control through line items of the budget	• Control of minutiae • Budgeting through an aggregation process • Emphasis on accounting and payment controls • Prior approval from the Ministry of Finance in most cases • General emphasis on inputs
Performance budgeting paradigm	• Emphasis on results or performance • Specification of results • Activity- or program-oriented classification • Emphasis on cost controls
Planning paradigm	• Emphasis on development programs and projects • Exploration of alternatives and application of quantitative techniques of analysis • Longer-term horizon • Program classification
Macroeconomic policy paradigm	• Containment of budget deficits • Moderation of expenditure rate of growth • Ensuring that budget outcome is congruent with intent
Fiscal consolidation paradigm	• Restructuring of government operations with emphasis on contracting out to private sector and nonprofit organizations • Reorganization of the civil service • Privatization of public enterprises • Benefit and entitlement reform
Corporate practice paradigm	• Creation of task-oriented agencies • Determination of global budgetary ceilings • Provision of managerial autonomy • Specification of results • Performance contract • Client orientation
Governance paradigm	• Transparency of government transactions • Accountability • Ethical practices

At the end of the 20th century, and as a result the cumulative advances made over the years, a set of beliefs emerged; it includes the following:

1. Financial management cannot and should not be considered in a disembodied fashion; rather, it should be considered as a part of the overall fabric of macroeconomic policies and setting and as a major instrument for the pursuit of social and economic goals of the society.
2. In furtherance of the preceding objective, the budget of the public body should be comprehensive and coterminous with the range of the activities pursued by that body and should be developed as a part of medium-term strategy. The process of budget formulation should be in conformity with rules specified for the purpose.
3. In order to consolidate the role of the civic society and with a view to promoting a participatory and inclusive decision-making process, adequate arrangements should be made to ensure transparency in all aspects of government transactions, to establish a framework of accountability through which governments can be made responsible for omissions and commissions and through which the public has opportunities to revoke policies when they are deemed to be inappropriate, and to establish a due process for the participation of the public.
4. As an extension of the preceding, a civic society should have organized legislatures that are representative and that have oversight powers for the financial conduct of a government. As an integral part of this arrangement there should be an independent judiciary with operational discretionary powers of its own. An independent and effective audit is a necessary feature.
5. There should be a collaborative framework between governments and the corporate sector and nongovernmental organizations. To the extent possible, service delivery should be diversified and the corporate sector and nongovernmental organizations should be utilized, on a competitive bidding basis, for service provision.
6. Government operations should rely on competitive bidding to secure policy and other inputs and to provide public services.
7. There should be extensive reliance on decentralization of financial decision making without adversely affecting the pursuit of macroeconomic stability. The framework of decentralization should ensure congruence between tasks and responsibilities, and powers, and agencies should be held responsible for performance. Central agencies should be responsible for steering and for the allocation of resources whereas the responsibility for the utilization of resources and performance will be that of the agencies.

8. A code of public conduct governing the political and professional class of administration should be established.
9. There should be a belief in the urgency of realizing the various ends described.

ASSESSING THE EXPERIENCE

The preceding set of beliefs have a universal appeal in both space and time; as such there is likely to be little debate about the desirability of a comprehensive budget or an accountable framework or a code of conduct governing the activities of government officials. It could be argued, however, that not all countries have legislative systems with adequate powers to regulate the finances of a country; similarly, it could be pointed out that effective audit is still evolving in many countries and that more progress remains to be achieved. It has to be recognized that the existence of institutions and operational systems does not necessarily generate an effective financial management system. Established Western democracies such as the United Kingdom and the United States can be said to have all the features enumerated in the set of beliefs stated. But it would be far-fetched to suggest that the systems in these countries are effective and that there are no issues. The problems arise for a variety of reasons. To ascertain these reasons, three basic questions need to be answered: What is the financial management expected to do? To what extent has it been successful in accomplishing the prescribed tasks? And how are the objectives and the working experience of the financial management machinery perceived by the citizens and the participants?

The system has acquired several dimensions; the most important are to serve the purposes of macroeconomic stability; to provide services within specified parameters of cost, time, and quality; and to ensure that there is no wastage of resources. In order to assess the effectiveness of the full financial management machinery, the instruments available to achieve the three major objectives are illustrated in Table 2.

A deeper examination of the instruments illustrated in the table shows that the immediate purposes served by them may be contrary to the needs of macroeconomic stability. Since the mid-1970s, the goal of macroeconomic stability has been mainly to reduce the size of budget deficits through efforts at reducing the rate of growth of expenditures. Medium term rolling expenditure planning, development plans, output budget systems, and accrual-based budget systems emphasized clarifying the financial requirements of continuing policies and the funds needed to provide services with some standards of quality and cost. In fact, if the emphasis is on performance, there is very little likelihood of moderating the growth of expenditure as standards of performance are based on assured levels of commensurate funding. Fundamental reviews of expenditure and zero-base bud-

TABLE 2 Objectives and Instruments of Financial Management

Objectives	Instruments	Remarks
Macroeconomic stability	• Medium-term fiscal policy • Medium-term rolling expenditure planning • Development plans • Specific strategies aimed at containing deficits • Fundamental expenditure reviews • Zero-based budgeting • Output budget systems • Target-based budgeting • Accrual-based budgeting system • Top-down budget techniques	• By far the most successful approach has used "specific strategies" including strict limits on budget deficits. As such, the benefits may not be of an enduring type. • Most developing countries have very little experience with output or accrual-based systems.
Service provision	• Performance or output budget system • Cost standards	• Standards remain, for the most part, entrenched to measure effort and not results or performance.
Prevention of wastage of resources	• Internal evaluation of programs and projects • Reengineering of work processes • Market tests and competitive tendering and bidding • Application of electronic data processing (EDP) technology to reduce processing costs	• The programs in all of the areas are too limited to have any significant impact on the growth of expenditure or prevention of waste.

geting have the potential of reducing the rate of growth, but neither of these techniques has been extensively used in the developing world. The only effective measure that has had frequent application is the use of specific strategies aimed at deficit reduction. Here again there is a major difference in the experiences of industrial and developing countries. In the industrial countries, new legislation enacted as a part of regional economic cooperation agreements (e.g., the Maastricht Treaty) had a major impact in that it forced the member countries to reduce the size of the deficit and, more important, to maintain it at that level. Moreover, limits on a gross public debt too induced an extensive reorganization of government machinery. In the United States, budget legislation and the agreements reached with the legislative branch enabled it, prior to the advent of the prosperous years in the late 1990s, to maintain reduced deficits. On the whole, the differences between industrial and developing countries in this regard comprise the following: First, the industrial countries undertook an extensive range of reforms including reengineering of the public sector, policy and legislative changes, program adjustments, and wage freezes and associated measures. In the developing world, the range of measures was more limited. Apart from privatization, most measures had only short-term impact. Second, the industrial countries undertook an extensive range of reforms including reengineering of the public sector, in which financial management was one component. The other components related to personnel management, procurement, and work processes in government. As a part of this effort, they established a financial management infrastructure that included (a) institutional requirements for fiscal responsibility; (b) programming expenditures over the medium term through multiyear rolling estimates; (c) formulation of global ceilings as a part of devolutionary budgeting; (d) a gradual, if discernible, shift from input management to output and performance-oriented management cultures; (e) greater reliance on information technology to facilitate transactions and to abridge the oversight process while contributing to decentralization; and (f) movement away from cash-based budgetary and accounting systems to accrual systems. These elements had a collective impact of changing the rules of the game. In the developing countries, more focus was on short-term adjustments, mostly at the margin, with the core remaining hollow and ineffective. The work processes remained more or less the same even after the introduction of information technology. In Latin American countries, where the application of technology was far more widespread than elsewhere, the benefits were limited to the payments and accounting areas, while the systems and approaches to budgeting continued in their previous mold. The absence of the infrastructure was the most striking difference with enduring impact on the systems. In the case of industrial countries, the infrastructure sustained a structural adjustment. In the developing world, it is a movement that is waiting to happen.

In regard to service provision, the industrial countries had little option but to develop performance and cost controls in a context where the service delivery moved, for all intents and purposes, into the nongovernmental sectors. As funding continued to be provided by government, they had to develop reliable standards and control measures, to extract compliance from the contractors. But this journey is still in its infancy. In the developing world, funding and provision of services continue to be in-house operations and are, therefore, managed, as with the rest of the public sector operations, primarily with reference to inputs. Similarly, in regard to the identification and wasteful use of resources, industrial countries have taken to greater utilization of evaluations and market tests. This has yet to become a widespread practice. In both, however, attention to waste is often a seasonal activity resorted to in the context of a major financial scandal, or expression of discontent by legislatures, or where the cases are so egregious that even the lay public are informed about them.

At a practical level, the experience of both industrial and developing countries shows that the introduction of new techniques of financial management is not necessarily followed by a change in the management philosophy. As William James noted, "When we look at living creatures . . . one of the first things that strike us is that they are bundles of habits." This would appear to be particularly applicable to the category of finance managers. In developing countries, the introduction of information technology has remained, except in a clutch of Latin American countries, as a mechanical processing adjunct to the obsolete administrative machinery. Moreover, experience also shows that ministries of finance & offices of Management and Budget continue to be intrusive and continue to engage in activities that are more appropriately handled at the level of the spending agencies.

In some cases, the introduction of innovations has contributed to unintended consequences and to paradoxical results. In many developing countries, aid-financed projects and programs have remained, for the most part, as enclaves, intended to serve the needs of donors, rather than the recipient counties. More significantly, the existence of dual systems—one indigenous to the country and another transplanted at the behest of the donor—has contributed to an enduring form of dyarchicical government, and a substantial erosion in the credibility of the receiving government. Elsewhere, as a part of the program of application of information technology and in furtherance of the objectives of macroeconomic stability, payments were centralized to be managed by the central agencies. Although it was conceived as a short-term measure to keep the proclivities of the spending agencies under check, it became a durable feature, in turn contributing to a further loss of financial conscience in the spending agencies. In the industrial countries, the system of devolutionary budgeting contributed to a further accumulation of powers in the central agencies and to a corresponding reduction in the financial autonomy of the agencies. The absence of consultative procedures has exacerbated the problem of interrelationships between central and spending agencies. These paradoxical results remind us of what Bertrand Russell (1956: 12) remarked more than four decades ago: "The point of philosophy is to start with something so simple as to seem not worth stating, and to end with something so paradoxical that no one will believe it."

In both worlds, the practice of circumvention has been extensive and provided yet another illustration of the remark of the late Chicago economist Frank Knight, who observed, "Man seeks to be inherently both a law maker and law breaker." Thus, where balanced budget laws were enacted, they were so drafted as to be tautological in that inflows were equivalent to the outflows. What constituted inflows was left delightfully vague, leaving ample room for maneuvre and facilitating a nominal compliance with laws, while violating their spirit. In other cases, where there were limits on annual borrowing, extensive resort was made to the issue of informal IOUs: Incurrence of unpaid bills, change of effective dates of payment, unbundling approaches to avoid funding ceilings, carryovers, expenditure offsets are but a few of the selected practices intended to avoid them.

RETROSPECT AND PROSPECT

The Oxford philosopher R. G. Collingwood made the point that in any given historical period there are deep lying assumptions that contemporaries share, not even conscious of them as assumptions, so taken for granted are they, and that these are sometimes not accepted by later generations. Such a watershed is now emerging where the assumptions of those engaged in financial management may begin to be questioned. The assumptions, as noted earlier, differed, depending on the professional discipline of those engaged in analysis.[1] The overwhelming dependence of economists on financial management as an allocative mechanism, the assumptions of the management scholars on managerial autonomy as a panacea for all practical problems, the view of the accountants that a move away from cash to accrual systems would induce a massive awareness among the practitioners and the public alike leading to improved policies, the belief of the technology experts that the introduction of information technology would contribute to major transformation in the way in which governments work, and finally the emphasis of international financial institutes on the building up of administrative infrastructures are valid in their own assumptions, but their habit of not recognizing the subtle interrelatedness among the various elements of financial management and not relating the prescriptions for change with the areas where change were needed has contributed to the present situation, in which it is necessary to review the approaches again.

Experience shows that there is a broad systemic inadequacy in dealing with the major problems. As the preceding analysis shows, the available instruments have not had the capacity to meet the growing requirements of macroeconomic stability, service delivery, and prevention of waste in the use of resources. This inadequacy was further compounded by the slow and frequently inept implementation of the budget innovations. There was little consistent follow-up, and when the systems did not deliver the results, the lack of realism in anticipating the results was ignored and new avenues were explored instead. In other cases, the techniques suffered from spotty implementation and the experimentation did not go beyond the central or federal government. Increasingly, however, a greater part of the central budgets were devoted to transfers to the state and local governments.

Such increased transfers coupled with an inadequate machinery raised additional issues about the capacity and credibility of financial management systems. It should be noted in extenuation that many developing countries were confronted with a long list of issues and necessarily, in the process of prioritizing, only those that were of immediate consequence, such as exchange rate, interest rate, and financial sector reform, were taken up for implementation; the systemic issues, including those of financial management, were added onto the pile to be addressed later.

Looking into the Future

The preceding situation cannot be continued into the next millennium as it will only mean a continuation of problems that are likely to be compounded further. To that extent, more vigorous efforts and more comprehensive efforts are clearly indicated. In undertaking these efforts, the following general postulates have to be recognized:

All financial management systems hereafter have a need both to be transparent and to be more accountable. An explicit factoring in of these needs may add to the complexity of the systems and thus to their cost, but is deemed to be necessary to serve the broader purposes of the society.

Governments would pay attention to the utilization of information technology in all their operations and more specifically in the area of financial management. Such an introduction would be accompanied by a rationalization of the existing administrative processes.

Governments would develop a collaborative framework to work with the corporate and nongovernmental organizations and would encourage the latter to seek more effective methods for the provision of government funded services.

The changing portfolio of expenditures at the level of central government and the consequent reliance on state and local governments for delivery of some services require a well-coordinated framework of management within a system of multilevel decision making.

In the context of growing globalism, greater flexibility would be needed in fiscal policies. In turn, this requires a financial management machinery that can anticipate situations and that can better manage uncertainty while fostering necessary confidence among the investors.

The preceding postulates, it is now recognized, would have greater influence in determining the form and content of government financial management. The machinery of financial management would also need to reconcile the differing needs.

Major Challenges

Reconciling the Different Strands

The task of financial management is to reconcile the different strands that now dominate it. In the absence of a framework that reconciles them, financial management would continue to have major internal weaknesses that would plague its effectiveness. Forging an integrated management requires that one would have to be a painter of murals and miniatures. The landscape has to be so detailed as to pay attention not merely to the rhinoceros that is dominating the scene but also to the small chirping bird that sits on its horn. In the case of financial management, such attention to detail should include the task of reconciling different perspectives in regard to the following six areas: (a) concerns of the legislature and the needs of the executive; (b) representative institutions and social control; (c) needs of macroeconomic stability and the factors governing the delivery of services; (d) compliance with rules and the need for administrative flexibility; (e) needs of central agencies and those of spending agencies; and (f) control needs of governments and administrative needs of the corporate and nongovernmental sectors.

During recent decades, the nature of economic decision making was such that there was a gradual shift of power from the legislature to the executive. The growing number of extrabudgetary accounts, the approaches of legislative circumvention, the growth of outlays that were exempt from legislative appropriations, and the powers of the executive to incur debts and contingent liabilities have steadily eroded the traditional power of the purse function of the legislature. Further, the habit of legislatures of creating permanent legislation governing some categories of expenditure has exacerbated the delicate problem of expenditure balancing. These experiences collectively forced the legislatures into a defensive position. Moreover, the introduction of new public management philosophy has effectively reduced the role of the legislature. This has contributed to an imbalance in the relationships between the legislature and the executive, and a major challenge remaining to be addressed is to restore a semblance of balance in this area.

The issue also arises whether some form of social control is necessary to supplement the work of the representative institutions. Experience shows that because of the generally perceived ineffectiveness of representative legislatures, additional involvement by the community is taking place at the local level in the development of programs, award of contracts, and monitoring of implementation. It is quite likely that similar forms of collaboration would be developed at the level of central government in the future. The paradox of such development is that the credibility and the legitimacy of the representative institutions would be even less than before. The need then is to develop forms of social control without seriously affecting the stature of legislative institutions.

Yet another area in which three decades of experience shows an imperative need for reconciliation relates to the pursuit of macroeconomic stability, on the one hand, and the delivery of services at the street level, on the other. During periods of economic crisis, underfunding of services has seriously affected their quality and quantity. The issue, viewed in relation to the delivery of services, is the need for continuity and minimum of unpredictability. The macroeconomic picture is, however, full of uncertainties. What tools of planning and control would be appropriate in such a situation? This too is in need of further analysis.

Legislatures enact legislation and issue rules and regulations to strengthen the rule of law and the machinery of a civic and democratic society. On the other hand, the day to day administration of finances may require more of discretion, risk taking, and flexibility in management. The problem in many countries is the surfeit of legislation and rules, many of them outdated and frequently contradictory. They have so far promoted a compliant administrative culture rather than a management culture. Delegation of more powers and reduction in rules may be considered appropriate for the promotion of a management culture, although such an approach may be considered by critics as a reduction in the legislative power and further empowering of the administrative class.

Another area in which there has been little progress relates to the whole spectrum of relationships between the central agencies such as the ministry of finance or the office of Management and Budget and the spending agencies. It is now widely felt that this area remained relatively immune from the decentralization efforts and that, in fact, there has been a further concentration of financial decision making power in the central agencies. A balance is needed in this area and the need for more power for the pursuit of macroeconomic policies has to be tempered by a need for further delegation of powers to the executive agencies.

The growing network of relationships between government and the corporate sector has not been without problems. Governments perceive that they have been at the receiving end bearing all the risks while the benefits accrue to the corporate sector; the latter, for its part, nurses the view that there are far too many regulations to be complied with and that they have become routine instruments of governments. The truth is that this is an area of darkness where governments have yet to develop adequate financial instruments to guide the funded activities.

Technical Issues

In addition to the major philosophical challenges, there are three technical areas that require continued attention: improved policy planning; selection of a proper base for expenditure control, and adaptation to changing information technology.

It was expected that medium-term fiscal planning, with more focus on rolling expenditure forecasting, would facilitate policy formulation and implementation. In practice, however, many developing countries did not introduce medium-term expenditure planning replacing their exiting system. Rather, it became an additional exercise intended more to win the approval of the international financial institutions. Moreover, much of it was in the nature of projections rather than a detailed analysis of program dynamics and their impact on the magnitude of overall outlays. Consequently, the costs of programs remained unknown and the needs of policy formulation remained unmet. It is necessary, however, that greater attention be paid to these aspects so that the techniques can serve policy purposes and illuminate the nature of the public debate.

The anchor of expenditure control too remained in a state of continuous flux, leaving a number of questions on the utility of the techniques employed. Traditionally, the emphasis was on personnel strength, reflecting the belief that once the staff strength was determined, the rest would lend itself to better control. The introduction of development plans; the focus on yardsticks of expenditure in social sectors, such as education; and the application of new public management philosophy under which the power to determine staff strength and pay scales was delegated to agencies put an effective end to this type of control. The anchor was consequently shifted to running costs, and now to the global determination of expenditure ceilings. As a short-term approach, global ceilings have been effective, but over the medium term, a more reliable instrument that reflects careful planning and that eschews the traditional one-size-fits-all approach is needed.

Information technology too has been rapidly changing. Mainframes ceased to be relevant and the network of personal computers, with adequate transitional arrangements, is the order of the day. More revolutionary changes are likely in the future.

The task in all these areas is to ensure that there is continuous adaptation to the changing requirements—a task that is likely to give little respite to those engaged in public financial management. There may be no such thing as a perfect or grown-up system: It has to mutate itself in the full knowledge of what that mutation will bring and how it will meet the needs of the day.

REFERENCES

Damrosch, David (1995). *We Scholars: Changing the Culture of the University.* Harvard University Press, Cambridge, Mass.

Premchand, A. (ed.) (1998a). Symposium on management of public finances: Recent organizational and systemic adjustments. *Journal of Public Budgeting, Accounting and Financial Management. 10*(1,2).

Premchand, A. (1998b). Umbrella themes obscure real problems: An appraisal of recent efforts to improve financial management. *Public Budgeting and Financing.* (Fall): 72–88.

Russell Bertrand (1956). *Logic and Knowledge.* Allen and Unwin, London.

NOTE

1. Excessive specialization and the consequential habit of not paying any attention to the other aspects has contributed to a conceptual segregation, in turn leading to cultural segregationism that is prevalent among economists, accountants, management specialists, not to mention those specializing in budget law. It is suggested that recent trends in academic research confirm this type of segregationism. For an interesting discussion of these aspects see Damrosch (1995).

7

Changes and Administrative Reforms in Local Government Budgeting

Jerry A. Gianakis
Department of Public Administration,
University of Central Florida,
Orlando, Florida

This chapter seeks to summarize recent changes that have occurred in local government budgeting in the United States (administrative reforms in other countries are addressed in other chapters of this volume) and to identify trends that may engender changes in the near future. The term *administrative reform* connotes conscious, purposive change in the management processes of an organization—here, a change in the formal budget processes and budget formats of local governments that is rationally designed to achieve a given end or to optimize a specific value. By this definition, the structures and formats of local government budgeting systems have changed very little since the definitive reforms that occurred in the first quarter of the 20th century. Line-item budgets persist, and, despite periodic experiments with alternative formats designed to facilitate policy development and implementation processes or to optimize the operations management function of budgeting, the goal of fiscal control continues to dominate (Wildavsky, 1978).

The early budget reforms, however, were less the product of rational planning than the outcomes of the interaction of distinct political movements pursuing what were often contradictory goals in a specific socioeconomic context. The formal resource allocation process of a jurisdiction simply reflects the nature of the political system in which it occurs (Wildavsky, 1988), and, thus, all changes in budgeting are ultimately the products of dynamic, uncertain, and multifaceted policy-making processes. This suggests that the formal elements of the budgetary process can remain the same while the nature of the resource allocation process changes considerably. It also means that generalizations regarding local government budgeting are very tenuous, given what is often the highly idiosyncratic nature of local political cultures. Even within the local government organization, the budget process is characterized by several distinct but interdependent decision-making processes—focusing on issues of balance, expenditure mixes, revenue sources, process design, and budget execution, and typically involving different sets of actors pursuing separate goals (Rubin, 1997)—that cause it to resemble more closely a "garbage can hierarchy" (Cohen et al., 1972) than a classically rational administrative system. The complexity of the field of public budgeting is also manifested by the broad range of disciplines involved in its study (Caiden, 1990).

Thus, this chapter will also review selected, salient changes in the nature of local government budgeting that are precipitates of political, social, economic, and technological trends, as well as substantive reforms that have occurred in related administrative processes. These changes and reforms are briefly reviewed, in the context of the factors that produced them, in the following:

1. *Results-oriented budgeting.* Results-oriented budgeting (ROB)—also called *outcomes-oriented budgeting* and *entrepreneurial budgeting* (Cothran, 1993)—is a cornerstone of the "reinventing government" (Osborne and Gaebler, 1992) movement, and it represents a conscious, purposive attempt to reform public budgeting and public management in general. The reinventing government movement, founded by public management practitioners, seeks to introduce private sector management methods, incentives, and controls in public management. Public managers do not enjoy the same autonomy to use their expertise in the pursuit of policy goals as their private sector counterparts. ROB calls for the loosening of line-item controls on inputs, in order to facilitate the attainment of outcomes. Accountability for public resources is maintained by holding managers responsible for the attainment of substantive policy goals. This approach clearly requires the measurement of policy outcomes, and the development of performance measurement systems and performance-based budgeting formats constitute corollary reforms.

2. *Enhanced policy function of budget office.* This change captures the impact of a variety of trends. First, the budget office typically serves as the clearinghouse for the performance data required by ROB formats. To date, performance measurement systems would seem to have been more widely adopted than formal ROB systems, and they may serve as a substitute for the development of ROB in the face of the staying power of line-item budgets. Second, the Internet

and low-cost microcomputers have given citizens convenient access to their local governments. They are able to voice complaints and comment on budget allocations, and the budget office also serves in a clearinghouse capacity here. Technology has also altered the nature of some services, often necessitating a reallocation of resources that is handled through the budget office. Technology has also given budgetary personnel more time to analyze policy initiatives as it has relieved them of the more mundane tasks associated with budgeting. Fourth, tax limitations and the reversal in the increase in intergovernmental support have meant that local governments must husband their resources more effectively and look to existing revenue allocations to fund new initiatives. Finally, privatization of service delivery necessitates the negotiation and monitoring of performance contracts, and this responsibility often falls to the budget office; indeed, many performance measurement systems have been adopted specifically to support contract development and monitoring.

3. *Biennial budgeting.* An extended budgeting horizon is required if the budget office is to assume more responsibility for policy planning, coordination, and analysis. State laws tend to limit the possibilities for multiyear budgeting, but annual budgeting can still be conducted in the context of a longer planning period. The advent of "competitive Federalism" (Shannon and Kee, 1989) and greater reliance on own-source revenues have made local governments more sensitive to the need to manage revenues and develop tax bases. These ends clearly require an extended planning horizon. User-friendly software has made supportive forecasting models more accessible to local government budgeters.

4. *The professionalization of the budget office.* The Government Finance Officers Association (GFOA) has instituted a Certified Public Finance Officer Program, which consists of five examinations designed to assess the knowledge required of a practicing public finance officer and which contains a continuing education requirement of 30 hours per year for continued certification. There remains the possibility that such a program will be developed specifically for budget officers. The GFOA also administers a Distinguished Budget Award Program for budgets that meet the majority of its criteria. More recently, the National Advisory Council on State and Local Budgeting (cofounded by the GFOA and seven other organizations) developed 59 recommended budget practices spanning each phase of the resource allocation process and centered on a goal-driven approach to budgeting. These criteria and recommendations reinforce the trends outlined, but this one-size-fits-all approach to budgeting may not be sensitive to local idiosyncrasies. In any case, the GFOA is not in the same position to enforce its standards and recommendations as is the Governmental Accounting Standards Board (GASB), which is able to enforce its accounting and financial reporting standards through its influence on the bond ratings of local governments.

5. *Emphasis on identifying costs.* The GASB's new accounting model (described in more detail elsewhere in this volume) requires that local govern-

ments account for the value of their fixed assets,such as infrastructure and capital facilities. Although the move to full accrual accounting does not directly impact the budget process, a reported deficit in unrestricted net assets could cause resources to be directed to capital and infrastructure maintenance and replacement simply by highlighting these needs. Local governments must reallocate resources to meet emerging needs in the face of revenue restrictions, and the new reporting model promises to be more responsive to management's need for cost information to support reallocation decisions. Cost information is also required to evaluate privatization options.

These changes and reforms are clearly interrelated in that they are driven by common macrotrends, or one makes the other desirable or more feasible. The preceding list is designed to focus the discussion of budget reforms and changes, and alternative ways of organizing the topics are obviously possible. Each of the five areas is reviewed in greater detail, and an attempt is made to assess the problems and prospects of lasting change. The chapter closes with a short analysis of the ways in which the budget process and the budget office can contribute to efforts to optimize the allocation of local government resources.

Research on budgeting tends to follow budget practice, so this chapter does not represent a comprehensive view of the research literature on the subject. The review of current trends in local government budgeting and the prospects for their future routinization is based on conversations with budget and financial management professionals and attendance at practitioner conferences. It is hoped that the findings of this review can serve as a source for future research.

RESULTS-ORIENTED BUDGETING

The traditional line-item budget persists in local government because it is simple to understand and involves only a few calculations to adjust last year's allocations; potentially divisive policy issues are pushed into the background and less value-laden line items become the focus of attention; the line-items apply equally well to the range of service departments; it is the product of a fragmented, bottom-up process in which service managers are able to apply their substantive expertise in ways that do not confuse elected officials; and the line items typically parallel the chart of accounts and support the accounting control function (Wildavsky, 1978). Reform formats each address perceived shortcomings of the line-item budget. Performance budgeting focuses on service activities rather than line items and seeks to optimize efficiency by highlighting costs per service unit. The Planning-Programming-Budgeting System (PPBS) manifestation of program budgeting focuses on policy goals and seeks to optimize policy outcomes through the application of analytical techniques. Zero-base budgeting employs decision packages through which managerial hierarchies can rank order service level alternatives in an effort to reallocate resources. The top-down PPBS format featured in the administration of President Lyndon Johnson requires consensus on a broad range of policy goals, and the political power necessary to pursue these goals proved fleeting. Zero-base budgeting pursues policy development from the bottom up but, like PPBS, requires an analytical capacity and extensive paperwork. The service units required by performance budgeting are difficult to define for many local government services, and the identification of real costs is also often difficult. In addition, the three reform formats all require the collection of output or outcome measures, and these are also difficult for many services to develop.

Various budget formats have been championed by various reformers depending on whether they pursued efficiency, effectiveness, or economy in government, and many have been implemented to deal with specific allocation issues (Rubin, 1998, 1999). Results-oriented budgeting is also rooted in an ideology that calls for the adoption of marketlike management systems for public organizations. Proponents of ROB contend that private sector management systems are inherently superior to public sector processes, although it is an open question whether the private sector was the teacher or the pupil in the development and application of management control systems during the reform period (Rubin, 1993). The various reform groups at the turn of the 20th century all shared a concern with controlling government expenditures, hence, the ubiquity of the line-item format. But ROB proponents hold that controls placed on public managers' use of inputs—or the factors of production (Wilson, 1989)—constrain their capacity to use their expertise to achieve improvements in policy outcomes. They favor the loosening of line-item controls, and they redefine control as accountability for the efficient and effective achievement of policy goals.

ROB is the budgeting manifestation of the "new public management." Implicit in this model is the idea that public sector managers should act as policy "entrepreneurs" (although ROB would seem to focus on the efficient and effective pursuit of policy goals, thus reflecting a reincarnation of the politics/administration dichotomy) and adopt the same self-interested motivation that characterizes private sector managers (Terry, 1998) (although proponents would argue that public managers are similarly motivated now, but these lead to perverse effects in control-oriented, hierarchical bureaucracies). This is held by critics to be destructive of the pursuit of the public interest (the definition of which is acknowledged to be elusive and dynamic) and the notion of public service in general (Terry, 1998). The failure of the field of public administration to define effectively the role of the expert in a democratic society (largely because of its own use of various manifestations of the politics/administration dichotomy) has left practitioners vulnerable to attacks from those riding the crest of the global "triumph of capitalism" and the economic boom ostensibly made possible by the private sector's "liberation management." The interests of managers, owners, and customers may dovetail neatly in a narrowly defined private sector system in which each group pursues its own self-interest, but the definition of collective action is more than the aggregation of private interests. ROB also suffers from the same defect as the other reform formats: namely, the lack of suitable measures of policy outcomes.

ROB proposes to use outcome measures to maintain accountability in the face of enhanced managerial autonomy. The research literature has developed a range of criteria for acceptable outcome measures, some of which clearly conflict with others (Bouckaert, 1993), but there has been less progress in developing actual measures that meet these criteria. The GASB is in a position virtually to mandate that local governments collect outcome measures (at potentially high costs) through its Service Level and Accomplishments reporting model, but it cannot simply mandate the creation of useful measures. Without feasible outcome measures, ROB gives managers more flexibility to pursue policy goals that are developed on the basis of self-interest. Theoreticians with more sensitivity to the public nature of public management identify enhanced citizen participation in the policy-making process as a preferred form of accountability (King and Stivers, 1996).

Program budgeting left behind an appreciation of the communicative benefits of a formal mission structure for public programs, performance budgeting focused on the utility of cost data, and zero-base budgeting highlighted the need to institutionalize resource reallocation processes. ROB has benefits from this legacy, as well as from practitioner demands for greater flexibility in using resources, political pressures for the reallocation of public resources, and the technological improvements that have made the structure of the chart of accounts less salient in budgeting. But its characterization of public management as private management that just does not work quite right and its dependence on program performance measures that have yet to be developed for many services make its possible implementation questionable.

ENHANCED POLICY FUNCTION OF BUDGET OFFICE

Many local governments are making their budget documents and processes accessible to citizens through the Internet. Others maintain a centralized citizen complaint or comment capacity on the Internet. The budget department is often the clearinghouse for this information: incorporating suggestions into budget presentations to policymakers; forwarding complaints to service departments and monitoring responses; or compiling comments and turning them into policy recommendations. The budget department mediates between citizens and policymakers and service departments because the budget document is the most visible expression of public policy, and it is shared by all of the departments that the local government organization comprises. Technology is making possible a form of direct democracy for which there exist no institutional arrangements, and budget departments may be meeting this need. This trend will call for a broad range of analytical skills from budgeters and will make the budget department more influential in the policy-making process. Technology has also helped budgeters with the record keeping and expenditure tracking aspects of budgeting and has made analytical techniques more accessible.

Technology has also forced some local government services to redefine themselves. For example, new building materials and the proliferation of smoke detectors and sprinkler systems have greatly reduced the threat of building fires; fire departments are redefining their service as prevention, inspection, and emergency medical service. This redefinition requires a realignment of line-item expenditures, which inevitably attracts the attention of policymakers in the traditional line-item budget process (along with requests for new positions). Budget departments are called upon to build bridges to service departments in order to provide for a smooth reallocation process.

In addition to the reallocations within departments caused by new technologies, revenue limitations, reductions in intergovernmental aid, and the demands of "competitive Federalism" have necessitated reallocations among departments. Fundamental questions regarding the size and scope of government are also being debated. Service departments are no longer simply competing for their "fair share" of annual revenue increases; rather they are competing to maintain their service domains and their relative shares of shrinking budgets. This competition engenders the same "game playing" and political machinations that characterize the traditional budget process, but issues of missions and service level policies are gaining greater salience. This gives the budget office greater prominence in the policy-making process, because the budget process is the only administrative process in the local government organization that couples the various service departments to one another. Hence, it is there that basic issues of missions and the ways these contribute to the general welfare of the community will be discussed. At least, it is there that the collective expertise of the public organization will be brought to bear on these issues.

Program performance measurement systems—regardless of whether they are used in a formal results-oriented budgeting system—assist in this process. Central management can use these data to weight the impacts of services on the general welfare of the community, which serves as a common "bottom line" for the various service departments of the public organization. Service managers can place their own services into a wider framework. This approach allows for the rational analysis of policy options that can inform the political process. Once again, the outcome measures employed for many public programs are weak, but the very process of developing the measures can help develop the focus on a common bottom line. This can enhance the capacity of the management staff of the local government organization to employ its collective expertise to optimize resource allocations; this argument is further developed later.

Budget departments are also serving as links among jurisdictions. Reductions in intergovernmental aid and the proliferation of special districts have made local governments more cognizant of the need for regional approaches to economic development and have necessitated the negotiation of interlocal agreements to achieve economies of scale in service delivery. These horizontal intergovernmental relationships have created new roles and responsibilities for finance professionals, and local government budgets will be increasingly influenced by these relationships. The necessity for intergovernmental coordination in service delivery will create pressures for a long-term perspective in policy development and resource allocation, and this issue is also addressed later.

The trend to the privatization of service delivery will also enhance the substantive policy role of the budget office. Finance professionals will negotiate contracts and, hence, service levels. The monitoring and enforcement of contracts will often fall to the budget office, particularly when the privatization effort results in the elimination of the department that was previously responsible for the service. Once again, private firms usually require a long-term contract, and this requirement will result in an extension of the policy planning horizon and create pressures for multiyear budgeting.

The enhanced policy role of the budget office is an emerging phenomenon. The rational consideration of policy options in the budget process has been a goal of many budget reformers, whether they have sought greater efficiency in the delivery of public services or an expansion of the role of government. This is apparent from the nature of the budget formats presented as alternatives to the traditional line-item budget. These previous reform formats have been defeated by flaws inherent in their design (e.g., the lack of suitable units of analysis in the case of performance budgeting) or by the nature of the political environment in which they were to be implemented (e.g., the difficulty in assembling the political power required for the top-down PPBS model). However, the enhanced policy role described here is more the potential product of trends and pressures in the environment of local governments than it is the result of conscious, deliberate reform (although the National Advisory Council on State and Local Budgeting supports these developments with recommended practices; see later discussion). Hence, this policy role may be a long-term trend rather than a short-term response to specific problems or opportunities.

BIENNIAL BUDGETING

An enhanced policy function in the budget office and the effective use of outcome-oriented performance measures will require an extended planning horizon and a longer budget cycle. Many state statutes prohibit local governments from using a biennial budget cycle that does not require that a balance between revenues and expenditures be achieved on an annual basis. Indeed, Rubin (1998) contends that state statutes have constrained budget reforms in general on the local level; not only are such laws restrictive, but they are slow to change in response to budgetary advances and local needs. However, if Rubin (1999) is correct in her suggestion that changes in budgeting tend to arise in response to specific issues or problems facing individual governments in specific contexts, pressures for biennial budgeting seem to be building.

First, local governments have become more cognizant of the need to maintain and develop their economic bases as they become increasingly dependent on own-source revenues. Annual appropriations to operating agencies tend to occur within an investment framework that employs an extended planning horizon. The annual capital budget typically emerges from a 5- or 6-year capital improvement program plan, in order to schedule multiyear projects and arrange for their financing and to meet the planning needs of private developers. The biennial budget is simply an extension of this multiyear planning horizon to the formal budget process.

Second, the privatization of service delivery often requires the use of multiyear contracts, in order that private firms can recover their initial capital investments. As privatization increases, a greater percentage of local government expenditures will escape the annual budget process. Third, budget cutbacks resulting from tax limitations or new councils are more effectively handled within a multiyear framework. As described earlier, cutbacks cannot be made on the same across-the-board, incremental basis that typically characterizes the distribution of gains in times of revenue growth, because essential services soon fall below acceptable levels and pressures for wholesale reallocations build. Decisions regarding which services will be eliminated are best made within the framework of an extended planning horizon that permits the application of analytical techniques to determine their impacts in economic base and revenue sources. A new city council in one city with which the author is familiar became enamored with zero-base budgeting because the members were elected on a cutback platform; the city administrators were able to trade the implementation of a zero-base budget process for biennial budgeting so that they could rationalize the service reductions, as well as deal more effectively with the paperwork demands of the zero-base process.

Until recently, the budgeting computer programs and data base management systems available to local governments were difficult to adapt to local practices, partly because they were based on private sector budgeting systems and concepts. The capability of these systems to control positions individually was particularly weak. The diffusion of user-friendly microcomputer programs has freed budget analysts from the more mundane tasks associated with budgeting and expenditure tracking, and they have more time available for analysis of long-term expenditure and revenue trends, as well as for the construction of econometric models of the local economic base. Supporting analytical and statistical software is also readily available.

The need to report revenues and expenditures to the state at the end of each fiscal year is less of a problems than the widespread requirement to balance the budget on an annual basis. But the salient issue here is whether the participants approach the resource allocation process with a multiyear perspective, and the development of this perspective in the culture of the public organization is the real substance of the reform. For example, budgeters can engage in a zero-base analysis of one-fourth of the organization's services each year of a 4-year planning cycle that features annual appropriations. Thus, the nature of the budget process can change and not manifest any formal structural changes; indeed, a formal administrative reform is often adopted to substitute for real substantive change.

THE PROFESSIONALIZATION OF THE BUDGET OFFICE

The changes outlined here indicate that it is becoming increasingly more difficult for local government budget offices to retreat to a simple "publishing function," in which they merely collect the budget requests of the various agencies that the organization comprises and ultimately assemble them into a budget document with little offered in the way of substantive guidance, policy direction, or analysis and evaluation. Some progress has also been made in codifying the elements of a good budget document, formalizing the role of the budget office, and identifying the skills required of budget analysts. A framework for the development of a profession of budget analyst is beginning to emerge.

In 1984, the Governmental Finance Officers Association implemented its Distinguished Budget Presentation Awards Program, in which professionals evaluate the budget of other jurisdictions in regard to criteria in four areas: the policy orientation of the document, the extent to which the document manifests a framework of sound financial planning, the capacity of the budget to serve as a guide to operations management, and its functionality as a communications tool. This program is complemented by the GFOA's awards program for financial reporting. The GFOA also sponsors a Certified Public Finance Officer (CPFO) program that comprises five examinations designed to assess the knowledge required of a practicing public finance officer, as well as a continuing professional education requirement. Given the demands of the new accounting model described later, the same knowledge may prove useful to budget analysts, or a similar program may eventually be designed for them.

In 1995, the GFOA partnered with seven other professional organizations to form the National Advisory Council on State and Local Budgeting. Three years later the council produced 59 specific recommended budget practices for state and local governments designed to encourage a goal-driven approach to resource allocation. The recommended practices promote the linkage of the formal budget process with other management activities and emphasize that annual resource allocation decisions should occur within a long-range financial and substantive service planning perspective. The practices are organized on the basis of four broad principles: broad goals should be established to guide government decision making; management policies and service plans should be established to support the pursuit of these goals; the annual budget must be consistent with these goals; and performance must be continuously evaluated and adjustments in goals made as needed. These principles clearly reflect the trends outlined.

Professional budgeters are generally favorably disposed to having their jurisdiction's budget characterized as "distinguished" by their professional association. The addition of "certified" to their respective resumes may also be a desirable goal. However, the GFOA does not have the authority or power to force local jurisdictions to adopt their budget standards or training requirements. The GASB is able to encourage local governments to adopt its accounting and reporting standards as a result of its capacity to influence the interest rates that they pay to borrow funds. This power may also ultimately force local governments to adopt the GASB's Service Efforts and Accomplishments (SEA) reporting standards. However, reforms should be sensitive to the context in which they are adopted, and it is an open question whether professional organizations should have the power to force local governments to adopt specific reforms. The recommendations of the NACSLB would seem to be general enough to allow for local idiosynrasies, but established accounting and reporting standards—designed to meet the informational needs of private sector investment institutions and the financial establishment—can often compromise the ability of local governments to meet service needs in light of local political culture and managerial capacity (Gianakis and McCue, 1999). Despite the establishment of the GASB, the public sector accounting model is still rooted in the standards developed by the Financial Accounting Standards Board, and efforts to force these "square pegs" into the "round hole" of public sector management can engender perverse externalities.

Professionalism in budgeting has clearly come to be defined as the systematic analysis of policy goals and the employment of an extended planning horizon in the resource allocation process. The basis for the active participation of public finance professionals in the long-term, goal-driven budget process described by the NACSLB recommended practices constitutes an additional normative issue. It is suggested here that the application of an extended planning horizon to the resource allocation process is the essence of professionalism in public finance, in that the maintenance of the long-term financial viability of the organization is the elemental responsibility of public, as well as private sector, finance professionals. Citizens and elected officials can suffer from a myopia that allows them to sacrifice financial viability for current gain or to recast current private gain as providing for the general welfare, the former because they can ultimately "vote with their feet" and the latter because the next election constitutes their planning horizon. What is sought here is the attainment of a long-term "structural balance" between policy goals and economic capacity (Proctor, 1992). This is not to say that there exists one best set of policy goals that will protect the revenue bases of the jurisdiction and optimize the development of its economic base—only that the professional public organization should inform the annual budget process with those issues. It should also apply its analysis and expertise as an integrated organization rather than as a collection of agencies that merely reflect the policy differences in the community. The application of collective expertise allows the public organization to see beyond parochial private gains. Every local government manager must be part finance professional, because if the financial viability of the organization as a whole is not maintained, revenues to fund short-term political goals become increasingly scarce. This issue is developed further after the following section.

EMPHASIS ON IDENTIFYING COSTS

Traditional budgets do not provide clear information regarding the costs of specific services. First, each individual service may not be a distinct budget entity, and individual budget entities may house a variety of services; thus, the simple identification and isolation of services and their inputs can be problematic. Second, capital outlays are listed in the budget in the year in which the purchases are planned, and the costs of capital items are not usually depreciated over the useful lives of the items. Budgets often list pension fund expended rather than the amount incurred as a cost of providing the current service. Ancillary costs, such as training, appear as 1-year expenditures, but these costs should be prorated over the career of each employee in order to identify the true annual cost of providing the targeted service. Fifth, budgets do not ordinarily allocate administrative and service overhead to individual services. Internal service funds may facilitate the allocation of service overhead, but the bases of these allocations are often controversial.

In order to evaluate privatization options, local governments must know the real costs they are currently incurring to provide the service. Analysts can then determine what costs can be avoided through privatization, and whether the contract price yields real economies. The imposition of fees and charges for selected services requires the same cost information. Pressures to impose user fees and to privatize mean that local governments must become more aware of their costs. Budgeters must complement their focus on the planned expenditures for individual line items with analyses of the true costs of identifiable services; this was an end of traditional performance budgeting and is currently being explored through activity-based budgeting.

The finance function has traditionally focused on the acquisition and disposition of financial resources, at least in regard to general fund revenues and expenditures. The GASB's new accounting model features the full accrual basis for general fund accounting, which will require local governments to account for their economic assets as well as their financial assets. The value of infrastructure and other general fund assets will be depreciated over their useful lives in annual reporting statements. Once again, the GASB can virtually mandate these changes through its indirect influence on the interest rates paid by local governments to borrow funds. Although this model does not mandate the accounting of the total costs of providing specific services, it will create a "cost consciousness" that could hold implications for budgeting.

The GASB's proposed Service Efforts and Accomplishment reporting model will surely create direct pressure to account for the costs of services. The potential danger here is that budgeters become virtual accountants, and the resource allocation process is ultimately reduced to a cost-benefit calculus. Local government financial reporting and accounting professionals generally oppose the SEA model, partly because of the costs of maintaining the data and housing the necessary analytical capacity, but also because of the perception that it will put them too close to the policy-making process. The costing and performance measurement responsibilities enunciated by the GASB will fall to the budget department, and these will enhance its policy-making role.

Accrual accounting and the SEA reporting model are designed to meet the information needs of potential lenders, in that they allow comparisons to be made among jurisdictions. Currently, two different jurisdictions can submit identical year-end financial reports though their potential financial condition may be vastly different as a result of unreported differences in the age of their core infrastructure or the results achieved through identical spending in given service areas. This spotlight can clearly influence allocation decisions. The psychological impact on policymakers of a reported deficit in unrestricted net assets under the new accounting model may create pressures for the reallocation of general fund operating expenditures. Public works and public utilities departments may be in a position to ask for additional revenues for projects and equipment to upgrade and expand infrastructure. This will place additional pressures on the resource allocation process. The idea that there are no value-free budgeting systems may be extended to accounting systems. Sometimes these spending pressures will be justified—for example, when infrastructure maintenance has been neglected or long-term investment curtailed to meet short-term needs—but comparisons among jurisdictions can be misleading when they ignore local idiosyncrasies. Hence, the SEA model and the new accounting model both contain extensive provisions for explanatory information.

The reduction of costs through the pursuit of technological efficiencies should be the hallmark of professional public management. In addition to the lack of knowledge regarding costs, public sector managers face disincentives when they contemplate technological efficiencies; these revolve on the budget issue of "Spend it or lose it." If service managers retain savings, they can raise service levels, but if policymakers are happy with existing service levels, they can appropriate the savings and reallocate them elsewhere. The decision-making perspectives of service managers must encompass the welfare of the community as a whole, because they must pursue technological efficiencies within a framework of allocative efficiency.

A confluence of pressures is making cost information increasingly important, and, until the optimal perspective can be developed among service managers, it is likely that those pressures will bear on the centralized budget department.

BUDGETING AND OPTIMAL RESOURCE ALLOCATIONS

The end of all budget reforms is better resource allocation decisions. V. O. Key (1940) pointed out long ago that the definition of the best mix of public expenditures is ultimately a function of political values, and budgeters cannot determine that mix simply on the basis of structured analysis. Aaron Wildavsky (1988, 1961) has demonstrated that there is no value-neutral budget process: That is, budget processes themselves reflect political values and make possible the exercise of political power by different groups. Indeed, the early budget reformers did not share the same goals: Some groups sought a larger, more effective government; others wanted a smaller, more economical government; and others tried to enhance the efficiency of government through the adoption of businesslike methods. Even if the reformers could agree on "conscious, purposive reforms," however, the mix of resource allocations would still be open to contention, and no single budget process or format would serve to optimize that mix.

The optimality of the mix of resource allocation decisions is a function of the quality of the political process, and here, once again and even more obviously than in the case of budget processes, the nature of the political process is the ultimate expression of public values. An emerging and increasingly salient issue in the public policy-making process is the fact that influence and power have shifted from the formal political and electoral institutions to the professional bureaucracies at all levels of government (Wilson, 1989; Lowi, 1969). This growing reliance on professional expertise is rooted in the complexity of public issues and the increased demands for collective action in specific policy areas. One result has been the fragmentation of the policy-making process as policy-making in distinct areas becomes dominated by different groups of experts and those with a vested interest in the outcomes. These developments are seen by many as threatening the core values of democracy, and if these are to be preserved, either this process must be reversed or the policy-making process that has moved to the public organizations must be made more accessible and democratic. The former option may be impractical given the complexity of modern society, and the latter may not be less feasible at the distant federal level; that may be one of the reasons for the political popularity of the current devolution of collective action to the state and local levels.

The typical local government organization is the most highly differentiated organization that can still be addressed as a single organization. The executive agencies of the federal government are so highly fragmented that one cannot speak of a single "umbrella" public service organization, and the various executive agencies of state governments take on characteristics of both the federal government and the typical local government—usually as a function of the number of separately elected executive agency heads. The local government organization features a legitimate, single executive officer, but the executive must often defer to the expertise of the agencies that compose the organization because of the wide range of substantive service areas that it houses. Hence, it is difficult to take a holistic, deliberative approach to resource allocation decision making, and agencies use their respective areas of expertise to compete for resources rather than to optimize the resource allocation scheme.

If the key to optimizing resource allocations is to improve the political process, two broad goals should be pursued. First, the public agencies must be made more accessible to the broad range of citizens in order that their needs can be enunciated to those who possess the knowledge and capacity to meet them. Second, the public organization itself must engage the community as an integrated political institution rather than as a loose collection of atomistic political actors. It is an inescapable fact that political power exists within the public bureaucracy, and efforts to shield this power from politics have served to constrain democratic values. More politics must occur within the professional bureaucracy in order that that power can be exercised responsively and responsibly. This calls for less politicization among the professional agencies that constitute the public organization in order to enhance its capacity to act in that manner.

A new dialogue would seem to be emerging regarding the community-building roles of public administrators and the need that they directly engage the public (King and Stivers, 1998). However, the need to build the managerial capacity of the local government organization to act is receiving less attention. The "new public management" focus on serving the "customers" of particular agencies would seem to reinforce the centrifugal forces that characterize highly differentiated organizations. The budget process becomes salient in this regard, because it is only during the formal budget process that the various agencies that the public organization comprises need acknowledge that they are members of a single organization. Individual agencies can interact with the centralized personnel, data processing, and finance functions as if they were components of their own agencies. The budget process should be designed to function as a centripetal force within the public organization and enhance the managerial capacity of the organization as a whole.

The payoff from budget reforms does not result directly from the tools, techniques, and formats designed to address specific resource allocations problems, but rather from the use of the formal budget process as a vehicle for developing the managerial capacity of the organization. Hence the earlier suggestion that the benefits of performance measurement systems do not necessarily arise from the performance data and their application in the resource allocation process, but from the process of developing the measures and the communication function that they serve within the public organization. As a result of the highly differentiated nature of local government organizations, their substantive expertise will be housed in and exercised by the management of the agencies that compose the organization; this is as inescapable as the fact that this expertise yields political power. The productive use of this power depends on the decision-making perspective adopted by those who exercise it. The heads of service agencies must base their decisions on what is best for the organization and the community rather than what is best for their individual agencies. Once again, this is not to say that "what is best" be dictated by the public organization, but rather that its expertise and resulting power be employed in a process that manifests democratic values.

The zero-base budget process can function to enhance overall managerial capacity, particularly if it is coupled with an outcome-oriented performance measurement system to describe the impacts of alternative decision packages. This format forces managers to think about how their and other programs contribute to a common "bottom line"—namely, the general welfare of the community as a whole. Of course, it is a simple matter to interpret the general welfare in terms of one's own service area, but in this scenario managers are not compelled to do so. Agency staff should also be involved in the development of financing and revenue alternatives, the capital project selection processes, economic development programs, and technical matters in which they have a vested interest, such as revenue forecasting. Performance problems and operational issues could be addressed by ad hoc, temporary groups that comprise personnel from a variety of agencies. These activities might not yield better decisions in the short run, but the process of inclusion will develop the broader managerial decision-making perspectives on which the budget process depends. Expertise will be at the disposal of a more democratic process rather than vested interests, and this will yield better resource allocation schemes in the long run.

It may also prove feasible to operationalize a definition of the general welfare that cuts across substantive service areas. The pursuit of efficiency is a value that all managers have in common; the public expects it from all areas of expertise, and it is why policy-making power has devolved to managers. However, efficiency has no meaning apart from the attainment of some substantive goal—that is, efficiency for what? The fact that this answer differs among substantive service managers contributes to the centrifugal forces that characterize local government organizations. But there can be no long-term efficiencies unless the long-term financial viability of the organization is maintained (Gianakis and McCue, 1999). This is not to say that there is only one way of optimizing the financial viability of the organization; there are a variety of alternative courses to protecting revenue bases and developing economic bases. This issue operationalizes "the general welfare" in more concrete terms, and it constitutes a common goal that is less vulnerable to insular definitions.

This review leaves open the issue of how to draw the citizens into the professional organization, because it is beyond the scope of this chapter. However, this is an important issue because without such participation the professional organization is ultimately dictating its own policy preferences to the public, and it may be more desirable that this is done by a fragmented organization in a piecemeal fashion. It is suggested here that the same rigid, hierarchical, bureaucratic structures that encourage insular decision-making perspectives by local government service agencies (as well as internally among their management staffs and operational personnel) are the same structures that limit public access. Indeed, they are designed for that purpose, but if political power made its way into the public organization, public participation must follow in order for democracy to be preserved. Citizens will be able to gain access to and deliberate the broad range of policy areas if that range is represented in all of the parts of the public organization. Ironically, bureaucracy must be given more power if democracy is to thrive (Behn, 1998; Meier, 1997).

CONCLUSION

Budgeting tends to look very much as it did 75 years ago because budgeting reforms arise in response to distinct response allocation problems in specific socioeconomic and political contexts; when these problems pass, local governments often revert to traditional budgeting, which features detailed line items and emphasizes a control function (Rubin, 1999). The resulting reforms are the products of the confluence of a variety of macroenvironmental trends, as well as conscious choices in the design of the budget process that invariably reflect political values. This is not to say that no progress has been made in budgeting practice, because these experiments serve to expand the administrative tools available to local governments to deal with future problems (Rubin, 1999). However, less progress has been made in identifying what a budget process should look like in light of the problems and issues that a given jurisdiction is facing.

Budget reforms should add value to the resource allocation process—that is, they should be designed to optimize the allocative efficiency of the budget. In the present context of intergovernmental revenue cutbacks, tax limitations, and increased demands for services, a local government budget process that simply duplicates the previous year's allocation represents a retreat from the pursuit of allocative efficiency. Admittedly, the definition of an allocatively efficient budget is ultimately a political question, but this chapter has sought to develop a definition for budgeters based on the responsibilities of the professional finance officer: namely, to provide a process that facilitates the pursuit of allocative efficiency, and to maintain the long-term financial viability of the jurisdiction. These can serve as standards to evaluate reforms in the present macroenvironment of local government budgeting.

Biennial budgeting should be implemented by local government managers even if it is not formally adopted by elected officials, although its long-term prospects are enhanced if they do. The need to maintain the economic base of the jurisdiction means that short-term resource allocation decisions must be made within the context of their long-term effects. Economic development efforts and capital programming must be considered in the budget process, and these demand analytical processes that the annual process precludes. Time and analysis also allow substantive program managers to develop technological efficiencies in their service delivery systems, and these ultimately have allocative effects. Biennial budgets can help to rationalize cutbacks and reallocations so that an optimal level of allocative efficiency can be maintained. The long-term prospects of a jurisdiction are threatened if allocative efficiency is severely curtailed, because residents will disinvest in the community and weaken its economic base.

Cost data are also necessary for the pursuit of technological and allocative efficiencies, and this reform has been virtually mandated by the new accounting model. The difficulties in allocating service and administrative overhead and identifying the true costs of providing local government services will add a new technical dimension to budgeting, and this will complement the increased professionalization of the budget office. However, if enhanced professionalism comes to be defined in purely technical terms, the policy role of the budget office could be compromised. If the budget office is to serve as a center for the pursuit of efficiency in the resource allocation process, it must be seen as working in tandem with substantive service managers rather than as simply exercising a control function centering on costs. Finance officers, for example, have objected to the GASB's efforts to implement Service Efforts and Accomplishment reporting, partly because they do not see such data as an integral part of the financial accounting profession.

Performance outcome measures have the potential to serve both allocative and technological efficiencies, but the prospects for identifying useful measures for the broad range of local government services appear to be limited. The costs of maintaining comprehensive performance measurement systems may also be prohibitive, and this is another basis for the resistance of finance professionals. It has been suggested here that the very process of identifying missions, goals, objectives, and outcome measures for substantive service areas can serve as a vehicle for enhancing the collective capacity of the substantive service managers of a local government to pursue allocative efficiency as an integrated team. This has been presented as the administrative reform that would contribute most productively to allocative efficiency in light of the pernicious effects of the centrifugal forces generated by the highly differentiated local government organization. However, this scenario calls for a more political, policy-oriented role for the budget office—one that is becoming increasingly difficult to avoid.

The "wild card" of allocative efficiency is citizen participation. It is impossible to optimize the pursuit of multiple service demands within a budget constraint if one does not know what those demands are or what the real budget constraint is. The results-oriented budget concept seeks to develop a market for policy outcomes and to hold managers accountable for achieving policy goals, but the lack of meaningful measures has severely curtailed its capacity to do so. In addition, market competition would augment the centrifugal forces that characterize multiservice local governments, and the decision premises of service managers would inevitably be reduced to narrow self-interest.

In the absence of outcome measures, accountability controls must be moved back to inputs, but controls should take the form of active citizen participation in the policy-making process rather than rigid, ex post controls on spending. Without rigid line-item controls managers have the autonomy to apply their expertise in the pursuit of policy goals, as well as to put it at the disposal of the policy-making process. It is essential, however, that this collective expertise engage the public as a single integrated organization pursuing allocative efficiency and long-term financial viability, in order to prevent its constituent parts from being appropriated by narrow special interests.

Reform of the resource allocation process cannot be reduced to technique. If budgeting is both a technical and a political process (Rubin, 1997), budgeters must become better politicians as well as better technicians if technical expertise is to serve democracy. The public organization that houses the technical expertise necessary to pursue allocative efficiency must also be made accessible to the process that defines it.

REFERENCES

Behn, Robert D. (1998). What right do public managers have to lead? *Public Administration Review. 58*(3): 209–224.

Bouckaert, Geert (1993). Measurement and meaningful management. *Public Productivity and Management Review. 17*(1): 31–44.

Caiden, Naomi (1990). Public budgeting in the U.S.: The state of the discipline. In *Public Administration: The State of the Discipline* (Naomi B. Lynn and Aaron Wildavsky eds.). Chatham, Chatham, N.J.

Cohen, Michael, March, James, and Olsen, Johan P. (1972). A Garbage-can model of organizational change. *Administrative Science Quarterly. 17* (1): 1–25.

Cothran, Dan A. (1993). Entrepreneurial budgeting: An emerging reform. *Public Administration Review. 53*(5): 455–461.

Gianakis, Gerasimos A., and McCue, Clifford P. (1999). *Local Government Budgeting: A Managerial Approach.* Quorum, Westport, Conn.

Key, V. O. (1940). The lack of budgetary theory. *American Political Science Review. 35*(4): 1137–1140.

King, Cheryl S., and Stivers, Camilla (eds.) (1998). *Government Is Us: Public Administration in an Anti-Government Era.* Sage, Thousand Oaks, Calif.

Lowi, Theodore J. (1969). *The End of Liberalism.* Norton, New York.

Meier, Kenneth J. (1997). Bureaucracy and democracy: The case for more bureaucracy and less democracy. *Public Administration Review. 57*(3): 193–199.

Osborne, David, and Gaebler, Ted (1992). *Reinventing government.* Addison-Wesley, Reading, Mass.
Proctor, Allen J. (1992). New directions in budgeting and financial planning. *Government Finance Review.* (December): 15–19.
Rubin, Irene S. (1993). Who invented budgeting in the United States? *Public Administration Review. 53*(5): 438–444.
Rubin, Irene S. (1997). *The Politics of Public Budgeting,* 3rd ed. Chatham, Chatham, N.J.
Rubin, Irene S. (1998). *Class, Tax, and Power: Municipal Budgeting in the United States.* Chatham, Chatham, N.J.
Rubin, Irene S. (1999). Presentation at the April, 1999 *National Conference of the American Society for Public Administration.* Orlando, Florida.
Shannon, John and Kee, James E. (1989). The Rise of Competitive Federalism Public Budgeting and Finance 9(4): 5–20.
Terry, Larry D. (1998). Administrative leadership, neo-managerialism, and the public management movement. *Public Administration Review. 58*(3): 194–200.
Widavsky, Aaaron (1961). Political implications of budget reform. *Public Administration Review. 21*(3): 183–190.
Widavsky, Aaron (1978). A budget for all seasons? Why the traditional budget lasts. *Public Administration Review. 38*(6): 501–505.
Wildavsky, Aaron (1988). *The New Politics of the Budgetary Process.* Harper-Collins, New York.
Wilson, James Q. (1989). *Bureaucracy.* Basic Books, New York.

8

Changes and Reforms in Tax and Public Revenue Systems

John R. Bartle
Department of Public Administration, University of Nebraska at Omaha, Omaha, Nebraska

Reform can be approached from either the normative perspective—how *should* policy be changed—or the positive perspective—how *will* policies be changed. This chapter gives several normative recommendations in the hope that scholars and practitioners of taxation will consider and discuss them. The positive perspective is probably more interesting, yet surely more hazardous. However, a central theme of this chapter is the prediction that U.S. taxes will change in the future in response to pragmatic rather than ideological concerns. This prediction is justified by historical patterns of tax reform in America. The normative recommendations made here or elsewhere will only come to pass if political, economic, and social forces converge to make them viable.

This chapter outlines trends in U.S. taxation in the 20th century with an attempt to identify reforms from both the positive and normative perspectives that may affect the 21st century. The first section gives the background to the development of the major taxes in this nation. These taxes are individual income taxes; corporate net income taxes; payroll taxes; general sales taxes; excise taxes on tobacco products, alcoholic beverages, and motor fuels; and the property tax. The next section looks at recent trends at federal, state, and local levels, followed by a discussion of each major tax and reforms that are likely to be considered. A concluding section follows.

BACKGROUND

All major federal and state taxes were adopted during the 20th century. Before 1909, the federal government relied entirely on excise taxes and customs duties, although an income tax had been used during the Civil War and death taxes were levied sporadically. Now taxes on income and payrolls constitute 92 percent of federal tax collections. At the turn of the 20th century, over half of state tax revenues were from the property tax and none was from a tax on income. Now less than 2 percent is from the property tax and almost 40 percent is from income taxes. Local governments were, and still are, heavily reliant on the property tax, although local taxes on income and consumption have gone from 0% to 21 percent of tax revenue (Pechman, 1987; Aronson and Hilley, 1986).

The federal corporate income tax was adopted in 1909 and the federal individual income tax in 1913. The individual income tax rates ranged from 1 percent to 7 percent when initially adopted. During the First and Second World Wars, these marginal rates rose to as high as 77 percent and 94 percent, respectively, and the federal corporate rate rose to 53 percent during 1942–1949. In the year 1999 individual rates ranged from 15 percent to 39.6 percent and corporate rates from 15 percent to 39 percent. The federal payroll tax was first imposed in 1937 as a part of the Social Security Act of 1935. Initially, rates were 1 percent on both employer and employee for the retirement portion of Social Security. In 1999, the tax rates on both employer and employee for the retirement portion were 5.6 percent, plus 0.6 percent for disability insurance, and 1.45 percent for hospitalization insurance (Medicare), for a total combined rate of 15.3 percent.

Some state individual income taxes were created in response to the federal adoption in 1913, but 17 were adopted later in the 1930s and 10 between 1961 and 1971 in part as a result of pressures to reduce property taxes. The same general trend applies to state corporate income taxes. In 1999, all states but Alaska, Florida, Nevada, South Dakota, Texas, Washington, and Wyoming levied an income tax (New Hampshire and Tennessee taxed only dividends and interest). Local income taxes are a relatively recent development. The first local income tax was passed in Philadelphia in 1938 (Rodgers and Temple, 1996).[1] By 1994 an estimated 4111 of the 86,750 local governments in the United States used this tax. Fourteen states authorize local governments to tax income; in three of these (Arkansas, Georgia, and Virginia) no governments currently exercise that authority. In three others (California, New Jersey, and Oregon), taxes are levied on employer payrolls in certain cities. Although corporate and individual income taxes account for only slightly more than 2 percent of local revenues, in some cities they constitute half or more. Among the largest 50 cities, Cleveland, Columbus, Cincinnati, Toledo, Philadelphia, Detroit, Kansas City, and Saint Louis all raise large portions of their revenue from income and earnings taxes (U.S. Department of Commerce, 1995).

Most states adopted general sales taxes in response to the Depression. Mississippi was the first state to do so, in 1930, and by 1938, 24 states had adopted this tax. Ten more states and the District of Columbia added it between 1947 and 1966, and another 11 did so between 1960 and 1969. Since 1944 the general sales tax has been the largest tax source for state and local governments (Aronson and Hilley, 1986). The five states still without a sales tax are Alaska, Delaware, Montana, New Hampshire, and Oregon. The first local sales tax was adopted in New York City in 1934. The number of states authorizing local governments to use the sales tax rose from 1 in 1950 (Mississippi) to 12 in 1963, 25 in 1970, and 31 in 1994 (Rodgers and Temple, 1996). Among cities over 500,000 in population, Dallas, Houston, San Antonio, El Paso, Phoenix, Seattle, San Jose, and San Diego derive more than 20 percent of their revenue from this tax (U.S. Department of Commerce, 1996).

The federal government began taxing liquor and snuff shortly after the adoption of the Constitution, although these taxes were repealed in 1802. Taxes on alcoholic beverages and tobacco were reinstituted during the Civil War (Pechman, 1987). All 50 states and the District of Columbia also tax cigarettes and other tobacco products, beginning with Iowa in 1921, followed by 7 other states during the 1920s, and 34 other states and the District of Columbia in the 1930s and 1940s. Thirty-two states and D.C. directly tax alcoholic beverages, and 18 states do so indirectly in their operation of liquor stores. Most of these laws were passed shortly after the repeal of Prohibition. The federal government began taxing diesel fuel in 1928, gasoline in 1932, and aviation-related fuels in 1970 (Pechman, 1987). All 50 states and D.C. have a gasoline tax; 44 of those adoptions occurred between 1921 and 1929 as the automobile became widely used. These taxes are not widely used at the local level. They constitute less than $5 per capita and are authorized in fewer than 10 states (Mikesell, 1999).

The property tax is one of the oldest and most widely used tax in the United States. In the 19th century, it was a fairly comprehensive tax on wealth, as most wealth was either real property or tangible personal property. As the economy moved away from its agrarian basis, the tax also changed. Now it is mainly a tax on real property and limited types of personal property, such as business machinery, equipment, and inventories, and in some states, automobiles and boats. Although it is used most intensively at the local level, 43 states and D.C. tax some forms of property, such as bank shares, capital stocks, and intangibles (ACIR, 1995). As a wealth tax it is flawed, as it taxes only certain types of wealth and does so on the basis of the gross, rather than the net, value. Further, the property tax is expensive for governments to administer, as it requires property valuation by assessors. Political pressures work against accurate and up-to-date assessment, and for some governments, assessment quality is low (Mikesell, 1993, 1999). Despite this, the real estate component of the tax has the desirable features of taxing an immobile factor of production and taxing landowners who benefit from certain locally provided services such as public safety, roads, and sewers and sanitation. Many premature obituaries of the property tax have been written. Although it is used less intensively than it was 30 years ago, the property tax will survive well into the 21st century, and probably beyond.

With one exception, therefore, the major forces shaping the development of tax policy during the 20th century were external events: the Depression, Prohibition, World War I and World War II, and the advent of the automobile and the airplane. The only reform that was attributable to ideological changes was the 16th Amendment, which permitted the federal income tax. Granted, this was the most important change during this decade, but its unique development suggests that most U.S. tax reform is pragmatic in nature, responding to wars, economic crises, social restrictions, and technological changes. Tax reform has been pragmatic rather than ideological. It seems likely that this pattern will continue.

MAJOR CHANGES

This section focuses on revenues, and to a lesser degree, expenditures of federal, state, and local governments since 1986. In the aggregate, total government receipts as a percentage of gross domestic product (GDP) grew from 27.9 percent in 1986 to 30.1 percent in 1996, and to 31.2 percent in 1998. In per capita terms, total receipts increased by 69 percent from 1986 to 1996, slightly faster than the 65.9 percent increase in per capita income and faster than inflation (35.2 percent).[2] Federal receipts grew slightly faster than the state-local total (Executive Office of the President, 1999).

The trend in total government expenditures is quite different. Total government expenditures fell from 30.8 percent of GDP in 1986 to 29.9 percent in 1996 and 28.7 percent in 1998. In per capita terms, total government spending increased by 54.3 percent from 1986 to 1996. Federal spending accounts for this change, as state and local spending has increased.[3] Combined with the federal revenue increase, this has caused a movement from deficits to surpluses at the federal level. State-local spending outpaced both inflation and personal income.

Recent Trends in Federal Government Finances

As Table 1 shows, federal receipts grew by 74.2 percent between 1986 and 1996, slower than state revenue during this period (82.6 percent) but faster than local revenues (68.0 percent). Federal receipts are dominated by the individual income tax (48.1 percent of total receipts) and the payroll tax (31.4 percent). Payroll tax rates increased in 1990, and certain individual income tax rates increased in 1993.

TABLE 1 Federal Receipts Per Capita, 1986–1998

	1986	1996	1998	Percentage Change 1986–1996	1998 Percentage of Total
Total Receipts	3,146.09	5,479.33	6,369.99	74.2%	100.0%
Individual income tax	1,427.24	2,475.27	3,065.45	73.4%	48.1%
Corporation taxes	258.25	647.93	698.03	150.9%	11.0%
Social insurance taxes	1,161.15	1,920.94	2,115.55	65.4%	33.2%
OASDHI and Railroad Retirement	1,043.20	1,796.30	1,997.84	72.2%	31.4%
Unemployment insurance	98.56	107.79	101.68	9.4%	1.6%
Other retirement	19.39	16.85	16.03	–13.1%	0.3%
Excise taxes	65.67	95.97	80.15	46.1%	1.3%
Alcohol	23.84	27.23	26.69	14.2%	0.4%
Tobacco	18.77	21.85	20.93	16.4%	0.3%
Telephone	9.57	15.97	18.17	66.9%	0.3%
Other excise taxes	13.49	30.92	14.36	129.2%	0.2%
Trust funds	68.98	107.72	133.22	56.2%	2.1%
Other receipts	164.79	231.51	277.59	40.5%	4.4%
Estate and gift taxes	28.46	64.82	89.07	127.8%	1.4%
Customs duties and fees	54.51	70.40	67.69	29.2%	1.1%
Miscellaneous receipts	81.83	96.29	120.82	17.7%	1.9%

Source: Executive Office of the President (1999).

These two sources grew at about the same rate as total federal revenue, and as state and local income taxes. Together with the corporate taxes, these two sources constitute over 90 percent of federal receipts. Corporate taxes have grown twice as fast as these other two sources. Corporate net income is highly volatile, so the upturn of the business cycle may in part explain this.

No other single source of federal revenue is more than 2 percent of the total. The growth of the excise taxes has been slow mainly because of declining consumption. Some of these tax rates increased during this period. Alcoholic beverage tax rates were increased in 1990, but have been stable since then. Tobacco rates increased steadily in the 1990s cigarette taxes increased from 16 cents per pack in 1989 to 34 cents in 2000 and will rise to 39 cents in 2002. All of the fuel tax rates have increased since 1989, but other excise taxes on vehicles, tires, guns, and sporting equipment have been stable during this period. The largest component of "trust fund receipts" are taxes on fuel earmarked for the trust funds for highways, airports and airways, and waterways. Tax rates for the taxes supporting the Airport and Airway Trust Fund were increased in 1997. Estate and gift taxes have also grown substantially despite stable rates.

Federal outlays increased more slowly than per capita income growth and only slightly faster than inflation. As Table 2 shows, a 10.4 percent decrease in defense spending, the second largest category behind Social Security, is part of the reason for this change. Other functions that decreased were international affairs, energy, agriculture, commerce and housing credit, and general government. Many of the human service functions increased faster than the total during this period, specifically education, training, employment, social services, health, Medicare, income security, and Social Security. These are likely to continue to grow. General science, space, and technology also increased faster than the average.

Recent Trends in State Government Finances

Table 3 shows that states draw revenue from four principal sources: taxes (43.3 percent), federal aid (21.5 percent), charges and miscellaneous revenue (13.5 percent), and insurance trust revenue (composed of employee retirement, workers compensation, and unemployment compensation, 19.6 percent). The most important taxes are those on general sales (14.4 percent), individual income (13.8 percent), and corporate income (3.0 percent). Of these three, individual income taxes grew at about the same rate as total revenues during this period, corporate income tax collections decreased slowly despite their high growth at the federal level, and sales taxes also grew slowly. This is a continuation of 50-year trend of reduced reliance on the sales tax and increased use of the individual income tax (ACIR, 1995). The slower sales tax collections happened despite 19 states' increasing their rates between 1989 and 1999. In part, this is attributable to the erosion of more than one-fourth of the sales tax base since 1979 as a result of shifting con-

TABLE 2 Federal Outlays Per Capita, 1986–1998

	1986	1996	1998	Percentage Change 1986–1996	1998 Percentage of Total
Total Outlays	4,050.98	5,884.51	6,113.80	45.3%	100.0%
National defense	1,118.10	1,002.12	993.18	–10.4%	16.2%
International affairs	57.88	50.89	48.50	–12.1%	0.8%
General science, space, and technology	36.71	63.01	67.40	71.6%	1.1%
Energy	19.18	10.71	4.70	–44.2%	0.1%
Natural resources and environment	55.78	81.50	82.86	46.1%	1.4%
Agriculture	128.63	34.54	45.16	–73.1%	0.7%
Commerce and housing credit	20.69	–39.49	3.75	–290.8%	0.1%
Transportation	115.00	149.20	149.21	29.7%	2.4%
Community and regional development	29.58	40.29	35.96	36.2%	0.6%
Education, training, employment, and social services	125.09	196.09	203.18	56.8%	3.3%
Health	146.98	450.16	486.28	206.3%	8.0%
Medicare	286.97	656.98	713.37	128.9%	11.7%
Income security	490.08	852.10	862.76	73.9%	14.1%
Social security	812.92	1,318.59	1,402.99	62.2%	22.9%
Veterans benefits and services	107.68	139.47	154.57	29.5%	2.5%
Administration of justice	26.88	66.17	84.47	146.2%	1.4%
General government	51.39	44.93	49.74	–12.6%	0.8%
Net interest	556.43	909.12	900.33	63.4%	14.7%
Undistributed offsetting receipts	–135.00	–141.86	–174.60	5.1%	–2.9%

Source: Executive Office of the President, 1999.

TABLE 3 State Revenue per Capita, 1986–1996

	1986	1996	Percentage Change ctg.	1996 of Total
Total Revenue	1995.93	3644.43	82.6%	100.0%
General revenue	1632.16	2904.50	78.0%	79.7%
Intergovernmental revenue	408.89	834.46	104.1%	22.9%
Federal	384.38	784.01	104.0%	21.5%
Local	24.50	50.45	105.9%	1.4%
Taxes	945.98	1577.14	66.7%	43.3%
Property tax	18.06	37.60	108.2%	1.0%
General sales	310.36	525.34	69.3%	14.4%
Motor fuels	58.43	97.96	67.7%	2.7%
Alcoholic beverages	12.70	13.82	8.8%	0.4%
Tobacco	18.45	27.66	49.9%	0.8%
Public utilities	24.90	32.47	30.4%	0.9%
Individual income	279.87	503.41	79.9%	13.8%
Corporate income	76.17	110.51	45.1%	3.0%
Motor vehicle license	31.85	47.80	50.1%	1.3%
Other taxes	115.19	180.57	56.8%	5.0%
Charges and misc.	277.29	492.90	77.8%	13.5%
Charges	124.39	253.54	103.8%	7.0%
Education	71.19	141.70	99.0%	3.9%
Hospitals	26.13	58.55	124.1%	1.6%
Transportation	10.69	18.18	70.1%	0.5%
Environment and housing	6.45	12.52	94.1%	0.3%
Other charges	9.91	22.59	128.0%	0.6%
Interest	73.61	107.89	46.6%	3.0%
Other misc. revenue	79.29	131.47	65.8%	3.6%
Special revenue	363.77	739.93	103.4%	20.3%
Utility revenue	12.06	14.77	22.5%	0.4%
Liquor store revenue	11.64	11.91	2.3%	0.3%
Insurance trust revenue	340.07	713.25	109.7%	19.6%
Debt outstanding	1027.54	1705.31	66.0%	

Source: U.S. Department of Commerce, 1997.

sumption patterns and state policy choices (Fox, 1998). Individual income taxes, on the other hand, have substantially higher revenue elasticities than all other taxes (Mikesell, 1999). Only 7 states increased their income tax rates during this period, while 10 cut them, yet revenues increased steadily. Corporate income tax rates were unchanged in 33 states and increased in only 6 (FTA, 1999; ACIR 1989). The only state to make a major change in its income tax during this period was Connecticut, which broadened its tax from one only on capital income to include salaries and wages. Most states reacted to the federal Tax Reform Act of 1986 by adjusting their income tax systems by broadening the tax base, reducing marginal rates, and raising personal exemptions and standard deductions. The net effect was to reduce state income tax liabilities for many low-income taxpayers, while also reducing the progressivity of state rate schedules (Fisher, 1996).

An important recent trend in state taxes is the very slow growth of the excise tax collections on tobacco, alcoholic beverages, and public utilities. The erosion of the political power of tobacco growers and companies has led to very substantial increases in cigarette tax rates. Thirty-six states and the District of Columbia increased their rate between 1989 and 1999, and the median rate rose from 20 to 34 cents per pack. Some states even doubled or tripled their rate; Maryland, for example increased its rate from 13 cents per pack in 1989 to 66 cents in 1999 (FTA, 1999; ACIR, 1990). However, falling tobacco consumption and a low revenue elasticity of the tax have kept revenue increases low. Tax rates on alcoholic beverages have lagged behind. From 1989 to 1999, only 14 states increased their tax on beer and only 6 of the 32 states and D.C. that directly tax liquor increased their rates (the other 18 states directly control liquor sales). As these taxes are unit taxes rather than ad valorem taxes, collections do not grow with inflation. Also consumption of liquor, which is taxed most heavily, has fallen relative to consumption of beer and wine, which are taxed at lower rates. States should be more vigilant about increasing these rates.

Tax collections from motor vehicle licenses grew at relatively slow rates during this period although 21 states increased their registration fees. State sales taxes on motor vehicles also increased in 21 states (ACIR, 1990; District of Columbia, 1999). Motor fuel tax collections prevented serious revenue erosion by rate increases. Thirty-six states increased their gas tax from 1989 to 1999, and the median rate rose from 16 cents per gallon to 20 cents (FTA, 1999; ACIR, 1990).

Charges replaced some of the slowdown in taxes. Over half of state charges are for education, which is almost entirely tuition and fees for higher education. The next largest category is hospital charges, which mainly arise from mental hospitals. Hospital charges cover 53 percent of expenditures, a much higher percentage than in the past. In 1996, revenues from air and water transportation covered 89 percent and 76 percent, respectively, of state expenditures in these areas. Education charges cover about one-third of expenditures, whereas revenues from charges for highways, housing, and natural resources, and parks and recreation are much lower relative to expenditures (Aronson and Hilley, 1986; U.S. Department of Commerce, 1997). Federal aid and insurance trust revenue grew fast, although this latter category is segregated from general revenues and so is not available to fund other spending. Interest earnings grew slowly, as did revenues from state utilities. Liquor store revenues barely increased, but cover 122 percent of expenses.

State debt outstanding increased at moderate rates during this period after doubling between 1980 and 1987. This reflects a rush of debt issuances prior to the adoption of the 1986 Tax Reform Act. The composition of state debt has shifted dramatically since 1949, when 85 percent of total debt was general obligation debt; by 1996 that fell to 26.5 percent. This has happened in part because in many states general obligation debt has constitutional limits or requirements for voter approval, unlike nonguaranteed debt. Some of the purposes of the nonguaranteed debt are higher education loans, hospital and university bonds, and mortgage revenue bonds.

Table 4 shows that over half of state direct spending is for two broad categories: education (21.2 percent) and public welfare (31.9 percent). In turn, the largest subcategories are higher education and vendor payments (largely to vendors of health care). These two categories have been trending sharply in opposite directions. This continued a 30-year trend of a decrease in the state and local share of spending on education and highways and an increasing share of spending on health and public welfare (Fisher, 1996). Other rapidly growing functions were health, corrections, and "other welfare" (principally administrative costs) and sewerage and solid waste. Slow-growing categories included cash assistance, "other transportation" (air, water, public transit, and parking), social insurance (unemployment benefit administration) and veterans' services, and interest. Library spending fell slightly.

Recent Trends in Local Government Finances

Table 5 shows the overall trend in local government revenue from 1986 to 1996. Overall, per capita revenue increased by 68 percent during this period, about the same rate of change as that of per capita income (65.9 percent), and faster than the rate of inflation (35.4 percent). Local revenue consists of four main categories: intergovernmental revenue, taxes, charges and miscellaneous revenue, and special revenue. The first two categories each constitute one-third of the total; charges and miscellaneous revenue (principally interest, special assessments, and sales of property) constitute 21 percent; and special revenue, 12 percent. Intergovernmental revenue as a whole grew at about the same rate as the total, but state aid increased much faster (74.5 percent) than did federal aid (19.7 percent). Taxes as a whole and the property tax in particular increased at the same rate as total revenues. The property tax dominates the local tax scene so much that it shadows the other taxes; however, some of the trends are revealing. As at the state level, there was some shifting away from local taxes on alcoholic beverages, tobacco, and corporate net income and toward motor fuels, motor vehicle licenses, and the individual income tax. The category of local revenue that increased the fastest during this period were charges. Interest revenue and utility revenue grew slowly. Insurance trust revenue (composed almost entirely of employee retirement revenue at this level) grew faster than the average.

The dominant role of the property tax in financing local government fell from 51.4 percent of total local general revenue in 1948 to 28 percent in 1981. This

TABLE 4 State Expenditures per Capita, 1986–1996

	1986	1996	Percentage Change	1996 Percentage Direct General Expenditure
General expenditures	1561.82	2847.17	82.3%	
Intergovernmental expenditures	547.40	949.94	73.5%	
Direct general expenditures	1014.42	1897.23	87.0%	
Education	241.67	401.70	66.2%	21.2%
Higher education	198.81	321.72	61.8%	17.0%
Elementary and secondary education	4.81	9.22	91.7%	0.5%
Other education	38.05	70.76	86.0%	3.7%
Libraries	1.08	1.06	−1.9%	0.1%
Welfare	233.35	605.68	159.6%	31.9%
Cash assistance	43.30	53.11	22.7%	2.8%
Vendor payments	147.51	462.34	213.4%	24.4%
Other welfare	42.54	90.22	112.1%	4.8%
Hospitals	70.93	109.56	54.5%	5.8%
Health	34.72	83.61	140.8%	4.4%
Social insurance and veterans	11.69	15.62	33.6%	0.8%
Highways	125.23	179.23	43.1%	9.4%
Other transportation	4.74	6.30	32.9%	0.3%
Police	13.80	24.50	77.5%	1.3%
Corrections	40.88	95.35	133.2%	5.0%
Protective inspections	11.27	17.94	59.2%	0.9%
Natural resources	28.61	46.39	62.1%	2.4%
Parks and recreation	7.19	11.55	60.6%	0.6%
Housing and community development	4.93	8.93	81.1%	0.5%
Sewerage	1.41	5.76	308.5%	0.3%
Solid waste	0	6.11		0.3%
Financial administration	23.93	46.71	95.2%	2.5%
Judicial and legal	15.46	30.57	97.7%	1.6%
General public buildings	3.98	6.84	71.9%	0.4%
Other administration	7.33	10.77	46.9%	0.6%
Interest	70.00	95.79	36.8%	5.0%
Salaries and wages	315.65	488.45	54.7%	

Source: U.S. Department of Commerce, 1997.

TABLE 5 Local Revenue per Capita, 1986–1996

	1986	1996	Percentage Change	1996 Percentage of Total
Total revenue	1803.37	3029.72	68.0%	100.0%
General revenue	1579.01	2673.42	69.3%	88.2%
Intergovernmental revenue	610.83	1019.59	66.9%	33.7%
Federal	84.76	101.42	19.7%	3.3%
State	526.07	918.16	74.5%	30.3%
Taxes	601.46	1020.04	69.6%	33.7%
Property tax	445.32	751.90	68.8%	24.8%
General sales	65.91	111.99	69.9%	3.7%
Motor fuels	1.30	3.18	144.6%	0.1%
Alcoholic beverages and tobacco	1.91	1.73	–9.4%	0.1%
Public utilities	16.69	27.54	65.0%	0.9%
Individual income	28.82	50.12	73.9%	1.7%
Corporate income	6.59	10.15	54.0%	0.3%
Motor vehicle license	2.36	4.10	73.7%	0.1%
Other taxes	32.56	59.33	82.2%	2.0%
Charges and miscellaneous	366.73	633.79	72.8%	20.9%
Charges	209.12	433.28	107.2%	14.3%
Education	27.31	45.80	67.7%	1.5%
Hospitals	68.57	131.97	92.5%	4.4%
Transportation	23.46	45.97	96.0%	1.5%
Environment and housing	61.37	140.84	129.5%	4.6%
Other charges	28.41	68.69	141.8%	2.3%
Interest	75.10	109.21	45.4%	3.6%
Other miscellaneous revenue	82.51	91.31	10.7%	3.0%
Special revenue	223.97	356.30	59.1%	11.8%
Utility revenue	169.83	255.10	50.2%	8.4%
Water supply	54.76	95.41	74.2%	3.1%
Electric power	86.59	124.37	43.6%	4.1%
Gas supply	13.65	14.28	4.6%	0.5%
Transit	14.83	21.04	41.9%	0.7%
Liquor store revenue	2.10	2.16	2.9%	0.1%
Insurance trust revenue	52.04	99.04	90.3%	3.3%
Debt outstanding	1705.51	2703.98	58.5%	

Source: U.S. Department of Commerce, 1997.

pattern held for all types of local governments. However, the property tax rebounded slightly, to 30 percent of revenue in 1992, again, for all types of local governments. School districts and townships are most reliant on the property tax, whereas municipalities and special districts least reliant (Fisher, 1996; ACIR, 1998). The burden of the tax on homeowners has varied and mirrors political changes. In 1958, the national average effective property tax rate on single-family residential property was 1.34 percent. It rose to 1.70 percent in 1966 and 1.98 percent in 1971 before many states adopted sales and/or income taxes in order to reduce state and local property taxes. In 1977 it was still high, at 1.67 percent, before falling to 1.26 percent in 1981 after the property tax rebellion. By 1987 it had fallen to 1.15 percent (ACIR, 1990, 1986). More recent figures from a different source indicate that this figure is about the same. National average effective property tax rates in 1998 ranged from 1.16 percent on high-valued residential property to 1.23 percent on low-valued property. Some of the highest states were New Jersey, New Hampshire, Illinois, Wisconsin, and Pennsylvania (Minnesota Taxpayers Association, 1999).

States use a variety of means to relieve property taxes, in particular for homeowners. Eighteen states and D.C. have an explicitly classified system, and in many other states assessment practices tend systematically to underassess homeowner property (Minnesota Taxpayers Association, 1999; Mikesell, 1999). In some cases, the benefit of classification and other property tax relief programs is quite high. One study found that in Louisiana, Hawaii, Massachusetts, and New York the effective tax rate on residential property is as little as one-fifth that on business property (Minnesota Taxpayers Association, 1999). Since 1989, nine states have adjusted their classification ratios to be more generous to homeowners, and six states did so to benefit business property (Minnesota Taxpayers Association, 1999; ACIR, 1990).

Another way to aid homeowners is to provide an exemption for some portion of assessed value or a tax credit. Twenty states do so, plus Rhode Island, which allows local exemptions. In some cases these programs can be quite generous. For instance, Louisiana exempts the first $7,500 of a home's value, but as assessment rates are 10%, this translates into $75,000 in market value. In Louisiana and five other states (Alabama, Florida, Hawaii, Indiana, and Idaho) these exemptions reduced gross local assessed value by more than 10 percent (Mikesell, 1999). Since 1989, 10 states have made these programs more generous and 2 have scaled them back (Minnesota Taxpayers Association, 1999; ACIR, 1990).

An even more explicit way to reduce the property tax is by use of a "circuit-breaker" payment, which gives either an income tax credit or a direct payment to homeowners and/or renters with low incomes and high property taxes. In 26 of the 35 states and D.C. that have a program, it is limited to narrow beneficiary groups such as the elderly, disabled, or blind. In nine other states and D.C., the program is available to all homeowners and/or renters. The median income limit among these states is $35,000, although these limits vary widely. It is interesting to note that D.C., Minnesota, and Wisconsin provide both a circuit-breaker and general homestead exemption or credit to homeowners.

These tools have been criticized for being complex and overly generous or for stimulating property tax increases (Bell and Bowman, 1987; Bartle, 1995; Fisher, 1996). All of these criticisms are accurate. From a normative perspective their main justification is that they serve as a valve to release the political pressure of the property tax that can lead to taxpayer revolts. As such, they are pragmatic measures that are likely to be adopted or increased as needed. However, they have a cost, as they either require an infusion of state funds or shift the tax burden to other property owners.

Property tax limits are a more general way to mute the impact of the tax. Research to date indicates that limits can be effective, at least initially, in slowing the growth of property tax revenues, and in some cases reducing revenues. However, they do so by inducing greater reliance on other local revenue sources, such as state aid and user fees. Some limits do seem to reduce local spending, and with it the quantity and quality of local services (Aronson and Hilley, 1986; Ebdon and Bartle, 1998).

The number of local governments with an income tax grew from 3517 in 1986 to 4111 in 1994. All of this growth occurred in the central states. Although there was no growth in the number of states authorizing an income tax, many states authorized additional local governments to use these taxes. Iowa added 318 school districts; Ohio 129 cities and school districts; Pennsylvania 53 municipalities and school districts; Kentucky 48 cities, counties, and school districts; Indiana 35 countries; Alabama 8 cities; and Michigan 3 cities (ACIR, 1995). Some major cities and counties increased their income or payroll rates during this period, in particular, New York, Los Angeles, Newark, Cincinnati, Scranton, Portland, Oregon metropolitan area, Lexington, Kentucky, Marion County, Indiana and Montgomery and Prince George Counties, Maryland. However, Philadelphia, Dayton, and Allen County, Indiana, decreased their tax rates on residents (ACIR, 1987, 1995). Thus the growth in local income tax revenue is attributable to increases in the number of governments levying the tax and the growth in income, rather than rate increases.

The number of local governments collecting sales taxes decreased from 6705 in 1986 to 6579 in 1994, although this change is almost solely attributable to a restructuring in Illinois in 1990 that repealed the sales tax authority of 1314 local governments and shifted collection of a portion of the sales tax to the state, with the state returning these funds to these local governments. Among the 30 other states with local sales taxes, the number of local governments using this tax increased. New local sales taxes were adopted for counties in Florida, South Carolina, and Iowa. Large increases occurred in the number of governments levying the tax in Arkansas (municipalities and counties), Nebraska (municipalities), North Dakota (municipalities), and Wisconsin (counties) (ACIR, 1995). During this period the combined state and local sales tax rate increased in many major cities.

Increases in the combined rate were due to increases in the state rate, the local rate, or both. For instance, California increased its state rate from 4.75 percent to 6 percent while local rates also increased in major cities such as Los Angeles, San Diego, and San Francisco. Local and state rates also went up in Arkansas, Florida, Texas, New Mexico, Oklahoma, South Carolina, and Tennessee (ACIR, 1987, 1986, 1995). A number of major cities now have combined rates over 8 percent: New York, Los Angeles, San Francisco, Chicago, Dallas, Houston, San Antonio, Seattle, New Orleans, Oklahoma City, Mobile, Nashville, and Memphis (District of Columbia, 1999; ACIR, 1995). Thus, the trend in local sales tax collections is exactly the opposite of that in the local income tax; as local sales tax rates increased in many cases, the number of governments levying the tax decreased.

Motor fuel taxes increased faster than any other local tax during this period. From 1985 to 1994, four more states (Alaska, Montana, New Mexico, and Washington) gave their local governments power to tax fuels, while Arkansas rescinded this power, raising from 13 to 16 the number of states allowing local governments this authority (ACIR, 1995, 1986). Most of the states that do so give the authority to counties, although Chicago and Honolulu collect fair amounts of motor fuel revenue. Local tax collections on alcoholic beverages and tobacco fell during this period. A small number of local governments tax these sources, so this trend is more specific to the states of Illinois, New York, Tennessee, Georgia, and Alabama (Rodgers and Temple, 1996). However, this trend does reflect the changes in consumption patterns discussed, as well stable unit tax rates.

Local governments in 40 states tax either the sales or gross receipts of public utilities (mainly natural gas, electric, and telephone companies). The collections from this source are largest for municipalities. Collections have been fairly stable, as is consumption of these services.

User charges in most functional areas other than education increased rapidly during this period, and also over a longer period of over 30 years (Fisher, 1996). This reflects in part a resistence to property tax increases as well as an increasing acceptance of benefits-based charges. In certain areas (water and air transportation, parking, sewerage) charges are close to covering local expenditures. In other areas (hospitals, sanitation, and parks and recreation) expenditures are substantially higher, but charges are increasing. Special districts, especially those providing utility services, collect the largest percentage of their revenue from user charges. Counties and municipalities are also high in this area, whereas townships and school districts are low (Downing and Bierhanzl, 1996; Fisher, 1996).

While charges have increased, utility revenues have slowed. Gas supply revenues were essentially stable as electric power and transit revenues increased slowly. Only water utility revenues increased at a rate comparable to that of total revenue. In large part, this slowdown is attributable to rates. For all of these utilities, expenditures increased faster than revenues over almost a 50-year period. Water supply revenues were only 88 percent of expenditures in 1996, compared to 149 percent in 1953 and 131 percent in 1973, indicating that general revenues are now used to subsidize consumption. Electric power revenues are 104 percent of expenditures and gas revenues are 108 percent, so these utilities are on a more self-funded basis. For transit, however, revenues are only 27 percent of expenditures, compared to 94 percent in 1953 (Aronson and Hilley, 1986).

Local debt outstanding increased relatively slowly after growing at very fast rates until the 1986 Tax Reform Act. As with state debt, the composition of local debt has shifted over a long period, but unlike state debt, that trend began to reverse itself recently. From 1949 to 1984 the percentage of local debt that was general obligation debt fell from 88.3 percent to 36.3 percent, but then increased to 40.2 percent in 1996. This trend began during the Depression as a way to work around state debt limitations on local governments. General obligation debt typically funds local infrastructure such as school building projects, water and wastewater, utilities, and roads. The increased nonguaranteed debt reflects such projects as industrial development bonds, housing, stadiums, and a host of other quasi-enterprise functions.

Table 6 shows trends in local government expenditures during the 1986–1996 period. Elementary and secondary education consumes by far the largest share of local spending (40.4 percent), and the rate of growth of this category is similar to that of the total. The fastest-growing categories were health, corrections, solid waste, and judicial and legal. Some of these increases were due to mandates and grants from federal and state governments, as these functions attracted significant attention during this period. Hospitals and police, the second and third largest categories of local spending, also increased faster than the average, probably for the same reasons. Spending growth was slowest for welfare cash assistance, natural resources, highways, and interest.

In the aggregate local spending did not change in major ways during this period. However, different types of local governments have differing spending responsibilities. Counties are responsible for the fast-growing functions of corrections, hospitals, health, and judicial and legal administration. The main functions for which cities are responsible (police, fire, education, sewerage, and parks and recreation) grew at average rates. The same is generally true of school districts, and most special districts. Townships are responsible for certain slow-growing functions, such as highways and fire, and so are probably under less fiscal pressure.

The Current Situation

Although antitax sentiment is a very powerful force constraining the adoption of new tax authority at all levels, recent developments do indicate some degree of movement. Sales and excise tax collections have been lagging, creating pressure for rate increases. Income tax collections have grown, helping to eliminate the federal deficit and allowing some states to cut their rates. Charges have increased in some areas but still offer opportunities for more revenue, as do local utilities. The

TABLE 6 Local Expenditures per Capita, 1986–1996

	1986	1996	Percentage Change	1996 Percentage Direct General Expenditure
General expenditures	1509.57	2617.00	73.4%	
Intergovernmental expenditures	16.68	30.90	85.3%	
Direct general expenditures	1492.89	2586.10	73.2%	
Education	632.82	1101.81	74.1%	42.6%
Elementary and secondary education	597.12	1043.81	74.8%	40.4%
Higher education	35.70	58.00	62.5%	2.2%
Libraries	11.15	20.50	83.9%	0.8%
Welfare	76.55	123.65	61.5%	4.8%
Cash assistance	34.95	48.40	38.5%	1.9%
Vendor payments	5.81	8.82	51.8%	0.3%
Other welfare	35.52	66.43	87.0%	2.6%
Hospitals	86.96	156.76	80.3%	6.1%
Health	29.78	67.80	127.7%	2.6%
Highways	79.55	118.91	49.5%	4.6%
Other transportation	24.05	41.00	70.5%	1.6%
Police	80.29	143.94	79.3%	5.6%
Fire	39.71	66.75	68.1%	2.6%
Corrections	21.16	46.05	117.6%	1.8%
Protective inspections	5.65	9.29	64.4%	0.4%
Natural resources	9.03	13.24	46.6%	0.5%
Parks and recreation	34.97	60.59	73.3%	2.3%
Housing and community development	41.88	76.51	82.7%	3.0%
Sewerage	53.78	87.22	62.2%	3.4%
Solid waste	24.20	49.31	103.8%	1.9%
Financial administration	25.42	38.60	51.8%	1.5%
Judicial and legal	23.13	46.53	101.2%	1.8%
General public buildings	13.05	20.12	54.2%	0.8%
Other administration	19.62	34.10	73.8%	1.3%
Interest	83.74	126.29	50.8%	4.9%
Salaries and wages	748.83	1198.95	60.1%	

Source: U.S. Department of Commerce, 1997.

property tax has stabilized after a flurry of cuts and limit impositions in the late 1970s and early 1980s and states have worked to moderate the tax on homeowners. As the property tax is the residual source of funds at the local level, future trends in its use will depend on the degree of discontent with the tax and its administration, and state willingness to reduce local taxes with state dollars. In general, spending on human service functions has increased disproportionately, while spending on transportation, natural resources, and, at the federal level, defense has grown more slowly.

ISSUES AND FUTURE IMPLICATIONS

Proposed reforms should be evaluated by commonly accepted goals of taxation. Four principles are particularly compelling. First, revenue structures should be equitable. Either the benefits-received principle or the ability-to-pay principle may be compelling. The benefits-received principle recommends the development of devices such as user fees and special assessments to make a more explicit connection in fiscal decision making. The ability-to-pay principle is most appropriate for redistributive programs. The second goal is economic efficiency. Fees that charge appropriate prices for goods previously provided free will increase economic efficiency. Also taxes and fees that internalize external costs, such as effluent taxes and solid waste disposal fees, will improve economic efficiency. Third, a good tax should have a high yield and be stable and predictable. In general, this can be achieved by broadening the tax base, thereby also improving horizontal equity, efficiency, and administrative simplicity. Fourth, a tax should be administered in a way that minimizes administrative and compliance costs in a way compatible with other goals. Fair administration is essential to establish credibility among citizens.

Perhaps the most important tax issue in the near future will be the sales tax. As electronic commerce grows, and with the continued reluctance to expand the tax to other forms of consumption such as services, the base of this tax will continue to narrow. State sales taxes are only 41.9 percent of total personal income, so there is ample opportunity to broaden the tax base (Fox, 1998). Broadening the base increases revenue productivity, equity, efficiency, and ease of administration. But this change will require states to row against the political currents, and that is not likely. Without base broadening, many problems will become apparent. The horizontal and vertical inequities of the tax will be exacerbated. Certain goods, such as clothing, furniture, and equipment, tend to be particularly sensitive to rate differentials (Mikesell, 1985). If consumers, seeking tax savings, shift their spending on these sorts of items, economic inefficiency, reduction of overall tax revenue, and further diminished perceptions of equity will result. Finally, the tax is no longer deductible from the federal income tax, so its burden is heavier. It is likely that in the near future the income tax will pass the sales tax as the largest state tax. It is tempting to predict that some of the states now with a sales tax but without an income tax will adopt the income tax and reduce or even repeal their sales tax. However, this list of states (Florida, Nevada, South Dakota, Texas, Washington, and Wyoming) does not include any that seems likely to do so soon. Instead, it is more likely that sales tax revenues will grow slowly, putting pressure on sales tax rates and state spending. As necessity is the mother of invention, income taxes will not be adopted in these states until they face dire situations.

Major reform of the federal individual income tax is frequently the subject of debate. It is impossible to forecast whether reform will occur, and, if it does, what form it will take. Current political pressures seem to be of two types: either to move toward a flat income tax or to move toward a more consumption-based tax. A combination of both is also possible. The political stars that aligned to pass the 1986 Tax Reform Act suggest two things: first, that major tax reform is infrequent, and second, that rather than originating at one end of the political spectrum, such reform requires the odd bedfellows of any political compromise. One plausible change is continued incremental movement in the direction of exempting contributions to savings, especially at the lower ends of the income scale, to the point where consumption is the main base of the federal income tax. Although this would narrow the base and decrease progressivity, it could improve the efficiency of the tax. Assuming that states follow the federal shift, this could help states tax the consumption base with a means much better than the current sales tax, helping them address that problem.

The payroll tax, as the source of funding for Social Security and Medicare, is highly unlikely to change or decrease until the pressure from the retirement of the "Baby Boom" generation is off. Still, adding a tax of over 15 percent on top of federal and state income tax rates easily makes the combined tax rate on labor income 50 percent or more for many taxpayers. Compared to some types of capital income, which are exempt or taxed at preferential rates under the income tax and not included in the payroll tax, the tax differential on labor income compared to that on capital income is large. Further expansion of the earned income credit or reduction of exemptions on capital income would be two ways to close this gap.

Although the federal corporate income tax has long been a favorite target of reformers, it lives on, riddled with complexity. There is a very good justification to integrate it with the personal income tax, although there are numerous practical difficulties. Methods of partial integration are similarly difficult. Corporate financial structures are probably too firmly entrenched to accommodate a major reform of this tax. State corporate income taxes are becoming increasingly problematic because of conflicting state rules regarding the calculation and apportionment of the income of multistate and multinational corporations (Pomp, 1998). Whereas the problems with current approaches to taxing business income are easy to see, workable alternatives are not. One alternative, a value-added tax, would require major reform at both federal and state levels that is not politically feasible at this time. Therefore, against the recommendations of many tax experts, corporate income taxes are likely to continue in their present form.

There will be a growing justification for allowing some local governments to use the income tax in the future. Counties in particular are increasingly funding redistributive services that are not logically related to the property tax, such as corrections, health care, welfare, hospitals, and courts. In Indiana and Kentucky counties are increasingly using the income tax, as all Maryland counties do. This change can be made with relatively little political fallout if states adjust their own taxes to accommodate counties.

As suggested in data presented earlier, when residential property taxes rise above 1.5 percent or so, the political opposition to the tax builds, although there already are several states where homeowners tolerate higher rates. Further, the tax is highly visible, assessment quality questionable, and its burden is high for farmers and seniors. For these reasons, it is likely to be a political itch that needs to be scratched every so often by any of the various property tax relief mechanisms. This is unfortunate, because many property tax relief devices tend to obscure the accountability for tax increases, which may in turn stimulate further increases. It also complicates administration and creates new inequities. Tax limits tend to be either ineffective or pernicious. Circuit-breakers are probably the best form of property tax relief, as they can be targeted and reduce the regressivity of the tax. Or states can simply grant additional sales or income tax authority to local governments to reduce the property tax.

It would make sense for counties to shift somewhat from the property tax to the income tax. Also, in five states (Arkansas, Florida, South Carolina, Iowa, and Wisconsin) the number of counties using the sales tax has substantially increased over the last dozen years. These trends should continue. Similarly, large cities are moving away from the property tax, and it seems likely that this trend will also continue. Six of the 24 largest cities collect more than 30 percent of their taxes from income or payroll taxes, and 8 collect more than 20 percent of their tax revenue from the sales tax. Central cities have unique responsibilities, and some revenue source other than the property tax is often needed to fill that gap. The future of the metropolis is hard to predict in an era of rapid technological change; however, it is likely that the property tax will be a smaller portion of revenues for many major cities.

Although the use of the property tax to finance schools has been an equity concern, it is likely to continue if for no other reason than that there is no better revenue source. The sales or income tax would create similar equity problems in their distribution of tax revenues among school districts. Many state governments have increased their share of the financing burden, but this conflicts with local control over decision making. As a result, the state share is likely to continue to increase some, but not greatly. Although increased federal aid to local schools makes sense at a theoretical level, the logistics and politics of aid distribution are overwhelming. One source that may well increase for schools is private foundation support. Whether this source can be enough to become significant is difficult to tell.

Excise taxes are likely to change in dramatic ways. Tobacco use is declining, and tax policy is one tool in that social change. It is possible that tobacco will be used so sparingly in the near future as to make its tax implications trivial. Consumption of alcoholic beverages will stay with us, as it has for many millennia, although social pressures against it may increase, leading to concomitant increases in tax rates. Despite their illegal status, narcotics are taxed in some states, and possible changes in this status for certain items, such as marijuana, may enhance revenue collections as the legalization of alcoholic beverages did after the repeal of Prohibition. Other "social bads," such as pollution, firearms, hazardous wastes, and chemicals, are likely to face new or increased excise taxes.

Transportation is likely to change dramatically in the near future. I suspect my grandchildren will be amused by pictures of my automobiles. Even if the internal combustion engine and surface transportation are common in the future, the gas tax (and other fuel taxes) may cease to exist. They do not create a close link between payment and resource use, as pavement damage is weakly related to fuel consumption and the social costs of congestion are not included. Technological advances already allow easy-to-administer tolls that can be calibrated to time of day, roads traveled, and weight of vehicle. The only good reason to retain fuel taxes for highways, or any other type of transportation, is to incorporate the social costs of pollution, and possibly the scarcity of fossil fuels. Aviation taxes are similarly flawed, taxing fuel, ticket values, international flights, and numbers of passengers, none of which is closely correlated with infrastructure costs or congestion. Despite current political opposition to change, rapid technological change in this area is likely to cause a reaction in tax policy similar to that 80 years ago.

Expansion of user charges is an attractive option. Charges are attractive for four reasons: They raise additional revenue, they create a link between the revenue and expenditure parts of the budget that can improve fiscal decision making, they provide public managers an indicator of the desirability of expanding or contracting service supply, and they can enhance efficiency by rationing services to those who value them enough to pay their cost. This approach does raise some issues of access to public services and therefore equity, and the administrative costs may be high. Recreation probably should rely more heavily on fees, especially during peak times and seasons. Also, more cities are charging for trash removal, thus encouraging recycling and reducing disposal costs. At the state level, highway fees cover a much smaller portion of their costs than do other forms of transportation, suggesting another revenue opportunity that would also level the playing field in transportation. Some states should increase higher education tuition, as its share of costs has also been dropping. Other possibilities for expansion of fee revenues include stormwater run-off, bridges, airports, and development charges.

Local utility services are recouping a smaller and smaller percentage of their costs, a change that suggests an opportunity to increase revenue. It makes much more sense for these to be self-funded than to draw property tax revenues to cover expenses. One exception is local public transit, which can justify its use of the property tax because it reduces traffic congestion.

Over the last half of the 20th century, state and local debt shifted toward nonguaranteed debt. The interest costs of these issuances are higher than that of guaranteed debt. Also these issuances are less public in the nature of their benefit. Although revenue bonds serve many legitimate purposes, governments would be wise to restrict their quasi-commercial activities, and with it their interest costs. Further, the impact of the elimination of the federal deduction for state and local interest would dramatically increase state and local interest costs. Federal debt is subject to much different influences and is currently manageable.

CONCLUSION

American tax policy is a collection of pragmatic compromises and balances. These can be upset as political or socioeconomic winds shift. Ideological purists attempting reform are likely to be disappointed. However, there will be many changes that will create fiscal tensions and require a rebalancing. Future shifts in the patterns of employment and commerce will be numerous and will have important impacts on the tax system. The taxes that are most likely to change are sales and excise taxes. Corporate income taxes are also in need of change, but this is less likely to occur. Individual income taxes will likely see some adjustments, but the basic structure should stay intact. The payroll tax is unlikely to change, and the role of the property tax may be further diminished, but it will live on.

NOTES

1. Rodgers and Temple (1996: 256) write, "Charleston, South Carolina adopted an income tax in the early nineteenth century but abandoned it. New York City adopted a local income tax in 1934 but repealed the ordinance in 1935 before any collections were made."
2. In this chapter, inflation measures are drawn from the fixed-weight GDP price deflators for total government purchases, federal government purchases, or state and local government purchases, as is appropriate.
3. State-local spending here does not include spending funded by federal aid.

REFERENCES

Advisory Commission on Intergovernmental Relations (ACIR) (1986). *Significant Features of Fiscal Federalism, 1985–86 Edition.* Advisory Commission on Intergovernmental Relations, Washington, D.C.

Advisory Commission on Intergovernmental Relations (ACIR) (1987). *Significant Features of Fiscal Federalism, 1988 Edition,* vol. 1. Advisory Commission on Intergovernmental Relations, Washington, D.C.

Advisory Commission on Intergovernmental Relations (ACIR) (1989). *Significant Features of Fiscal Federalism, 1989 Edition,* vol. 1. Advisory Commission on Intergovernmental Relations, Washington, D.C.

Advisory Commission on Intergovernmental Relations (ACIR) (1990). *Significant Features of Fiscal Federalism, 1990,* Vol. 1. *Budget Processes and Tax Systems.* Advisory Commission on Intergovernmental Relations, Washington, D.C.

Advisory Commission on Intergovernmental Relations (ACIR) (1995). *Significant Features of Fiscal Federalism, 1995.* Vol. 1. *Budget Processes and Tax Systems.* Advisory Commission on Intergovernmental Relations, Washington, D.C.

American Council on Intergovernmental Relations (ACIR) (1998). *Significant Features of Fiscal Federalism, 1995.* Vol. 2. *Revenues and Expenditures.* American Council on Intergovernmental Relations, Washington, D.C.

Aronson, J. R., and Hilley, J. L. (1986). *Financing State and Local Governments,* 4th ed. Brookings Institution, Washington, D.C.

Bartle, J. R. (1995). The fiscal impact of federal and state aid to large U.S. cities: an empirical analysis of budgetary response. *Public Budgeting & Finance. 15:* 56–67.

Bell, M. E., and Bowman, J. H. (1987). The effect of various intergovernmental aid types on local own-source revenues: The case of property taxes in Minnesota. *Public Finance Quarterly. 15:* 282–297.

District of Columbia (1999). *Tax Rates and Tax Burdens In the District of Columbia: A Nationwide Comparison.* Government of the District of Columbia, Washington, D.C.

Downing, P. B., and Bierhanzl, E. J. (1996). User charges and special districts. In *Management Policies in Local Government Finance,* 4th ed. (J. R. Aronson and E. Schwartz, eds.). International City/County Management Association, Washington, D.C.

Ebdon, C., and Bartle, J. (1998). Budget responses to local government tax limits in Nebraska: Who decides? Presented at the *Annual Conference of the Association for Budgeting and Financial Management.* Washington, D.C.

Executive Office of the President, Office of Management and Budget (1999). *Budget of the United States Government, Fiscal Year 2000, Historical Tables.* [http://w3.access.gpo.gov/usbudget/fy2000/hist.html].

Federation of Tax Administrators (1999) *State Rates and Structure.* [http://www.taxadmin.org/fta/rate].

Fisher, R. (1996). *State and Local Public Finance,* 2nd ed. Richard D. Irwin, Chicago.

Fox, W. F. (1998). Can the state sales tax survive a future like its past? In *The Future of State Taxation* (D. Brunori, ed.). Urban Institute, Washington, D.C.

Mikesell, J. (1985). Retail sales and use taxation in Minnesota. In *Final Report of the Minnesota Tax Study Commission. Vol. 2. Staff Papers* (R. D. Ebel and T. E. McGuire, ed.). Butterworths, St. Paul.

Mikesell, J. (1993). *City Finances, City Futures.* Ohio Municipal League Education and Research Fund.

Mikesell, J. (1999). *Fiscal Administration,* 5th ed. Harcourt Brace, Fort Worth, Tex.

Minnesota Taxpayers Association (1999). *50-State Property Tax Comparison Study, Payable Year 1998.* Minnesota Taxpayers Association, Saint Paul.

Pechman, J. (1987). *Federal Tax Policy,* 5th ed. Washington, D.C., Brookings Institution.

Pomp, R. D. (1998). The future of the state corporate income tax: Reflections (and confessions) of a tax lawyer. In *The Future of State Taxation* (D. Brunori, ed.) Urban Institute, Washington, D.C.

Rodgers, J. D., and Temple, J. A. (1996). Sales taxes, income taxes, and other nonproperty tax revenue. In *Management Policies in Local Government Finance,* 4th ed. (J. R. Aronson and E. Schwartz, eds.). International City/County Management Association, Washington, D.C.

U.S. Department of Commerce, Bureau of the Census (1987). *Government Finances in 1985–86.* U.S. Government Printing Office, Washington, D.C.

U.S. Department of Commerce, Bureau of the Census (1995). *Finance Data for Cities Having 300,000 Population or More: 1991–92.* [http://www.census.gov/govs/city/92cisum.txt].

U.S. Department of Commerce, Bureau of the Census (1996). *Finances of Individual City Governments Having 500,000 Population or More: 1993–94.* [http://www.census.gov/govs/www/city94.html].

U.S. Department of Commerce, Bureau of the Census (1997). *United States State & Local Government Finances by Level of Government: 1995–96.* [http://www.census.gov/govs/estimate/96stlus.txt].

9

Human Resource Management Change in State and Local Government

N. Joseph Cayer
School of Public Affairs,
Arizona State University, Tempe, Arizona

Sandra J. Parkes
Department of Political Science,
University of Utah, Salt Lake City, Utah

In an age of reinvention, technological advancements, and changing organizational demographics, public personnel administrators, particularly at the state and local levels, face many challenges. Given the complexity of the roles and functions of human resource managers, it is crucial to understand such challenges and the impact they may have on reform efforts.

Reform in state and local human resource management (HRM) practices is an ongoing, evolving process. Reform efforts seek to improve training, compensation, benefits, classification, and virtually all other practices of the field while maintaining the values of democracy and efficiency (Ban and Ricucci, 1993; Cayer, 1995; Rosenbloom, 1985). Many reform efforts within public personnel systems reflect reactions to social and political value changes and more general government reforms at many levels. Such efforts often act as catalysts for experiments or changes at the national level and are simultaneously affected by changes from the national level. HRM practices, to a large extent, mirror both social and political changes (Cayer, 1995; Rosenbloom 1985).

The roles and functions of state and local personnel departments are very complex and broad in scope. Often this complexity, and the challenges that accompany it, drives reform efforts. First, the roles and functions are complex because they are *political.* Personnel managers are often responsible for determining the allocation of government resources (Rich, 1982; Thompson, 1995). In addition, they must abide by rules and regulations set forth by the political system and policy process, and ultimately, their decisions may influence public policy. Public personnel administrators are expected to uphold the democratic values upon which our political system is based, while being held accountable to individual concerns within their organizations.

Second, the complex roles and functions of public personnel administrators are *constitutional.* Individuals in HRM must recognize the rights and privileges espoused within the Constitution in examining the way they deal with people. Administrators must consider equity, justice, public interest, rights, and the underlying values of the American government system and must be accountable and responsive to the public and employees within those established boundaries (Lee, 1992; Rosenbloom, 1995).

Third, the roles and responsibilities are complex because they are *legal.* The actions of HR managers generally are influenced and limited by precedents and court decisions (Cayer, 1998; Klingner, 1995: Rosenbloom, 1995). In addition, state and local governments may depend upon decisions made at other levels of government and often rely upon those other levels for a variety of resources (Hartman et al., 1998; Saltzstein, 1995).

Fourth, their complex roles and functions are *social* because decisions and actions made by HR managers often stem from the demands of citizens and/or the characteristics of their communities. Public interest frequently initiates reform efforts, and state and local personnel departments must pay attention to these forces within their communities.

Finally, the roles and responsibilities are complex because they are *organizational.* Public personnel administrators must work within political, constitutional, legal, and social constraints in the name of effective and efficient organizations (Ott, 1998). They must allocate resources in such a way as to maximize organizational effectiveness and productivity and not tip the balance away from adherence to public expectations.

Clearly, the nature and number of roles and responsibilities for public personnel management can lead to conflict, and ultimately to the need for change and reform. Because their roles and functions are diverse and potentially conflicting, it is easier to understand why reform efforts are often undertaken in an attempt to uphold myriad expectations.

It is important to understand the complexity of the roles and responsibilities of state and local personnel administrators in order that reform efforts can be better understood within the most appropriate context. This chapter reviews the background of human resources reform, current reform efforts at the state and local levels, their impacts, and future possibilities.

BACKGROUND

Within these political, constitutional, legal, social, and organizational contexts, reform attempts are made to maximize differing values at different times, to gain control over government bureaucracy, to make organizations more efficient, or to reinvent government (Ban and Ricucci, 1993; Cayer, 1995; Klingner, 1998). Traditionally, personnel reform focused on reducing or eliminating partisanship from personnel decisions and replacing it with merit based actions. Although some state and local level governments began experimenting with elements of reform before the national government created the civil service system in 1883, reform at the state and local levels mainly developed after the national reform. The Pendleton Act of 1883 and similar reforms in state and local personnel reflected the value of neutral competence current at the time (Ingraham, 1985).

Because government theoretically reflects political values of the citizens, reform is inevitable as values change. Difficulties emerge as the values and tendencies of bureaucratic organizations conflict with citizen interest in change. Bureaucratic organizations tend to be secretive and self-protective, whereas the public expects openness and responsiveness. Reform efforts historically reflect differing values and concerns of the times. Thus, 19th- and early 20th-century reforms attempted to correct the perceived problems of the time. The major problems revolved around spoils and patronage during the late 19th and early 20th centuries. Spoils and patronage also concerned conflicts over who controlled government personnel. Reformers also promised greater efficiency through their efforts. Because the reforms led to unintended consequences, new reforms arose to make the public service more responsive and more focused on the service it was supposed to deliver (Sayre, 1948). More recent reform efforts, such as reinvention and total quality management (TQM), reflect desires to reduce the size and cost of government and to make it more responsive to the citizenry through devolution of authority (Ban, 1997; Berman, 1994; 1997; Brudney et al., 1999).

State and local governments provided the original models for spoils, which the national government eventually embraced (Fish, 1905). After the national government adopted reform through the Pendleton Act of 1883, many states followed suit, creating their own civil services, including local governments in the reforms. Traditionally, states closely controlled the activities of local governments (some still do). Under what was called Dillon's rule, resulting from a court decision written by an Iowa justice, John Dillon, local governments receive their powers from and are subject to control by state legislatures and constitutions (*City of Clinton v. Cedar Rapids and Missouri River Railroad Company,* 1868). As such, local personnel functions were closely controlled by the states. Over the years, states have granted home rule powers to many cities so that they control their own destinies, but counties in most states still operate under provisions of the state constitutions or state legislatures.

New York led the states in using the 1883 national reform as a model by adopting a civil service law in the same year, and Wisconsin did so in 1884. Several other states adopted merit-based systems after the turn of the century: Illinois (1905), Wisconsin (1905), Colorado (1907), New Jersey (1908), and Ohio (1912). The exposure of corruption and the effects of spoils by such muckraking journalists as Lincoln Steffens (1904) stimulated much of the interest in reforming the system at the state and local levels.

The national government also stimulated reform in state and local government personnel systems through the grant-in-aid process and through mandates for participation in national programs. The Social Security Act of 1935 represents the largest step of the national government in influencing state and local personnel functions until that time (Aronson, 1974; Cayer 1986; Dresang, 1982). The legislation created numerous programs, many of which required state participation for implementation. The statute required that state employees involved in the nationally funded programs be covered by merit systems. To participate, states developed merit systems, often covering only those involved in the Social Security Act programs, but eventually states covered most of their employees and extended merit principles to local governments as well. Some states cover limited numbers of employees, but national government mandates make it difficult to avoid use of merit principles in most areas. Federal courts also influence the role of spoils in personnel activities (Hamilton, 1999).

During the 1970s, some state and local governments experimented with further reform of their systems and attempted to integrate them into the management system rather than using the independent commission model represented by the U.S. Civil Service Commission. Gradually, the reform reached the national level and President Jimmy Carter spearheaded the Civil Service Reform Act (CSRA) of 1978, which attempted to make the national personnel system more responsive to management. The 1978 CSRA stimulated many other states and local governments to act, and reform occurred across the country.

Although merit principles permeated the reform of personnel systems from the late 19th century on, the form they took varies greatly from one governmental unit to another (Chi, 1998). Although called merit systems, many do not live up to the appellation. Generally, state and local governments have some systemwide personnel system, although the system may not cover all employees. Texas is the only state with no centralized personnel agency (Mallory, 1996). At the local level, central personnel agencies are common, especially in council-manager cities, whereas counties reflect very mixed approaches (Tompkins and Stapczynski, 1999). In very small communities, the town/city manager may have the responsibility, or it may be combined with other functions in one office. Counties in many states divide personnel functions among commissioners or supervisors on the basis of their geographic representation. Because many county officers are elected, they often control their own personnel; that practice leads to very decentralized systems. Clearly, at the state and local levels, there are tensions among values about neutral competence, responsiveness, centralization/decentralization, and political realities that influence approaches to the personnel function (Daly, 1990; Klingner, 1998).

The early reform efforts spawned systems independent of the chief executive. In creating systems independent of political partisanship, the reformers insulated civil service systems from political accountability. These systems often took on a life of their own, justifying Wallace Sayre's lament that they represented a "triumph of technique over purpose" (Sayre, 1948). The insularity resulted in systems that often became more concerned with the process by which personnel management took place than with the reason for having personnel systems, i.e., to facilitate serving the public. The independence also resulted in some tendencies for personnel specialists to gain control over administrative processes (Ealy, 1981).

These legacies of traditional civil service resulted in systems that were ill prepared to adapt to the increasingly rapid societal changes and their impact on government entities. During the 1960s, pressures for opening the process of government and the employment of public servants to all segments of society arose. These changes challenged the traditional rigid and closed processes of personnel management. Changing demographics of the labor force resulted in more diverse organizations and the inevitable challenges in managing workplace diversity (Gossett, 1997; Guy and Newman, 1998; West, 1998).

The political realities of the 1970s included reducing the size of government and tax cutting, a trend that accelerated during the 1980s and continues through current times. Most planning in state and local government assumed continuous growth in need for personnel services. As tax and budget cuts became necessary, personnel administrators found themselves having to change assumptions and draw up plans for reductions in force instead of recruiting more employees (Anselmini, 1996; Ban, 1997). During the mid-1990s, efforts to reduce national government programs resulted in devolution of many program responsibilities to state and local governments with the result that they again had to employ people to provide the services, once again reversing their personnel planning. Increased privatization also emerged as a response to some of the changes in demands on the system (Chi, 1998; Kettl, 1997).

As discussed in Chapter 15, labor relations and collective bargaining became a reality for most state governments and many local governments in the 1960s and 1970s (Kearney, 1992). As with other changes, most state and local governments had to develop new ways of thinking with the emergence of employee unions and bargaining.

EFFORTS IN REFORM

As state and local governments develop new ways of thinking about services and specifically personnel practices, each chooses to embrace varying degrees of reform. The following are some of the more apparent changes in state and local personnel systems in recent years.

System Structure

State and local governments boarded the reinvention bandwagon during the late 1980s and 1990s; experiments with reform resulted. Some states, such as Florida and Georgia, adopted what appeared to be sweeping reforms (Ealy, 1981; Wechsler, 1994), and others (New York and City of St. Louis) took more modest approaches (Ban and Ricucci, 1994; Stein, 1994). In a 1996 survey by the National Association of State Personnel Executives, nine states and Puerto Rico reported that they were undertaking or continuing general personnel system reform. All the rest, except Nevada (a few did not report), indicated that they planned changes in various functional areas, with classification and compensation among the most common (Mallory, 1996). Common themes in the general reform are the decentralization of the personnel function and reduction of rigidity in civil service system rules and processes. Florida and Georgia went so far as to eliminate their civil service systems and replace them with new systems. Many critics suggest that the new systems really have not changed much in their operation.

Classification

In 1998 and 1999, 16 states created new classification systems, which include streamlined, broadbanded classes when possible in an attempt to make the system more useful. These new systems allow managers to redesign and reassign jobs more easily and to hire, promote, and retain the most qualified employees (Perspectives in Human Resources, 1999). States report that updating and refining of the classification systems are ongoing processes (Mallory, 1996). Many jurisdictions report efforts to reduce the number of classifications and simplify them to give managers and supervisors more flexibility in relating classifications to unit needs. The need for simplification and consolidation is clear when one considers that the state of New York has 7300 different classifications, California has 4500, and other states and municipalities have similar patterns (Ban and Ricucci, 1993; Chi, 1998). Even the state of South Dakota, with a small population, has over 500 classifications.

One of the major changes in classification is broadbanding, which groups jobs into "families" or categories based on similarities in career progression, basic skills, recruitment, training, or other characteristics (National Academy of Public Administration, 1991). Illinois, Minnesota, Missouri, and New Jersey are states that are proceeding with broadbanding experiments. These efforts increase the discretion of supervisors and managers and permit them to deploy their human resources more effectively. Such changes also reduce the need for spending money on maintaining outdated classification systems or in processing reclassification requests.

Compensation

Though pay is certainly the primary organizational reward, compensation does take many forms. Well-designed compensation systems serve many other purposes in the organization (Siegel, 1998): They serve management by providing a rational approach to structuring pay; they are instruments for fairness and motivation as well. Competitive compensation facilitates recruitment of individuals to the organization, helps retain them, and motivates them to perform in a manner in line with the organization's goals (Perry, 1995).

Traditional pay systems were tied closely to the classification system and were very rigidly implemented. As a result, they made it difficult for managers to use them as an effective tool for getting the work of the organization done. Many found the rigid pay plans demoralizing and demotivating (Cayer, 1996). Supervisors often resorted to reclassfying positions as a means of getting around the rules and awarding pay increases to high-performing employees. To overcome the problems of rigid structure, many state and local government employers now experiment with pay banding, giving supervisors and managers greater discretion in setting pay for individuals in their units (Boyd and Dickerson, 1990). Wyoming and South Carolina are experimenting with such systems (Selby and Russel, 1997), and an ICMA study in 1990 found that 46.2 percent of the municipalities surveyed and 37.3 percent of the counties surveyed used some form of pay banding (Boyd and Dickerson, 1990).

Many state and local governments also utilize merit pay or pay-for-performance systems to reward individual performance. Although these systems can be powerful performance motivators, they must be approached carefully. McCurdy and Lovrich (1999) explain that if performance is to be linked to pay, a comprehensive program must exist to educate managers on making those linkages. Additionally, it is important that employees understand the connection between pay increases and specific performance issues so that they are able to improve in the future (Perry, 1995).

Employee benefits are part of the total compensation package and play important roles in the welfare of the employee as well as in state and local government success in recruiting and retaining employees. Until the start of the 20th century, benefits for government employees were virtually unheard of, but since then they have become almost universal in the public sector. (Levine, 1993–94). Beginning with modest retirement pensions, benefits now represent a significant part of most state and local compensation costs. Benefits now cover health care and retirement as well as vacation, sick leave, disability, legal insurance, educational expenses, and employee assistance, among other types of compensation.

Some benefits are mandated by national law (e.g., Social Security, Unemployment Compensation, Workers' Compensation, and Family and Medical Leave). State and local governments offer the others at their discretion but usually feel forced to offer many because of competition for employees.

Along with competition in the labor market, changing demographics lead to changes in benefits programs. An aging work force and a more highly educated work force as well as other demographic changes result in the need for different types of benefits. Older workers require more health care options, whereas younger workers find flexible work schedules, support for educational expenses, child care help, and vacation and personal leave more important. Employee assistance and legal insurance along with elder care represent some of the newer benefits. Dual-career couples need a different array of benefits than the traditional one-worker family and domestic partner benefits have become a priority for many employees.

With the changes in benefits employees need, employers experiment with different approaches to accommodate them. Many state and local governments now offer cafeteria benefit plans or flexible spending accounts (Cayer and Volk, 1999). Although these plans usually require that employees be covered by health care and pension plans as a minimum, employees can choose other benefits they consider important. With dual-career couples, the health care plan may be redundant and the employee can opt out of it as long as he or she is covered by the spouse's plan. Under cafeteria plans and flexible spending accounts, employees are allotted a fixed sum to allocate to benefits and may distribute the funds as desired as long as the minimum coverage requirements are met; a small but growing number of state and local governments permit these options (U.S. Bureau of the Census, 1994). Dakota County, Minnesota's, FlexComp Plan is an example of a flexible benefits plan; it is being used as a model for many other jurisdictions, especially after it received an achievement award from the National Association of Counties in 1998 (Cayer and Volk, 1999). North Carolina adopted a flexible benefits program for all state employees in 1996 ("North Carolina," 1999).

The cost of funding benefits plans at the same time state and local governments experience pressure for holding down or cutting expenses creates a major challenge for personnel management. The cost of benefits, especially health care benefits, continues to increase. State and local governments are faced with finding ways to continue to offer the benefits while reducing their costs in doing so. The flexible spending accounts noted represent one way of reducing redundancy and eliminating spending on benefits of little value to particular employees. Traditional indemnity health care insurance has given way to managed care, in which health maintenance organizations (HMOs) and preferred provider organizations (PPOs) provide the service at a fixed contract cost to the employer as one way of reducing health care cost increases. Employers increasingly ask their employees to share some of the cost of the premiums for health care as well. Traditionally, the public sector paid the whole cost of health care plans. Now that has changed, and employer and employee both pay part.

Retirement plans have changed as well. Traditionally, state and local governments provided a specific retirement pension based on some formula using number of years of service, age, and/or other factors. Called *defined benefits plans,* they pay employees a fixed pension. Increasingly, employers use defined contribution plans in which employer and employee share in the cost of the plan by investing a percentage of the employee's salary into a retirement account. The pension paid to the employee upon retirement in a defined cost plan is a function of how much was invested and what the investment has earned. By sharing the cost, employers save money and employees find that these investments tend to perform better than the trust funds established for covering the defined benefits plans. In some cases, employees may choose approved financial advisers to manage their retirement accounts, thus increasing the flexibility of the plans.

Coalitions or consortia also help in cost cutting. By joining with other jurisdictions, local governments often can negotiate better terms for health care and pension plans because of the leverage they have in larger numbers of participants. Small governments, particularly, find these efforts helpful.

Recruitment, Selection, and Hiring

The quality of any public organization depends largely upon the ability of the personnel department to recruit, select, and hire competent, qualified employees. However, implementation of these complex practices does not occur without certain difficulties.

According to Witt and Patton (1999), recruitment entails the challenges of diversifying the work force and attracting highly qualified candidates for positions. If the recruitment process is poorly executed, personnel managers go into the selection process with a less than qualified applicant pool. A positive public image and word of mouth can help to create a favorable impression of public service and improve the applicant pool. In addition, many state and local governments are using more targeted advertising and technology to attract applicants to their organizations (Hamman and Desai, 1995).

The challenges of selection lie in making sure that selection criteria are job related and consistently applied, then identifying those applicants who are qualified for the position. Once those individuals have been identified, the personnel manager may use various processes in making a hiring decision (Hays, 1998). Typically, state and local governments use some form of testing, whether assembled or unassembled. The assembled test may be administered by paper and pencil or by computer. It may be a performance test to see whether the applicant actually can perform the activities essential to the position. The unassembled exam consists of careful review of documents that demonstrate the background of the applicant. Typically, resumes, transcripts, and applications provide the information for judging and ranking candidates. The unassembled exam is most commonly used for professional and management positions, although, the difficulties arising from use of written exams lead many employers to rely more heavily on unassembled exams for other positions as well. Interviews and assessment centers constitute other processes for selection decisions. Assessment centers permit observation of applicants in a variety of exercises to see how they perform and react to situations. Reference checks are used as well for many positions, especially professional and managerial positions.

Operating departments in state and local governments generally criticize the hiring process as being too cumbersome and lacking in timeliness. They need employees when they seek them and find it difficult to compete in the labor market with processes that take a long time. Some of the best practices now speed the process through decentralization of the process, flexibility, use of technology, use of alternatives to written exams, and continuous recruitment (Trice, 1999b). Decentralization makes sense because the hiring department knows much better than the central personnel department what is needed. Ohio has decentralized many of the personnel processes such as testing and hiring. Decentralization and flexibility go hand in hand. Many jurisdictions (such as Maricopa County, Arizona) no longer require strict adherence to a small number of eligibles from the eligibility list. Maricopa County requires the hiring agent to consider at least five names, but he/she may request more, including the full list of eligibles. The state of Wisconsin also has loosened restrictions.

State and local government employers use new technology in continuous efforts to improve their personnel functions. In the hiring process, potential employees can access information on-line about vacancies; Ohio even has videos that contain scenarios on the positions available on-line. Potential applicants can make realistic assessments about whether the positions actually meet their expectations and needs. The technology should lead to better fit of applicants. Applicants can submit applications and resumes on-line in increasing numbers of jurisdictions and can track the progress of their applications. In Michigan, for example, hiring managers can access applicant information and perform other selection processes, and new employees can sign up for benefits on-line ("Space-Age, 1998).

Alternatives to written exams such as qualifying resumes or other documents can speed the hiring process immensely. Along with alternatives, continuous recruitment, especially for high-turnover positions, can reduce the time needed for hiring decisions. Some people suggest discarding traditional applications completely and recommend use of resumes as a way of attracting good potential applicants who may be turned off by lengthy applications (Trice, 1999a). Once finalists are identified, they can be asked to answer pertinent questions or to fill out a form.

The Americans with Disabilities Act (ADA) requires employers to make reasonable accommodations for applicants and workers with disabilities. There continues to be a great deal of debate and litigation over who is disabled under the ADA and what constitutes reasonable accommodation. In 1999, the Supreme Court reviewed three employment-related ADA cases. The court that a disability should be considered in its treated state (*Sutton v. United Airlines, Inc.*, 1999; *Murphy v. United Parcel Service, Inc.*, 1999) and that a truck driver with monocular vision is not disabled per se (*Albertsons Inc. v. Kirkingburg,* 1999).

Affirmative action is the process of actively engaging in efforts to diversify the work force in terms of race, ethnicity, gender, and disability (Ricucci, 1998). Affirmative action requires proactive efforts to recruit applicants from protected groups so as to diversify applicant pools. These policies face a number of political and legal challenges. Opponents believe that the policies are a direct violation of the Civil Rights Act of 1964 and constitute reverse discrimination (Witt and Patton, 1999; DiNome et al., 1999).

In 1998, legislation was introduced to limit the federal government's ability to grant preferences in hiring and contracting. The legislation died in committee in the House of Representatives. On the state level, however, such legislation is gradually being introduced and implemented. The state of Washington, for example, followed California's earlier lead and passed a referendum, Proposition 200, to prohibit the state from giving preference to minorities in hiring, contracting, and education.

Training and Development

In order to facilitate continuing growth and development within organizations, it is important for personnel managers to increase the capabilities of employees (Carnevale, 1995; Van Wart, 1998). Training and development are increasingly recognized as keys to employee and organizational improvement. Training includes instructional experiences that are designed to develop skills and knowledge, to achieve organizational objectives, to facilitate organizational growth and change, and ultimately, to be applied in the workplace for the sake of organizational improvement (Bramley, 1996; Broad and Newstrom, 1992).

Particularly in public organizations where tax dollars are spent to train and educate employees, training dollars must be allocated wisely, and a return on the investment is often expected. As the composition of the work force changes and organizational reinvention and effectiveness are stressed, the notion of transfer of training has become more important than ever. Transfer of training is the "effective and continuing application, by trainees to their jobs, of the knowledge and skills gained in training, both on and off the job" (Broad and Newstrom, 1992: 6). There is a growing recognition of a transfer problem in organizations. As Peter

Bramley explains, "If the things learned during the training are to result in different ways of doing the job, then some thought must be given to the transfer process" (1996: 34).

It is increasingly important that personnel managers and trainers follow up with trainees after they have been trained, in order to examine both the perceived and actual outcomes of training efforts. This allows management to assess continually the needs of the individuals within the organization and to seek supplemental training where necessary.

In 1998, President Clinton signed the Workforce Investment Act (HR 1385) into law. The act consolidates several training programs into three state block grants and allows communities to establish one-stop employment and training centers. In addition, the law creates a system in which individuals can purchase training using vouchers from training accounts, creates state boards to evaluate training efforts, and requires states to have plans for training.

By focusing on outcomes of training and attempting to make training more accessible, personnel managers also focus on improving their capacity to recruit, develop, and maintain a high-quality work force. It is through these types of efforts that organizational improvement occurs.

Discipline

Even in the best managed organizations, problems requiring disciplinary action arise (Bruce, 1997). Sometimes, finding a balance between the rights and responsibilities of employees and employers can cause conflict. Such conflict may result in the need for mediation, due process, communication, union contracts, or disciplinary actions.

Effective discipline requires clearly stated and clearly understood policies that are uniformly applied. Additionally, timeliness is of the essence. Disciplinary actions must be specific and job related with explanations of why the employee is being disciplined and documentation of the activity that led to the discipline and the communication with the employee about the incident. Discipline that is perceived to be unfair will lead to further problems as resentment gives way to loss of morale and trust. Employees also need the opportunity to review any disciplinary action through an appeals process. In the public sector, this focus on justice, rights, and fairness can lead to the impression that public employees have an excessive amount of job security and may hinder management from disciplining employees aggressively (Hays, 1995). Complicating the issue, some systems focus on discipline as corrective action, and others view it as punishment (Bruce, 1997).

Progressive discipline is accepted widely by state and local governments and often is mandated by policy or court rulings. In progressive discipline, employees are informed of problems and provided the opportunity to correct them. If they do not respond to the counseling about the problem and warning of consequences of failure to correct it, increasingly severe disciplinary action is taken. Discipline progresses from counseling through oral and written reprimand, to varying levels of suspension, and finally to termination. There may be other steps and refinements through these steps such as suspension with pay or without pay. The discipline needs to be appropriate to the situation. Thus stealing may lead to termination without progressing through the other steps and the policy will state so.

Some state and local governments now use affirmative discipline, in which the employee enters into a contract with the supervisor or manager (Wise et al., 1999). The contract specifies the steps to be taken to remedy the situation and the consequences if the steps are not taken. In such a case, the responsibility for the situation rests squarely with the employee, who has the power to rectify the problem. Affirmative discipline, combined with progressive discipline, can be a powerful tool for dealing with problem employees.

Employers with collective bargaining have specific agreements on how disciplinary matters are to be handled. The agreements specify whether mediation, conciliation, or arbitration is to be used. Many state and local governments and their employee organizations or unions are experimenting with cooperative approaches to resolving disputes. Similarly, those without labor agreements to cover such matters have used alternative dispute resolution techniques, often employing counseling, conciliation, or mediation to resolve problems. Pinellas County, Florida, has used positive discipline effectively by employing a number of alternatives (Ricucci and Wheeler, 1987).

THE CHANGING FACE OF THE WORKPLACE AND POLICY

Personnel managers must consider a variety of policy changes in doing their work. Not only are they responsible for recruiting, developing, and maintaining the highest-quality work force, they must do this work within political, constitutional, legal, social, and organizational contexts that are constantly changing. As these environments change, legislation and procedures that influence the personnel system are developed and reformed. As policy, administrations, technology, and society change, organizations must also change. Demographic, technological, and organizational changes all entail unique and complex challenges for the public personnel manager.

Demographic changes require personnel managers to adapt to and recognize the unique skills and abilities of individuals within their organizations. As the American population grows, diversifies, and ages, public personnel managers must recognize and utilize the uniqueness of their employees in order to raise the quality of public service (Guy and Newman, 1998; West, 1998). Doing so often requires new ways of doing things.

Technology poses additional challenges that must be faced (Danziger and Gianos, 1998). Although it expedites processes and simplifies the workplace, it also allows employees and the public to be connected to the workplace from virtually anywhere. Personnel managers must consider carefully the interests of citizens and must be increasingly willing to allow employees to explore the possibility of job flexibility and even telecommuting, when the job allows such an arrangement.

Telecommuting can help to save travel time, office space, and the environment, all of which are important issues in public organizations trying to do more with less. Human resource (HR) managers must be more careful than ever, though, to maintain regular contact with telecommuters in order to clarify expectations continually and to reinforce organizational goals for the employee, and ultimately, the public. In California, for example, a 1990 law created a "telework" program, which has grown to improve management and employee effectiveness.

Many state and local personnel administrators are finding other innovative and resourceful ways to incorporate cutting-edge technology into their work. The Connecticut State Police, through the state's Department of Administrative Services Human Resource Business Center, are saving taxpayers a great deal of time and money by handling recruitment applications on the World Wide Web. In addition to serving as a cost-saving practice for the department, this resource has expanded the visibility of their department and range of applications worldwide (McKay, 1998).

Wisconsin's Department of Employee Relations has also implemented an Internet-based application system for information technology positions. Candidates are added to a database that is used by agencies and universities statewide to fill vacancies. Managers can use the database to identify those applicants with the necessary knowledge, skills, and abilities to fit the needs of each position (Lavigna, 1998).

State and local governments also use privatization as a way of delivering services as efforts to shrink government continue (Kettl, 1997). Privatization is the transfer of public responsibilities to private sector entities. Advocates of privatization argue that it will provide better service to citizens at lower cost. As such, privatization fits well with the trend toward shrinking the size of government. Privatization has been around for a long time in the form of contracting; governments contract for road construction, construction of buildings and facilities, purchase of supplies, and maintenance of equipment. In recent years, governments have extended the contracting process to delivery of services to citizens. Thus, many local governments contract for fire service, trash collection, and process serving, among other services. States now often contract with private firms for delivery of many health services, vehicle pollution inspections, and operation of prisons. Personnel systems contract for software to process applications, evaluate candidates, process payroll, provide benefits, and supply temporary workers.

Governments also may stop providing certain services on the basis of the argument that they really are not government's responsibility. In California after tax limits were passed by popular vote, some services were abandoned or severely diminished by state and local governments. For example, many library and park programs were cut or eliminated and the private sector began to offer them if they could earn a profit. During the 1990s, many people argued that many social services were the responsibility of religious and nonprofit organizations, not government, and many cuts were made with the expectation that the private sector would assume the responsibility.

Particularly popular among advocates of privatization are vouchers for services. Many people advocate the use of vouchers for education or housing; in this system, citizens would be eligible to receive a voucher and use it to pay for the service with any approved provider. The advocates argue that service is likely to be better and less costly because of the competition of the marketplace. Not everyone is comfortable with such dependence on the market, however.

Privatization has numerous implications for public personnel management. Managers must deal with morale problems, equity issues, unions, the need for new management skills, and monitoring (Kettl, 1997). Public employee morale usually is affected negatively when privatization occurs. Employees feel threatened and insecure, not knowing what is likely to happen to them. The employer finds itself needing to develop programs to communicate and reassure employees. Unions usually insist on participation in the decision making process as well, especially if any downsizing is to occur. Equity issues arise, especially in contracting, because employees of the private sector generally operate under policies and expectations different from those for public employees. Private sector employees do not have the same constitutional and legal protections as public employees. Pay and benefit packages may be very different for employees of the private contractor and even for people doing similar jobs.

Managers face many challenges in managing private sector delivery of public services. The government retains the responsibility for satisfying the citizens; thus, public managers need to develop the standards for service and see that they are met. This requirement adds a new dimension to the public employer's responsibility. Especially in contracting, the public organization needs to monitor the service and take action when standards have not been met. The personnel system becomes responsible for the training and development of employees to do these jobs effectively.

With downsizing, the use of volunteers has increased as well, offering still more challenges to state and local personnel managers (Brudney, 1998). Personnel managers need to be able to integrate the volunteers into the organization, oftentimes in the face of hostility from regular employees or their unions. Finding and selecting appropriate volunteers and making sure they have the necessary skills are problems as well. Monitoring volunteers is not easy, they often do not feel as constrained by the values of the organization or the authority structure because they are not being paid. Volunteers need training and constant communication. Managers also need to provide ways of recognizing their contributions to the organization. Ultimately, volunteers should be accountable to the government entity for which they volunteer, and that presents a challenge to personnel management.

Ethical behavior is an increasingly important aspect of personnel management. Public personnel managers must consider fairness, honesty, justice, and social responsibility as they make decisions and take actions within their organizations. Public perceptions of the public service and citizen support of it depend upon the behavior of public employees. If they do not demonstrate integrity in their actions, the public loses respect for the public service. To maintain the highest levels of integrity and ethics, personnel systems provide training along with monitoring of personal behavior.

Another area of increasing concern to personnel managers is the issue of violence. Violence in the workplace has become a major problem. The challenge for personnel is in protecting employees from violent acts and in providing services to help employees should violence occur. Most acts of workplace violence seem to stem from problems outside the workplace, although, some are the direct effects of some personnel action such as discipline. Many are carryovers of domestic problems and general stress brought to the workplace. Employers need to take precautions to provide security and should attempt to weed out potential problem employees in the selection and probationary processes. Employee assistance programs are important in providing counseling to those employed in offices where violence occurs so that they can recover from trauma.

CONCLUSION

Any reform effort can be justified by the fact that it is an attempt to improve the management of human resources at the state, local, and even national levels. The success of any reform effort will always lie in the eyes of those who are affected most directly by it. The field of HRM and the reform efforts that it must deal with are inherently political, constitutional, legal, social, and organizational.

In the public sector, managers have to think about many factors that go far beyond the walls of the organization. Law, the Constitution, ethics, fairness, demographic, and technological change, and employment and development of responsible public servants are all common considerations for the personnel manager.

The underlying complexities and issues that drive the need for reform are fundamental. As stated by Cayer (1995), the "basic dilemma is still one of balancing democratic control and responsiveness with management based on professional expertise unfettered by political partisanship." Despite reform efforts, the dilemma remains.

The future for public personnel management can only become more complicated. The expectations of citizens and elected officials will continue to increase demands on public personnel. At the same time, litigation will surely increase as employees and citizens alike look to the courts to right perceived wrongs. Personnel managers will always have to respond to the changing elements of the environment in which they work.

REFERENCES

Albertsons Inc. v. Kirkingburg, Docket #98-591 (June 22, 1999).

Anselmini, L. (1996). Downsizing and privatization. In National Association of State Personnel Executives. *State Personnel Office: Roles and Functions,* 3rd ed. Lexington, KY., The Council of State Governments.

Aronson, A. H. (1974). State and local personnel administration. In *Biography of an Ideal.* United States Civil Service Commission. Washington, D.C., Government Printing Office.

Ban, C. (1997). The challenges of cutback management. In *Public Personnel Management: Current Concerns, Future Challenges* (C. Ban and N. M. Ricucci, eds.). White Plains, N.Y., Longman.

Ban, C., and Ricucci, N. (1993). Personnel systems and labor relations: Steps toward a quiet revitalization. In *Revitalizing State and Local Public Service: Strengthening Performance, Accountability, and Citizen Confidence* (F. J. Thompson, ed.). San Francisco: Jossey-Bass.

Ban, C. and Ricucci, N. (1994). New York state: Civil service reform in a complex political environment. *Review of Public Personnel Administration. XIV* (Spring): 28–39.

Berman, E. (1994). Implementing TQM in state governments: A survey of recent progress. *State and Local Government Review. 26*(1):46–53.

Berman, E. (1997). The challenge of total quality management. In *Public Personnel Management: Current Concerns, Future Challenges* (C. Ban and N. M. Ricucci, eds.). White Plains, N.Y., Longman.

Boyd, K. J. and Dickerson, S. D. (1990). Local government personnel compensation and fringe benefits. *Baseline Data Report* 22, no. 3. Washington D.C., International City Management Association.

Bramley, Peter (1996). *Evaluating Training Effectiveness,* 2nd ed. London, McGraw-Hill.

Broad, Mary L., and Newstrom, John W. (1992). *Transfer of Training.* Reading, Mass. Addison-Wesley.

Bruce, W. M. (1997). Oppositional and correctional paradigms: Ways to study and practice employee discipline. *Public personnel Management: Current Concerns, Future Challenges,* 2nd ed. (C. Ban And N. M. Ricucci eds.). White Plains, N.Y., Longman.

Brudney, J. L. (1998). Utilizing volunteers in the workplace. In *Handbook of Human Resource Management in Government* (S. E. Condrey, ed.). San Francisco, Jossey-Bass.

Brudney, J. I., Hebert, F. T., and Wright, D. S. (1999). Reinventing government in the American states: Measuring and explaining administrative reform. *Public Administration Review. 59* (January/February): 19–30.

Carnevale, D. G. (1995). Human capital and high performance in public organizations. In *Public Personnel Administration: Problems and* Prospects, 3rd ed. (S. W. Hays and R. C. Kearney, eds.). Englewood Cliffs, N.J.: Prentice-Hall.

Cayer, N. J. (1995). Merit system reform in the states. *Public Personnel Administration: Problems and Prospects,* 3rd ed. In (S. W. Hays and R. C. Kearney, eds.). Englewood Cliffs, N.J., Prentice-Hall.

Cayer, N. J. (1996). *Public Personnel Administration in the United States,* 3rd ed. New York, St. Martin's Press.

Cayer, N. J. (1998). Public personnel and labor relations. In *Handbook of Public Administration*, 2nd ed. (J. Rabin, W. B. Hildreth, and G. J. Miller, eds.). New York, N.Y., Marcel Dekker.

Cayer, N. J., and Volk, W. (1999). Employee benefits: Creating an environment for excellence. In *Human Resource Management in Local Government: An Essential Guide* (S. F. Freyss, ed.). Washington, D.C., International City/County Management Association.

Chi, K. S. (1998). State civil service systems. In *Handbook of Human Resource Management in Government* (S. E. Condrey, ed.). San Francisco: Jossey-Bass.

City of Clinton v. Cedar Rapids and Missouri River Railroad Company, 24 Iowa 455 (1868).

Daley, D. (1990). The organization of the personnel function: The new patronage and decentralization. In *Public Personnel Administration: Problems and Prospects,* 2nd ed. (S. Hays, and R. C. Kearney, eds.). Englewood Cliffs, N.J.: Prentice-Hall.

Danziger, J. N., and Gianos, C. L. (1998). Anticipating and coping with technological change in the workplace, In *Handbook of Human Resource Management in Government* (S. E. Condrey, ed.). San Francisco, Jossey-Bass.

DiNome, J. A., Yaklin, S. M., and Rosenbloom, D. H. (1999). Employee rights: Avoiding legal liability. In *Human Resource Management in Local Government: An Essential Guide* (S. F. Freyss, ed.). Washington, D.C.: International City/County Management Association.

Dresang, D. L. (1982). Diffusion of civil service reform: The federal and state governments. *Review of Public Personnel Administration. 2*(Spring): 35–47.

Ealy, S. D. (1981). Reform of the Georgia state merit system. *Review of Public Personnel Administration. 1*(Summer): 33–50.

Fish, C. R. (1905). *The Civil Service and the Patronage.* New York, Longman, Green.

Gossett, C. W. (1997). Lesbians and gay men in the public sector work force. In *Public Personnel Management: Current Concerns, Future Prospects* (C. Ban and N. M. Ricucci, eds.). White Plains, N.Y., Longman.

Guy, M. E., and Newman, M. A. (1998). Toward diversity in the workplace. In *Handbook of Human Resource Management in Government* (S. E. Condrey, ed.). San Francisco, Jossey-Bass.

Hamilton, D. K. (1999). The continuing judicial assault on patronage. *Public Administration Review. 59* (January/February): 54–62.

Hamman, J. A., and Desai, U. (1995). Current issues and challenges in recruitment and selection. In *Public Personnel Administration: Problems and Prospects,* 3rd ed. (S. W. Hays and R. C. Kearney, eds.). Englewood Cliffs, N.J., Prentice Hall.

Hartman, G. S., Homer, G. W., and Menditto, J. E. (1998). Human resource management legal issues: An overview. In *Handbook of Human Resource Management in Government* (S. E. Condrey, ed.). San Francisco, Jossey-Bass.

Hays, S. W. (1995). Employee discipline and removal: coping with job security. In *Public Personnel Administration: Problems and Prospects,* 3rd ed. (S. W. Hays, and R. C. Kearney, eds.). Englewood Cliffs, N.J., Prentice-Hall.

Hays, S. W. (1998). Staffing the bureaucracy: Recruitment and selection. In *Handbook of Human Resource Management in Government* (S. E. Condrey, ed.). San Francisco, Jossey-Bass.

Ingraham, P. W. (1985). Politics and administration: The continuing relevance of an old issue. In *Public Personnel Policy: The Politics of Civil Service* (D. H. Rosenbloom, ed.). Port Washington, N.Y., Associated Faculty Press.

Kearney, R. C. (1992). *Labor Relations in the Public Sector,* 2nd ed. New York, Marcel Dekker.

Kemp, D. (1995). Telecommuting in the public sector. *Review of Public Personnel Administration. XV* (Summer): 5–16.

Kettl, D. F. (1997). Privatization: Implications for the public work force. In *Public Personnel Management: Current Concerns, Future Prospects* (C. Ban and N. M. Ricucci, eds.). White Plains, N.Y., Longman.

Klinger, D. (1990). Variables affecting the design of state and local personnel systems. In *Public Personnel Administration: Problems and Prospects,* 2nd ed. (S. W. Hays and R. C. Kearney, eds.). Englewood Cliffs, N.J., Prentice-Hall.

Klinger, D. E. (1998). Beyond civil service: The politics of the emergent paradigm. In *Handbook of Human Resource Management in Government* (S. E. Condrey, ed.). San Francisco, Jossey-Bass.

Lavigna, R. (1998). Wisconsin goes on-line. *State Personnel View.* (Winter): 3.

Lee, Y. S. (1992). *Public Personnel Administration and Constitutional Values.* Westport, Conn., Quorum Books.

Levine, C. (1993–94). Employee benefits: Growing in diversity and cost. *Occupational Outlook Quarterly.* (Winter): 39–42.

Mallory, L. D. (1996). Office of the state personel executive. In National Association of State Personnel Executives. *State Personnel Office: Roles & Functions,* 3rd ed. Lexington, Ky., The Council of State Governments.

McKay, J. (1998). "21st century technology helps Connecticut state police. *State Personnel View.* (Winter): 3.

McCurdy, A. H., and Lovrich, N. P. (1999). Maintaining a high-performance workforce. In *Human Resource Management in Local Government: An Essential Guide* (S. F. Freyss, ed.). Washington D.C., International City/County Management Association

Murphy v. United Parcel Service, Inc., Docket #97-1992 (June 22, 1999).

National Academy of Public Administration. (1991). *Modernizing Federal Classification: An Opportunity for Excellence.* Washington, D.C., National Academy of Public Administration.

Nigro, L. G. (1997). Public law in the changing civil service. In *Handbook of Public Law and Administration* (P. J. Cooper, and C. A. Newland, eds.). San Francisco, Jossey-Bass.

North Carolina flexible benefits program. (1999). *IPMA News.* (June): 5–6

Ott, J. S. (1998). Understanding organizational climate and culture. In *Handbook of Human Resource Management in Government* (S. E. Condrey, ed.). San Francisco, Jossey-Bass.

Perry, James L. (1995). Compensation, merit pay, and motivation. In *Public Personnel Administration: Problems and Prospects,* 3rd ed. (S. W. Hays and R. C. Kearney, eds.). Englewood Cliffs, N.J., Prentice Hall.

Perspectives in Human Resources (1999). *Arizona International Personnel Management Association Newsletter. 4*(2).

Rich, W. C. (1982). *The Politics of Urban Personnel Policy: Reformers, Politicians, and Bureaucrats.* Port Washington, N.Y., Kennikat Press.

Ricucci, N. M. (1998). A practical guide to affirmative action. In *Handbool of Human Resource Management in Government* (S. E. Condrey, ed.). San Francisco, Jossey-Bass.

Ricucci, N. M., and Wheeler, G. (1987). Positive employee performance: An innovative approach to employee discicpline. *Review of Public Personnel Administration. 8*(Fall): 49–63.

Rosenbloom, D. H. (1985). *Public Personnel Policy: The Politics of Civil Service.* Port Washington, N.Y., Associated Faculty Press.

Rosenbloom, D. H. (1995). What every personnel manager should know about the Constitution. In *Public Personnel Administration: Problems and Prospects,* 3rd ed. (S. W. Hays and R. C. Kearney, eds.). Englewood Cliffs, N.J., Prentice Hall.

Saltzstein, A. (1995). Personnel management in the local government setting. In *Public Personnel Administration: Problems and Prospects,* 3rd ed. (S. W. Hays and R. C. Kearney, eds.). Englewood Cliffs, N.J., Prentice Hall.

Sayre, W. (1948). The triumph of technique over purpose. *Public Administration Review. 8*(Spring): 134–137.

Selby, K., and Russel, S. (1997). Wyoming partners with South Carolina on new classification and compensation system. *State Personnel View.* (Summer): 3.

Siegel, G. B. (1998). Designing and creating an effective compensation plan. In *Handbook of Human Resource Management in Government* (S. E. Condrey, ed.). San Francisco, Jossey-Bass.

Space-age human resource technology. (1998). *State Personnel View.* (Winter): 1.

Steffens, J. L. (1904). *The Shame of the Cities.* New York, McClure, Phillips.

Stein, L. (1994). Personnel rules and reform in an unreformed setting. *Review of Public Personnel Administration. XIV*(Spring): 55–63.

Sutton v. United Airlines, Inc., Docket #97-1943 (June 22, 1999).

Thompson, F. J. (1995). The politics of public personnel administration. In *Public Personnel Administration: Problems and Prospects,* 3rd ed. (S. W. Hays and R. C. Kearney, eds.). Englewood Cliffs, N.J., Prentice Hall.

Tompkins, J. and Stapczynski, A. (1999). Planning and paying for work done. In *Human Resource Management in Local Government: An Essential Guide* (S. F. Freyss, ed.). Washington, D.C., International City/County Management Association.

Trice, E. (1999a). Timely hiring: Cater to your candidates and toss the applications. *IPMA News.* (June): 11–12.

Trice, E. (1999b). Timely hiring: Make your agency a best practice. *IPMA News.* (June): 10–11.

U.S. Bureau of the Census. (1994). *Statistical Abstract of the United States.* Washington, D.C., U.S. Government Printing Office.

Van Wart, M. (1998). Organizational investment in employee development. In *Handbook of Human Resource Management in Government* (S. E. Condrey, ed.). San Francisco, Jossey-Bass.

Wechsler, B. (1994). Reinventing florida's civil service system: The failure of reform. *Review of Public Personnel Administration. XIV* (Spring): 64–76.

West, J. P. (1998). Managing an aging workforce. In *Handbook of Human Resource Management in Government* (S. E. Condrey, ed.). San Francisco, Jossey-Bass.

Wise, C. R., Clemow, B., Murray, S., Boston, S., and Bingham, L. B. (1999). When things go wrong. In *Human Resource Management in local Government: An Essential Guide* (S. F. Freyss, ed.). Washington, D.C., International City/County Management Association.

Witt, S. L., and Patton, W. D. (1999). Recruiting for a high-performance workforce. In *Human Resource Management in Local Government: An Essential Guide* (S. F. Freyss, ed.). Washington, D.C., International City/County Management Association.

Workforce Investment Act. HR 1385 (1998).

10

Changing Roles and Duties Within Government's Human Resources Profession: Contemporary Models and Challenges

Steven W. Hays
Department of Government and International Studies, University of South Carolina, Columbia, South Carolina

Of all the administrative functions, human resources management (or personnel management—the two phrases will be used interchangeably) most certainly engenders the widest range of attitudes and emotions among practitioners and academicians alike. Since the 1960s, a seemingly interminable debate has raged over the appropriate role that public personnel management (PPM) should play in modern organizations. Opinions vary from those who believe that PPM holds the key to effective administrative reform to those who have written off the function as a hopelessly bureaucratic and ineffectual anachronism. Whereas some authors refer to human resource management as top leadership's new strategic partner in orchestrating change and innovation (Johnston, 1996; Perry, 1993), others launch blistering critiques that even include calls for the field's abolition. A widely circulated article in *Fortune* magazine, for example, offers the "modest proposal" that the typical personnel office should be "blown up. . . . Abolish it. Deep-six it. Rub it out. Eliminate, toss, obliterate, nuke it. Give it the old heaveho. . . . Turn it into road kill" (Stewart, 1996:34).

Although this latter suggestion might strike those of us who depend upon PPM to make our living as somewhat draconian, it is rooted in a legitimate set of complaints that are well known to students of management, both public and private. As it has been practiced for many decades, personnel management has not generally been part of the administrative mainstream. It has been preoccupied with narrow techniques and has consequently been perceived as an impediment to line managers. The personnel office was obsessed with control functions, emphasizing administrative minutiae that complicated the lives of other managers and failed to contribute to the accomplishment of organizational objectives. In the contemporary language of administration, personnel activities were not attentive to the requirement that all support functions be "value-added." Indeed, they appeared to reduce organizational effectiveness and deflect resources from mission-driven goals.

The contrasting view of personnel management is grounded in the simple premise that most of the administrative challenges and opportunities of the modern era revolve around *people* (i.e., employees). The attraction, retention, training, motivation, and development of workers all depend in large part upon activities that, for better or worse, are usually vested in the personnel department. To the extent that public personnel managers can elevate their performance and synchronize their activities with those of line managers, the personnel office can make a critical (if not essential) contribution to the achievement of organizational objectives. Consistent with this theme, much of the contemporary literature asserts that personnel managers are becoming (or have become) "partners" and even "architects" of management improvement and innovation (Ulrich, 1998). According to this perspective, the personnel profession is rapidly acquiring new competencies and assuming a wider array of responsibilities. A revolution is putatively taking place in personnel offices throughout the public and private sectors, shifting their traditional focus away from *control* activities and toward *service* to line managers.

That this chapter should begin with the classic juxtaposition of the two competing visions of personnel management is inherently ironic. It is truly a case of *déjà vu,* since an almost identical introduction would have been just as appropriate if this chapter were being written in 1969 rather than 1999. The key difference, however, is that the organizational and environmental conditions that prompted calls for changes in the personnel function in the 1960s are far more compelling and foreboding today. Most personnel offices *have* changed over the years, but whether or not they have changed *enough,* and whether or not they have the capacity to meet the daunting challenges of the 21st century are important questions that this chapter will attempt to address. After chronicling the most pressing environmental trends that are currently shaping human resources management, succeeding sections of the chapter summarize the types of responses that will be necessary for PPM to assume its rightful place as a positive force for change within modern public agencies. Likely impediments to this revised vision of the public personnel function are also discussed, along with references to recent developments that offer insights into PPM's possible future. The underlying theme is that PPM *must* transform itself, and that significant strides are being made. An implicit concern that permeates the chapter is that failure at this point in the field's evolution is not really an option: To fail now is to risk the extinction of personnel administration as a coherent organizational function.

FACTORS COMPELLING CHANGE

So much has been written about the turbulent environment of contemporary public administration (both in the general literature *and* in other chapters of this volume) that only a brief recitation of the catalysts for PPM's hoped-for transformation is necessary here. A concise summary of the most pressing challenges to, and failures of, public personnel systems appeared in the Volcker Commission (1989) and Winter Commission (Thompson, 1993) reports. Among the factors that have intensified the pressure on personnel offices are recurrent fiscal crises, a brooding and hypercritical public, rapid technological change, and fundamental shifts in labor demographics (Newland, 1984; Hays, 1996). The public's negative attitude toward government, coupled with revenue shortages (or at least an unwillingness among politicians to invest more money in the public service), have contributed to recruitment and retention problems for many public agencies. Meanwhile, the information revolution and a paucity of skilled workers in high-need areas have exacerbated government's inability to compete for human resources with the private sector. When these factors are combined with the systemic problems inherent in many "merit systems"—including painfully outdated personnel procedures and dysfunctional motivation and reward practices—the picture appears particularly bleak.

The collective effects of these factors are evident in the *reinvention movement* (RIGO), which singles out PPM as a primary target for reform. The RIGO agenda calls for a large number of specific alterations in the way that public personnel systems are organized and operated. Decentralization, privatization of some functions, debureaucratization, and importation of innovative personnel strategies from the private sector are common themes. There is no mystery as to why these goals have been identified for PPM, since each arises in response to acknowledged failings in most merit systems. At least until recently, the typical public personnel system was a highly centralized operation that focused more on process than on outcomes. Line managers were obliged to seek the personnel office's approval for most employee actions, including reclassifications, promotions, transfers, and reassignments. Burdensome procedures slowed the recruitment of new employees, and ex cathedra dictates restricted the ability of line managers to reward, punish, and otherwise supervise their subordinates. The presence of these traits exerted a profoundly negative effect upon management dating back to the 1960s, but the situation has become especially untenable within the current administrative environment.

In the opinion of virtually everyone, the rapidly changing and highly complex environment of public agencies calls for a *flexible* organizational response. Instead of adhering to an unyielding set of procedures, public organizations need the ability to alter course quickly, to adapt to circumstances, and to focus on strategic objectives. This requirement applies to all facets of the public personnel function but is especially apparent in regard to the changing nature of the work force. It has become a truism that today's workers are more diverse and demanding than those of the past, and that they confront a much greater challenge in refining and upgrading their job-related skills. Keeping such workers motivated is a significant dilemma, as is constructing adequate reward systems. Consistent with these trends, the concept of a *career* is quickly being transformed. Most workers do not expect to stay in any particular organization for an entire lifetime, or even for more than a few years. The labor market is *churning,* with skilled (especially "knowledge") workers peddling their skills to the highest bidders while organizations struggle with the decision to "make or buy" talent. Spending large sums of money on training and employee development might seem a waste of resources when the workers' commitment to their organizations is low. As a result, there is a strong likelihood that many organizations will increasingly buy the skills they need on a short-term basis by outsourcing or using temporary workers (Whittlesey, 1997). Within this context, the typical career system in public organizations—one based on narrow job classifications, routine promotion schedules, and intermittent raises—is laughably outdated.

One need not look far to find additional examples that emphasize the necessity for a responsive and flexible approach to the staffing function. Because of the infamous "bash the bureaucrat" tendency that has predominated in recent decades, both the intrinsic and extrinsic rewards of public employment have declined. In addition to being placed on the defensive by an unsympathetic press and public, civil servants have not generally had raise and fringe benefit packages that have kept pace with those in the private sector (Wooldridge and Wester, 1991). Government, which was once the model employer, has thus lost an additional edge in the struggle to compete with business and industry for workers. Moreover, some commentators argue that the ultimate objective of RIGO is to "deprivilege" (rather than to empower) civil servants by reducing their discretion and many of their job perquisites (Kearney and Hays, 1998). Relying upon traditional reward systems under such circumstances is not likely to yield much of a return. The situation calls for experimentation, innovation, and creativity, not the bureaucratic responses (such as predetermined longevity increases) that have characterized PPM for far too long.

In sum, a widespread consensus exists that the traditional approach to PPM has failed, and that sweeping changes are required to enhance the function's effectiveness. Not only must personnelists modernize their procedures and techniques, they must assume new roles in the internal dynamics of their organizations. At the risk of using a horribly jargonistic expression, PPM must evolve a new paradigm to parallel developments in the other areas of public management. And, because the personnel function sits at such a strategic junction in the internal life of organizations, efforts to improve the performance of other management functions depend in large part upon successful reform. Reinvention, reengineering, devolution, and all the other themes (and catchwords) of modern management ultimately depend upon the recruitment, retention, and development of competent and motivated employees. This situation represents an enormous opportunity for personnel managers to expand their responsibilities, increase their influence, and otherwise enhance their organizational image.

THE PERSONNEL FUNCTION'S NEW "PARADIGM"

Perhaps the best way to characterize the level of change that is required within PPM is to suggest that revolution, not just reform, is probably needed (Lee, 1993: 385–401). The essential task confronting PPM is nothing short of reversing the field's fundamental ethos. In other words, the personnel function must transform itself from a functionally based activity to one that emphasizes the provision of *services* to various groups of clients (Holt, 1994). This requires that the field's traditional embrace of control activities be loosened (or abandoned altogether) and that new operating strategies that promote a dramatically altered organizational role be devised.

Because this basic theme has dominated the relevant literature for so long, there is no shortage of ideas and opinions on how to accomplish the feat. Almost everyone seems to agree about the overall direction of reform. The first step in the reform process is to redefine *whom* and *what goals* the personnel office is supposed to serve. The accepted answer is that line managers and employees are PPM's primary clients. Once this concept has been internalized, then the personnel office's goals can be brought into conformity with those of the rest of the organization. Instead of following its own agenda—which typically encompassed a rather narrow concern for rule enforcement and protection of the merit system from political manipulation—the personnel office would expand its horizons beyond departmental boundaries. The goals and objectives of the wider organization would be the primary determinants of the personnel office's priorities.

To accomplish this transformation, personnelists must abandon their century-old preoccupation with *policing* the personnel system. Control activities must be supplanted by *supporting* actions that are responsive to the needs of the managers and workers who are ultimately responsible for accomplishing the organization's objectives. In contrast to past practice, personnel offices are urged to pay less attention to inputs and give much greater emphasis to outputs (as has supposedly been done for many years in the areas of budgeting and finance). Thus, for example, the field's traditional obsession with such concerns as eligibility requirements, test scores, job posting restrictions, and position questionnaires (to name but a few) would be replaced by a more commonsense approach to the staffing function. In effect, there would be far less emphasis on personnel "techniques," an ambition that has been expressed since the 1940s with Wallace Sayre's famous criticism that PPM represents "the triumph of technique over purpose" (1948). Practitioners must learn to act *strategically,* to link their activities with the broader goals of the organization, and to assess each procedure on the basis of its contribution to the agency mission. By altering its philosophical foundations in this manner, PPM would no longer be viewed as the "protector" of the personnel system, but as a *facilitator* (Copper et al., 1998: 284; Whittlesey, 1997). Or, as suggested by a different author, the personnel managers' internal role would be transformed from that of "regulators and enforcers" to "partners" of line managers (Santry, 1996).

Making the dramatic transition from policeman to servant of line managers is clearly no sport for the short-winded. No one thinks that the changes will occur easily, yet cause for optimism can be found in the wide consensus that exists concerning the major guideposts along the road to reform. Suggestions concerning needed changes inevitably concentrate on at least two interrelated change strategies: *decentralization* and *simplification.*

Decentralization represents the linchpin of the reform effort. Because centralization and its corresponding "bureaupathologies" (e.g., excessive red tape, undue emphasis on process, time delays) are viewed as major causes of PPM's current disease, delegation of personnel authority is considered the most promising cure. The key to successful change is to "give agencies latitude to design human resource policy to match organizational strategies and missions" (Perry, 1993: 62). As is also true within other management fields that are being reinvented, the concept of "local autonomy"—be it intraorganizational or geographical—is perceived as an essential prerequisite to management improvement. Centralized offices are expected to stop managing details and to "steer at arm's length" (Loffler, 1997: 71). By permitting line managers to exercise discretion over most human resource decisions, operating units can tailor the personnel system to their individualized needs. A state personnel system might thereby delegate authority to each state agency to define positions, to recruit and select personnel, and to assign and reassign employees as necessary without superfluous bureaucratic interference from the central office of human resources (or "OHR," which has become the favored name for most public personnel departments). The resulting flexibility permits public managers to eliminate unnecessary administrative practices, to expedite decision making, and to ensure that important personnel decisions are linked to the unit's objectives.

Simplification, in turn, refers to the ongoing effort to purge public personnel systems of redundant, inconsistent, inefficient, and overly complex procedural requirements. All policies and procedures should be reviewed in order to determine whether they promote or impede the accomplishment of organizational goals and to assess whether or not they are user-friendly. Within recent years, for instance, many time-honored vestiges of the past have been jettisoned once they were scrutinized in the light of current demands for a flexible and responsive personnel system. The rule of three—which confines the appointing authority's discretion to just the top three candidates on any civil service screening examination—has been replaced in most jurisdictions by much more lenient guidelines (e.g., a rule of 20 is now common). Similarly, the antiquated requirement that applicants for civil service jobs specify the *exact* job for which they are applying has been eliminated in all but the most inertia-bound jurisdictions. Instead, the qualifications of applicants are automatically matched to any openings that might be available. Because the objective today is to attract talented workers to the public service, unreasonable impediments are targeted for revision or abolition.

A complementary goal of simplification is to make the personnel system *transparent* to everyone both inside and outside the organization. From the perspective of the employees and supervisors, personnel policies should be clear, concise, and not unduly burdensome. Changing one's health insurance status, for instance, should not require two or more visits to a distant personnel office, both of which must occur only in the month of October (believe it or not, this type of requirement is not uncommon). Likewise, the progressive discipline code should provide a succinct delineation of employee rights and responsibilities that is readily understood by anyone with a minimal education. Similarly, potential employees should not have to jump through a large number of procedural hoops in order to identify vacancies or to file applications. In the past, accessing jobs in the public sector was often akin to unraveling the recipe for Coca-Cola. With the advent of procedural simplification, the worst examples of such procedures should quickly dissipate.

NEW ROLES AND RESPONSIBILITIES FOR THE PUBLIC PERSONNEL MANAGER

Obviously, the transformation of PPM that is sketched out here will require an equally stunning revision in the roles and responsibilities of personnel managers. Given the profession's long-term fixation with a limited number of control and service functions, most personnel practitioners have been trained to be *specialists*. Especially when employed in large state or urban human resources offices, personnel managers are typically hired and socialized to perform in a highly differentiated organizational setting. Specialization by narrow functional areas—such as training, testing, counseling, classifying, compensation, and employee relations—fosters a restricted professional outlook that inhibits communication and understanding between personnelists and line managers. Moreover, it unnecessarily complicates the decision-making process by forcing managers to deal with a different representative of the personnel department for each major type of problem that arises. In addition to fragmenting service delivery, specialization impedes the acquisition of a more holistic perspective on one's role in the broader organization. Nurturing a strategic outlook in such a setting is nearly impossible.

In order to implement the upgraded role envisioned for PPM successfully, personnelists will need to acquire new attitudes *and* new skills. Whether or not they are up to this challenge is a legitimate concern, since personnel offices have not traditionally attracted the "best and brightest" of all civil servants. Hope lies in the fact that, with the expansion of PPM's role (and, not incidentally, stature) within the organization, personnel offices will begin to become magnets to fast-track managers who are seeking interesting career challenges.

A brief look at the types of roles that the next generation of personnel professionals will (ideally) be asked to assume reinforces this notion. The transformation from narrow specialist to strategic partner with line management offers personnelists the opportunity to engage in a wide array of activities that have not typically been within their purview. Given the unprecedented demands of contemporary public management and the high expectations that have been articulated for PPM, personnel professionals may have the chance to contribute to organizational missions in the following ways (Hays and Reeves, 1984; Johnston, 1996; McCarthy, 1991).

Facilitating the Technology Revolution

According to most experts on the subject, one of the highest priorities of all organizations, both public and private, consists of managing the changes imposed by the information and technology revolutions. This represents a special dilemma to PPM because the salary structure within government makes it extraordinarily difficult to recruit and retain workers with advanced information-processing skills. Additionally, public agencies have been embarrassingly slow in responding to the impacts of technology on the way that government does business. According to Albert Hyde (1999), "The next chapter of internet development, the massive advances in knowledge management and the huge impacts of technology-based learning will fossilize most of what is done in HR today." Yet, despite these shortcomings, it is the personnel departments that will be expected to *lead* the change movement (Johnston, 1996). The implications are obvious. In addition to posing challenges in the areas of recruitment and retention, OHRs must work to devise training strategies that can help existing employees harness the technological tools upon which future work will depend. Employee development activities thus become critically important, as do the design and implementation of programs aimed at keeping workers motivated when the threat of quick obsolescence is prevalent.

Lead the Search for Best Practices

Another facet of PPM's role in helping organizations to cope with change is the need to search out and adopt promising innovations that are discovered in other public jurisdictions or in the private sector. At the risk of hyperbole, it might be suggested that the late 1990s and early 2000s represent the most exciting era in the history of management (perhaps excluding the Industrial Revolution). The amount of experimentation is so great, and the rate of change so dizzying, that simply "keeping up" is an enormous challenge. Large quantities of resources can be saved by organizations that keep an alert eye out for useful new management tools that can be transported into their own settings.

Human resource executives have the potential to interject themselves into the organizational mainstream by assuming leadership roles in the search for best practices. What better way to demonstrate the relevancy of the personnel office to line managers than to show them a way to do their jobs more efficiently? Abundant examples of successful innovations are readily available to any personnel executive with sufficient curiosity (and/or motivation) to look. Expedited hiring of applicants through the on-line screening of credentials (the "resume data base"), competency-based learning strategies that yield more "bang per buck" for training expenditures, flexible salary schemes (most notably, broadbanding) that enable public agencies to reward deserving employees, in-house programs to develop and retain information technology (IT) workers (NASPE, 1999), and creative employee recognition programs that encourage customer service and enhance worker motivation (e.g., "on-the-spot" bonuses in which supervisors are empowered to write checks of up to $500 to recognize employees who make exceptional contributions in public service) represent just the tip of the iceberg.

The personnel office's strategic position within the organization, coupled with an aggressive effort among professional organizations to disseminate information about management innovations, make the OHR a potential idea factory. Two of the most useful sources of information in this regard are the National Association of State Personnel Executives (NASPE) and the International Personnel Management Association (IPMA). NASPE, whose infrastructure is supported by the Council of State Governments, bestows annual Rooney Awards for human resource innovations in state and local government and maintains a web site that describes the programs that are thus recognized. This effort to publicize and transport best practices is co-sponsored by the IPMA, which also encourages innovation through a variety of complementary programs (including a benchmarking project, an internet e-mail network, and a highly articulated publications program).

Information Broker

Except in very small and/or poorly managed jurisdictions, the personnel office has always had access to important information that is potentially useful to line managers. Merely by maintaining employee records, tracking personnel actions (promotions, terminations, etc.), and conducting exit interviews, personnel executives sit at the crossroads of a number of important data streams. If used properly, this information can provide valuable assistance to decision makers. The simplest data system can be applied to work force projections in order to predict shortages and bulges in various job categories. This type of information enables the organization to act strategically, i.e., to operationalize a plan *now* to address a problem that will not actually surface for several years. Similarly, the systematic analysis of exit interview data is an extraordinarily rich source of employee feedback. Supervisory problems or other dysfunctional situations can often be highlighted through such techniques and thus point the way to possible resolution.

To the extent that the OHR assumes an even more aggressive posture in the collection and analysis of information, its impact upon strategic planning and decision making can be compounded. Dilemmas such as skyrocketing health care costs, workers' compensation claims, grievances, and turnover may all be alleviated (to widely varying degrees) through carefully crafted analyses and tailored administrative responses. When one considers that nearly 70 percent of any public agency's budget is devoted to salaries and related human resource expenses, the potential for personnel offices to play instrumental roles in cost reductions and improved efficiencies becomes evident.

One of the information-gathering strategies that holds the most potential is the *social audit* or *employee attitude survey*. Especially in this era of a supposed motivational crisis among public servants, attitude surveys have become common fixtures in many jurisdictions. In addition to soliciting input concerning gripes and suggestions, these instruments play a role in assessing the workers' levels of organizational commitment and job satisfaction. Because both of these phenomena are strongly correlated with turnover, absenteeism, grievances, and the like (not to mention a hypothesized connection to productivity), properly conducted surveys can serve as barometers of an organization's internal condition. Personnel offices that employ such information to fashion appropriate remedies (or at least recommendations to agency management) rarely suffer for the effort. In fact, the effective use of this type of feedback to an organization's leadership can catapult the personnel office into a new role as "diagnostician" (Cawsey, 1980; Dillon, 1975).

Employee Motivation and Development

Although line managers will ultimately carry the lion's share of responsibility for motivating their subordinates, many of the impediments to job satisfaction are structural. That is, they are less attributable to supervisory behavior than to the character of the career system and the organization's approach to recognizing and rewarding performance. Relatedly, one of the chief irritants among many workers is the performance evaluation process. Classic complaints about merit systems concentrate on the fact that they function as seniority systems (i.e., longevity is rewarded, not performance), that they discourage productivity by ignoring superior effort, and that performance appraisals are rife with favoritism and subjectivity.

Whereas the personnel office may not ever be able to resolve all of these problems, it certainly carries some of the responsibility for making structural adjustments in the appraisal and reward systems. Insofar as the appraisal process is concerned, the general consensus seems to be that public organizations need to do a better job of assessing outputs and pay less attention to behavior and traits (see the Daley chapter in this volume). Some experts are so disgusted with the traditional evaluation practices that they recommend the abolition of individual appraisals and the utilization of group output measures (this proposal is, of course, one of the foundations of Deming's total quality management). Whatever the "solution," the fact remains that PPM needs to recognize the flaws in the appraisal process and seek creative solutions. Any progress in this regard will certainly elevate the personnel office in the eyes of both managers and employees.

A comparable situation exists in regard to compensation, classification, and career systems. Narrow job classifications are blamed for the mind-deadening nature of much public work, and for such related maladies as restricted career paths, slow salary progression, and limited promotional opportunities. As should be apparent from the preceding discussion, this situation is simply unacceptable in today's management world. Fortunately, the technology of compensation and career management has progressed to the point that these ancient problems are no longer fixtures in every merit system. Indeed, progressive personnel systems have made significant strides in moving toward *rank-in-person* career systems (in which employees are not tied to narrow job classes but can be assigned according to their talents and desires). A related measure—broad salary bands that permit much greater compensation flexibility—at least provides public managers with a fighting chance to recognize, reward, and utilize their human resource talent. Any jurisdiction that has not yet considered the application of one or more of these innovations probably contains a personnel office that does not assume the next role that is discussed.

Policy Initiator and Implementer

Implicit in the preceding discussion is the notion that personnel managers ought to play a central role in agency leadership. Because of their control over important internal functions and their access to critical information, personnelists can legitimately take their place at the management table. By helping line managers to resolve recurring problems or to avoid pitfalls that might be looming on the horizon, they can transcend departmental boundaries and improve their organizational stature. Whereas PPM was rarely a policy initiator in the past, the future demands that personnel offices be much more proactive in proposing, drafting, and implementing new policies and programs. To do so requires a change in "mind-set" for both personnel practitioners and line managers. Simply stated, the new paradigm of personnel management must be internalized by both groups. The immediate task is to convince those who practice PPM that a proactive and strategic approach to the field is both possible and desirable. Once they have learned this lesson and experienced a few successes, then the line managers will likely be a much easier group to persuade.

RELEVANT STRATEGIES FOR CHANGE

Even Pollyanna would probably have doubts about the personnel profession's ability (or perhaps willingness) to emerge from its cocoon spontaneously. Despite the presence of many stresses and inducements, radical change in any setting is usually slow and painful. Before proceeding far down the road to reform, at least three types of adjustments will need to be made in the typical merit system. First, safeguards will be required to ensure that the personnel system's basic goals are not perverted in the stampede toward decentralization. Second, human resource specializations will have to be redefined or abandoned altogether. Finally, structural alterations within personnel departments will almost assuredly be demanded in order to accommodate emerging roles and functions.

Safeguarding Traditional Value: Benchmarking Human Resource Outputs

Up to this point in the discussion no mention has been made of the fact that some of the trends and proposals being discussed are at least slightly controversial. It is important to recognize that the proposed paradigm for PPM is not endorsed by everyone in the political and management communities for some very legitimate reasons. When public personnel systems were initially modernized during the late 19th and early 20th centuries, they were centralized because the lure of patronage proved to be too strong a temptation for many politicians. Centralization, along with extensive sets of rules and guidelines, were the antidote to the political disease that almost always plagued unprotected merit systems. Consequently, calls for decentralization and "debureaucratization" of the civil service raise in some minds the fear that political manipulation and abuse will soon follow. Whereas the traditional merit system putatively emphasized the values of expertise, neutrality, and competence, the revised model clearly advances such values as responsiveness, accountability, and "efficiency." It would be naïve to assume that these differing value schemes can coexist in harmony, and that some values will not ultimately be sacrificed in the pursuit of alternative societal objectives. One of the better-known characterizations of the changing value structure within PPM is that, unless merit systems are very careful, reform will become "politicization masquerading as executive accountability" (Thompson, 1995).

Those who are pessimistic about the consequences of reform hope to preserve some of the merit system's traditional values. The essential conundrum is figuring out how to create a decentralized system that empowers line managers to perform most staffing functions without abandoning centralized control measures altogether. A related worry is that, in a highly decentralized personnel system, balkanization will result. In each agency or department independent personnel systems that lack coherence and continuity will evolve. The quality of leadership in each agency will then dictate how the personnel system operates. Some may perform in a completely professional and competent manner, but others may fall victim to co-optation as agency leaders and/or politicians use civil service positions for unintended (i.e., partisan) purposes.

Potential responses to these dilemmas are not difficult to find (although they will certainly not satisfy every critic). The most obvious solution is for the central authority to retain some measure of control and influence over those to whom staffing authority is delegated. This can be accomplished in a relatively unobtrusive fashion through the use of *performance standards* or *benchmarks.* Instead of requiring preapproval of staffing decisions or enforcing stringent procedures, decentralized OHR can be held accountable to operating standards that are predetermined, measurable, and carefully audited. The human resource function is already the most heavily "benchmarked" facet of management (Brecka, 1995; Struebing, 1996), so Herculean efforts will not be necessary to put effective control measures into place. Personnel practices that are most commonly targeted include the presence of formal job analysis protocols, validated tests for selection, linkage of compensation to productivity measures, absenteeism and turnover rates, availability and use of a formal grievance procedure, routine employee attitude surveys, and various cost/benefit calculations (e.g., number of personnel managers per worker). Another promising idea is to develop benchmarks relating to the personnel office's success in aligning human resource goals with the organization's strategic plan. If this can be engineered, then "the notion of *control through service*" may be attainable (Weule, 1999). By formally integrating the OHR's performance standards with the organization's mission, the personnel function might ultimately be able to demonstrate its contribution to the "bottom line." This has been successfully accomplished in the private sector (Becker and Gerhart, 1996), where effective personnel offices have been shown to enhance organizational profitability.

Although benchmarks are a seductively simple "solution," they suffer from a few recognized shortcomings. Because of the lack of profit or other tangible measures of accomplishment in many government settings, output measures are notoriously "mushy" and/or difficult to establish. Moreover, critics argue that political considerations can never be eliminated from the decision calculus: Whoever has the greatest influence will have a disproportionate ability to set performance standards. It has also been demonstrated that administrators who are being evaluated on the basis of quantifiable benchmarks have a huge incentive to "cook the books" or to focus *only* on that which is measured to the exclusion of other considerations (Walters, 1994). For these reasons, the identification and measurement of performance standards in any field require an enormous amount of both science and art.

From Specialist to Generalist

As has been noted, the myopia that characterized the personnel profession of the past is largely attributed to excessive job specialization. Spending 40 hours per week doing nothing but classifying jobs or scoring tests tends to narrow a person's perspective and harden resistance to change.

A more eclectic approach to personnel management has long been perceived as an expeditious way to enhance interaction and understanding between human resource and line managers (Hocker, 1964). When functioning as generalists, personnelists become jacks-of-all-trades in providing an array of support services to operating managers. Under one configuration, for example, a single representative from the personnel office might be assigned to a large subunit of the organization (a bureau, department, or section). The person may even be physically located within the relevant work group and be available to serve in a variety of capacities. The role can involve such tasks as interpreting personnel policies and procedures for supervisors, advising and counseling workers regarding career development or other topics, and untangling unpleasant interpersonal problems. Depending upon the level of his/her expertise, the generalist might also assist managers in formulating and implementing productivity-improvement programs (Hays and Reeves, 1984: 85–86). In effect, the personnelist functions as a member of the line manager's staff, although he/she retains responsibility for enforcing the generic policies of the central personnel office (to the extent that they exist).

Although not excessively common, the generalist approach to the human resource function is now expanding at an unprecedented pace. Many private corporations, for instance, maintain elaborate developmental programs to train their personnel managers as generalists. Job rotation and cross-functional assignments are used by such entities as General Electric (Stockman, 1999) and Andersen Consulting (Hunter, 1999) to expand their personnelists' competencies. Transferring the employees among a variety of both staff and line positions helps them to acquire a richer set of skills and a far more comprehensive understanding of the organization's mission. The personnelists spend time not only in all functional areas of the human resources office, but in front-line jobs that put them in face-to-face contact with clients, workers, and supervisors. The resulting integration of perspectives and skills enables these individuals to function as internal *consultants* (Hunter, 1999).

The state of South Carolina's Office of Human Resources has adopted the personnel generalist model as part of its mission to emphasize service over control. All of the individuals who once were employed in various specializations (classifiers and employee relations specialists, for the most part) have been cross-trained and retitled as "personnel consultants." Each consultant is assigned a small number of state agencies, and each is expected to provide "one-stop shopping" for almost all interactions between the central office and the agency personnel department. In addition to problem solving and consulting on the entire range of staffing issues (recruitment, testing, evaluation, etc.), the consultants play an instrumental role in helping to elevate the quality of personnel management that is available in each agency. They participate in upper-level decision making and even have a hand in selecting the individuals who are hired to serve as agency personnelists. Through strategies of this type, the human resources function can be both decentralized and modernized simultaneously. The results to date appear extraordinarily promising, a fact that was acknowledged when *Governing magazine* rated South Carolina's OHR as the nation's best (it was the only state to receive a grade as high as A– on the human resources "report card").

Structural Accommodations

As a corollary of the movements described, personnel departments will obviously require structural alterations to accommodate their new roles. With the advent of the personnel generalist/consultant, internal units that are organized on the basis of functional specializations lose their relevancy. In fact, the continued presence of such departmental divisions represents a tall barrier to the broader view of the personnel function that is being fostered in the modern era. Thus, OHRs of the future are likely to be far less structured than is presently the case. The new organizational form will need to be more organic; i.e., the personnel office should be flatter, more open, and more fluid. Some routine functions, such as recruiting and testing, might well be effectively outsourced. This will free the personnel professionals to pursue the more meaningful assignments that have been forecast, including partnering with line managers to pursue strategic objectives. To the extent that the OHR is divided into subunits, they would best be organized around *outputs* rather than inputs. Thus, there might be an increasing reliance upon "skill centers" (Roussel, 1995) or other units that concentrate upon improving managerial competencies, employee development, information technology, or other desired ends.

According to one author, the emerging organizational model looks "like a three-legged stool" (Johnson, 1999: 44). The first leg contains all of the old specializations, but now they are conceived as a "service center" that processes paperwork efficiently and tries to assist line managers with their technical human resource needs. The second leg is a "center for excellence" that is responsible for training, employee development, and other long-range strategies to enhance organizational performance. The final leg consists of a pool of generalists ("business partners," in the language of the private sector) who provide consultative services to other managers and who are responsible for conducting employee attitude surveys and otherwise monitoring the internal health of the agency (Johnson, 1999). Interestingly, the South Carolina OHR that was mentioned has an internal structure that is remarkably similar to the one just described. Because it is so new, and because other models are so rare in the public sector, it is not yet possible to render a judgment as to the design's effectiveness. On a commonsense level, however, the three-legged format is certainly consistent with the trends that have been forecast for PPM.

HOW FEASIBLE IS THIS TRANSFORMATION?

Anyone who is familiar with the recent history of merit systems will probably react to this chapter with a healthy dose of caution, if not cynicism. As mentioned, the themes embodied in the present reform movement have been advocated for at least 30 years. Those of us who have witnessed only fitful changes in the operation of some merit systems over this lengthy period may be forgiven for our pessimism. We know all too well the conditions and attitudes that may impede reform.

Other than the natural inertia that occurs in any organization, there are at least four reasons why the reforms detailed may not be enthusiastically adopted in large numbers of jurisdictions. The first problem is simply one of *capacity.* The revised personnel system will count on line managers to perform most staffing functions, but this assumes that the empowered individuals will have the requisite knowledge and skills to do a decent job. Unless sufficient training precedes the delegation of authority, the line managers may be no better (or even worse) than their predecessors at screening, choosing, evaluating, and otherwise maintaining the work force. And, given the government's poor record in terms of training and employee development (Carnevale, 1995), there is inadequate evidence that most public personnel systems are truly ready to be decentralized. Another capacity issue arises from the fact that personnel offices have been especially hard-hit by the downsizing trend within government. Simply stated, many OHRs may be too busy merely trying to keep up with their old responsibilities to entertain the notion of systematic reform (Hays, 1996: 291).

A closely related concern arises from the conditions that prevail in many of the nation's *85,000* public jurisdictions. A large percentage of these cities, counties, and special jurisdictions are too small, poor, and/or inattentive to support modern personnel systems. In fact, many of the nation's public personnel managers are actually city clerks, assistant city managers, or other employees who handle the PPM chores on a part-time basis. Within such settings, the personnel function is usually very underdeveloped. In jurisdictions that lack even a systematic recruitment or evaluation program, it is unlikely that the person responsible for the civil service "system" will engage in creative reform. Human resource activities are so basic and backward in these jurisdictions that developments in the broader field of PPM simply pass them by.

Another dilemma stems from the inadequate "state of the art" that exists among the various personnel techniques. Although significant improvements have been made over the years, much additional work needs to be done in many facets of human resources practice. This phenomenon is especially apparent in employee selection (where test validity persists as a major challenge) but also extends to such areas as incentive systems (where fixation with merit pay tends to discourage experimentation with other formats) and performance evaluation (where rating scales are still popular, despite copious literature proving that they are notoriously unreliable). The risks associated with decentralizing the personnel function are compounded by uncertainty over the *quality* and *effectiveness* of the techniques on which the field depends. Whether or not personnel systems are transformed structurally, greater attention clearly needs to be paid to refining PPM's techniques.

The final impediment relates to the values conflict that was discussed earlier. Although some personnelists may resist reform for all the wrong reasons (i.e., self-protection, territoriality, fear of change), others harbor honest reservations about the long-term implications of dismantling merit systems. Personnel practitioners are caught in the middle of an epic struggle between competing values. Professionalism, neutral competence, and expertise are being challenged by pressures for accountability and responsiveness. PPM's dilemma is to balance these competing demands and to achieve an equilibrium that everyone can live with. This sometimes requires them to make difficult personal and professional choices. Does one turn a blind eye to the politicization of career appointments in order to satisfy other demands? What does one do when ordered to delegate staffing authority to an agency that is known to be incapable of exercising it responsibly? Resistance to "reform" under such circumstances might be the choice that some personnel managers make. Whether or not that course of action is right or correct is more a matter of conscience than of public policy. For this reason, the foot dragging of personnel practitioners may occasionally appear to be warranted among some observers.

CONCLUSION

In summary, no one should expect an instantaneous transformation of public personnel systems. The change process will undoubtedly be slow and measured. Mistakes will occur, horror stories will surface, and detours will be taken. About the only conclusion that can be drawn with certainty is that the general direction of the reform movement is set. Like it or not, merit systems are targeted for debureaucratization and decentralization. More and more line managers will find themselves newly empowered with authority over human resource decisions. How they utilize that power will probably dictate further advances—or retreats—on the reform front.

REFERENCES

Baill, Barbara (1999). The changing requirements of the HR professional. *Human Resource Management. 38* (Summer): 171–176.

Brecka, Jon (1995). Human resources is top benchmarking process. *Quality Progress.* (April): 17–19.

Brecker, Brian, and Gerhart, Barry (1996). The impact of human resources management on organizational performance: progress and prospects. *Academy of Management Journal. 4:* 779–801.

Carnevale, David (1995). Human capital in high performance public organizations. In *Public Personnel Administration: Problems and Prospects* (S. Hays and R. Kearney, eds.). New York, Marcel Dekker.

Cawsey, T. (1980). Why line managers don't listen to their personnel departments. *Personnel.* (January-February): 11–20.

Cooper, Phillip, Brady, Linda, Hidalgo-Hardeman, Olivia, Hyde, Albert, Naff, Katherine, Ott, Steven, and White, Harvey (1998). *Public Administration in the Twenty-First Century.* Harcourt Brace, Fort Worth.

Dillon, John (1975). A new role for personnel: monitoring superchange. *The Personnel Administrator. 20* (November): 20–22.

Hays, Steven (1996). The 'state of the discipline' in public personnel administration. *Public Administration Quarterly. 20* (Fall): 283–304.

Hays, Steven, and Reeves, T. Zane (1984). *Personnel Management in the Public Sector.* Allyn & Bacon, Boston.

Hocker, M. (1964). The personnel generalist: an aid to management problem solving. *Personnel Administration.* (March–April): 39–50.

Holt, Blake (1994). Benchmarking comes to human resources. *Personnel Management. 26* (June): 32–41.

Hunter, Robert (1999). The 'new HR' and the new HR consultant: developing human resource consultants at Andersen Consulting. *Human Resource Management. 38* (Summer): 147–155.

Hyde, Albert (1999). Personal Communication. September 9.

Johnson, Carla (1999). Changing shapes: as organizations evolve, HR's form follows its functions. *HR Magazine.* (March): 41–48.

Johnston, John (1996). Time to rebuild human resources. *The Business Quarterly. 61* (Winter): 46–52.

Kearney, Richard and Hays, Steven (1998). Reinventing government, the new public management, and civil service systems in international perspective. *Review of Public Personnel Administration. 18* (Fall): 38–54.

Lee, Robert (1993). *Public Personnel Systems.* Aspen, Gaithersburg, Md.

Loffler, Elke (1997). Personnel management in German public administration. *Review of Public Personnel Administration. 17* (Summer): 69–81.

McCarthy, Joseph (1991). Riding the third wave. *Personnel Journal. 70* (April): 34–39.

National Association of State Personnel Executives (NASPE) (1999). Human Resource Benchmarking Project. [http://www.ipma-hr.org/tests/bpITOR.hrm].

Newland, Chester (1984). Crucial issues for public personnel professionals. *Public Personnel Management.* (Summer): 15–45.

Perry, James (1993). Strategic human resource management. *Review of Public Personnel Administration. 13* (Fall): 59–71.

Roussel, Charles (1995). Promises to keep: affecting organizational transformation. *HR Focus. 72* (April): 13–15.

Santry, Kerry (1996). Bridges says workers of the future must flex and change with the needs of the job market. *Management Journal. 36* (Spring): 36–39.

Sayre, Wallace (1948). The triumph of technique over purpose. *Public Administration Review. 8* (Spring): 134–137.

Stewart, Thomas (1996). Taking on the last bureaucracy. *Fortune Magazine.* (June).

Stockman, James (1999). Building a quality HR organization at GE. *Human Resource Management. 38* (Summer): 143–146.

Struebing, Laura (1996). Group's clients most often use benchmarking for human resource improvements. *Quality Progress.* (April): 20–22.

Thompson, Frank (1993). *Revitalizing State and Local Public Service.* Jossey Bass, San Francisco.

Thompson, Frank (1995). The politics of public personnel administration. In *Public Personnel Administration: Problems and Prospects* (S. Hays and R. Kearney, eds.) Prentice-Hall, Englewood Cliffs, N.J.

Thornburg, Linda (1993). Yes, Virginia, HR contributes to the bottom line. *HR Magazine. 38* (August): 62–66.

Ulrich, Dave (1998). The future calls for change. *Workforce.* (January): 87–91.

Walters, Jonathan (1994). The benchmarking craze. *Governing.* (April): 33–37.

Volcker Commission (1989). *Leadership for America: Rebuilding the Public Service.* National Commission on the Public Service, Washington, D.C.

Weule, Daniel (1999). Personal Communication. September 7.

Whittlesey, Fred (1997). The future of human resources management. *ACA Journal.* (Spring): 12–15.

Wooldridge, Blue and Wester, Jennifer (1991). The turbulent environment of public personnel administration: Responding to the challenges of the changing workplace of the twenty-first century. *Public Personnel Management.* (Summer): 207–223.

11

Changes and Reforms in Public Labor-Management Relations

Richard C. Kearney
Department of Political Science,
East Carolina University, Greenville,
North Carolina

As embodied in the terms of the National Labor Relations Act (NLRA) of 1935 (also known as the Wagner Act after its leading proponent in the U.S. Senate), labor relations and collective bargaining in the United States are legally premised on adversarial, zero-sum assumptions. The NLRA does not directly apply to the public sector, but its basic assumptions and procedures prevail in most state collective bargaining statutes and in Title VII of the federal Civil Service Reform Act (the federal labor relations statute). One important result is that, until very recently, precious few meaningful reforms or innovations had been developed and disseminated under the constraining language of the NLRA and similar public sector labor relations statutes.

Beginning in the early 1990s, however, the corporate search for greater competitiveness, productivity, and profits in a time of enormous economic and technological change led to widespread interest in restructuring organizations and their authority systems (Kochan and Useem, 1992). Corporate downsizing, reorganization, and reengineering have flattened hierarchies and altered authority relationships. Traditional adversarial relations between labor and management have been supplemented or replaced by a variety of cooperative mechanisms in a surprisingly large number of firms (almost 80 percent of Fortune 500 companies with unions, and about 60 percent of those without unions, according to Eaton and Voos, 1992).

The public sector has not been immune to the vast changes occurring in technology and corporate thinking. Recurring fiscal problems, citizen hostility, and the reinventing government phenomenon have exerted their own pressures on public organizations at all levels of government. One consequence is that a growing number of public organizations have also begun to experiment with new forms of worker participation and empowerment.

The movement from adversarial relations in collective bargaining environments, and from unilateral management decision making in nonunion settings, to a cooperative, participative approach to making organizational decisions represents a profound transformation. All of the major reforms in labor-management relations in both the public and private sectors during the 1990s were responses to this transformation from adversarial to cooperative relations. These reforms involve conflict resolution and problem solving in collective bargaining, contract administration, many other aspects of the workplace.

After an overview of the legal environment and literature on labor-management cooperation in the private sector of the United States, this chapter examines the shift from traditional confrontational, zero-sum approaches to labor relations in the public sector to more participative, cooperative models. Various mechanisms for cooperative approaches will be examined at all levels of government. The chapter concludes with an analysis of the potential impacts and implications of the transformation for labor-management relations in the future.

BACKGROUND

There are many forms of labor-management cooperation, running the gamut from informal management consultation with employees to formal mechanisms for joint decision making. In this chapter, the emphasis is on participative decision making in unionized settings. Participative decision making (PDM) is defined as meaningful employee participation in organizational decision making wherein there is an operative, formal vehicle for the exercise of employee voice and where employee views and decisions are given serious consideration (Kearney and Hays, 1994). Among the mechanisms for PDM are quality circles, total quality management (TQM), labor-management committees (LMCs), employee involvement programs (EIPs), and quality of work life (QWL) programs.

Interest in participative approaches in the private sector arises from the growing recognition that as the venerable human resources model of administrative has asserted since the 1940s, employees are the organization's most important asset and should be treated accordingly. The model envisions bottom-up authority structures and participatory decision-making strategies. Few organizations in the corporate world took this model seriously until the 1980s, when external competitive pressures and widely heralded Japanese management innovations spurred an interest in employee involvement programs. Today, adoption of PDM programs is "quite widespread" in the private sector (Osterman, 1994), with up to 50 percent of large firms adopting it in one form or another (Delaney, 1996: 47).

An extensive literature has developed on private sector employee participation, including its antecedents, designs, results, and impacts and the role of unions. Generally, the evidence is positive concerning PDM's effects on productivity of the individual and the firm, job satisfaction, personal growth and development, and willingness to change (Kearney and Hays, 1994). Individual benefits are believed to contribute, directly and/or indirectly, to desired organizational outcomes. For example, where PDM enhances worker satisfaction with the job, increases commitment to the job, and reduces alienation, it may then produce less turnover, fewer absences, lower sickness and accident rates (Kolarska and Aldrich, 1980; Schwochau et al., 1997: 381), and stronger commitment to the organization (Verma and McKersie, 1987; Straw and Heckscher, 1984; Morris and Steers, 1980).

Organizational benefits of PDM include improved ability of employees to perform technical tasks (Mohrman and Lawler, 1988: 47) and to respond positively to a rapidly changing environment (Gabris and Kenneth, 1986). The findings are less conclusive concerning the impacts of PDM on organizational efficiency and productivity (Wagner, 1994), although there is growing evidence that organizational performance is enhanced (Levine, 1995; Doucouliagos, 1995). Participation has civic and social value as well. It "can stimulate the development of civil society because it encourages individuals to develop and practice habits that are critical to self-sufficiency, self-rule, and . . . individual responsibility" (Delaney, 1996: 46). In other words, PDM can help stimulate responsible self-government. Because employees clearly desire to participate in workplace decisions (Rogers, 1994; Dunlop Commission, 1994), and employers believe that organizational benefits also accrue from participation programs, the number of such programs is likely to grow in the future.

Perceived obstacles to the proliferation of labor-management participation programs are the language of the NLRA that defines labor organizations and two widely cited National Labor Relations Board (NLRB) decisions grounded on that definition. During the 1920s and early 1930s, prior to legalization of full collective bargaining and labor rights for private sector unions, many employers resisted unions through various strong-arm tactics, including the firing of organizers and the use of strike-breaking "goon squads." Others discouraged unions more subtly by adopting "representation plans" that established committees of employee and management representatives to meet on workplace concerns. The representation plans were forced on workers by management, which strictly reserved its prerogatives in making important decisions. Unions viewed these plans as "subterfuges used by employers to mask virulent antiunionism and preclude employees from exercising their right to collective bargaining" (Kelly, 1998: 465). A related tactic was the "company union," created and essentially operated by an employer in the guise of a legitimate labor union.

To prevent such corporate evasions, the NLRA defined a *labor organization* as one "in which employees participate and which exists for the purpose . . . of dealing with employees concerning grievances, labor disputes, wages, rates of pay, hours of employment, or conditions of work" (Section 2([5])). The language further provided that it is an unfair labor practice for an employer to "dominate or interfere with the formation or administration of any labor organization or contribute financial or other support to it" (Section 8([a])([2])). Federal case law and NLRB decisions have found that labor-management committees and similar devices established by employers are "labor organizations" under the NLRA, and therefore illegal because they are created and dominated by the employer (see *Electromation* 309 NLRB 990 ([1992])). Therefore, to be legal, employee participation programs must be established and operated with a substantial degree of independence from management control (i.e., with the cooperation of a union) (see Delaney, 1996: 44–46).

The NLRA is widely viewed as a deterrent to labor-management participation programs that do not have substantial union involvement. However, recent court and NLRB interpretations of the act provide exceptions that appear to permit employers to establish participation programs in the absence of unions so long as sufficient decision-making authority is granted to employees (Delaney, 1996: 52–53). For example, supervisors are excluded from the definition of employee in the NLRA, thereby effectively excluding them from collective bargaining. As organizational hierarchies are flattened and team-based work groups gain responsibility for making decisions, more and more employees fit one or more of the criteria of the NLRA definition of *supervisor,* particularly those who are engaged in professional positions involving independent judgment. In sum, the NLRA does not preclude PDM, but it does not facilitate it, either.

In the private sector, not surprisingly, unionized workers are significantly more likely to be involved in PDM programs than are nonunion workers (Cooke, 1990; Eaton and Voos, 1992; Osterman, 1994). In principle, and contrary to the conventional wisdom, unions tend not to be opposed to participation programs. Levine (1997) suggests that because unions are usually able to protect jobs, organized employees may be more willing to assume the risks of a PDM program than their nonunion peers. Moreover, it is in the interest of unions to support participation efforts that aim to improve product and service quality and efficiency, because if such programs are successful, they may lead to higher wages and benefits. Research shows that negative outcomes tend to occur when unions decide *not* to get involved in participation programs. Union opposition to PDM chills employee interest in the program and increases the odds of program failure (Allen and Van Norman, 1996).

In contrast to the rich literature and scholarly research in the private sector, most of the published work on public sector labor-management participation has been anecdotal, with a pronounced tendency to sing the praises of participation experiments loudly. Little systematic or comparative research has appeared in the professional journals. This is largely a consequence of the relatively recent occurrence of the PDM phenomenon in government. However, insofar as the union role in PDM is concerned, government is the playing field where most of the future action will be witnessed.

Organized labor has a much greater presence in government than in the private sector. As of January 1998, 43.4 percent of local employees and 30.5 percent of state employees were represented by a union, compared to only about 9 percent of private sector workers (US BLS, 1999). The heaviest representation is for fire fighters, teachers, police, and sanitation workers, in that order. Some of the fastest organizing growth, however, is in health care occupations. And whereas private sector unionization has been declining since its peak in 1954, public employee unions generally maintained their membership levels during the 1990s.

Thirty-six states grant some or all of their local government workers collective bargaining rights through statute or gubernatorial executive order, and 29 provide collective bargaining rights to state employees. Not surprisingly, union density is much greater in states that are bargaining-friendly. For instance, 75 percent of state employees are covered by collective bargaining contracts in Connecticut, compared to only 7.6 percent in Virginia; 83 percent of Hawaii's local government employees are under contract, versus only 8.1 percent in South Carolina. Federal sector labor relations are embodied in Title VII of the Civil Service Reform Act. Approximately 59 percent of federal employees are represented in bargaining units. However, because of the inability of bargaining representatives to negotiate salaries and benefits and the absence of union security provisions such as the fair share arrangement, only 32 percent of qualified (represented) federal employees belong to a union and pay dues. However, the U.S. Postal Service and a handful of other federal entities have their own statutory or administrative framework that permits negotiation of pay and benefits. In the case of the Postal Service, several unions average membership levels of around 90 percent of employees in the bargaining unit. Generally, state and local employees have labor and collective bargaining rights that are as strong as those provided for private sector workers under the NLRA, with the major exception of the right to strike. All federal employees, and most state and local workers, are prohibited from going on strike. Certain categories of "nonessential" employees are permitted to strike in 10 states, subject to a variety of required—and lengthy—preliminary procedures.

As noted, the NLRA is not entirely irrelevant to public sector labor relations, because much of its language is replicated in state labor relations statutes. Moreover, the adversarial spirit of private sector labor relations was carried over to the public sector with the NLRA principles and procedures that were inserted into statutes. Hostility and deep-rooted distrust have characterized collective bargaining and contract administration in most government jurisdictions. As the National Commission on the State and Local Public Service (1993: 384) observed, "For far too long an adversarial climate . . . has predominated. It is a climate that can stifle innovation and government's ability to get the job done." Contract negotiations are not infrequently obstructed by game playing and lengthy delays, in a process that can play out over many months or even be counted in years. Once a contract is in place, destructive, adversarial interactions between union and management representatives can result in an expanding backlog of grievances, both trivial and serious. In such an environment, sustained cooperative behavior is virtually impossible.

The federal government's collective bargaining law is even more constraining than the NLRA in terms of scope of bargaining. As noted, federal unions, with only a handful of exceptions, are prohibited from negotiating wages and benefits. Compensation is determined for General Schedule (GS) employees by the president and Congress, after receiving recommendations from the President's Pay Agent. Wage Board employees (trade and blue-collar workers) are paid the "prevailing rate," based on Bureau of Labor Statistics salary and wage survey data and recommendations made by area wage committees. A restrictive management rights clause in Section 7106 of Title VII of the CSRA further prohibits or discourages cooperative endeavors in such important areas as performance standards, seniority issues, contracting out, reductions in force, and most agency rules and regulations (however, President Clinton's Executive Order 12871 of 1993 broadened the scope of bargaining to require negotiations on topics that were previously treated as "permissive" under the CSRA, including position assignments and the technology and methods for performing work). Little assistance has emerged from the Federal labor Relations Authority (FLRA), the administrative apparatus for federal labor relations (US GAO, 1991). However, as described in more detail later, "partnering" initiatives (facilitated by an expansion in the scope of bargaining through the aforementioned presidential executive order) are now required of all federal agencies through reinventing government policy. Despite predictable adjustment problems spawned by a long history of highly adversarial relations, many interesting and successful programs have been established throughout the agencies.

Despite the fact that as many as 26 state bargaining laws are modeled on the NLRA, they are generally more amenable to PDM approaches. Under some state bargaining laws, cooperative ventures may be developed and implemented rather informally, outside the confines of the negotiated contract, so long as the state equivalent of the NLRB—typically called the Public Employee Relations Board—approves. In other states, a structure for PDM may be established through collective bargaining. For example, Illinois and its largest state employee union (AFSCME) have used joint labor-management committees and quality involvement committees since 1975 to tackle issues such as employee health and safety, expedited grievance procedures, and drug testing (Ball, 1996: 26). Through joint union and management involvement in establishing and operating such committees, employee rights are not usurped.

There were isolated experiments with various types of labor-management cooperation in federal, state, and local government in the 1960s and 1970s, including productivity bargaining in a handful of cities (an early form of gainsharing) and labor-management committees in the Internal Revenue Service (IRS) and other federal agencies. But the adoption of PDM and related ventures picked up pace in government in the 1980s and accelerated further in the 1990s. In addition to expanding the scope of bargaining, Executive Order 12871 directed federal agencies to construct labor-management partnerships for the collaborative solving of workplace problems. By 1996 almost 90 percent of federal agencies were actively "partnering" (Lane, 1996: 41). Although no comprehensive data exist on the extent of PDM approaches in state and local workplaces, anecdotal reports indicate increasingly broad adoption of partnerships, PDM, and other cooperative arrangements.

MAJOR CONCEPTS, ISSUES, AND CHANGES

The major changes and reforms in public sector labor-management relations today are basically concerned with resolving conflicts and solving problems in collective bargaining and contract administration and, more generally, in the workplace. The emerging paradigm for addressing conflicts and problems involves PDM and other cooperative approaches. Unions, in particular, desire greater employee participation in decision making. Public managers, for their part, are increasingly willing to share some elements of decision-making responsibility with employees (Freeman, 1996).

The receptivity of public managers to employee and union participation emerges from two key factors. First, the history of labor-management relations in government, although sometimes stormy, is much briefer and not as replete with extreme adversarial encounters as is the history of union-management relations in the private sector. With the glaring exception of President Reagan's mass dismissal of 12,000 striking federal air traffic controllers in 1981, hardly any federal, state, and local government employees have lost their jobs since the 1970s as a result of union organizing or job actions. Traditional civil service projections have, of course, contributed to job security. The highly adversarial relations that prevailed in many public jurisdictions during the early years of unionization and collective bargaining gradually moderated in most cases, as union and management roles and expectations stabilized and matured.

Second, public managers and those who work for them share important characteristics and interests. Many of them are, or consider themselves to be, public service professionals who work for the public interest. Research has rather consistently shown that public employees are motivated by different, less-economic incentives than their private sector peers (Perry and Wise, 1990). Public employees at all levels are engaged in work intended to benefit the public as a whole, and to help solve problems and improve conditions in important public concerns such as health care, public education, and criminal justice. Program success and productivity gains can translate into compensation increases for all public employees and special recognition for managers. Private sector personnel are employed to pursue profits and the interests of owners and shareholders. In the corporate setting, the pursuit of profits often causes serious divisions between the ranks of management and workers. Another distinction is that labor and management in government share key enemies: namely, spoils politicians, bureaucrat bashers, and hostile public opinion. The commonality of interests and enemies of public managers and workers makes cooperation more feasible than in the private sector. Nonetheless, three important conditions must be met if PDM and similar vehicles are to transport their passengers successfully to the desired destinations.

Conditions Necessary for Successful PDM

The first condition for successful PDM is a firm foundation of trust and mutual respect. Constructing such a foundation has been particularly difficult in the private sector, where management-designed schemes for employee "participation" are still, at times, smoke screens for warding off unions. In both business and government, union leaders sometimes fear that participation efforts originated by management are actually intended to manipulate workers and their unions, and that, no matter what their true intent might be, such approaches might weaken collective bargaining and grievance systems as well as employee commitment to the union. Even in settings in which cooperative arrangements are well established, union members and their leaders tend to be less enthusiastic about them than managers (Eaton, 1994; Juravich et al., 1993). But suspicion and doubts also infect midlevel managers, who feel particularly threatened by their potential loss of authority, and even their jobs, when PDM programs are introduced (Lawler and Mohrman, 1985).

Where a negative or hostile labor relations environment has prevailed, trust and respect must be constructed from the ground up. This is not a simple task, and failures have been reported. The U.S. Postal Service's history of confrontational relations in the context of an autocratic management style, rigid work rules, and something much less than ideal working conditions has made meaningful cooperation between unions and management very difficult to achieve (US GAO, 1994). Similarly, a labor-management partnership program in Miami, Florida, was adopted in the context of low employee morale, high levels of conflict, and a "chaotic" labor relations climate that included serious internal divisions in the ranks of both labor and city management (Bryson et al., 1999). After several years, major problems remained.

In other cases significant progress has been reported in converting hostile and adversarial labor-management relationships to a productive and cooperative state. The San Francisco Bay Area's Union Sanitation District was burdened by low morale, lack of trust, and an adversarial climate, but a far-reaching change effort directed by the district's general manager opened up direct communication lines between union and management representatives, facilitated much less contentious contract negotiations, and achieved a number of improvements in operations and problem solving (Berzon et al., 1999).

The second condition for successful, sustained PDM programs is a strong level of commitment by both management and employees. A sufficient level of attention, time, and resources must be invested in the program if it is to have an opportunity to work over the long haul. Managers at all levels, from agency and department heads to front-line supervisors, must be able to work closely with union leaders from the president down to the shop steward. The organization itself should commit financial and human resources to special training in problem solving and interpersonal skills for key individuals.

The federal experience illustrates the salience of commitment to successful PDM. One of the earliest interest-based, cooperative approaches is attributable to the Department of Health and Human Services and the National Treasury Employees Union (NTEU). The parties began a sustained interest-based relationship in the early 1980s for the purpose of resolving Equal Employment Opportunity (EEO) cases, then extended the process into resolving grievances and unfair labor practice allegations. Sufficient resources were committed to train negotiation team members and to train supervisors and employees in how to implement the products of collaborative bargaining through labor-management committees (Marshall et al., 1999). Many other positive outcomes of PDM have been recorded in the federal sector (US Secretary of Labor's Task Force, 1996: 13–25). However, various partnerships were reported to be struggling in 1997–1998 because of a lack of commitment from top managers and a "general distrust of the idea of co-management" ("Partnerships Posing Problems," 1997).

Devoting resources to training, skills, and procedural aspects of labor-management cooperation is essential, but the level of commitment must be much deeper and more profound than mere attention to technical concerns if PDM is to succeed over the long term. Sincere, sustained commitment from top-level officials is particularly important, but it is not easy to secure in public sector jurisdictions in which newly elected officials or their appointees fail to maintain the collaborative policies adopted by their predecessors, or where budget problems drive reductions in force or cutbacks in employee compensation. An example of positive and sustained leadership commitment to collaborative undertakings is found in Peoria's experience with labor-management cooperation on health care cost containment. The city council, union leadership, and city administration evidenced a "commitment of leadership, training, and neutral third party facilitation" that helped the parties move beyond their existing adversarial atmosphere in 1993 to a more positive decision-making environment (Parsons et al., 1998). Peoria is just one case among many that illustrate the critical importance of genuine, continuing commitment by top labor, management, and elected officials to PDM in local government (Bell and Litscher, 1998; Hirokawa et al., 1999).

The third condition for successful PDM is that both parties must be committed to finding win-win, interest-based solutions to problems and conflicts. The win-win concept, which has drawn increasing levels of positive attention in a wide variety of settings since the 1980s, may be traced to the work of Walton and McKersie (1965), who originated the concept of "integrative bargaining." Defined as negotiations that involve a cooperative search for mutual interests and gains that ends with both parties "winning," integrative bargaining was later popularized by Fisher and Ury's (1981) *Getting to Yes,* where it is referred to as "principled" or "interest-based" negotiations. Integrative bargaining is contrasted with conventional distributive bargaining, which is adversarial, competitive, and zero-sum.

Examples of successful win-win negotiations have been accumulating. Federal agencies, acting under the instructions of the National Performance Council, have developed partnerships premised on interest-based negotiations to resolve contract and workplace disputes and to address a wide variety of other problems. The IRS-NTEU relationship stands out for the level and scope of its activities. In addition to the EEO, grievance, and ULP collaborations noted, other partnership experiments in the early 1980s involved NTEU in redesigning an incentive pay system and soon led to joint development of a gainsharing program for 10,000 employees. IRS and NTEU have also cooperated through quality circles, quality improvement teams, and TQM, addressing everything from minor workplace irritants to the redesign of entire operating systems (Ferris and Cooper, 1994). Win-win expectations apparently drive the IRS-NTEU relationship. One might assume that since the partnering continues, expectations are being realized.

Win-win in Wisconsin state government has occurred since 1992 in the context of "consensus bargaining" by management with the 27,000-member Wisconsin State Employees Union. Among the benefits attributed to the Wisconsin approach are more cooperative labor-management relations, reduced time to settle contracts, and "a more positive and closer labor-management relationship." The foundation for consensus bargaining is "the belief that both parties can be winners" (Bell and Litscher, 1998). Interest-based programs have been described in a variety of other settings, including Ramsey County, Minnesota (Brainerd, 1998); Peoria, Illinois (Parsons et al., 1998); and Portland, Maine (Peightal et al., 1998). Interesting experiments have been recorded in the public schools, which, in a growing number of locations, are struggling for survival in the context of intense public criticism and private alternatives. A suburban Sacramento, California, school district with a history of highly adversarial relations developed a successful interest-based approach with the assistance of the state public employee relations board (Wishnick and Wishnick, 1993). Successful cooperative programs are also described in the Hawaii schools (Hirokawa et al., 1999). An interesting approach receiving attention in some school districts is site-based management, in which teachers and administrators jointly determine rules, procedures, and policy for a particular school through collaborative processes that are linked to collective bargaining (Rubin and Rubin, 1997). Although systematic data have not yet been collected and published, it is quite likely that win-win programs similar to those described here are under way in a large proportion of collective bargaining jurisdictions.

Techniques for PDM

Many different, but related tools or mechanisms have been developed for achieving the positive participation of unions and management in making organizational and individual decisions. The earliest roots of PDM may be traced to efforts in manufacturing industries to improve productivity by involving workers. Scanlon plans, named after Joseph Scanlon, their initial proponent, were among the first efforts to establish union-management committees to develop ideas and proposals for reducing production costs, with a portion of the savings to be shared by workers (Kochan, 1980: 428–430). Cooperative union-management relationships also developed approximately three decades ago with the purpose of addressing health and safety issues. The enactment of the Occupational Health and Safety Act of 1970 created strong incentives for labor-management cooperation on health and safety. A third precursor of contemporary labor-management participation was quality-of-work-life programs, which first appeared in the early 1970s and were actively promoted by the National Commission on Productivity.

Health and safety committees and quality-of-work-life team approaches continue to be found in federal, state, and local jurisdictions. However, many of the most popular collaborative mechanisms today evolved from the quality circle movement of the early 1980s. Quality circles (QCs) are small groups of employees who meet regularly to develop suggestions for improving work procedures, interpersonal interactions, product quality, or other concerns. Their major contributions have been identified as boosting employee and organizational performance by improving employees' attitudes, behavior, and job effectiveness (Ouchi, 1981; Griffin, 1988). QCs soon functioned widely in government at all levels, but their use tailed off by the end of the 1980s. Unions were not major players in the QC movement, but they have been key participants in certain individual quality efforts (e.g., the IRS-NTEU Joint Quality Improvement Process). A related tool for cooperation and participation is the process improvement team (PIT), which consists of large numbers of employees assembled on a temporary basis to attack a specific designated problem. PITs have been used extensively at Department of Defense installations (GERR Special Report, 1990).

The major quality initiative of the early 1990s was total quality management

(TQM). Principally propelled by management, TQM embraces a participative decision-making strategy that focuses on continuous product and service improvement, prevention of errors, and customer satisfaction. Various cooperative strategies may be employed under TQM to involve and empower employees and, in bargaining jurisdictions, their unions (Levine, 1992; Verma and Cutcher-Gershenfeld, 1996: 223–227).

Another vehicle for participative decision making is gainsharing. Related to profit sharing in the private sector and isolated "productivity bargaining" experiments in the 1970s and 1980s, gainsharing plans distribute to bargaining unit members a portion of dollars saved from work rule changes, process improvements, and other efficiencies. Gainsharing arrangements are typically negotiated by the union and management and placed in the collective bargaining contract. For example, in Philadelphia transit workers negotiated a 3.5 percent pay increase in exchange for $18 million in health care cost savings, and in Michigan state prison guards agreed to a plan in which increases in the cost of groups health insurance were pegged to wage increases (lower insurance cost growth translated into larger pay increases) (Walters, 1994). Interest in similar gainsharing arrangements grew throughout the 1990s.

Probably the most widely adopted strategy for structuring participation is the labor-management committee (LMC). A LMC involves cooperative efforts between a union and management to resolve troublesome problems or issues that are not or cannot be attended to through collective bargaining. IRS and NTEU pioneered the LMC in the federal government and continue to use it successfully in a variety of contexts. There are strong similarities between LMCs and the partnership councils (also known as labor-management partnerships) called for in all federal agencies by Clinton's Executive Order 12871. Both approaches, for example, push decision making to as low a level of the organizational hierarchy as feasible, and both employ win-win principles. Indeed, the name of the game is not as important as the way it is played. Most of the initiatives that represent something relatively new and promising in labor-management relations are the ones that involve meaningful participation in decision making.

However, a much longer-lived technique for resolving contract disputes and other disagreements between labor and management deserves mention, because it, too, employs the principles of "Getting to Yes." Alternative dispute resolution (ADR) has taken the form of mediation, fact finding, and arbitration for many years in public sector labor relations. Since the 1990s ADR has been increasingly applied to resolving conflicts between and among public employees, supervisors, citizens, and other stakeholders outside the courtroom and collective bargaining processes. The use of ADR in federal agencies was codified and encouraged by the Administrative Dispute Resolution Act of 1990 and the Negotiated Rulemaking Act of 1990. A great many possible procedures are possible, all of them incorporating significant interest-based negotiating principles (Bingham, 1996). ADR is not uncommonly applied to grievance resolution in the public sector. One of the major benefits of ADR is to discourage or weed out frivolous or "frequent filer" complaints that constipate conventional grievance processes, thereby saving significant amounts of time and financial resources.

Carnevale (1993) describes one ADR approach in the U.S. Postal Service's Oklahoma City area. The program, called Union-Management Pairs (UMP), is based on teams consisting of one representative each from management and the National Association of Letter Carriers union. The UMPs interact with union stewards and front-line supervisors to settle contract disputes or violations quickly at the lowest possible level of the organization. Results have been impressive, with the number of formal grievances dropping from more than 1100 before the program was initiated to fewer than 10 after adoption. The U.S. Merit Systems Protection Board (MSPB) adopted an ADR policy in 1987. The rate of early settlement for grievance appeals leaped from 18 percent in 1985 to 50 percent throughout the 1990s (US MSPB, 1999: 10). An ADR approach in the Postal Service's Lansing, Michigan, Mail Sorting Center helped eliminate nearly all of a 2000-grievance backlog within 1 year and, through jointly established training sessions for all supervisors and stewards, has helped keep the grievance inflow rate at a greatly reduced level (Verma and Cutcher-Gershenfeld, 1996: 230–232).

Impediments to Participative Decision Making

If, as the foregoing implies, PDM is the wave of the future in public sector labor-management relations, why has it not been adopted in a larger number of bargaining jurisdictions? It is because several major obstacles are poised to seal the doom of participation initiatives. Most of them have been noted. The NLRA premise of adversarial relations between labor and management casts legal and structural barriers in the path of PDM in those jurisdictions that are modeled on private sector law. The expansion of the federal scope of bargaining by Executive Order 12871 is helpful, but significant exclusions that would be useful topics for PDM remain. In conjunction with an imbalance in bargaining power associated with the prohibition against negotiating union security provisions and wages and benefits, these factors tend to discourage collaboration and win-win expectations.

An even greater disincentive to PDM is the legacy of mutual suspicion and distrust between managers and union leaders at all levels of government. Management's almost innate distrust of and discomfort with unions is amplified by a fear of losing authority and control in the workplace (Levine, 1992:110–111), particularly among middle managers. But cooperation with employees requires cooperation with employee organizations. Union leaders themselves, many of whom cut their teeth on fighting management, fear that consultative and participation proposals by management are wolves dressed up in sheep's clothing who will seek to obtain concessions, eliminate jobs, weaken union power, and even displace the union as the voice for employees.

Collaboration requires the placing of PDM and conventional collective bargaining within their respective spheres of responsibility. Traditionally, unions have fulfilled their organizational purpose by representing members of the bargaining unit in collective bargaining, grievance, and other dispute resolution procedures. Collective bargaining continues under collaborative ventures. PDM opens up a new interactive arena, but which problems and issues should be addressed with interest-based approaches and which should be hammered out at the bargaining table? This dilemma also presents role conflicts for labor and management representatives, who must try to make the transition back and forth from adversarial interactions to cooperation. As one union official said, "Its hard to represent someone who's being screwed in the morning and then flip the switch and be buddies with management in the afternoon, when we are still angry" (quoted in Ban, 1995: 144). Should the union designate "partnership stewards" for cooperative activities with management and "grievance stewards" for traditional adversarial relations? Clearly a separation of roles should be maintained, with issues suitable for cooperative resolutions assigned to PDM and conventional differences of opinion involving wages, benefits, and working conditions settled at the bargaining table (Reeves, 1997).

Implementation of PDM techniques requires a significant and sustained commitment of time and resources. The U.S. system of democratic governance is not especially well suited to long-term commitments. Elected officials come into office with their own agendas, looking to make a difference. Functioning PDM efforts may present a tempting target for breaking with past initiatives. Appointed officials at all levels of government come and go rapidly, typically with little or no interest in championing existing programs such as PDM. The finite nature of collective bargaining, which is usually structured in terms of a 2- or 3-year contract, discourages a long-term perspective (Lobel, 1992). And variable economic situations can disrupt PDM, particularly when budget shortfalls arise. PDM is not a quick fix for the problems that beset labor-management relations. It requires years of persistent effort and hard work for PDM programs to overcome a history of stormy interactions and the weighty objects thrown in their path by the vicissitudes of American government and politics.

CONCLUSION

Effective organizations of the future will be those that have the capability to respond and adapt to a rapidly changing environment. This is just as true for government agencies and departments as it is for firms and nonprofits. An adaptive organization—sometimes referred to as a high-performance organization—requires flexible work designs and processes so that human and financial resources can be applied as needed to cope with a variable environment. A traditional key role of unions has been to limit management authority so that members of the bargaining unit are not treated arbitrarily or unfairly. This has been accomplished through restrictive collective bargaining contract provisions that effectively reduce the scope of management authority, such as well-defined work rules and procedures, staffing requirements, and seniority rules. The dominant approach in the traditional union-management venue consists of adversarial encounters at the negotiating table and challenges to management interpretation of the contract through the grievance system. Today, an organization attempting to function effectively and efficiently within such a traditional labor-management environment is in a highly disadvantageous position. As management's reluctant partner, the traditional union can stymie adaptive endeavors by assiduously working to the contract, litigating, and frequently grieving management actions. Government can hardly be "reinvented" under such circumstances.

The clear and pressing need is for true partnering through teamwork, cooperative problem solving, and participative decision making. Despite the substantial impediments in the path to their adoption and successful implementation, these labor-management innovations hold a great deal of promise for redefining the workplace of the future. Unions continue to exhibit a strong profile in the public sector. If government is to be reinvented, the unions must be major players. It will be extremely difficult for unions to play a positive role in reinventing government and public work if they blindly adhere to the practices of the past. As Sulzner (1997: 166–167) has observed, unions need to show that they have a purpose other than enhancing the private, economic interests of their members. Management, too, must forgo a measure of authority and autonomy when participative decision-making programs are adopted. Cooperation, after all, is unlikely to be effective if it is mandated. Where present, unions must be positively engaged. Given the marked commonality of interests, all participants are required to make certain concessions for the good of public service.

The potential payoff from successful PDM is substantial. It promises to improve the quality of public services at all levels of government and to enhance the climate of labor-management relations and the quality of work life for involved employees (Kearney and Hays, 1994). Mutual gain undertakings also have potentially broader implications for reestablishing and elevating civic and social values (Delaney, 1996). Participation in workplace decisions may encourage citizen-employees to intensify their levels of political and civic participation and could lead, ultimately, to improved self-governance. More pragmatically, it is one of the few options available for improving government productivity and service quality as we enter the 21st century.

REFERENCES

Allen, Robert E., and Van Norman, Kathleen L. (1996). Employee involvement programs: the noninvolvement of unions revisited. *Journal of Labor Research. XVII* (Summer): 479–495.

Ball, Carolyn (1996). Is labor-management cooperation possible in the public sector without a change in the law? *Journal of Collective Negotiations. 25*(1): 23–30.

Ban, Carolyn (1995). Unions, management, and the NPR. In *Inside the Reinvention Machine.* Donald F. Kettl and John J. DiIulio, eds. The Brookings Institution, Washington, D.C.

Bell, Martin, and Litscher, Jon E. (1998). Consensus bargaining in Wisconsin state government: A new approach to labor negotiation. *Public Personnel Management. 27* (Spring): 39–50.

Berzon, Judith R. et al. (1999). Reinventing local government together. [www.alliance.napawash.org].

Bingham, Lisa B. (1996). Negotiating for the public good. In *Handbook of Public Administration,* 2nd ed. (James L. Perry, ed.). Jossey-Bass, San Francisco.

Brainerd, Richard (1998). Interest-based bargaining: labor and management working together in Ramsey County, Minnesota. *Public Personnel Management. 27* (Spring): 51–68

Bryson, William et al. (1999). The Miami story: The pros and cons of the cooperative process. [www.alliance.napawash.org].

Carnevale, David G. (1993). Root dynamics of alternative dispute resolution: an illustrative case in the U.S. Postal Service. *Public Administration Review. 53* (Sept.–Oct.): 455–461.

Cooke, William N. (1990). Factors influencing the effect of joint union-management programs in employee-supervisor relations. *Industrial and Labor Relations Review. 43* (July): 587–603.

Delaney, John T. (1996). Workplace cooperation: Current problems, new approaches. *Journal of Labor Research. XVII* (Winter): 45–61.

Doucouliagos, Chris (1995). Worker participation and productivity in labor-managed and participatory capitalist firms: A meta-analysis, *Industrial and Labor Relations Review. 49* (October): 58–77.

Dunlop Commission (1994). *Report and Recommendations of the Commission on the Future of Worker-Management Relations.* U.S. Department of Labor, Washington, D.C.

Eaton, Adrienne E. (1994). The survival of employee participation programs in unionized settings. *Industrial and Labor Relations Review. 47* (April): 371–389.

Eaton, Adrienne E., and Voos, Paula B. (1992). Unions and contemporary innovations in work organization, compensation, and employee participation. In *Unions and Economic Competitiveness* (Paula B. Voos and Lawrence Mishel, eds.). Armonk N.Y. M. E. Sharpe.

Ferris Frank, and Cooper, Richard (1994). Two views of one agency: The IRS and NTEU: National treasury employees union. *The Public Manager. 23:* 27–31.

Fisher, Roger and Ury, William (1981). *Getting to Yes.* Penguin Books, New York.

Freeman, Richard B. (1996). Through public sector eyes: employee attitudes toward public sector labor relations in the United States. In *Public Sector Employment in a Time of Transition* (Dale Belman, Morley Gunderson, and Douglas Hyatt, eds.). IRRA, Madison, Wis.

Gabris, Gerald T., and Kenneth, M. (1986). Personnel reforms and formal participation structures: The case of Biloxi merit councils. *Review of Public Personnel Administration. 7* (Summer): 99–114.

GERR Special Report (1990). *Employee-Management Cooperation in the Federal Service: A Selective Look.* Bureau of National Affairs, Washington, D.C.

Griffin, Ricky (1988). Consequences of quality circles in an industrial setting: A longitudinal assessment. *Academy of Management Journal. 31*(2): 338–358.

Hirokawa, Rhoda et al. (1999). Implementing statewide bargaining and cooperation at the local level. [www.alliance.napawash.org].

Juravich, Tom, Harris, Howard, and Brooks, Andrea (1993). Mutual gains? Labor and management evaluate their employee involvement programs. *Journal of Labor Research. 14* (Spring): 165–185.

Kearney, Richard C., and Hays, Steven W. (1994). Labor-management relations and participative decision making: Toward a new paradigm. *Public Administration Review. 54* (Jan.–Feb.): 44–50.

Kelly, Eileen P. (1998). Historical perspectives on ideological and legal challenges to labor-management participation efforts. *International Journal of Organization Theory and Behavior. 1*(4): 459–479.

Kochan, Thomas A. (1980). *Collective Bargaining and Industrial Relations: From Theory to Policy and Practice.* Richard D. Erwin, Homewood, Ill.

Kochan, Thomas A., and Useem, Michael, eds. (1992). *Transforming Organizations.* Oxford University Press, New York.

Kolaraska, L., and Aldrich, H. (1980). Exit, Voice, and Silence: Consumers' and Managers' Responses to Organizational Decline. *Organizational Studies.* (March): 41–58.

Lane, Cathie M. (1996). Bittersweet Partnerships. *Government Executive.* (February): 41–44.

Lawler, Edward E., III, and Mohrman, Susan A. (1985). Quality circles after the fad. *Harvard Business Review. 85* (Jan.–Feb.): 65–71.

Levine, David I. (1995). *Reinventing the Workplace: How Business and Employees Can Both Win.* The Brookings Institution, Washington, D.C.

Levine, Marvin J. (1992). Labor and management response to total quality management. *Labor Law Journal. 42* (February): 107–116.

Levine, Marvin J. (1997). The union role in labor-management cooperation. *Journal of Collective Negotiations. 26*(3): 203–222.

Lobel, Ira B. (1992). Labor-management cooperation: A critical view. *Labor Law Journal. 42* (May): 281–289.

Marshall, June et al., (1999). Federal experience in interest-based bargaining. [www.alliance.napawash.org].

Mohrman, Sue A., and Lawler, Edward E. (1988). Participative managerial behavior and organizational change. *Journal of Organizational Change Management. 1*(1): 45–59.

Morris, James, and Steers, Richard (1980). Structural influences on organizational commitment. *Journal of Vocational Behavior. 17:* 50–57.

National Commission on State and Local Public Service (1993). *Hard Truths/Tough Choices.* Nelson A. Rockefeller Institute of Government, Albany, N.Y.

Osterman, Paul (1994). How common is workplace transformation and who adopts it? *Industrial and Labor Relations Review. 47*(2): 173–188.

Ouchi, W. (1981). *Theory Z.* Addison-Wesley, Reading, Mass.

Parsons, Patrick A., Belcher, Jerry, and Jackson, Tom (1998). A labor-management approach to health care cost savings: The Peoria experience. *Public Personnel Management. 27* (Spring): 23–38.

Partnership posing problems (1997). *Government Executive.* (August): 6.
Peightal, Patricia et al. (1998). Labor-management cooperation: City of Portland, Maine. *Public Personnel Management. 27* (Spring): 85–92.
Perry, James L., and Lois R. Wise (1990). The motivational bases of public service. *Public Administration Review. 50* (May/June): 367–373.
Reeves, T. Zane (1997). Labor-management partnerships in the public sector. In *Public Personnel Management: Current Concerns, Future Challenges,* 2nd ed. (Carolyn Ban and Norma M. Riccucci, eds.). Longman, New York.
Rogers, Joel (1994). Talking union. *The Nation. 259* (December 26): 784–785.
Rubin, Barry M., and Rubin, Richard S. (1997). A heuristic model of collaboration within labor-management relations. *Journal of Collective Negotiations. 26*(3): 185–202.
Schwochau, Susan et al. (1997). Employee participation and assessments of support for organizational policy changes. *Journal of Labor Research. XVIII* (Summer): 378–401.
Straw, Ronnie J. and Heckscher, Charles C. (1984). QUs: New working relationship in the communication industry. *Labor Studies Journal. 8* (Winter): 261–274.
Sulzner, George T. (1997). New roles, new strategies: Reinventing the public union. In *Public Personnel Management: Current Concerns, future Challenges,* 2nd ed. (Carolyn Ban and Norman R. Riccucci, eds.). Longman, New York.
U.S. Bureau of Labor Statistics (1999). *The Employment Situation* (October, 1999): 1–25.
U.S. G.A.O. (1991). *Federal Labor Relations: A Program in Need of Reform.* U.S. Government Printing Office, Washington, D.C.
U.S. G.A.O. (1994). *U.S. Postal Service: Labor-Management Problems Persist on the Workroom Floor.* GAO/GGD 94-201A, Washington, D.C.
U.S. Merit Systems Protection Board (1999). *Building a Foundation for Merit in the 21st Century.* U.S.M.S.P.B., Washington, D.C.
U.S. Secretary of Labor's Task Force (1996). *Working Together for Public Service.* U.S. Government Printing Office, Washington, D.C.
Verma, Anil, and Cutcher-Gershenfeld, Joel (1996). Workplace innovations and systems change. In *Public Sector Employment in a Time of Transition* (Dale Belman, Morley Gunderson, and Douglas Hyatt, eds.). IRRA Press, Madison, Wis.
Verma, Anil, and McKersie, Robert B. (1987). Employee involvement: The implications of noninvolvement by unions. *Industrial and Labor Relations Review. 40* (July): 556–568.
Wagner, John A. (1994). Participation effects on performance and satisfaction: A reconsideration of research evidence. *Academy of Management Review. 19* (April): 312–330.
Walters, Jonathan (1994). The trade-off between benefits and pay. *Governing.* (December): 55–56.
Walton, Richard E., and McKersie, Robert B. (1965). *A Behavioral Theory of Labor Negotiations.* McGraw-Hill, New York.
Wishnick, Yale S., and Wishnick, T. Kathleen (1993). Collective bargaining and educational reform: Establishing a labor-management partnership. *Journal of Collective Negotiations. 22*(1): 1–11.

12

Developmental Performance Appraisal: Feedback, Interview, and Disciplinary Techniques

Dennis M. Daley
Department of Political Science and Public Administration, North Carolina State University, Raleigh, North Carolina

Performance appraisal is a conscientious effort at formally, rationally, and objectively organizing our assessments of others. In doing so, it is focused on the task of enhancing job-relatedness. Eliminating measurement and rating errors and structuring the decision-making process itself in order to accomplish this are the dual foci of appraisal research.

As a decision-making tool, performance appraisal is designed to structure the assessment process positively. By formally focusing attention solely on the objective, job-related criteria for assessing performance, the manager is provided with the means for making appropriate decisions that rationally contribute to the organization's and individual's effectiveness and well-being.

When the modern civil service reform movement switched its attention from preventing political interference as a means for assuring "good government" to developing administrative techniques, research first focused on selection and then on performance rating. The performance appraisal process became the means for aiding in decisions on pay, promotion, training, retention, reassignment, reinstatement, demotion, and dismissal and for validating personnel selection techniques (Landy and Farr, 1980).

The purposes in which performance appraisal can be employed are numerous. However, these can be grouped into two broad categories—judgmental and developmental (Cummings and Schwab, 1973). Although both developmental and judgmental appraisals have enhanced productivity as their goal, they approach it in two quite distinct fashions. A developmental approach coaches and mentors an employee. Its goal is improvement through process or means. A judgmental approach rewards and punishes. Its goal is also improvement; however, it aims to achieve this through the specification of desired results or ends.

Judgmental appraisal follows the management systems or command and control model of authority and is quite explicitly linked to extrinsic rewards (and punishments). For the most part, judgmental approaches are intricately tied to pay-for-performance. This has proved to be an important limitation on their use among public sector agencies. Even where valid appraisal instruments are used by adequately trained supervisors, the failure to reward can undermine the entire system.

The failure to invest in adequate reward systems and training (especially a problem among public sector agencies) has proved to be a disincentive in using a judgmental approach. In addition, a judgmental role interferes with a supervisor's need to create trust and teamwork among employees. Developmental appraisal is seen as means by which supervisors can engage in "score keeping" while maintaining a strong organizational commitment among employees.

DEVELOPMENTAL APPRAISAL

Developmental methods take an employee's basic competence for granted (the coordination of recruitment and selection with position or job analysis techniques is deemed sufficient to handle this). Hence, developmental appraisals focus on adding value to the employee. They are humanistic in nature and operate on an intrinsic motivational level (although developmental opportunities may also entail substantial present or potential extrinsic rewards). More specifically, the performance appraisal serves as an action device or needs assessment instrument triggering employee training (Herbert and Doverspike, 1990). Linking appraisal to training can prove difficult even in conjunction with the most objective appraisal instrument (Daley, 1983, 1987).

Development focuses on an individuals' potential rather than his or her current level of skills and capabilities. Hence, it is essential in such assessments to consider the question of growth for what? Whether viewed from an organizational or individual perspective, the goal toward which this potential is directed needs examination. Organizationally, the need for developing this potential must be determined. Basically, will the organization accrue some benefit from developing an individual's potential? The human resources aspects of an organization's strategic planning process should serve to provide the answers to these questions. If an organization is to provide an employee with enhanced skills and abilities, it is important that the organization perceive what reward it expects to receive from this process.

Individuals hope to receive feedback for improving their performance from the appraisal process. They also do not generally perceive an objective assessment as threatening. To a great extent this latter attitude can be attributed to the relatively high opinion individuals tend to hold of their own abilities. There is even some evidence for managers seeking out negative comments (Ashford and Tsui, 1991).

This desire for objective appraisal is, however, intricately tied to an individual's sense of self-identity. In addition, individuals are keenly aware that most appraisals are used for allocating highly desired extrinsic rewards. All of these factors combine to set the stage for an array of potentially divisive individual-organizational conflicts (Mohrman et al., 1989; Murphy and Cleveland, 1995).

DEVELOPMENT AND JUDGMENT

Individuals desire development and rewards; organizations desire to develop and reward their employees. Unfortunately, the information necessary for achieving one of these goals may hinder achievement of the other. If individuals detail their weaknesses so that they can receive needed training in order to improve their performance, they may in the process lose out on valued rewards. Obversely, in order to allocate rewards efficiently among employees, organizations may miss out on important considerations that vitally affect their future (Longenecker and Nykodym, 1996).

Where a substantial degree of employee loyalty and trust exists, appraisal systems may successfully merge judgmental and developmental purposes. Such appraisal systems rely upon objective measures chosen through a highly participative, almost consensual supervisor-employee understanding (Mikkeisen et al., 1997).

Clearly, it may not be possible to mix judgmental and developmental purposes in the same appraisal process (Cascio, 1982; Hyde and Smith, 1982). Cognitive research has long indicated that managers are influenced by the purpose of the appraisal in making their judgments (Landy and Farr, 1980; Meyer et al., 1965; Mohrman and Lawler, 1983; Murphy and Cleveland, 1995; Daley, 1992) The purpose for which an appraisal is to be used shapes and frames a manager's assessment of an individual. Even with the most objective appraisal instruments the criteria take on a more subtle and specific perspective.

Use of multiple appraisals is one suggested solution to this dilemma (Meyer, 1991). Instead of employing one appraisal and using it willy-nilly for a multitude of purposes, each specific purpose can be the focus of a separate appraisal process. Yet, even here it is important to maintain employee perceptions that the systems are indeed independent of one another—an almost impossible condition (Cummings, 1973). Even so, an organization in establishing a performance appraisal process may have to choose between serving judgmental and developmental purposes.

The validity of appraisals completed with one goal in mind is questionable when they are subsequently used in the assessment of another. Even if the measurement factors employed were to remain identical, supervisors might assess them differently in light of a different purpose they were being asked to assess. In contrasting developmental and judgmental purposes with the extent of agency investment in the performance appraisal process Balfour (1992) found few distinctions. Investment was found to make for virtually no significant difference among employee attitudes. The judgmental attitudes predominated regardless of whether an agency emphasized developmental purposes or not.

Separate, multiple appraisals have been proposed as a possible solution. However, the increased costs and workload envisioned under a scheme of multiple appraisals are formidable. Would the potential benefits of multiple appraisals be worth such efforts? Even if separate appraisals were introduced, would managers and employees perceive them as indeed being separate and distinct?

FEEDBACK

Feedback is integral to the performance management process. Whether judgmental or developmental purposes are the focus of the management process, feedback is an essential mechanism for their working. Without an adequate means for informing employees of their performance, desired changes in motivation and productivity cannot occur.

Performance management feedback can take place in a number of ways. However, the primary means through which feedback occurs is through the performance appraisal interview. The appraisal interview is a formal meeting of employee and supervisor that is explicitly devoted to the discussion of the employee's job performance. Preparations necessary for properly conducting an appraisal interview along with the requisite interviewing skills for carrying it out are, therefore, important elements in the supervisor's job domain.

Feedback is an essential component in the learning cycle. It also plays a pivotal role in the performance management process. The feedback from the performance management process serves as a productivity tool for managers; it provides employees with an indication of how they are doing.

From an organizational perspective, feedback serves as a means for enhancing productivity. It helps to convey to the worker the message of what is to be done. Feedback on job performance is a vital mechanism for the organization in other ways as well. It can be a means for clearing up misunderstandings and for providing supervisors with a better picture or sense of what is going on. Under a "worst-ease scenario," feedback represents the organization's good faith effort at assisting poor performers in their improvement.

From an employee perspective, feedback is itself a means of intrinsic motivation. The feeling of accomplishment derived from doing a job and doing it well can be quite stimulating. It helps foster a sense of craftsmanship that can rather mystically transform an ordinary job into a professional calling.

Research studies, conducted in a number of settings and under widely differing circumstances, link feedback to increased productivity and enhanced worker motivation (Ilgen et al., 1979; Greiner et al., 1981: 158–160; Yeager et al., 1985; Alexander et al., 1984; Murphy and Cleveland, 1995). In addition, feedback is also found to be an important element in the theory of goal setting (Locke et al., 1981; Roberts and Reed, 1996).

There is relatively clear evidence that employees seek out feedback on their performance (Ashford and Cummings, 1981; Longenecker and Gioia, 1988; Ashford and Tsui, 1991). However, the desire for feedback is tempered by considerations of what impression it may make on those being asked. The act of seeking feedback itself marks and makes more vivid the substantive nature of feedback being requested than would otherwise be the case. The request for feedback serves to spotlight the performance itself uniquely (Ashford and Tsui, 1991; Morrison and Bies, 1991).

Psychologically, there is a heuristic tendency to take a specific piece of good or bad performance as an example of an individual employee's normal or typical work. Although an employee may see such vividness as desirable when performance has been good, employees whose work has been marginal or even bad are less likely to want that drawn to the attention and into the long-term memories of their supervisors.

There are a number of ways other than interviews with which to provide employee feedback vis-à-vis job performance. One of the various notions entailed in the term *critical incidents* suggests the immediate feedback of examples of good and bad behavior to the employee. This is also advocated in all the basic "management by walking around" schemes (Ouchi, 1981; Pascale and Athos, 1981; Peters and Waterman, 1982). Of course, this is not a new concept; it can be traced back, at least, to Frederick Taylor's (1911) recommendation that his functional teachers (foremen) step in immediately whenever they saw an employee performing a task incorrectly and demonstrate how to do it right.

For feedback purposes, the performance appraisal interview is the next most often advocated method after the critical incident approach. Although it lacks the immediacy of the critical incident technique, it compensates for this with a more measured or well-rounded evaluation of employee job performance. Examining an individual's efforts over an entire management cycle allows a more balanced picture of his or her entire performance to be drawn, and under less hasty circumstances.

The performance appraisal interview is a formal meeting of employee and supervisor devoted entirely to a discussion of the employee's job performance. This can be an exciting or traumatic experience—for both the employee and the supervisor.

Objective appraisals, especially those employing a management by objectives (MBO) approach, are explicitly built around a participative management concept. Although such participative approaches are designed to encourage positive employee-supervisor interactions, even in these systems the appraisal interview often proves difficult. For the most part, performance appraisal systems involve judgmental rather than developmental purposes. As a result, feedback is often focused on what can only be deemed questions of the individual's personal worth and identity rather than topics addressing means for assisting the employee in improving performance.

The feedback process can involve important consequences for the entire organization. Systems in which feedback is seen to be positively linked to goals are also likely to be viewed as being more concerned with the attainment of those goals. Hence, organizational support, supervisory effectiveness, and even the usefulness of the MBO technique itself are all accorded a greater degree of efficacy when used in conjunction with an adequate means of employee feedback. In addition, individual job satisfaction is enhanced when feedback is provided (Aplin and Schoderbek, 1976; Roberts and Reed, 1996).

Supervisory training in the art of providing feedback is an essential requirement, especially as few individuals exhibit a natural talent in this area. In fact, it is the lack of training in this process that substantially contributes to supervisors' sense of unease when faced with the need to conduct a management interview. Simulations, role playing exercises, and behavioral modeling can all be used to train supervisors to conduct management interviews (Martin and Bartol, 1986).

Ideally, training should include both supervisors and employees. They should be apprized of their individual roles and ways they interact with one another. This also provides them with an understanding of or an expectation as to what the appraisal interview entails. Training should include not only the mechanics of the appraisal system; i.e., job analysis, setting of performance standards, ways to use the forms, etc., but the behavioral skills for motivation as well (Pajer, 1979).

INTERVIEW PREPARATION

The performance interview should not just happen. It is an important management tool requiring careful preparation and planning. The tendency, in part because it is an often unpleasant experience for both supervisors and employees, is to treat the interview as an ad hoc event. This only contributes to and perpetuates its undesirable features and reputation for failure.

The physical and psychological situation in which the interview is to occur must also receive serious consideration. Attribution theory indicates that situational circumstances have important interpretational effects on the performance management process (Knowlton and Mitchell, 1980; Feldman, 1981; Lord and Smith, 1983; DeVader, et al. 1986). The purposes for which a management interview is intended as well as the conditions or environment in which it occurs are intricate parts of the assessment process. A number of other employee, supervisory, job, and organizational factors can also be seen to affect the interview (Clement and Stevens, 1986).

The purpose underlying the use of the performance appraisal influences how employees as well as supervisors approach the process. The distinction between a judgmental and a developmental process is not trivial. Different purposes lead to different assessments. Even when an objective appraisal instrument is employed, the supervisor approaches its terms and behavioral anchors in light of the specific purpose it is viewed as serving.

The characteristics of individual employees can be significant factors in determining performance ratings. The extent to which employees are actually experienced in doing a job may matter as much as or more than their actual level of job performance. Newer employees may be allowed greater latitude than those who "should know better." In addition, the personal needs of an employee can play a role in the assignment of ratings. A higher rating may be needed to build up an employee's confidence; a lower rating than objectively warranted may serve to instill caution or humility.

Similarly, the experience an individual has as a supervisor can also be an important factor. More experienced supervisors are often more comfortable with the employee-supervisor relationship. When it comes to performance appraisals, they are often more at ease in exercising their authority and in fulfilling their responsibilities. In addition, they possess a greater experiential base vis-à-vis employee performance with which to guide their assessment of job behavior. The development of specific skills in conducting the performance management process, including interviews, is also a factor. Finally, the personal and organizational needs the supervisor brings to the table may also play a substantial role.

In addition to an employee's performance in a job, the nature of the job itself can influence the appraisal and interview process. Numerous job- or position-related factors can influence the way an individual's performance is assessed. How routine are the tasks performed? Do individual employees have clear perceptions of their job role? How new is the position? The answers to questions such as these help frame the environment for the appraisal process and set the tone in which the interview is conducted.

Organizational culture and climate help shape the entire process from beginning to end. The time available in which to actually conduct the interview (which is influenced by the number of interviews to be conducted) sets the boundaries on what topics can be adequately covered. Finally, organizational or personal politics may be involved.

Preparation for an employee interview should be continuous. Keeping a critical incident log on individual employee performances can greatly aid in this task. This also enables the supervisor to respond with feedback immediately—correcting errors and acclaiming successes. Although critical incident logs entail additional paperwork and suffer from many of the problems commonly associated with essay appraisals, they can also help prevent the introduction of rater errors into the management process (Pajer, 1979).

Preparation for the interview should also actively include the employee. Advance notice as well as the scheduling of a mutually convenient time are important considerations. Both the supervisor and employee need sufficient time prior to the actual interview that both can conscientiously analyze and evaluate the employee's performance (Pajer, 1979).

For the feedback interview itself, Robert Pajer (1979) recommends that supervisors prepare a script of what it is they want to accomplish in the interview. Although is unnecessary and perhaps even counterproductive to follow such a script rigidly, it provides a structured outline with which to assure that the interview covers all the important points.

In terms of developmental opportunities, supervisors should have an assessment of not only the employee's needs but the organization's capability for meeting and resolving them. Specific plans for employee development set a positive tone in an interview. This is an especially important consideration when indicating to employees "areas in need of improvement." In such circumstances it is absolutely essential, as well as legally required, to provide accompanying corrective actions.

Finally, the physical location where the interview is conducted must be taken into consideration. The physical conditions pertaining to the interview should be chosen so that they help reduce the stress inherent in the performance appraisal process.

Employees do not want to experience an appraisal interview, even one with a developmental focus, in a crowd. An enclosed office space that assures privacy is called for under these circumstances. Even within this setting it is important to put the employee at ease—if that is the desired message the supervisor wishes to convey. Instead of confronting an employee from across a desk, using a more informal conversational arrangement can work better. In addition, the interview should be free of interruptions, either by a phone or by unexpected visits (Pajer, 1976).

INTERVIEW TECHNIQUES

Having set the tone for the interview, the supervisor begins by providing a general assessment of the employee's performance evaluation. Each distinct dimension is then examined with the employee being afforded opportunities to participate in the discussion. It is important that the interview remain an open process. The interview is a means for managers to obtain additional information on organizational and individual performance. Maintaining an open process in which the "conclusions" are still subject to change can assist in enhancing organizational effectiveness. Even what are initially deemed as "self-serving excuses" may, in fact, turn out to be valid arguments that fairness and justice demand be taken into consideration.

Hence, conducting a performance interview calls upon the supervisor to employ a number of interpersonal communications skills avidly. First, the style in which a supervisor chooses to conduct an interview is an important determinant of what follows (Clement and Stevens, 1986). Norman R.F. Maier (1958, 1976) distinguishes three interview styles—tell and sell, tell and listen, and problem solving—with a preference for the last. These approaches run the gamut from judgmental to developmental.

The tell and sell approach sees the supervisor as a judge handing down a sentence. Communications is centered on convincing the employee to accept the verdict. This is an authoritarian style. It assumes that employees appreciate such frank and honest appraisals. However, unless employees respect their supervisors (and trust the organization), hostility and the development of evasive behavior can result.

The tell and listen style attempts to integrate the judgmental pronouncement of the management evaluation with a hearing of employee grievances by the supervisor. Unfortunately, in a tell and listen format the listening is viewed more as a means for allowing the employee to "let off steam" than as a legitimate means for redressing grievances. However, even this limited listening can help to reduce employee stress.

The listen component of the interview is used symbolically to express the organization's acceptance of the employee as a member. In essence, even when the specific message is negative, the tell and listen style is designed to convey a sense of belonging and job security. This long-term commitment implied by a tell and listen approach can reduce resistance to change.

Since the supervisor is free to change the evaluation as well as to convey information to others in the hierarchy, the process remains somewhat open. This ability to change the evaluation can also help enhance the supervisor's standing with employees.

The problem-solving approach is an example of a developmental, participative application. It is the interview style preferred by Norman Maier as well as most other management scholars; it is also the style most favored by employees.

The problem-solving approach is designed to be a true discussion of job performance focusing primarily on stimulating employee development.

ACTIVE LISTENING

The problem-solving style involves the employment of active listening skills by the supervisor. Although this approach can contribute to employee growth, organizational problems may not necessarily be solved or solved in the manner anticipated by the supervisor.

Active listening is a technique that encompasses a wide range of verbal and nonverbal communication skills (Kikoski and Litterer, 1983; Bolton, 1986; Clement, 1987; Murphy, 1987; Kikoski, 1998). They are all aimed at creating an environment that is conducive to an employee-supervisor dialog and assists in the effective interpretation of that dialog.

As Robert Bolton (1986) notes, active listening is designed to suspend the behavioral barriers that inhibit communications. Dialogs are hindered by an array of premature judging, solution sending, and avoidance habits. Individuals reply before they have received the complete message. Unfortunately, the complexities of modern American society have instilled these actions. Although they are basically defensive mechanisms for coping with a modern world, their indiscriminate application is harmful.

Instead of listening to what is being said, individuals are engaged in evaluating the incoming messages before they have even been completely transmitted. English grammar, unlike that of such languages as German, does not force the listener to await the verb at the sentence's end in order to evaluate the meaning of the sentence's message. Individuals are also likely to respond during this process in such a manner as to affect the remainder of the message transmission: i.e., to cause the sender to change or abruptly end the message. In addition, individuals may choose to ignore the content of the message either because they prefer not to deal with it or because they deem it unimportant in comparison to what they want to say.

Nonverbal skills focus on demonstrating the listener's participation in the conversation qua listener. Physically, individuals position themselves to catch the speaker's message. The listener must treat the message very much as if it were a ball being tossed or pitched to him or her and keep attention focused on it. Such attending skills entail both posture and natural body motions. Ignoring physical distractions is also an important consideration (Bolton, 1986).

Specific verbal skills are designed to aid the listener in receiving the message and in interpreting it. These skills include those that fall into the more traditional area of deliberative communications. The translation or interpretation of the main or substantive message is the focus of attention and analysis (Bolton, 1986).

Other verbal skills—following and reflective—focus on the medium in which the message is transmitted. Although not focusing on the message's substantive content, they can be just as important. These skills are used to interpret the additional messages that emphasize, reinforce, or negate the substantive message being sent.

Following skills begin with sizing up the sender's state and then providing the appropriate climate for receiving the message. This consists of providing the attentive silence—physical and psychological—in which to listen to the message. Questions should be infrequent and open-ended. Questions are designed to clarify and encourage the conversation; they are not meant to serve as analytical vehicles (Bolton, 1986).

Reflective skills aid in the interpretation of the message. The speaker's message is paraphrased in the listener's own words in order to aid understanding and to verify its content of the speaker. The speaker's emotions need to be interwoven with the spoken message. Reflective skills serve as a reality check; they also convey the important notion of "message received" back to the sender (Bolton, 1986).

THE DEVELOPMENTAL APPRAISAL AND THE DISCIPLINARY PROCESS

Although viewed as a negative phenomenon, discipline is a form of development. Although disciplinary actions only involve a very small portion of the work force, their repercussions can be explosive. Because discipline affects the individual's basic existence through the imposition of financial punishments or termination, it is a highly emotional phenomenon that psychologically ripples out across the entire work force. It is this greater, shadow effect that an organization must be careful about. Like the criminal justice system upon which it is modeled, the disciplinary process must place its primary emphasis on the overall perception of justice. The outcome of the specific case is, to a great extent, only a secondary concern.

In contrast to the criminal justice process, an organization's disciplinary process is voluntarily accepted by the employee. The employee is always free to quit (or, as the case may be, pursue countercharges in the legal system).

Disciplinary systems exist to enforce work rules that the organization deems necessary for its proper functioning. The organization also has a disciplinary system because its focus is not to savage but to salvage the employee. Although some offenses are so severe that termination is the only recourse, most are minor infractions by otherwise valuable employees. Hence, the purpose of discipline is not to punish but to modify behavior (Odiorne, 1987).

Because of this, it is necessary that all disciplinary cases be based on well-documented incidents. The standards of evidence used must be objective and specific. Needless to say, they must also be work-related. It is also important that a disciplinary infraction be accompanied by a statement outlining the appropriate corrective action. This prevents discipline from being imposed when the problems being dealt with are really remedial training or coaching. The adherence to such standards helps establish the fairness of the disciplinary process.

The need to establish job-related documentation for undertaking disciplinary action gives rise to its association with the performance appraisal process. Although focused on negative behavior, discipline fits in with both judgmental and developmental approaches to performance appraisal. The ultimate consequences of disciplinary action are clearly judgmental in nature. The requirement to include suggested corrective action provides a developmental cast. However, a developmental approach to appraisal would most likely prefer that disciplinary cases be dealt with separately.

A separate disciplinary reporting process can be established. This would be triggered at the occurrence of a critical incident. Only at this point would a file be "opened" and a record of the specific event be made. If no other events occur or successful corrective action is undertaken, the file can become "inactive" or "closed" (legally all records must be preserved to document organizational behavior).

The fairness of a disciplinary process is attested to more by the procedural safeguards that exist than by the substantive cases it deals with. Because individual cases may include special circumstances and be subject to privacy restrictions, employees will focus on the due process accorded in determining their acceptance of the process. Hence, consistency in rule application and uniformity of treatment are essential. Equity is the key.

As a practical matter, enforcement needs to occur as soon after a disciplinary event as possible. The rule violated needs to be clearly identified along with the reason the rule exists. This clearly reinforces the importance of the relationship between the undesired behavior and the disciplinary consequences. Otherwise, intervening events may serve to mute this relationship or even be seen as moderating it. This will result in a weakening of the disciplinary process.

Similarly, the work rules must apply to all. There cannot be separate, more lax standards for high performers. Geniuses and stars may indeed be different from us mere mortals, but as long as they live and work with us, they need to abide by the common rules. High performers serve as role models. We want their better attributes and successes emulated rather than their worse.

Effective disciplinary processes usually incorporate a strategy of progressive discipline. In essence a code of work rules is promulgated. Potential infractions dealing with undesired work behavior in such matters as attendance, performance, personal conduct, safety and security, and general abuse are identified along with the penalty (or range of penalties) that will be imposed for first, second, and subsequent incidents. Although some serious infractions lead to automatic termination, most focus on remedial efforts to salvage the employee and change undesirable work behavior. Penalties for repeated offenses of even minor infractions merit progressive, harsher disciplinary action (Odiorne, 1987; Finkle, 1995).

The conduct covered under the work rules may vary from minor irritants such as tardiness and absenteeism (which become substantial problems when repeated) to breaches of safety procedures that place the lives of employees and the public at risk. It is this variation that requires the introduction of progressive or graduated responses.

Where progressive disciplinary systems are employed, each offense includes a "statute of limitations" in order to prevent earlier incidents from being used to harm salvaged employees. These "expiration dates" can vary with the seriousness of each individual infraction. In essence such a system functions similarly to insurance points for car drivers.

Progressive discipline often starts with an informal warning or verbal counseling. With an informal warning the employee is told what needs correction, but no record is made in the employee's file. Verbal counseling places a written notice that an oral warning was made into the employee's file. It documents the nature of the violation discussed and the date of the occurrence. It should also include the employee's response—acceptance or denial of the action (Finkle, 1995; Knierim, 1997).

More serious or repeated offenses can result in a formal written warning that is included in the employee's personnel file. This would document the full nature of the violation, counseling that has occurred, and expected behavioral improvements. It would also outline the consequences for the employee if he or she fails to correct that behavior. For more serious situations, suspension with pay (a strong indication that the organization still values the employee) is designed to force the employee to take time out and think about the situation (Finkle, 1995; Knierim, 1997).

Ultimately, the disciplinary process may involve the use of either suspension without pay or termination. Suspension without pay imposes a financial penalty. The loss of pay is designed to remind the employee of the hurt and seriousness that failure to reform can entail. Finally, termination may be necessary where reform has failed or the transgression is egregious (Finkle, 1995).

Progressive discipline is applied to specific actions and is designed to correct them. When an employee who has been subjected to progressive discipline for one type of behavior exhibits a new disciplinary problem, it is necessary to begin the process anew. Each type of infraction is dealt with separately. To lump all disciplinary infractions together creates an "out to get me" impression among employees and negates any successful or good faith efforts.

Organizations often develop or negotiate "price lists" that detail each infraction and the range of appropriate penalties. This gives supervisors with guidelines and employees with prior notice.

Finally, all disciplinary systems need to be monitored and periodically reviewed. The organization must monitor its imposition of disciplinary penalties in order to assure itself and its employees that they are being correctly implemented. Supervisors must be trained in the use of the disciplinary system and monitored in its use. In addition, the system needs periodic review of the work rules to be sure that they still serve a meaningful, work-related purpose (Finkle, 1995).

In administering disciplinary penalties a supervisor needs to be aware of how they fit into the organizational culture for similar offenses and its fairness. As an aid supervisors may maintain an informal record that is not a part of an employee's official file. This record can include memos of discussions and proposed solutions. If such notes are kept, the employee should be aware of exactly what they are and what they include. These are not secret dossiers (Knierim, 1997).

Computer technology allows for the construction of expert systems to aid and guide supervisors in making disciplinary decisions. An expert system consists of a series of menus linked in the form of a decision tree. At each step the supervisor is prompted with a set of questions and real-world job-related examples of their meaning. The supervisor's decision generates the next computer screen menu and its set of appropriate options.

The Florida Department of Highway Safety and Motor Vehicles employs an expert system in its disciplinary process. Many positive effects are noted in this respect. The expert system gives the supervisors a much more useful and user-friendly "manual." Since the system has the support of top management and helps document the supervisor's actions, it fosters greater confidence. Finally, it also assures more consistent and appropriate responses to specific cases (Berry et al., 1998).

CONCLUSION

Objective appraisal systems can serve both judgmental and developmental interests. In either case training in their use is imperative. Although the appraisal process will always engender a degree of fear and uncertainty among employees, developmental appraisals (especially if disciplinary matters are handled with a separate reporting system) alleviate much of this. The positive focus on employee growth helps create a shared interest in employee and supervisor.

For a developmental appraisal system to function properly, it is necessary that supervisors be trained in providing feedback. Whereas feedback is a continuous process, the performance appraisal interview is the formal, summary forum in which it occurs. Both supervisor and employee must be trained in communications skills to reap the full advantages.

Finally, discipline is development. Although it certainly has a negative connotation, it is important to see it not as punishment but as corrective training. Still, it might be wise to handle disciplinary actions in a separate reporting system.

REFERENCES

Alexander, L.R., Helms, Marilyn M., and Wilkins, Ronnie D. (1984). The relationship between supervisory communications and subordinate performance and satisfaction. *Public Personnel Management. 18*(4) (Winter): 415–429.

Aplin, John C., and Schoderbek, Peter P. (1976). MBO: Requisites for success in the public sector. *Human Resources Management. 15* (Summer): 30–36.

Ashford, Susan J., and Cummings, L.L. (1981). Strategies for knowing: When and from where do individuals seek feedback. *Academy of Management Journal.* 161–165.

Ashford, Susan J., and Tsui, Anne S. (1991). Self-regulation for managerial effectiveness: The role of active feedback seeking. *Academy of Management Journal. 34*(2) (June): 251–280.

Balfour, Danny L. (1992). Impact of agency investment in the implementation of performance appraisal. *Public Personnel Management. 1*(1) (Spring): 1–15.

Berry, Frances Stokes, Berry, William D., and Foster, Stephen K. (1998). The determinants of success in implementing an expert system in state government, *Public Administration Review. 58*(4) (July/August): 293–305.

Bolton, Robert (1986). *People Skills: How to Assert Yourself, Listen to Others, and Resolve Conflicts.* Simon & Schuster, New York.

Cascio, Wayne F. (1982). Scientific, legal, and operative imperatives of workable performance appraisal systems. *Public Personnel Management. 11*(4) (Winter): 367–375.

Clement, Ronald W. (1987). Performance appraisal: Nonverbal influences on the rating process. *Review of Public Personnel Administration. 7*(2) (Spring): 14–27.

Clement, Ronald W., and Stevens, George E. (1986). The performance appraisal interview: What, when, and how? *Review of Public Personnel Administration. 6*(2) (Spring): 43–58.

Cummings, Larry L. (1973). A field experimental study of the effects of two performance appraisal systems. *Personnel Psychology. 26:* 489–502.

Cummings, Larry L., and Schwab, Donald P. (1973). *Performance in Organizations: Determinants and Appraisal.* Scott, Foresman, Glenview, Ill.

Daley, Dennis M. (1983). Performance appraisal as a guide for training and development: A research note on the Iowa performance evaluation system. *Public Personnel Management. 12*(2) (Summer): 159–166.

Daley, Dennis M. (1987). Performance appraisal and the creation of training and development expectations: A weak link in MBO-based appraisal systems. *Review of Public Personnel Administration. 8*(1) (Fall): 1–10.

Daley, Dennis M. (1992). *Performance Appraisal in the Public Sector: Techniques and Applications.* Quorum, Westport, Conn.

DeVader, Christian L., Bateson, Allan G., and Lord, Robert G. (1986). Attribution theory: A meta-analysis of attributional hypotheses. In *Generalizing from Laboratory to Field Studies* (Edwin A. Locke, ed.). Lexington Books, Lexington, Mass.

Feldman, Jack M. (1981). Beyond attribution theory: Cognitive processes in performance appraisal. *Journal of Applied Psychology. 66:* 127–148.

Finkle, Arthur L. (1995). The practice of employee discipline. In *Handbook of Public Personnel Administration: A Review of State and Local Government Initiatives* (Jack

Rabin, Thomas Vocino, W. Bartley Hildreth, and Gerald Miller, eds.). Marcel Dekker, New York.

Greiner, John M., Hatry, Harry P., Koss, Margo P., Millar, Annie P., and Woodward, Jane P. (1981). *Productivity and Motivation.* Urban Institute, Washington, D.C.

Herbert, Glenn R., and Doverspike, Dennis (1990). Performance appraisal in the training needs analysis process: A review and critique. *Public Personnel Management. 19*(3) (Fall): 253–270.

Hyde, Albert C., and Smith, Melanie A. (1982). Performance appraisal training: Objectives, a model for change and a note of rebuttal. *Public Personnel Management. 11*(4) (Winter): 358–366.

Ilgen, Daniel R., Fisher, Cynthia D., and Taylor, M. Susan (1979). Consequences of individual feedback on behavior in organizations. *Journal of Applied Psychology. 64*(4) (August): 349–371.

Kikoski, John F. (1998). Effective communication in the performance appraisal interview: Face-to-face communication for public managers in the culturally diverse workplace, *Public Personnel Management. 27*(4) (Winter): 491–513.

Kikoski, John F., and Litterer, Joseph A. (1983). Effective communication in the performance appraisal interview. *Public Personnel Management. 12*(1) (Spring): 33–42.

Knierim, Alny (1997). Employee Discipline Troubleshooter HRNET@cornell.edu listserve. Alexander Hamilton Institute.

Knowlton, William A., Jr., and Mitchell, Terence R. (1980). Effects of causal attributions on a supervisor's evaluation of subordinate performance. *Journal of Applied Psychology. 65*(4): 459–466.

Landy, Frank J., and Farr, James L. (1980). Performance rating. *Psychological Bulletin. 87:* 72–107.

Locke, Edwin A., Shaw, K.N., Saari, L.M., and Latham, Gary P. (1981). Goal setting and task performance. *Psychological Bulletin. 90:* 125–152.

Longenecker, Clinton O., and Gioia, Dennis A. (1988). Neglected at the top—executives talk about executive appraisal. *Sloan Management Review. 29*(3): 41–47.

Longenecker, Clinton O., and Nykodym, Nick (1996). Public sector performance appraisal effectiveness: A case study. *Public Personnel Management. 25*(2) (Summer): 151–164.

Lord, Robert G., and Smith, J.E. (1983). Theoretical, information processing, and situational factors affecting attribution theory models of organization behavior. *Academy of Management Review. 8:* 50–60.

Maier, Norman R.F. (1958). Appraisal on the job: Three types of appraisal interviews. *Personnel. 54*(2) (March/April): 27–40.

Maier, Norman R.F. (1976). *The Appraisal Interview: Three Basic Approaches.* University Associates, La Jolla, Calif.

Martin, David C., and Bartol, Kathryn M. (1986). Training the raters: A key to effective performance appraisal. *Public Personnel Management. 15*(2) (Summer): 101–109.

Meyer, Herbert H. (1991). A solution to the performance appraisal feedback enigma. *Academy of Management Executive. 5*(1) (February): 68–76.

Meyer, Herbert H., Kay, Emanuel, and French, John R.P., Jr. (1965). Split-roles in performance appraisal. *Harvard Business Review. 43* (January-February): 123–129.

Mikkelsen, Aslaug, Ogaard, Torvald, and Lovrich, Nicholas P. (1997). Impact of an integrative performance appraisal experience on perceptions of management quality and working environment: Findings from a state enterprise in Norway. *Review of Public Personnel Administration. 17*(3) (Summer): 82–98.

Mohrman, Allan, and Lawler, Edward E., III (1983). Motivation and performance appraisal behavior. In *Performance Measurement and Theory* (Frank Landy, F. Zedeck, and Jeannette Cleveland, eds.). Erlbaum, Hillsdale, N.J.

Mohrman, Allan M., Jr., Resnick-West, Susan M., and Lawler, Edward E., III (1989). *Designing Performance Appraisal Systems: Aligning Appraisals and Organizational Realities.* Jossey-Bass, San Francisco.

Morrison, Elizabeth Wolfe, and Bies, Robert J. (1991). Impression management in the feedback-seeking process: A literature review and research agenda. *Academy of Management Review. 16*(3) (July): 522–541.

Murphy, Kevin J. (1987). *Effective Listening: Hearing What People Say and Making It Work for You.* Bantam Books, New York.

Murphy, Kevin R., and Cleveland, Jeanette N. (1995). *Understanding Performance Appraisal: Social, Organizational, and Goal-Based Perspectives.* Sage, Thousand Oaks, Calif.

Odiorne, George S. (1987). *The Human Side of Management: Management by Integration and Self-Control.* Lexington Books, Lexington, Mass.

Ouchi, William G. (1981). *Theory Z. Addison-Wesley,* New York.

Pajer, Robert (1979). *Employee Performance Evaluation: A Practical Guide to Development and Implementation for State, County, and Municipal Governments.* Office of Personnel Management, Government Printing Office, Washington, D.C.

Pascale, Richard T., and Athos, Anthony O. (1981). *The Art of Japanese Management.* Simon & Schuster, New York.

Peters, Thomas J., and Robert H. Waterman (1982). *In Search of Excellence.* Harper & Row, New York.

Roberts, Gary E., and Reed, Tammy (1996). Performance appraisal participation, goal setting and feedback: The influence of supervisory style. *Review of Public Personnel Administration 26*(4) (Fall): 29–60.

Taylor, Frederick (1911). *The Principles of Scientific Management.* W. W. Norton, New York.

Yeager, Samuel J., Rabin, Jack, and Vocino, Thomas (1985). Feedback and administrative behavior in the public sector. *Public Administration Review. 45*(5) (September/October): 570–575.

13

Using Strategic Planning to Manage Strategically in the Public Sector

Frances Stokes Berry
Askew School of Public Administration and Policy, Florida State University, Tallahassee, Florida

Public sector organizations face an environment of change and choice. That's the simple reason many of them turn to strategic planning to help navigate their complex terrains. The widespread recession of the early 1990s has given way to a robust U.S. economy, but the public mood to hold down the size of American government has been embraced by leaders across political persuasions. Managers are asked to do more with fewer dollars and downsized staff. Performance measurement and accountability, devolution of policy and administration to the state and local governments, changing technology and the Internet, and increased contracting out for government services are all aspects of the environmental forces that prompt a focus on mission and strategic thinking for governments at all levels. Strategic planning has become a commonly used process for organizational leaders to address what government should be doing and how it can be done most effectively and efficiently.

Although many models of strategic planning exist (Bryson and Roering, 1996), the most widely used processes include the following common elements: conducting an environmental assessment of societal trends and policy directions, clarifying the organization's missions, identifying internal and external stakeholders or customers the organization serves, articulating strategic issues that must be addressed for the organization to be successful, and developing concrete actions to resolve those strategic issues. Whereas many people focus on the importance of the planning document itself, the constructive dialogue and learning that should take place during strategic planning may be as important as the specific plan produced through the process. Thus the overall purpose of the strategic planning journey is to enable managers to think and act more strategically in accomplishing the organization's mission, not just to produce a concrete plan.

Strategic planning may be viewed skeptically by managers, especially those who have seen traditional planning documents gather dust on shelves. But strategic planning can be distinguished from prior planning efforts in several ways. First, a hallmark of strategic planning is considering the organization in the context of its external environment, whereas traditional planning gave little attention to an outward focus. In the strategic perspective, identifying stakeholders and gathering information from stakeholders to use in the decision-making process represent a fundamental change from traditional planning. Second, traditional planning was often short-term, whereas strategic planning in the public sector generally uses a 5-year framework. Third, traditional planning was primarily developed and written by planners serving in a staff function without significant input by line managers; strategic planning emphasizes the involvement of senior line managers in developing the elements of the plan as well as involving managers from all levels of the organization in implementing the goals and strategies. Fourth, traditional plans incorporated goals and objectives but often without action plans for implementation. Effective strategic plans include feasibility assessments and steps for putting the plan into action. Finally, increasingly strategic plans are being integrated into the budgeting and quality management systems used by organizations to improve organizational performance rather than serving as stand-alone planning documents.

Public managers use strategic planning for many reasons. In general, they want to be more proactive in dealing with issues and move away from crisis-oriented management, but a variety of factors lead to the adoption of strategic planning. In a national survey of state agency leaders (Berry and Wechsler, 1995), the top managers cited the following reasons: (a) mandates from the governor or federal agencies—"We were told to do it"; (b) their own perceived need to set a clear mission and directions for the agency; (c) prior positive experience of the chief executive with strategic planning in another organization; (d) fiscal stress and the need to resolve competing pressures to allocate resources; and (e) a desire to emulate good business practices. Other writings on strategic planning (e.g., Bryson, 1995; Anthony, 1985) highlight these additional factors: (a) responding to the governmental accountability movement, which requires multiple-year planning with specific outcome measures and data; (b) needing to refocus mission and services with a newly hired leader or a new group of board members; (c) wanting to learn more about what clients and customers think of an agency's services and products; (d) searching for a process to help build an organization's capacity to think strategically and deal with changing demands; and (e) needing to communicate among geographically dispersed units of an agency. Thus managers receive signals from a variety of quarters to adopt strategic planning (Berry, 1994).

After the introductory material, this chapter covers five topics. First, a range of definitions of strategic planning is outlined. Then a brief history of the development and use of strategic planning in the public sector is presented. Some of the primary models for strategic planning in organizations and in communities are next described. Fourth, an assessment of how strategic planning was integrated into other public sector management reforms in the 1990s is presented, as well as the lessons we are learning from those integrated efforts. A brief Conclusion completes the chapter.

WHAT IS STRATEGIC PLANNING?

Bozeman and Straussman (1990: 54) assert that there are three major features of a strategic approach in managing an organization: defining goals and objectives, developing an action plan that mediates between the organization and its environment, and designing effective methods of implementation.

John Bryson's widely used strategic planning model defines *strategic planning* as "a disciplined effort to produce fundamental decisions and actions that shape and guide what an organization (or other entity) is, what it does, and why it does it. These decisions typically concern the organization's mandates, mission, product or service level and mix, cost, financing, management or organizational design" (Bryson, 1994: 155).

Berry and Wechsler (1995: 159) define strategic planning as a systematic process for managing the organization and its future direction in relation to its environment and the demands of its external stakeholders. Strategic management involves taking the strategic planning process and extending it into an ongoing management paradigm of anticipating and managing organizational change and environmental uncertainty. It also helps organizations deal with uncertain futures by defining goals and strategies for achieving them.

A more entrepreneurial definition of strategic management is expressed in *Creating Public Value. Strategic Management in Government,* in which Moore (1995) asserts that managers who operate from a strategic management perspective primarily create public value. In this view, managers are agents who help define what would be valuable for their programs and agencies to do instead of merely developing means of carrying out mandated services. Managers engage the politics surrounding their organization to help define public value and reengineer how their organizations operate instead of expecting stability in policy and management styles. Moore (1995: 23) goes on to assert that managers have functions that they must serve to be effective: (a) judging and articulating the public value of their mission and purpose; (b) managing outward, toward politics, to invest their purposes with legitimacy and support; and (c) managing downward, toward improving the organization's capabilities for achieving the desired purposes.

The common features of these definitions are that strategic planning should encourage agency leaders to align their organization more closely with its environment and develop a clearer focus on the agency's mission and goals. The written plan should be action-oriented and focused on measuring and achieving results. Overall, the process and the plan should help organizations deliver their services more effectively and ensure accountability to the public.

BACKGROUND AND DEVELOPMENT OF STRATEGIC PLANNING

Strategic planning has been imported into the public and nonprofit sectors from the private sector. Peter Drucker's (1959) early work showed that long-range planning is not equivalent to forecasting. Alfred Chandler, in the widely read *Strategy and Structure* (1962), defined strategy as a "determiner of the basic long term goals of an enterprise and the adoption of courses of action and the allocation of resources necessary for carrying out these goals" (Bracker, 1980). Mintzberg's *The Structuring of Organizations* (1979) reinforced the view that strategy mediates between the organization and its environment, and organizations should structure themselves according to the type of environment in which they exist. Global competition, uneven business cycles, technological advancements, and rapid environmental change led corporations to use strategic planning to anticipate and adapt to change. Igor Ansoff's *Corporate Strategy* (1965) was an early prescriptive process-dominated book that defined and extolled the Harvard policy model for corporate America. Other private sector models of strategic planning (Bryson and Roering, 1996) included stakeholder management (Freeman, 1984), portfolio management (Wind and Mahajan, 1981), competitive analysis (Porter, 1980), and strategic issues management (Ansoff, 1980).

By the late 1970s and 1980s, articles critical of early corporate strategic planning processes appeared, often lamenting similar pitfalls: a lack of management commitment, excessive concern with financial data and forecasting, dominance by staff rather than responsible managers, failure to develop true strategic choices, and planning processes that were too elaborate and unsubstantive (e.g., Steiner, 1979; Wilson, 1994). Broader-based strategic management approaches were developed to address these weaknesses, and more focus on strategic issues and processes for developing strategy appeared in the literature.

Early writers on strategic planning and management in the public sector highlighted the differences in strategic management in the public and private sectors and noted that the public sector presents some special obstacles to strategic planning and management. (Ring and Perry, 1985; Klay, 1989; Bozeman and Straussman, 1990). Both policy vagueness, often due to competition among coalitions in the policy-making process, and incompatible program goals frustrate establishing clearly articulated strategies for results. Public sector decision making is generally incremental; thus strategies are more likely to be emergent and based on minor changes to existing strategies rather than radical departures from current policies. Decisions may also be more process-oriented than strategy-driven in some clear-cut direction. Public organizations face a wide range of stakeholders, and their power in the policy process can be substantial. Thus stakeholder management takes on an added urgency for the strategic manager who lives in a world of fragmented power and multiple constituencies. In the public sector, time constraints for realizing strategies are often greater as a result of electoral cycles and the short tenure of agency heads. Ring and Perry (1985) sum up strategic management in the public sector this way:

> In many respects, strategic management in the public sector entails the management of discontinuity. Coalitions are unstable, political tenure is brief, agendas change constantly. Successful public sector managers act to minimize discontinuity and bridge the gaps that it leaves in its wake.

STRATEGIC PLANNING APPROACHES AND PROCESSES

A prodigious amount of information has been written on strategic planning for public and nonprofit agencies (e.g., Olsen and Eadie, 1982; Bryson, 1995; Nutt and Backoff, 1992; Kemp, 1993) and numerous models developed on the strategic planning process. Most of the models include specific steps: clarifying the organization's mission and purpose, scanning the organization's environment for information on opportunities and threats, getting feedback from stakeholders or customers, articulating the key issues facing the organization, and developing plans to address these issues.

Although an effective strategic planning process for an organization is always designed uniquely for that organization to meet its particular needs, a "generic" and fairly comprehensive strategic planning model can be described. This model builds from the Harvard policy model and includes the identification of strategic issues and the development of implementation plans; the steps in this model were found to be commonly adopted by the 50 states (Berry and Wechsler, 1995) and were also used by the Southern Consortium of University Public Service Organizations in their curriculum *Results-Oriented Government* (Southern Growth Policies Board, 1997), which has been widely used in training public sector managers. A generic strategic planning process and an elaboration of each step in the process are described in detail in the following section.

Step One: Plan for the Strategic Planning Process

Planning for strategic planning begins with discussion of what the agency wants to gain from strategic planning, and why it is undertaking the process. A planning process that is geared primarily to creating a consensus on an agency's mission, vision, and strategic issues may look very different from a process whose key objective is to restructure and downsize the agency, and different still from a process designed to avert the organization's imminent demise. Although all the purposes do not need to be articulated, there should be a fairly clear sense of what the agency hopes to gain from the strategic planning experience. This information is valuable to devise an appropriate planning process and to communicate to other organizational members why the process is being initiated, thereby ideally reducing the negative gossip surrounding a new strategic planning process, which inevitably assumes the worst-case scenario behind its introduction—often staff cuts and organizational downsizing. Such gossip leads to poor staff morale and pessimism about the process from the beginning.

Generally the planning is done with a "steering team" of people from inside the agency who oversee the planning process throughout its life. If there is an outside consultant, she will also be a member of the steering team. Less commonly, a few key stakeholders are also invited to help set the parameters of purpose and design. The agency director appoints the head of the planning committee, who may be the organization's chief planner, a deputy director, or a senior program manager with management and problem-solving skills. The team members should represent the major units in the organization, including district or other geographical offices, depending on the organization's structure. The steering team should stay small, no more than 8 to 10 members, unless there is a convincing reason for expansion.

The steering team decides on which strategic planning approach is to be used, whether to use an outside consultant (and for what aspects of the process), and how to manage and staff the process. Many organizations find that engaging an outside consultant can help the organization stay focused on the process and can provide an experienced facilitator for the larger group meetings when the strategic planning issues are discussed. Experienced consultants can also give advice on fine-tuning the planning process as unexpected problems or delays arise to keep the process productive and carry it through to its conclusion. Finally, the timeline and key dates for retreats and other core meetings of senior management staff as well as the products to be created by the process are all responsibilities of the steering group.

Step Two: Clarify the Organization's Mission, Values, and Vision

Every organization is unique, just as are the individuals that make it up, but the leadership literature is clear that inspiring a shared vision of an organization's purpose is a primary job for the organization's leader (Kouzes and Posner, 1987). Staff and stakeholders have to know what an organization's purpose and values are, to be able to help get the organization there. Thus the articulation of the organization's mission and values is frequently an early step in the strategic planning process that provides key parameters to guide the rest of the deliberations.

The mission statement is a clear, succinct statement of the organization's purposes and goals. It defines the agency's reasons for existence and the key roles that it will contribute to society's well-being. Questions the mission might address include the following: Whom do we serve? What are the reasons we exist and our main purposes? What were the problems that we were created to help address? How do we see our existence as making a difference in society? What makes us unique and distinctive? The mission statement should be short enough that people can memorize it. It should be jargon-free and written in bold, plain language that the citizen on the street would understand. (See Table 1 for examples of well-constructed mission statements.)

TABLE 1 Examples of Well-Constructed Mission Statements

Florida Department of Corrections
The mission of the Florida Department of Corrections is to protect the public, provide a safe and humane environment for staff and offenders, work in partnership with the community to provide programs and services to offenders, and supervise offenders at a level of security commensurate with the danger they present.
City of Goose Creek, South Carolina
The City of Goose Creek seeks to serve the needs of citizens for a safe, secure and healthy environment and facilitates planned and managed growth and economic development. The City fulfills its mission by ensuring that the highest quality of essential services are provided and by serving as a forum for identifying and addressing the needs of the community. The City assumes a leadership role in determining the future direction of the community.

An organization's values, simply put, are what it cares about and the concepts that it stands for. Values help define the organization's culture and expectations about how people are treated, how services are delivered, and how work is done. Values should drive decisions, and value statements should be widely disseminated to people throughout the organization to link the mission of the organization—its reasons for existing—with its values as to how that mission will be achieved. There may be an incongruence between the values articulated by the organization's leadership and the values perceived by staff and stakeholders. This contributes to a lack of credibility, loss of trust, and stakeholder dissatisfaction (Southern Growth Policies Board, 1997: Unit 6-2) but may also help motivate change.

The organizational vision is a description of what the organization should look like "once it has successfully implemented its strategies and achieved its full potential" (Bryson, 1995: 35). In this regard, the vision statement builds from the organization's mission, values, core strategies, and expectations of how it will operate and what it will contribute to society. The vision articulates a view of a realistic, credible, attractive future that in many ways is better than the current state of affairs. Bryson (1995) notes that some organizations may find the visioning process difficult and prefer to conduct it near the end of the strategic planning process after people have a more vivid understanding of their common view of the organization's future. Or it may serve a useful purpose in rounds two or three of the strategic planning process. For organizations whose staff are highly motivated by their public service mission and who have a focused mission, the process of visioning and producing a vision statement can be invigorating and helpful early in the process.

The dialogue concerning what makes up the organization's primary reasons for existing, or its key purposes, starts the process of thinking strategically. In general, public agencies tend to be characterized by goal ambiguity and lack of a clear mission (Rainey, 1983; Ring and Perry, 1985), and evidence mounts that this ambiguity can be a hindrance in effective strategic management. Public agencies with considerable goal ambiguity tend to have a difficult time strategizing and implementing management innovations (Wechsler et al., 1998). Studies across a range of programs and functional areas support the view that establishing a clear mission and goal does have salutatory effects on the agency's effectiveness. Kaufman (1995) finds that agencies that identify a primary mission objective, one that is based on the part of the agency's ideal vision that it is committed to provide, tend to be more successful in using outcome results and integrating them into the agency's planning and management. A study of Michigan schools and their mission statements (Weiss and Piderit, 1999) finds that the content of the mission statements is related to the subsequent performance of the students and the schools; the authors conclude that mission statements do matter. Finally, in their theory of effective organizations, Rainey and Steinbauer (1999) cite mission clarity and focus as a core element, a conclusion supported by numerous other studies (e.g., Osborne and Gaebler, 1992; Behn, 1991).

Step Three: Identify Stakeholders and Assess Their Views and Needs

Your organization's stakeholders are those individuals and organizations that are affected by your work and that can affect your organization. Stakeholders may also be those people who directly use your organization's services and products, in which case they may be called *customers* (following common private sector language) or *clients*. Typically, a public sector organization has a large number of stakeholders, some of whom may be more important than others and some of whom may have conflicting views and interests regarding the organization. Often the stakeholder analysis may assess external and internal stakeholders separately. External stakeholders include citizens, clients receiving services, other public sector agencies in the policy process that interact with the program, vendors, the legislature, the elected executive, media, and suppliers. Internal stakeholders directly receive input and services from other organizational staff. Their concerns frequently identify inadequate administrative processes, often related to inefficient work processes, human resource management problems, cumbersome procurement rules, missing technology deployment, and inadequate information management processes.

Why are stakeholder concerns so important? Stakeholders judge the quality and effectiveness of the organization on the basis of their own criteria, which may be different from the professional standards that organizational staff use in assessing their work. In the private sector, quality is defined by the customer, who will not buy services he doesn't like. In the public and nonprofit sectors, organizational success is increasingly also measured by the satisfaction of stakeholders. For example, in Florida's strategic planning process, agencies must develop outcome measures for their programs. Most agencies now include measures taken from customer satisfaction surveys as indicators of their program's success or failure. Organizational leaders need to know what their customers' criteria are as they develop performance measures for their organization. External assessments also help guard against the organization's becoming too removed from their external environment, can help identify strategic issues, and provide insight into the organization's mission and values.

To conduct a comprehensive stakeholder analysis, the strategic planning team must identify the internal and external stakeholders, assess their relative importance and interest in the organization, survey or interview them to determine their expectations and assessments of the organization, and summarize the findings by stakeholder category. Ideally, the same general questions can be asked of all stakeholder groups, for example: What are their expectations of the organization? What do they see as opportunities and challenges for the organization? What do they think makes the organization unique or distinctive? How do they rate the organization's performance? In what areas do they think the organization needs to improve? Do they believe the mission statement adequately captures the organization's purposes? The findings can then be compared across the categories of stakeholders to uncover patterns of similar and conflicting views about how the organization is doing and what its future direction should be. Another advantage of this type of organizational assessment is that it helps to educate the participating stakeholders about the organization's mission and duties and send a message of openness, responsiveness, and improvement.

Step Four: Understand Your Organization's Environment: Assess the External and Internal Environments

A fundamental reason for engaging in strategic planning is to align or fit the organization with its external environment; thus getting information about and from the external environment is critical to a successful planning process. Bryson (1995: 86) aptly notes that the external and internal assessments

> allow the strategic planning team to see the organization as a whole in relation to its environment. This is usually one of the singular accomplishment of strategic planning—an ability to see the organization as a whole in relation to its environment keeps the organization from being victimized by the present. Instead the organization has a basis for *reasoned* optimism in that difficulties may be seen as specific rather than pervasive, temporary rather than permanent and the result of factors other than irremediable organizational incompetence.

The stakeholder analysis in step three is one type of feedback from the external environment. In step four, information is gathered that can help assess the organization's strengths and weaknesses, opportunities and threats (SWOT analysis). This includes an external environmental scan of facts and information on political, economic, social, technological (also called PESTS—Bryon, 1995), and other trends, as well as an internal assessment of the organization's strengths and weaknesses.

The External Environmental Scan

The purposes of the external environmental scan are to uncover issues and trends that may impact the organization's future work and to help develop the managers' capacity to think beyond the organization's boundaries. Implications based on these data are then used in identifying strategic issues and developing strategies to address the organization's key issues. Topics often included in environmental scans are changing demographics of current and potential client groups, and of the organization's work force; community, state, and national "hot topics" that point to underlying social conditions that the organization might address; economic, revenue, or funding trends that may affect the organization; political, cultural, social, and international issues and trends; new technologies and work environment issues; policy and management innovations at the local, state, or federal levels that might affect the organization; and competition from other organizations for similar services and products that the organization produces. Although the environmental scans need not relate everything to the organization, clearly the intent is to provide different views of the organization's environment to spur managers to think beyond the status quo.

Some organizations develop alternative future scenarios that the organization may need to address to make the information apply concretely to the organization and make it more accessible for managers to ponder (Bryson, 1995). Other organizations develop short briefing reports with key facts to use as input for thinking about what the organization should be addressing over the next 5 years (Stern, 1999). Results can also be captured in short oral briefings presented early in a strategic planning retreat to place the planning discussion inside the broader social and political context.

The Internal Environmental Assessment

The internal assessment focuses on the organization's strengths and weaknesses and helps identify the organization's current core competencies and capacities that can be mobilized to fulfill its mission and address external opportunities and threats. Internal assessments include factual data on the organization's culture, services, finances, work force, technology, and structure, as well as a determination of what is working well and what is not up to par.

Three categories of organizational resources can be usefully documented (Bryson, 1995: 90) in this process: inputs (budgets, personnel, and demand for services and products), the organization's current strategies, and performance measures, or outcomes information. Many organizations have ample input data and can quantify what their staff salaries and levels, travel and administrative costs, and client or service demands are. There may be fewer quantifiable data on what the organization's performance and outcomes are, with data on activities and outputs more likely to be available than data on outcomes—to what extent the organization is making a difference in addressing its mission and program purposes. With the increasing linkage of strategic planning and budgeting, most public organizations are facing demands for performance measurement data that capture both outputs and outcomes. The internal assessment can help identify what data the organization routinely collects and where the gaps are. This information also feeds into the development or improvement of management information systems that the organization uses or needs to build, so that performance data can be routinely collected and reported to managers and key stakeholders.

An important part of the internal assessment is to articulate what the organization's current strategies are to advance its mission. Remarkably, often agency leaders and staff have never really considered what strategies they are pursuing until faced with this question. In the context of the internal assessment, managers attempt to determine, Are the strategies this organization pursuing working or not? Numerous processes for SWOT analysis can be used. Bryson (1995) gives clear examples of the "organizational highs, lows and themes" exercise; the snowball method; and other process methods for soliciting and compiling SWOT assessments.

Finally, short internal and external assessments can profitably be conducted on a regular basis, say quarterly, as part of an effort to keep abreast of changes that should be addressed immediately, instead of waiting for an annual or biennial planning process. Integrated into a weekly staff meeting, the SWOT analysis can highlight emerging issues that weren't previously considered in the organization's strategies or can assist the organization in flexibly adjusting strategies incrementally as subtle changes develop that the organization should capitalize on or counter immediately. Also, as the organization's performance measures and information systems become fully developed and integrated into decision making, they assist in determining when adjustments to the organization's programs need to be made.

Step Five: Identify Strategic Issues

Issues in strategic management can be seen as analogous to problems in problem solving (Nutt and Backoff, 1992). They stake out the area that calls for a strategic response from the organization. Strategic issues can be framed as a question and as a challenge that the organization can address—How can the organization stabilize and increase the financial resources available to it?—instead of as a problem—How can we deal with a budget deficit? A challenge is more likely to encourage broader brainstorming for ways to resolve the issue and keep optimism high that solutions can be found and implemented. The specific framing of a strategic issue affects the resources and strategies that might be used to deal with it and thus makes it more likely that certain actions will be viewed favorably by the leadership team.

How does the planning group identify strategic issues? The stakeholder and SWOT analyses will highlight issues that face the organization. Future scenarios of how the organization might develop (Eden and Ackerman, 1998; Nutt and Backoff, 1992) can pinpoint strategic issues that emerge from the assessment of the difference between where an organization presently is and where its possible future may take it. Discussions of what is preventing the organization from achieving its mission (and values and vision) or what would promote achieving the mission suggest strategic issues.

Strategic issues involve conflicts or tensions for the organization and imply that multiple options (or strategies) could be adopted to address them. But the leadership team determine whether the issue is a strategic one for the organization. If the organization cannot do anything to effect resolution of the issue, it is not a strategic issue for that organization. If the issue will be resolved shortly and affects only one program or unit, then again, it is not likely to be a strategic issue, as these generally cut across program functions or units. If it is identified as a potential future strategic issue, through discussion of future scenarios that may develop, then it should be tracked and kept on the organization's radar screen without taking action at the current time.

The leadership team is best advised not to select strategic issues superficially without careful assessment. The assessment might include the following (Southern Growth Policies Board, 1997): What is the issue? Why is it an issue? Who says it is an issue, and how do we know it is an issue? And what are the consequences of not doing anything about it? Bryson (1994: 165) suggests a three-step written issue statement be developed for each potential strategic issue: Step one describes the issue and frames it as a question that the organization can do something about. Step two lists the factors (often from the SWOT analysis) that make it a fundamental policy question. Effective strategies build on strengths and opportunities and overcome or counter weaknesses and threats. Step three considers what will happen if the strategic issue is not addressed. If there are no or only small consequences, this is not a a strategic issue for the organization. But if catastrophic consequences might result from inattention to the issue, then the issue is clearly highly strategic. Thus the identification of strategic issues is a step that identifies the parameters of the organization's primary strategic attention to ensure survival and effectiveness—in short, to ensure a good fit with its environment.

Step Six: Develop Goals, Objectives, Performance Measure, and Action Plans

Once strategic issues have been identified, organizational goals and objectives can be developed to help flesh out the direction the organization wants to take. Goals are broad-based, issue-oriented statements that focus actions toward clearly defined purposes; goals are often tied to specific strategic issues. Sample goals from the North Carolina Economic Development Board include the following: Build a high-growth economy in all parts of the state, Achieve high wages and high incomes for North Carolina's work force, and make North Carolina a world renowned center for entrepreneurship (Southern Growth Policies Board, 1997).

After goals are established, objectives can be specified. These spell out the short-term and individual accomplishments that will lead to the overall goal achievement. Objectives should be linked directly to goals and should be written as measurable, time-based statements of action and expected results.

Strategic plans that have performance measures incorporated into their goals and objectives are increasingly common in the public sector (Brudney et al.,

1999) and provide clear targets or benchmarks against which their organization's performance can be judged. Some agencies gather data by regions and use their best performing region as their target performance; other agencies may set incremental percentage increases in performance based on some trend data from past performance or expectations based on new technology or process improvement. Without prior year data on program outputs and outcomes, setting targets is at best an imprecise science.

Performance measures became more important in strategic planning in the late 1990s as they often link strategic planning objectives to performance-based budgets. Typically organizations use two broad types of performance measures: output and outcome measures. Output measures capture the actual goods or services delivered by an organization, such as the number of persons screened for disease, lane miles of roads paved, or number of students graduating. Outcome measures go beyond activity measures to address the "So what?" question. What difference did the program make? What are the public benefits that result from the program? Examples of outcome measures include water quality after treatment, client satisfaction with programs, and rate of highway deaths (see Walters, 1998; Newcomer, 1997, for further information on developing effective performance measures). Performance measures are used to assess progress in meeting goals and objectives and represent a quantifiable way to indicate accountability for what the organization is accomplishing. Monitoring and reporting measurement information on a regular basis are steps that help managers keep track of how well their units are doing and ensure that performance information is available for the budgeting and decision-making cycles. To the extent possible, performance information should also be incorporated into individual and unit level performance appraisals as well as into performance contracts for outside vendors.

Step Seven: Devise and Assess Strategies

Strategies are specific courses of action that an organization undertakes to achieve a specific goal or objective. Ideally, strategies should effectively link the organization to its environment and move it toward accomplishing its mission, help it overcome the obstacles and threats that the SWOT analysis uncovered, and identify positive, doable solutions to the strategic issues selected in step five. Discussions on selecting goals and objectives also lead to consideration of strategies, and some organizations may want to fold steps six and seven into one step.

In developing strategies, it is best to use a set of questions systematically to help the group stay on task. These questions might include the following: What are the barriers and opportunities to achieving the goal or objective under consideration? What practical alternatives (strategies) can be used to meet the goal or objective (encouraging brainstorming or other group processes to develop lots of options)? What would be the major steps to implement these strategies? These questions prevent the group from quickly reaching consensus on one solution without a full discussion of how the issue can be addressed and encourage the group to keep prominently in mind how to move from where the organization currently is to where they want it to be.

Once strategies are identified, they can be evaluated by asking five questions: Does the strategy reflect the organization's vision and mission? Is there a high likelihood that the strategy will achieve the desired goal or objective? Is the strategy feasible politically and is it realistic in terms of costs and organizational staffing and other resources? Will the strategy be accepted by key stakeholders? And is the strategy compatible with other organizational strategies? In short, strategies should be politically acceptable, technically workable, and legally and morally defensible (Southern Growth Policies Board, 1997).

Generally in the literature there has been a distinct preference for deliberate strategy formulated in advance of implementation and written in the annual strategic plan rather than for emergent strategy, whereby managers on the front lines devise solutions to problems. Mintzberg (1987) has criticized organizations' heavy reliance on deliberate strategy making as detrimental to effective strategy making. Instead, Mintzberg asserts, strategy can be formed (emergent strategy) as well as formulated (deliberate strategy), and he argues that emergent strategy, a strategy crafted by the involved manager to fit the specific situation, may be more critical to an organization's success than deliberate strategy alone. Emergent strategy promotes flexible responses to ever changing environments. Environments do not change in predictable ways, so the real challenge in crafting strategy is to detect the often subtle changes that will undermine the program, products, or services in the future. These subtle changes can only be picked up by people who are attuned to existing patterns and are able to identify changes that may really matter. To manage strategy, then, says Mintzberg (1987: 73), "is to craft thought and action, control and learning, stability and change," and not rely totally on deliberate strategy, often developed by people in the organization who are far removed from where the service or product is delivered.

Mintzberg and Waters (1985) develop a typology of real-world strategies that organizations undertake. In addition to deliberate and emergent strategies, they note increasing evidence that two middle-ground types of strategy—umbrella and process strategy—are used by organizations. In the umbrella strategy leaders define boundaries for organizational actions and then let managers maneuver within those boundaries. In the process strategy, organizational leaders may determine who participates in and how the strategic planning process is structured but leaves the content of the strategy to participants in the planning process. In both of these strategies there is some central vision, but middle- to lower-level managers are also free to respond to the intricacies of their environments to innovate and try new strategies to achieve goals. Both the umbrella and process strategies may be found frequently in the public sector in organizations that have a framework for their plan or specify the process elements to be used in planning but delegate the specific strategy development to line managers.

Step Eight: Implement and Build Commitment to the Plan

The implementation of the plan and the decisions on the organization's strategic directions must be carried out if the planning process is to make any difference to the organization's performance. Thus implementation should be planned consciously and strategically. If the plan developers are not the plan implementers, more education and communication about the plan's elements and purposes are required than if the primary implementers are the authors of the plan. In any case, the implementers should be given an opportunity for input into how the plan will be carried out. Decisions have to be made on the number of strategies and the parallel timing of beginning different strategies so activities are coordinated and strategic changes do not overtax the organization's resource and managerial capabilities. Linking the strategic plan to existing operational plans and budgets is one way to begin the implementation. In this process, "action" plans that spell out the order and timing of the major activities, assignment of lead responsibility, and time and resources estimated for successful completion can be developed. Gantt and Program Evaluation Review Technique (PERT) charts or other planning formats for project management can be adapted to managing the implementation of the key strategies.

Managers can learn from the lessons of successful policy implementation and organizational change management, highlighted in the following "implementation proverbs": Develop coalitions of internal and external stakeholders to assist with particular strategies. Try to achieve early successes so organizational members see that change is possible and that the planned activities led to intended purpose. Celebrate success to reward employees and show clear incentives for undertaking the effort involved in organizational change. Promote the development of a "learning organization" in which managers regularly assess program service and delivery changes. Finally, work to maintain the spirit of the planning process—oriented to strategic thinking and building a more united management team throughout the organization.

Step Nine: Evaluate and Monitor the Plan

Evaluation is the feedback loop that enables the organization to determine whether the plan and process are working and to answer the broad question, Have the planning and the resulting strategic thinking produced the actions planned and performance levels expected? Evaluation is important to refining and institutionalizing effective strategic planning. Assessment also helps individuals and organizations learn from past actions and take corrective steps to improve their strategies and actions.

Three different types of monitoring and evaluation should be undertaken (Southern Growth Policies Board, 1997). First, performance measures should be tracked so that actual outcomes and outputs can be compared against targeted expectations. Organizations should establish a systematic process to report and interpret performance measures. Since different audiences (e.g., elected officials, clients, citizens, and managers) have different information needs, reports should be tailored to each audience. A broader assessment of the organization's performance might address the following questions: Is our work consistent with our mission statement? Are we meeting our stakeholder expectations? Are we meeting our goals and objectives performance targets?

Second, the strategic planning process itself should be assessed to determine what impact the planning process had, what worked well, what refinements are needed, and how often the planning process should be revisited. And finally, the organization may want to adopt an ongoing environmental scanning process that would enable it to keep up with changing social and political conditions, technology, and stakeholder views that might affect the assumptions on which the organization's plan is based. There are numerous ways to set up an ongoing environmental scanning process; Bryson (1995) and Stern (1999) provide a variety of detailed examples.

Strategic planning is generally presented as a step-by step process, but in practice, it is not a linear process. Some steps may be passed over, some taken out of turn, and some repeated if a consensus is not formed on how to proceed. The mission and values may be addressed early, as described, or may be created after the stakeholder and environmental analyses have been completed. In some organizations, the vision of the future may be close to the last step after the inductive work of defining issues and environmental constraints and opportunities is complete. Bryson (1995) offers sound advice on how to gauge where your organization should begin the process, particularly if it has undergone planning processes in the recent past. Public organizations are often mandated to revise their strategic plans annually, but they may fully revisit their strategic plans only every 2 or 3 years and make incremental adjustments in the intervening years.

Other Strategic Planning Models

Several other strategic planning processes have gained acceptance and widespread use among public and nonprofit agencies; these are reviewed briefly to highlight differences and additions to the generic strategic planning model outlined.

Bryson's Strategy Change Cycle and Planning Process Probably the most widely used strategic planning model is John Bryson's strategy change cycle model (Bryson, 1995). Its contents clearly influenced the generic strategic planning model discussed previously. His model integrates many of the strengths of individual business models—such as the Harvard policy model, stakeholder management, and strategic issues management—in a model tailored for the public and nonprofit sectors. Bryson gives more attention to the legal mandates than does the generic model described and goes into more detail on plan implementation. His 10-step strategic planning process is as follows (Bryson, 1995: 23) (see Figure 1 on pg. 281 for graphic presentation):

Step One: Initiate the strategic planning process.
Step Two: Identify organizational mandates.
Step Three: Clarify organizational mission and values.
Step Four: Assess the internal and external environments (including SWOT analysis).
Step Five: Identify the strategic issues facing the organization.
Step Six: Formulate strategies to manage these issues.
Step Seven: Adopt the strategic plan.
Step Eight: Establish an effective organizational vision.
Step Nine: Develop an implementation plan.
Step Ten: Reassess strategies and the planning process.

Bryson's book contains detailed examples of processes from three organizations that help frame some of the dilemmas faced in group planning and give practical advice on how to carry out a strategic planning process.

Alliance for Government Process The handbook *Creating High Performance Organizations* (Popovich, 1998: 51) by David Osborne's Alliance for Redesigning Government presents a simple but straightforward public sector model consisting of four steps:

1. Clarifying your purpose
2. Understanding the environment
3. Engaging stakeholders
4. Building commitment to change

This model underscores the belief that taking a strategic view does not require an elaborate or highly formal planning process and offers a basic approach to strategic planning without all the bells and whistles of the more comprehensive models.

Drucker Foundation Organizational Assessment Process Emphasizing the theme of organizational assessment and reinvigoration, the Drucker Foundation has developed a four-step strategic planning process designed for nonprofit organizations or small public sector agencies with volunteer boards of directors responsible for organizational governance. The *Drucker Foundation Self-Assessment Tool,* their handbook, urges organizations to "focus on changing lives and building communities" (Stern, 1999: 9), using the following five questions to guide assessment and plan development:

1. What is our mission?
2. Who is our customer?

3. What does the customer value?
4. What are our results?
5. What is our plan?

Their assessment process is broken into three phases: Phase one is preparing for self-assessment, which includes designing the planning process, selecting the assessment team and facilitator for the process, and conducting the environmental scan of internal and external data. Phase two is conducting the self-assessment process, in which the board of directors reviews the information from the first phase; determines the mission, vision, and values of the organization; identifies key issues and strategies for addressing the issues; and develops a draft report of the process. The final phase focuses on developing the objectives, action steps and budget for the plan for final board approval.

Examples of Strategic Planning Processes in the Public Sector.

FEDERAL GOVERNMENT. The current federal strategic planning process was legislatively enacted in the Government Performance and Results Act (GPRA) of 1993, although the first agency strategic plans were due to Congress until 1997. The strategic plans were required to have a comprehensive agency mission statement, well-specified goals and objectives and strategies for achieving them, some environmental assessments (particularly concerning factors that might affect the achievement of the agency goals and objectives), stakeholder input, and a plan for evaluating programs and making revisions to the strategic plan. The plans are based on a 5-year time framework, although the budget cycle is annual. Agencies are also required to establish annual performance plans that set out performance goals measured in objective, quantifiable measures and to submit annual performance reports that compare the actual performance of each program to the performance goals set out in the strategic plan (for more information on GPRA, see Radin, 1998; Wholey, 1999; U.S. General Accounting Office, 1997).

STATE GOVERNMENT. Two different approaches to strategic planning—but each a commonly adopted model—are illustrated by the strategic planning processes used by the states of Oregon and Florida. First the Oregon model, which used a state board of citizens to develop goals and strategies, is discussed, then the Florida model is described. In the early 1980s, Oregon experienced a long and deep recession. In response Governor Goldschmidt invited more than 150 business and community leaders to create a one-time strategic plan for the state on economic development issues. Working primarily in a series of committees that addressed problem areas, the report—*Oregon Shines: An Economic Strategy for the Pacific Century*—identified three strategic initiatives: a superior work force, an attractive quality of life, and an international frame of mind. The legislature also created the Oregon Progress Board to monitor "benchmarks" (quantifiable measures related to the initiatives) to assess how effectively the state was moving toward the Oregon Shines vision. By 1995 the state had undergone a remarkable economic recovery with a diversified economy and low unemployment and high growth rates, and the Oregon planning process won praise and awards (Kissler et al., 1998). In 1996, Governor Kitzhaber appointed another committee to lead the strategic plan's revisions, but this time around, regional meetings were held to involve a much broader and larger group of citizens. Several studies have concluded that the Oregon process has been successful (Kissler et al., 1998; US GAO, 1993); the General Accounting Office report noted that Oregon administrators pointed to the consensus on statewide goals that developed from a diverse set of stakeholders participating in the strategic planning process as a significant outcome. Oregon Shines represents a model in which the plan is updated every 5 to 10 years and is driven by business and citizen views rather than state agency staff. Strategic planning with an emphasis on economic development and use of a one-time task force have been the most common single-policy strategy planning processes used by the states.

Florida's strategic planning process is more typical of statewide planning processes that cover all program areas and is generally coordinated from the Governor's office or the Budget Office. The process was fully implemented in 1992; the "ultimate goal of strategic planning [in Florida] is to focus on the quality of services provided and the results or benefits of these services to Floridians" (Executive Office of the Governor, 1997: 3–11). The Florida process steps are similar to the generic planning model and Bryson's strategy change cycle, presented earlier (see Fig. 2). The process begins with a stakeholder analysis, SWOT analysis, and internal and external environmental assessment. The organization's mission and values are reconsidered each year in light of these assessments. Each strategic issue is identified and defined as an issue that "significantly impacts the health, safety or welfare of the public," and if not addressed will probably lead to undesirable results of a threat, a missed opportunity, or both. Strategic goals and objectives and strategies (the method for achieving the goal and objectives) are developed for each strategic issue. The strategy includes action plans and innovations designed to achieve the agency's goals and objectives. Strategy development is followed by plan implementation and performance evaluation. Detailed performance output and outcome measures are integral to the plan. Strategic planning was a key part of Governor Chiles's administrative reforms that formed a plank in his campaign platform for his successful Florida gubernatorial run in 1990 (Berry et al., 1999).

LOCAL GOVERNMENT. At the local government level, Kemp (1992) found that traditional planning practices are quickly being replaced by strategic planning processes. A 1998 survey (Berman, 1998) found that 52 percent of cities of more than 50,000 had used community-based strategic planning in the past year. But a greater variety of strategic planning projects and processes appear in local governments than at the state or federal levels. "Many of the strategic planning prac-

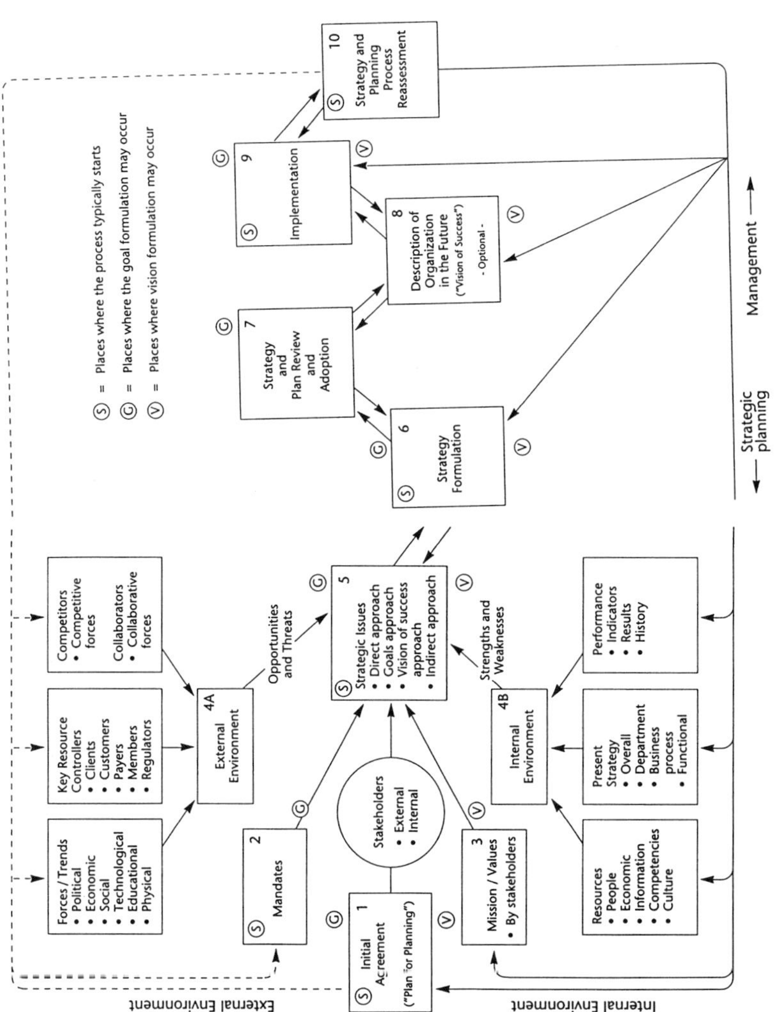

FIG. 1 The 10-step strategy change cycle.

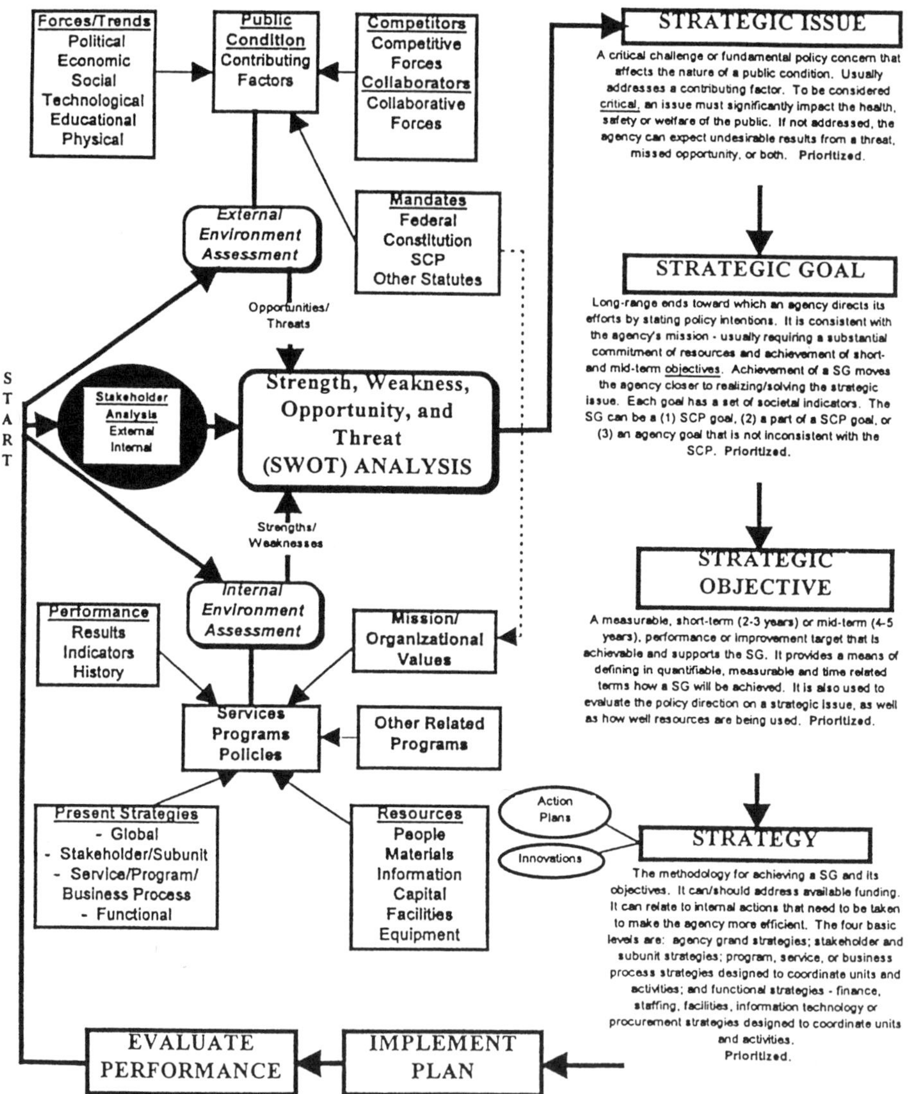

FIG. 2 Florida strategic planning process.

tices in local governments have been diverse, fragmented, and piecemeal in their development and application. For the most part, each local government is doing its own thing in this dynamic and rapidly evolving planning discipline," wrote Roger Kemp (1992: 6), himself a city manager, in a book that profiles 17 city strategic planning efforts. Many local governments use a strategic planning model similar to Florida's or the generic model described earlier for their annual agency planning. But local governments are also more likely to use community-based strategic planning models than are other levels of government. Several examples of local-level strategic planning processes are presented next.

Community-based strategic planning aims to build a broad consensus among citizens, businesses, and organizations in the community to develop collective responses to the community's problems. Communities often find they must develop effective networks of policy understanding and shared resources to be effective in dealing with their complex problems. Some examples can illustrate this logic. To deal effectively with high crime rates, communities must involve the local police officers, schools, neighborhood associations, public interest groups, churches, and citizens. To bolster community economic development, local governments (e.g., cities, counties, special districts) must coordinate their efforts with universities and community colleges, business groups, and intergovernmental policy organizations that support local economic development. Thus whereas effective *agency* strategic planning involves its stakeholders, *communities* have even more reason to reach out to its diverse stakeholders so that the solutions developed reflect their diverse needs and backgrounds. If the strategic planning process has been productive and well managed, those stakeholders can be mobilized to help implement the solutions.

The steps used in community-based strategic planning processes often appear very similar to those described in our generic model. One author (Berman, 1998: 107) notes four distinctive phases of community-based strategic planning:

1. The decision to initiate the process and the selection of a leadership team
2. Data collection (such as SWOT analysis and environmental scans)
3. Development of a mission, vision, and values statement and the identification of strategic issues, goals, strategies, objectives, performance measures, and target dates for implementation
4. Implementation of recommendations

Again, the process steps for developing this information are similar to those of other strategic planning models, but the process is characterized by a broad base of participants from the community rather than just elected or agency leaders. Another emphasis of community-based strategic planning is the use of values and community visions as a guiding metaphor for subsequent planning work. Indeed, a popular community-based strategic planning process, called *community visioning,* focuses on articulating core values and a shared vision of the diverse participants. Examples of community visioning projects are detailed in Kemp (1992).

The American Assembly process has been used for over 30 years to build consensus among a broad-based stakeholder group on a major policy issue. Typically the American Assembly used for local and regional issues has five steps (deHaven-Smith and Wodraska, 1996). First, approximately 75 participants are identified and brought together to discuss a specific issue and make recommendations as to what should be done to address it. The participants should represent diverse backgrounds, associations, and fields of expertise and have an interest in the community or policy issue under consideration. Second, prior to convening the assembly, experts write background papers that provide a framework and information about the topic. Third, during the assembly, the participants are divided into small groups of 7 to 10 people who meet for four discussion periods over 3 consecutive days. An experienced facilitator leads each group discussion. The ideas generated in the groups are written on flip charts so there is a complete record of each group's ideas, findings, and recommendations on the issue. These group data are then consolidated into a draft report, which is reviewed by the full assembled group on the last day of the assembly. Finally, recommendations in the report and amendments from participants are voted on and adopted before the assembly adjourns. Thus the assembly process could be used as the first stage in a strategic planning process to identify solutions and strategies that might address an issue or policy problem by using broad-based citizen input. The strategic plan would be written as a follow-up activity after the assembly meeting(s).

The next section discusses how strategic planning processes have been integrated into broader management reforms to create strategic management processes for the changing public sector organization.

THE INTEGRATION OF STRATEGIC PLANNING AND BROADER MANAGEMENT REFORMS

In the two decades since strategic planning was introduced into the public sector, strategic management has evolved from a framework that placed central focus on strategic planning (Bryson and Roering, 1996) to a more comprehensive framework in which strategic planning drives related quality and performance management initiatives (Berry and Wechsler, 1995). Strategic management is a systems view of organizational performance emphasizing the alignment of strategy and the organization's mission with its budgeting, decision making, stakeholder management, and other management processes. In short, strategic management works to integrate the planning outcomes throughout the organization, affecting the organizational structure, the motivational and reward systems, the data collected, the attention paid to clients and stakeholders, and the organizational culture.

Among the administrative reforms most compatible with strategic planning are performance measurement and the introduction of performance-based budgeting. At the state level, 47 of 50 states adopted some type of performance-based budgeting during the 1990s; 16 of those states had legislation that explicitly linked their agency strategic planning process to the development of performance measures based on the agency's mission and goals (Melkers and Willoughby, 1998). In Florida, for example, no new budget requests can be made to the governor without showing how that request fits into achieving the agency's strategic plan (Berry and Flowers, 1999). In Texas, a state that has been widely recognized as having an integrated approach to performance measurement, the state agencies use 6-year strategic plans, including mission, goals, objectives, strategies, and output and outcome measures, to support their budget requests. At the federal level, also under GPRA, performance-based management integrates strategic planning with output and outcome performance measures (Wholey, 1999).

Administrative reforms in the 1990s at all levels of government were heavily influenced by the "reinventing" government movement. In *Reinventing Government* (1992) Osborne and Gaebler develop 10 principles they argue should drive government reform if it is to be effective. The principles include (a) a focus on mission, (b) a results orientation, (c) decentralization of administration, (d) meeting of customer needs and use of their standards for quality assurance, and (e) injection of competition and incentives for lower costs in government programs. A 1999 study of state governments provided evidence that state administrators tend to adopt a "package" or group of reinventing government reforms (Brudney et al., 1999); interestingly, strategic planning was cited as the most widely implemented reform of this group, lending credence to the assertion that it both is widely used and is becoming more integrated into broader management reform efforts. Other widely adopted management reforms included customer service training, quality improvement programs, outcome measurement including using benchmarking and customer satisfaction measures, and decentralized decision making. Likewise, strategic planning in the private sector is no longer viewed as a stand-alone process. Studies (Wilson, 1994) show there is an increased emphasis on the external environment at the same time newer methodologies and techniques are incorporated into the expanded strategic planning/management process, including benchmarking, total quality management, scenario planning, and core competencies analysis.

As organizations go through multiple cycles of strategic planning, the leadership becomes more aware of the organizational culture and structure that promote, and more often hinder, achievement of strategic goals. Some of these traits might include "turf" concerns that lead to infighting over changes, bureaucratic and centralized decision making, risk aversion to innovation and change, inefficient service delivery processes, and poor communication. Private sector writings have clearly established the link between corporate culture and performance (Kotter, 1988; Wilson, 1994), and public sector research also establishes that these organizational issues can impede effective organizational performance (Rainey, 1991). Thus organizations may become more interested in using management techniques such as total quality management, process reengineering, cultural assessment, and organizational change strategies to help develop a broader strategic management process supportive of the strategic plan's initiatives.

Improving organizational performance is a major theme in public management, and several prestigious awards recognize outstanding high-performing organizations. Strategic planning systems are highlighted in each of these awards. In Florida, the Governor's Sterling Award is awarded annually to outstanding private and public sector agencies that meet rigorous criteria (similar to the U.S. national Malcolm Baldridge National Quality Award) for high performance. Strategic planning is one of seven core categories (i.e., leadership, strategic planning, customer and market focus, information and analysis, human resource focus, process management, and business results) that agencies must possess to be seriously considered for the award (Florida Sterling Council, 1999). Both the strategy development process (environmental assessment, strategic objectives, and systematic refinement of the process) as well as the strategy deployment process (action plans, performance measures, and evaluation efforts) are integral to the evaluative criteria for strategic planning in this assessment process.

CONCLUSION

This chapter has provided an overview of the development and use of strategic planning in the public sector, and its evolution from an isolated planning process to an integral part of strategic management. Details on the specific models and steps in the strategic planning process have been covered. Elsewhere arguments have been made that strategic planning and strategic management approaches do not work in the public sector. Mintzberg's (1994) critique of strategic planning is equally harsh to the private and public sectors, asserting that strategic planning tends to reinforce a unitary, centralized hierarchical mode of decision making that is antithetical to the types of flexible, decentralized decisions organizations must make in a changing environment. But little empirical support for this finding has been produced in the public sector, and some research finds opposing evidence (Huang, 1997; Huang and Berry, 1995; Brudney et al., 1999). Another criticism of strategic planning is that it precludes organizations from taking action that falls outside the plan; simply put, emergent strategy is stifled by deliberate strategy articulated in the plan. Mintzberg (1987) argues that the plans and the implementation must come together in the person who knows the details of the program so intimately that she can take action and manage change. The 1990s models of strategic planning tried to address flexibility by creating a broad framework and allowing many decisions on particular strategies to be developed by middle-and lower-level workers in organizations. This helps to integrate sound emergent strategy into the organization's more deliberative strategy making to promote responsiveness and flexibility. Evidence mounts that managers believe strategic planning has been useful to their organization's effectiveness (Berry and Wechsler, 1995; Huang and Berry, 1995). One study of strategic planning in the Florida Department of Corrections (Huang and Berry, 1995) found that nearly all the managers

(94 percent) expressed commitment to the strategic planning process and made positive assessments of its organizational impacts.

Strategic planning may have begun as a management fad imported from the private sector, but it has demonstrated both real staying power and results in the public sector. The simplistic linear strategic planning processes of 15 years ago have been reborn as flexible adaptive processes tailored to the specific needs and capabilities of the leaders and agencies that adopt them. Clearly, good leadership and persistent attention to making strategic planning an integral part of the strategic management process can promote more effective organizations and help create public value.

REFERENCES

Ansoff, H. I. (1965). *Corporate Strategy.* McGraw Hill, New York.

Ansoff, H. I. (1980). Strategic issue management. *Strategic Management Journal. 1*(2): 131–148.

Anthony, W. P. (1985). *Practical Strategic Planning: A Guide and Manual for Line Managers.* Quorum Books, Westport, Conn.

Behn, R. D. (1991). *Leadership Counts.* Harvard University Press, Cambridge, Mass.

Berman, E. (1998). *Productivity in Public and Nonprofit Organizations: Strategies and Techniques.* Sage Publications, Thousand Oaks, Calif.

Berry, F. S. (1994). Innovation in public management: The adoption of state strategic planning. *Public Administration Review. 54*(3): 322–329.

Berry, F. S., Chackerian, R., and Wechlser, B. (1999). Administrative reform: Lessons from a state capitol. In *Public Management Reform and Innovation* (G. Frederickson and J. Johnston, eds.). University of Alabama Press, Tuscaloosa.

Berry, F. S., and Flowers, G. E. (1999). Public entrepreneurs in the policy process: Performance-based budgeting in Florida. *Journal of Public Budgeting, Accounting, and Financial Management. 11*(4): 585–624.

Berry, F. S., and Wechsler, B. (1995). State agencies' experience with strategic planning: Findings from a national survey. *Public Administration Review. 55*(2): 159–167.

Bozeman, B., and Straussman, J. D. (1990). *Public Management Strategies: Guidelines for Managerial Effectiveness.* Jossey-Bass, San Francisco.

Bracker, J. (1980). The historical development of the strategic management concept. *Academy of Management Review. 5*(2): 219–224.

Brudney, J. L., Hebert, F. T., and Wright, D. S. (1999). Reinventing government in the American states: Measuring and explaining administrative reform. *Public Administration Review. 59*(1): 19–30.

Bryson, J. M. (1994). Strategic planning and action planning for nonprofit organizations. In *The Jossey-Bass Handbook of Nonprofit Leadership and Management* (Robert D. Herman and Associates, eds.). Jossey-Bass, San Francisco.

Bryson, J. M. (1995). *Strategic Planning for Public and Nonprofit Organizations.* Jossey-Bass, San Francisco.

Bryson, J. M., and Roering, W. D. (1996). Strategic planning options for the public sector. In *Handbook of Public Administration* (James L. Perry ed.). Jossey-Bass, San Francisco.

Chandler, A. D., Jr. (1962). *Strategy and Structure: Chapter in the History of the Industrial Enterprise.* MIT Press, Cambridge, Mass.

DeHaven-Smith, L., and Wodraska, J. R. (1996). Census-building for integrated resources planning. *Public Administration Review. 56*(4): 367–371.

Drucker, P. F. (1959). Long-range planning. *Management Science.* (April): 238–249.

Eden, C., and Ackerman, F. (1998). *Making Strategy: The Journey of Strategic Management.* Sage Publications, Thousand Oaks, Calif.

FL Executive Office of the Governor (1997). *Instructions to State Agencies on Developing State Agency Strategic Plans.* FL Executive Office of the Governor, Tallahassee, Fla.

Florida Sterling Council (1999). *The 2000 Sterling Criteria for Organizational Performance Excellence.* FL Sterling Council, Tallahassee, Fla.

Freeman, R. E. (1984). *Strategic Management: A Stakeholder Approach.* Pittman, London.

Hammer, M., and Champy, J. (1993). *Reengineering the Corporation: A Manifesto for Business Revolution.* Harper Business Books, New York.

Huang, C. J. (1997). The effects of strategic planning: Perceptions of the Florida state managers. Doctoral dissertation, submitted to Florida State University, Tallahassee, Florida.

Huang, C. J., and Berry, F. S. (1995). *Strategic Planning in the Florida Department of Corrections.* FL Department of Corrections, Tallahassee, Fla.

Huang, C. J., and Berry, F. S. (1998). Impacts of strategic planning: The experience of florida state agencies. A paper presented at the *59th National American Society for Public Administration Conference,* Seattle, Washington.

Kemp, R. L. (1992). *Strategic Planning in Local Government: A Casebook.* American Planning Association Planners Press, Washington, D.C.

Kissler, G. R., Fore, K. N., Jacobson, W. S. Kittredge, W. P., and Stewart, S. L. (1998). State strategic planning: Suggestions from the Oregon experience. *Public Administration Review. 58*(4): 353–360.

Klay, W. E. (1989). The future of strategic management. In *The Handbook of Strategic Management* (J. Rabin, G. Miller and W. B. Hildreth, eds.). Marcel Dekker, New York.

Kotter, J. P. (1988). The leadership factor. Free Press: New York.

Kouzes, J. K., and Posner, B. Z. (1987). *The Leadership Challenge.* Jossey-Bass, San Francisco.

Kaufman, R. (1995). Megaplanning: The changed realities; Part 1, P & J, Dec: 8–14.

Melkers, Julia, and Willoughby, Katherine (1998). The state of the states: Performance-based budgeting requirements in 47 out of 50. *Public Administration Review. 58*(1): 66–73.

Mintzberg, H. (1979). *The Structuring of Organizations: A Synthesis of the Research.* Prentice-Hall, Englewood Cliffs, N.J.

Mintzberg, H. (1987). Crafting strategy. *Harvard Business Review.* (July/August): 66–75.

Mintzberg, H. (1994). *The Rise and Fall of Strategic Planning.* Free Press, New York.

Mintzberg, H., and Waters, J. A. (1985). Of strategies, deliberate and emergent. *Strategic Management Journal. 6*(2): 257–272.

Montanari, J. R., Daneke, G. A., and Bracker, J. S. (1989). Strategic management for the public sector: Lessons from the evolution of private-sector planning. In *The Handbook of Strategic Management* (J. Rabin, G. Miller and W. B. Hildreth, eds.). Marcel Dekker, New York.

Moore, M. H. (1995). *Creating Public Value: Strategic Management in Government.* Harvard University Press, Cambridge, Mass.

Newcomer, K. N. (ed.) (1997). *Using Performance Measurement to Improve Public and Nonprofit Programs.* New Directions for Evaluation, No. 75. Jossey-Bass, San Francisco.

Nutt, P.C., and Backoff, R.W. (1992). *The Strategic Management of Public and Third Sector Organizations.* Jossey-Bass, San Francisco.

Olsen, J.B., and Eadie, D.C. (1982). *The Game Plan: Governance with Foresight.* Council of State Planning Agencies, Washington, D.C.

Osborne, D., and Gaebler, T. (1992). *Reinventing Government: How the Entrepreneurial Spirit Is Transforming the Public Sector.* Addison Wesley, New York.

Popovich, M.G. (ed). (1998). *Creating High Performance Government Organizations.* Jossey-Bass, San Francisco.

Porter, M. (1980). *Competitive Strategy: Techniques for Analyzing Industries and Competitors.* Free Press, New York.

Radin, B.A. (1998). The Government Performance and Results Act (GPRA): Hydra-headed monster or flexible management tool? *Public Administration Review. 58*(4): 307–315.

Rainey, H.G. (1991). *Understanding and Managing Public Organizations.* Jossey-Bass, San Francisco.

Rainey, H.G., and Steinbauer, P. (1999). Galloping elephants: Developing elements of a theory of effective government organizations. *Journal of Public Administration Research and Theory. 9*(1): 1–32.

Ring, P.S., and Perry, J.L. (1985). Strategic management in public and private organizations: Implications of distinctive contexts and constraints. *Academy of Management Review. 10*(2): 276–286.

Southern Growth Policies Board (1997). *Results-Oriented Government: A Public Sector Training Curriculum in Strategic Planning and Performance Measurement.* Southern Growth Policies Board, Research Triangle Park, N.C.

Steiner, G.A. (1979). *Strategic Planning: What Every Manager Must Know.* Free Press, New York.

Stern, G.J. (1999). *The Drucker Foundation Self-Assessment Tool: Process Guide.* Jossey-Bass, San Francisco.

U.S. General Accounting Office (1993). *Performance Budgeting: State Experiences and Implications for the Federal Government.* General Accounting Office, Washington, D.C.

U.S. General Accounting Office (1997). *The Government Performance and Results Act: 1997 Government-wide Implementation Will Be Uneven.* GAO/GGD-97-109. Government Printing Office, Washington, D.C.

Walters, J. (1998), *Measuring Up.* Governing Books, Washington, D.C.
Wechsler, B., Berry, F.S., Park, W.S., and Tao, J. (1997). Determinants of strategic choice: Proactive, political and defensive models. A paper presented at the *Fourth National Management Research Conference at the University of Georgia,* Athens, Georgia.
Weiss, J.A., and Piderit, S.K. (1999). The value of mission statements in public agencies. *Journal of Public Administration Research and Theory. 9*(2): 193–223.
Wholey, J.S. (1999). Performance-based management: Responding to the challenges. *Public Productivity & Management Review. 22*(3): 288–307.
Wilson, I. (1994). Strategic planning isn't dead—it changed. *Long Range Planning. 27*(4): 12–25.
Wind, Y., and Mahajan, K.R. (1981). Designing products and business portfolios. *Harvard Business Review. 59:* 155–165.

14

Productivity Improvement and Public Management

Marc Holzer and Kathe Callahan
Graduate Department of Public Administration, Rutgers University, Newark, New Jersey

IMPORTANCE OF PRODUCTIVITY TO PUBLIC ORGANIZATIONS

A challenge confronting many public administrators today is how to run a productive organization with limited resources and oftentimes an overburdened work force. After years of bureaucrat bashing and headlines that criticize the ability of the public sector to provide goods and services effectively and efficiently, the public has come to expect and demand "more for less." And with the increased expectation of doing more with less, public organizations find themselves subject to greater public scrutiny.

According to Siedmann (1984), "The American public's love-hate relationship with its government produces demands for services, assistance, and protection while denigrating the people, processes, and costs necessary to meet those demands." From the outside, government appears to be the "problem," an argument politicians use to great advantage as they bemoan "large government" and berate the growth of public spending. But viewed from the inside, the services, the accomplishments, the problems solved are only some of those that society demands from its public servants. Government is a necessary, productive sector, providing important, critical services that meet society's needs, services we take for granted: Our mail is delivered, our garbage collected, our streets protected, and our children educated.

Some services are appropriate only to government. Public safety, public health, and public highways are necessary to the very existence of our society. Just as the armed services have replaced the private armies of feudal eras, today police, criminal justice, fire, and emergency services are virtually all publicly funded, publicly operated, and publicly controlled. We assume that our streets and highways must be public, that our parks must be open to all our citizens, and that our public schools will educate all applicants. As protector of our common assets, such as water and air, public sector water systems have replaced polluted private wells, public sector sewage systems have superseded polluting septic systems, and public sector regulations have sharply decreased air pollution. As protector of our rights, government is the locus for programs of affirmative action, human rights, and legal protections for individuals and businesses. Our society simply could not function without a wide range of public services.

Some services are problem-solving systems of last resort, missions at which other sectors of our society have failed. In these instances government is charged with solving unpleasant or unprofitable societal problems that the private sector (despite arguments for privatization) has turned away from or abandoned as unprofitable. Our society has high expectations that public servants will "solve" such difficult problems as municipal transit, public education, and health care for the uninsured—all of which the private sector has abandoned to its public counterparts. By default, public assumption of private responsibilities continues over the full spectrum of our society's services.

Government agencies run thousands of other enterprises that were once private but are now public or publicly subsidized, such as colleges and universities, airports, terminals, wholesale markets, theaters, and parks. When private outputs become public problems, government is called upon to compensate for those unanticipated or unpleasant consequences. If toxic industrial waste leaches out of landfills or pollutes our air, we turn to government to clean up the problems of poisoned waters and acid rain. If manufacturing workers are displaced as plants close and move to areas of lower labor costs, those workers become public responsibilities—for unemployment and retraining in the short term, and often for health care and financial support in the long term. If individuals violate the law, they often become the long-term responsibility of the criminal justice system.

We take good government for granted. Some services are visible and familiar. Many others are equally necessary, but virtually invisible. Public servants quietly provide many of the critical linkages a complex society requires. As regulators, they oversee the fiscal health of our banks and the quality of much of our food. As arbitrators they attempt to settle disputes before they enter the court system. As mechanics and engineers they safely maintain our basic systems of water supply and sewage. As extension agents they help our farmers be more productive. As lab workers and statisticians they help determine the causes of mysterious epidemics. As technicians they monitor the quality of our air and water. There are thousands of such jobs, each of which contributes to the productivity of public, and ultimately private, organizations and individuals.

THE DEVELOPMENT OF PRODUCTIVITY CONCERNS/AWARENESS IN PUBLIC ORGANIZATIONS

Despite the stereotypes and the broad range of services that we call upon its members to provide, the public sector is often innovative, entrepreneurial, and savvy—using state-of-the-art methods to improve efficiency and quality, to achieve outcomes as promised. As Osborne and Gaebler (1992) conclude in *Reinventing Government,* "We were astounded by the degree of change taking place . . . public sector institutions—from state and local governments to school districts to the Pentagon—are transforming the bureaucratic models they have inherited from the past, making government more flexible, creative, and entrepreneurial."

Perhaps Osborne and Gaebler should not have been so "astounded." There has been, and continues to be, a great deal of work within the public management community as to how to improve the processes of service delivery. There are many examples of innovation within the public sector, many productive applications of knowledge, many confirmations of more efficient and higher-quality services. *Reinventing Government* is just one of the latest rediscoveries of that work. As Poister concludes: "Despite the negative perceptions of the public bureaucracy that prevail in some quarters, successes are routinely scored by administrative agencies at all levels of government. These range from single episodes of satisfactory interactions with individual clients to the effective implementation of new programs and the development of innovative policies, strategies and treatments" (Poister, 1992).

At the state level, for example, New York state's Management and Productivity Program has saved over $1 billion since 1982. At the county level, Streib and Waugh (1991) have found considerable confidence in the administrative and political capacities of counties to design, implement, finance, and manage effective programs. At the local level, Ammons (1991) identified 35 jurisdictions and 39 officials as reputational leaders in local government productivity and innovation. And the Local Government Information Network (LOGIN) contains a database of over 50,000 cases of innovative, entrepreneurial accomplishment at the state, county, and municipal levels.

Hard evidence that "government works" can be found in state, county, and municipal awards programs. Each year thousands of projects are nominated for formal recognition by associations of their peers such as the National League of Cities, the U.S. Conference of Mayors, the American Society for Public Administration, the National Association of Counties, and the International Personnel Management Association. After rigorous, objective scrutiny, hundreds receive awards as models of problem solving and revitalization. They have accomplished what government's critics demand: entrepreneurial actions by public servants to improve public services and save public tax dollars. Those successes in federal, state, and local agencies directly counter assumptions that public servants care little about operational efficiency and effectiveness.

Some of government's successes can be measured in the terminology of business: dollars saved, units of service delivered, rate of errors. But other—less tangible and just as important—are virtually unique to the public sector: national inspiration, individual optimism, level of literacy, sense of security, mastery of like skills, fostering of the arts. Public sector award programs recognize both dimensions of success, "bottom line" and "quality of life."

At Rutgers University, the Exemplary State and Local Awards Program (EXSL) sponsored by the National Center for Public Productivity (NCPP) (http://newark.rutgers.edu/~ncpp) is designed to encourage productivity, creativity, and innovation in state and local government. This nationwide program, established in 1989, recognizes public initiatives that are designed to improve the quality of government services and operations. EXSL provides evidence of tangible accomplishments through productive public management: enhanced efficiency, capacity, and quality-of-life outcomes throughout the public sector. Since 1989 EXSL has presented 140 awards through a peer review process in collaboration with the Section on Management Science and Policy Analysis of the American Society for Public Administration. Awards are made to projects and programs that produce significant cost savings, measurable increases in quality and productivity, and improvements in the effectiveness of government services. Programs chosen are highly rated on program outputs, impact on quality of life of population served, cost-effectiveness, client support/satisfaction, innovative nature, obstacles or encumbrances that had to be overcome, nature of the problem addressed, degree of difficulty, and transferability or ability to serve as a model for other programs.

The Innovations in American Government Awards: A Program of the Ford Foundation and the John F. Kennedy School of Government at Harvard University (http://ksgwww.harvard.edu/innovat/) strives to identify and celebrate outstanding examples of creative problem solving in the public sector. Since its inception in 1986, the program has recognized 180 innovative programs that are examplars of public sector innovation—because of what they have accomplished and how they have accomplished it. Harvard selects 25 semifinalists, of which 10 receive major awards, "on the basis of the creativity involved in the innovation, the significance of the problem it undertakes to solve, the program's value to the clients who benefit from it, and its transferability to other jurisdictions."

The Rutgers and Harvard awards are evidence that significant improvements in the quality of services to the public have occurred when public employees have been empowered to undertake quality-improving, problem-solving initiatives. The creative, quality-oriented accomplishments that government's critics often call for are actually evident in virtually all parts of the public sector. They address society's most difficult-to-solve problems, producing high-quality outcomes—especially improvement in clients' lives, such as providing no-cost medical care for the indigent, unclogging court calendars, installing pollution and flood controls, expanding the supply of decent housing, increasing critical services to senior citizens, and rehabilitating youthful and older offenders. Awards are evidence that producing public services is not only difficult work—but anonymous work. Often only those at the very top are recognized. It is, however, just as important—if not more important—to recognize the people, the problem solvers who make government work.

MAJOR THEORETICAL CONCEPTS AND MANAGERIAL ISSUES/STRATEGIES

Successful problem-solving projects—award-winning or routine—are not the "commonsense" solutions typically posed by politicians, voters, corporate critics, and the media: "cut the fat" or "cutback management," "economize" or "privatize," "work harder" or "work smarter," "businesslike management" or "Japanese management." If only such straightforward adages were what public organizations need, then government's efficiency would not be at issue.

But simple prescriptions are not very useful. They are based on popular misperceptions of public management. They are contrary to the complex problem-solving processes governments (or private organizations of comparable size) require in order to address our society's most difficult-to-solve problems such as crime, pollution, or homelessness. Rather, the provision and improvement of services, in government or in the most profitable private sector firms, are complex and require hard, detailed work.

As a function of this organizational and analytical momentum, today to produce public services the best public organizations have developed multiple, reinforcing capacities. Award-winning government agencies typically apply quality management principles, use measurement as a decision-making tool, invest in human resource development and organizational learning, adapt new technologies, and develop partnerships—with the private sector, with other governmental and nonprofit agencies, and between management and labor. We have found those approaches to be consistently apparent in award-winning cases, as illustrated in Figure 1.

Each emphasis improves the utilization of resources (i.e., tax dollars, labor, energy, capital) in order to organize internal capacities, which produce outputs

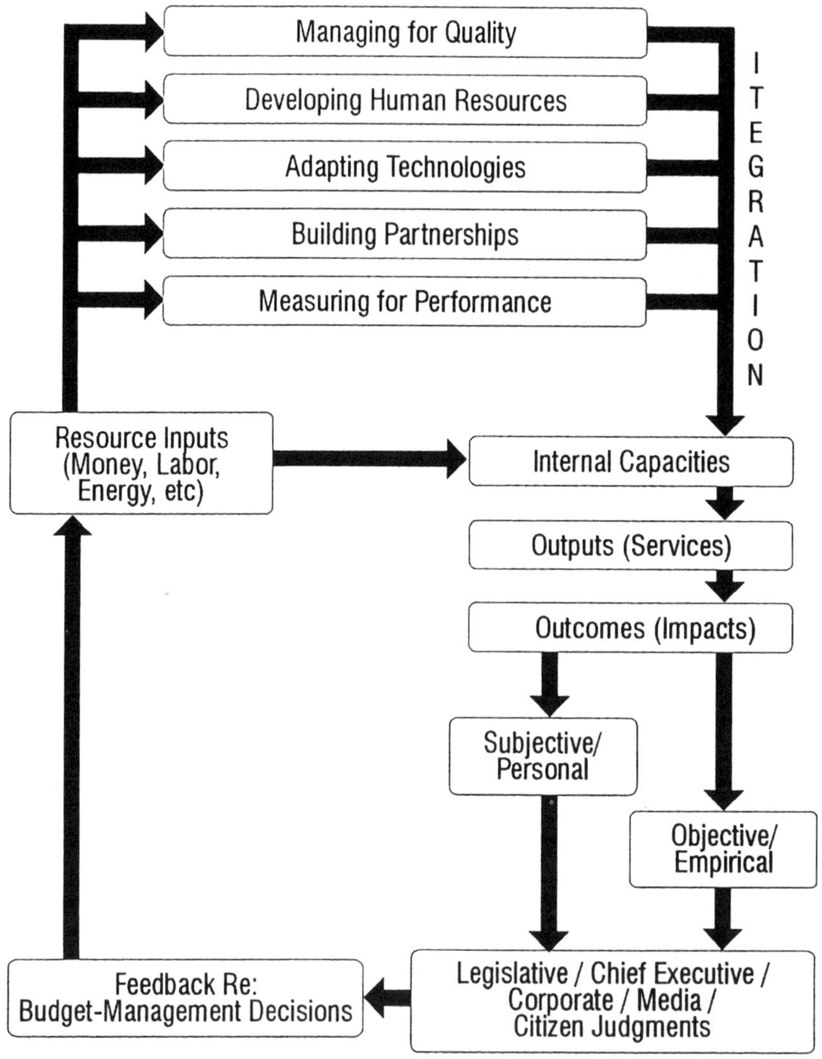

FIG. 1 Productivity improvement: A multifaceted approach.

(i.e., services) leading to expected outcomes (i.e., the impacts of those services) more efficiently and effectively.

Within the context of Fig. 1, productivity, then, is the ratio of outputs and outcomes (work done, products distributed, services rendered, impact achieved) to inputs. Productivity improvement is related to favorable changes in that ratio. Expectations of productivity improvement in the public sector must be tempered by recognition that there are differences between various ratios (or definitions) of improvement and that several of the five possibilities discussed in the following represent difficult circumstances that any organization—private or public—would be hard pressed to meet. In each of the five emphases, award-winning government has successfully responded to challenges the private sector would have considered impossible or unprofitable to confront.

1. Doing the same with less: Resource inputs decline, but outputs/outcomes are expected to remain constant. This represents a cutback management situation in which management is forced to respond productively when confronted with budget cutbacks in real dollars. For example, faced with a cutback in staff, a state mental health facility may reorganize, allowing for the same level of services with more efficient use of remaining staff.
2. Doing more with the same resources: Although resource inputs remain constant, public servants may be asked to improve outputs/outcomes. Many critics of government, particularly elected officials, argue this case. They often expect "quick fixes" based on limited perspectives or critiques by groups external to the agency. For example, they might propose that each social services worker increase applications processed by 25 percent. This might be a reasonable goal but cannot be implemented instantly, only as better management of inputs improves outputs.
3. Doing much more with much less: In the most difficult case, resource inputs may decline substantially, but government is pressured to improve outputs/outcomes substantially. Some elected officials and private sector critics advocate this scenario. It is, however, almost always based on an unreasonable and naive assumption, that is, that waste is of enormous proportions. Without the ability to invest in improved capacities, while maintaining adequate services to all applicants, this case is less reasonable than 2.
4. Doing much more with a little more: If some resource inputs can be increased moderately, then outputs/outcomes may improve substantially. This is a more likely case, as it allows for continued modest investments in improved productive capacity. But in the short run, a true productivity program is more likely to experience temporarily decreasing productivity—constant outputs while inputs increase modestly to allow for improved internal capacities, which increase outputs at a later stage. For example, in a state correctional facility investments in training, buildings, and equipment may be necessary in year 1 prior to improved correctional services in year 2.
5. Doing somewhat less with much less: If some inputs decline substantially, then public managers are challenged to limit the decline in outputs/outcomes. Although the output-to-input ratio is apparently increas-

ing, drastic cutbacks in resources often result in cutbacks in services, which fall most heavily on those citizens least likely to have alternatives. In a situation of deep cutbacks a municipal college, for example, may be forced to cut psychological counseling services to students—most of whom are unlikely to be able to purchase such services privately.

Management for Quality

Quality improvement in government, particularly state and local government, is not a recent phenomenon. Comprehensive productivity-quality improvements have long been characteristic of government in an environment of increasing demands and reduced resources (Poister, 1992). In many cases, what were formerly "productivity" projects are now redescribed (or repackaged) as "quality" efforts. Many of these, such as dramatic improvements in vehicle maintenance at the New York City Department of Sanitation, were described as "productivity" improvements prior to the total quality management (TQM) movement.

The Local Government Information Network (1999) data base, for example, contains more than 650 examples of programs with a quality component dating back through the 1980s. In 1993 West, Berman, and Milakovich (1993) estimated "that twenty-five percent of all cities over 25,000 population used TQM in at least one functional area . . . most often police work, parks and recreation services, personnel management, and budgetary reporting."

Although not new, then, quality management has become a fundamental element of the reinventing government movement. Just as the private sector is shifting from bureaucratic to customer-responsive management approaches in order to remain competitive in a global marketplace, government is becoming more quality-conscious to meet the challenges posed by privatization and to meet the public's view of themselves as customers, deserving of the highest-quality services.

In the continuous search for improved methods, the public service is more than willing to consider, and then often borrow and adapt, concepts that have become popular among their private counterparts. For instance, *quality* has been a corporate buzzword, and the quality movement in government draws heavily on decades of industrial quality improvement work in the private sector, such as that of Deming (1986) and Juran (1988). Seven factors typically serve as the framework for quality improvement efforts in the public sector:

Top management support
Customer focus
Long-term strategic planning
Employee training and recognition
Employee empowerment and teamwork
Measurement and analysis of processes and products
Quality assurance

Top Management Support

The commitment of top management is a necessary first step in disseminating quality improvement values throughout the organization. Leaders must be committed to achieving excellence. That commitment is more than just a "signal." Nor is it superficial "lip service." Quality-oriented changes will only result from basic reorientations of an organization's culture, and change of that magnitude must start with changes in behavior at the top as a model throughout the hierarchy. Leaders must be willing to relinquish some of their control and become facilitators of change (Hunt, 1993). Quality-oriented leaders in the public sector are also committed to the creation of an ethical climate in terms of the dissemination of quality improvement values throughout the organization.

Customer Focus

Public sector organizations often have a captive clientele. Traditionally, many agencies (and service providers) took the individuals they interacted with for granted—students in a classroom, welfare recipients in a waiting room—rather than viewing them as clients with particular needs. Forward-looking public organizations, however, have adopted a different model, citizen-as-customer, through which they consciously identify obstacles to improved client services and then work to solve those problems. They respect and respond to customers. As Hunt (1993) argues, successful organizations engage in open, continuous, two-way communication with their customers and utilize ongoing measures of customer satisfaction to alter and improve their services and processes.

Long-Term Strategic Planning

Government must often react to changes in its environment—budget cutting, a decreased tax base, an unfunded mandate, a change in elected officials. Those are all environmental constants, and adept public managers have developed excellent coping skills for maintaining their balance. But the most effective top officials have also undertaken deliberate planning to anticipate and then steer change in a productive, quality-enhancing direction.

Employee Training and Recognition

The highest quality goals of the most well-intended public sector leaders will remain unfulfilled if organizations are not prepared to produce. And the prerequisite for any productivity-quality effort is the preparation of the most important, most expensive organizational elements—its human resources. If employees are to produce at higher levels of quality, then the training that is prerequisite to service delivery must also be delivered at high levels. Although training is one of the first targets of policy- and management-level budget cutters, exemplary programs do not sacrifice that capacity-building investment for short-term savings. Quality-improving organizations must continuously upgrade work force skills.

Employee Empowerment and Teamwork

Producing quality is almost never the effort of only one individual. High-quality services are produced by teams, and those teams are empowered to solve problems. Teams recognize the reality of interdependence: Individual service providers function only within a support system of many colleagues who are often invisible to the service recipient. Hospital medical personnel are dependent not only on each other (doctors, nurses, technicians), but on intake, maintenance, billing and food staff, as well as volunteers. Teachers are similarly dependent on personnel in transportation, maintenance, pupil personnel services, and administration. And problems of quality in a hospital, school, or other public organization are best solved by those closest to the problem, including staff in both line (direct providers) and support (indirect providers) roles.

Measurement and Analysis of Processes and Products

Quality-enhancing public sector programs value feedback. They establish a data collection system, continually measure their internal and external outputs/outcomes (Fig. 1), analyze those measures for indications of problems, and then approach those problems as opportunities for improving service delivery.

Quality Assurance

Measurement and analysis are useful in providing a relative approach, that is, a process of benchmarking against past performance in pursuit of continual improvement. But a capacity for measurement and analysis against an objective, external benchmark such as a professional standard or the performance standards of other, similar organization is also important. Assuring quality means assuring that those standards are met.

Development of Human Resources

Quality management requires public sector managers who are willing to rethink human resource management. In a society with higher, quality-oriented expectations, the traditional bureaucratic, hierarchical management style is insufficient. Yet too many organizations, public and private, fail to utilize or maintain their expensive human capital intelligently. The reason for this is simple: It is difficult and it takes a lot of time and effort. The easiest way to increase productivity, in the short run, may be to introduce new technology or mechanize a process. However, the more enduring, but more difficult, way to improve productivity is to develop each worker's individual capacity and desire to function at the highest level possible.

Award-winning programs provide evidence that, in practice, "people approaches" are just as important as procedural, fiscal, or technological factors in improving productivity and the quality of services provided. The most successful public organizations recognize that productivity is dependent upon people who deal with clients, operate equipment, enter data, and solve unanticipated problems. People are the foundation on which the successes of every public organization rest.

The enlightened management of human resources is particularly important in the public sector because government's most extensive and expensive investments are people; most public organizations devote from 50 to 85 percent of their budgets to employee salaries and benefits. Because those "human resources" have complicated needs, responsive public organizations have adopted enlightened human resource practices, rejecting an authoritarian, bureaucratic style. Public organizations have often recognized that a productive organization is humane, structured around not only the task but its members and their human needs. They understand that the art of leadership inheres in inducing people to work well for the organization by grasping and responding to their needs.

We have found that, rather than taking a simple-minded, out-of-date approach to the management of complex human assets, productive public organizations confirm a multidimensional approach. They are systematically addressing the contemporary problems of human resource management:

Recruiting the best and brightest
Providing systematic training
Recognizing diversity
Building services by building teams
Providing employee assistance
Balancing employee and organizational needs

Recruiting the Best and Brightest

To provide high-quality, responsive service to their citizens, government agencies must hire highly talented and skilled public servants. Thus, personnel recruitment—the very beginning of the system of human resource management—is both a problem and an opportunity that the the most forward-looking jurisdictions have recognized and addressed. They begin by attracting the very best people to public sector careers.

Providing Systematic Training

Recruitment is only the first step in improving an organization's capacity to deliver services. Effective team efforts also require effective, ongoing training. High-performing public organizations have developed responsible models for the next step: helping prepare employees to perform.

Recognizing Diversity

Although service delivery is often dependent on cooperation among service providers, valuable contributions by personnel eager to solve problems are often stifled by the problems of discrimination and bias.

Building Services by Building Teams

The most productive agencies recognize that more productive services are achieved not by isolated individuals working alone and competing with each other, but by teams working cooperatively and supporting their colleagues. Thus, successful programs often build programs that maximize the strengths of employees while compensating for their weaknesses.

Providing Employee Assistance

Employees often suffer crises in their personal lives. Medical care, addiction, marital crises, abuse, and financial stress are examples of stresses may overflow into the workplace, impinging on productivity. Enlightened, high-performing organizations recognize that relatively small investments in helping employees overcome those problems will improve employee morale and loyalty and, just as important, result in substantial savings or cost avoidance to the organization.

Balancing Employee and Organizational Needs

Classical management concepts often assume a tension between employee and employer. Tight rules, systems, and supervision are necessary to limit counterproductive discretion, dishonesty, and laziness. Employees view the organization as an enemy, and vice versa; work is merely an interruption in their leisure time, and a great deal of energy is wasted attempting to sidestep those constraints. Organizations can be minimally productive under such assumptions but almost never produce at high levels of productivity and quality. Rather, organizations that work at high levels also work as partners with their employees. They recognize that performance is limited by burdensome rules, avoidable travel, and unavoidable health problems or personal stress.

Adapting Technology

Motivated, trained employees are only part of the productivity and quality improvement "formula." Each individual needs to be supported by reliable, up-to-date technologies. Advanced technologies are as important to the public as to the private sector. Both sectors need powerful computer and information systems, automated and rapid communications, energy-saving and security-enhancing devices, and an almost limitless menu of "hardware and software." To meet these needs, government often relies on off-the-shelf products developed by the private sector.

But when adequate products are not available, the public sector has taken the initiative to pioneer new systems. Government employees have invented lasers, solid-state technology, the basic design of most commercial and military aircraft, instrument landing systems, the first modern computer, titanium (and other stronger and lighter materials), the computed tomography (CT) scan, plastic corneas, advanced fishing nets, nuclear power, Teflon, wash-and-wear fabric, resuscitation devices, and plastic wrap (Public Employees Roundtable, 1987–1996).

Profiting from government's large up-front investments in such products, business has taken these products to the market. The National Aeronautics and Space Administration (NASA) (1997), for example, has a continuing program to help the private sector exploit innovations resulting from the space program. Sometimes government shares in those profits through licensing or royalty arrangements. Typically, however, the public sector and public servants receive neither royalties nor sufficient recognition.

Technologies that make possible improved performance are not limited to "high-tech" or computer applications. They apply to roads and sewers as much as they do to satellites and smart bombs. In as mundane an area as refuse collection, for example, departments of sanitation in New York City; Scottsdale, Arizona; and other localities have developed and applied productive technological changes, sometimes patenting those innovations.

The development and adaptation of technology for applied problem solving are often initiated by local or state governments. They are also functions of deliberate, goal-oriented efforts. Public Technology, Inc., for example, is devoted to the development and diffusion of productive technologies for state and local government.

Productive public agencies utilize technology to improve services to the public through overlapping approaches:

Provision of open access to data
Automation for enhanced productivity
Delivering on the public's demands
Cost-effective applications
Cross-cutting techniques

Provision of Open Access to Data

One obstacle to effective government, as well as to confidence in government, is lack of access to information. Citizens and businesses are often frustrated, angered, and alienated by difficulties in obtaining necessary information as to eligibility, deadlines, status, demographics, user fees, and requirements. Electronic kiosks and computer websites have vastly improved access to and exchange of information.

Automation for Enhanced Productivity

Automation is often thought of as reducing employment. Many award-winning cases, however, demonstrate that the creative application of automated programs can help overburdened agencies make better use of the "people power," improving both their effectiveness and their benefit/cost ratios.

Delivering on the Public's Demands

The majority of technology-based improvements in government are increments in quality. More award-winning uses of technology are primarily linked to better quality rather than to other factors. Although saving money is often an important corollary consideration, in some cases the public is clearly demanding clean water or improved skills, and significant investments may be necessary to accomplish those goals.

Cost-Effective Applications

Government's best technological practices are models for saving both time and money. Just as private citizens and the private sector seek to reduce downtime, the public sector has the same agenda, reducing unproductive travel time or waiting time.

Cross-Cutting Techniques

Some jurisdictions do more than just seek and adapt technologies. They develop and apply comprehensive approaches to the management of tangible assets, incorporating both low-tech and high-tech approaches.

Building of Partnerships, Not Privatization

Despite "businesslike" innovations in quality, human resources, and technology, the rush to privatize government has seemingly gained unstoppable momentum. Touted regularly by politicians and emphasized by the media, it is now virtually an unquestioned assumption.

The logic of privatization proponents is that turning over services to the private sector—through contracts or through abandonment—produces large savings with virtually no loss of quality or reduction in service levels (Savas, 1992). Proponents of privatization "have lived by the mantra that anything government can do, business can do better" (Katz, 1991). Advocates hold that outsourcing can deliver a much greater portion of services that are now public. Privatization is marketed as a solution that will (Savas, 1992):

—lower costs, while improving quality
—allow economics of scale
—allow public versus private comparisons of cost and performance

—prevent large start-up costs
—provide access to specialized skills and training
—promote flexibility in the size and mix of services
—make it possible to hire and fire as necessary
—allow for experimentation in different modes of service provision
—reduce dependence on a single supplier
—bypass inert bureaucracies
—allow quicker response to new service areas

But skeptics hold that many services are necessarily government's responsibility, and a public-to-private shift will not automatically enhance productivity in a jurisdiction or department. (Barnekov and Raffel, 1992). They and other critics suggest questions the public manager needs to answer when considering whether to privatize in order to enhance productivity (Stahl, 1988). To what extent is privatization likely to

—interfere with accountability?
—degrade responsiveness?
—reduce services?
—lower employee morale?
—result in incomplete contracts?
—produce cost overruns?
—lower quality at the expense of quantity?
—place short-term profits over long-term planning?
—negate the service ideal inherent in public service?
—provide opportunities for graft and corruption?
—duplicate services?

A recurring theme in the privatization literature is that what makes a difference is competition between the sectors, not privatization itself, and that private monopolies are no better than the public ones (Donahue, 1984). According to Savas (1992), cost-saving competition will, for instance, encourage innovation by allowing for experimentation in different modes of service provision, bypassing inert bureaucracies and allowing quicker response to new service areas.

Thus, privatization is only one form of competition, but a form limited to the private sector; an equally productive alternative is an expanded form of competition in which public organizations are competitive bidders. Some cities, such as Phoenix and Indianapolis, have pioneered public-private competition, and in head-to-head competition with private bidders public organizations have often won those bids.

Although competition is certainly an important assumption, it is not the only paradigm. The "flip side" of competition—cooperation—is also an essential productivity enhancement strategy, and one that is very often overlooked in the shadow of pressures for privatization. Yet joint public-private initiatives are options to which innovative public officials often turn, and cooperative arrangements for service provision are increasingly evident as the public sector seeks creative ways to stretch resources.

In contrast to privatization, these relationships are joint problem-solving efforts, or partnerships, which may be initiated by either "side." Some of the more successful public agencies, for example, have recognized working alliances between the work force and management; between levels of government and between neighboring local governments; and between government and citizens, government and corporations, government and not-for-profits. These innovations have proved to be effective arrangements aimed at improving government service and cutting costs. Because they represent the ability to think and act outside the rigid but familiar "bureaucratic box," they can be essential for pooling resources and improving productivity in an increasingly resource-scarce atmosphere.

EXSL and other best practice cases highlight different forms of partnerships that enhance productivity improvements in public organizations. Award-winning programs often occur in one of four types of relationship:

Community partnerships—citizens and volunteers
Public sector partnerships
Private sector partnerships
Not-for-profit partnerships

Community Partnerships—Citizens and Volunteers

Government's partners are most often the citizens it serves. Sometimes they coproduce services because they are required to by law: maintaining a sidewalk, carrying garbage to the curb, driving children to school. But, if afforded the opportunity, citizens are often eager to contribute their time and creative energies and to cooperate with service agencies.

Public Sector Partnerships

Government agencies often serve the clients of other agencies. Cooperation between those agencies is important in minimizing costs, especially when the "products" of one agency become the "workload" of another.

Private Sector Partnerships

Joint public-private ventures may strengthen government's capacity to deliver services by

—providing donations of personnel or equipment
—supplementing such services as schools, parks, and libraries
—jointly developing strategies to ameliorate emerging problems, such as homelessness or crime
—stimulating economic development

Private partners generally expect their investment, typically donations of personnel and equipment, to provide at least some indirect return, such as a better educated labor force, a safer neighborhood in which to do business, or a stimulus to economic development. But the private partner may also begin to act as a public-serving institution, directly investing for the general public good rather than for any specific, short-term bottom line gain.

Not-for-Profit Partnerships

The public sector has a long history of cooperative relationships with the nonprofit sector, particularly in the field of health and human services.

Measurement for Performance

Although public servants produce necessary public services, their agencies have not always built a capacity for measurement that can highlight both progress and the need for critical investments. Faced with competing demands and expectations public sector agencies confront issues that seem to defy measurement. Without the pressure of competition or the "unforgiving bottom line" of profit and loss, governmental agencies are likely to ignore performance measurement as they focus on more pressing issues (Ammons, 1996). In light of the growing emphasis on controlling costs, maintaining accountability, and reducing the size of government, performance measurement has become a priority in many state and local agencies.

Performance measurement provides government with a means of keeping score on how well their various departments and operations are doing. As Hatry notes, scorekeeping is essential:

> Unless you are keeping score, it is difficult to know whether you are winning or losing. This applies to ball games, card games, and no less government productivity. . . . Productivity measurements permit governments to identify problem areas and, as corrective actions are taken, to detect the extent to which improvements have occurred (Hatry, 1978).

Measurement of performance has always been implicit in questions as to outputs and outcomes: Is crime up? Are the streets cleaner? Is the air quality better? How well are our children doing in school? In short, Is a program producing as promised? The answers to such questions are important. They can provide feedback that influences decisions to allocate or reallocate public sector resources, to set or change priorities. Such decisions are made internally by public managers, chief executives, and legislators. They are substantially influenced externally by feedback from citizens, public interest-advocate groups, private businesses, and their elected or media surrogates. Each of these actors—internal or external—holds opinions as to service priorities.

Following the "subjective" arrow in Fig. 1, however, opinions as to the allocation of scarce public resources are often based on vague assessments of efficiency and efficacy, judgments that are typically subjective and "soft." They may be formed from a critical incident of success or failure. They may be grounded in a rumor. They may be a function of a personal experience.

But following the "objective" arrow in Fig. 1, performance measurement offers an opportunity to develop and present "hard" data instead. Measurement provides an opportunity to present evidence that the public sector is a public bargain; to highlight the routine, but important, services that public servants quietly provide; to respond to the public's sometimes angry questions, and implicit suggestions, dispassionately. Measurement, then, helps to move the basis of decision making from personal experience to measurable accomplishment (or lack thereof). Data about levels and trends of outputs and outcomes, and associated benefit/cost ratios, help defend, expand, or improve a program, rather than proceeding from relatively subjective, political decisions based on circumstantial (if any) evidence. Measurement helps objectively answer such questions as, Is an organization doing its job? Is it creating unintended side effects or producing unanticipated impacts? Is it responsive to the public? Is it fair to all, or does it favor certain groups, inadvertently or deliberately? Does it keep within its proper bounds of authorized activity? In short, is it productive?

In the process of providing answers to those questions, productive governments stress the following:

Establishing goals and measuring results
Estimating and justifying resource requirements
Reallocating resources
Developing organization improvement strategies
Motivating employees to improve performance

In the course of a measurement effort several processes occur:

1. High-performing public organizations monitor the production of "internal" services that contribute to the efficient and effective production of "external" services for clients. Such internal (or invisible) services as maintenance, training, and auditing are necessary prerequisites to the production of outputs.

2. Outputs are measurable as services provided in terms of such factors as quantity (How many clients are served? How many units of service are delivered?) and quality (Are the services delivered to certain standards? What is the error rate?)

3. *Output,* however, is a narrow term that limits interpretations of productivity improvement. If managers are to make better decisions as to resource allocation and reallocation, then they need measures not only of outputs, but of *outcomes*—the services' results, such as improvements in a client's quality of life or ability to maintain employment.

A productive agency must, therefore, monitor and improve productivity at all three stages, internal services, external services, and outcomes, and communicate those measures clearly and honestly to the public. Fortunately, the tools are available. Performance measurement is fairly well developed as a set of tools for making better decisions within public organizations. Managers who are responsible for day-to-day management now often have access to information that helps them implement public policies effectively and efficiently. A substantial body of research demonstrates that measurement of public services is conceptually sound and feasible. For example, the Government Accomplishment and Accountability Task Force of the American Society for Public Administration has produced an extensive *Performance Measurement Training* manual (1996).

Overall, then, a measurement program, which requires substantial expertise and careful planning, can ask, and begin to answer, such questions as the following.

In terms of program performance:

How much of a service is provided?
How efficiently are resources used?
How effectively is a service provided?

In terms of effectiveness indicators for performance:

What is the intended purpose of the service?
What are the unintended impacts of the service?
How effective is the service in preventing problems?
Is the service adequate?
Is the service accessible?
Are clients satisfied with services?
Are services distributed equitably?
Is a product durable?
To what extent is a service provided to clients in a dignified manner?

In terms of desirable characteristics of performance measures:

Is a service significant?
Is the service appropriate to the problem being addressed?
Is performance quantifiable?
Are services readily available?
Are services delivered in a timely manner?
Are services delivered in a relatively straightforward manner?
Is a measure of performance valid?
Is a measure acceptable?
Is performance measured completely?
Are measures accurate?
Are measures reliable?

Public managers and policymakers have the performance measurement tools to help carry out their responsibilities to deliver and improve services, as promised, in at least eight different ways:

–Establishing goals and measuring results
–Estimating and justifying resource requirements
–Reallocating resources
–Developing organization improvement strategies
–Motivating employees to improve performance
–Controlling operations
–Predicting periods of work overload or underload
–Developing more sophisticated capacities for measurement (Hatry and Fisti, 1992)

Establishing Goals and Measuring Results

"Holding programs accountable" is a popular political prescription. But accountable for what? To the extent goals are vague, the public will be neither satisfied nor informed as to progress (or lack thereof). The best public programs specify goals, treat those goals as planned targets, and match results with plans. Such comparisons facilitate accountability.

Estimating and Justifying Resource Requirements

Budgets are estimates of resource requirements. Traditionally, they are based on past expenditures and "guesstimates" as to future needs. But fiscal planning can be accomplished more systematically and quantitatively. Justifications as to expenditures can be more precise, more objective, and more factual to the extent that they are the products of measurement.

Reallocating Resources

Measurement contributes to more productive resource allocation decisions. It may help save substantial sums by developing and evaluating benefit-cost linkages. It may help reduce costs by highlighting lower-cost alternatives.

Developing Organization Improvement Strategies

Measures can help bring problems into focus. Once clear, problems can then be addressed in a more systematic manner, such as overcoming obstacles, targeting services, and planning for anticipated problems. In short, measurement can help prevent disappointments and surprises.

Motivating Employees to Improve Performance

Motivation is often a function of measurement. Setting reasonable, measurable goals can create an expectation that those goals can be reached. Displaying progress toward goals, or just measuring present against past performance, often induces members of the work force to work in positive directions, taking pride in moving the trend lines in the "right" directions: more output, higher quality, more effective outcomes.

Multiple Opportunities for Improvement

Exemplary progress often results from multiple approaches to the improvement of public performance. Public sector improvement programs operate under many labels. The program's name, however, is less important than its substance: comprehensive productivity improvement in an environment of increasing demands and reduced resources. Such programs improve performance systematically, by integrating advanced management techniques and, in the best cases, institutionalizing productivity improvement initiatives.

A Step-by-Step Strategy

Complementing the improvement factors of Fig. 1, public sector performance improvement programs typically follow a multiple-step strategy (Holzer, 1995):

Step 1 Clarifying goals and obtaining support: Productivity programs must agree upon, and have commitments to, reasonable goals and objectives; adequate staff and resource support; and organizational visibility. The full cooperation of top management and elected officials is a prerequisite to success.

Step 2 Locating models: As productivity is an increasing priority of government, existing projects can suggest successful paths and ways to prevent potential mistakes. Models can be found through computer networks, the professional literature, and conferences.

Step 3 Identifying promising areas: As a means of building a successful track record, new productivity programs might select as targets those functions continually faced with large backlogs, slipping deadlines, high turnover, or many complaints. Because personnel are the largest expenditure for most public agencies, improved morale, training, or working conditions might offer a high payoff. Organizations might also target functions for which new techniques, procedures, or emerging technologies seem to offer promising paybacks.

Step 4 Building a team: Productivity programs are much more likely to succeed as bottom-up, rather than top-down or externally directed, entities. Productivity project teams should include middle management, supervisors, employees, and union representatives. They might also include consultants, clients, and representatives of advocacy groups. If employees are involved in looking for opportunities, then they are likely to suggest which barriers or obstacles need to be overcome; which tasks can be done more efficiently, dropped or simplified; which workloads are unrealistically high or low.

Step 5 Planning the project: Team members should agree on a specific statement of scope, objectives, tasks, responsibilities, and time frames. This agreement should be detailed as a project management plan, which should then be updated and discussed on a regular basis.

Step 6 Collecting program data: Potentially relevant information should be defined broadly; it may include reviews of existing data bases, interviews, budgets, and studies by consultants or client groups. A measurement system should be developed to collect data on a regular basis, and all data should be supplied to the team for regular analysis. The validity and usefulness of such information should be constantly monitored.

Step 7 Modifying project plans: On the basis of continuing team discussions of alternative approaches and data, realistic decisions must be made about program problems, opportunities, modifications, and priorities. For instance, could a problem best be solved through the more intensive use of technology, improved training, better supervision, or improved incentives?

Step 8 Expecting problems: Projects are more likely to succeed if they openly confront, and then discuss, potential misunderstandings, misconceptions, slippages, resource shortages, client and employee resistance, and other topics. Any such problem, if unaddressed, can cause a project to fail.

Step 9 Implementing improvement actions: Implementation should be phased in on a modest basis and without great fanfare. Those projects that are highly touted, but then do not deliver as expected, are more likely to embarrass top management (and political supporters), with predictable consequences. Those that adopt a low profile are less likely to threaten key actors, especially middle management and labor.

Step 10 Evaluating and publicizing results: Measurable success, rather than vague claims, is important. Elected officials, the press, and citizen groups are more likely to accept claims of success if they are backed up by hard data. "Softer" feedback can then support such claims. Particularly important in providing evidence of progress are timely data that reflect cost savings, additional services, independent evaluations of service levels, client satisfaction, and reductions in waiting or processing times.

As with any other generic recipe, this model should be modified and adapted to a specific organizational context. Real cases will always be slightly different from the model; in some cases one or two steps would be missing because of the organizational and cultural assumptions of the situation; in other cases several steps can be combined in one. Still, because the steps of the model are analytically distinguishable, the model is useful for analyzing real organizations and programs to highlight the strengths and illuminate the weaknesses of cases under discussion.

Overall, then, the most innovative and productive public agencies do not simply execute one good program. Rather, they integrate advanced management techniques into a comprehensive approach to productivity improvement. They institutionalize productivity improvements by identifying, implementing, measuring, and rewarding major cost savings and performance enhancements in their agencies. They benchmark their efforts against those of similar organizations across the nation. They have a client orientation. Perhaps most important, productive programs are built on the dedication, imagination, teamwork, and diligence of public servants.

IMPACT/IMPLICATIONS OF PRODUCTIVITY IMPROVEMENT ON THE PUBLIC MANAGEMENT PROFESSION

Government does solve problems. From preserving natural resources to ensuring the safety of farmers, from providing short-term housing for the homeless to instilling responsibility in teenage fathers, the problems addressed by government are multiple and complex. And virtually all state and local governments are confronting existing and emerging problems with far fewer resources than they had a decade ago.

Good things are happening in the public sector. Creative solutions to pressing problems are implemented on a daily basis. We do not, however, hear enough about the positive accomplishments. The failures of government are what dominate the air waves, the headlines, and the water cooler conversations. We would prefer to see a middle ground established where both the good and the bad aspects of government are honestly portrayed and openly discussed. Constructive dialogue and positive examples can provide opportunities for bad programs to become good and for good programs to become great.

If citizens only hear about the failures and inefficiencies of the public sector, they will believe that government is incapable of doing anything right. Citizens will expect less, and public servants may actually end up giving less when the dominant perception is "it can't be done." A self-fulfilling prophecy emerges, and society eventually gets what it expects, and possibly what it deserves. If as citizens we believe in government unresponsiveness, that is most likely what we will get—unresponsive government. However, if we believe that government is responsive, or at least has the potential to be responsive, and we work with and support our public servants, then we are more likely to get better government. If as citizens we become involved in the process of government, in a proactive manner, our expectations, as well as the performance of the public sector, will markedly increase.

The people who work in government are dedicated to the public service and dedicated to improvement of the quality of life of their fellow citizens, in spite of seemingly insurmountable odds. They deserve to be commended for their efforts rather than criticized and condemned. People who work in government are different from people who work in the private sector. Intrinsic rewards, such as recognition, and acknowledgment that they are "doing the right thing," are far greater motivators than money and a corner office with a view. We should, therefore, try consciously to acknowledge and reward the accomplishments of these individuals. The criticism they suffer on a daily basis, even from the clients they serve, only serves to undermine their ability to perform and function effectively.

Successes are routine, yet they are taken for granted and rarely acknowledged. We expect our mail to be delivered on time and our garbage to be collected on a regular basis. The school bus should arrive promptly at 7:35 so we can leave for work on time. And of course the public highways have to be in good repair and the public transportation systems have to be operating on schedule so we actually get to the office on time. It is when these systems and services do not work that we become vocal complainants. For the most part, when they do work, we remain silent.

The substantial research and experience with public sector productivity programs in scores of federal, state, and municipal agencies are sufficient to dispel misconceptions that executives care little about operational efficiency and effectiveness. It is true that some managers have given up trying to improve productivity or have given in to low expectations. But a more comprehensive view indicates that, as policy implementers who are on board for the long term, many managers and executives are professionally committed to productivity improvement. Their commitments are at least as strong as those of transient policymakers, and their innovations are at least as promising and sophisticated as those proposed by their sometimes condescending corporate critics.

Overall, then, we might conclude that in a fairly permanent era of fiscal stress, commitment, professionalism and intangible support are relatively more important than fiscal resources—either as budgetary pressures or as slack resources. This is an optimistic situation, for intangible resources, that is, professionalism and commitment and support, are easier to generate and tap than are finite, limited dollars.

This argument can lead to further hypotheses. Despite budget cuts and limited resources

—If public servants are treated as committed professionals who want to do the right things
—If internal innovators consciously seek to build support within the agency, the broader organization, and the political-client environment
—If public administrators receive enlightened political support
—If they are treated as administrative professionals on a par with their private sector colleagues
—If they are allowed to become less bureaucratic
Then
—more productive innovations will be developed and implemented.

EXSL and other "best practice" awards are particularly important because it has never been more clear that government is under pressure not just to be productive—or efficient and effective in the most straightforward meaning of the term—but to pull back from a broad range of public responsibilities: to privatize such basic functions as education, police, corrections, sanitation, airports, and information systems.

Our society is at a critical juncture. The public is losing patience with what it perceives to be unproductive government. Two roads seems to diverge. Under the broad banner of "privatization," one seemingly straight and sunlit road is a set of optimistic promises, defined by the argument that the private sector can deliver necessary public services more effectively, even at lower cost. The myth is that government is neither businesslike nor adaptive.

The other road, perhaps winding and less well lit, is composed of pragmatic responses to the weakening of public support—a set of solutions proposed by the public service to improve services to the public. The reality of productive government is distinctly different from the myth. There are some bureaucratic horror stories—just as there are in private sector bureaucracies. But beneath the surface of the stereotypes are many dedicated public servants and many hard decisions quietly made to save money, stretch resources, reorder priorities, invent, and innovate. Government *is* often businesslike, *does* often tap all types of expertise, and *can* often deliver as promised.

To the extent the first path is chosen, the public service will be smaller, weaker, and less enticing as a career choice. To the extent the public is convinced that by way of the second option the public sector can deliver services, efficiently and effectively as promised, then the public service will become a more promising career path.

Is there, then, a future for the public service in an era of privatization? The answer is likely to be yes, under several optimistic scenarios as the record of public sector successes helps to rebuild public support:

1. The privatization highway becomes a dead end as reality sets in: Contractors do not deliver as promised, costs to the public rise quickly, and wages drop precipitously. As a quick fix, privatization fades, although contracting remains an option for creative, productive public decision makers.

2. Government competes successfully with the private sector. Competition has been sold to the public and policymakers as the primary means to achieving efficiency. But only one form of competition—privatization (or private versus private)—has been assumed. Competition can certainly improve organizational performance. But in linking competition to privatization the former concept has been defined too narrowly. We ought to consider "government as competitor" as an expanded set of approaches to the problem of public productivity.

3. Internal competition within government is adopted as the best of both worlds. Recognizing the importance of public control of public services, competition without privatization becomes an acknowledged alternative. Agencies or units of government compete to provide services that are appropriate only to public sector delivery systems.

Evidence from public sector productivity programs in scores of federal, state, and municipal agencies should begin to dispel misconceptions that executives care little about operational efficiency and effectiveness. But a more sophisticated view indicates that, as policy implementers who are on board for the long term, many managers and executives are professionally committed to performance improvement. Their commitments are at least as strong as those of transient policymakers, and their innovations are at least as promising and sophisticated as those proposed by their sometimes condescending corporate critics.

If public servants are treated as administrative professionals on a par with their private sector colleagues, and if they are allowed to become less bureaucratic as suggested by the Gore and Winter reports (1993), then more innovative programs and initiatives will be developed and implemented. Public servants will act more as creative entrepreneurs, less as bureaucratic civil servants. And the public sector will, in the public's perception, be more businesslike, more deserving of the public's tax dollars.

A public sector that holds the public's confidence is very much within our grasp. Hummel suggests that *public servant,* with more professional connotations, should replace *bureaucrat,* with its negative connotations (Hummel, 1984). Of course, the public service can neither mandate nor manipulate that change. But that substitution of terms, as evidenced by common usage, should be the measure of our success in transforming government. To the extent performance improves, so will image. To the extent image changes, so will language. *Bureaucrat* will slowly give way to *public servant. Bureaucracy* will slowly give way to *public service.* And the public will feel confident in turning to its public organizations for solutions to society's problems.

CONCLUSION

If government is to continue to improve its productivity *and* to counter the rush to privatization, it must address critical issues of human resources, technology, partnerships, and measurement.

Human Resource Issues

In pursuit of performance, government's best practices suggest a set of typical people-oriented diagnostic questions that should be asked by and of managers:

Can employees have a voice in decisions that affect them? These might include joint labor-management committees, quality circles, or vertically integrated problem-solving task forces.

Does management create an environment that workers feel part of? Indicators of a participatory, fear-free workplace are open information, open doors, and an atmosphere in which risk takers are not punished for the inevitable failures.

Are people involved in looking for improvement opportunities? Employees are often the first, best (and cheapest) sources for identifying barriers and obstacles to overcome, tasks to be done more efficiently, work that might be dropped, shortened, or simplified.

Are employees challenged by work that uses their skills, abilities, and intelligence? Most employees feel they can operate at higher levels of responsibility and are willing to do so if given appropriate opportunities. Appropriate training should be available to upgrade skills and enhance knowledge.

Does management provide support and assistance to employees coping with problems? A yes to that question presumes that managers and employees are adequately trained, adequately equipped, and adequately informed.

To the extent these questions are answered, public servants will be more efficient and effective, agencies will deliver promised services, and citizens will find that their work force is a valuable, productive asset.

Technology Issues

Adopting new technologies can be as simple as using a fax machine to provide up-to-date information on the employment status of noncustodial parents, as creative as using existing bar code technology to monitor recycling compliance, or as complex as setting up an interstate fingerprint identification system to track offenders. Public employees have no shortage of such ideas, and they freely "put them on the table" when asked. But in comparison to employees in the private sector they do suffer from a shortage of capital to invest in productive innovations.

The public sector could apply many more productive, cost-saving, quality-enhancing technological innovations if funding were available. The innovations mentioned were typically accomplished with minimal funding by private sector standards. But they were successful despite the "handicaps" by which public agencies are typically limited: the political nature of the budget process, multiyear delays in approving requests for capital investments, and prohibitions on reinvesting savings in their own agencies.

If government is to be more businesslike, then the private sector has to support its public counterparts in raising funds for comparable investments in technology: state-of-the-art computers, comfortable buildings, and timely information systems. Despite the technological creativity high-performing agencies evidence, it is unrealistic to expect many governments to be able to squeeze expensive investments from budgets that are declining in real dollars. That is, government must be allowed to overcome a blatant double standard in which the private sector is expected to make capital investments necessary to do its jobs, but the public sector is starved for the capital investments that would help support the public infrastructure that businesses need to be profitable: transportation to work and market, public schools for a developing work force, water and sewers for a developing economy.

Partnership Issues

Creative partnerships—with other levels of government, with the private sector, with nonprofit agencies—illustrate how a wide range of stakeholders can develop, deliver, and sustain public programs. Partnerships are formed to address complex social issues that one agency alone could not possibly handle and to reduce, and if possible eliminate, the fragmentation and duplication that exist in the service delivery system. All of these partnerships realize cost savings and at the same time tangibly improve the quality of services provided.

Innovative partnerships of the public and private sectors, and across agencies, departments, levels, and even branches of the government, serve as models for significantly higher levels of accomplishment once we begin to think outside the normal bureaucratic box. Federal, state, and local governments need to encourage and support effective partnerships that improve service delivery, reduce expenses, and overcome fragmentation and duplication of government functions. When permitted to approach problem solving creatively, public servants can create exciting programs, producing more productive, more responsive government.

Measurement Issues

Measurement-based best practices are becoming models for the entire public sector. Working from the premise that measurement of performance and financial management are intertwined, the Government Accounting Standards Board (GASB) has stated that the goal of service delivery would be well served if debates about service allocation and resource utilization were guided by objective criteria (Fountain, 1997). GASB has made major progress toward the development and widespread use of objective measures in municipal budgets and fiscal reports. The impetus for this effort has been widespread concern that lack of such data undercuts the efforts of the government to communicate information about its efficiency and effectiveness; that the financial reports of governmental entities do not go far enough in providing "complete information to management, elected officials and the public about the 'results of the operations' of the entity or its programs" (Fountain, 1992). The National Center for Public Productivity (1997) and other organizations, through the support of the Sloan Foundation, are developing pilot projects that provide a results-oriented, citizen-driven basis for performance improvement in the public sector.

REFERENCES

Ammons, David (1996). *Municipal Benchmarks: Assessing Local Performance and Establishing Community Standards.* Sage Publications, Thousand Oaks, Calif.

Ammons, David N. (1991). Reputational leaders in local government productivity and innovation. *Public Productivity and Management Review. 15*(1): 19–43.

Barnekov, Timothy K., and Raffel, Jeffrey (1992). Public management of privatization. In *Public Productivity Handbook* (Marc Holzer, ed.). Marcel Dekker, New York.

Deming, William E. (1986). *Out of the Crisis.* MIT Center for Advanced Engineering Study. Cambridge, MA.

Donahue, J.D. (1984). *The Privatization Decision: Public Ends, Private Means.* Basic Books, New York.

Fountain, Jay (1992). *Service Effort and Accomplishment Project,* 1st ed. Government Accounting Standards Board, Norwalk, Conn.

Fountain, Jay (1997). *Service Effort and Accomplishment Project,* 2nd ed. Government Accounting Standards Board, Norwalk, Conn.

Government Accomplishment and Accountability Task Force (1996). *Performance Measurement Training.* American Society for Public Administration. Washington, D.C.

Hatry, Harry (1978). The status of productivity measurement in the public sector. *Public Administration Review. 38:* 28.

Hatry, Harry, and Fisk, Donald (1992). Measuring productivity in the public sector. In *Public Productivity Handbook* (Marc Holzer, ed.). Marcel Dekker, New York.

Holzer, Marc (1995). Building capacity for productivity improvement. In *Competent Government: Theory and Practice* (Arie Halaclirni and Marc Holzer, eds.). Chatelaine Press, Burke, Va.

Hummel, Ralph (1984). *The Bureaucratic Experience.* St. Martin's Press, New York.

Hunt, David V. (1993). *Quality Management for Government.* ASQC Quality Press, Milwaukee.

Juran, J.M. (1988). *Juran on Leadership for Quality.* McGraw-Hill, New York.

Katz, J.I. (1991). Privatizing without tears. *Governing Magazine.* 38–42.

Local Government Information Network (LOGIN) (database). William C. Norris Institute, St. Paul, Minnesota.

National Aeronautic and Space Administration (NASA) (1997). *Technology Transfer Program.* Office of Technology Applications, Washington, D.C.

Osborne, David, and Gaebler, Ted (1992). *Reinventing Government.* Addison-Wesley, Reading, Mass.

Poister, Theodore H. (1992). Productivity monitoring: Systems, indicators, and analysis. In *Public Productivity Handbook* (Marc Holzer, ed.). Marcel Dekker, New York.

Public Employees Roundtable (1987–1996). *Unsung Heroes* (newsletter). Public Employees Roundtable, Washington, D.C.

Savas, E.S. (1992). Privatization and productivity. In *Public Productivity Handbook* (Marc Holzer, ed.). Marcel Dekker, New York.

Siedman, Elizabeth. (1984). Of games and gains. *The Bureaucrat.* (Summer): *13:* 4–8.

Stahl, O.G. (1988). What's missing in privatization? *The Bureaucrat. 17:* 41–44.

Streib, Gregory, and Waugh, William L. Jr. (1991). Administrative capacity and the barriers to effective county management. *Public Productivity and Management Review. 15*(1): 61–70.

West, Jonathan P., Berman, Evan M., Milokovich, Michael (1993). Implementing TQM in local government. *Public Productivity and Management Review. 17* (2): 175–189.

15

Measuring Government Performance

Kathryn E. Newcomer
Department of Public Administration,
George Washington University,
Washington, D.C.

"Managing for results"—the watchword for public managers leading their programs into the 21st century—typically signifies the adoption of performance measurement systems in public programs. Monitoring progress made toward achieving program goals requires systematic measurement; however, although collecting data on performance may be a useful tool, it is no guarantee of improvement in management. As public managers across the world have found, creating organizational cultures supportive of the use of performance data in management and allocation decisions also presents a significant challenge.

Performance measurement is the label given to routine measurement of program inputs, outputs, and/or outcomes undertaken by agencies within governments and the nonprofit sector to meet demands for documentation of program performance (Wholey and Hatry, 1992). During the last three decades of the 20th century a number of managers at all levels of government in countries around the world developed and implemented performance measurement systems to address demands that they document government performance.

The increased demand for data documenting the performance of public programs is in part a sign of the information age, in that information technology has facilitated the processing of unprecedented amounts of program data more efficiently than ever before. Routine reporting of program performance also reflects the widespread desires of citizens and their elected officials for more transparent, entrepreneurial, and efficient government (Osborne and Gaebler, 1992).

Faced with ardent citizen demands to see what value they receive for their taxes, a large number of local governments in the United States started measuring performance in the mid-1970s. Through experimentation with this management tool, local government officials have found that they can use performance measures to inform decision making in a wide variety of arenas, including strategic planning, budgeting, and contractor monitoring, as well as to report to the public on program performance. Table 1 lists applications for performance measures that have been documented in local governments across the United States. However,

TABLE 1 Local Government Processes That May Incorporate Performance Measures

Processes That Use PMs	Literature Addressing Each PM Use
Strategic Planning	Glazer (1991); Tigue (1994); Willoughby & Melkers (1996); Dupont-Morales & Harris (1994); Tuck and Zaleski (1996); Jackson (1993)
Policy Analysis	Leithe (1997)
Budgeting	Glazer (1991); Dupont-Morales & Harris (1994)
Performance Reports/(SEA)	Blessing (1991); GASB (1994); Hatry, et al. (1990); Marshall (1996); Tracy (1996); Tracy & Jean (1993)
Citizen Surveys	Epstein (1988); Epstein and Olsen (1996); Alter (1995); Chan (1994); Osborne and Gaebler (1992)
Benchmarking	Hatry, et al. (1990); Tracy & Jean (1993); Tracy (1996); Fischer (1994); Bruder and Gray (1994); Ammons (1996)
Program and Performance Monitoring	Newcomer (1996, 1997); Epstein (1988); Perrin (1998); Wholey and Hatry (1992); Aristigueta (1997); Willoughby & Melkers (1996)
Personnel Appraisal	Benowitz and Schein (1996); Tigue (1994); Chan (1994)
Contractor Monitoring	Lemov (1998); Katz (1991); Osborne & Gaebler (1992)
Performance Auditing, Evaluation	Heaton et al. (1993)

Source: Bernstein (1999: 31).

although the list of possible uses is impressive, there is little documentation of the efficacy of these efforts in improving public management.

Implementing and using performance measurement systems require much more of managers than technical measurement skills. In fact, experience in government jurisdictions across the world has shown that effective use of performance measurement to improve program management presents managers with complex communication, analytical, political, and measurement challenges. The U.S. federal government adopted performance measurement as a management tool later than many other governments. During the late 1990s managers in U.S. federal agencies were coping with demand and supply challenges regarding performance measures, and their struggles provide instructive lessons for other public managers.

This chapter provides an overview of the origins and deliberations of performance measurement efforts in the U.S. federal government and draws upon the American experience to identify the challenges and opportunities this management tool presents for public managers. The first section describes the political context that has shaped performance measurement efforts in the U.S. federal government. Then what we have we learned about the challenges managers face in designing and using performance measurement is reviewed. And in the third section, current and evolving issues that affect the effectiveness of performance measurement efforts are discussed.

THE POLITICAL CONTEXT SHAPING DEMANDS FOR PERFORMANCE MEASUREMENT

Demands for data documenting program performance have originated from citizens and from both executive and legislative branches in governmental jurisdictions across the world. As Fig. 1 displays, factors facilitating adoption of performance measurement efforts, as well as those inhibiting their effective use, reflect directives, incentives, and relationships both within and outside government.

Factors Facilitating Performance Measurement

Chief executives and their budget offices have issued requirements that performance measures accompany budget requests in jurisdictions across the world. Initiatives in the U.S. federal government aptly illustrate typical consequences of executive's embracing performance measurement as a top-down management reform tool. The U.S. Office of Management and Budget (OMB) started asking agencies to include performance measures in federal agency budget requests in 1992. OMB's commitment to performance measurement has been reflected in revisions to the primary budget guidance, OMB Circular A-11, that require that budget requests include performance measures, OMB staff training on performance measurement, and active "Spring Reviews on Program Performance," which started with the FY 1997 budget process.

Facilitating:

Internal Factors:

- ☆ Executive Branch Initiative
  - Budget Calls for Non-Financial Performance Measures
- ☆ Legislation
  - Laws affecting All Programs, e.g. Government Performance and Results Act
  - Laws Requiring Performance Measures for Specific Programs

Pressures from Environment:

- ☆ Citizens Demands for Evidence of Program Results
- ☆ Success Stories from Other Jurisdictions and Other Countries
- ☆ Accounting Profession Use of Performance Auditing

Inhibiting:

Internal Factors:

- ☆ Insufficient Authority and/or flexibility to Execute Needed Change
- ☆ Mixed Signals from Legislative Committees on Use of Measures in Budget Process
- ☆ Multiple Calls for Measurement in Different Laws and Executive Directives
- ☆ Complex Relationships among Service Delivery/Regulatory Partners
- ☆ Unclear Expectations about Use of Performance Data
- ☆ Unclear Expectations about Incentives/Punishment for Performance

Pressures from Environment:

- ☆ Citizen Expectations of Clear Evidence of Program Results
- ☆ Anxiety about Comparing Performance across Jurisdictions
- ☆ Lack of Comparable, Reliable Data Collection Procedures across Jurisdictions

FIG. 1 Pressures on public managers to measure program performance.

OMB has also facilitated agency sharing about methods for developing performance measures within three interagency councils chaired by the deputy director for management at OMB. Subcommittees within the Chief Financial Officer's Council, the President's Council on Integrity and Efficiency (the Inspectors General of the major agencies), and the President's Management Council (the chief operating officers of the major agencies) were tasked with facilitating the exchange of information about how to develop performance measures. Specific revisions to OMB guidance on contracting for goods and services, Circular A-123, were also made to highlight the need for managers to provide performance data supporting their contracting decisions.

A focus on measurement of program results also accompanied the executive initiative coordinated by Vice President Gore and initiated by President Clinton on March 3, 1993, commonly known as the National Performance Review (NPR). A key element of the NPR was to develop recommendations for carrying out "mission-driven, results-oriented management."

NPR highlighted the need to focus on and measure performance in many of the reforms they sponsored. For example, it called for agency streamlining plans, whose purpose was to identify ways of reducing the size and increasing the efficiency of government. Managers were called to make performance-related decisions in downsizing efforts. The focus on improving processes, such as procurement and personnel, was designed to improve results through freeing federal managers to focus on mission, less encumbered with procedural restraints. Performance measurement was tied to demonstrating that more can be accomplished with less when processes are improved. However, it should be noted that cutting (red tape, staff, etc.) was clearly the dominant message of the initial NPR efforts, rather than measuring.

The Clinton administration also called for "performance contracts" to be signed by various parts of government. For example, presidential-agency performance agreements were signed by President Clinton and six department heads during his first term in office. These agreements identified a small number of fairly specific objectives for each agency and pressed agency heads to focus on results and to envision how they would be measured. Agency performance agreements signed within agencies called upon leadership of bureaus and programs within agencies to develop data on results to inform decision making. And a few performance partnerships between federal agencies and states and communities were forged to force all parties to identify ways to measure performance for accountability purposes. The political climate in the United States during the 1990s was supportive of giving states more responsibility for administering and funding governmental programs, so the balance of power in the federal-state partnerships was negotiable.

Many initiatives within the legislative branch of the U.S. federal government have required federal managers to measure performance. Three important pieces of legislation that contained across the broad requirements for agencies to measure performance were passed in the 1990s. The legislative call for the provision of performance data in agency financial statements was first made in the Chief Financial Officers Act (CFO) of 1990. The CFO act, which describes agency responsibilities for financial management, requires reporting of measures of nonfinancial program results. Reporting requirements for performance data in financial statements first discussed in the CFO act were then expanded in the Government Management Reform Act of 1994.

The CFO community has been further sensitized to their role in measurement by ongoing conversation about the need to develop nonfinancial measures of program results within the accounting community. Policy guidance from the Federal Accounting Standards Advisory Board (FASAB) acknowledges the importance of performance measurement; FASAB's Statement of Recommended Accounting and Reporting Concepts, Number 2, recommends that a Statement of Program Performance Measures should include measures for each of the major programs operated by the reporting entity (FASAB, 1994: 23). An indication of the seriousness of the FASAB effort was the frequency of discussion about performance measures in FASAB forums during the 1990s.

Perhaps the most important legislative initiative in the U.S. federal government was the Government Performance and Results Act of 1993 (GPRA), which required all agencies to draft strategic plans by 1997, to set performance goals by FY 1999, and to report on actual performance by FY 2000. Recognizing that measuring and reporting on program performance presented an incredibly complex management challenge, GPRA also specified that pilot projects were to be established in at least 10 departments and agencies. The law specified that the pilot projects were to represent a range of government functions, from military and foreign affairs to regulation, research, and development, to processing of claims and providing benefits. Of the 25 major government functions that OMB identified, only 2 (direct delivery of health care and electric power generation and distribution) lacked pilots; in other words, there were pilots in virtually every federal endeavor. Agency heads (anxious to illustrate their compliance with the act) volunteered over 70 individual program or component organization pilot projects.

The U.S. General Accounting Office (GAO) was required by GPRA to report on the efforts of the pilots, and in fact, the GAO published well over 20 reports on efforts undertaken by agencies to comply with GPRA (for example, see GAO, 1994, 1995, 1996, 1997, 1998, 1999). Many of the GAO reports synthesize lessons learned by agencies preparing their first strategic plans with performance goals, and their first performance plans. These documents provide superb guidance on design of performance measurement systems.

Fig. 2 presents a model for performance measurement efforts provided by the GAO that reflects the intent of GPRA but provides useful guidance for man-

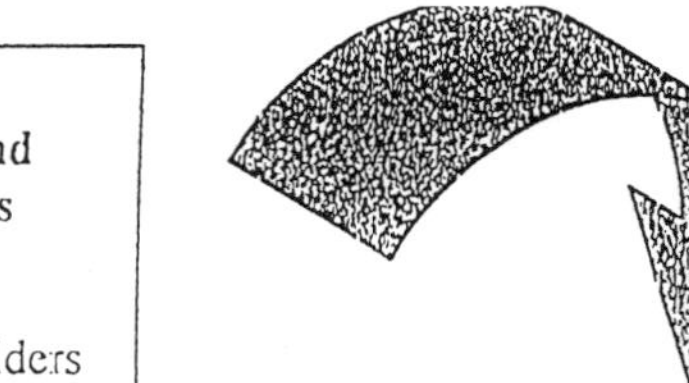

FIG. 2 A model approach to performance measurement: key steps and critical practices. *Source:* U.S. General Accounting Office (1900).

agers charged with implementing performance measurement in any jurisdiction. As illustrated, the basic steps envisioned by GPRA include defining a program's mission and performance objectives, identifying appropriate measures, collecting the data, reporting the data, and building capacity and incentives to ensure the usefulness of the entire endeavor.

Since GPRA was passed in 1993, dozens of federal laws have been passed that require performance measures in specific policy arenas. Members of Congress gradually became knowledgeable about the espoused benefits of securing performance data and were impressed by success stories about performance measurement reforms in other countries and in local governments within the United States. When they were reauthorizing existing policies and programs, they inserted requirements for performance measurement. For example, the Adoption and Safe Families Act of 1997 required the development of outcome measures to be used in allocating federal funds to state agencies involved in child welfare. A large number of federal and state officials are involved in securing the health and safety of children who become wards of the state. All of these key stakeholders have had to be consulted so that they can reach consensus on which measures to use in evaluating program performance. The 1997 statute specified that this consultative process be completed by May 1999, a target that was deemed by all concerned to be far too optimistic and was met with only tentative recommendations. Selection of performance measures is usually difficult, and it can be especially contentious when the allocation of federal grants is driven by those measures.

Factors Inhibiting Use of Performance Measurement

Despite apparent political support for performance measurement, there are some real pressures working against managers striving to design and implement useful performance measurement systems. OMB initially emerged as the prime mover in urging federal managers to develop performance measures, but OMB did not provide technical assistance to agencies as they struggled in their performance measurement efforts. Recognizing the diversity across programs in the sorts of measures that may be appropriate, OMB encouraged creativity in agency measurement strategies. However, agency staff, accustomed to following OMB directives, found that the challenge of developing measures raises uncertainty about what measures will be perceived as best.

Another difficulty has stemmed from the views and abilities of the OMB staff tasked with working with the agencies on performance measurement. Moving to results-oriented management entails a real change in perspective for budget oversight staff as well as program managers. Within OMB performance measurement oversight responsibilities were given to budget examiners who were accustomed to budgeting as usual. Although attempts have been made to help budget examiners become knowledgeable about performance measurement, affecting the roles played during budget negotiations requires real cultural change.

The Clinton administration, through OMB and NPR, advocated results-oriented management, but the managers were not convinced that they would be granted sufficient authority or flexibility to change their way of doing business. In addition, GPRA was passed unanimously at midnight with very few members of Congress present, so knowledge of the law spread quite slowly across the Congress. Although some in Congress have shown interest in the law, there has been only spotty interest exhibited by the all-important appropriation committees. Budgeting as usual seemed to proceed during the 1990s, with little evidence that performance measures have much effect on allocation decisions.

In addition, federal managers accurately recognized the lack of real coordination among the executive and legislative actors requesting performance data as well as a lack of recognition by the requestors of the sort of resources that are required for agencies to design and support useful measurement systems. Many line managers have voiced the concern that they will have to meet different expectations for performance measures for different oversight offices within their agencies, resulting in duplicative and contradictory efforts.

Congressional fervor for leaner, more efficient government also sent an important message to managers coping with demands for performance report cards during the late 1990s. Systematic use of performance measurement could provide useful data to inform budget cutting. Uncertainly about how performance data might be used presents perhaps the most difficult challenge to developing performance measurement systems. Some measures that might effectively guide internal decision making may provide data that managers would not want made public come budget time. Given a choice about the use of limited resources to measure performance, data that will support budgetary requests will likely win out against internally useful, yet potentially damaging measures.

Experience within the U.S. federal government has revealed how challenging it is to secure agreement among the diverse stakeholders on the selection of measures for programs in which there are multiple service delivery partners. The vast majority of U.S. federal programs are intergovernmental, in that they involve federal, state, and local governmental agencies and, in some cases, even nonprofits in service delivery. The extensive level of dialogue among service delivery "partners" surrounding performance measurement in intergovernmental programs has highlighted the very different views held by stakeholders about what should be measured and how the measures should be used.

Relatedly, there is anxiety within agency staff about measuring outcomes that may be beyond their control. In many programs, from providing job training to welfare mothers to increasing troops to prevent the outbreak of war, it is difficult to establish a causal link between the government effort and the eventual outcome for the individual or society served. As the U.S. General Accounting Office reported, careful planning and time-consuming dialogue are required to facilitate experimentation with performance measurement for federal programs in which the federal government has quite limited control (GAO, 1998). And in some cases it is simply impossible to measure program outcomes in the sort of real time that GPRA and other statutes requiring performance measures require. For example, programs that are intended to prevent homelessness or the spread of acquired immunodeficiency virus (AIDS) are unlikely to find accessible data. Foreign assistance programs present more examples of situations in which many factors are beyond the control of federal program managers, yet the U.S. Agency for International Development requires outcome measures for programs as diverse as nuclear safety assistance to Russia and municipal services reform in Kenya.

Citizen expectations seem to rise when performance measurement efforts are undertaken as rapidly as anxiety about the consequences of not meeting performance targets rises among public managers. Unclear and/or inflated expectations among politicians as well as citizens affect the manner in which public managers approach performance measurement. Local governmental experience in the United States has demonstrated that managers fear publicizing some data, such as ambulance response times, because invidious comparisons across cities or counties may be drawn. Comparisons of performance data across jurisdictions may in fact be quite dubious as a result of differences in measures and measurement procedures across jurisdictions, and even across agencies within the same government. Questions about the reliability of data collection and of data across countries certainly plague the World Bank and other international assistance organizations as they have adopted performance measurement for their projects.

In sum, there are many pressures on public managers to measure government performance stemming from governmental initiatives and from the current political environment. Once governments adopt performance measurement, managers are expected to measure the results of their programs, identify realistic yet laudable performance targets, and communicate clearly to both politicians and the public how well their programs are performing. In many cases differences in expectations between the managers and those receiving performance reports may exist. So what guidance may be provided to managers tasked with measuring and reporting on program performance?

MEETING CHALLENGES IN USING PERFORMANCE MEASUREMENT

Designing and implementing performance measurement systems that will provide data on how well programs track against the agency's mission are challenging politically, as well as resource-intensive. There are four sets of challenges to managers: communication, analytical, measurement, and political. As illustrated in

Fig. 3, these challenges might be envisioned as hurdles that managers must clear as they attempt to use performance measurement to improve management.

Communication Challenges

Clear, effective communication among relevant stakeholders is essential for successful performance measurement efforts. Managers must communicate clearly and frequently with program staff, clients, and other stakeholders; legislative committees; budget officials; and other public and nonprofit agencies with whom they work. Securing agreement among the key stakeholders regarding agency mission, a strategic plan, strategic objectives, and performance measures should be step one. If performance measures do not track an agency's strategic objectives, it will certainly be difficult to use them to manage effectively.

Within agencies multiple offices are typically involved with designing and implementing performance measurement systems, so effective intraagency communication is crucial. In some agencies policy staff work on strategic plans and budget staff work on the performance measures. In other agencies, a comprehensive planning office linked to the budget office may undertake the entire effort. Ensuring effective communication among offices tasked with performance measurement in separate bureaus within large agencies may also present imposing communication challenges. Both extensive vertical and horizontal communication channels in large government agencies simply render clear communication about sensitive measurement issues more difficult.

An important objective of GPRA was to empower program managers to participate in the development of the program mission statement, goals, and performance indicators. With the involvement of agency chief financial officer (CFO) and budgetary staff, and OMB budget examiners, it should not be surprising that confusion arose over ownership of measurement efforts. The issue of where stewardship over the performance measurement process is located is important. If control over the process is located in financial management offices, it may be difficult to ensure that measures are line manager–friendly. This dilemma reflects the issue of the intended use of the performance measures. If the budget office develops measures specifically to accompany budget requests, it is very likely that the measures will not serve line managers' internal needs. And if there is not buy-in by the line managers who play key roles in data collection, again problems may ensue.

The key finding of virtually all observers of performance measurement exercises is that the support of top political leadership in an agency is essential to ensure the success of the system. If political appointees simply give performance measurement efforts lip service, chances are that line managers will as well. Support from political leaders is needed for the immense efforts that managers will need to expend to consult stakeholders about selection of appropriate measures

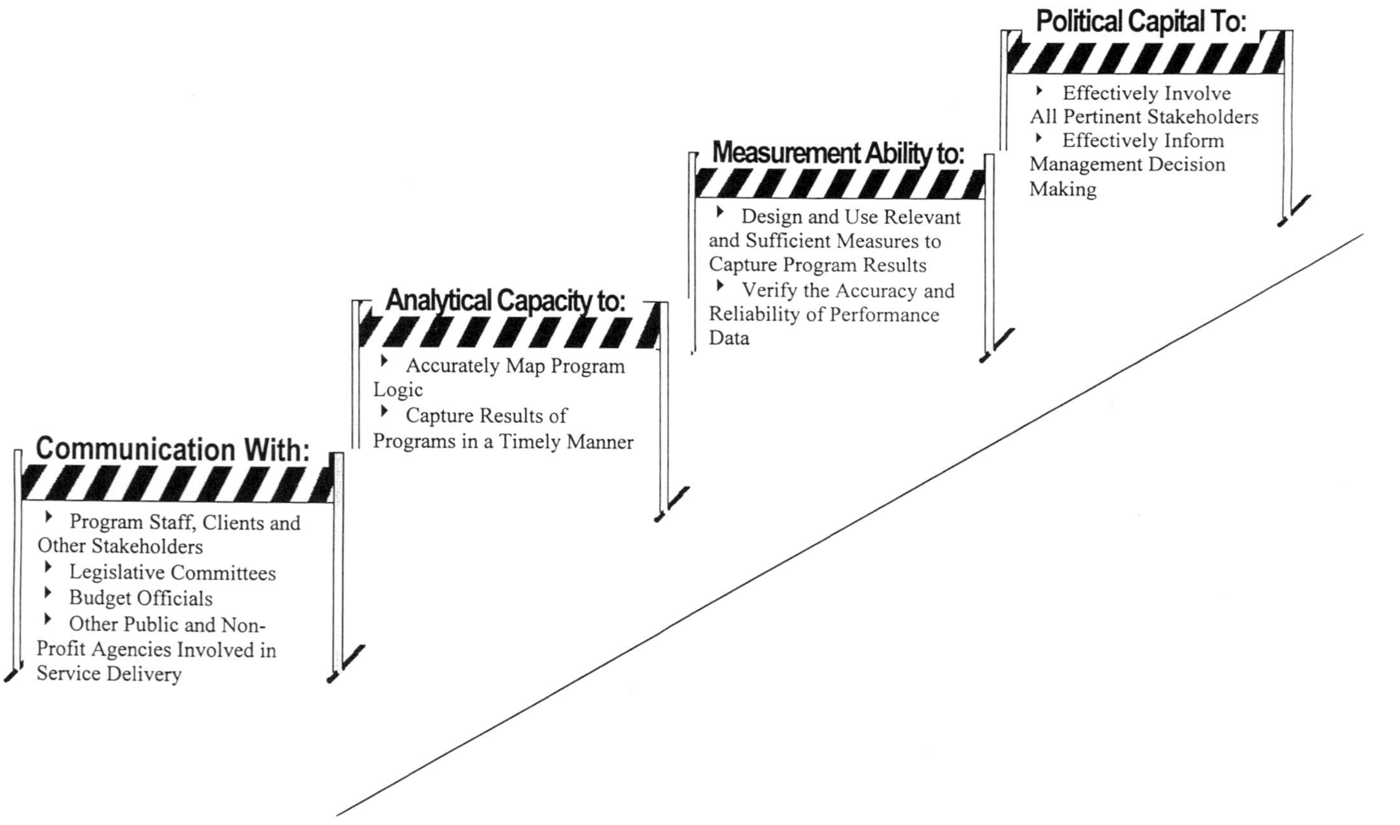

FIG. 3 Challenges to use of performance measurement to improve management of public programs.

and their use. And headquarters must communicate clearly with managers in the field regarding expectations and resources for performance measurement.

Analytical Challenges

The analytical capacity to map program logic accurately and to conceptualize appropriate outputs or outcomes to measure is a second fundamental challenge for those charged with measuring performance of public programs. Program performance is not an objective reality waiting to be measured. Performance is a socially constructed reality (Berger and Luckmann, 1967). Determining what to measure tends to be a political challenge, but clarifying the logic underlying a program should precede discussions about appropriate measures.

Traditionally inputs, or the resources allocated to the delivery of programs, have been measured to track programs. Dialogue about what to measure in this results-oriented management era has tended to focus instead on program outputs and outcomes. Table 2 displays commonly used definitions of inputs, outputs, and outcomes, as well as performance targets. Counting outputs, such as the number of persons served by programs or the number of firms inspected, is fairly straightforward. The more interesting issues arise when politicians require managers to measure program outcomes, or results.

Program logic models, the analytical tools that social scientists have long advocated for use in evaluating the effectiveness of public programs, are especially useful for informing performance measurement deliberations. Logic models are graphic presentations of the theoretical linkages between program inputs

TABLE 2 Program Inputs, Outputs, Outcomes, and Goals

Inputs: measures of what an agency or manager has available to carry out the program or activity; i.e., achieve an outcome or output. These can include: employees, funding equipment or facilities, supplies on hand, goods or services received, work processes or rules.

Output: a tabulation, calculation or recording of a program activity or effort that can be expressed in a quantitative or qualitative manner, such as number of cases opened and number of children immunized.

Outcome: an assessment of the results of a program compared to its intended purpose, such as number of cases with convictions.

Performance goal: a target level of performance expressed as a tangible, measurable objective, against which actual performance can be compared, including a goal expressed as a quantitative standard, value or rate, e.g., "Improve maternal and child health on tribal reservations to meet 98% of the national standards for healthy mothers and children by 2004."

Source: The Government Performance and Results Act of 1993.

and activities and their intended outcomes (see McLaughlin and Jordan, 1999). Factors external to the program, usually called *contextual* or *mediating factors,* that may affect the ability of a program to produce intended outcomes are also included in the model. Fig. 4 presents a basic program logic model that identifies the components typically included in such representations.

Program logic models are tools that may facilitate communication about the potential for programs to have intended outcomes and about the different sorts of outcomes likely to result from program efforts. For example, intermediate outcomes are typically fairly immediate reactions to program activities, such as satisfaction with training or with medical care. Actions undertaken by local governments in response to federal outputs such as regulations may also be considered intermediate outcomes. Long-term outcomes are typically the results that public programs seek such as healthy people and safe water and air.

Fig. 5 displays a completed program logic model of a needle exchange program that highlights the impact the factors outside program management's control can have on the desired outcomes of the program. For example, levels of private donations and coordination with other social service agencies can affect the ability of the needles exchange program even to perform their basic service, and the availability of other intravenous drug use prevention programs in the area affects the number of drug users in need of services. When assessing performance of needle exchange programs such factors should be taken into account.

Mapping out expected relationships between program activities and outcomes can raise important questions requiring study. GPRA specifies that agencies should apply systematic studies, or program evaluations, to probe presumed linkages between activities and outcomes and to investigate instances in which performance targets are not met. Performance measurement, even when outcomes of programs are routinely measured, does not address questions about how or why programs are effective. Similarly, the measurement process does not provide explanations for low performance.

Through developing comprehensive program logic models program staff can identify factors that also effect change in the outcome variables of interest, such as infant mortality rates or illicit drug use. Trends in these relevant contextual factors may be measured to help program staff anticipate trends in the outcomes they wish to effect.

The periods that are most appropriate for tracking both intermediate and longer-term outcomes can be analyzed through modeling and can help program management understand how the timing of program activities relates to trends in outcomes. Timing is crucial for most program interventions, and a better appreciation of the time required for interventions to affect on outcomes may be crucial. Cyclical variation in outcomes also deserves attention as program managers seek to understand trends in program performance.

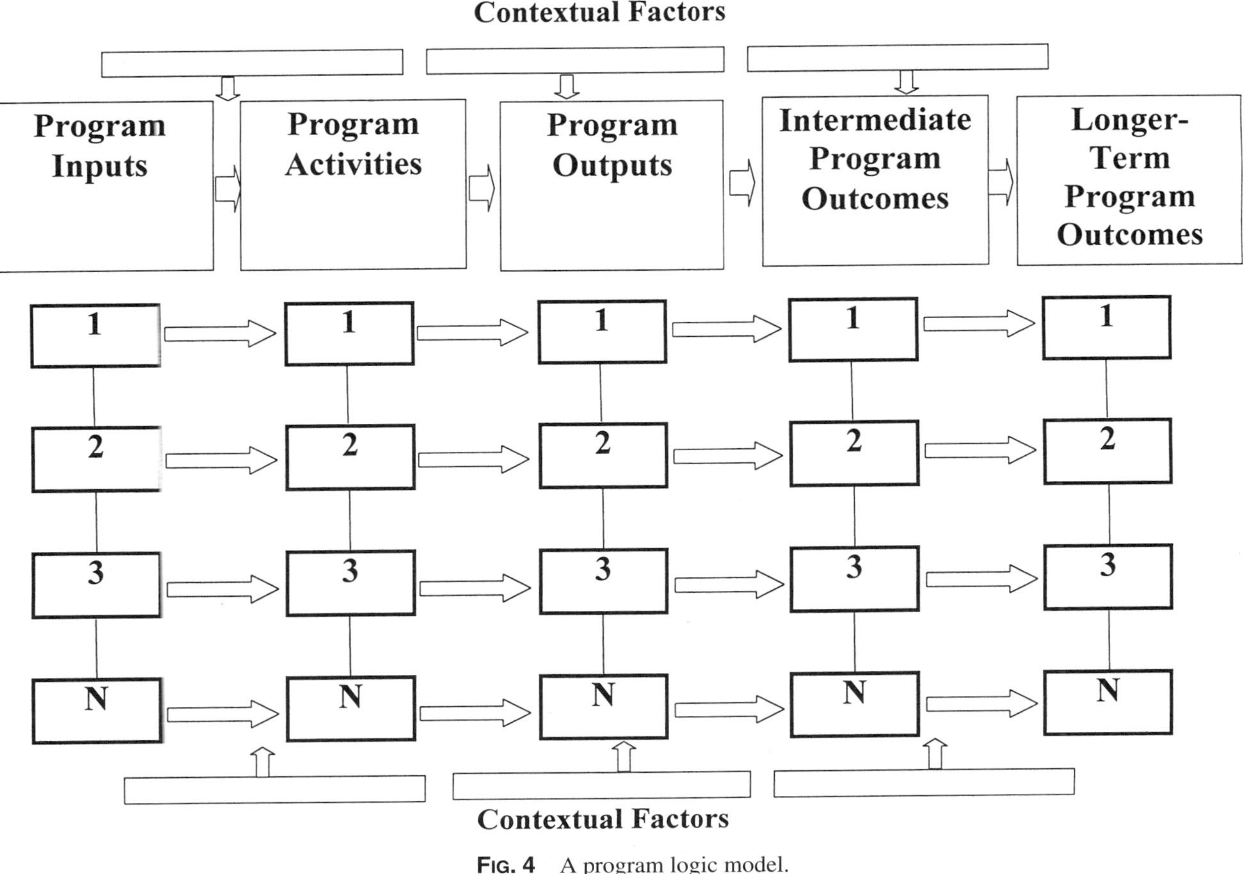

FIG. 4 A program logic model.

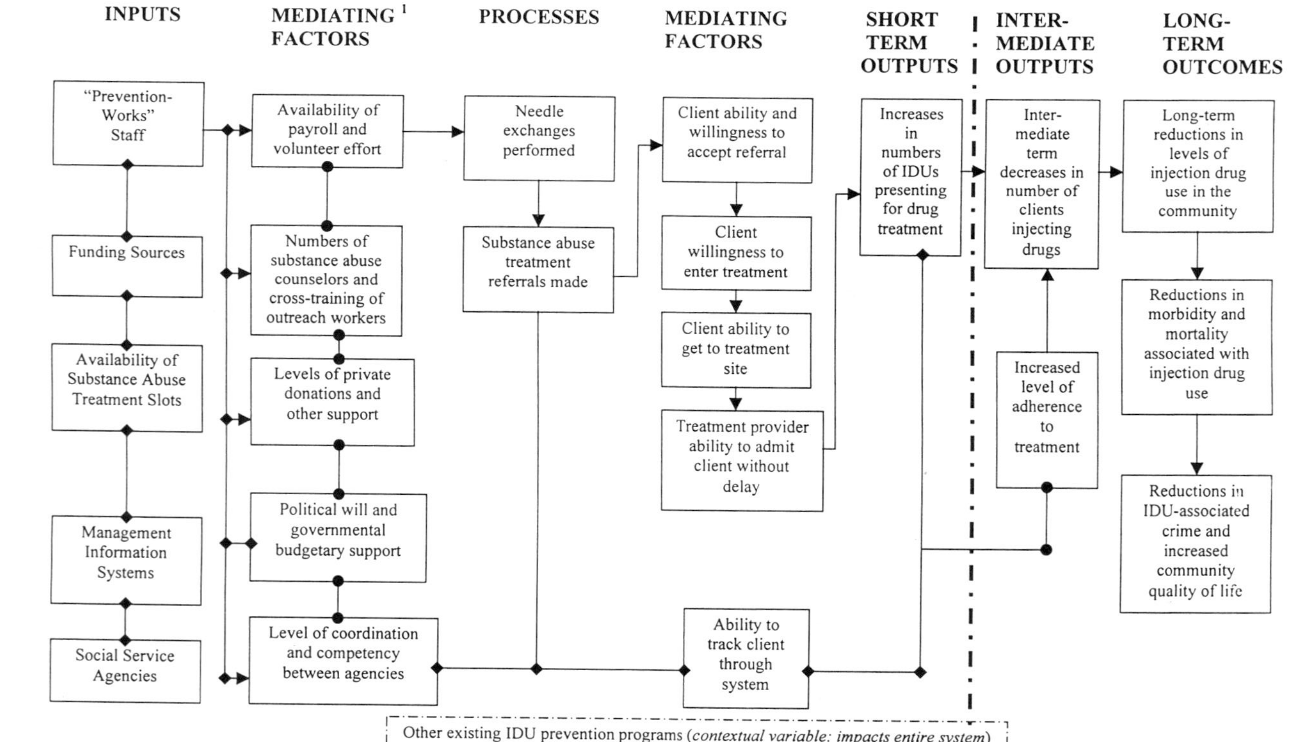

[1] "Mediating Factors" are those which, given variations in levels of their intensity and scope, will positively or negatively affect relevant processes. The red vertical dotted line indicates the point beyond which it would be impractical for *PreventionWorks* to conduct an effective and affordable evaluation.

Fig. 5 Program logic: prevention works as gateway to substance abuse treatment.

Measurement Challenges

The ability to design and use relevant and sufficient measures to capture program performance depends on analytical capacity but extends further as staff responsible for performance measurement must also know how to verify the accuracy and reliability of performance data. There are many criteria that are applied to performance measures; Table 3 summarizes the criteria most often cited by users of performance measurement systems. The criteria are categorized under the three basic rules for evidence applied by the U.S. GAO and most other governmental U.S. audit agencies: evidence must be relevant, competent, and sufficient. Performance measures must be clearly linked to program mission and perceived as such by the public (relevant). The measures must accurately and consistently measure what program staff and other stakeholders believe they measure in a timely fashion (competent). And a relatively complete and balanced set of measures should be used to capture program performance in a manner that is not overly costly, yet is inclusive enough to protect against unintended consequences.

The old adage "What gets measured gets done" may well apply to performance measurement efforts, so it is important that those selecting performance measures not adopt only measures that are accessible and relatively inexpensive without considering how their collection may affect priorities of program staff.

Within the U.S. federal government the Department of Transportation (DOT) received praise for the first performance plan it submitted to the Congress

Table 3 Desirable Attributes of Useful Performance Measures

Relevant
- Clearly linked to program mission
- Perceived as legitimate by citizens
- Understandable
- Not overly vulnerable to factors outside control of program

Competent
- Accurately measuring the criterion of interest
- Capable of being validated
- Verifiable
- Reliable measurement procedures
- Comparable across relevant jurisdiction
- Measurable within allowable time for frame

Sufficient
- Capturing a balanced set of dimensions
- Measuring a reasonable number of dimensions (complete)
- Measuring an adequate number of dimensions to guard against unintended consequences
- Reasonable cost

in 1998. Table 4 displays a brief excerpt from the DOT performance plan that illustrates the qualities that earned praise. Performance measures were linked clearly to major strategic goals, and a set of measures were used to assess progress on a set of outcome goals for each strategic goal. DOT also provided justification for the measures selected and discussed strategies that were under way to help them make progress on each performance goal. Although the performance measures appearing in Table 4 are outputs rather than outcomes, their relationship to the outcome goal seems fairly logical and reasonable.

Political Challenges

Finally, performance measurement efforts will only be successful if there is sufficient political capital to involve the pertinent stakeholders throughout planning and measuring processes, and to convince the pertinent political leaders that the performance data should be used to guide managerial decision making. Political capital is also needed to ensure the ongoing resource commitment needed for support and maintenance of performance information systems. For example, even when resources are available to develop new information systems, will there be

TABLE 4 Illustrative Performance Measures for U.S. Department of Transportation

Strategic goal: mobility (*Shape America's future by ensuring a transportation system that is accessible, integrated, efficient, and offers flexibility of choices*)
Outcomes: Progress in achieving the Department's strategic goal of mobility will be measured at the end of FY 1999 against the following outcome areas

Outcome goal	Performance indicator
1. Improve the structural integrity of the transportation system.	• Percentage of national highway system pavement with acceptable ride quality • Percentage deficient bridges on the national highway system • Percentage of airport runway pavements in satisfactory condition • Percentage of availability of marine aids to navigation • Percentage of availability of locks and related navigation facilities of the St. Lawrence Seaway • Average age of bus and rail transit fleet

Source: U.S. Department of Transportation, (1999: 27).

ongoing resources to support modification of the systems and to train agency staff adequately to enable them to support and use the data? Will the systems actually provide the useful performance data in a politically useful time frame? Such questions imply great foresight and planning capabilities, as well as long-term resource commitment from political leadership.

Cultural receptivity to the use of performance measures presents a related challenge. The organizational culture within most public agencies is process-oriented, reflecting the predominant emphasis upon procedural and legal accountability within the U.S. government (Light, 1996). Years and entire careers dedicated to monitoring processes tend to render agency staff somewhat impervious to total revamping of management. Negative experiences with past management reform efforts such as Planned–Programming–Budgeting–Systems (PPBS), management by objectives, and total quality management—efforts with ephemeral effects—have left many middle and upper managers within the federal establishment with skeptical outlooks. A "wait and see" attitude toward performance measurement and management is fairly common, and such skepticism is compounded if there are not clear and consistent signals from top political and career leaders that an agency will institutionalize performance measurement systems. The sort of cultural change that is required to release public managers from a process-oriented mentality is rather fundamental, and such change requires leadership commitment, time, effective training, and consistent reinforcement.

Incentives provided within organizations in a consistent manner across suborganizational entities can help in such cultural change. However, effective incentive systems require both the will and the knowledge to provide incentives consistently to encourage and reward setting ambitious performance targets, for example. Experimentation with incentives to identify what works in specific program contexts is needed, and organizational support for such trial-by-error learning is needed. Moving from a blame-oriented approach to accountability to a reward-for-results accountability system requires a learning culture in which risk taking is supported by stable and supportive agency leadership.

Incentives from key actors outside agencies, such as the OMB, the GAO, and congressional appropriations, authorization and oversight committees, are also needed to encourage the sort of trust required for the development and use of performance measurement systems. Those intimately involved in the design of GPRA assumed that federal agencies would develop effective performance measurement systems through an iterative learning process, not through an overnight conversion. Local governmental experience with performance measurement has also shown that implementation of useful systems takes time, and expectations should not be overly high during development stages.

Since the implementation of the vast majority of federal programs in the United States involves the cooperative actions of federal, state and local, and even nongovernmental organizations, the success of performance measurement systems depends upon collaboration among many partners and is subject to the vicissitudes accompanying highly complex joint ventures. Clarity in expectations regarding responsibility and accountability for jointly provided programs with quite diverse customers and in quite diverse contexts is a valuable yet costly political commodity.

EVOLVING ISSUES FOR PERFORMANCE MEASUREMENT

Expectations of public management and about the desired role for government in the 1990s were dynamic and fairly consistent across the world. Calls for privatizing, outsourcing, and contracting out public service delivery echoed across the world as well as across the United States as desires to mimic entrepreneurial management practices in the private sector captivated politicians and members of the public. Interestingly, the more dispersed the responsibility for the provision of public services, the more crucial the role clarity in expectations of all involved plays. Changes in both the role and the size of government and in the availability of resources from the environment directly affect the likelihood that performance measurement efforts will improve public management.

Performance measurement will not fade away as previous management reform efforts in the United States did, since it has been required by law for the entire federal government, as well as for many local governments. There are, however, many interesting issues as yet unresolved surrounding the use and usefulness of performance measurement, including performance measurement in cross-cutting program areas, an appropriate interface between performance measurement and program evaluation, and relationships between performance measurement and performance budgeting and between performance measurement and human resources management.

Performance Measurement in Cross-Cutting Program Areas

The problems addressed by the U.S. government are complex and multifaceted, and there is simply inadequate understanding of the causes of many. Over time different governmental agencies at different levels have developed programs to address these problems. Thus, there are many programs offered to address unemployment, teenage pregnancy, infant mortality, flow of illicit drugs into the country, and domestic violence—to name a few.

Different programs within different agencies may offer different solutions to similar problems, or similar solutions to slightly different problems, or even similar solutions to similar problems. These programs are labeled *cross-cutting programs,* and in an era marked by calls for downsizing and greater efficiencies in program delivery, they may be politically vulnerable. Performance measurement offers the opportunity for such programs explicitly to clarify and improve their relationships with other programs; it may also make indefensible redundancies more visible.

If performance measurement efforts are institutionalized within governments, eventually politicians and public managers will receive performance data documenting cross-cutting programs and will have to address the political issues raised.

An Appropriate Interface between Performance Measurement and Program Evaluation

"Assessment, through objective measurement and systematic analyses, of the manner and extent to which federal programs achieve intended objectives" is the definition of program evaluation provided in GPRA. Program evaluation is clearly viewed as a complementary analytical tool to support performance measurement in government within GPRA. Program evaluations can address questions about why and how programs achieve or fail to achieve their objectives. The program evaluation field also includes many other useful studies, such as needs assessments for programs, assessments of the compliance of program implementation with statutory guidance, and cost-effectiveness of different program interventions.

Theoretically, there are clear benefits to using program evaluations to accompany performance measurement. However, program evaluation requires resources and the political will to spend them on evaluation. Performance measurement efforts may pave the way to increase the use of program evaluation in government since performance data may be used to identify interesting questions for further study and may make politicians more accustomed to receiving empirical data on programs. On the other hand, politicians may not feel that program evaluations are necessary as long as outcomes are routinely reported, thus reducing the likelihood that evaluations will be used to answer the questions raised but not addressed by performance measurement efforts.

Performance Measurement and Performance Budgeting

Performance measurement does not imply nor necessarily result in performance budgeting; however, it does provide support for this approach to budgeting. GPRA requires agencies' annual performance plans to link performance goals to the program activities of their budget requests directly. In other words, performance goals are to be linked to budget accounts. As a 1999 GAO report acknowledged, the federal budget account structure was not created as a single, integrated framework, but developed over time to respond to specific needs, and budget accounts and program activities within the accounts vary from agency to agency (GAO, 1999). At least in the U.S. federal government, linkage between performance goals and measures and budget accounts varies greatly from agency to agency. There is really no evidence yet that the linkages will facilitate performance budgeting at the federal level. And experience at the state level with performance budgeting during the performance measurement era of the late 20th century does not inspire optimism (Newcomer, 1997). Whether performance measurement efforts will lead to performance budgeting remains an open question.

Performance Measurement and Human Resources Management

How should performance measurement efforts be coordinated with performance appraisals for public managers? That question arises naturally when program performance is measured, but there is no easy answer. There are virtually no successful models, and research on incentives for performance among public managers offers little guidance on effective means for linking program performance with personnel rewards systems. However, some experimentation has started (GAO, 1998), and it is likely that linkages will continue to stimulate theorizing and testing in the 21st century.

CONCLUSION

The measurement and reporting of program performance are management tools that became extremely popular in countries across the world during the 1990s. Demands for data documenting the performance of public programs arose from citizens, executives, and legislatures, and success stories in other jurisdictions prompted elected officials to have high expectations of the benefits of performance measurement efforts.

A lack of clarity in expectations among public managers regarding how performance measures may be used presents a significant constraint inhibiting the effective use of such measures to inform managerial decision making. Experience in a variety of governmental jurisdictions has shown that managers face complex communication, analytical, political, and measurement challenges in designing and implementing performance measurement systems. Yet despite these challenges, opportunities for using performance measurement to improve public management are endless, and the momentum carrying performance measurement forward seems quite strong.

Although many governments have experimented with performance measurement, several issues remain unresolved: how performance measurement should be used to clarify the performance of programs in cross-cutting program areas, how program evaluation should be most effectively used to support performance measurement efforts, and how performance measurement should be linked effectively with performance budgeting and with human resources management.

NOTES

1. Mediating factors are those that, given variations in levels of their intensity and scope, positively or negatively affect relevant processes. The vertical dotted line indicates the

point beyond which it would be impractical for Prevention Works to conduct an effective and affordable evaluation.

REFERENCES

Alter, A.E. (1995). Silicon valley civics. In *Accountability for Performance: Measurement and Monitoring in Local Government* (D.N. Ammons, ed.). (pp. 139–145).

Ammons, D.N. (1995). *Accountability for Performance: Measurement and Monitoring in Local Government.* Internation City/Count Management Association, Washington, D.C.

Ammons, D.N. (1996). *Municipal Benchmarks: Assessing Local Performance and Establishing Community Standards.* Sage, Thousand Oaks, Calif.

Aristigueta, M.P. (1998). *Managing-for-Results in the States.* University of Southern California, Washington, D.C.

Armey, Richard (1997). Testimony on Government Performance and Results Act by the House Majority Leader. House Government Reform and Oversight Committee. February 12.

Benowitz, P.S., and Schein, R. (1996). Performance measurement in local government. In *Government Finance Officers Association, Municipal Year Book 1996.* Government Finance Officers Association, Chicago, pp. 19–23.

Berger, P.L., and Luckmann, T. (1967). *The Social Construction of Reality.* Anchor Books, Garden City, N.J.

Bernstein, D.J. (1999). Local government performance use: Assessing system quality and effects. Doctoral Dissertation Proposal, George Washington University.

Blessing, L.J. (1991). Reporting of government performance indicators for assessment of public accountability. Doctoral Dissertation, Arizona State University. UMI Dissertation Abstracts (order #9124788).

Bruder, K.A., Jr., & Gray, E.M. (1994). *Public-Sector Benchmarking: A Practical Approach.*

Campbell, Glenn R. (1996). DHHS releases innovative performance measurement tool: Announces managed Medicare initiative to rate plan quality. *Managed Healthcare.* May, 15.

Chan, A. (1994). Managing a government like a business: The Sunnyvale system. *Government Finance Review. 10*(2): 7–11.

De Lancer, P.D. (1997). Performance measures as knowledge and innovation: An elaborated model explaining utilization. Doctoral dissertation, Rutgers, The State University of New Jersey. UMI Dissertation Abstracts (order #9806876)

Dupont-Morales, J.A., & Harris, J.E. (1994). Strengthening accountability: Incorporating strategic planning and performance measurement into budgeting. *Public Productivity and Management Review. XVII*(3): 231–239.

Epstein, J., & Olsen, R.T. (1996). Managing for outcomes: Lessons learned by state and local government. *The Public Manager. 25*(3): 41–44.

Epstein, P.D. (1988). *Using Performance Measurement in Local Government: A Guide to Improving Decisions, Performance, and Accountability.* National Civic League Press, New York.

Epstein, P.D. (1992). Get ready: The time for performance measurement is finally coming! *Public Administration Review. 25*(5): 513–519.

Executive Office of the President (April, 1998). New government—a new federal state partnership. [http://www.whitehouse.gov/WH/Publications/html/briefs/iv-3-plain.html]

Fischer, R.J. (1994). An overview of performance measurement. *Public Management. 76*(9): S-2–S-8.

Glazer, M. (1991). Tailoring performance measurement to fit the organization: From generic to germane. *Public Productivity and Management Review. XIV*(3): 303–319.

Governmental Accounting Standards Board (GASB) (1994). *Concepts Statement No. 2: Service Efforts and Accomplishments Reporting.* Governmental Accounting Standards Board, Norwalk, Conn.

Governmental Accounting Standards Board. (1994). *Service Efforts and Accomplishments Report, No. 2 of Concepts Statements of the Governmental Accounting Standards Board.* Governmental Accounting Standards Series, No. 109-A. Norwalk, Conn.

Governmental Accounting Standards Board and the National Academy of Public Administration (GASB/NAPA). (1996). *Survey on the Use of Performance Measures by State and Local Government Entities.* CT: Governmental Accounting Standards Board. Norwalk, Conn.

Governmental Accounting Standards Board and the National Academy of Public Administration (GASB/NAPA) (1997). *Report on Survey of State and Local Government Use and Reporting of Performance Measures-First Questionnaire Results.* Governmental Accounting Standards Board, Norwalk, Conn.

Hatry, H. (1996). Tracking the quality of services. In *Handbook of Public Administration* James L. Perry, ed. Jossey-Bass, San Francisco.

Hatry, H.P. (1996). Tracking the quality of service. In *Handbook of Public Administration* 2nd ed. (J. Perry, ed.). Jossey-Bass, San Francisco, pp. 537–554.

Hatry, H.P. (1998). Performance measures and decision making. Presented at the *Managing for Performance Conference.* Austin, Tex., May 1998.

Hatry, H.P. (2000). *Performance Measurement*: Getting Results. The Urban Institute, Washington, D.C.

Hatry, H., et al. (1987). Program analysis for state and local governments, 2nd ed., The urban institute. In Implementing Performance Measurement in Government, (J.L. Leithe, ed.). Government Finance Officer Association, Chicago.

Hatry, H.P., Gerhart, C., and Marshall, M. (1994). Eleven ways to make performance measurement more useful to public managers. *Public Management. 76*(9): S-15 to S-18

Hatry, H.P., Fountain, J.R., Sullivan, J.M., and Kremer, L. (1990). *Service Efforts and Accomplishments Reporting: Its Time Has Come—an Overview.* Governmental Accounting Standards Board, Norwalk, Conn.

Heaton, J.D., Savage, L.J., and Welch, J.K. (1993). Performance auditing in municipal governments. *The Government Accountants Journal. 42*(2): 51–56.

Henderson, Lenneal J., Jr. (1995). GPRA: Mission, metrics, meaning, and marketing. *The Public Manager.* Spring.

Jackson, P.M. (1993). Public service performance evaluation: A strategic perspective. *Public Money & Management, 13*(4): 9–14.

Katz. J.L. (1991). Privatizing without tears. *Governing. 4*(9): 38–42.

Kimm, Victor J. (1995). GPRA: Early implementation. *The Public Manager.* Spring.

Koskinen, John (1997). Testimony on Government Performance and Results Act by the Deputy Director for Management, Office of Management and Budget. House Government Reform and Oversight Committee. February 12.

Kravchuk, Robert S., and Ronald W. Schack (1996). Designing effective performance-measurement systems Under the Government Performance and Results Act of 1993. *Public Administration Review.* July, 348–358.

Leithe, J.L. (1997). *Implementing Performance Measurement in Government.* Government Finance Officers Association, Chicago.

Lemov, P. (1998). Measuring performance, making progress. *Governing. 11*(4): 54–58.

Light, Paul C. (1993). *Monitoring Government: Inspectors General and the Search for Accountability.* Brookings Institution, Washington, D.C.

Likierman, A. 1993. Performance indicators: 20 early lessons from managerial use. *Public Money & Management. 13*(4): 15–22.

McLaughlin, J.A. and Jordan, G.B. (1999). Logic models: A tool for telling your program's performance story. *Evaluation and Program Planning. 22:* 65–72.

National Performance Review (1997). *Best Practices in Performance Measurement.* National Performance Review, Washington, D.C.

National Performance Review. (1997). *Serving the American Public: Best Practices in Performance Measurement.* National Performance Review, Washington, D.C.

National Performance Review (1998a). Performance Partnerships, Washington, D.C. [http://www.npr.gov/library/fedstat/26f2].

National Performance Review (1998b). Performance Partnerships Summary and Guiding Principles, Washington, D.C. [http://www.npr.gov/library/fedstat/2572.html].

Newcomer, Kathryn E. (1996). Evaluating public programs. In Handbook of Public Administration (James L. Perry, ed.). Jossey-Bass, San Francisco.

Newcomer, K. (1996). Evaluating public programs. In *Handbook of Public Administration,* 2nd ed. (J.L. Perry, ed.). Jossey-Bass, San Francisco.

Newcomer, K. (1997). Using performance measurement to improve programs. In (K. Newcomer, ed.). *Using Performance Measurement to Improve Public and Non-Profit Programs, New Directions for Evaluation.* Number 75. Jossey-Bass, San Fracisco, pp. 5–14.

Newcomer, Kathryn E., and Bernstein, David J. Government Performance and Results Act: Lessons learned for local government and intergovernmental relations. Paper presented at the *1998 Annual Conference of the American Society for Public Administration,* Seattle, Washington, May 1998.

Newcomer, Kathryn E., and Amy Downey (1997–1998). Performance-based management: What is it and how do we get there? *The Public Manager.* Winter.

Osborne, D., and Gaebler, T. (1992). *Reinventing Government: How the Entrepreneurial Spirit is Transforming the Public Sector.* Addison-Wesley, Reading, Mass.

Perrin, B. (1998). Effective use and misuse of performance measurement. *American Journal of Evaluation. 19*(3): 367–379.

Poister, T.H., and McGowan, R.P. (1984). The use of management tools in municipal government: A national survey. *Public Administration Review. 44*(3): 215–223.

Reaching Public Goals: Managing Government for Results Resource Guide (1996).

Scheirer, M.A., Schediac, M.C., and Cassady, C.E. (1995). "Measuring the implementation of health promotion programs: The case of the Breast and Cervical Cancer Program in Maryland. *Health Education Research: Theory & Practice. 10:* 11–25.

Shediac-Rizkallah, M.C., Cassady, C.C., Scheirer, M.A. et al. (1996–1997). Linking implementation to outcomes: Evaluation of a community-based breast and cervical cancer screening program. *International Quarterly of Community Health Education. 16:* 5–22.

Tigue, P. (1994). Use of performance measures by GFOA members. *Government Performance Review. 10*(6): 42–45.

Tracy, R.C. (1996). *Development and Use of Outcome Information: Portland, Oregon.* American Society for Public Administration, Washington, D.C.

Tracy, R.C. and Jean, E.P. (1993). Measuring government performance: Experimenting with service efforts and accomplishment reporting in Portland, Oregon. *Government Finance Review. 9*(6).

Tuck, N., and Zaleski, G. (1996). Criteria for developing performance measurement systems in the public sector. *International Journal of Public Administration. 19*(11,12): 1945–1978.

U.S. Advisory Commission on Intergovernmental Relations (1996). *Intergovernmental Accountability: The Potential of Outcome-Oriented Performance Management to Improve Intergovernmental Delivery of Public Works Programs.*

United States Code Section 1115(e) (1998). Performance plans. Washington D.C. [gopher://pula.financenet.gov:70/00/docs/legis/gpra93.gop].

U.S. General Accounting Office (1997). Governmentwide Implementation Will Be Uneven, Washington, D.C.

U.S. General Accounting Office (1998a). Agencies' Annual Performance Plans Can Help Address Strategic Planning Challenges, Washington, D.C.

U.S. General Accounting Office (1997). Agencies Strategic Plans Under GPRA: Key Questions to Facilitate Congressional Review, Washington, D.C.

U.S. General Accounting Office (1997). Critical Issues for Improving Federal Agencies' Strategic Plans, Washington, D.C.

U.S. General Accounting Office (1996). Effectively Implementing the Government Performance and Results Act, Washington, D.C.

U.S. General Accounting Office (1997). Agencies Strategic Plans Under GPRA: Key Questions to Facilitate Congressional Review, Washington, D.C.

U.S. General Accounting Office (1999). Major Management Challenges and Program Risks: A Government wide Perspective. Washington, D.C.

U.S. General Accounting Office (1997a). Managing for results: analytic challenges in measuring performance, HEHS/GGD-97-138. Washington, D.C.

U.S. General Accounting Office (1998). Managing for results: Measuring program results that are under limited federal control, GAO/GGD-99-16. Washington, D.C.

U.S. General Accounting Office (1999). Performance budgeting: Initial experience under the results act in linking plans with budgets. GAO/AIMD/GGD-99-67.

U.S. General Accounting Office (1998). Performance management: Aligning employee performance with agency goals at six results act pilots. GAO/GGD-98-162. Washington, D.C.

U.S. General Accounting Office (1998). The Results Act: An Evaluator's Guide to Assessing Agency Annual Performance Plans GAO/GGD-10/1/20. Washington, D.C.

U.S. General Accounting Office (1997b). The Statutory Framework for Improving Federal Management and Effectiveness, Washington, D.C.

U.S. General Accounting Office (1998b). The Statutory Framework for Performance-Based Management and Accountability, Washington, D.C.

U.S. General Accounting Office (1997). Using the Results Act to Address Mission Fragmentation and Program Overlap, Washington, D.C.

U.S. Office of Management and Budget (1995). Budget of the United State Government, Fiscal Year 1996. Washington, D.C. Executive Office of the President.

U.S. Senate, Report 103-58 (1993). Government Performance and Results Act of 1993: Report of the Committee on Governmental Affairs, United States Senate. Washington, D.C.

Weber, Edward P. (1998). "A Wish List for 21st Century Environmental Policy: Decentralization, Integration, Cooperation, Flexibility, and Enhanced Participation by Citizens and Local Governments." *Policy Studies Journal. 26*(1): xx–xx.

Wholey, J. & Hatry, H. (1992). The Case for Performance Monitoring. *Public Administration Review 52*(6): 604–610.

Wholey, J. & Newcomer, K. (1997). Clarifying Goals, Reporting Results. In *Using Performance Measurement to Improve Public and Nonprofit Programs, New Directions for Evaluation.* Jossey-Bass, San Francisco, CA.

Wholey, Joseph S., (1997). *Trends in Performance Measurement: Challenges for Evaluators, Evaluation for the 21st Century: A Handbook.* Eleanor Chelimshky and William R. Shadish, eds.). Sage Publications. Thousand Oaks, CA.

Willoughby, K.G., & Melkers, J. (1996). The State of the States: Performance-based Budgeting Legislation. Presented at the 1996 American Evaluation Association Conference.

16

Ethics and Public Management

Donald C. Menzel
Division of Public Administration, Northern Illinois University, DeKalb, Illinois

Do managers of public organizations have to be ethical in order to have good government? Perhaps, although it might be argued that if good government can be achieved with morally mute managers, that is, managers who do not feel it is their responsibility to promote ethics or morality in government, then it may still be possible to have government that gets the job done efficiently, effectively, and economically. A chilling possibility? Perhaps. But now consider the opening question rephrased somewhat. Would we have good government if public managers were unethical? Probably not—perhaps definitely not. Conventional wisdom suggests to us that good government—here defined as government that gets the right things done right—cannot be peopled by men and women who either are lacking in ethical or moral values or fail to act (govern or manage) on the basis of those values.

Government, of course, is not in the business of producing ethics (Thompson, 1985). It is in the business of producing public goods and services such as justice, transportation, air and water quality, consumer and occupational safety, national security, and protection from the misfortunes of age, poverty, or race, to name a few. Thus public managers and elected officeholders are charged with providing and producing those collective goods and services deemed necessary and desirable that are often not provided by private sector firms or organizations in a cost-efficient or effective manner. But why then do so many people, managers included, believe that ethical government is so important? The answer is disarmingly straightforward—without ethical government, the production of necessary and desirable public goods and services is not possible. Or, as is so commonly illustrated in the experiences of undemocratic and developing countries, the costs and consequences are so great that whatever goods and services are produced are often not affordable by the vast majority of the population.

This seemingly undeniable law linking ethics, public management, and government has not always been so undeniable or even noteworthy in the United States. Indeed, as Americans enter the 21st century and as we move past the Clinton-Lewinsky scandal and impeachment imbroglio, there is reason to wonder whether or not such a law really exists in the governance of the nation. Do public managers and elected officeholders understand the vital linkage between ethics and good government? Does anyone care whether they do? Or are we entering an era of "anything goes" governance so long as somebody will pay for it?

These controversial questions provide a frame of reference for this chapter, and an effort is made to respond to them. Appropriate responses, however, cannot be offered without first taking stock of the historical record of the evolution of ethics and public management in the United States. The record begins with the fingerprints left by the Founding Fathers in Philadelphia in 1787.

VISIONS OF AN ETHICAL AND DEMOCRATIC GOVERNANCE

There is no question that the Founding Fathers believed that a democratic government would require leaders with impeccable moral and ethical credentials. It was expected that those who occupied public office, whether appointed or elected, would demonstrate the highest degree of integrity and conduct themselves in honorable ways. A democratic government—one that is open and accessible to popular will and thought—could only be achieved by morally committed men and women. As Louis C. Gawthrop so aptly notes in *Public Service and Democracy,* the 55 men who gathered in Philadelphia to draft the Constitution for a new republic wove a garment threaded with ethical values and moral virtues. These values "constituted an indivisible presence in all of the practical and pragmatic decisions made concerning the structure and functions of the new government" (1998: 38).

A cursory examination of the historical record—the Constitution and the Federalist Papers—to identify the framers' expectations of the qualifications one must possess to hold public office suggests that, beyond age and residency requirements, members of Congress (especially the Senate) should have "stability of character" and be "truly respectable." "No government, any more than an individual," Madison cautioned, "will long be respected without being truly respectable" (Federalist no. 62).

A morally imbued constitution required nothing less than morally imbued officials to ensure that a true democracy would prosper. Still, the framers were somewhat schizophrenic inasmuch as they recognized a darker side of the human spirit—ambition, greed, and revenge. In Federalist Paper no. 6, Alexander Hamilton asserts that in creating a government of the people we must not forget that "men are ambitious, vindictive and rapacious." James Madison (Federalist no. 51) shared Hamilton's view, arguing that "ambition must be made to counteract ambition." Checks and balances, the separation of powers among the three branches of government, and the division of power between the national government and the states (federalism) were put forward as the structural means to "counteract ambition." And, as Madison so eloquently proclaimed, "In framing a government which is to be administered by men over men, the great difficulty lies in this: you must first enable the government to control the governed; and in the next place oblige it to control itself" (Federalist no. 51).

GOVERNMENT OF THE PEOPLE AND BY THE PEOPLE

The framers' seemingly contradictory views of human nature and the need for government conducted by ethically and morally upright persons gave way a generation later when Andrew Jackson (1828–1836) occupied the White House. Jacksonian democracy, as historians dubbed it, meant that the common man could lay claim to a job in the federal government; and, perhaps most importantly, that the credentials for this claim were neither the possession of moral character or workplace competency; rather, the claim was rooted in political and personal connections. Thus the "spoils system," whereby those who won political office rewarded their friends and supporters, came into existence.

Patronage politics was to dominate much of American government—city, state, and national—for the next 50 years. Even during the Civil War, President Lincoln spent much of his time receiving and responding to federal job seekers. Government by "incompetent" and "immoral" and "unethical" officials approached epidemic proportions by the end of the 19th century. American courthouses and state capitols became breeding grounds for the corrupt and ambitious. In New York City, for example, the Boss Tweed gang and a string of Tammany Hall political successors handed out jobs and dollars with impunity. Among the more famous personalities was the New York state senator and ward boss George Washington Plunkitt, son of Irish-American immigrants, who entered politics and government to amass and lose a fortune in his lifetime (1842–1924). Senator Plunkitt's ethics, "I saw my opportunity and I took it," or more appropriately, lack of ethics, eventually became the anathema of government reformers.

Despite the lively condition of big city political machines and patronage government in the 1880s and 1890s, change and reform got under way with the passage of the Pendleton Act of 1883 (also known as the Civil Service Act). This new federal law aimed to inject "merit" and "political neutrality" into the operations of the national government and presumably lead to a modern civil service imbued with an ethical impulse. Joining the reformers, the then–Princeton professor Woodrow Wilson (1887) called for "a civil service cultured and self-sufficient enough to act with sense and vigor." Wilson's clarion call included a separation of politics from administration, contending that "administration lies outside the proper sphere of politics." The result of civil service reform, Wilson argued, is "but a moral preparation for what is to follow. It is clearing the moral atmosphere of official life by establishing the sanctity of public office as a public trust."

ADMINISTRATION, SCIENCE, AND ETHICS

Wilson's plea to remove the running of government from the "hurry and strife" of politics in order to have effective and moral government required two additional considerations: that the field of administration be viewed as a "field of business" and that efforts be undertaken to build a "science of administration." These pronouncements, when taken together, provide the first embryonic definition of public management and, as the industrial age roared into the 20th century, found an intellectual home with the emergence of the "scientific management" movement founded by Frederick Taylor.

Taylor, an engineer who believed that America suffered enormously from inefficiencies in the factory and government, advocated "one-best-way" to accomplish work and introduced tools such as time-and-motion studies to find that one best way. The application of scientific management principles in industry and government, Taylor argued, would lift America out of its wasteful and unproductive habits to the benefit of all. Taylor's "siren call" resonated well with good government reformers and the movement to create an impartial, merit-based civil service. Inefficiency, after all, was closely identified with corruption and other misdeeds so prevalent in America's cities and states. Moreover, in creating a "neutral" cadre of public servants to carry out the work of government, the proper emphasis would be placed on work processes, not personal or political friendships.

A science of administration and Taylorism, as the "scientific management" school became known, came to be the dominant paradigm in the evolution of public management and administration. The ethics associated with this paradigm was instrumentalism (getting the job done right benefits the greatest number) and found overt expression in the evolution of the city management profession. Staunton, Virginia, appointed the first person ever with the title of city manager in 1908. The city manager was expected to be politically neutral and competent to know how to get the city's streets repaired and sewer and water lines working properly. This separation of management from politics was exactly what Wilson had in mind, and the fact that the prevailing ethic was utilitarian was not especially concerning to anyone. Indeed, utilitarianism fit very well with a work ethos. It also fit very well with the evolution of the City Managers' Association,[1] which was established in 1914, although it should be noted that the association recognized early on that it was very important for its members to embrace a strict code of ethics.[2]

THE RISE OF THE MORALLY MUTE PUBLIC MANAGER

The efforts described to turn administration or management into a scientific practice began to waiver with the onset of World War II but still stirred the imaginations of managers and organizational theorists well into the 1960s. Science, progress, and modern management, inextricably interwoven, had become dogma by the late 1930s (Stillman, 1991). The war effort, its scale and planning and execution, gave a new reality and thinking to public management. The politics-administration dichotomy floundered under the reality of policymakers who administered wartime programs and administrators who were heavily involved in policy-making. Planning, coordinating, and executing programs and policies were not driven by scientific principles but by the necessity to get the job done quickly, efficiently, and effectively. And, with the advent of the destructive potential of nuclear weapons, many began to question whether progress needed to be redefined.

The war years certainly contributed to a proactive management style and led to the "golden years" of working in the federal government in the 1940s and 1950s. Gone was some of the intellectual baggage but not all, especially the identity of public managers as "neutrally competent" problem solvers. Neutrality, as epitomized through local, state, and federal civil service, had grown larger than the Wilsonian legacy of removing partisanship from government work. In conjunction with the ethic of utilitarianism and Weberian norms of impartiality and hierarchy, neutrality meant that public servants had either no claim to values (personal, social, political), especially insofar as they might enter into the carrying out of one's official duties, or at best, as professionals, could make an argument for a preferred course of action but must fall into line once the policy decision was made by organizational or political superiors. The result of these influences was the appearance, if not the reality, of amoral management or, put more kindly, morally mute management—neither of which is desirable.

Indeed, as public managers and public organizations became more sterile morally and ethically, a movement was launched to do something about it. In the late 1960s at the height of civil unrest and diminishing confidence in the ability of the United States to become a "Great Society,"[3] a group of young academics gathered in upstate New York at a retreat called Minnowbrook and put forth a call for a "new" public administration: one in which administrators and managers accepted responsibility for promoting social justice and equity. This value-infused movement was seen by many as an antidote to the perilous plight of morally mute public management.

For a variety of reasons, the "new" public administration did not have as great an impact on public service as some had hoped. Its proactive posture made many managers and public officials question whether or not it was proper for non-elected officials to be so presumptuous in defining the public interest. After all, is that not the responsibility of legitimately elected officeholders?

NO ROAD, LOW ROAD, OR HIGH ROAD ETHICS?

There's a saying, "If you don't know where you're going, then any road will get you there!" These words may have some relevance to the role and place of ethics in public management during the past several decades. The tumultuous 1960s may have come to a close with a quest to make public managers more relevant morally and ethically, but then there was Watergate—and the aftermath. The secret White House tapes revealed a president who not only conspired with others to cover up a politically motivated break-in of the Democratic Headquarters at the Watergate Hotel, but had a moral and ethical compass that seemed ajar, if not altogether spinning aimlessly in the breeze of power seeking and holding.

President Nixon's resignation in 1974 spawned a wave of legislative initiatives in Washington and the states to prevent wrongdoing in government and punish those who choose to break the law. State after state enacted ethics laws and established ethics boards or commissions, with some given substantial powers to investigate alleged cases of wrongdoing by public officials. At the federal level, Congress moved with dispatch to enact the Ethics in Government Act of 1978, a law that, among other things, created the U.S. Office of Government Ethics and the now-infamous independent counsel, whose broad investigatory powers were put on display in Kenneth Starr's investigation of President Clinton's financial and personal affairs.

These presumably meritorious efforts to legislate the ethical behavior of local, state, and federal officials, including high-ranking appointed public managers and often front-line members of the government work force, have produced dubious results. There is precious little empirical evidence that ethics laws, ordinances, or boards have given us good government (Menzel, 1999; Williams, 1996). Indeed, there is even a suggestion that ethics legislation allows public officials to employ the lowest common denominator in deciding right and wrong behavior. That is, by stating in law what are punishable offenses, lawmakers have given elected and appointed officeholders the opportunity to define ethics as "behaviors and practices that do not break the law." Stated in the vernacular, "If it's not illegal, it's okay!" This approach has been appropriately labeled by John Rohr, a noted ethics scholar, as the "low road" to ethics. The low road features compliance and adherence to formal rules. "Ethical behavior," Rohr (1989: 63) asserts, "is reduced to staying out of trouble" and results in "meticulous attention to trivial questions."

But is the low road the only road? It is certainly arguable that it is the "best" road. In fact, many public administration ethics scholars believe it is even a poor substitute for "no road." What then might be a more agreeable or desirable alternative? The "high" road to ethics behavior for public managers, Carol Lewis argues in *The Ethics Challenge in Public Service,* is the path of integrity. "Relying on moral character," she argues, "this route counts on ethical managers individually to reflect, decide, and act" (1991: 10). This approach blends accepting responsibility for one's behavior with honorable intentions and personal integrity, that is, adherence to moral and ethical principles.[4] But whose morals and whose principles should one adhere to? Herein lie the challenge and difficulty of the high road.

The legislative flurry to enact ethics laws in the 1970s, as described earlier, is regarded by some as an important step forward. However, insofar as this step fosters the low road of compliance to ethical behavior, it may actually be a half-step at most. To be sure, ethics scholars such as Carol Lewis, Terry Cooper, and John Rohr are not advocating a blanket repeal of ethics laws and ordinances in America. Rather, they are calling for an awakening, perhaps a reawakening, of what might be referred to as the "moral sense" that inheres in every human being.[5] A tall order? To be sure. Indeed, one that is fraught with real world challenges that were amply illustrated in the decade of the eighties.

ISSUES AND CHALLENGES OF THE 1980s

The thrashing around to find an appropriate ethical road for public managers and elected officeholders to follow both improved and worsened with the "me" generation of the 1980s. Scandals on Wall Street, in the U.S. Department of Housing and Urban Development (HUD), and in the White House with the Iran-Contra affair, to identify the most well known and notorious, sent many peoples' ethical compasses spinning wildly. Why would inside traders on Wall Street use their knowledge to skim off thousands and thousands of dollars? Why would a federal agency seem to be owned by the highest bidders? And, why would an American president, especially one so well liked, lie to the American public about selling arms to an unfriendly regime (Iran) to raise money for an insurgency in another part of the world thousands of miles away?

The answer to the first set of questions is greed with some overtones of Plunkitt ethics—"I saw my opportunity." The Wall Street and HUD scandals clearly involved men and women of ambition and avarice. Some observers believe that these incidents were merely symptomatic of the "me" generation. Neither government officials nor private sector managers and CEOs seemed immune to the question, What's in it for me?

Lying, as in the Iran-Contra affair, was equally troublesome and symptomatic of a moral malaise that seemed to be gaining ground in America. This particular scandal was especially disturbing because the chain of command from the president through his top security advisers and eventually Lieutenant Colonel Oliver L. North seemed to be an unbroken lie bound together by patriotism, duty, and blind loyalty. As Lieutenant Colonel North explained to Congress, "Lying does not come easily to me. But we all had to weigh in the balance the difference between lies and lives." That President Reagan actually lied is arguable, however, given the congressional testimony of Admiral John M. Poindexter, the president's national security adviser.[6] Admiral Poindexter, testifying before a joint Senate and House hearing in July 1987, said: "I made a very deliberate decision not to ask the president [about whether or not arms should be sold to Iran to raise money for the Nicaraguan Contras to fight the Communist-controlled Nicaraguan government] so that I could insulate him from the decision and provide some future deniability." In other words, Admiral Poindexter deliberately withheld information from President Reagan about the money for arms transactions that Congress had specifically legislated against.

The ethical angst of the 1980s spilled over into the world of public management as well, so much so that a number of countermeasures were initiated. One was the promulgation in 1984 of a Code of Ethics by the American Society for Public Administration (ASPA).[7] ASPA was established in 1939 by men and women of the New Deal generation to promote professionalism and ethical behavior in public service. But it took more than 40 years to build a consensus needed to enact a code. Another countermeasure was the recognition by many schools of public affairs and administration that it was time to develop and include ethics courses in their curricula. By the end of the 1980s, 40 schools had added an ethics course to their graduate program of study (Menzel, 1997). A related initiative was taken by the National Schools of Public Affairs and Administration (NASPAA) in 1989 when a new curriculum standard on ethics was promulgated. Schools seeking accreditation since that date must demonstrate that their programs "enhance the student's values, knowledge, and skills to act ethically."

Scholarship on administrative ethics also expanded significantly in the 1980s as evidenced by the number of ethics books and journal articles appearing in print. Authors such as Burke (1986), Cooper (1982, 1984, 1987), Denhardt (1988, 1989), Gawthrop (1984), and Rohr (1989) made important contributions, especially to ethics theory. Additionally, the International City/County Management Association published an influential volume, *Ethical Insight, Ethical Action* (Keller, 1988), and the *Public Administration Review* published insightful articles by Cooper (1987), Hart (1984), Frederickson and Hart (1985), Chandler (1983), and Thompson (1985).

These collective efforts by individuals and professional associations constituted a major push to ensure that men and women who entered and advanced in the public service could contribute to ethical government as well as to competent government. Whether or not these results have been achieved remains an important but mostly unanswered question as we enter the 21st century. In fact, the pluralistic nature of these initiatives in combination with the rethinking of administration and management in the 1990s may have diffused the presumed desirable outcomes.

ADMINISTRATION AS MANAGEMENT: ETHICAL IMPLICATIONS

This chapter has largely assumed that public administration and public management mean essentially the same thing, i.e., getting the job done, and therefore, any discussion of ethics is relevant to either. During the past several decades, however, the meaning of managing and administering public programs and organizations has sufficiently changed to make it necessary to rethink what it means to be a public manager or administrator and to reassess the ethical implications associated with each.

But what are the changes? And where did they come from? The most important changes were the enlargement of management as an operating concept and practice in public affairs and the diminution of administration as an operating concept and practice. One might go so far as to say that public administration in its most traditional fiduciary sense has been cast aside in favor of a public management defined as business management. Echoes of Woodrow Wilson's assertion that administration is a field of business administration? Perhaps. Another important change was the erosion of the meaning of *public* in public service.

Where Has the Public Gone in Public Administration?

When institutions of higher education began to recognize the importance of educating men and women for public service careers, the line between governmental and nongovernmental employment was fairly clear. Thus the rise of master of public administration (M.P.A.) degree-granting programs was a response to the need to supply city, state, and national governments with talented and capable administrators. The M.P.A. degree, however, was supposed to convey more than competency on its holder; it was presumed that its recipient understood why competent administration was essential in a democracy and why he or she, in giving competence to administration, was also serving the public interest. Normative commitments to promoting democratic governance and the public interest explain precisely why a graduate degree in public administration was not called a master's degree in government administration (M.G.A.).[8]

Nonetheless, times change and over the past 30 years it has been increasingly difficult to separate public sector employment from private sector employment—not to mention the enormous growth of third-party-sector employment (nonprofits and quasi-public agencies). The result, some believe, has been an unwitting redefinition of the M.P.A. degree to emphasize competency only.

H. George Frederickson in *The Spirit of Public Administration* (1997) eloquently and persuasively argues that this approach is wrongheaded and potentially dangerous. A democracy, he contends, requires a democratic administration, i.e., one in which managers and workers are competent *and* morally committed to serving the public. Redefining administration as management poses some risks and prompts concern with regard to "managerial" ethics, especially the utilitarian views described next.

New Public Management

As noted, the 1980s witnessed a renewal of interest in public sector ethics issues and problems. This decade also witnessed the steady blurring of private/public sector lines, unending bashing of bureaucrats and bureaucracy by the media and republican presidents (remember it was Ronald Reagan who quipped, "Washington is not the solution to our problems; it is the problem"), and a steadily growing belief in the application of private sector management tools to public sector management problems (quality circles, total quality management, team building, etc.). Thus, when the former city manager Ted Gaebler and the management consultant David Osborne published *Reinventing Government* in 1992, the stage was set for even more dramatic change in our thinking about administration and management. The "reinvention" movement, as it is often called, was galvanized when the Clinton administration assumed office. In October 1992, the administration released the *National Performance Review*, a document that embodied the spirit and soul of reinventing government per Osborne and Gaebler, by promising to turn the federal government into a government that "works better and costs less."

The "new public management" would require men and women who steer organizations—not row them; empower citizens and coach workers through teamwork and participation; thrive on and promote competition; reject rule-driven organizations in favor of mission-driven organizations; seek results, not outcomes; put customers first; foster enterprising and market-oriented government; and embrace community-owned government. New public managers (NPMs) are also likely to find the privatization of public goods and services an attractive alternative and adopt new management tools such as benchmarking, strategic planning, reengineering, and total quality management as the situation warrants. This new way of thinking about management casts public managers into the forefront of getting the job done for Americans in an economical and cost-effective fashion. The era of the administrator who responds to citizen requests and demands rather than meeting the customer's needs, fixes problems when they arise rather than preventing them before they become uncomfortable, and promotes the public interest per the new public administration or some other value set is over.

But what are the implications for ethical behavior and practices under the new public management?[9] Advocates are certainly not encouraging NPMs to break the law or engage in unethical management practices or behavior. Rather, they are mostly silent about the place of ethics or morality in public management.[10] This silence has not gone unnoticed and has caused some observers to worry a great deal about what might be ahead. Professor Larry Terry (1993: 393–394), an outspoken opponent of new public management, believes that NPMs go too far in embracing entrepreneurial values such as "autonomy, a personal vision of the future, secrecy, risk-taking, domination, coercion, and a disrespect for tradition." A colleague, H. George Frederickson (1997: 22), also worries that NPMs' acceptance of utilitarianism, much as in years past when the tenets of science were believed well suited to public administration, will reduce the public interest to the "sum of atomistic individuals." A public interest so defined is, essentially, no public interest, only competing interests. Furthermore, Frederickson cautions against the downside of turning citizens into customers, which may result in a collective escape from responsibility and diminish civil discourse as individuals and groups vie against one another to extract promises and favors from government. He is equally concerned about the effect of the reinvention movement and privatization on public affairs.

> Government . . . is being reinvented to put together public-private partnerships, "empower" citizens with choices, and so on. In sum, it is now fashionable to degovernmentalize on the promise of saving money and improving services. If previously governmental functions are shifted to the private sector or are shared, it is a safe bet that corruption will increase. It is no small irony that government is moving in the direction of privatization at the same time that there is a rising concern for governmental ethics. (1997: 171)

Professor Louis W. Gawthrop (1999) has also been outspoken about the risks of debureacratizing government and treating public service as merely work. In *Public Service & Democracy,* Gawthrop (1998: 17) is unrelenting in his concerns:

> We are faced with a new reality in which the citizen has been reinvented into the customer; interest groups—broadly defined to include private-sector contractors, suppliers, and so on—have been re-designated stakeholders, and, most significantly, public servants have been recast in the mold of entrepreneurs. In the process of reconfiguring public bureaucracies, however, little attention is being given to how this new reality conforms to the ethical-moral values and virtues that are deeply embedded in our democratic system.

This new reality represents a break from the old but no less reassuring reality of the administrator as a detached, dispassionate rational provider of objective information and advice to elected bosses. Good men and women with good intentions who allow themselves to be seduced by a sense of duty as competent purveyors of neutral information became neither moral nor immoral actors. Rather, they became amoral, and, in this capacity, they can contribute little to ethical or democratic governance. Notions of faith, hope, and love, Gawthrop contends, are not "generally recognized as significant components of public administration in America today. Instead, it is the logic of utility that still provides the basic rationale for the classical management tenets of efficiency and control" (1998: 87).

Despite the enormous influence of the old and new management realities, Gawthrop is an optimist, not a pessimist, about public service, ethics, and democracy. A moral impulse, he contends, must suffuse bureaucracy and democracy if the common good, as promised by a democratic society, is to be achieved. But from where could and should a moral impulse radiate? From the public? Elected officeholders? Administrators? Gawthrop places his confidence in administrators if and only if they can break out of "the habits of the self-serving good which allow public servants to pursue a procedural, quasi-ethical life" (1998: 139). In other words, an ethical life rooted in procedural correctness—avoiding conflicts of interest, disclosing financial information relevant to one's office-holding, and conducting public affairs in the sunshine—is, in Gawthrop's view, a hollow ethical life at best. At worst, a procedural, quasi-ethical life produces a "government of persons without fault, operating in a society without judgment, through the ministrations of a Constitution without a purpose" (1998: 139).

Ethics is morality in action, he believes. It is, therefore, a mistake to separate morality and ethics, as is often done. Ethics defined only as compliance—"Tell me what is right; what is wrong; what is legal; what is not permissible"—is also unacceptable. It is imperative that public administrators and managers understand that ethics is morality in action and that there is a moral dimension of democracy.

One other issue that may be amplified considerably by NPMs is the challenge of managerial discretion. As John Rohr notes, this is an enduring issue in public affairs that remains an unsolved problem. Put as a question, "How can a democratic regime justify substantial political power in the hands of people who are exempt by law from the discipline of the ballot box?" (Rohr, 1998: 6). Rohr has dared to "solve" this unsolved problem in *To Run a Constitution* (1986), the oath of office, he asserts, legitimates a degree of professional autonomy for the public manager and "can keep this autonomy within acceptable bounds" (1998: 69). The oath of office, he reminds the reader, is more than a mere promise; it is a morally binding commitment to uphold the Constitution. As such, he argues, it is a "statement of professional independence rather than subservience" (1998: 72). The oath guides autonomy and deters public managers from becoming maximizing bureaucrats.

As appealing as Rohr's solution might appear, it is not without its problems. For example, not all public managers take an oath of office. Public managers in the U.S. government are, but not all state or local public managers are sworn to uphold the Constitution. Then there are public managers who manage nonprofit organizations or organizations that are quasi-public. These managers may not take an oath as well. Finally, there is the bleak reality that managers who do take an oath of office do not understand Rohr's contention that the oath places self-imposed limits on the exercise of managerial discretion.

ETHICS AND PUBLIC MANAGEMENT IN THE FUTURE

This chapter has presented a historical portrait of the evolution of ethics in public administration and management in the American experience. Unfortunately, it will remain an unfinished portrait given the changes in our thinking about organizing and managing public organizations. These changes are in no small measure exacerbated by the forces of privatization, globalization, computerization, and the rapidly moving world of information technologies.

The threat of the resurrection of the morally mute manager is real and must be taken seriously. The new public management movement described has yet to define itself ethically or morally. Or, in the worse case, it has redefined itself as a pernicious brand of moral muteness that reduces citizens to customers and public service professionals to businessmen and businesswomen whose major task is to make citizen-customers satisfied with what they want and receive from government (Frederickson, 1999). This pathway, as Gawthrop reminds us, is certainly not a pathway to the common good. It even raises the question of whether or not such an approach can avoid the worse pitfalls of unethical behavior and practices in government.

Do managers of public organizations have to be ethical in order to have good government? Without question. Public managers who do not understand why the public cannot be removed from their job descriptions or why being competent in one's work is not sufficient to being a good manager are dangerous and should be encouraged to ply their trade in those occupations that do not demand more than competency from them. Perhaps President John F. Kennedy's view of ethical government best captures what is needed: "The ultimate answer to ethical problems in government is honest people in a good ethical environment. No web of statute or regulation . . . can hope to deal with the myriad possible challenges to a man's integrity or his devotion to the public interest (Lewis, 1991: 14).

NOTES

1. The City Managers' Association changed its name in 1924 to the City Management Association and again in 1969 to the International City Management Association and again in 1980s to the International City/County Management Association.
2. The code was first adopted in 1924 and revised in 1972 and 1998.
3. President Lyndon B. Johnson promised Americans that a great society was possible—

hence programs to stamp out injustice, poverty, pollution, illiteracy, and so forth were fashioned during his administration and largely continued during Nixon's first term of office.

4. The "high road" approach of character and integrity is a virtues approach to ethics that has a history that goes back to the writing of Aristotle.
5. James Q. Wilson makes a persuasive argument in *The Moral Sense* that human beings possess a basic sense of right and wrong much like the senses of taste, smell, sight, touch, hearing.
6. One point of view is that President Reagan had tacitly given his approval of such rogue operations even though he did not have specific information about what was happening.
7. The American Society for Public Administration has more than 10,000 members who are drawn primarily from city, state, national, and nonprofit organizations. Academics in public affairs and administration are also typically members. Additionally, members of private sector firms can join the society since membership is not limited to governmental or nonprofit agencies or academic institutions. The society has a diverse membership base, which explains in part why it took more than 40 years for a consensus to develop on the contents of a code of ethics.
8. One well-known school, the Wharton School of Business at the University of Pennsylvania, actually did grant a master's degree in governmental administration.
9. For a spirited discussion of the new public management, see the Symposium on Leadership, Democracy, and the New Public Management in the *Public Administration Review,* vol. 58 (May/June) 1998.
10. There is not a single reference to "ethics" in *Reinventing Government.*

REFERENCES

Burke, John P. (1986). *Bureaucratic Responsibility.* The Johns Hopkins Press, Baltimore.

Chandler, R.C., (1983). The problem of moral reasoning in American public administration: The case for a code of ethics. *Public Administration Review. 43:* 32–39.

Cooper, T.L. (1982). *The Responsible Administrator: An Approach to Ethics for the Administrative Role.* Kennikat Press, Port Washington, N.Y.

Cooper, T.L. (1984). Citizenship and professionalism in public administration. *Public Administration Review. 44:* 143–149.

Cooper, T.L. (1987). Hierarchy, virtue, and the practice of public administration: A perspective for normative ethics. *Public Administration Review. 47* (July/August): 320–328.

Denhardt, Kathryn G. (1988). *The Ethics of Public Administration: Resolving Moral Dilemmas in Public Organizations.* Greenwood, New York.

Denhardt, Kathryn G. (1989). The management of ideals: A political perspective on ethics. *Public Administration Review. 49* (March/April): 187–192.

Frederickson, H. George (1997). *The Spirit of Public Administration.* Jossey-Bass, San Francisco.

Frederickson, H. George (1999). Public ethics and the new managerialism. *Public Integrity. 1* (Summer): 265–278.

Frederickson, H.G. and Hart, D.K. (1985). The public service and the patriotism of benevolence. *Public Administration Review. 45:* 547–553.

Gawthrop, L.G. (1998). *Public Service and Democracy.* Chatham House, Chappaqua, N.Y.

Gawthrop, L.G. (1984). *Public Sector Management, Systems, and Ethics.* Indiana University Press, Bloomington.

Gawthrop, L.G. (1999). Public entrepreneurship in the lands of Oz and Uz. *Public Integrity. 1* (Winter): 75–86.

Hart, D.K. (1984). The virtuous citizen, the honorable bureaucrat, and 'public' administration. *Public Administration Review. 44:* 111–120.

Keller, Elizabeth (ed.) (1988). *Ethical Insight, Ethical Action.* International City/County Management Association, Washington, D.C.

Lewis, Carol W. (1991). *The Ethics Challenge in Public Service.* Jossey-Bass, San Francisco.

Menzel, Donald C. (1997). Teaching ethics and values: A survey of graduate PA/A programs in the U.S. *PS: Political Science & Politics. 30* (September): 518–524.

Menzel, Donald C., with Carson, K.J. (1999). A review and assessment of empirical research on public administration ethics: Implications for scholars and managers. *Public Integrity. 1* (Summer): 239–264.

Osborne, David, and Gaebler, T. (1992). *Reinventing Government.* Addison-Wesley, Reading, Mass.

Rohr, John A. (1986). *To Run a Constitution.* University Press of Kansas, Lawrence.

Rohr, John A. (1989). *Ethics for Bureaucrats: An Essay on Law and Values,* 2nd ed. Marcel Dekker, New York.

Rohr, John A. (1998). *Public Service, Ethics and Constitutional Practice.* University Press of Kansas, Lawrence.

Stillman, Richard J., II (1991). Preface to public administration. St. Martin's Press, New York.

Terry, Larry D. (1993). Why we should abandon the misconceived quest to reconcile public entrepreneurship with democracy. Public Administration Review. 53

Terry, Larry D. (1998). Administrative leadership, neo-managerialism, and the public management movement. *Public Administration Review. 58* (May/June): 194–200.

Thompson, Dennis F. (1985). The possibility of administrative ethics. *Public Administration Review. 45:* 555–561.

Williams, Russell L. (1996). Controlling ethical practices through laws and rules: Evaluating the Florida Commission on Ethics. *Public Integrity Annual.* Lexington, Kentucky: Council of State Governments.

Wilson, James Q. (1993). *The Moral Sense. 2:* 197–222. The Free Press, New York.

Wilson, Woodrow (1887). The study of administration. *Political Science Quarterly. 56* (December 1941).

17

Win-Win Public Management

Stuart S. Nagel
Political Science Department
University of Illinois, Urbana, Illinois

Public management, or the management of government agencies, involves many controversial issues. Some relate to procedures and other relate to substance.

Procedural issues include (a) the role of ideology versus technology, (b) choice among applicants and personnel recruitment, (c) rewarding of performance in personnel administration, (d) tax sources in revenue raising, and (e) responses to the deficit in financial management.

Substantive issues include socialism versus capitalism as an economic policy issue, population control versus reproductive freedom as a social policy issue, environmental protection versus economic development as a technology policy issue, and presidential versus parliamentary government as a political policy issue.

WIN-WIN ANALYSIS

All these issues can be analyzed from a win-win or superoptimizing perspective. Such a perspective can enable conservatives, liberals, and those having other major viewpoints to come out ahead of their best initial expectations simultaneously.

For example, in the minimum wage controversy, both liberals and conservatives endorse the goal of paying a decent wage and the goal of not overpaying to the point where some workers are unnecessarily laid off because their employers cannot afford the new higher minimum. Liberals, however, give relatively high weight to the first goal and relatively low but positive weight to the second goal, and vice versa for conservatives.

The liberal alternative in the minimum wage controversy might be $4.40 an hour and the conservative alternative might be $4.20 an hour. The liberal alternative would thus score higher on the "decent wage" goal, and the conservative alternative lower. On the goal of "avoiding overpayment," the liberal alternative would score lower, and the conservative alternative higher. This real data would thus provide a classic trade-off controversy.

The object in this example is to find a solution that is simultaneously better from a liberal perspective than $4.40 an hour and better from a conservative perspective than $4.20 an hour. One such superoptimum solution would be to provide for a minimum wage supplement by the government of 22 cents an hour to each unemployed person who is hired. The worker would receive $4.41 an hour, but the employer would pay only $4.19 an hour.

The liberal-labor interests would be getting more than their best expectation of $4.40 an hour, and the conservative-business interests would be paying less than their best expectation of $4.20 an hour. The government and taxpayers would be benefiting by virtue of (a) the money saved from otherwise providing public aid to unemployed people; (b) the money added to the gross national product, which provides income to others, increases taxes, and creates an increased base on which to grow in subsequent years; (c) better role models for the children of people who would otherwise be unemployed; and (d) an upgrading of skills if qualifying for the wage subsidy means business has to provide on-the-job training and workers have to participate.

PROCEDURAL ISSUES

The Role of Ideology Versus Technology

Public administration is the study of methods for improving and understanding how governmental programs are implemented, especially in terms of personnel, financing, and accountability. This chapter systematically analyzes some recent developments in Chinese public administration. It uses a win-win or superoptimizing perspective that emphasizes methods whereby all major sides and viewpoints in a dispute or dilemma can come out ahead of their best initial expectations.

Table 1 analyzes the problems of ideology versus technology in Chinese public administration. From the establishment of the People's Republic of China to about 1980, the emphasis was on ideology in evaluating alternative ways to implement governmental programs. That meant referring to Mao, Marx, and Lenin or interpreters of them. The result in personnel management was to emphasize hiring on the basis of ideological loyalty and Communist party enthusiasm

TABLE 1 Ideology versus Technocracy in Chinese Public Administration[a]

	Criteria	
	C	L
Alternatives	Efficiency and effectiveness	Equity
C *Technocratic*	+	−
L *Democracy and equalitarian ideology*	−	+
N *Compromise*	0	0
SOS or Win-Win Both simultaneously	++	++

[a]Public administration especially refers to personnel management and public finance. In the context of personnel management, ideology in the 1970s emphasized Communist party loyalty. In the 1980s, technocracy meant modern automation in tax administration. In the context of public finance, ideology in the 1970s emphasized heavy taxes on the rich and on profit-making activities. In the 1980s, technocracy meant modern automation in tax administration. The SOS alternative for personnel management might emphasize loyalty to worthwhile Communist ideals such as equity and merit in the distribution of government jobs, rather than irrelevant party loyalty or mathematical skills. The SOS alternative for public finance might emphasize taxation to stimulate entrepreneurial development for the benefit of the economy, rather than confiscatory taxes or mindless automation. C, conservative; L, liberal; N, neutral; SOS, superoptimum or win-win solution.

rather than technical skills. From about 1980, an increased emphasis was placed on knowledge of economics in administering a business program, of engineering and physics in administering an energy program, or of other substantive fields for other programs.

In terms of Table 1, the basic alternatives are ideology, technocracy, and a compromise between the two. Equity was the stated key goal of those supporting the ideology alternative; it was, however, often only a lip-service goal since personal status was the real goal. Efficiency and effectiveness were the stated key goals of those supporting the technocracy alternative. They too were often only lip-service goals; personal status was actually the goal of those with technocratic skills.

In the late 1980s, more emphasis was placed on public administration as practiced in the United States, Western Europe, and countries with American-trained professors and practitioners in public administration. That emphasis recognizes the importance of equity in governmental programs, including postal systems, elementary schools, urban transportation, and other services that take a loss in providing services to the poor and many other people in order to provide better access and equity. That emphasis also recognizes the importance of efficiency and effectiveness as manifested in the use of decision analysis, operations research, management science, and other such generalist techniques to supplement the substantive expertise in business administration, engineering, physics, and other relevant substantive specialties.

Striving for both equity and efficiency simultaneously is associated with the superoptimizing idea of enabling both ideologists and technocrats to come out ahead of their best initial expectations. With regard to personnel, an enlightened public administration approach talks in terms of quality of opportunity to apply for and meet the entrance requirements in government positions. At the same time, high-quality standards, designed to promote efficiency and effectiveness, are set. The broadened perspective on public finance may emphasize income taxes to provide equity but sales and other consumption taxes as an efficient way of collecting large sums of money.

Choice Among Applicants in Personnel Administration

Table 2 looks at a classic personnel recruitment problem. Applicant A does well on the first goal but not so well on the second goal, although above a minimum threshold. Applicant B does well on the second goal but not so well on the first. The traditional recruitment approach might be to hire applicant C, who is a compromise in the sense of falling in the middle on both goals. The superoptimizing solution (SOS) alternative might be to hire applicant A in order to obtain the benefits of his or her high quality on goal 1 but provide on-the-job training to raise applicant A on goal 2 to a level close to that of applicant B. Applicant B would be hired with on-the-job training if the nature of the skills were such that it would be easier to train on goal 1 than on goal 2.

TABLE 2 Superoptimizing Applied to Personnel Recruitment[a]

Alternatives	Criteria G1	G2
Applicant A	+	–
Applicant B	–	+
Applicant C	0	0
SOS or win-win Hire A with OJT	++	++

[a]G1, goal 1; G2, goal 2; OJT, on-the-job training.

Applicant A does best on goal 1, but applicant B does best on goal 2. There is thus a trade-off that needs to be resolved.

The usual way of resolving such a trade-off would be to decide which goal is more important. One would then hire the better applicant in terms of the more important goal. The SOS alternative might be to hire the applicant who does better on the characteristic that is harder to train for. That might be the less important goal. That applicant would then be given on-the-job training (OJT) to improve in relation in the other goal. The result might be that the applicant hired would become the better person on both goals.

Another SOS alternative might be to hire the applicant on the more important goal but provide training on the other goal. The result might be that the one hired improves enough on the other goal that his or her total score exceeds that of the applicant not hired, regardless of which goal is considered more important.

That is the essence of an SOS solution, namely, to be the winning alternative regardless of whether one uses the goals and weights of any major groups, perspective, or ideology.

Rewarding of Performance in Personnel Administration

Table 3 deals with the conflict between the conservative or elitist desire to reward especially high performance versus the liberal or democratic desire to have many people rewarded even if lower goals are achieved. The SOS alternative might be to ask for even higher performance than the conservatives or elitists are advocating but to provide subsidized facilitators to enable more people to achieve those high performance levels. The subsidized facilitators might include skills upgrading and the introduction of new technologies.

TABLE 3 Elitism versus Democratic Sharing in Rewarding Performance[a]

	Criteria	
	C	L
Alternatives	Elitism	Democratic sharing
C *Reward high performance*	+	
L *Winners of lower goals*	−	+
N *Reward moderate performance*	0	0
SOS or win-win Ask for higher performance but with subsidized facilitators	++	++

[a]C, conservative; L, liberal; N, neutral; SOS, superoptimum or win-win solution.

The issue here is how to reward performing well in public administration.

The conservative approach is mainly to reward those who do especially well, thereby creating a small elite at the top. The liberal approach is to broaden the definition of doing well so there are more winners of the rewards that are available.

If the conservative approach gives big rewards to the top 10 percent and the liberal approach gives small rewards to the top 50 percent, then the neutral approach might give moderate rewards to the top 30 percent.

The SOS approach might determine that the top 10 percent operates at a level of 8 on a 1–10 scale. The SOS approach might say that everyone who gets a score higher than 8 will be rewarded, but the SOS approach provides many facilitators to enable a high percentage to score better than an 8, maybe even more than 50 percent.

Facilitators especially relate to subsidies to upgrade the skills of public administrators so they can perform better than an 8 on a 1–10 scale. Facilitators might also include introducing new technologies that enable public administrators to be even more productive, especially if they are trained with the new skills needed to use the new technologies.

Tax Sources in Revenue Raising

Table 4 provides an SOS approach to tax sources. The conservative alternative emphasizes sales taxes, which disproportionately bear on the poor. The liberal alternative emphasizes income taxes, which disproportionately bear on the rich. A compromise is to enact both taxes but with neither producing as much revenue as

TABLE 4 A Superoptimum Solution Approach to Tax Sources[a]

	Criteria	
	C	L
Alternatives	Stimulating investment	Ability to pay
C *Sales tax*	+	–
L *Income tax*	–	+
N *Other or both*	0	0
SOS or win-win Decreases tax rates but increase total taxes with well-placed subsidies	++	++

[a]C, conservative; L, liberal; N, neutral; SOS, superoptimum or win-win solution.

might be needed. The superoptimizing perspective seeks to increase both kinds of taxes in order to have sufficient funding for necessary governmental programs. The key element is a superoptimizing approach (as reflected in the policies of both Ronald Reagan and Bill Clinton) to produce a system of well-placed subsidies and incentives so that total taxes will increase even if the tax rate is lowered.

Conservatives tend to emphasize taxes on consumption such as the sales tax or the value-added taxes. Liberals tend to emphasize taxes on income, especially progressive income taxes, whereby the rates are higher on higher incomes. The neutral position is to have both sales taxes and income taxes, but with the sales tax rates lower than conservatives advocate, and the income tax rates lower than liberals advocate.

Both conservatives and liberals recognize the need for some tax money to support the government activities they like. The superoptimum solution then is not to abolish all taxes, that would be undesirable to both conservatives and liberals if it meant abolishing the government activities they endorse. Likewise, the neutral position may result in a decrease in the government activities endorsed by conservatives and those endorsed by liberals.

The SOS alternative involves substantially decreasing both kinds of tax rates while increasing the total tax revenue by increasing the gross national product (GNP) tax base. That can be partly done by well-placed tax breaks and subsidies to encourage greater national productivity.

Responses to the Deficit in Financial Administration

Table 5 involves the important financial management problem of dealing with annual deficits and a large and possibly increasing national debt. The conservative alternative to dealing with a deficit tends to decrease domestic spending and increase consumption taxes. The liberal alternative tends to decrease defense spending and increase income taxes. The neutral alternative is eclectic. It seeks to increase spending, but spending designed to upgrade skills and introduce new technologies that will pay off in terms of a larger gross national product. It may use selective tax reductions with strings attached in order to reward productivity-increasing activities. This kind of perspective is especially associated with the public finance aspects of Japan's and the former West Germany's industrial policy. It is also associated with newly industrializing areas of the Far East, including South Korea, Taiwan, Hong Kong, Thailand, and South China.

A fuller statement of the conservative goal might be to have a strong national defense and to stimulate investment through low taxes on the relatively rich. A fuller statement of the liberal goal might be to have strong domestic policies, for example, related to education and housing and to stimulate consumption through low taxes on the relatively poor.

The SOS involves a reduction of taxes in the form of tax breaks designed to stimulate greater productivity. Likewise, the SOS involves an increase in spending

TABLE 5 Dealing with the Deficit[a]

	Criteria	
	C	L
Alternatives	Defense and investment	Domestic and consumption
C −Domestic spending *+Taxes on poor*	+	−
L −Defense spending and *+Taxes on rich*	−	+
N −Both spend *+Taxes on both*	0	0
SOS or win-win +Spending −Taxes	++	++

[a]−, reduce under "Alternative"; +, increase under "Alternative."

in the form of targeted subsidies designed to stimulate productivity. The increased productivity means an increased gross national product, which means an increased base on which to apply the national tax rate. Thus the tax rate can drop and still increase tax revenue and thereby make more money available for government spending, including defense, domestic programs, deficit reduction, and more well-placed subsidies.

SUBSTANTIVE ISSUES

Socialism Versus Capitalism as an Economic Policy Issue

The changes that are occurring in Eastern Europe and in many other regions and nations of the world provide an excellent *opportunity* to apply systematic policy analysis to determining such basic matters as how to organize the economy, the government, and other social institutions. Population control and land reform are highly important problems, but they may not be as basic as reconstituting a society.

Alternatives

Table 6 analyzes the fundamental issue of *socialism versus capitalism* in the context of government versus private ownership and operation of the basic means of production in industry and agriculture. The essence of socialism in this context is

TABLE 6 Government versus Private Ownership and Operation[a]

	Criteria							
	C Goal	L Goal	L Goal	L Goal	L Goal	N Total	L Total	C Total
Alternatives	High productivity C = 3 L = 1	Equity C = 1 L = 3	Workplace quality C = 1 L = 3	Environ-mental protection C = 1 L = 3	Consumer protection C = 1 L = 3	(neutral weights)	(Liberal or socialistic weights)	(Conser-vative or Capitalistic Weights)
C Alternative Government ownership and operation (socialism)	2	4	2	2	2	24	32*	16
L Alternative Private ownership and operation (capitalism)	4	2	2	2	2	24	28	20*
N Alternative some govt. and some private	3	3	2	2	2	18	24	18
SOS Alternative 100% Govt. own and 100% private operation	>3	>3	>3	>3	>3	>30	>39**	>21**

[a]C, conservative; L, liberal; N, neutral; SOS, superoptimum or win-win solution.
*Best alternative on total before considering the SOS Alternative.
**Best alternative on total after considering the SOS Alternative.

government ownership and operation of factories and farms, or at least those larger than the handicraft or garden size, as in the Soviet Union of 1960. The essence of capitalism is private ownership and operation of both factories and farms, as in the United States of 1960. The neutral position or middle way is to have some government and some private ownership and operation, as in Sweden of 1960. The year 1960 is used because that is approximately when the Soviet Union began to change with the advent of the leadership of Nikita Khruchchev. The United States also underwent big changes in the 1960s with the election of John F. Kennedy.

Table 6 refers to government ownership-operation as the liberal or left-wing alternative, as it is in the United States and in the world at least since the time of Karl Marx. The table refers to private ownership-operation as the conservative or right-wing alternative, as it is in the United States and elsewhere at least since the time of Adam Smith. In recent years in the Soviet Union and in China, those favoring privatization have been referred to as *liberals,* and those favoring retention of government ownership-operation have been referred to as *conservatives.* The labels make no difference in this context. The object of Table 6 is to find a superoptimum solution that more than satisfies the goals of both ideologies or groups, regardless of their labels.

Goals and Relations

The key capitalistic *goal* is high productivity in terms of income-producing goods substantially above what it costs to produce them. The key socialistic goal is equity in terms of the sharing of ownership, operation, wealth, and income. Other goals that tend to be more socialistic than capitalistic, but are less fundamental, are (a) workplace quality, including wages, hours, safety, hiring by merit, and worker input; (b) environmental protection, including reduction of air, water, radiation, noise, and other forms of pollution; and (c) consumer protection, including low prices and goods that are durable, safe, and high in quality.

Going down the *productivity* column, the liberal socialistic alternative does not score so high on productivity for a lack of profit-making incentives and a surplus of bureaucratic interference in comparison to the capitalistic alternative, assuming the level of technology is held constant. The empirical validity of that statement is at least partially confirmed by noting that the capitalistic countries of Japan and the former West Germany are more productive than their socialistic counterparts of the former East Germany and China, although they began at approximately the same level as of 1945 at the end of World War II. Going down the *equity* column, the liberal socialistic alternative does score relatively high. By definition, it involves at least a nominal collective sharing in the ownership and operation of industry and agriculture, which generally leads to less inequality in wealth and income than capitalism does.

On the goals that relate to the *workplace, the environment, and consumers,* the socialists traditionally argue that government ownership-operation is more sensitive to those matters because it is less profit-oriented. The capitalists traditionally argue that private ownership-operation is more sensitive in competitive marketplaces in finding high-quality workers and increasing the quantity of one's consumers. The reality (as contrasted to the theory) is that without alternative incentives or regulations, both government managers and private managers of factories and farms are motivated toward high production at low cost. That kind of motivation leads to cutting back on the expenses of providing workplace quality, environmental protection, and consumer protection. The government factory manager of the Polish steelworks may be just as abusive of labor as the private factory manager of the U.S. steel company. Likewise, the government factory managers in the state factories of China may be just as insensitive to consumer safety and durability as their monopolistic counterparts in the American automobile industry.

A Superoptimum Solution

As for how the *superoptimum solution* operates, it involves government ownership, but with all the factories and farms rented to private entrepreneurs to develop productive and profitable manufacturing and farming. Each lease is renewable every year, or less often if necessary to get productive tenants. A renewal can be refused if the factory or farm is not being productively developed, or if the entrepreneur is not showing adequate sensitivity to workers, the environment, and consumers.

As for some of the *advantages* of such an SOS system, it is easier not to renew a lease than it is to issue injunctions, fines, jail sentences, or other negative sanctions. It is also much less expensive than paying subsidies. The money received for rent can be an important source of tax revenue for the government to provide productive subsidies elsewhere in the economy. Those subsidies can be especially used for encouraging technological innovation-diffusion and upgrading of skills and for stimulating competition for market share, which can be much more beneficial to society than either socialistic or capitalistic monopolies. The government can more easily demand sensitivity to workers, the environment, and consumers from its renters of factories and farms than it can from itself. There is a conflict of interest in regulating oneself.

This SOS alternative is *only available to socialistic countries* like the former USSR, China, Cuba, North Korea, and others since they already own the factories and land. It would not be economically or politically feasible for capitalistic countries to move from the conservative capitalistic alternative to the SOS solution by acquiring ownership through payment or confiscation. In this example socialistic countries are in a position to decide between socialism and capitalism by compromising and to wind up with the worst of both possible worlds. That means the relative unproductivity of socialism and the relative inequity of capitalism. The socialistic countries are also in a position to decide between the two basic alternatives by winding up with the best of both possible worlds. That means retaining the equities and social sensitivities of government ownership, while having the high productivity that is associated with profit-seeking entrepreneurial capitalism. It would be difficult to find a better example of *compromising versus superoptimizing* than the current debate over socialism versus capitalism.

Population Control Versus Reproductive Freedom as a Social Issue

Ideology and Technocracy

As of the 1970s, the People's Republic of China was seeking to resolve public policy problems largely by consulting the *ideological* writings of Karl Marx, Mao Zedong, and their interpreters. As of the 1980s, government agencies in China were seeking to become more professional by way of the introduction of personnel management, financial administration, and other bureaucratic ideas from the West, some of which are actually a throwback to Confucian bureaucracy.

Thus ideology became offset by *technocracy.* What we were seeing may fit the classic Hegelian and Marxist dialectic of thesis, antithesis, and synthesis. Ideology represented the prevailing thesis in the 1970s, whereby population control might be analyzed by reading Marx and Mao. Technocracy represented the antithesis in the 1980s, whereby population control might be analyzed by reading biological literature.

The 1990s may represent a superoptimum synthesis of the best, not the worst, of both possible worlds. It may draw upon the idea of having *goal-oriented values* from the ideological thesis, as contrasted to rejecting values as being unscientific or not objective. Values and goals may be quite objective in the sense of being provable means to higher goals, or in the sense of demonstrating that certain alternatives are more capable of achieving the goals than others.

The 1990s may also draw upon the idea of *empirical proof* based on observable consequences, rather than ideological labels of socialism or capitalism. It is empirical proof that also makes sense in terms of deductive consistency with what else is known about the world, rather than mindless technical number crunching without thinking about how the results might fit common sense. Being technical does not necessarily mean being effective in getting the job done efficiently and equitably, and that is what should really count in governmental decision making.

The win-win solution involves a synthesis of goals to be achieved (the ideological element and systematic methods for determining which alternative or alternatives best achieve those goals (the technical element). The true dialectic is dynamic not only in the sense that a thesis leads to an antithesis, which leads to a higher-level synthesis. It is also dynamic in the sense that a synthesis does not stagnate, but becomes a subsequent thesis to be resynthesized by a new antithesis into a still higher level of analysis. There may be policy evaluation methods that are even more effective efficient, and equitable.

TABLE 7 Superoptimizing Analysis Applied to the China Excess Population Problem[a]

	Criteria				
	C Goal	L Goal	N Total	L Total	C Total
Alternatives	Small families	Reproductive freedom	(neutral weights)	(liberal weights)	(conservative weights)
C Alternative *Strict one-child policy*	4	2	12	10	14*
L Alternative *Flexibility about family size*	2	4	12	14*	10
N Alternative *One child with exceptions allowed*	3	3	12	12	12
SOS Alternative —Causes of excess children	5	5	20	20**	20**

[a]Relevant causes of excess children in the China population context include the need for adult children to care for their elderly parents, which could be better handled through social security and/or jobs for the elderly; the need for extra children to allow for child mortality, which could be better handled through better child health care; the need for male children in view of their greater value, which could be better handled through providing more opportunities for females; the lack of concern for the cost of sending children to college, which could be better handled through a more vigorous program of recruiting rural children to college; it is not a superoptimum solution to provide monetary rewards and penalties in this context because the monetary rewards for having fewer children enable a family to have more children; the monetary punishments for having more children stimulate a family to have still more children to provide offsetting income; the monetary rewards and punishments are made meaningless by the simultaneous policies that are increasing prosperity in rural China. C, conservative; L, liberal; N, neutral; SOS, superoptimum or win-win solutions.

*Best alternative on total before considering the SOS Alternative.

**Best alternative on total after considering the SOS Alternative.

Those are the methods that are hinted at in various places in this chapter where *superoptimum solutions* are explicitly or implicitly mentioned. Such solutions enable conservatives, liberals, and advocates of other major viewpoints to come out ahead of their best initial expectations simultaneously. Traditional optimizing involves finding the best alternative or alternatives in a set. SOS analysis involves finding an alternative that is better than what conservatives previously considered the best and simultaneously better that what liberals previously considered the best, using conservative and liberal values.

Alternatives, Goals, and Relations as Inputs

Table 7 can be used to illustrate what is meant by superoptimizing policy analysis, whereby those having all major viewpoints can come out ahead of their best initial expectations. The table relates to excess population, rather than the population problem. This is so because most of China's so-called *population problem* does not relate to a surplus of people, but rather to a shortage of production. Some of the population problem (at least in the short run) may, however, relate to a strain on China's current resources that can be lessened by lessening the number of consumers.

The *alternatives* are listed on the rows. The conservative alternative (in the sense of being the most regulatory) is to try to enforce a strict one-child policy. The liberal alternative (in the sense of allowing the most freedom) is to be completely flexible on family size. This alternative also may conform most closely with Marxist ideology, which tends to view population control as a capitalistic idea designed either to increase the population of the poor (in order to have a reserve army of unemployed people) or to decrease the population of the poor (out of fear that the poor will overwhelm the middle class). Those two Marxist views tend to nullify each other, possibly leading one to the conclusion that there is no Marxist view on population policy. The compromise position between conservative regulation and liberal freedom is to have a one-child policy, but with various exceptions such as allowing a second child if the first is a daughter or allowing a second child among rural but not urban people.

One of the key *goals* of the regime is to allow only small families, given the tremendous burden on the Chinese economy and government services of a billion people reproducing at a rate greater than about one child per family. Even one child per family would mean substantial short-run population growth. This would occur because people are living longer in China. If one simplifies the arithmetic by saying that if the 500 million males marry the 500 million females and have one child apiece within the next few years, then the population goes from a billion to 1.5 billion. That increase of half a billion is more people than every country of the world currently has with the exception of China and India. The rich may not get richer, but the highly populated get even more highly populated. The second key goal is reproductive freedom. Even the conservatives recognize that interfering with reproductive freedom makes for a lot of antagonism toward the government.

Thus both goals are endorsed by both conservatives and liberals in China, but Chinese conservatives place relatively more emphasis on small families, and Chinese liberals place relatively more emphasis on reproductive freedom.

The *relations* between the alternatives and the goals are shown on a 1–5 scale in which 5 means highly conducive to the goal, 4 means mildly conducive, 3 means neither conducive nor adverse, 2 means mildly adverse, and 1 means highly adverse to the goal. We have here a classic trade-off, even more so than the previous three tables. A strict one-child policy is good on small families, but bad on reproductive freedom. Flexibility on family size is good on reproductive freedom, but bad on small families. The compromise alternative is middling on both, as are compromises in general. This compromise is better than the worst on both small families and reproductive freedom. It is clearly not better than the best expectations on either goal.

Finding a Superoptimum Package of Policies

In many public policy problems, the superoptimum solution involves well-placed subsidies and tax breaks. Well-placed *tax breaks* are meaningless in a Communist society. Under communism, people do not do much direct tax paying (especially income taxes) as they do in Western societies. Instead the government is supported by paying people less than they are worth in their government jobs. The difference is a hidden tax. Ironically this fits well the Marxist idea of surplus-value exploitation of labor. It is an easy form of tax to collect, but it does not allow for the use of tax breaks as incentives.

China has tried subsidizing small families by giving *monetary rewards* to those who have small families and monetary punishments to those who do not have them. The effect has been almost the opposite of the government's intent. The subsidies to small families have in many instances increased their income so they can now afford to have more children. Having a monetary punishment or reduced salary may even motivate parents to have an additional child to help produce more income to offset the reduced salary. Also, moving simultaneously toward a more prosperous free market (especially in farm products) has enabled many rural people now to have more children and not be bothered by the withdrawal of subsidies or other monetary punishments.

A kind of superoptimum solution may make a lot more sense for dealing with the China population problem. It could provide small families and reproductive freedom simultaneously. Doing so requires looking to the causes of having additional children and then trying to remove or lessen those causes. One cause is a need to have children who will support parents in their *old age*. Adopting a more effective social security system helps eliminate or lessen that cause.

Another cause is having additional children as backup because the *death rate* is so high among rural Chinese children prior to age 5. Various forms of pediatric public health can make a big difference such as giving shots and using effective remedies to prevent life-jeopardizing infant diarrhea and dehydration.

A third cause is the widespread feeling that female children are worthless in terms of bringing honor to the family. One therefore keeps trying until at least one son is born. That cause can be substantially lessened by the new moves in China toward much greater *opportunities for females* to become lawyers and doctors and enter other prestigious occupations. In China, women's liberation has facilitated birth control, whereas in the United States birth control has done more to facilitate women's liberation.

Environmental Protection Versus Economic Development as a Technology Issue

As an example, the field of environmental policy involves both conservative and liberal approaches. Conservatives emphasize the role of consumers and the marketplace in restraining business from engaging in socially undesirable acts such as causing pollution. Liberals emphasize the role of the government in restraining pollution. Conservatives are especially interested in the goal of economic development, which may be interfered with by governmental restraints. Liberals are especially interested in the goal of a cleaner environment, which may not be achieved so effectively by relying on selective consumer buying.

A neutral compromise approach might involve giving business firms partial subsidies to adopt antipollution devices. Doing so would involve some requirements for receiving the subsidies, but less interference than regulation and fines. Doing so would help promote a cleaner environment, but there still might be evasions by business in view of the extra expense and trouble in complying.

A win-win policy alternative instead might emphasize subsidies to universities and research firms to develop new processes (that relate to manufacturing, transportation, energy, and agriculture) that are both less expensive and cleaner than the old processes. Those new processes then would be adopted by business firms because they were more profitable, not because the firms were being forced or subsidized to do so.

The new processes thus would achieve the conservative goals of profits and economic development, even better than retaining the present marketplace. Such a win-win policy also would promote the liberal goal of a cleaner environment, even better than a system of regulation, and without the expense of a continuing subsidy for adopting and renewing antipollution devices.

A specific example of such an environmental win-win policy has been finding a substitute for aerosol propellants and air-conditioning freon that is more profitable to manufacturers and simultaneously less harmful to the ozone layer, which protects against skin cancer. Another specific example is developing an electric car, which saves money on gasoline and maintenance, while not generating the exhaust pollution of internal-combustion cars. Developing hydrogen fusion or solar energy also may produce less expensive and cleaner fuel for manufacturing processes.

Win-win policies may be capable of achieving both conservative and liberal goals in theory, but not in practice. To be meaningful policies, they may have to satisfy various kinds of feasibility. For example, is the policy of developing solar energy for manufacturing feasible technologically? Is there sufficient funding available to subsidize the needed research if the private sector is not willing, as a result of the risks, to spend the large amount of money needed or to wait out the long interval if payoffs do occur?

Is there insurmountable political opposition from liberals who do not like government subsidies to make business more profitable? What about the opposition from conservatives who do not like government involvement in developing a research agenda? Is the program feasible administratively in terms of built-in incentives, or does it require a lot of obtrusive monitoring? Does the program violate some constitutional rights? Does the program make provision for workers and firms that might be displaced if the policy is adopted?

Win-win policies may involve creativity, but developing them is becoming easier as a result of experience with the ideas. We now have many different approaches that can serve as a checklist in leading one to a win-win policy. For example, expanding the resources available can enable conservatives to have more money for defense and liberals to have more money for domestic programs. The government sometimes can be a third-party benefactor in providing vouchers to enable both landlords and tenants, and also merchants and consumers, to come out ahead.

One also can deal with problems such as abortion by getting at the causes. These causes consist of unwanted pregnancies that could be lessened through more effective abstinence programs and birth control. Thinking in terms of the goals to be achieved, rather than the alternatives to choose among, can stimulate win-win policies. So can thinking in terms of increasing benefits and decreasing costs.

Other approaches deal with early socialization of widely accepted values, technological fixes like nonpolluting hair spray, and contracting out of government activities to private firms (which do well as a result of both the profit motive and quality specifications in the contract). Further approaches may involve combining (rather than compromising) alternatives, developing a package with something for each major viewpoint, having international economic communities, adopting a gradual or incremental win-win policy, and arranging for big benefits on one side and small costs on the other.

Presidential Versus Parliamentary Government as a Political Policy Issue

The fundamental political science dispute between parliamentary and presidential governments is applicable to all countries.

The Alternatives

The conservative position is generally to support presidential government because it yields greater stability, which conservatives like. The liberal position is to support parliamentary government largely because it is more responsive and liberals have traditionally been more interested in responsiveness, at least with regard to economic issues (although not necessarily with regard to civil liberties issues). The neutral position is to try to find a middle position, which is not so easy. One can make it easier to remove the president through impeachment, but that has never been done. One can try to give parliamentary government more stability by saying that a two-thirds vote is required to bring down the prime minister rather than a mere majority vote, but that has never been done. One can have a presidential government with short terms and no provision for reelection to get more responsiveness. One can likewise have long terms for members of parliament in order to get more stability.

The Goals

The conservative goal should be referred to as *continuity,* not as stability. *Stability* sounds like stagnation. *Continuity* implies growth, but smooth growth rather than jerky growth. *Continuity* can imply change, but change in accordance with some kind of predictability based on previously developed trends. The key liberal goal is responsiveness, which is broad enough to include more than just electoral responsiveness. This could be an example of raising one's goals so as to broaden the notion of responsiveness, as in broadening the notion of unemployment and broadening the notion of continuity.

The Superoptimum Solution

The SOS is to say that the structure is not especially important as to whether one has a chief executive who is chosen directly by the people or indirectly by the people through the parliament. What is needed is a constitutional or statutory commitment of the chief executive and the government in general to responsiveness and stability (see Table 8).

Responsiveness. Responsiveness goes beyond merely reading the public opinion polls in order to get reelected. Responsiveness in the traditional political context has meant ease in throwing the government out of power. That is more a process designed to bring about responsiveness than responsiveness in itself. Responsiveness should mean, for example, that the government is sensitive to people who are displaced as a result of new technologies or reduced tariffs; for example, the government is responsive to their need for new jobs. A government is much more responsive if it sees to it that displaced workers find new jobs even though the president is a president for life and cannot be thrown out of office than

TABLE 8 Presidential Versus Parliamentary Government[a]

Alternatives	Criteria				
	C Goal	L Goal	N Total	L Total	C Total
	Continuity	Responsiveness	(neutral weights)	(liberal weights)	(conservative weights)
C Alternative Presidential government	4	2	12	10	14*
L Alternative Parliamentary government	2	4	12	14*	10
N Alternative Compromise	3	3	12	12	12
SOS Alternative Right to continuous economic growth, right to upgraded work	5	5	20	20**	20**

[a]The first part of the SOS alternative is to provide a constitutional right to continuous economic growth, backed up by appropriate governmental institutions such as a ministry of international trade and industry. This alternative is especially related to the goal of upward continuity, rather than stagnating stability. The second part of the SOS alternative is to provide a constitutional right to upgraded skills, backed by appropriate governmental institutions, including a separate government agency to administer skills-upgrading programs. This alternative is especially related to the goal of responsiveness to the needs of adult voters to be more valuable in the economy, rather than the responsiveness that is associated with rapid turnover of government personnel.

is a government in which the prime minister can be replaced in 10 percent of the parliament states a desire to get rid of him. Responsiveness should mean that when people are hurting, the government does something about it other than changing prime ministers.

Stability. On the matter of stability, we do not want stability. We want continuity. We want continuous growth. Growth is change, not stability. We want statutes and constitutional provisions that will require the government, regardless of whether it consists of Republicans or Democrats, to engage in policies that guarantee about 6 percent growth per year. We do have a 1946 Employment Act and a 1970 Humphrey-Hawkins Act that say unemployment should not rise above 3 percent, or that inflation should not exceed 3 percent. Such laws mean nothing because they have no provision for enforcement. Worse, they have no provision to achieve those goals. They are the same kind of fiat as King Canute's asking the waves to stop—a goal that can be achieved by the Army Corps of Engineers' building appropriate dams, but not simply by issuing of a "There shalt not be" statement.

A Pair of Constitutional Provisions

The SOS thus would be a set of statutes or a pair of statutes (or better yet, a pair of constitutional provisions).

Continuous Economic Growth. Continuous economic growth would be approximately 6 percent growth a year. That is a minimum. There is nothing wrong with doing better than that, even if it is jerky, one year 10 percent, another year 6 percent, another year 12 percent. That sounds very unstable, but neither conservatives nor liberals would object to that kind of instability. Nobody is likely to object to having a highly unstable income of $1 million one year, $20 million the next. When people talk about instability they mean jumping from positive to negative, or positive to zero, not from very high positive to positive and back.

Upgrading Skills. The second statute or constitutional right is an obligation to displaced workers to be retrained and/or relocated. This is like two new constitutional rights. Traditional constitutional rights have related to free speech, equal protection, and due process. Modern constitutional rights have related to social security, minimum wage, safe workplace, and more recently clean air. What we are proposing is a constitutional right to economic growth and to relocation if one is a displaced worker; the word *relocated* sounds like moving a person from one city to another. We are also talking about upgrading skills so one can get a better job without moving to another city. Instead of talking about the right to relocation, we should talk about the right to upgraded work. It is not the right to work. That phrase has been ruined by the connotation of a right not to be in a union. A problem with the concept of the right to upgraded work is that there is nothing in that concept that confines it to displaced workers, although that is not necessarily bad. Perhaps all workers should have a right to upgraded work, but especially those who have no work at all as a result of technological change or tariff reductions. If there were really a meaningful right to economic growth and upgraded work, that kind of SOS would score high on continuity. To emphasize that, we need to talk about continuous economic growth. The upgraded work part especially relates to responsiveness.

Making Those Rights Meaningful

A key point is that those rights are not meaningful by merely being stated in statutes or constitutions. They are also not meaningful if someone who feels he has been denied one of those rights can sue Congress or the president. They are made meaningful by establishing institutions like a ministry of international trade and industry that has a mandate, a budget, personnel, and subunits that are meaningfully relevant to promoting continuous economic growth. One could establish a separate government agency to enforce the right to upgraded work. The rights become meaningful when there are institutions to enforce them, not just words in a statute or a constitution. The courts cannot enforce them; that requires specialized administrative agencies. The courts can enforce due process by reversing convictions that violate due process. The courts can enforce free speech and equal protection by issuing injunctions ordering the police to cease interfering with speakers or marchers, or ordering the schools to cease operating segregated classrooms. The courts have no power to award well-targeted subsidies or tax breaks needed for economic growth and upgraded work. That requires appropriate administrative agencies.

The presidential versus parliament issue has recently taken on some new importance in certain countries.

1. In *Israel* it is being proposed as a way of getting out of the paralysis of the parliament's being controlled by small political parties that can disrupt a parliamentary coalition by withdrawing. With a president chosen at large, there would be an institution that could govern without undue influence of small political parties.

2. The issue has come up in *Yugoslavia,* where the president would be, and has been three people: one Serbian, one Croatian, and one Slovenian or from one of the other republics. The country operated in roughly that way, although more at the vice-president level, for 30 years. It did not hold the country together. What held the country together was the Communist party, which collapsed, as did the country.

3. It came up in *France* under DeGaulle, partly for the same reasons as in Israel, namely the instability of coalition government in parliament. The instability is different, however, from that in Israel. In Israel the parliament could be destabilized by a political party that has 2 seats of more than 100 seats that decides to withdraw its support from the government. In France the destabilization occurred

because there were five political parties, each of which had about 20 percent of the representation, when one of the relatively large political parties decided it did not like the government, the government would collapse. Both France and Israel have strong public administration people who carry on regardless of what is happening with parliament. But they do not make policy as parliament or a president would. France now has a compromise system in that they still have a prime minister but also have a president.

A bigger issue that relates to separation of powers is the independence of the judiciary, although that is not a presidential versus parliamentary issue. It involves all three branches of government. Another, bigger issue is related to the conflict between coordinated government and political parties that cannot get along. That situation is more apparent when one has a president of one party and a parliament of another party, as the United States did in the 1990s. That can lead to more paralysis than a parliamentary form of government that keeps changing as a result of the changing coalitions. Thus the idea that presidential government provides some kind of stability and coherence that parliamentary government does not is quite untrue in the case of the United States. And it would probably be the same of other countries where it is possible for the president to be of one party and the parliament to be another party.

It happened in France with Mitterand as a Socialist president and parliament dominated by conservative parties. France cannot experience the paralysis the United States can, because they do not have a true presidential system. It is a compromise, and Mitterand may not even have any veto power over what parliament passes. He is like an elected Queen Elizabeth to some extent, although more than that, partly because of his personality as of 2000, the situation is reversed in the sense that there is a conservative President Charic in France with a Social Democratic Parliament. The Soviet Union also had both a president and a prime minister, but the president was very explicitly a figurehead whereas the French president is supposed to be more vigorous, especially by virtue of national election. The Soviet president was chosen by the parliament largely for ceremonial purposes.

CONCLUSION

Professors and government people in developing countries like China and the Philippines cannot afford the luxury of super-optimum solutions. Instad, they should perhaps be satisfied with something substantially less (that point sometimes implied that superoptimizing was too complicated except for people trained in computer science, mathematics, statistical analysis, operations reearch, and other sophisticated methodologies).

After the conference presentations, however, the consensus generally was that those method are largely irrelevant. Mathematical statistical methodologies are often irrelevant because they emphasize what is measurable rather than what is important. They can sometimes be even harmful if they cause paralysis or an overemphasis on unnecessary measurement and data. The prerequisites for superoptimizing analysis are basically knowledge of the key facts relevant to the problem; awareness of such political concepts as "conservative" and "liberal"; an understanding of such decisional concepts as "goals," "alternatives," "relations," "tentative conclusions" and "what-if analysis"; and some creativity in developing superoptimum solutions. That kind of creativity is enhanced by possession of the first three prerequisites. It is also made easier by having access to case studies like those discussed so that one can learn from the experience of other groups or individuals in developing superoptimum solutions.

Developing nations are generally or at least often able to afford super-optimum solutions because they are not expensive. If they are expensive, they may still be well worth investing the funds needed. The United States and other developed countries have less need for superoptimum solutions than developing countries do. The United States can probably go for a whole generation without developing any innovative ideas or coming close to solving any of its policy problems. If that happened, the United States would still have a high quality of life because it has such a well-developed cushion to fall back on. Developing countries, on the other hand, cannot afford to be satisfied with merely getting by. Doing so will put them further behind regions that are advancing rapidly, including Japan, Korea, Hong Kong, and Singapore.

In that context, superoptimum solutions are like free speech. Sometimes people in developing countries say they cannot afford free speech because it is too divisive. After they become more developed, then they can allow opposition parties and abolish one-party systems with presidents for life. The reality is that they need free speech to stimulate creative ideas for solving their policy problems. Those problems need solutions much more than the policy problems of well-developed countries.[1]

NOTE

1. For further details on win-win analysis, see Stuart S. Nagel (1997), *Super-optimum solutions and win-win policy: Basic concepts and principles* (Quorum Books: Westport, Conn, 1997); Stuart S. Nagel (1998), *Public policy evaluation: Making super-optimum decisions* (Ashgate: London, England, 1998); and Stuart S. Nagel (1998), *Policy within and across developing countries* (Ashgate: London, England, 1998).

18

Privatization Policy and Public Management

Van R. Johnston
Department of Management,
University of Denver, Denver, Colorado

Paul Seidenstat
Department of Economics,
Temple University, Philadelphia,
Pennsylvania

During the decade of the 1980s both the pressures of declining revenue growth and the rising costs of producing services spurred American state and local governments to seek more effective means to control costs and, in the case of infrastructure, to finance capital improvements. A variety of government management experiments or innovations were initiated with the objectives of increasing productivity and containing costs. One of the key reform methods was the privatization of government services.

Privatization is considered to be: "any process aimed at shifting functions and responsibilities, in whole or in part, from the government to the private sector" (United States General Accounting Office, 1997). A marginally different emphasis defines privatization as "the transfer of ownership, control, or operation of an enterprise or function from the government/public sector to the private sector" (Seidenstat, 1996). The increased utilization and emerging reality of privatization are noted by its inclusion in the dictionary for the first time in the 1980s.

BACKGROUND

Notification that the public sector paradigm for delivering services to citizens was going to shift was delivered on June 6, 1978, with the passage of Proposition 13 in California. Reducing the availability of local property taxes dramatically, this citizens' initiative placed a heavy fiscal burden on public sector managers to become much more efficient, innovative, creative, and frugal. The pressure to do so was immediate and clear. The tax revolt, as it has come to be called, was born. It eventually spread across the country. In Massachusetts, it was called Proposition 2.5. In Colorado it was Amendment 1.

Proposition 13 was also a harbinger of a significant shift in the ideological orientation of the nation. This was manifested in the same year, 1978, by deregulation of the airlines by the Democratic president, Jimmy Carter. This policy adjustment was designed to bring about more competition in the industry. Therefore, it was reasoned, efficiency would increase and prices would decrease, providing more and cheaper service to customers. Efficiency and economy were clearly increasing concerns in both the public and private sectors (Halachmi, 1994-ab; Halachmi and Boydston, 1994).

Ronald Reagan was elected and applied his much more conservative brand of administration and economics (Reaganomics) from 1980 to 1988. George Bush continued this focus until 1992. This was a boom period for conservative economics, manifested primarily in terms of increasing deregulation, growth of privatization (Linowes, 1987), and outsourcing in the public sector; and mergers, acquisitions, hostile takeovers, and leveraged buyouts in the private sector. As the decade of the 1980s came to a close, and we moved into the 1990s, the goals of efficiency and economy were reflected in reinventing government (Osborne and Gaebler, 1992; Gore, 1993, 1994) in the public sector and reengineering (Martin, 1993) in the private sector.

A managerial adaptation to improving efficiency and economy in both sectors was total quality management (TQM). Pressure for fiscal conservatism was coming from citizens through their initiatives; [both Democratic and Republican presidents—Carter, Reagan, Bush, and Clinton (with Vice President Gore heading up the National Performance Review)—and the reengineering/merger/acquisition/hostile takeover turbulence of the private sector were influenced by that pressure.] There were also increasing demands and pressures for quality and productivity from the international dimension—the North American Free Trade Agreement (NAFTA), the new European Union (EU), and the Asia-Pacific Economic Cooperation (APEC) forum (McGowan and Wittmer, 1999).

Privatization became the primary strategy of public sector managers and leaders as they struggled to cope with an imposed paradigm shift (Kuhn, 1970) toward fiscal retrenchment (Johnston, 1996-abc). As the new efficiency (output over input) model unfolded, citizens found their effectiveness (output over standards, liberal or conservative) based services being increasingly limited. In a sense, they were being treated more as customers (Johnston, 1995a), but they did not appear to have many choices about quality to make (Johnston, 1995b). Governance concerns were increasing as well (Johnston, 1990).

Privatization involves two functions: provision (financing and policy-making) and production (actual production of the service, or implementation) (Kolderie, 1986). Some argue that the distinction can be hard to make in reality and that therein lies a threat to our constitutional rights (Sullivan, 1987); therefore, we need to beware of the limits of privatization (Moe, 1987). Privatization also involves two dimensions: total private sector control and operation of a government organization or a much more common and popular limited form of privatization such as contracting out, which is also known as *outsourcing*.

PRIVATIZATION OPTIONS

Privatization can be packaged in a lot of different ways. Table 1 shows various privatization options.

Contracting Out

Contracting out is clearly the predominant form of privatization in use today. By 1993, over 75 percent of state agencies were employing this version of privatization. Local governments are following the same pattern. In contracting out, government agencies maintain overall control and ownership but contract with private firms to deliver the service or services involved. Contracting out is used extensively in trash collection, transportation, street repairs, corrections, health, education, data processing and administrative services, building maintenance, social services, and general services.

TABLE 1 Privatization Options

Contracting out (outsourcing)
Franchising
Load (service) shedding
Public-private partnerships
Grants, subsidies, and vouchers
Asset divestment
Competitive contracting (managed competition)
Volunteer services
Total privatization

Among the primary reasons for the emerging dominance of contracting out as a form of privatization are the following: Control and cost savings are the goals. Contracting out can enhance available expertise and provide access to state-of-the-art equipment. It is also chosen as a privatization option for sharing risk, solving labor problems, generating additional services, solving practical problems, and getting more rapid implementation (Siegel, 1999).

Better performance can flow from the market environment familiar to private sector operators and from the existence of the profit motive. Private sector managers are accustomed to competitive pressures for cost containment and good product quality. Moreover, they can avoid the cost-elevating forces of monopsonistic input suppliers and inflexible civil service and union rules. Profit-based compensation arrangements and powerful financial incentives for private managers can induce improved performance.

Relating managers' pay to profitability can lead to more emphasis on innovative ways to produce, incorporating new technology, dispensing with "red tape," and making timely decisions. It is also far easier to change managers for poor performance than to engage in the much more complex, time-consuming, and disruptive traditional processes of removing public managers.

Public sector unions are opposed to contracting out. They see it as a threat to their jobs. It is not unusual for private contractors to pay lower wages to their employees. This can be translated into narrower job definitions or more limited services for citizens and customers. In an attempt to leverage their positions, agreements can be made for requiring private pay to equal that of public employees. This would create questions of economy and efficiency with regard to private contracts. Experience has also shown that there can be substantial costs involved in gathering data for, and actually monitoring, contractor performance (Siegel, 1999).

It should be mentioned, however, that governments themselves expend substantial resources in monitoring their own operating departments. Budget and central management office personnel are deeply involved in overseeing in-house performance. Further, union wages can be substantially higher than the private market level as a result of political clout of the union.

It is important for any government organization considering contracting out to be certain that there will be viable competition for the service contract. Failure to do so will leave the agency or jurisdiction vulnerable to cost increases. Market model behavior (Johnston, 1995a) is significantly different from that in the traditional public sector model and, if not monitored and controlled adequately, can lead to rapid cost escalation. Also in accordance with market logic is the practice of creaming or skimming. Private contractors tend to screen for highly profitable and easy to accomplish tasks, leaving the rest for government; that tendency can lead to skewed analysis of performance according to which sector renders the service sets (Johnston, 1990).

In order to be able to monitor private sector contracts adequately, agencies and jurisdictions should make sure they keep relevant qualified expertise in-house for the services they contract out. At a minimum, this will permit appropriate monitoring. Should a dearth of contractors evolve, with the predictable surge in prices, then the agency would also be able to reassume the delivery of the service itself. With the increasing prevalence of contracting out, maintaining at least basic in-house expertise should be considered to be simple insurance against potentially turbulent market vicissitudes.

A prime area for future government attention is in increasing the skill level of government employees in the contracting arena. To improve the negotiation, agreement, and supervision of contracts, public agencies often use private consulting firms that specialize in this work.

Contracting out tends to separate the provision (policy-making and financing) and production (implementation or delivery of services) functions. Citizens can find themselves with increasingly less control over the services they receive. Gaining satisfaction for grievances due to lessened service becomes more complex as well. On the other hand, under private operation there is less likely to be favoritism or penalizing behavior toward citizen-customers motivated by political considerations.

Although there is increasing effort being made to detect and control contract-based service, monitoring is not considered to be a strength of government agencies (Carver, 1989). Among the services deemed most appropriate for contracting out are those that have clear specifications and can be simply measured and reasonably monitored (Donahue, 1989).

Government can improve its performance with contracting out by establishing performance standards. This can be done in-house or by use of related applicable standards developed by professional or trade organizations. Utilizing several indicators for given services will allow agencies to prepare meaningful and relevant guidelines for performance measurement, especially where complex services are delivered and the review needs to be more sophisticated.

Standards involve an outcome-based system of evaluation. Clearly, government buyers of contract services must become smarter shoppers. They must not only set clear performance standards but also build into the contract strong financial penalties and financial rewards for not reaching, or for achieving, the preset standards, as appropriate. The process of setting standards forces the contracting agency to think through what it really wants to accomplish.

There are several key components in performance-based contracts:

1. Results are to be specified. Methods of achieving these results should be left to the discretion of the vendor.
2. Financial incentives and penalties can spur performance. For example, several state highway departments give bonuses for completing a road

project ahead of schedule and extract financial penalties when a project goes overtime.

3. Monitoring is a full-time job and can benefit by using sophisticated data collection and analysis techniques. Often it may be cheaper and more effective to hire an outside contractor to do the monitoring.

Governments also need to get to a stage where service alternatives are evaluated as well. Some experimentation has also been done with in-house contracting. This can be a very viable option when employees are valued but market forces indicate that government production costs more than alternative private sector service delivery. Yet another strategy available for public sector providers is to employ multiple private contractor producers, assuming appropriate scale.

An approach that government should explore more significantly in the future is building multiple agency-based organizations to contract with private sector contractors. This would permit public providers to utilize their increased market leverage optimally to reduce costs. Standards and contract monitoring would be managed more efficiently and effectively under such an arrangement as well.

Franchising

Franchising involves turning over a government service to a private sector organization. Government can decide to hold back some operational control in the deal and may even require that its standards of service be achieved. An example would be a local governments franchising trash collection routes to one or more private companies.

The governmental entity actually load sheds trash collection (load shedding is discussed in the next section); it retains certain control functions and the right to determine the standards for quality involved in delivering the service. Franchising is increasingly significant as a privatization alternative.

It is becoming more commonly understood and accepted that without some sort of meaningful competition within agencies, efficiency is not likely to be enhanced. Realizing that efficiency and economy are increasingly prized in the age of privatizing, outsourcing, reinventing, and reengineering, the federal government has decided to experiment with infusing competition into its organizational systems. In 1995 five pilot franchise funds were initiated in an attempt to explore franchising as a means to improve efficiency on the one hand and productivity on the other.

As public managers begin to think and behave more along market model lines, it becomes increasingly clear that agencies have a lot of different kinds of resources. There is value in the training of agency personnel and in agency equipment that, for instance, may be based on technology or in capital projects and investments. Payroll functions utilize both human and nonhuman resources. Telecommunications and office systems efforts have franchising potential as well.

Under the concept of franchising, we begin to see agency managers attempt to become more competitive by selling the use of their property and other assets. Other agencies, for instance, can pay for the use of various business or government-based systems. It would not be uncommon to find franchising efforts to be involved in data processing, conference facilities, payroll, or even travel. Slack capacity is the typical target of franchising. By selling underutilized facilities, agencies can generate competitive, marketlike conditions and reduce their operating expenses by generating a franchising sort of revenue stream.

Franchising is based upon a contractual infrastructure. It is focused on replacing part of the public sector production model. It works best where win-lose competition is avoided and where bargaining and negotiation, or ideally even problem solving, can be attained. A principal, for example, a government unit contracting its services or equipment to other units, could deal with multiple agents—other agencies that are seeking to reduce their costs by contracting the services or equipment rather than purchasing the equipment or doing the work themselves. An agent organization could even purchase a variety of services and equipment from a variety of organizations. Arie Halachmi is one scholar who is studying the emerging franchising phenomenon in an attempt to develop a new theory based on principal-agent perspectives (Halachmi, 1996).

Load (Service) Shedding

Load shedding is also known as *service shedding.* It is considered to be the most complete form of privatization when production and financing of the service are turned over to a private firm. Another form of load shedding is dissociation: ceasing to render a service. It is not unusual for a government to keep its capital assets when converting a service to private operators. In the classic case of trash collection, preserving assets such as trucks would permit the government to resume operations if the firm's services are inadequate or if the rates rise as a result of lack of competitive bidding.

Public-Private Partnerships

Public-private partnerships are typically based on contractual agreements that specify the roles and activities of both private and public partners. Government is the provider. The private company is the producer. A classic example of this type of privatization dealing with social services would be the case of human immunodeficiency virus (HIV) control. The private organization would actually operate the program while the government agency provided the needles and educational documents.

Grants, Subsidies, and Vouchers

Government payment (provision) by means of grants, subsidies, and vouchers is the most market-oriented form of privatization. A government agency could provide payment directly to a private producer as a grant or subsidy. The recipient of the service, or the consumer, may have more limited choice here because of the dearth of private producers receiving the grants or subsidies. Typical recipients of these forms of privatization are hospitals, museums, and universities.

Vouchers typically give the consumers of services more choice, assuming there are competing suppliers. Under this format, one receives a check or voucher to pay for a certain type of service. Typical state and local government vouchers target job training, social services, and Medicaid. The federal examples would focus on housing, food stamps, and Medicare.

Asset Divestment

Asset sales or divestment can take many forms. A government agency can sell outright to a private buyer, with no restrictions. Or restrictions can be placed on a purchase; a private operator, for instance, could be required to continue to operate a recreation facility. In some cases, where the private purchaser has the option, a service may even be discontinued. It is even possible for private providers to substitute other assets they own to continue a service after buying public property that it may choose not to utilize.

Competitive Contracting and/or Managed Competition

Competitive contracting, or managed competition, is a different form of contracting out. Under this model agencies, or subunits thereof, bid on contracts that are also available to private bidders. Part of a service may be kept in-house and the rest outsourced. Or all of it could be contracted out—if the internal bid is less competitive than that of the private vendor. If the internal bid turns out to be more competitive, the service could still be provided entirely from within the agency, but on a contract basis.

Volunteer Services

Citizen volunteers, such as school crossing guards, contribute another alternative to traditional government provision and production of services. Sometimes nonprofit organizations are involved; on other occasions they are not. Government supervision, in any event, is usually involved. Other examples of volunteer activities include educational assistance, food delivery support for the poor, and neighborhood crime watches.

Total Privatization

Examples of total privatization of a government service or organization, such as a prison or hospital, are more rare. They involve taking over the actual operation of the organization. Often there are problems involved that may or may not be overcome. In the case of a for-profit prison, for example, there are concerns about dilemmas such as awarding time off for good behavior by the privatized organization where the owner-operator is making money by keeping jail cells full. This is a classic conflict of interest.

Take the case of a large privatized state hospital such as University Hospital in Denver, Colorado. After only 18 months as a private corporation, and after significant improvement of its efficiency, effectiveness, professionalism, and financial position the Colorado State Supreme Court found this case of total privatization to be unconstitutional, noting that it had a duty to take care of the indigent, that its personnel system had not been adjusted legally, and that it could not simply give away taxpayer-supported capital investments to a private corporation (Johnston, 1999). Similarly, contracting with private firms or nonprofit organizations to operate an entire school system, as was the case in Baltimore and in the Boston area, did not prove to be effective, especially since union contracts were left intact.

PRIVATIZATION ISSUES

The arguments for and against privatization are usually dealt with on two levels: First are the ideological arguments. Then come the practical reasons for privatizing.

The ideological case for privatization is typically made as follows: Privatization can stimulate the economy and lower taxes. Government is better when it is smaller. Private firms are more efficient than government agencies. Government should not provide or produce services when there are private companies available to do so. Private managers are better than government administrators. Governments are less efficient than private firms. Monopolistic government agencies do not have adequate incentives to manage well (O'Brien, 1989).

The practical arguments for privatization are usually easier to see and measure. They are typically oriented toward reducing the costs of delivering services. They become increasingly significant when considering the following: improving government operations, meeting short-term project needs, lowering the costs involved in service delivery, adjusting for resource limitations, and improving service quality (O'Brien, 1989).

Some warn about the increasing dangers of "sector blurring" and the "twilight zone" (Bozeman, 1987; Moe, 1987): whether individuals would be likely to fall between the cracks and receive less than optimal treatment as citizens receiving services from government or as customers from private firms. Increasing numbers believe that substantial benefits and significant values and protections can be lost in the transition (Thompson, 1983; Kolderie, 1986; Moe, 1987; Sullivan, 1987; Donahue, 1989; Palumbo and Maupin, 1989; Johnston, 1990, 1995a).

Privatization and Sovereignty

Sovereignty is a particularly significant issue that goes to the heart of many privatization cases. Typically, privatization does better when the case deals with discrete, packageable units of service that approximate private sector functions. Government provides defense and safety and security that are reflective of the medieval social contract between the nobility and the vassals. As translated by our governance history, then, there are certain attributes inherent in a sovereign that can and do become problematic in privatization efforts.

Some also consider these to be "publicness" checks. They include the following: Sovereigns have legitimate rights to enforce their will, usually as a function of politics, *governance,* and law. Technically they cannot do wrong. In order to be sued, they have to give permission. They can disavow debts. Technically, they cannot go bankrupt, as private firms can. Sovereigns can declare war. By eminent domain, the sovereign government can take private property for government use (Moe, 1987). Sovereignty clearly, then, casts a different lens on the private versus government organization.

Conditions Required for Success

In order to achieve the objectives set forth in a privatization initiative, certain environmental factors must be present. These factors include political support, managerial/political leadership, and a supportive private market structure. Overcoming the bias toward the status quo protected by the stakeholders who receive monopoly rent is essential. A strong case must be made for change. The case must speak to the benefits to be received with a provision/production arrangement in comparison to the costs that may have to be incurred. Legislative and voter support offers the opportunity to move in the privatization direction and to allow the new structure a fair chance to demonstrate its advantages.

The full support of political leaders, especially in the executive branch, greatly enhances the chance of success. Not only is this support required for the approval of change, but often enthusiastic and careful backing of the effort is necessary to sustain it. Well-prepared and ardent political leaders are often needed to overcome the inertia of the status quo.

To achieve the required objectives requires more than political support and strong leadership. To achieve the maximum benefits of privatization, the private sector should be structured such that alternative suppliers exist to compete in providing the service in the case of load shedding; can compete for contracts in the case of contracting out or franchising; or can supply services in the case of vouchers. Without competition, privatization might simply consist of substitution of a private monopoly for a government monopoly.

Cautions and Pitfalls

Several cautions must be exercised, and pitfalls prevented, when contracting out. Where there is little competition in the private sector prior to privatization, a viable bidding process may not take place, with the result that the savings anticipated or the quality improvement desired may not be achieved. Changing public monopoly to private monopoly is not the answer. Even where there is competition and the bidding is spirited, the contract must be carefully drafted and monitored; especially in service categories where output is ill-defined and relevant costs are hard to measure, vague contracts may lead to less than optimal results and enforcement may not be effective.

Also, a reasonable contract period may be required for the vendor to demonstrate results, especially for social services, in which achievement of desirable outcomes may take years. During the span of this long contract, the government may not be able to rebid even if performance is marginal.

Undesirable outcomes could also occur during the contract period or at the time of rebidding. The private supplier may not perform according to the contract because of strikes, other work stoppages, significant business interruption or cessation, or bankruptcy. The contracting government agency must be prepared to find an alternative supplier or to resume operation itself. Where large capital investments in plant and equipment are necessary for operations, the government must be wary of disinvesting itself of back up equipment in case it has to resume operation.

Maintaining operations is a particularly vital issue when infrastructure is involved. The public sector must have contingency plans to take over. Essential services such as waste water treatment, airport operations, and water treatment must not be interrupted.

In monitoring, and at the rebidding phase, there is also the danger that the provider and beneficiary coalition may subvert the public interest. The experience of contracting out social services in Michigan illustrates the problem. In quick order, the evaluation of services and the interpretation of the "needs" of client beneficiaries became heavily influenced by providers. "For their part, self-interested bureaucrats and legislators cannot fail to see the opportunities for developing mutually beneficial relationships with contractors" (DeHoog, 1984).

Abuse of the public trust and favoritism in awarding contracts to political friends are always possibilities. Public officials who let contracts may eventually work for the contractor. A case in point is a Fairfax County, Virginia, episode in which the Fairfax County Park Authority selected a company to build golf facilities at two parks. Shortly after the contract was let, a board member of the authority quit to work for the contractor as a "$500 per day consultant" (Lipton, 1996). Large contracts may even be let without competitive bidding. For example, the Washington, D.C., school board hired a firm to handle a $21-million contract to operate school cafeterias without competitive bids (Vise, 1996).

Reliance on bidder competition and aggressive public watchdog activities are essential to prevent undue influence of suppliers on the contracting process. "Sweetheart" contracts, guaranteed contract renewal, and collusion among bidders are always a threat to undermine the potential advantages of privatization.

Several critics of contracting out point to the history of widespread corruption when several large cities undertook contracting in the 19th century. Political favoritism, bribery, and the toleration of poor contractor performance were documented in New York City, Chicago, and Detroit. Adler traces the problem to the existence of personal incentives for the public servant who does the hiring. "The (private) entrepreneur is interested in performance and nothing else. The public servant may trade performance for a personal gain" (Adler, 1996).

Privatization's Supporters and Detractors

The forces supporting privatization include owners in the private sector, managers and workers in the private sector, taxpayers, antigovernment ideological groups, and prospective private vendors. Those who defend government's right and ability to deliver government services include the following: public administrators, employees, and unions; elected officials; recipients of government services; current private vendors; and progovernment ideological groups (Seidenstat, 1996).

Among those primarily critical of privatization are the following organizational opponents: the American Federation of State, County and Municipal Employees; the American Bar Association; the National Sheriffs Association; and the American Civil Liberties Union (Donahue, 1989). There are others who raise questions about whether profit-seeking private sector organizations succeed at the expense of broader public sector values. They wonder about the fundamental issues and processes involved in safety, legal rights, politics, and creaming or skimming easy and/or profitable ventures (Palumbo, 1986; Kautsky, 1987; Donahue, 1989; Palumbo and Maupin, 1989).

Criteria for Public Activities and Organizations

Nagel provides the following as decision criteria to be involved in determinations regarding what should be public as opposed to private sector organizations. *Effectiveness* deals with how well a private firm would deliver a public service or achieve a public function. *Efficiency* measures cost per unit. *Predictable rules and procedural due process* are typically provided by government agencies that have constitutional duties versus private firms that have different guidelines.

Political feasibility is the test that is passed when both liberals and conservatives support a particular course of action. *Public participation* is a normal process provided by public as opposed to private organizations (Nagel, 1989). These are criteria that help in determining the appropriateness of privatization ventures.

Privatization and Entrepreneurial Ethics

When public sector decision makers decide to privatize, to change the provision and production relationships, the rules of the game change. The customer-based market model becomes more predominant, and the sovereignty-based governance system is deemphasized. The force driving change is a demand for increased economy and efficiency. Traditional government has not been given credit for frugal administration. Leveraged by voter approval, debt limitations across the country were enhanced by the surge of reinventing, reengineering, TQM, and the other conservative change-oriented forces. Public sector managers and elected officials responded by opting for privatization and entrepreneurship as a method for coping, surviving, and, at times, even thriving (Johnston, 1995ab; Johnston, 1996abc).

Entrepreneurial behavior usually stimulates innovation and creativity, elements government was perceived to be lacking. With the increase of privatization and reinvention over the last several years, however, there has been enough entrepreneurial behavior with corresponding negative impacts to cause many to look at entrepreneurship in the public sector more analytically. It can be said that entrepreneurs have giant egos, are opportunists, behave waywardly, and are domineering and selfish (de Leon, 1996). They may, however, also provide progress toward organizational productivity in the turbulent environment we now experience.

If catalytic entrepreneurial behavior is deemed to be necessary, then it should be more optimal to design jobs, organizational structures, and reward systems both to support and to control such behavior. Harnessed, it works for the good of the organization and its human capital, and for its citizen/customers as well. Allowed to get out of hand, however, it can become unethical, predatory, and destructive. It is increasingly incumbent upon public managers to guide the behavioral performance of their entrepreneurs, professionals, and other employees. Professional organizations and scholars are now providing assistance in this increasingly significant values-based arena.

CONCLUSION

Privatization has become a very important tool for public managers and policymakers. Following the advice of Osborne and Gabler (1992) to "steer, not row," the public sector decision makers can utilize the special advantages and market-oriented management approach of private firms to produce public sector goods while maintaining control of the provision of these outputs. In the process, costs can be contained and quality of output can be enhanced.

Multiple forms of privatization are available on a continuum, ranging from complete load shedding or full privatization to contracting out. Each method may have certain advantages and limitations. The specifics of a given situation such as type of service, availability of vendors, and seriousness of service breakdowns would dictate the policy device to be employed.

Whichever mode of privatization is adopted, it is clear that the key issue affecting the efficacy of the device is the ability to inject competition. Part of the criticism of the performance of public agencies in rendering services is related to their monopoly status. Suboptimal performance is what motivates government officials to play the privatization card. However, simply employing private producers in one form or another without ensuring that there will be vigorous competition in securing the contract or in performing the service may not be an improvement-oriented strategy. Governments that have injected competition into bidding for government work or have allowed the operating agencies to compete typically saw a significant reduction in operating costs and an improvement in service delivery when the agency was able to reform itself and win the contract.

If used in the right circumstances, a competition-enhanced privatization process that specifies a clear-cut performance contract and offers aggressive and careful monitoring of performance will evolve. Privatization will become increasingly effective and its use will spread. Forces opposing privatization will find their position weakened. Public opinion will become increasingly benign regarding the concerns about the consequences of moving toward increased utilization of private producers.

Privatization, when used as a management tool, is in the tradition of the pragmatic American approach to public management. As success is achieved and the environment becomes more friendly, "management by privatization" will become more common. As we experiment with this tool, more creative and imaginative applications are likely to emerge.

REFERENCES

Adler, M. (1996). In city services, privatize and beware. *New York Times*. April 7, DF9.

Bozeman, Barry (1987). *All Organizations Are Public: Bridging Public and Private Organizational Theories*. Jossey-Bass, San Francisco.

Carver, R.H. (1989). Examining the premises of contracting out. *Public Productivity and Management Review*. *13*(1): 27–40.

DeHoog, R.H. (1984). Theoretical perspectives on contracting out for services. In *Public Policy Implementation* (G.C. Edwards III, ed.). JAI Press, Greenwich, Conn., 227–259.

de Leon, Linda (1996). Ethics and entrepreneurship. In Privatization and entrepreneurial management (Van R. Johnston, Symposium ed.). *Policy Studies Journal 24*(3): 495–510.

Donahue, John D. (1989). *The Privatization Decision: Public Ends, Private Means.* Basic Books, New York.

Gore, Al, Jr. (1993). *From Red Tape to Results: Creating a Government That Works Better and Costs Less.* United States Government Printing Office, Washington, D.C.

Gore, Al, Jr. (1994). The new job of the federal executive. *Public Administration Review. 54*(4): 317–321.

Halachmi, Arie (1994). The political economy of outsourcing. In *The Enduring Challenges In the Public Management: Surviving and Excelling in a Changing World* (A. Halachmi and G. Bouckaert, eds.). Jossey-Bass, San Francisco. 220–246.

Halachmi, Arie (1996). Franchising in government: Can a principal-agent perspective be the first step towards the development of a theory? In Privatization and entrepreneurial management (Van R. Johnston, Symposium ed.). *Policy Studies Journal. 24*(3): 478–494.

Halachmi, Arie, and Boydston, R. (1994). The political economy of outsourcing. In *Public Budgeting and Financial Management* (A. Kahn and B. Hildroth, eds.). Kendall Hunt, Dubuque, Iowa, pp. 3–13.

Johnston, Van R. (1990). Privatization of prisons: Management, productivity and governance concerns. *Public Productivity and Management Review. 14*(2): 189–201.

Johnston, Van R. (1995a). Caveat-emptor: Customers vs. citizens. *The Public Manager-The New Bureaucrat. 24*(3): 11–14.

Johnston, Van R. (1995b). Increasing quality and productivity: Strategic planning, TQM, and beyond. In (Arie Halachmi and G. Bouckaert, eds.). *Public Productivity Through Quality and Strategic Management* IOS Press, Washington, D.C., pp. 83–97.

Johnston, Van R. (1996a). The entrepreneurial management transformation: From privatization, reinventing and reengineering: To franchising, efficiency and entrepreneurial ethics. In Privatization and entrepreneurial management (Van R. Johnston, Symposium ed). *Policy Studies Journal. 24*(3): 439–443.

Johnston, Van R. (1996b). Optimizing productivity through privatization and entrepreneurial management. In Privatization and Entrepreneurial Management (Van R. Johnston, Symposium ed.). *Policy Studies Journal. 24*(3): 444–463.

Johnston, Van R. (Symposium ed.) (1996c). Privatization and entrepreneurial management. *Policy Studies Journal. 24*(3): 439–510.

Johnston, Van R. (1999). Privatization lessons for hospitals and prisons. In *Contracting Out Government Services* (Paul Seidenstat, ed.). Praeger, Westport, Conn.

Kautsky, W.L. (1987). *Privatization-an Analysis.* Colorado Department of Corrections, Colorado Springs.

Kolderie, T. (1986). The different concepts of privatization. *Public Administration Review. 14*(2): 189–201.

Kuhn, Thomas (1970). *The Structure of Scientific Revolutions.* University of Chicago Press, Chicago.

Linowes, D.F. (1988). *Privatization: Toward More Effective Government.* President's Commission On Privatization. United States Government Printing Office, Washington, D.C.

Lipton, E. (1996). Fairfax investigates ex-park authority official's work for bidder. *The Washington Post.* July 26, B01.

Martin, J. (1993). The impulse to reengineer. *Governing. 6*(6): 26–30.

Mc Gowan, Robert P., and Wittmer, Dennis (1999). Gaining a competitive edge: Economic development strategies for state and local governments. *Public Administration Quarterly. 22*(3): 301–314.

Moe, Ron C. (1987). Exploring the limits of privatization. *Public Administration Review. 47*(6): 453–460.

Nagel, Stuart S. (1989). *Higher Goals for America.* University Press of America, Lanham, MD.

O'Brien, T.M. (1989). *Privatization in Colorado State Government.* Colorado Office of the State Auditor, Denver.

Osborne, David, and Gaebler, Ted (1992). *Reinventing Government: How the Entrepreneurial Spirit Is Transforming the Public Sector.* Addison Wesley, New York.

Palumbo, Dennis J. (1986). Privatization and corrections policy. *Policy Studies Review. 5*(3): 598–605.

Palumbo, Dennis J., and Maupin, P. (1989). The political side of privatization. *Journal of Management Science and Policy Analysis. 6*(2): 25–40.

Seidenstat, Paul (1996). Privatization: Trends, interplay of forces, and lessons learned. In Privatization and entrepreneurial management (Van R. Johnston, Symposium ed.). *Policy Studies Journal. 24*(3): 464–477.

Siegel, Gilbert B. (1999). Where are we on local government service contracting? *Public Productivity and Management Review. 22*(3): 365–388.

Sullivan, H. J. (1987). Privatization of public services: A growing threat to constitutional rights. *Public Administration Review. 47*(6): 461–467.

Thompson, D.L. (1983). Public—private policy: An introduction. *Policy Studies Journal. 11*(3): 419–426.

United States General Accounting Office (1997). *Privatization Lessons Learned by State and Local Governments.* GAO/GGD 97–48. United States Government Printing Office, Washington, D.C., 46.

Vise, D. (1996). Dispute over food service bid could imperil effort to cut jobs, costs. *The Washington Post,* July 25, A01.

19

Economic Development Policy and Public Management

Kuotsai Tom Liou
Department of Public Administration,
University of Central Florida, Orlando,
Florida

Economic development has become one of the top public policies emphasized by many state and local governments in the United States for the past several decades. The increasing interest in economic development policy has to do with the changing domestic and international political and economic environment. In the domestic environment, the changes are related to the economic recession, the rise of tax revolt, the federal budget deficit, and the cutback of federal aid, which have forced local governments to find additional resources for their communities. In the international environment, the globalization of the world economy, the increase of foreign investment, the end of Cold War, and the advancement of communication technologies have provided local governments many opportunities to seek new markets and enhance the development of their communities.

Recognizing the importance of economic development, policymakers and public managers have worked closely with business and community leaders to develop and implement various policies and programs to promote local economic growth and diversity as well as to improve the overall quality of life in their communities. The policies and programs developed have addressed such areas as industrial recruitment, business formation and retention, community development, international development, high-technology development, and cluster industries development. The implementation of these policies and programs has called for changes and improvement in public management practices, ranging from strategic planning and management to organizational and institutional arrangement, operational improvement and excellence, financial assistance and incentive, technology enhancement, and probusiness attitudinal development.

The purpose of this chapter is to examine the development of regional and local economic development policy and the changes in public management to promote economic development.[1] The chapter begins with discussions about the important role of government in economic development and the rise of economic development policy. It follows with an overview of the evolution of economic development policies and approaches that have been emphasized for the last several decades. Finally, it emphasizes the importance of improving public management to promote economic development and reviews major activities and changes that have been introduced to support economic development.

THE ROLE OF GOVERNMENT IN ECONOMIC DEVELOPMENT

The important role of government in the modern economic system has been well recognized and accepted in the literature of public finance, development economics, and political economy. For example, after reviewing the related literature, Stern (1991: 250–251) identifies five different arguments for governmental intervention in the economy: a concern for market failure, which arises from sources such as externalities, public goods, and imperfect information; a concern for prevention or reduction of poverty and improvement of income distribution, which may result from imperfect market situations and unlimited competition; the assertion of a right to certain facilities or goods, which include general education, health, and housing; the importance of paternalism, which relates to such issues as pensions and drugs; as well as the rights of future generations, which are related to concerns about the environment.

Similarly, Liou (1998a) promotes five major roles of government in the study of post-Mao Chinese economic reforms: government as a promoter of growth, which involves in developing and implementing growth policies in agriculture and industrial sectors; government as a manager of the economy, which emphasizes macroeconomic management of inflation and unemployment; government as a distributor of income, which prevents unfair distribution of resources among various classes and regions; government as a regulator of industry, which focuses on the balance between economic growth and protection of natural environment and individual rights and benefits; and government as a protector of citizens and business, which promotes a safe environment without political interruption and social unrest.

The issue of government involvement in economic growth has been further emphasized and debated in the literature of national and international economic development. The issue of debate is not whether state or government should be involved in economic development, but what the appropriate role of government might be in promoting growth and development. For example, the neoclassical theories of development emphasize the role of foreign trade and investment and the importance of a free market in stimulating competition during the development process (e.g., Galenson, 1985; Haggard, 1990; Wade, 1990, 1992). They suggest that the problems of less developed countries (LDCs) result from extensive government intervention in promoting import-substitution policies that limit the scope of industrialization. They explain that one of the major factors contributing to the success of East Asian newly industrialized countries (NICs) is the adoption of export-oriented policies that encourage the process of technological adaptation and entrepreneurial maturation. They recognize the role of state in the process of development but emphasize a passive and limited role of government in such activities as maintaining stability and providing physical infrastructure.

The statist approach to economic development emphasizes the role state or government plays in developing and implementing industrialization policy to promote economic development. The state can be an important substitute (and the only substitute) for market coordination, which is very important, but often fails, at the initial stage of economic development for many developing countries. The statist arguments of development indicate that the successful experience of NICs is related not only to the operation of the free market but also to the active role of government in directing public and private resources to change the structure of their economy (Johnson, 1982; Ho, 1981; Wade; 1990). For example, in East Asian economies, their governments played a major role in managing economic development when policymakers promoted economic development as the top priority of public policies and usually established one major agency to be in charge of analyzing the market condition for necessary governmental intervention. Public officials in these countries have to formulate and implement strategic policies to boost specific industries. (e.g., Johnson, 1982; Amsden, 1989; Wade, 1990).[2]

In addition, recent studies of economic structure adjustments in developing countries and economic reforms or transitions in postsocialist nations focus on the issue of governmental involvement in economic development. With regard to the structural adjustments, researchers (Haggard and Webb, 1993; Rondinelli and Montgomery, 1990) emphasize the importance of the administrative and political functions of the state and government in the successful implementation of an adjustment program or a reform policy. Similarly, many studies of economic transitions in postsocialist countries (e.g., Fisher and Gelb, 1991; Fisher et al., 1996; Liou, 1998b) emphasize the issue of stabilization in the process of economic transformation and identify the important role and involvement of government to assure the success of the transition. Comparing the reform experience in China and Eastern European countries, for example, most of the studies point out that among the major factors contributing to China's success are the gradual reform approach and stable environment emphasized by the Chinese government (Liou, 1999a).

The previous arguments for the involvement of government in economic activities and development are also recognized and accepted in the United States. For example, in a mixed economic system, government plays a protector role in establishing and maintaining social and legal orders to assure market operations and plays a promoter role in investing and maintaining public infrastructures such as roads and bridges, police and fire protection, and public education. On the other hand, government also plays a regulator role in reducing undesirable consequences of market activities such as environmental regulation and plays a distributor role in encouraging economic and social equity among disadvantaged groups such as females and minorities.

With regard to economic development, federal agencies have focused on the increase of overall national productivity and assistance to economically distressed and poor communities. In general, federal development efforts consist of both place- and people-related programs (Levy, 1990). Place-related development programs and organizations include the Area Redevelopment Administration (which was later replaced by the Economic Development Administration), the Appalachian Regional Commission, the Urban Renewal Program (replaced by Community Development Block Grants), and the Department of Housing and Urban Development. People-related programs and organizations include the Manpower Development and Training Act, the Comprehensive Employment and Training Act, the Jobs Training Partnership Act, the Small Business Administration, and the Department of Labor.

The involvement of federal programs in local economic development has been scaled back significantly because of the changes in economic and political environments since the 1970s. The changes refer to the turbulence of the U.S. economy in the 1970s, the recessions of the early 1980s, the rise of federal budget deficits, the conservative ideology of the Reagan administration, and the cutback of federal aid to states and localities. Federal agencies today operate less as mass suppliers of certain goods and services and more as facilitators, brokers, and agents. In a 1996 study of the federal role in economic development, the National Academy of Public Administration proposed a new approach to assist economic development needs, which stresses the importance of federal government "to help states and localities learn through better information, leverage all available resources, and link multiple federal initiatives to assist local communities (NAPA, 1996: ix).

The changes in federal roles and programs have forced state and local governments to expand their own efforts in economic development policies and programs (e.g., Blakely, 1994; Eisinger, 1988; Levy, 1990; Luke et al., 1988; McGowan and Ottensmeyer, 1993; Reese, 1994). On the one hand, these governments have experienced continuing fiscal difficulties and challenges, such as the increasing difficulties in raising adequate revenues (because of the impact of tax revolts) and the increasing demand for public services (because of the cutback of federal social programs). On the other hand, local officials have become actively involved in economic development promotion activities as they have recognized many business development opportunities resulting from changes in the advancement of communication technology and the globalization of the world economy. The formal change refers to the development of telecommunication systems and web-based Internet services, which significantly reduce the barriers of time and distance among business communities. The latter change has to do with the increase of foreign trade and investment in the United States, the end of the Cold War, and the development of many postsocialist countries, which provide additional businesses and markets for the local economy growth.

The involvement of state and local governments in promoting business development has been supported by researchers of regional economic development. For example, Bartik (1990) uses the market failure approach to explain the importance of regional economic development policy. The approach has such strengths as allowing a wise use of government resources because it focuses on what private markets are unable to do and leading to goals that are measurable in the common currency of dollar benefits. The limitations of the market failure approach consist of the lack of precise information about the magnitude of some nonmarket benefits, nonconsideration of distributional effects of regional economic development policies, and overlooking of the benefits and costs of one region's policies in relation to other regions. In the absence of federal government involvement, however, Bartik (1990: 368) believes that "encouraging regional governments to pursue regional efficient policies is likely, on average, to increase the efficiency of the national economy."

STAGES AND APPROACHES OF ECONOMIC DEVELOPMENT POLICY

Recognizing the increasing activities in state and local economic development, researchers have studied many categories of development policies, programs, and strategies emphasized for the previous decades (e.g., Blakely, 1994; Clark and Montjoy, 1998; Clarke, 1986; Eisinger, 1988; Luke et al., 1988; Reese, 1994; Waits, 1998). For example, Clark and Montjoy (1998: 169–170) summarize economic development programs in terms of four types of activities: (a) subsidizing traditional inputs such as capital (e.g., direct loans and loan guarantees, tax-example bond financing, development corporations), land (e.g., land banking, site development provision), and labor (e.g., low-cost/mass production, and high-quality/lean production); (b) lowering political costs of doing business, including tax abatements and incentives, and limitations on the regulatory environment; (c) promoting entrepreneurial activities of market development (e.g., export promotion, research and dissemination) and business services (e.g., policy planning, R&D support and consortia); and (d) developing attractive social amenities (e.g., arts, environment) and improving distressed areas (e.g., enterprise zones). Focusing on state economic development, Mary Jo Waits (1998) identifies similar development strategies and activities in four phases: (a) industrial recruitment (i.e., attracting plants through low costs, cheap labor, low taxes, financial subsidies, minimal regulation); (b) business formation, focusing on creating jobs through the provision of a talented work force, technology, physical infrastructure, quality of life, tax and regulatory policy); (c) period of refinement and reinvention to improve program and policy accountability, performance, and quality; and (d) new directions of global competitiveness, which emphasize interrelationships among firms and clusters (groups of firms) and identify specialized cluster resources to attract, retain, and develop firms to build into clusters.

Considering all the issues discussed the author has identified four different approaches of economic development: industrial recruitment, business formation and retention, international business development, and cluster industry development. Despite their different focuses, these approaches are not mutually exclusive and public officials may consider the combination of several approaches at one time.

Industrial Recruitment

The first approach of economic development is the recruitment of outside businesses to relocate or expand within their regions and communities. The industrial recruitment approach, also known as *smokestack chasing,* was emphasized by state and local governments in poor and less industrial regions (such as southern states) to recruit large manufacturing companies and plants from more developed regions (such as northern states). This approach assumes that the recruitment of mass-production factories is the best strategy to promote local economic growth and increase number of firms and jobs in a short time. The approach did not consider the type of jobs and industries being recruited and did not evaluate the impact, especially social and noneconomic aspects, of these jobs and industries on their communities.

The industrial recruitment approach emphasizes the use of governmental incentives and subsidies as the major strategy to attract those large and established firms. The strategy of relocation incentives and subsidies, also known as *supply-*

side polices (Eisinger, 1988), focuses on changes in the supply condition of companies by reducing their operational costs of capital and labor. The major components of the supply-side strategy are such governmental programs and activities as tax-reducing policies, debt financing, labor market deregulation, pollution control incentives, subsidized training, and free land.

The role of government in the industrial recruitment approach tends to be reactive and limited. Reacting to businesses' relocation and expansion decision, state and local governments prepare their inducement packages to show their comparative advantages among competing regions and communities. The comparative advantages, however, are only marginal and limited, as they are based on the manipulation and changes of public policies. Under industrial recruitment, government follows and supports private business development decisions, and governmental programs and activities are limited to specific companies and specific conditions.

The traditional industrial recruitment approach was later criticized as ineffective in terms of the impact on business location decisions and on local economic conditions. Many researchers of economic development found that governmental financial assistance and tax incentives, which became available in almost all communities, were not considered by business leaders among the top factors in making their decisions on plant expansion or firm relocation (Smith and Fox, 1990). In addition, they noticed that the large manufacturing firms recruited tend to employ relative unskilled, low-wage workers; that tendency does not have significant impact on local tax base and may have a negative impact on the local natural environment.

Business Formation and Retention

The second approach of economic development is related to new business formation and old business modernization in the local market. Unlike the industrial recruitment approach, the business formation approach attempts to improve regional and local economic growth by strengthening internal economies and businesses. This approach, also known as *home-grown development,* focuses on small indigenous firms and emphasizes activities to develop new businesses locally and to retain, modernize, and expand existing local firms.

The business formation approach takes a comprehensive strategy to promote regional and local economic development. In addition to supply-side policies and programs, state and local governments consider a broad range of factors and activities, both internal and external to firms, to improve business development environment and conditions. The new approach, also known as *demand-side policies,* emphasizes the importance of public policies in discovering, expanding, developing, or creating new markets for local goods and services. The business formation approach consists of activities such as assisting in talent/work force development, improving technology advancement, improving physical infrastructure, providing capital assistance, addressing tax and regulatory policy, and improving quality of life.

The role of government in the business formation approach is more active than it is in the industrial recruitment approach. Policymakers and public managers at state and local levels adopt a proactive attitude and the public-private partnership strategy to develop new policies and programs to assist business development. The proactive attitude requires governments to help identify investment opportunities for the private sector. Governments need to assess the strengths and weaknesses of their development environment and develop strategic targets and criteria for governmental assistance. In addition, the proactive role of government also leads to an emphasis on the public-private partnership strategy in economic development, which calls for the participation, support, and coordination of business, nonprofit, and community organizations in the process of economic development.

One example of this new approach to business formation is the promotion of high-tech industries in local communities (e.g., Research Triangle in North Carolina, Route 128 in Massachusetts, Silicon Valley in California). Public officials are interested in developing high-tech industries because of the prestige and potential benefits of high-value jobs associated with high-tech development. Many state and local governments work together to support efforts to attract, retain, or encourage new high-tech firms. These development efforts include investment in university-based research centers, development of a skilled labor force, provision of venture capital financing programs, and arrangement of development and production infrastructures such as business incubator facilities (Blakely, 1994).

Another example of the business formation approach is the emphasis on small business development. Policymakers recognize that small firms and service industries provide more employment opportunities for the community and a more diverse and stable economic base even though these firms and industries are generally related to low-skill, low-paying jobs (Waugh and Waugh, 1990). To assist small firms, state and local governments provide financial and technical assistance programs to improve their operations and to further their development. Examples of financial assistance programs are government-guaranteed loans, special tax districts, and assistance in grant application and fund-raising projects. The technical assistance programs include the support of small business development centers in providing management training, counseling, consulting, and research services to small firms.

International Business Development

The third approach to economic development is the active involvement of state and local governments in international business development activities. Policymakers in these governments are increasingly involved in international business development as a result of the increasing difficulties of their financial condition and the continuing expansion of a global economic market (Fosler, 1988; Kline, 1983, 1984a, 1984b; Kurdrle and Kite, 1989; Liou, 1993; Luke and Caiden, 1989; McIntyre, 1983; Neuse, 1982; Noponen et al., 1997). As explained previously, state and local governments are experiencing fiscal difficulties because of internal factors such as the cutback of federal programs, the impact of tax revolts, and the threat of plant closings and relocations. The advance in communication technologies, the increase of foreign investment, and the end of the Cold War have made it possible for state and local officials to think about global business opportunities and to act on local economic development programs.

In general, state and local international business development activities refer to three areas: increasing exports to other countries, attracting foreign direct investment in local businesses, and encouraging tourists from other countries to visit local communities. To promote international business development, policymakers have adopted traditional development policies and programs such as financial incentives and technical assistance to reduce the cost of business operations. In addition, many of them have also emphasized new policies and programs to assist business in market development such as opening and expanding overseas offices, arranging governors' and mayors' overseas trips, providing information on trade fairs and exhibits, and holding trade seminars or conferences.

Similarly to the business formation approach, in this strategy government plays a proactive role and emphasizes a public-private partnership approach to promote international business development. In many cases, policymakers provide leadership to encourage and assist local businesses to consider and participate in international business activities; often they also have to mobilize political resources to convince local communities to change conservative attitudes and to embrace foreign businesses and international activities. In addition to the advocate role, state and local governments need to evaluate their economic base from a global perspective, assess the capacities of public and private institutions, and develop a community-based, public-private cooperative international development program.

Finally, on the basis of both empirical analyses and attitudinal surveys, many studies of foreign direct investment in the United States have reported that traditional public policy and promotion incentives are not major factors in foreign business local decision, (Ajami and Ricks, 1981; Coughlin et al., 1990, 1991; Little, 1978; Luger and Shetty, 1985; McConnell, 1980; Sokoya and Tillery, 1992; Woodward, 1992). Instead, researchers have pointed out the importance of such factors as regional market demands, better service consideration, and attractive political climate and public attitude. To promote a positive business climate for international development it is thus important for public employees, community leaders, and business people to understand cultures, markets, languages, and government structures of other countries. Some types of cross-cultural training are certainly important and necessary to the better understanding of these issues.

Industry Cluster Development

The last approach to economic development is related to cluster-based industry development. This approach is based on Michael Porter's study of competitive advantage (Porter, 1990): that regional clusters of related industries, rather than individual firms or single industries, are the source of economic growth. The industry clusters are geographical concentrations of industries that share needs for common talent, technology, and infrastructure through colocation.

The idea of industry cluster development is related to, but significantly different from, the traditional theory of regional agglomeration economies (Doeringer and Terkla, 1995). The traditional agglomeration theory emphasizes the reduction of the costs of firms in a common location through positive externalities, such as lowering transaction and transportation costs with the same industry and among industries, as well as sharing the benefits of public goods such as public infrastructure and public research and development support. While enjoying positive externalities, the theory of competitive advantage promotes economic dynamics in the clustering process. In other words, unlike the static nature of the traditional agglomeration economies (i.e., cost advantages remain the same through time), the competitive advantage theory depends on dynamic factors constantly evolving as a result of continual innovation and the transfer of new knowledge within clusters of firms (Doeringer and Terkla, 1995).

The industry clusters development approach differs from the conventional development approaches in many ways (Waits, 1998: 195–200). For example, the cluster development approach emphasizes a new economic competitiveness, which is based on the changes in global economic environment and technological advancement. Unlike the traditional approaches of targeting individual firms, the cluster approach defines the customer differently and focuses on clusters or groups of firms that foster increased regional and local business activities. In addition, the cluster development approach measures success in new, more comprehensive ways. Emphasizing the interdependence of many different parts of the community, the cluster approach attracts, retains, and develops firms to build clusters that increase the number of high-quality jobs and the growth of exports as well as to provide a higher standard of living and higher per capita income.

Government in industry cluster development plays an intelligent partner role, creating the civic capacity to mediate and facilitate the cluster development process and fostering an environment that encourages collaboration among competing firms (Doeringer and Terkla, 1995; Waits, 1998). As an intelligent partner to the private sector, state and local government have to focus strategically their intelligence gathering, resources, and attention on identified industry clusters or sectors. *Civic capacity* is the capacity of communities and their governments to provide a civic climate that enhances dynamic efficiency. To create high civic capacity, policymakers again need to emphasize the public-private partnership strategy and develop long-term policies to address such important issues as education, labor-management relations, and regulation.

CHANGES AND CHALLENGES IN PUBLIC MANAGEMENT

The importance of public sector management to economic development is well documented in the literature of economic development. At the national and international levels, researchers (Keating, 1998; Liou, 2000a) claim that good governance is critical to economic and social development, especially for developing and economic-transition countries. The traditional literature of administrative reform focuses on activities to improve the operational efficiency and effectiveness of public organizations, including rules, procedures, and implementation methods. The new approach of public management reform (sometimes called *new public management*) expands the traditional concern with operational efficiency to the broader issues of governance. The new approach covers both structural and cultural changes in the public sector. The structural changes refer to policies of decentralization and devolution, privatization, and contracting out, as well as regulatory improvement and deregulation. The cultural changes introduce the spirit of competition and choice (between public and private organizations), the respect toward clients and citizens, and the value of accountability for results.

Similar arguments that support the importance of public management to regional economic growth have been emphasized by researchers of state and local economic development (Blakely, 1994, Luke et al., 1988). To promote economic development, public officials have to pay attention to both managerial and policy issues that are closely related to economic development. On the managerial activities, they need to adopt a proactive approach to establish a strategic economic development plan to prepare for a long-term goal of growth and diversity, to emphasize a public-private partnership approach to arrange various institutions to be responsible for the implementation of economic development policies and programs, and to use new ideas and modern techniques to overcome bureaucratic problems and improve operational excellence for better customer service.

On the policy issues, public officials need to mobilize limited local resources to provide financial assistance programs for business development and have to develop specific criteria and procedures for the application of financial assistance in order to prevent political misuse of public funds and to maximize the effectiveness and efficiency of financial assistance programs. In addition, they need to provide leadership in negotiating with local community and business groups to address concerns about negative outcomes of economic development (e.g., environmental and traffic deterioration) and to develop a positive and probusiness climate to welcome both domestic and international business development opportunities.

The specific activities and issues involved in economic development management and policy are further discussed in the following sections.

Economic Development Planning

To achieve the goal of increasing jobs, local governments and community groups must play a proactive, not a reactive, role in assessing their resources and designing alternative development strategies to promote economic activities (Bergman, 1981; Blakely, 1994). The important aspect of the proactive role is for local governments to emphasize planning function and activities in their assessment of short- and long-term effects of their development strategies. Planning is not only necessary, but the key to assure the success of local economic development.

In recent years, policymakers and public managers have emphasized a new strategic planning approach to deal with the changes in economic, political, and social environments and to assure the success of economic development in their communities (Liou, 1998c). Proponents of strategic planning (e.g., Eadie, 1983; Sorkin et al., 1984) often emphasize the difference between strategic planning and conventional public planning in terms of key characteristics of strategic planning. For example, they maintain that strategic planning is more oriented toward action, results, and implementation; promotes broader and more diverse participation in the planning process; and especially places more emphasis on understanding the community in its external context (via an environmental scan or the SWAT analysis) than conventional public planning. Although challenging these differences, planning researchers did agree that strategic planning has become an important technique in the area of economic development to help local communities develop a program of action based on public-private partnership (Kaufman and Jacobs, 1987:31)

Recognizing the importance of strategic planning, researchers of local economic development (e.g., Black, 1991; Friedman and Darragh, 1988; Morgan and England, 1996; Morrison, 1995; Reed and Blair, 1993; Sorkin et al., 1984) have recommended the following issues/steps for policymakers and public managers in their consideration of applying strategic planning to improve the effectiveness of local economic development policies or programs:

1. Analysis of the local economic base (i.e., environmental scan): examining major elements of local communities to understand their internal and external opportunities and constraints. The key elements include demographic elements (e.g., population trends, household size, income levels and trends, ethnic/minority groups); economic elements (e.g., major employers and future prospects, cost and availability of financing; inflation, interest, and employment rates); governmental factors (e.g., tax system and trends, infrastructure conditions,

capital improvement plans, political power, intergovernmental relationships, extent and quality of public services; business and development regulation); physical elements (e.g., climate, geographic location, land availability and quality, density, environmental conditions and constraints); and specific competitive environment (e.g., recognition of competing communities, understanding of competitive approaches, and analysis of competitors' strengths and weaknesses).

2. Identification of key stakeholders and establishment of some shared values, vision, and mission: establishing a steering committee to build the basis for a strong public-private partnership to support economic development. The steering committee should include such members as policymakers (e.g., county chairperson, mayor, city manager); public managers (e.g., planning and finance director); business leaders (e.g., chambers of commerce representatives, representatives of local banks and utility companies); representatives from the local school district, community college, and university; and citizens and neighborhood representatives. These members need to work together to establish some shared values of their community (e.g., level of community growth, quality of community life); vision of the community (i.e., community's hope for future), and a mission to summarize the community's plans for development (e.g., mission statement to explain the purpose and nature of community economic development).

3. Development of goals, objectives, and strategies (action plans): developing goals, objectives, and strategies of economic development through the preparation of an action plan. Economic development goals should indicate what the community would like to become or achieve in respect to the economic analysis and shared mission, which should be realistic, well understood, and may be classified in terms of the time required (i.e., long-range, intermediate-range, and short-range goals). Objectives should quantify the goals and establish a timetable for completion. Strategies refer to specific actions required to achieve the development goals and objectives. The action plans also need to include the evaluation of goals and objectives (e.g., through SWOT analysis) and the examination of priorities, costs, and benefits of each strategy.

4. Implementation, monitoring and evaluation of programs and results: involving the implementation, monitoring, and evaluation of the development plan. The implementation plan should include not only the community development goal and objectives, specific strategic actions, expected results, and action plans, but also the outline of task assignments, a time line, and a list of resources required. The monitoring process involves the designation of a specific entity with resources to assess specific implementation targets within specified periods. The evaluation process considers measurement of economic development goals, selection of evaluation criteria, and assessment of the overall effect of an economic development plan.

The success of applying the strategic planning model for economic development (and other public policies) depends on the careful consideration of the unique environment of the individual community and the leadership and support from the community (Bryson, 1988, 1989; Bryson and Roering, 1987; Streib, 1992). The benefits associated with the application of strategic planning in many organizations include, helping these organizations think strategically, clarifying future direction, dealing effectively with rapidly changing circumstances, building teamwork and expertise, and improving cooperative relationships between elected officials and public managers. In addition to these common items, local governments will also receive some specific benefits that are associated with the application of strategic planning concepts and processes in economic development programs. These benefits include at least four interrelated aspects: (a) a proactive approach—helping the communities be proactive in relation to their economic conditions and develop appropriate policies and programs based on the consideration of community characteristics, strengths, and weaknesses; (b) the coordinating function—providing a well-organized framework to coordinate all the key players in the development process; (c) a balanced development—offering opportunities for different stakeholders to raise their interests and concerns in the development process and producing a win-win situation for everyone involved in the process; and (d) the long-term considerations—helping community leaders understand not only the current needs but also the future trends and letting policymakers think of long-term investment in community human resources and consider trade-offs between short-term loss and future gains.[3]

Organizational Arrangement and Operational Improvement

Closely related to the planning issues discussed previously, many organizational and operational issues of economic development are also critical to the success of state and local governments' development programs. In fact, policymakers and public managers have generally incorporated the organizational and operational issues in their strategic planning for economic development. For example, the strategic economic development planning process usually requires changes in organizational arrangements to deal with new challenges in the environment and to achieve new missions and goals of the development program and planning. The implementation and monitoring stages of the strategic planning process especially emphasize the importance of improving operations and activities.

The organizational process for economic development entails the selection of appropriate organizational models for development. It is important for community leaders to recognize advantages and disadvantages of various organizational models for economic development. Three of the models are the full public-funded model (e.g., local government economic development department and redevelopment agency, regional economic development districts), the public-private partnership model (e.g., a local development corporation), and the pure private nonpolitical model (e.g., a private nonprofit local development cooperation) (Morrison, 1995).

The selection of an appropriate organization model for economic development is based on the consideration of the advantages and disadvantages of each model and the general environment of local conditions. First, there is no single best way to organize for managing economic development, and each model has its advantages and disadvantages. For example, the popular model of public-funded economic development agency is good in terms of providing public funding, tax incentives, and regulatory reliefs. On the other hand, this model may face such challenges as statutory limitation and philosophical arguments against using public funds for private gain. The environment of local conditions includes the physical (e.g., available resources) and attitudinal (pro- or antibusiness climates) components of local communities as well as the stages or approaches of local development policies (e.g., industrial recruitment, business formation).

On the basis of these considerations, state and local officials have made various organizational arrangements to promote economic development. For example, in Florida, the state government has reorgnized the Department of Commerce into a nonprofit organization, "Enterprise Florida," to promote statewide business development activities. Local governments in Florida have developed various public-funded or nonprofit organizations to coordinate local and regional economic development activities. In central Florida, the Mid-Florida Economic Development Commission provides services to coordinate the economic development efforts of the mid-Florida counties of Orange, Osceola, Lake, and Seminole and to encourage business development through industry diversity and job placement and creation in the Metro Orlando area. Each county and city government, in turn, has also established an independent office of economic development to assist business development and expansion in their communities. The trend today is to emphasize a public-private partnership approach to develop an organization that incorporates such characteristics as probusiness attitudes, professional and technical ability, and political acceptability and trustworthiness.

Closely related to the organizational arrangement, efforts to improve government operations on economic development have also been emphasized in recent years as a result of the reinventing government movement (Osborne and Gaebler, 1992). The new movement calls for, among other things, the application of managerial techniques from the private sector to address such bureaucratic problems as fragmentation, unresponsiveness, ineffectiveness, and resistance to change. The new movement especially emphasizes such concepts as accountability, quality, and performance measurement in the improvement of public service delivery.

For economic development programs, the operational improvement consists of such activities and issues as one-stop business development centers, regulatory improvement, and economic development evaluation. The one-stop center provides an integrated function of coordinating all types of useful business information valuable to business communities. The regulatory improvement attempts to remove flaws and problems associated with the business development process. The evaluation of economic development focuses on the issue of accountability and performance and examines not only numbers of jobs or firms created but also numbers of good-quality jobs created, types of firms/industries recruited, and overall impact on community quality of life.

Moreover, the operation improvement aspect of economic development has also been related to the use of modern techniques in the promotion of business development activities. One good example of this technology advancement is the use of web sites for many local economic development organizations to market their communities actively. Through the Internet, local governments are able to connect all the web sites of public agencies, private firms, and nonprofit organizations that are related to business development activities and provide easy access to the public and the business community. In many business conferences, local governments are also distributing a specially designed CD-ROM to participants and the interested public to establish good public relations and offer more information on community development.

Economic Development Financing

The evaluation of economic development approaches and stages in the preceding section indicates the importance of government financial support in assisting and promoting many different business development activities. The issue of economic development financing today does not concern whether local governments should provide financial support for development, since most local governments and communities provide some kinds of financial programs and incentives to attract new companies or retain existing firms. The issue of financing economic development is really a question of what type of financial support is appropriate for each community. In general, local governments have used three types of government financial programs to promote economic development (Liou, 1999b).

1. Financial services and guarantees—providing some direct financial services and guarantees to promote business development. Government involvement in this type of debt financing is based on the understanding that some businesses may have problems receiving financial support from traditional financial agencies because of the risks associated with their businesses. The risks may be related to the nature of business (e.g., high-tech), the location of the business (e.g., rural areas, distressed communities), or the background of the business owners (e.g., minority entrepreneurs). This type of government financial support uses such tools as direct loans to private business, issuance of bonds, cash contributions to projects, shared equity in projects, loan guarantees, and subsidies.

2. Tax incentives—changing tax structure and base to encourage business development. Government tax incentives are of three general types: broad-based tax incentives, targeted tax incentives, and selectively applied tax incentives (Hy

and Waugh, 1995). Related to the state's business tax structure, broad-based incentives are offered to all firms in the state as a low tax rate, credits, exemptions, and deductions permitted for business activities. Targeted incentives are extended to businesses located in a specific geographic region (usually an economically depressed area) to promote growth and job creation. Targeted incentives may apply to such areas as free enterprise zones and tax increment financing districts. Selectively applied incentives, such as tax abatement, are provided to some desired businesses to promote growth and development in that specific industry (e.g., high-tech). Both tax increment financing and tax abatement are related to changes in the local property tax base and assessment.

3. General services investment—investing financial resources to improve the operations and services related to business development (closely related to the operational improvement issue discussed previously). This type of financial support includes centralized management services, employee training/retraining, consolidated/one-stop permit issuance, a modified zoning process, relaxed environmental regulations, improved public safety services, and improved public infrastructure and facilities (e.g., streets, parks). Emphasis on this type of financial service is based on the premise of the new development approach: creating a good social environment to attract business development.

The issue of economic development financing has generated arguments about the appropriateness and implementation of many government financial programs (Bingham et al., 1990). Despite various incentive forms or programs, most evaluations of economic development programs conclude that state and local financial incentive programs have little influence on either the level or the distribution of economic growth, especially when compared with the impact of market factors (Bartik, 1991). For example, past studies of the effect of taxation on economic development have produced conflicting results because of different methodologies, measures of economic growth, data sources, and periods used and covered. Recent studies of the effectiveness of tax policies, using improved techniques and data, have produced empirical evidence to support the effect of tax policy. But researchers report that the effect of tax policy on economic development is only modest across interstate and intermetro areas, and much more pronounced within metro areas (Bartik, 1992; Phillips and Goss, 1995).

The interest in using public funds to support business development is usually based on political considerations. Policymakers and public managers have found that tax and financial incentives are easy to control and manipulate when comparing them with other determinative factors in economic development decisions such as the size of local markets and the quality of the local labor force. In many cases, policymakers enact tax incentives not on the basis of rational economic analysis, but as a defensive measure against regional competition (Grady, 1987). In addition, researchers argue that many of the traditional financial incentives simply transfer money from the public sector to successful firms and move these firms from place to place and do little to help those in need (Rubin, 1998; Wolman and Spitzley, 1996). Robinson-Barnes and Waugh (1998) point out that the provision of tax incentives has resulted in three negative outcomes: First, the tax incentive programs are counterproductive because they have caused intergovernmental competition. Next, targeted tax incentives may be ineffective and unfair because they often overlook opportunities in localities not typically targeted. Finally, many of the financial incentive programs fail to incorporate human resource development components in their overall development strategy.

To capitalize on the benefits of the financial incentives and to prevent many of the problems associated with them, researchers have suggested several principles and guidelines for policymakers to use with tax incentives to promote economic development (Ihlanfeldt, 1995). For example, they emphasize that (a) tax incentives should be accompanied by specific programs that seek to mitigate the unwanted side effects of economic growth; (b) tax incentives should be part of a comprehensive state economic development program containing carefully crafted supply-side and demand-side policies (i.e., a balanced approach); (c) tax incentives should be general, not specific, i.e., made available to all firms that satisfy eligibility criteria, rather than acting as bait to lure a particular company; (d) tax incentives should be targeted to firms in basic industries because their benefits will exceed their cost; (e) tax incentive programs should contain provisions to reduce potential revenue losses; (f) performance evaluation methods should be adopted for periodically monitoring the costs and benefits of each tax incentive; and (g) efforts should be made to publicize tax incentives and other economic development programs to ensure that companies are aware of them.

Leadership Support and Influence

Policymakers and public managers play an important leadership role in shaping and implementing economic development policy and programs. As explained, these public officials (both elected and appointed officials) have been very interested in economic development policy because of the potential benefits of increasing community economic growth, diversifying local economic structure, and creating value-added high-quality jobs. In fact, they have been actively involved in policies and programs of planning and financing economic development, have made institutional arrangements or rearrangements to identify specific agencies or organizations to be responsible for economic development activities, and have removed bureaucratic problems and regulatory barriers to improve operational effectiveness for better business service. In addition, the leadership from these officials is especially valuable in three aspects: building community consensus and support, promoting probusiness attitude and climate, and resolving the issue of equity development.

First, communitywide political support is critical to the success of any economic and business development activity (e.g., recruiting, retention, expansion) as many economic development policies and programs require the investment of public funds (e.g., tax and financial assistance). However, commonly citizens and interest groups have different interests and concerns in the development of their communities. For example, many citizens and groups are concerned about negative effects of economic development (e.g., environmental deterioration, traffic congestion) and are interested in slowing and limiting developmental activities. In addition, they may also have a very narrow view of the selection of various development projects and consider them only from a short-term perspective.

To build community support, public officials must show their leadership and human skills in interacting with concerned citizens, community groups, and business leaders to generate consensuses on the development mission, goals, and plans (Luke et al., 1988). Their communication ability is very important in understanding different views and concerns of other groups and in conveying to such groups their vision of the community development. Strong negotiation and collaboration skills are necessary for them to handle groups with conflicting values and to build coalitions among groups with similar goals and strategies. The final item on the agenda is convincing stakeholders and groups to develop a long-term-oriented, communitywide, win-win development policy.

Closely related to the issue of community consensus building, the second challenging issue for public officials is the promotion of a probusiness climate in their community and organizations. The business climate entails both formal policy positions and assistance and informal attitudinal support of business development. From the perspective of formal policy positions, public officials want to make sure that their communities and organizations will prepare and approve a comprehensive business development package to address such issues as tax policies, financial assistance programs, regulatory policies and relief, infrastructure assistance, and availability of technical and training programs. As discussed previously, there are different arguments and considerations about the issue of using public funds to support private business development, and public officials have to use their leadership and political skills to overcome opposing arguments and mobilize local resources to establish probusiness policies and programs.

In addition to the formal policy positions, public officials also have to pay attention to the informal social and organizational attitudes toward business development. The attitudinal support is important to the recruitment of foreign direct investment (FDI), as studies have shown that the attractive U.S. attitude toward foreign investment is one of the top 10 motivations affecting location decisions among foreign companies (e.g., Ajami and Ricks, 1981; Sokoya and Tillery, 1992; Tolchin and Tolchin, 1988). The attitudinal issue is especially important in the case of Japanese-affiliated investment because of the lack of understanding between the American public and Japanese firms. For example, a public opinion survey showed that more Americans (64 percent of the respondents) believe that Japanese investments in the United States pose a threat to U.S. economic independence than that European investments do (37 percent), even though Europeans invest more in the United States than do Japanese (Miko and Weilant, 1991: 15). In the study of perceptions of FDI of business and professional people in Montana, Karahan, Lee, and Akis (1995) noticed that positive perceptions about FDI dropped about 8 percent for Japanese FDI (i.e., from 65 percent for all FDI to 57 percent for Japanese FDI). It is interesting to note that in the study public officials especially showed a larger percentage drop (16 percent, from 73 percent to 57 percent) in their attitude toward Japanese FDI than did businesspersons and chamber of commerce and economic development organizations, 7 percent and 8 percent, respectively. To improve social and organizational attitude, it is important for public officials to promote multicultural understanding and provide some types of cross-cultural training programs to community groups and public employees (Chadwin et al., 1995: 520).

Finally, public officials should play an important role in addressing many equity issues related to economic development. As Rubin (1998) has indicated, the public sector has experienced many problems in traditional economic development policies and programs. For example, with regard to the issue of using public funds for business development, Rubin (1998: 303) explains that traditional economic development has encountered the following problems. "The public sector is caught in a game that requires it to subsidize the very businesses that do not need the money"; "The public sector obscures the costs, costs that produce few net benefits, while ballyhooing only the visible monuments of success"; and "As a result limited public funds for economic development end up simply moving firms from place to place and do little to help those in need."

Concern about equity issues in economic development has been evidenced in the location decisions of many companies, both domestic- and foreign-owned firms. Many studies of domestic industrial development (Markusen et al., 1987; Reginald, 1983) have reported a negative association between communities with a higher African American population and plant location. With regard to direct investment by foreign firms, Cole and Deskins (1988) also observed similar negative findings in site location and employment patterns of Japanese auto firms in America. These potential inequality and discrimination problems, even when unintentional, will no doubt result in serious antibusiness and anti–foreign investment attitudes among local communities.

Rubin emphasized a model of equity economic development to resolve many problems of the traditional economic development approach. The equity economic development model argues for "the use of incentives as tools to repair deteriorated neighborhoods, provide jobs to those in need, and increase aggregate income within neighborhoods of deprivation" (Rubin, 1998: 303–304). In the equity development approach, public officials need to take a leadership role to convince community and business groups that local governments have the ethical obligation to address many problems associated with the destruction of many inner-city neighborhoods and that the role of public involvement in economic development is to create new wealth that directly benefits those in need. Rubin suggests that governments can use community-based development organizations as the delegate agency to oversee private economic renewal efforts within poor communities so that they can coordinate economic development efforts with social service programs.

CONCLUSION

Focusing on the relationship between economic development and public management, this chapter examines the role of government in the process of economic development, reviews various stages and approaches of local economic development policies, and analyzes many changes and challenges of public management activities that are important to promoting economic development. The stages of economic development policy consist of such approaches as industrial recruitment, business formation and retention, international business development, and industry cluster development. These different approaches, although not mutually exclusive, require the assistance of government in planning various supporting roles and policies and in providing various development programs and strategies.

The challenges for public management are to make necessary changes in the economic development planning process, institutional arrangements, and operational improvements to offer high-quality services to business communities and to attract new development activities. In addition, public officials have to play a leadership role in dealing with efficiency and equity issues related to economic development financing issues and in establishing probusiness attitudes in local communities and organizations and overcoming many cultural and social problems associated with economic development.

The close relationship between economic development and public management as emphasized in this chapter provides strong arguments for the need for and importance of improving or reforming public management practices to increase business development opportunities and to promote local economic growth. The relationship between the two is a continuing process of learning, practicing, and changing that certainly requires further study.

NOTES

1. Focusing on the experience in the United States, this chapter examines the relationship between economic development policy and public management activities at the local level. For information about the linkage between economic development and public management at the national levels, see Liou (2000a).
2. In its study of Asian economic growth, the World Bank (1993) indicated that the high-performance Asian economies (HPAEs) were successful in getting the basics right, including stable marcoeconomy, superior accumulation of physical and human capital investment, effective and secure financial systems, limiting of price distortions, open-

ness to foreign technology, and assuring agricultural development policies. In addition, the governments of the HPAEs have also intervened, systematically and through multiple channels, to promote development: targeting and subsidizing credit to selected industries, protecting domestic import substitutes, subsidizing declining industries, establishing and financially supporting government banks, establishing firm- and industry-specific export targets, and developing export marketing institutions.

3. In addition to common problems of strategic planning (see Mintzberg, 1994), researchers (Liou, 2000b; Reed et al., 1987) have identified several challenges associated with the application of strategic planning in economic development, including at least four aspects of problems or limitations: the assumption of strategic planning, the context of public organizations, the problems of a citywide/communitywide approach, and the reality of political considerations and solutions.

REFERENCES

Ajami, R. A., and Ricks, D. A. (1981). Motives of non-American firms investing in the United States. *Journal of International Business Studies. 12* (Winter): 25–34.

Amsden, A. H. (1989). *Asia's Next Giant: South Korea and Late Industrialization.* Oxford University Press, Oxford.

Bartik, T. J. (1992). The effects of state and local taxes on economic development: A review of recent research, *Economic Development Quarterly. 6* (February): 102–111.

Bartik, T. J. (1991). *Who Benefit from State and Local Economic Development Policies?* W. E. Upjohn Institute for Employment Research, Kalamazoo, Mich.

Bartik, T. J. (1990). The market failure approach to regional economic development policy. *Economic Development Quarterly. 4* (November): 361–370.

Bergman, E. (1981). *Citizen Guide to Economic Development in Job Loss Communities.* Center for Urban and Regional Studies, Chapel Hill, N.C.

Bingham, R. D., Hill, E. W., and White, S. B. (eds.) (1990). *Financing Economic Development: An Institutional Perspective,* Sage, Newbury Park, Calif.

Black, H. (1991). *Achieving Economic Development Success: Tools That Work.* The International City/County Management Association (ICMA), Washington, D.C.

Blakely, E. J. (1994). *Planning Local Economic Development: Theory and Practice,* 2nd ed. Sage, Thousand Oaks, Calif.

Bryson, J. M. (1989). *Strategic Planning for Public and Nonprofit Organizations.* Jossey-Bass, San Francisco.

Bryson, J. M. (1988). A strategic planning process for public and non-profit organizations. *Long Range Planning. 21* (1): 73–81.

Bryson, J. M., and Roering, W. D. (1987). Applying private-sector strategic planning in the public sector. *Journal of the American Planning Association. 53* (1): 9–22.

Chadwin, M. L., Rogers, S. E., and Kim, P. S. (1995). Dealing with *Them:* Preparing state and local official for the cross-cultural challenge. *Public Administration Review. 55* (6): 517–521.

Clark, C., and Montjoy, R. (1998). Globalization and the revitalization of U.S. economic competitiveness: Implications for economic development policy. In *Handbook of Economic Development* (K. T. Liou, ed.). Marcel Dekker, New York, pp. 151–182.

Clarke, M. K. (1986). *Revitalizing State Economies: A Review of State Economic Development Policies and Programs.* National Governors Associations, Washington, D.C.

Cole, R. E., and Deskins, D. R., Jr. (1988). Racial factors in site location and employment patterns of Japanese auto firms in America. *California Management Review. 31* (1) (Fall): 9–22.

Coughlin, C. C., Terza, J. V., and Arromdee, V. (1990). State government effects on the location of foreign direct investment. *Regional Science Perspectives. 20:* 194–207.

Coughlin, C. C., Terza, J. V., and Arromdee, V. (1991). State characteristics and the location of foreign direct investment within the United States. *The Review of Economics and Statistics. 73:* 675–683.

Doeringer, P. B., and Terkla, D. G. (1995). Business strategy and cross-industry clusters. *Economic Development Quarterly. 9* (3): 225–237.

Eadie, D. C. (1983). Putting a powerful tool to practical use: The application of strategic planning in the public sector. *Public Administration Review. 43* (5): 447–452.

Eisinger, P. K. (1988). *The Rise of the Entrepreneurial State: State and Local Economic Development Policy in the United States.* University of Wisconsin Press, Madison.

Fisher, S., and Gelb, A. (1991). The process of socialist economic transformation. *Journal of Economic Perspective. 5* (4): 91–105.

Fisher, S., Sahay, R. and Vegh, C. A. (1996). Stabilization and growth in transition economies: The early experience. *Journal of Economic Perspectives. 10* (2): 45–66.

Fosler, R. S. (ed.) (1988). *The New Economic Role of American States: Strategies in a Competitive World Economy.* Oxford University Press, Oxford.

Friedman, S. B., and Darragh, A. J. (1988). Economic development. In *The Practice of Local Government Planning,* 2nd ed. (F. S. So and J. Getzels, eds.). ICMA, Washington, D. C., pp. 287–329.

Galenson, W. (ed.) (1985). *Foreign Trade and Investment: Development in the Newly Industrializing Asian Economies.* University of Wisconsin Press, Madison.

Grady, D. O. (1987). State economic development incentives: Why do state compete? *State and Local Government Review. 19* (Fall): 86–94.

Haggard, S. (1990). *Pathways from the Periphery: The Politics of Growth in the Newly Industrializing Countries.* Cornell University Press, Ithaca, N.Y.

Haggard, S., and Webb, S. B. (1993). What do we know about the political economy of economic reform? *The World Bank Research Observer. 8* (2): 143–168.

Ho, S. (1981). South Korea and Taiwan: Development prospects and problems in the 1980s. *Asian Survey, 21:* 1175–1196.

Hy, R. J., and Waugh, W. L., Jr. (1995). *State and Local Tax Policies: A Comparative Handbook.* Greenwood Press, Westport, Conn.

Ihlanfeldt, K. R. (1995). Ten Principles for State Tax Incentives. *Economic Development Quarterly. 9* (4): 339–355.

Johnson, C. (1982). *MITI and the Japanese Miracle.* Stanford University Press, Stanford, Calif.

Karahan, R. S., Lee, J. B., and Akis, S. (1995). Attitudes toward foreign direct investment in the rural United States: The case of Montana. *International Journal of Management, 12*(1): 78–82.

Kaufman, J. L., and Jacobs, H. M. (1987). A public planning perspective on strategic planning. *Journal of the American Planning Association. 53* (Winter): 23–33.

Keating, M. (1998). *Public Management Reform and Economic and Social Development.* OECD, Paris.

Kline, J. M. (1984a). The international economic interests of U.S. states. *Publius. 14* (4): 81–94.

Kline, J. M. (1984b). The expanding international agenda for state governments. *State Government. 57* (1): 2–6.

Kline, J. M. (1983). *State Government Influence in U.S. International Economic Policy.* D.C. Health, Lexington, Mass.

Kudrle, R. T., and Kite, C. M. (1989). The evaluation of state programs for international business development. *Economic Development Quarterly. 3* (4): 288–300.

Levy, J. M. (1990). *Economic Development Programs for Cities, Counties and Towns,* 2nd ed. Praeger, New York.

Liou, K. T. (ed.) (2000a). *Administrative Reform and National Economic Development.* Ashgate Publishing, Aldershot.

Liou, K. T. (2000b). Applying strategic management to economic development: Benefits and challenges. *International Journal of Public Administration 23* (9): 1621–1649.

Liou, K. T. (1999a). Strategies and lessons of China's post-Mao economic development. *Policy Studies Review. 16* (1): 183–208.

Liou, K. T. (1999b). Local economic development financing: Issues and findings. *Journal of Public Budgeting, Accounting, and Financial Management. 11* (3): 387–397.

Liou, K. T. (1998a). The role of government in economic development: The Chinese experience. *International Journal of Public Administration. 21* (9): 1257–1983.

Liou, K. T. (1998b). *Managing Economic Reforms in Post-Mao China.* Praeger, Westport, Conn.

Liou, K. T. (1998c). Strategic planning and economic development: Concepts and issues. *Public Administration Quarterly. 22* (3): 267–276.

Liou, K. T. (1993). Foreign direct investment in the United States: Trends, motives, and the state experience. *American Review of Public Administration. 23* (1): 1–17.

Little, J. S. (1978). Locational decisions of foreign direct investors in the United States. *New England Economic Review.* (July/August): 43–63.

Luger, M. I., and Shetty, S. (1985). Determinants of foreign plant start-ups in the United States: Lessons for policymakers in the Southeast. *Vanderbilt Journal of Transnational Law. 18:* 223–245.

Luke, J. S., and Caiden, G. E. (1989). Coping with global interdependence. In *Handbook of Public Administration* (J. L. Perry, ed.). Jossey-Bass, San Francisco, pp. 83–93.

Luke, J. S., Ventriss, C., Reed, B. J., and Reed, C. M. (1988). *Managing Economic Development: A Guide to State and Local Leadership Strategies.* Jossey-Bass, San Francisco.

Markusen, A., Hall, P., Glasmeier, A. (1987). *High Tech America.* Allen & Unwin, Boston.

McConnell, J. E. (1980). Foreign direct investment in the United States. *Annals of the Association of American Geographers. 70* (2): 259–270.

McGowan, R. P., and Ottensmeyer, E. J. (1993). *Economic Development Strategies for State and Local Governments.* Nelson-Hall, Chicago.

McIntyre, J. R. (1983). The role of state governments as international economic actors. *Southern Review of Public Administration.* (Winter): 465–488.

Miko, C. J., and Weilant, E. (eds.) (1991). *Opinions '90.* Gale Research, New York, p. 15.

Mintzberg, H. (1994). *The Rise and Fall of Strategic Planning.* The Free Press, New York.

Morgan, D. R., and England, R. E. (1996). *Managing Urban America,* 4th ed. Chatham, Chatham House Publishers, Chatham, N.J.

Morrison, D. (1995). *Economic Development: A Strategic Approach for Local Governments.* The International City/County Management Association, Washington, D.C.

National Academy of Public Administration (NAPA) (1996). *A Path to Smarter Economic Development: Reassessing the Federal Role.* Washington, D.C.

Neuse, S. M. (1982). State activities in international trade. *State Government. 55* (2): 57–64.

Noponen, H., Markusen, A., and Driessen, K. (1997). Trade and American cities: Who has the comparative advantage? *Economic Development Quarterly. 11* (1): 67–87.

Osborne, D., and Gaebler, T. (1992). *Reinventing Government.* Addison-Wesley, Reading, Mass.

Pammer, W. J., Jr. (1998). Linking economic development to strategic planning: Issues for community problem-solving. In *Handbook of Economic Development* (K. T. Liou ed.). Marcel Dekker, New York, pp. 239–256.

Phillips, J. M., and Goss, E. P. (1995). The effect of state and local taxes on economic development: A meta-analysis. *Southern Economic Journal. 62* (2): 320–333.

Porter, M. E. (1990). *The Competitive Advantage of Nations.* The Free Press, New York.

Reed, B. J., and Blair, R. (1993). Economic development in rural communities: Can strategic planning make a difference? *Public Administration Review. 53* (3): 88–92.

Reed, C., Reed, B. J., and Luke, J. (1987). Assessing readiness for economic development strategic planning: A community case study. *Journal of the American Planning Association. 53:* 521–530.

Reese, L. A. (1994). The role of counties in local economic development. *Economic Development Quarterly. 8* (1): 28–42.

Reginald, S. (1983). Business said to have barred new plants in largely black communities. *New York Times.* February 15.

Robinson-Barnes, C. J., and Waugh, W. L., Jr. (1998). The logic and pathologies of local and regional economic development strategies. In *Handbook of Economic Development* (K. T. Liou, ed.). Marcel Dekker, New York, pp. 215–228.

Rondinelli, D. A., and Montgomery, J. D. (1990). Managing economic reform: An alternative perspective on structural adjustment policies. *Policy Sciences. 23:* 73–93.

Rubin, H. J. (1998). Partnering with the poor: Why local governments should work with community-based development organizations to promote economic development. In *Handbook of Economic Development* (K. T. Liou, ed.). Marcel Dekker, New York, pp. 301–322.

Smith, T. R., and Fox, W. F. (1990). Economic development programs for states in the 1990s. *Economic Review.* (July/August): 25–35.

Sokoya, S. K., and Tillery, K. R. (1992). Motives of foreign MNCs investing in the United States and effect of company characteristics. *The International Executive. 34* (1): 65–80.

Sorkin, D. L., Ferris, N. B., and Hudak, J. (1984). *Strategies for Cities and Counties: A Strategic Planning Guide.* Public Technology, Washington, D.C.

Stern, N. (1991). Public policy and the economics of development. *European Economic Review. 35* (2/3): 241–254.

Streib, G. (1992). Applying strategic decision making in local government. *Public Productivity and Management Review. 15:* 341–354.

Tolchin, M., and Tolchin, S. (1988). *Buying into America: How Foreign Money Is Changing the Face of Our Nation.* Times Books, New York.

Wade, R. (1992). East Asia's economic success: Conflicting perspectives, partial insights, shaky evidence. *World Politics. 44:* 270–320.

Wade, R. (1990). *Governing the Market: Economic Theory and the Role of Government in East Asian Industrialization.* Princeton University Press, Princeton, N.J.

Waits, M. J. (1998). Economic development strategies in the American states. In *Handbook of Economic Development* (K. T. Liou, ed.). Marcel Dekker, New York, pp. 183–213.

Waugh, W. L., Jr. and Waugh, D. M. (1990). The political economy of seduction: Promoting business relocation and economic development in nonindustrial states. In *Public Policy and Economic Institutions* (M. J. Dubnick and A. Gitelson, eds.). JAI Press, Greenwood, Conn.

Wolman, H., and Spitzley, D. (1996). The politics of local economic development. *Economic Development Quarterly. 10* (2): 115–150.

Woodward, D. P. (1992). Locational determinants of Japanese manufacturing start-ups in the United States. *Southern Economic Journal. 58* (3): 690–708.

World Bank (1993). *The East Asian Miracle: Economic Growth and Public Policy.* Oxford University Press.

20

Deregulation Policy and Public Management

John P. Tuman, John Hindera,
Danielle Roth-Johnson
Department of Political Science, Texas Tech University, Lubbock, Texas

Since the mid-1970s, policymakers in the United States have embraced the concept of deregulation. Hoping to spur competition and increase efficiency, the federal government has dismantled economic regulations[1] in airlines, telecommunications, trucking, banking, and utilities (Quirk, 1990; Krause, 1994; Glasberg et al., 1998). Although federal authorities have taken the lead in the area of economic regulatory reform, state and local governments have been active as well. Toward that end, states have deregulated[2] land use, education, and utilities. In comparative terms, the U.S. commitment to economic deregulation has been far more extensive than that in nearly every other industrialized country (Vogel, 1996; Daugbjerg, 1997).

The shift toward economic deregulation has been paralleled by efforts to reform the public service. In 1989, the Volcker commission recommended that the federal government deregulate personnel and compensation rules, introduce merit-based incentives for employees, and give supervisors more flexibility in management decisions. Formed in the early 1990s, the Winter commission and Vice President Gore's National Performance Review echoed many of the concerns raised by the Volcker commission, while calling for broader reforms in federal and state government. For their part, state and local governments have also shown strong interest in deregulating the public service. Subnational governments throughout the United States have focused primarily on privatization, although some state legislatures also express a desire to deregulate personnel rules (DiIulio, 1994:3; Fuhrman and Elmore, 1995; Neemec, 1997; GAO, 1998).

The Federal government and states are also reforming the basic framework of social regulation. In the area of environmental policy, for example, federal and state authorities are increasingly relying upon market-based incentives to facilitate compliance with environmental standards. In addition, policymakers are redesigning regulations to promote industry self-reporting and to replace strict standards with rules that are more flexible. Governments have incorporated similar concepts in several other areas of social regulation, including health and safety regulations in the workplace.

Deregulation of the public service has important implications for public management. Reform may lead to the elimination of some roles for public agencies. However, even in a liberalized economic environment, there is an ongoing need for agencies to fulfill certain types of functions. Vendors who subcontract for the provision of public goods must still be monitored by public agencies to ensure quality and efficiency. Similarly, the use of market-based solutions to reduce emissions will not obviate the need for government action as much as it requires changes in the functions of the agencies that protect the environment.

Although there is significant debate about reform, the effects of deregulation on public management are not well understood. The recent policy literature has focused almost exclusively on the economic impact of deregulation. By contrast, comparatively less attention has been given to the relationship between deregulation and public administration.[3] In this chapter, we seek to this fill this gap in the literature. In what follows, we explore the implications of deregulation for public management, focusing primarily on the federal level. The first section examines administrative deregulation. In this section, we analyze the different paths to administrative reform, contrasting regulatory reform in certain areas with privatization. Next, we look at recent efforts to reform social regulation, focusing on environmental policy. In the Conclusion, we discuss the broader implications of deregulation.

ADMINISTRATIVE DEREGULATION

The Evolution of Administrative Regulations: An Overview

Regulation in the federal bureaucracy springs from a number of different sources. Some agencies have created their own internal regulations. For example, standard operating procedures (SOPs) are now widely used in public organizations as a means of standardizing and regulating decision-making processes within the agency. These rules help to maintain consistency and accountability. On the other hand, some claim that SOPs reduce innovation and limit the capacity of agencies to adjust rapidly to changes in their internal and external environments.

Many regulations emanate from organizations that are external to bureaucracy. In an effort to address public concerns over the accountability of bureaucracy, the Congress has generated a large share of administrative regulations. Ethics, civil service, and procurement laws have had a large impact on employment relations and government purchasing throughout the public sector (Burke, 1994: 64–65; Horner, 1994: 88–90). In addition, when the Congress formulates laws, it often includes agency mandates that are lengthy, detailed, and intended to reduce the discretionary power exercised by agency staff (Garvey and DiIulio, 1994).

Although the role played by courts has varied over time, judicial review of administrative decision making has grown in recent years. This has stemmed, in part, from laws that require federal agencies to use decision-making criteria patterned on legal procedures. Historically, judicial oversight also grew in response to the increase in administrative decision making, particularly in the domains of social policy and environmental regulation. As one step in ensuring that agency decisions were fair and within the scope provided for by relevant statutes, judges began reviewing administrative decision making, ultimately producing a new body of administrative law and regulation.

Unions representing public employees have also been important external sources of regulation. In 1998, nearly 40 percent of all federal employees were covered by collective bargaining agreements negotiated by public sector unions (Table 1). The rate of coverage is somewhat higher among state and local government employees (Bureau of Labor Statistics, 1999: Table 3). Because wage determination and employment at the federal level are excluded from the scope of col-

TABLE 1 Public Sector Unionization, Federal Level 1997–1998

	1997	1998
Total employment:	3,217,000	3,269,000
Total union members[a]:	1,030,000	1,105,000
Percent of total employed:	32%	33.8%
Total represented by unions[b]:	1,266,000	1,299,000
Percent of total employed:	39.4%	39.7%

[a]The data refer to members of a union or an employee association similar to a union.
[b]The data refer to members of a labor union or an employee association similar to a union as well as workers not affiliated to a union but whose jobs are covered by collective bargaining.
Source: Bureau of Labor Statistics (1999: table 3).

lective bargaining (Mills, 1994: 308), public sector unions have focused on technology, performance evaluation, and grievance resolution. Unions have also lobbied the Congress for the maintenance of regulations concerning personnel, budgets, agency missions, and employment levels (AFGE, 1999a).[4] To the extent that these laws remain intact, managers have difficulty linking compensation to job performance.

Unions have also lobbied to maintain rules that impose layoffs or staff reductions on employees with less service (Garvey and DiIulio, 1994:23). The frequently cited problem here is that managers are forced to impose layoffs on workers who are more efficient in favor of more senior employees whose performance is questionable. Because public unions openly support seniority rules, managers often view organized labor as an obstacle to the achievement of higher performance.[5]

Reforming Public Service

Many analysts have called for sweeping reform of the federal bureaucracy, including extensive privatization of services. Advocates of the midrange approach argue for regulatory reform in certain areas. In this section, we contrast both alternatives. The section on regulatory reform focuses on two areas that have been singled out in much of the literature: procurement policies and employment relations.

Regulatory Reform: Federal Procurement Policies

The federal government spends hundreds of billions of dollars annually on goods and services procured from private vendors. Created in 1974 and housed in the Office of Management and Budget (OMB), the Office of Federal Procurement Policy (OFPP) is charged with the responsibility of implementing procurement regulations for all executive agencies. The OFPP implements the Federal Acquisition Regulations System (FAR), which "is established for the codification and publication of uniform policies and procedures for acquisition by all executive agencies." (FAR, 1999: Subpart 1.011). These regulations, along with the occasional OFPP Policy Letters, have a large impact on government purchasing practices.

A number of policy goals are incorporated into the FAR. These include paying lowest price for high-quality goods and services; reducing the threat of corruption; creating an open, fair, and competitive process for bidders; and satisfying certain equity considerations and promoting social values.[6]

Critics of the federal procurement process have raised a number of objections to the current regulatory regime. Of these criticisms, two issues stand out. First, the FAR and other procurement regulations promulgated for specific agencies are extremely long and complex. Even though contracting and acquisitions personnel may receive training through their agencies and the Federal Acquisition Institute, the time and resources that staff must invest in remaining up-to-date in acquisitions rules are, in fact, considerable.[7]

Second, the current process does not specify clear guidelines for evaluating the past performance of vendors. A 1992 OFPP Policy Letter directs agencies to take past performance into account.[8] Similarly, subsection 1.102-2(3) of the 1999 FAR states, "When selecting contractors to provide products or perform services, the Government will use contractors who have a track record of successful past performance or who demonstrate a current superior ability to perform." Despite placing emphasis on past performance, however, the FAR does not indicate what, exactly, constitutes *adequate* past performance. Nor do the regulations state how past performance of vendors should be weighed against other criteria for selection (of which there are many). In this context, managers have expressed concerns that the evaluation of performance process will become subjective and inconsistent (Kelman, 1994:125).

Some analysts have argued that the procurement process could be simplified considerably. Kelman (1994), for example, advocates a system that would permit selected offices to experiment with elimination of procurement rules. Under this proposal, a multimember evaluation committee would make procurement decisions and provide a written justification for their selection of one bidder over others. All decisions would become part of the public record. Presumably, this system would make corruption more difficult (by using multimember boards) and also raise efficiency. In addition, a common rating system could be incorporated into the procurement process.

Regulatory Reform: Employment Relations in the Federal Bureaucracy

The U.S. Office of Personnel Management (OPM), along with the U.S. OMB and the Equal Employment Opportunity Commission (EEOC), administer a large body of regulation that has a significant impact on employment relations in the federal bureaucracy. One area singled out for reform is deregulation of the public employment relationship. As noted, some analysts have argued that deregulation of the public workplace could result in substantial gains in efficiency and quality of service delivery.

The hypothesized effects of employment regulation in the federal bureaucracy are straightforward. First, the General Schedule (GS) and other civil service regulations undermine the use of compensation as a mechanism to improve performance. Managers are unable to establish a salary structure that would allow them to recruit and retain talented employees.[9] Supervisors are generally prohibited from using contingent compensation to reward employees who exhibit superior performance (Horner, 1994). Second, as noted, public managers also have too little discretion over hiring, promotion, and discipline. Particularly in the area of promotion and retention, civil service regulations protect the seniority rights of employees, regardless of their performance.

The empirical evidence regarding the effects of employment regulation on performance is not conclusive.[10] It is beyond the scope of this chapter to assess the evidence. However, as Klingner (1996) has argued, the new management paradigm—which is widely shared within the public sector—assumes that the personnel regulations do, in fact, limit the performance of public agencies. Yet despite pressure for change in employment regulations at the federal level, the majority of employment regulations remain extant.

The absence of deregulation does not mean that the public workplace has been isolated from broader changes occurring in U.S. employment relations. There are strong indications that managers at all levels of government have been given more freedom to create a "flexible" work force. In particular, managers increasingly are given authority to meet staffing requirements through the use of employees not covered by civil service regulations (e.g., "exempt" positions), while also increasing use of temporary employees and outside contractors (U.S. Merit Systems Protection Board, 1994; Klingner, 1996). Some estimates suggest that the number of subcontracted employees working for federal projects is more than twice the size of the federal work force.[11] In addition, the use of flexible workers gives managers latitude to tie compensation to performance.

The growth in temporary and "contingent" employment in the public sector has significant implications for performance. Many agencies have probably experienced some productivity gains and cost reductions by using a more flexible work force. These benefits may be relatively short-lived, however. In the first place, permanent employees often feel threatened by the growth in subcontracting, temporary employees, and other flexible work arrangements. This, coupled with the generally negative rhetoric about the public sector, may have an adverse impact on morale levels and productivity of the permanent work force. Second, in those cases in which temporary jobs have filled gaps created by staff reductions of permanent positions, the long-run costs to the organization may, in fact, be higher. Managers who survive downsizing bear the burden of training. This burden often increases if there is a large turnover in the temporary work pool. Moreover, as the size of the permanent staff declines, the remaining employees and mid-to upper-level managers may suffer from gaps in their knowledge of agency mission and other issues, ultimately creating inefficiencies at the agency level (Peters and Savoie, 1994).

A more comprehensive approach might aim to raise efficiency through changes in the content of some employment regulations. This strategy would involve linkage between outcomes (collective or individual performance) and compensation, while making concessions to unions and employees in the area of employment and conflict resolution. The starting point for such a strategy is the recognition that reforms negotiated with (and supported by) unions and employee associations are more likely to be implemented successfully than reforms implemented unilaterally by managers (Argyris and Schon, 1996; Worley et al., 1996).

Under what conditions would unions and employees support change? Although public unions are often viewed as obstacles to reform, organized labor appears willing to give political endorsement to some changes in employment regulations. For example, public unions support giving employees more training and authority so that they can raise efficiency and service. They also, in principle, seem willing to accept a flattened hierarchy, the use of broader job descriptions, and some merit-based incentives. In exchange, they would like the government to reduce subcontracting, maintain employment security and seniority rights, and increase training (see AFGE, 1999b, 1999c; AFSCME 1999b). These proposals are not entirely dissimilar to labor-management initiatives that have raised performance in the private sector.[12] What this suggests, then, is that it is possible to transform the public workplace through negotiated changes without a full-scale deregulation of employment relations.

Privatization

As a mechanism for reforming the public service, privatization represents the most radical choice available to policymakers. In recent years, the federal government has considered privatization. To date, privatization at the federal level has been limited. However, state and local governments have been more active, using privatization in corrections, social services, higher education, and transportation (Council of State Governments, 1997: 1). Proponents of privatization suggest that many of the inefficiencies created by administrative regulation of the public workplace can be prevented completely through the privatization of some parts of the public service delivery. The mode of privatization open to governments, however, plainly varies (see Stein, 1990). Some governments may choose to contract out services to a single private vendor; others may opt for divestiture or managed competition to accomplish their goals (Stein, 1990: 76–79; General Accounting Office, 1998).

The regulatory and legal environments in place at the timing of privatization have been important factors shaping implementation. For example, provisions in intergovernmental support agreements between states and localities (or between the federal government and states) may constrain the ability of governments to change service providers. Similarly, affirmative action laws tend to restrict the pool of eligible vendors. Policymakers might also be constrained by collective bargaining agreements if privatization entails staff reductions in a unionized workplace.

The experience of U.S. states and foreign governments indicates that building political support for privatization is necessary from the outset of the process (Wellenius and Stern, 1994: 45–46; General Accounting Office, 1998). Building such support is complicated by the fact that the potential beneficiaries of privatization (e.g., consumers) represent a large, dispersed, and often unorganized group. However, the interests potentially opposed to reform—such as unions, workers, and even public managers—tend to be in smaller, well-organized groups that can be mobilized into collective action.[13] Mitigating resistance to reform is therefore not only desirable but also necessary. For both unionized and nonunionized workplaces, policies that address work force transition issues can certainly help to build support for privatization. These may include, for example, agreements that permit collective bargaining to continue after the unit has been transferred to private management; agreements that guarantee employment levels will not be reduced dramatically through privatization; and retraining and adjustment services for workers who lose their jobs (Wellenius and Stern, 1994: 45–46; General Accounting Office, 1998; Tuman, 1999).

Regardless of mode of reform chosen by policymakers, the implementation of privatization may paradoxically lead to "reregulation" or new forms of regulatory activity (Vogel, 1996: 2–3). To ensure the efficient delivery of high-quality services, administrators must collect data on costs and quality, monitor compliance with service agreements and regulations, and review customer complaints.[14] Monitoring may be necessary to guarantee that savings from privatization are measured and used appropriately on deficit reduction, tax relief, or service improvements. Regular performance evaluations send a clear signal that vendors must correct deficiencies—but such monitoring and enforcement activities require adequate resources that may not be available to public agencies.

Depending on the type of privatization plan implemented, governments often find that service markets must be regulated to promote competition. For example, if there is a monopoly or oligopoly in local service markets, governments may have to lessen the entry barriers for new firms. Once again, however, the challenge for policymakers is to find adequate resources to subsidize start-up and other costs.

REFORMING SOCIAL REGULATIONS: A FOCUS ON ENVIRONMENTAL POLICY

Environmental Regulation: An Overview

Since the early 1970s, the federal government has approved many new social regulations.[15] These rules encompass a number of different policy domains; environmental regulation, in particular, has assumed increased importance within the broad set of social regulations.

The justification for environmental regulations stems from economic theories that conceive of pollution as an "externality" (Coase, 1960). The concept of externalities focuses attention on the incentive structure of firms to deal with pollution in private markets. Firms create pollution while they produce goods and services, but they do not sell pollution in the marketplace. Therefore, if firms are assumed to behave as income maximizers, they have no incentive to address pollution; in the absence of regulation, they will move to "externalize" the costs of pollution on society. Through the threat of fines and other sanctions, government regulation can transform the incentive structure in private markets, making pollution a potentially costly activity that can reduce the income of the firm.[16]

Although the concept of externalities provides an important justification for government action to protect the environment, regulation has also grown as a result of public concern about environmental degradation. Popularized by such books as Rachel Carson's *The Silent Spring,*[17] as well as by media coverage of toxic waste dumps, water pollution, and other problems, the environment has come to occupy an important place in the consciousness of the American electorate. Indeed, public opinion surveys indicate that although the proportion of respondents "somewhat satisfied" with environmental protection increased between 1993 and 1999, up to two-thirds remain "extremely concerned" about safe drinking water and other environmental problems (Gallup Organization, 1999). Significantly, of those surveyed in 1999, 67 percent stated that they would prefer to protect the environment even if it meant reducing economic growth (Gallup Organization, 1999).[18] Given public concern over pollution, policymakers recognize the ongoing need for environmental protection, while disagreeing about the specific mechanisms used to clean up the environment.

Deregulation and Environmental Policy

Throughout the 1980s and early 1990s, federal environmental policy emphasized the importance of direct regulation of polluters, achieved principally through monitoring and enforcement of environmental standards. Although the Environmental Protection Agency (EPA) rarely enforced the most severe penalties provided for in the law, environmental regulations have drawn much attention, both in the popular press and in policy circles. The criticisms of the EPA's traditional "command and control" approach to environmental regulation are by now well known. Some analysts emphasize the effects of strict environmental standards on the competitiveness of industry and on the price of consumer goods (e.g., Weidenbaum, 1992). Others have suggested that the standards established by EPA are too inflexible and are difficult to implement, let alone to achieve. While acknowledging positive effects of environmental regulations, Gunningham and Grabosky (1999: 7) argue that it is not always technically feasible to enforce the standards associated with the traditional approach to regulation.

The Clinton administration has taken steps to reform environmental regulations. One initiative seeks to expand a program that allows companies to trade pollution rights, particularly in the area of open-air emissions (Clinton, 1995; EPA, 1998). First adopted in the 1990 amendments to the Clean Air Act, this program permits companies that exceed mandated reductions in emissions to sell emission rights to other companies. States that adopt the federal model receive automatic EPA approval; companies that participate may assume increased responsibility for tracking of emissions and compliance. Presumably, then, this program creates market-based incentives to reduce pollution, while decreasing the costs to federal authorities of monitoring and enforcement.

A second approach is to give industries more flexibility to meet environmental standards, along with reducing paperwork and streamlining the process of monitoring and compliance. By 1998, for example, the EPA had already eliminated over 1000 regulations that were deemed obsolete. The agency was also encouraging partnerships with states to allow industries to report through Internet services, thereby reducing costs and time. Beyond these initiatives, regulatory flexibility has also involved allowing industries more time to comply with existing standards if they agree to invest in pollution abatement technologies and exceed federal emission standards in the future (EPA, 1998). At the same time, EPA is now working with stakeholders—including state governments, industries, and labor and environmental organizations—to explore different approaches to achieve a continuous reduction in pollution.[19]

Deregulation is affecting the role and function of the EPA in significant ways. Under the new guidelines, the primary responsibility of the EPA's regional field staff has shifted away from monitoring to providing assistance and information on compliance to regulated industries. In addition, industry now plays a more important role in the process of regulation. First, the officials who promulgate regulations now consult industry and state government representatives at a much earlier stage in the process of writing new rules (EPA, 1998). Second, EPA is now seeking to promote more "consensus-based rulemaking" by engaging in negotiations with industries over specific rules.

Environmental policy deregulation has generated debate. Supporters argue that regulatory flexibility and market incentives will actually increase industry compliance with pollution regulations, while permitting the government to strike a balance between economic growth and environmental protection. Critics of deregulation point out that pollution trading and other market-oriented incentives allow emissions to continue at high levels in some areas, with serious consequences for public health. In addition, there is concern that by emphasizing negotiation and consultation with industry, the EPA's policy will lead to the "capture" of the field staff by the industries they are supposed to be regulating. The effects of capture, although varied, include the possibility that regulations and enforcement activities will increasingly reflect the priorities of corporate actors.

CONCLUSION

Deregulation enjoys support in a variety of different policy circles. Despite this, the degree of deregulation at the federal level has clearly varied. As noted, very little progress has been made in the area of administrative deregulation. By contrast, the Clinton administration has reformed many social regulations, including environmental policies. The reasons for this outcome are unclear. Future studies should attempt to explain the variation in reform in administrative and social regulations.

Although many analysts have argued for a comprehensive deregulation of the federal bureaucracy, the results of this analysis suggest that selected reforms might be more appropriate, and then only in certain areas. The most prominent areas that might benefit from reform include federal procurement and employment relations in the federal bureaucracy. We have suggested that changes in employment relations, in particular, should be negotiated with unions (where they exist) and implemented with the active support of employees. The same applies to privatization, which represents the most radical path toward transforming the public service.

A broader implication concerns the relationship between deregulation and organizational capture. Policies that foster negotiation between regulators and industry can help to promote better regulatory compliance. Nevertheless, deregulation programs that allow industry unchecked access to the processes of rule making, monitoring, and enforcement may lead to the capture of field staff and officials at higher levels in public organizations. This is not an intractable problem. Nevertheless, reformers who seek to extend the EPA model to other areas of social regulation need to develop procedures to check organizational capture.

NOTES

1. In the political science and economics literature, regulation is often defined as a set of laws and rules placed by government on citizens, firms, or government itself. Regulation generally falls into three categories (OECD, 1998): (1) *social regulation,* which is designed to promote workplace safety, health, and environmental protection, or equity, or civil rights; (2) *economic regulation,* intended to influence competition in the marketplace, entry (or exit) for firms, and pricing; and (3) *administrative regulation,* rules governing employment, procurement, budgeting, monitoring, and information collection. The focus of this chapter is on administrative regulation.
2. We follow Wilson's (1994: 45) definition of agency deregulation: "Deregulation means allowing public agencies to operate in a regime where, to the greatest extent possible, they are judged by outcomes (what they achieve) and not inputs (who they hire, where they operate, and how they negotiate contracts)." As noted later, the key question is *how* governments might create a regime in which public agencies are judged by outcomes.
3. For exceptions to this trend, see the essays in DiIulio (1994).
4. The American Federation of State, County and Municipal Employees (AFSCME) has also pursued an active legislative agenda at the federal, state, and local levels. See AFSCME (1999a).
5. As noted later, this view ignores that fact that there is sufficient "space" for compromise among public unions, agency managers, and legislators.
6. Recent efforts include policies promoting use of environmentally sound and energy-efficient producers and small businesses (including businesses owned by historically

disadvantaged groups). See Office of Federal Procurement Policy, Policy Letter No. 92-04 (November 2, 1992), and Policy Letter No. 95-01 (October 28, 1995). For a general overview, see also Kelman (1994).

7. The importance of continuous training and minimal education requirements is recognized in Office of Federal Procurement Policy, Policy Letter 97-01 (September 12, 1997), which established specific tasks for the Federal Acquisition Institute and implemented a number of mechanisms to improve the training and skills base of acquisitions personnel.
8. See Office of Federal Procurement Policy, Policy Letter No. 92-05 (November 30, 1992).
9. Horner (1994: 88) suggests that the Federal Employees Pay Comparability Act (1990) gave managers limited discretion to use bonuses to recruit and retain employees in some limited circumstances. More recent efforts at "broad-banding" have also had a minor impact, while leaving the underlying regulatory framework intact.
10. The evidence adduced in many studies is far from conclusive. See, for example, Cohen and Eimicke (1994); Perry, Wise, and Martin 1994; Horner (1994).
11. Estimate by Paul Light, Brookings Institute, as cited in AFGE (1999c).
12. In recent years, private sector unions have agreed to contingent compensation and the use of work teams in exchange for guarantees that firms will maintain investment, employment stability, and seniority rights (Tuman, 2000). Firms that have followed this trajectory have experienced modest gains in productivity.

    To be sure, there are important differences between public and private sector unions. Whereas private sector unions can ratify changes through collective bargaining agreements, public unions (at the federal level) would have to support legislation making statutory reforms. In both sectors, however, unions strive largely for the same goal: maximizing wages, subject to an employment constraint. Therefore, the underlying logic of compromise is similar for unions, regardless of whether they are located in the private or public sector.
13. Group support for privatization is a necessary, but not sufficient condition for change. As Quirk (1990) has noted, the ideology of individual legislators is another factor that has shaped deregulation efforts in the United States.
14. The assumption that private firms are naturally more efficient than public agencies is open to question (Goodsell, 1994). The fragmentary evidence indicates that some private contractors have been plagued with problems of mismanagement, abuse, and even billing of federal and local authorities for services that were not rendered. For examples, see Klingner (1996).
15. For a definition of social regulation, see note 1.
16. Coase suggests that private parties may move to address externalities if cooperation is not hampered by high transaction costs and if property rights are well defined. As one can see, the transaction costs of identifying the parties directly (or indirectly) involved in pollution are potentially high, making it an unsuitable candidate for private solutions.
17. For an exploration of the impact of Carson's writings on the environmental movement, see Marco, Hollingworth, and Durham (1987) and Hynes (1989).
18. The willingness of the public to accept some economic costs in exchange for environmental protection has been consistent over time. Since the Gallup Organization

first asked the question in 1984, over two-thirds have consistently stated that they wanted a clean environment even if it meant accepting less economic growth. In addition, well over half of Republicans and Democrats in 1999 identified themselves as being "environmentalists."

19. This approach has found support in the scholarly literature on environmental policy. For example, Gunningham and Grabosky (1999) argue that policymakers ought to combine traditional regulations with market incentives to improve environmental performance. In their view, public officials should recognize that various stakeholders—including financial organizations, and environmental and consumer groups—can play an important role in pressuring corporations to reduce emissions. Importantly, they also suggest that the specific mix of policy mechanisms employed to control pollution should vary by industry. In some industries, it is appropriate to rely mainly on traditional regulations; in others policymakers can use market incentives and pressure from environmental interest groups to achieve a reduction in emissions.

REFERENCES

American Federation of Government Employees (AFGE). (1999a). Position Papers. Washington, D.C.

American Federation of Government Employees (AFGE) (1999b). Contracting Out. Washington, D.C.

American Federation of Government Employees (AFGE) (1999c). Federal Pay—General Schedule Position Paper. Washington, D.C.

American Federation of State, County and Municipal Employees (AFSCME) (1999a). Legislative Agenda. Washington, D.C.

American Federation of State, County and Municipal Employees (AFSCME) (1999b). Of the People, by the People, for the People: How to Make Government Work Better and More Efficiently. Washington, D.C.

Argyris, Chris, and Schon, Donald A. (1996). *Organizational Learning.* II. *Theory, Method and Practice.* Addison-Wesley, Reading, Mass.

Bureau of Labor Statistics, U.S. Department of Labor (1999). Table 3: Union affiliation of employed wage and salary workers by occupation and industry. [http://stats.bls.gov/newsrels.htm].

Burke, John P. (1994). The ethics of deregulation—Or the deregulation of ethics? In *Deregulating the Public Service: Can Government Be Improved?* (J. J. DiIulio ed.). The Brookings Institute, Washington D.C., pp. 62–84.

Carson, Rachel (1962). *The Silent Spring.* Fawcett, Greenwich, Conn.

Clinton, William (1995). State of the union address. Reinventing environmental regulation. January 25, 1995. [http://es.epa.gov/program/exec/environ.html#over.]

Coase, Ronald H. (1960). The problem of social cost. *Journal of Law and Economics. 3:* 1–44.

Cohen, Steven, and Eimicke, William (1994). The overregulated civil service. *Review of Public Personnel Administration. 14*(2): 10–27.

Council of State Governments (1997). *Private Practices: A Review of Privatization in State Government.* Council of State Governments, Lexington, KY.

Daugbjerg, C. (1997). Policy networks and agricultural policy reforms: Explaining deregulation in Sweeden and re-regulation in the european community. *Governance. 10*(2): 123–140.

DiIulio, John J., ed. (1994). *Deregulating the Public Service: Can Government Be Improved?* The Brookings Institution, Washington, D.C.

Environmental Protection Agency (1998). Statement of Regulatory and Deregulatory Priorities. Washington, D.C.

Federal Acquisition Regulations System (FAR) (1999). Including amendments through August 31, 1999.

Fuhrman, Susan H., and Elmore, Richard F. (1995). The evolution of deregulation in state education policy. *Teachers College Record. 97*(2): 279.

The Gallup Organization (1999). Environmental concern wanes in 1999 Earth Day poll: Americans still care, but more likely to see progress. [http://www.gallup.com/poll/releases/pr990422.asp].

Garvey, Gerald J., and DiIulio, John J. (1994). Sources of public service overregulation. In *Deregulating the Public Service: Can Government Be Improved?* (J. J. DiIulio, ed.). The Brookings Institute, Washington, D.C., pp 12–36.

General Accounting Office (1988). *Privatization: Questions State and Local Decisionmakers Used When Considering Privatization Options.* General Accounting Office, Washington, D.C., Report No. GAO/GGD-98-87.

Glasberg, Davita Silfen, Skidmore, Dan, and Akard, Patrick (1998). Corporate welfare policy and the welfare state: Bank deregulation and the savings and loan bailout. *American Journal of Sociology. 103*(5): 1453–1462.

Goodsell, Charles T. (1994). *The Case for Bureaucracy: A Public Administration Polemic.* Chatham House, Chatham, N.J.

Gunningham, Neil, and Grabosky, Peter (1999). *Smart Regulation: Designing Environmental Policy.* Oxford University Press, New York.

Horner, Constance (1994). Deregulating the federal service: Is the time right? In *Deregulating the Public Service: Can Government Be Improved?* (J. J. DiIulio, ed.). The Brookings Institute, Washington, D.C., pp. 85–101.

Hynes, H. Patricia (1989). *The Recurring Silent Spring.* Pergamon Press, New York.

Kelman, Steven (1994). Deregulating federal procurement. In *Deregulating the Public Service: Can Government Be Involved?* (J. J. DiIulio, ed.). The Brookings Institute, Washington, D.C., pp. 102–128.

Klingner, Donald E. (1996). Beyond civil service: The politics of the emergent paradigm. Unpublished paper. College of Urban and Public Affairs, Florida International University, Miami.

Krause, George A. (1994). Economics, politics, and policy change: Examining the consequences of deregulation in the banking industry. *American Politics Quarterly. 22*(2): 221–243.

Marco, Gino, Hollingworth, Robert M., and Durham, William, (eds.) (1987). *Silent Spring Revisited.* American Chemical Society, Washington, D.C.

Mills, Daniel Quinn (1994). *Labor-Management Relations,* 5th ed. McGraw-Hill, New York.

Neemec, Richard (1997). Electricity deregulation and the municipals. *California Journal. 28*(2): 4.

OECD (1998). *Report on Regulatory Reform.* Paris.

Perry, James, Wise, Lois R., and Martin, Margo (1994). Breaking the civil service mold." *Review of Public Personnel Administration. 14*(2): 40–54.

Peters, B. Guy, and Savoie, Donald J. (1994). Civil service reform: Misdiagnosing the patient. *Public Administration Review.* September/October: 418–425.

Quirk, Paul J. (1990). Deregulation and the politics of ideas in congress, In *Beyond Self-Interest* (J. J. Mansbridge, ed.). University of Chicago Press, Chicago, pp. 183–206.

Stein, Lana (1994). Personnel rules and reform in an unreformed setting. *Review of Public Personnel Administration. XIV*(2): 55–60.

Stein, Robert (1990). *Urban Alternatives: Public and Private Markets in the Provision of Public Services.* University of Pittsburgh Press, Pittsburgh.

Stigler, G. J. (1971). The theory of economic regulation. *Bell Journal of Economic Management 2*(1).

Tuman, John P. (1999). Organized labor and the politics of telecommunications privatization: A comparative analysis of Argentina and Mexico. Paper presented at the Annual Meeting of the Southwestern Political Science Association. San Antonio, March.

Tuman, John P. (2000). Government labor policy, wage bargaining, and productivity in the North American Automobile industry: A comparative analysis. In *The North American Auto Industry Study* (Sidney Weintraub and Chris Sands, eds.). Center for Strategic and International Studies, Washington, D.C.

U.S. Merit Systems Protection Board (1994). *Temporary Federal Employment: In Search of Flexibility and Fairness.* Government Printing Office, Washington, D.C.

Vogel, Steven K. (1996). *Freer Markets, More Rules: Regulatory Reform in Advanced Industrial Countries.* Cornell University Press, Ithaca, N.Y. and London.

Weidenbaum, Murray (1992). Return of the 'R' word: The regulatory assault on the economy. *Policy Review. 5:* 40–43.

Wellenius, Björn, and Stern, Peter A. (1994). Implementing reforms in the telecommunications sector: Background, overview, and lessons. In *Implementing Reforms in the Telecommunications Sector* (Björn Wellenius and Peter A. Stern, eds.). The World Bank, Washington, D.C., pp. 1–64.

Wilson, James Q. (1994). Can the bureaucracy be deregulated? Lessons from government agencies. In *Deregulating the Public Service: Can Government Be Improved?* (J. J. Dilulio, ed.). The Brookings Institute, Washington, D.C., pp. 37–61.

Worley, Christopher G., Hitchins, David E., and Ross, Walter L. (1996). *Integrated Strategic Change: How OD Builds Competitive Advantage.* Addison-Wesley, Reading, Mass.

21

Looking Back, Looking Forward: What Did Reinvention Do?

Patricia W. Ingraham and
Donald P. Moynihan
Department of Public Administration,
Syracuse University, Syracuse, New York

The longest-running reform effort of the U.S. federal government defies easy summary. The reinvention movement,[1] like the government it addresses, is a sprawling and cluttered phenomenon, full of ideas and suggestions but apparently without a coherent or unified vision. This chapter considers the way in which this movement evolved, its successes, and its shortcomings.

What becomes apparent in considering the history of reinvention is that public sector reform is inextricably tied to politics. This is true throughout the reform process: in the design and packaging of ideas, in the "selling" of the ideas to political constituencies, in the "buying" (or not) of these ideas, in the implementation of these ideas and in the criteria used for judging their success. The movement has struggled to establish a solid legislative base for its reforms, relying to a great extent on nonlegislative action and ultimately on the willingness of federal workers to absorb its ideas. The inescapable union between reform of the government and politics is a constant theme throughout this chapter and shall be highlighted in the first section, which offers an account of the evolution of reinvention.

A consistent thematic keynote for reinvention has been the artificial simulation of private sector conditions and outcomes. A host of public administration scholars have worked to emphasize that government is different, and economists have provided support to this claim, largely emphasizing the more negative aspects of bureaucratic structure and behavior.[2] Reinventors have accepted the proposition of difference, and their solution has been to reduce the "difference" factor as much as possible, trying to simulate private sector–like environment. The urge to create private sector–like conditions for public organizations runs through many of the staples of the reinvention toolbox: customer service, downsizing, performance-based organizations (PBOs), decentralized operations, measurable goals, and empowered workers. With many of these efforts, reinvention has encountered inherently nonprivate dilemmas. Private-sector organizations, according to the conventional wisdom, have the marketplace to provide a guiding framework for their decisions, defining a clear link between the goal of the organization and the associated methods. Reinvention efforts have illustrated that this linkage may be disjointed in the public setting. This can be seen when discussing downsizing and customer service, two of the National Performance Review's (NPR's) clearest successes. Questions arise about the nonstrategic and largely political nature of the downsizing, and the dilemma between prioritizing government service to a customer as opposed to a citizen.

Despite the apparent success of reinvention in some areas, it has struggled to establish a basis by which its efforts, or the efforts of individual government agencies, may be judged. Different measures of reinvention success are considered: the levels of trust in government, the satisfaction of government employees, and the acceptance of specific measures of outcomes and outputs. It is clear that no single measure captures the ability to govern, and it may be argued that a more balanced approach will need to be more than the sum of the evaluation criteria mentioned.

If the reinvention movement has relied on the power of rhetoric, that does not deny the fact that it has in many ways proved itself an effective learner capable of developing and refining the direction of reform. Despite the achievements of reinvention, there remain substantial areas of concern that need to be addressed. Most pressing are the need to clarify what good performance means and to link different definitions of performance. In addition, the handling of the human resource function in the downsized and reinvented government is an issue that will require close attention in the future. The changes required demand vision and significant political support to establish a legislative basis for the reinvented government. Despite the claim to have shaped a government that is ready for the 21st century, the reinvention movement has limits, especially in the context of other reform movements across the world, that are too readily apparent. Reinvention has always been overly reliant on the will of Congress and actual agency workers to succeed, and it has been unable to develop a radical and comprehensive blueprint for governance in the 21st century.

THE EVOLUTION OF THE REINVENTION MOVEMENT

Reinvention has been characterized as more of an evolution than a revolution, marked by a series of identifiable phases during which it adapted to the changing political environment. Although the leadership of Vice President Gore has been a constant throughout the reform process, the focus, scope, and goals of reinvention have changed significantly. The details of this evolution are considered in greater detail by other authors (Ingraham et al., 1997; Kettl, 1994, 1998; Kettl and DiIulio, 1995).

Focus on Process

The first phase of reinvention might be regarded as its least political period. Under the mantra of "Creating a Government That Works Better and Costs Less" (National Performance Review, 1993), the National Performance Review was formed. Themes of customer service, empowerment of employees, reinvention labs, downsizing, and cutting red tape were first articulated at this point. The first report produced over 384 recommendations that focused largely on process issues. The keynote pieces of legislation for this period are the 1994 Federal Acquisition Streamlining Act, which made procurement processes more flexible, and the 1994 Federal Workforce Restructuring Act, which legislated for the downsizing of the federal work force. During this period, the National Performance Review was oriented to improving performance by making government operations more efficient: performance was to be improved by focusing on *how* government performed its tasks, rather than questioning the rationale for government intervention in the particular task.

In this first phase, the Clinton administration launched its effort to include labor in the reform process. In October 1993, President Clinton signed Executive Order 12871, Labor-Management Partnerships, which established the National Partnership Council. The council is made up of representatives of the largest federal employee unions, political appointees from federal agencies, and representatives of management groups. The council reports to the president on the status of labor-management partnerships in the federal government. It attempts to improve these partnerships by highlighting examples of good practice and by providing information to agencies and unions on ways to improve communication and coordination between labor and management.[3] If the political aim of the partnership was to cement union buy-in to administration reform initiatives, it has not succeeded. Unions have been largely skeptical of any proposed overhaul of the federal personnel system, and the council certainly does not appear to have generated any enthusiasm for a "reinvented" government. Unions have not seen rapid enough action on the perceived widening pay gap between the private and public sectors. It is the pay issue, rather than any goodwill generated by the partnership council, that will determine whether unions provide the support necessary to give any proposed personnel legislation a realistic chance of succeeding.

Reinvention laboratories also originated during this first period. Designated labs were units within agencies that were given top-level support for experimenting with new ways of performing their function, unconstrained by the usual regulatory limitations. The initiative began in April 1993, when the Vice-President asked the heads of various federal agencies to nominate labs in their areas. The labs remain a very identifiable part of reinvention, with over 300 different units across the federal government clearly representing the reinvention principles of less red tape, strong customer focus[4] and empowered employees. The multiplicity of labs makes it impossible to gain an overall understanding of the width and depth of reforms initiated. It appears that simplification of classification and compensation procedures is among the most popular lab innovations (Thompson and Ingraham, 1996). Other popular reforms undertaken by labs have been related to the use of information technology, procurement simplification and financial management (U.S. General Accounting Office, 1996: 32). Lab employees found that they often did not need regulatory waivers to implement the reforms that they wanted, in which case the status of the lab was of more symbolic than legal value. In cases in which waivers were needed, they were not always immediately forthcoming. Perhaps in response to this, President Clinton issued a memorandum in April 1998 to all agency heads that substantially streamlined the granting of waivers to staff, a significant step in delivering on the promise of empowerment for front-line employees.

Focus on Function

With the advent of the "Republican revolution" in 1994, when the conservative Republican party gained control of Congress, the political environment shifted dramatically. In terms of government reform, improving processes and streamlining the work force were no longer an adequate response to a Congress that favored the elimination of government intervention where feasible. The extreme end of the Republican revolution (calls for the elimination of the Department of Education, for example) gradually became more muted, as the White House co-opted a less radical version of the House Republican principles in its expansion of the scope of National Performance Review. Reinvention now not only examined how government did its job, but also questioned what functions government was involved in. This period was characterized by a series of public sector reforms that complemented the traditional Republican party distrust of the federal government. Making government better became equivalent to making it smaller, through reduction of regulations, elimination of central functions, contracting out, privatization, and devolution of powers to state and local government. Reinvention became a reference point for the major themes (raised by Republicans, but finally defined in Clintonian terms) of the period: The era of big government was declared over and the era of balanced budgets had just begun.

Focus on Results

The most recent phase of reinvention occurred in the context of the presidential aspirations of Vice President Gore. If the keynote for the first phase was process, and for the second phase function, then this period was characterized by focusing on the results of good governance, making these results relevant to the public, thereby increasing public confidence in government. Improving process and reducing functions rarely make headlines and do not conspire to produce an inspiring image for a politician. The political imperative for reinvention at this point was to relate its achievements to an electoral audience in a tangible way, hence the increased emphasis on focusing on "getting results that Americans care about." The widened scope of the movement was reflected in the change of its official title from the National Performance Review to the National Partnership for Reinventing Government.

While maintaining themes such as customer service and empowerment of front-line employees, the Blair House Papers, published at the beginning of the second Clinton term, was an effort to widen the reinvention strategy to a broader level. A series of short essays on different aspects of reinvention, the House Papers were to be the "little red book" for reformers. The papers presented "lessons learned" from the first phase of reinvention, including service delivery (with a strong emphasis on customer service), building of partnerships, and ways to "do more with less." Up to this point the fruits of reinvention were mainly seen at a fragmented level, either in terms of improving specific processes, e.g., procurement, or a reform of a (typically front-line) unit of an agency, e.g., through reinvention labs. The Blair House Papers conceptualized reinvention as a blueprint for better government for entire agencies.

Included in the list of Blair House Paper rules was the concept of performance based organization (PBO). Based on the United Kingdom's Next Steps initiative, PBO status was proposed for public organizations that had a clarity of operation similar to that of private organizations (but were not immediate privatization candidates). Legislation was proposed to give them the flexibility to operate according to a commercial model (National Performance Review, 1997: 42). The president's FY 2000 budget proposed nine organizations for PBO status (U.S. Office of Management and Budget, 1999: 50). Like other reinvention proposals requiring legislation, PBO candidates have failed to get the political support necessary to be brought to life. In fact, only two PBO's have received congressional approval, the Office of Student Financial Assistance at the Department of Education and the Patent and Trademark Office in the Department of Commerce.

Also significant in this period was the designation of High Impact Agencies: the 32 agencies that have the greatest level of direct contact with the public and are thus seen as the most important agencies if reinvention is to create a sense of renewed public trust in government. These agencies have committed to defining a series of concrete and measurable goals that they will reach by 2001. The broader goal is to make these agencies more customer-oriented and focused on specific results. High impact agencies are further discussed in the section, Performance Goals.

Legislative Weakness and Fragmentation

Any attempt to legislate bureaucratic change is inevitably tied to the politics of reform, and the high-profile leadership of Vice-President Gore guaranteed the politically charged nature of reinvention. As a result reinvention struggled to generate significant reforms that required legislative approval. On different occasions the White House proposed civil service reform legislation that died a quiet death in congressional committees. The clearest legislative successes associated with reinvention occurred in its first phase, with the politically neutral Acquisition Streamlining Act and the less-than-inspiring Workforce Restructuring Act. The most significant legislation directed to public sector management in the 1990s almost certainly was the Government Performance and Results Act of 1993, a congressional initiative. After 1994, government reformers faced a situation in which the executive branch was in the hand of the Democrats and the Congress was Republican-controlled. Given what appeared to be increasing bipartisanship, this was not an atmosphere conducive to an engaged approach to constructively redesign government and meet the evolving challenges of governance. At the same time other industrialized nations, at varying rates, started to move beyond the bureaucratic model of governance, most notably New Zealand, the United Kingdom, and Australia. The U.S. political system appeared unsuited to digesting models of radical or rapid change and was characterized as a "laggard" in its reform efforts (Aucoin, 1995).

Another factor that should be considered when trying to understand the lack of governmentwide legislative change is the fragmented nature of the personnel function of the U.S. federal government. Given the number of exceptions to civil service rules, it is less relevant to speak of reforming a "civil service" in the United States than it is in other countries. Since the Civil Service Reform Act of 1978, this tendency toward fragmentation and allowance of significant discretion for leading agencies has been widened (Ingraham and Moynihan, 1999). A decreasing number of U.S. federal government employees work under standardized government rules. It is increasingly the norm that the rules they work under are devised at the agency level. A good example of the extent of this fragmentation is the fact that less than one-third of the 38,000 permanent full-time federal employees hired in 1994 entered through regular civil service recruiting and hiring practices, nearly 70 percent entered through excepted or special hiring means (Kettl et al., 1996: 17). Reinvention has continued this tradition of giving leading agencies increased freedom from general civil service rules, urging greater personnel discretion be delegated to the agency level. More recently, the performance based organization concept, which proposes significant managerial discretion for businesslike agencies, became a priority of the White House.

Clearly the impact and focus of reinvention have been shaped by the political expediencies of each of its phases. At a more general level, it has been handicapped by its inability to gather the legislative support necessary for its most significant proposals. This has forced reinventors to adopt a "what can be done" rather than a "what needs to be done" approach to government reform. The advantage of this approach is that the movement discovered that many of the barriers to better performance in government were self-imposed and could be eliminated without need for congressional approval. Reinvention has achieved many of its goals through Executive Orders, for instance. It may be argued that a nonlegislative basis for change weakens the potential of reinvention to have a lasting impact on the way that the federal government does its job. This makes success dependent on the willingness of the federal worker to embrace its principles. Without the tools necessary for rapid restructuring of the federal service, reinvention has been characterized as a "gardening" approach to reform, conducive to gradual, bottom-up change (Thompson and Sanders, 1997). This approach makes the success of reinvention uncertain and incremental; however, where reinvention does succeed in integrating itself into an organizational culture there is likely to be greater employee ownership of the reform principles than could be achieved by legislation alone.

REINVENTION SUCCESSES

The reinvention movement has proposed myriad reforms, with varying degrees of success. Some have been largely noncontroversial and clearly improved matters. These are usually in the name of red tape reduction, as reinventors have consistently called for a less labored approach to process issues. A good example are regulations concerning government procurement. Because of the 1994 Federal Acquisition Streamlining Act government employees may now purchase items using a government credit card. Larger and more controversial issues are areas of less clear consensus. In this section we examine two more controversial areas of reinvention, continually cited as successes by reinventors.

Strengthening Customer Service

An explicit focus on customer service and customer satisfaction has been absent from previous definitions of government performance. The traditional focus on efficiency implies good performance as the largest result for a given application of resources (Simon, 1997), an essentially technical and process-oriented measure of performance. Customer service is an outcome and service-oriented measure of performance. The citizen as a taxpayer expects efficiency whereas the customer as a benefits receiver, in a more narrowly defined and specific role, expects good service. Executive Order 12862, Setting Customer Service Standards. (September, 1993), begins with the statement. "Putting people first means ensuring that the Federal Government provides the highest quality service possible to the American people." From this perspective, taking a step beyond the traditional process orientation means that the federal government needs to pay attention to the manner in which it delivers services, tailoring service provision to the desires of benefit recipients. Public organizations lack the natural link between making customers happy and organizational survival that is part of the private sector. Mandating a customer orientation (including measurable customer standards and customer satisfaction surveys) is an effort to enable government agencies to generate a more direct link with the service recipient and is viewed as being closely related to increasing public confidence in government (National Performance Review, 1997b: 2).

Perhaps more than any other single reinvention initiative, customer service has permeated the consciousness of government agencies. Employees believe that there is considerable focus on dealing with customers:

Seventy-five percent say that there are service goals aimed at achieving customer expectation

Forty-five percent believe that there are well-defined systems for linking customer feedback/complaints to agency planning and decisions

Forty-three percent agree that employees receive training and guidance in providing high-quality customer service (National Partnership for Reinventing Government, 1998).

Clearly the message of customer service is getting through, making federal employers think about the results of their actions in terms of impact on the recipients of services. There has been some concern that a customer orientation is being developed at the expense of citizenship, or that government has certain relationships with the recipients of its service that may make a customer focus inappropriate (federal prisoners and interest groups are two examples that raise different types of concerns). However, the emphasis on customer service has served to highlight that governmental action is most tangibly represented for the citizen through the quality of services received from the public sector. In this sense, putting the customer first, an element of worldwide government reform, is a different type of social contract with the citizen, one that ought to complement, rather than replace, more traditional ideas of the relationship between the government and its citizens.

Downsizing

Another area in which reinventors can claim measurable levels of success is downsizing. In his 1993 Memorandum on Streamlining, the President encouraged agencies to make the personnel reductions, but to use involuntary reductions in force (RIF) as a last resort. Ultimately the President got his wish: The cuts were made, with few RIFs and largely through contract by-outs and early retirements. NPR originally envisioned that the federal work force could be reduced by 252,000 over a 5-year period; the 1994 Federal Workforce Restructuring Act raised this number to 272,900. From the time the Clinton administration took power the civilian work force was reduced by 365,000; in 1998 the government work force as a percentage of the civilian work force was smaller than it had been at any time since 1933 (U.S. Office of Management and Budget, 1999: 46, 49).

In terms of numbers of employees, the downsizing program was a complete success, but reservations remain. The federal government failed to downsize in a strategic manner in two ways. The first concern is the lack of systematic consideration of the matter of the employees who should have been retained and those who should have been involuntarily separated. The desire for large personnel cuts through voluntary separation left individual employees—rather than the agencies involved—in the driving seat in terms of deciding who left and who stayed. Ultimately this produced a profoundly nonstrategic approach to downsizing. A survey of federal workers by the U.S. Office of Personnel Management found that employees certainly did not perceive that downsizing had any particular strategic vision beyond budget reduction. Only 22 percent agreed that "the installation's downsizing/reduction was well thought out from the perspective of how the work would continue to get done" (U.S. Office of Personnel Management, 1998: 9). The evidence suggests that rather than concentrating on using the downsizing process as a method of selective retention of the most able performers, most downsizing decisions were motivated by short-term budget reductions. This produced an "across-the-board" approach to downsizing rather than a strategic human resources management approach (1998: 1).

Downsizing by voluntary methods may be interpreted as a largely political calculation, aimed at appeasing Democratic supporters and some of the most necessary allies on government reform: the public service unions. A more generous interpretation is that this approach was aimed, at least in part, at maintaining employee morale. Although voluntary reductions may have been more successful at achieving this goal than any alternative option, there was still considerable uncertainty among the remaining employees as to their future in the downsized organization. Just 24% of employees in 1998 felt that their future with government was certain (1998: 15) and few management and employees surveyed felt that they had been adequately involved in downsizing decisions.

The second way that reinvention struggled with downsizing was in failing to make it fit into a larger vision of a redefined and improved government model. Reinvention rhetoric articulated that downsizing was part of a unified vision that would make the government cost less while making it work better. However, federal workers had serious reservations on this perspective, with only 10% agreeing that downsizing/reduction had produced an organization that was more productive and much better equipped to do its job (U.S. Office of Personnel Management, 1998: 29). Just 33% of managers/supervisors and employees said that they felt that top management, in carrying out its downsizing, analyzed what it wanted and why (1998: 29). In many cases workers are expected to maintain the same workload, despite the loss of personnel, raising concerns about the long-term sustainability of such an approach. Declines in performance will not announce themselves as a sudden phenomenon but are more likely to emerge slowly. Just 27% of managers and supervisors and 31% of employees surveyed believed that there were enough workers to get the job done (1998: 29).

If reinvention did have a strategy for tying downsizing to better performance, it appears to have been nothing more sophisticated than the indirect "cheese-slicer" approach to promoting performance. The logic of this approach is that forcing agencies to maintain previous functions with fewer resources will require employees to work harder and innovate to maintain standards. There is some support to the claim that this approach is working. Downsizing has forced government workers to reevaluate how they do business, according to 53% of managers, supervisors, and employees (1998: 13). A 1996 General Accounting Office report on reinvention labs found that downsizing "both stimulated the type of reforms the Vice President contemplated and made it more difficult to implement them" (U.S. General Accounting Office, 1996: 5). A more recent report (U.S. General Accounting Office, 1998) examined the attitudes of workers in the downsized components of NASA, HUD, OPM, DOI, and the GSA. The general conclusion was that downsizing had not severely impacted performance, although further downsizing was regarded as undesirable. Officials gave three reasons why performance had been maintained amid downsizing:

- Refocusing of missions—including outsourcing or eliminating of functions
- Reegineering of work processes
- Building and maintaining of employee skills

The main lessons that agency officials had learned from the actual downsizing process were the following:

- Open communication between employees and management is essential; employee input should be solicited in planning any downsizing process.

- People should be treated with compassion and must know that they are valued by the agency.
- There must be no favoritism though management may be reluctant to let some people leave.
- Buy-outs need to be planned and targeted to prevent a sudden loss of expertise.
- Critical skills must be backed up by more than one person (GAO, 1998: 11).

Perhaps a key lesson learned from downsizing is that despite its nonstrategic nature, it has forced employees to innovate and increase productivity, to do more with less. However, one should be wary of recommending downsizing as a method of improving performance on a continuous basis. The longer-term effects of downsizing are uncertain, and most likely deleterious. Such effects include shifting the traditional public employment contract, reducing the prospects of a job for life in the public sector. More serious are the unmonitored loss of some of the government's most able performers through the nonstrategic downsizing process, and the negative long-run impact that the loss of this expertise and institutional memory will have on public sector capacity and performance.

HOW DO WE JUDGE REINVENTION? HOW HAS REINVENTION JUDGED ITSELF? TRUST, EMPLOYEE SATISFACTION, AND PERFORMANCE

One of the unique features of organizational redesign of government agencies is that unlike private sector reform, public sector change is regarded as an issue appropriate to debate in the political domain. On the basis of different perceptions, political actors can, and will, offer different interpretations as to the success or failure of efforts to change government. Given that the *goals* of reformers may be open to disagreement (consider the different understanding of the term *political responsiveness* between a politician and a bureaucrat), there should be no surprise at wide disagreement over the outcomes achieved.

This is an issue that goes beyond the particularities of reinvention and is relevant to all efforts that try to judge the public sector. However, the multiple goals and shifting priorities characteristic of reinvention make the movement extremely difficult to judge and understand. Ingraham (1983) offers a checklist for public policy design: correct problem identification, correct causal theory and policy, correct target identification, internal consistency and consensus. The mercurial and multifaceted nature of reinvention suggests that it would not fare well when judged according to these criteria. NPR advocates might argue, with some justification, that reinvention represents something broader than a single policy or piece of legislation; at its best it represents an attitude and culture of performance and should be judged in those terms.

Another consideration when approaching the success or failure of policy design, including reform efforts, is an understanding that policies can have unrealistic expectations and produce unanticipated consequences. In terms of public sector change, discussions of reform provide opportunities for complaint on every conceivable aspect of government. This is exacerbated by the fact that the political preface to reform is grounded in a public debate on "what's wrong with Washington." Good management for the sake of good government is not regarded as a "sexy" issue. Reformers, even with the best of intentions, hope to channel the natural frustrations with the entire system of government as a springboard to bureaucratic reform. Jimmy Carter's promise to remove "deadwood" from the "Washington Marshmallow" is the classic, and textually confusing example. Carter's Civil Service Reform Act (CSRA) was the most comprehensive piece of federal-agency reform since the Pendleton Act[5] but was deemed a failure by many because its apparent contribution was minimal. The CSRA suffered because it was billed as the antidote to all that was wrong with bureaucracy—such expectations failed to consider that many of the characteristics of bureaucracy arise because they are part of an entrenched bureaucratic culture and an even more entrenched larger political system.

Having established the difficulty in judging the success or failure of public management reform, it is worth examining the manner in which it is possible to judge reinvention and the criteria by which reinvention judges itself. Three different measures emerge—public trust in government, employee satisfaction, and achievement of performance goals.

Trust

The goal of America@Its Best, the National Partnership for Reinventing Government's vision for the future, is to restore trust[6] in America's government by providing

Best value for each taxpayer dollar
Best service for each customer and regulated business
Best workplace for its employees
Best legacy for our future

The first question that needs to be addressed is whether trust makes sense as a goal of public management. Ideally, the public would have justifiable faith in public agencies. However, this is often not the case for a number of reasons (discussed later), and it is worth considering whether public agencies should reform themselves according to the goal of increased public trust. Trust is an ambiguous concept, an easy tool of political rhetoric, difficult to translate into practical prescriptions, problematic from a public managers' perspective, and alluring for politicians who discuss public management.

As demonstrated in Table 1, the public's perceptions of government are often contradictory. The American public tend to distrust the concept of government in the abstract and subsequently give it poor performance ratings. When asked about specific services or agencies, individuals are far more positive in their opinions. It is also unclear whether the performance of the bureaucracy is at the root of, and should be responsible for, distrust of government. It appears that low opinions of politicians and the perceived lack of leadership take the brunt of the blame for the public disenchantment with government. Are such opinions the basis of an indictment of bureaucracy?

A complementary argument based on the preceding and other (Bok, 1997) findings is that the public's view of government is often ill-informed, unrelated to actual performance and should not be regarded as a barometer of performance. Indeed the public's reaction to the federal government may be more influenced by ideological baggage, a sense of distance, attitudes toward politics, and the economy than the actual performance of government. As noted, citizens are usually positive about specific services received by the federal government. Individual bureaucrats or agencies, therefore, are in a weak position to enhance the *overall* perception of government, as this perception is largely influenced by factors beyond their control. Managers and reformers may, however, find a more reliable measure of organizational effectiveness when opinions about specific service provisions—from actual beneficiaries—are used. From this perspective, the reinvention bias toward customer satisfaction may be a more reliable performance barometer by which public agencies can judge their efforts than abstract notions of trust or distrust in government.

A final argument about the use of trust as a yardstick centers around broader social changes. Such changes, which bureaucrats and politicians are largely powerless to stop, are driving the declining trust of government and other societal institutions. Ingelhart (1997; Abramson and Inglehart 1998) has argued that prosperity promotes "postmaterialist" values; these values emphasize the centrality of the individual and reject an unquestioning view of authority. Whereas low-income countries maintain a culture of deference toward government, higher-income countries, such as the United States and Western European nations, have seen declining trust in various institutions, including government. Together, these arguments would not see the decline in trust of government as especially remarkable, reflective of performance or a crisis for governance.

Public trust of the public sector may be most relevant in terms of the government's role as employer. In recruiting employees, the public service will be at a disadvantage if it is perceived as an unrewarding place to work. Public attitudes are also relevant to public management in a customer survey format, whereby are opinions solicited in terms of specific elements of governmental service provision, linking with the reinvention emphasis on customer service. However, given the weak links between the public perception and actual performance of government,

TABLE 1 Sorting Out the Contradictions—Public Perception of Government

- Americans give government poor performance ratings; 74% believe that government does a poor job managing its programs and providing services; 64% agree that when a program is run by government it is generally inefficient and wasteful. When asked about how government performs specific tasks, e.g., caring for the elderly, the ratings do not move up substantially.
- Performance is closely related to trust; 70% of those who give the government a fair or poor rating basically distrust government, and 76% of those who are satisfied with government performance basically trust government.
- When asked about the performance of individual government agencies, Americans are much more positive. Approval ratings for individual agencies have, as a rule, improved in the last decade. Virtually all agencies that the public were queried about received a higher than 50% approval rating, and many had approval ratings of 70 or 80% and higher. This is not a new finding; citizens tend to have positive reactions to any actual interactions with government services (Goodsell, 1994: 37), and when asked about specific government agencies, tend to offer the highest approval to the services they interact with most regularly (Kettl, 1998: 35).
- Public desire for government services and activism has remained nearly steady over the past 30 years.
- Distrust of government is strongly connected to people's feelings about the overall state of the nation.
- By a margin of 67% to 16% the public has more trust in federal workers than in elected officials to do the right thing.
- Of those with an unfavorable opinion of government 40% offer complaints about political leaders as their reason for the negative view. This is considerably more than the 24% who offer critiques of the way government does its job, the 14% who cite complaints about government policies, and the 13% who say that government is uncaring.
- The same point is largely confirmed by a Hart-Teeter poll (1997) that found that citizens who exhibited a high degree of distrust were expressing their low regard for elected officials. Perceptions of wasteful spending (16%) and excessive size of government (15%) are dwarfed by complaints about politicians (33%), who are described as dishonest, self-interested, and partisan.
- With regard to comparison to other nations, the level of trust in government is similar to that in European countries. When asked, "Would you say you basically trust the Government, or not?" the U.S. level of trust was 40% (compared with a European average of 41%), and the level of distrust was 56% (compared to the European average of 45%).

Source: Unless otherwise noted, data from Pew Center for People and the Press (1998).

politicians should be wary of using an abstract barometer of public trust as an indicator of the success of governmental efforts.

Employee Satisfaction

The Reinvention emphasis on employee empowerment reflects (or should reflect) a Theory Y (McGregor, 1960) approach to federal employment. Through empowering, reducing the level of red tape, and making the federal government a more dynamic place to work, reinvention should be providing a clear benefit to employees. Therefore it is logical to focus on levels of employee satisfaction, attitudes toward the workplace and the reinvention process. Measuring employee attitudes also gives indicators as to the enduring effects of reinvention and the extent to which it has integrated itself into the federal employee culture. Reinvention has begun to focus on this area and commissioned a cross-government poll of employee attitudes toward various aspects of their job, in particular their attitude toward reinvention (National Partnership for Reinventing Government, 1998).

Federal employees responded favorably in a number of areas. In general federal employees are largely satisfied with their jobs (62% regard themselves as being satisfied with their jobs) and working conditions, including supervisory understanding of personal employee responsibilities, respect for differences among employees, and access to electronic sources of information. The reinvention emphasis on teamwork appears to be matched by workers, 59% agree that teams are used to accomplish organizational goals; 60% agree that a spirit of cooperation and teamwork are used to accomplish organizational goals; and 45% of whom respond that employees in different work units participate in cross-functional teams. However, teamwork seems to occur in spite of, rather than because of, central direction. Only 37% of employees believe that they are rewarded for working together in teams.

Employee surveys also raise areas that must be of concern to reinventors. Perhaps the most striking is that only 35% of government employees feel that their organization has made reinvention an important priority, suggesting that it has not yet embedded itself into the wider culture of federal employees. With regard to the success of cutting red tape, there appeared to be a mixed perspective:

54% agree that the use of government credit cards for small office purchases has been implemented in their organization

37% agree and 36% disagree that their organization is working to streamline its regulatory program

20% believe that their organization has implemented simplified travel arrangements

64% do not agree that their organization has streamlined the process for hiring employees

Another area of mixed responses are employee views of their value in the organization. This is reflected in questions about their perception of how they are treated within the federal system, and the equity of that system in treating of its employees. 51% feel that "At the place I work, my opinions seem to count," and 46% are satisfied with their involvement in decisions affecting their work. 42% are satisfied (and an equal percentage dissatisfied) with the recognition they receive for doing a good job. With regard to empowerment, only 30% of employees believe that creativity and innovation are rewarded. With regard to accountability and equity of treatment, only 32% of employees believe that recognition and reward are based on merit, 44% disagree that corrective actions are taken when employees fail to meet performance standards.

A very striking result is ambiguity that federal employees have about the concept of performance in the workplace. Only 26% of employees feel they understand how good performance is defined in their organizations, despite the acknowledged emphasis on service goals and customer requirements and generally favorable attitudes toward managers (57% believe that managers are effective in communicating the organization's mission, vision, and values) and supervisors (54% agree that their immediate supervisor has organized their work group effectively to get the work done; 52% believe that overall their supervisor/team leader is doing a good job). Therefore, despite the presence of specific goals in the customer service areas and a largely favorable attitude toward management and supervisors, employees do not have a clear concept of what "good performance" means and how they can meet that standard. This is perhaps the most telling insight that consultation with federal employees has revealed and should be a component of any reform effort of the federal government.

Performance Goals

An increasing concern of reinvention has been to package its efforts in a way the public may understand and relate to. The "High Impact Agency" initiative has set itself the goal of providing "results that Americans care about," making the efforts of performance management accessible to the general public. Thirty-two high-profile agencies that have direct contact with the public were asked to commit themselves to a series of concrete and measurable targets that they would reach within 3 years.[7] The fruits of reinvention (more realistically the fruits of the Government Performance and Results Act, or GPRA) were thereby to be judged by these agencies' capacity to make, and keep, promises on performance goals.

As with other standards of judging government performance, it is appropriate to ask whether performance measurement is a credible benchmark. Such a debate essentially centers on the validity of GPRA, from which reinvention borrows its goal measurement. GPRA mandated that all federal agencies construct a series of documents that would define goals and track success in reaching these goals. Each agency is obliged to develop a medium-term strategic plan, an annual performance plan that details specific and measurable goals for the year ahead, and a performance report that examines the agency's performance in the previous year against its preset goals. On the basis of the information provided by the individual performance plans, the Office of Management and Budget has begun to construct a governmentwide performance plan that is presented as part of the president's budget proposal for the first time in 1999.

In principle there can be few objections to GPRA and its aims for providing greater strategy, transparency, and accountability in agency performance and decision making. Potential for failure arises from two areas: assumptions of rationality in the decision-making process and ability of the federal government to make outcome commitments on matters they only partially control.

Performance measurement has real merit if it can be integrated into the decision-making process. This assumes that the decision-making process is rational and that decision makers will make constructive use of performance information, defying traditional notions of how decisions are made. It should be remembered that the recent history of governmental reform is strewn with the carcasses of attempts to import greater rationality into the planning/budgeting process (performance budgeting, PPBS, zero-based budgeting). GPRA appears to have at least partially learned the lessons of these previous failures, attempting to acknowledge the political elements of decision making by explicitly providing a strong role for Congress and stakeholders. However, it remains to be seen whether this will be adequate insurance against the political nature of decision making. The U.S. legislative process was not designed to produce clear goals; performance goals will work if the whole method of decision making, *throughout the political process,* changes. Reforms such as GPRA do not fail because they are bad ideas. They fail because they attempt to tame the political animal, and the political animal will not be tamed. Blame will fall on the shoulders of administrators for not truly implementing the process, for not trying hard enough. That the success or failure of such efforts rests solely with administrators rests on two assumptions: that it is a largely technical process and that administrators have complete decision-making authority. The first assumption is debatable; the second is—and should be—incorrect. Decision making is political, a value-laden process, suitably the domain of politicians. The fate of performance measurement efforts rests to a large degree on politicians[7] signaling that the process by which they make decisions will be affected by the performance information generated.

The second likely danger to performance goals is federal agencies' promising what they cannot deliver. Is the federal government really in a position to make promises on outcomes? Other players in the private, nonprofit, and local government area may have greater control of these outcomes. This is illustrated by the increasing emphasis on developing partnerships with state, local, nonprofit, and private actors to deliver services (U.S. Office of Management and Budget, 1999). Although the federal government may be *involved* in myriad services, the reality is that they control very few of these services directly. Government at the central level is increasingly concerned with regulation and overseeing of services rather than with direct service delivery (U.S. General Accounting Office, 1999b). If outcome goals are not met, the federal government can fairly shrug its shoulders and say, "Not my fault." Although there has been an emphasis on developing accountability within service delivery partnerships, the fact that multiple actors perform the tasks makes it difficult to assign responsibility to any one party, allowing accountability to fall between the different actors (Kettl, 1998: 49; U.S. General Accounting Office, 1999b).

Even if the government directly controls service delivery, the wisdom of outcome measurement remains questionable. Outcomes will inevitably be affected by a range of factors and unforeseen events that will vary with different issues (with the economy likely to be a common influence on the achievement of outcomes). Such factors are not under the control of the public sector. In New Zealand the government was radically reformed up the basis of principles of responsibility, transparency, and clear lines of accountability. Annual contracts between ministers and their agency head clearly delineate goals and allocate responsibilities between actors. However, agencies are judged by outputs rather than outcomes; the logic is that public servants can justifiably be held responsible for outputs, but not outcomes.[8] In the U.S. context, GPRA allows agencies an opportunity to explain why they failed to meet their goals (essentially the opportunity to articulate the excuse of extenuating circumstances), providing a potential escape valve for nonperformers.

RHETORIC AND SELF-AWARENESS

Even if trust is a poor measure of governmental performance, reinvention may be astute in trying to address the issue. For years the perception of the federal government as a lazy bureaucracy wrapped in red tape was fueled by simpleminded political rhetoric. If reinvention is to some degree bluster, it is at least bluster aimed in the other direction. It builds on the traditional notion of large and wasteful government, but it portrays its efforts in terms of creating a dynamic public sector rather than eliminating the public sector. The result may be that a more positive image of the federal government will permeate the national consciousness. However, the relationship between rhetoric and reality may be just as tenuous as that of bureaucrat bashing. The underlying tensions that frame many of the problems of government have not disappeared and cannot be reinvented away.

Efforts to shift the tone of the discussion on government performance to a more positive note has marked reinvention as an unusual type of government reform. In part, it has tried to portray the government in a more positive light to generate credit for the efforts of reformers. Reinvention discussions of positive performance in government are inevitably linked with a reinvention initiative. The fact that reinvention is in the position to make such efforts is indicative of other qualities of the movement that make it unusual. Unlike other reform efforts that were built around a single report or the goal of passing a particular piece of legislation, reinvention was guaranteed a semipermanent existence as long as Vice President Gore remained in the White House. Reinvention legislative initiatives have passed and failed at various times, but reinvention itself has remained. This status has allowed reinvention the capacity, unique among reform movements in the United States, to develop as a learning organization. Reinvention has evolved and matured, reshaping itself on the basis of its achievements and its political environment. It has proved itself adept at gathering ideas for reform from different forums: the private sector, state and local governments, governments in other countries, federal government workers themselves, and, to a lesser extent, academia. As a movement it has been able to select and present these ideas as options for the reform of government, consistently championing the concept of change, even as the breadth and type of these ideas evolved considerably. In 2000, reinvention resembled an internal government think tank with powerful executive branch political support and a spotty record on actual implementation of its ideas. Given the traditional lack of interest that the Office of Management and Budget has had in the actual management of the federal government and the declining role of the Office of Personnel Management, the reinvention movement filled a niche as the White House's public sector management organization.

LOOKING TO THE FUTURE

Linking Performance and Incentives

Reinvention has skillfully included the work of GPRA in the reinvention tent in the form of High Impact Agencies. By doing so it has embraced a particular definition of performance, one that is specific, measurable, output- and outcome-based, and organization-focused. The GPRA definition stands in contrast to the individualist approach that the 1978 Civil Service Reform Act, in which performance was defined between supervisor and employee and disconnected from organizational goals and public reporting (Ingraham and Moynihan, 2000). Neither the GPRA nor the CSRA definitions of performance will, in themselves, guarantee strong performance. The individualist approach could conceivably create an organization of excellent workers but does not provide a mechanism for the direction of their efforts. In practice, individual evaluations and pay for performance have not fared well, as a result of evaluation grade inflation. Every year from 1991 to 1996, at every level of the federal employment schedule, less than 1 percent of employees received anything less than a "fully successful" rating (U.S. Office of Personnel

Management, 1998b: 68). On the other hand, the GPRA approach to performance might be successful at defining and measuring goals, but without strong individual performance, it may be succeeding only in specifying poor performance.

The main challenge for reinvention is to realize that these approaches are complementary in an integrated approach to performance. At the individual level employees need to be motivated and have the capacity to perform well. They also need to understand the general goals of the organization and the manner in which their task contributes to that goal. This suggests that an organization needs to integrate its human resource function with a strategic management perspective so that there is coherence between the action of the individual and the goals of the organization. Reinvention has shown an openness to an emphasis on both the individual (through the language of empowerment and the offer of regulatory waivers to staff) and the organization (through High Impact Agencies and PBOs). It has also started to look at the links between these two approaches. In one reinvention discussion paper and in Vice President Gore's speeches, there has been discussion of personnel reform that would try to establish these linkages (Friel, 1999). The linkage between an individual's pay and performance, a central tenet of the 1978 reform, has reemerged, but with a more organizational emphasis. Pay for performance is still important, say reinventors, but performance evaluation must be widened to include variables that clearly contribute to organizational performance. Implementing such an approach would be a step toward allowing federal agencies to establish the linkages among the organizational, intermediate, and individual levels in a tangible way. However, reinventors have been unsuccessful in their past attempts to convince Congress of the need to reshape the personnel conditions of the federal government. Although Congress has established a coherent framework for organizational performance in GPRA, it has failed to consider the capacity needed to make this framework significantly improve performance.

The Human Resource Function and Capacity

The unwillingness of Congress to examine personnel reform, and to make the link between personnel reform and overall performance, is an issue that is unlikely to disappear. This is because there is good reason to believe that a large number of managers in the federal government do not, as it stands, have the capacity or inclination to manage the human resource function successfully. This problem arises for a number of reasons. The first is that managers are simply not experienced with exercising a great deal of discretion over employees. Related to this point is the fact that the culture of a particular agency, and the federal system in general, determines that formal and informal incentives direct supervisors to make personnel decisions based on a short-run perspective, even when that course conflicts with the best use of human resources in the longer term (U.S. Merit Systems Protection Board, 1998: 2). For instance, if a vacant post is not filled immediately, is runs the risk of being downsized in the budgeting cycle. Another example of this short-run perspective is that managers try to fill vacancies as quickly as possible, often using inservice replacements, at the expense of getting the best available candidate. Further, the training needs of employees are not carefully assessed or tied to development plans. Part of the problem arises from the fact that the U.S. federal system has traditionally promoted managers on the basis of their technical qualifications. It is no surprise then that mangers usually tend to do far better with the technical aspects of these jobs rather than with personnel matters.

The efforts of reinvention, in terms of downsizing the number of supervisory personnel and through the delegation of the personnel function, have increased the number of personnel decisions left to supervisors. With more personnel decisions, there is a greater likelihood of having too little time to consider how to build organizational capacity over the longer term (U.S. Merit Systems Protection Board, 1998: 10). The reduced role of the Office of Personnel Management has meant that it has been up to agencies and supervisors to make many of the personnel policies for its employees. Given that the culture and training of most federal supervisors have not prepared them for making long-term decisions on human resources, a problem arises. The centrality of a strategic human resource policy, integrated with efforts toward performance improvement, has been increasingly acknowledged in the private sector, in other reforming countries, and among observers of the U.S. government (U.S. General Accounting Office, 1999: 23–25, 100–110, Ingraham et al. 2000). However, the conditions that would foster the development of such a strategic policy do not appear to be present in the U.S. federal government. Given this fact, it is likely that some combination of two different options is likely. One would be some degree of recentralization of the human resource function within either the Office of Management and Budget or the Office of Personnel Management. The other would be to change the system of incentives for federal supervisors to increase their understanding of the importance of, and ways to deal with, personnel issues. Without such action there promises to be uneven implementation of the human resource function and underutilization of employee capacity.

CONCLUSION

Have the efforts of the reinvention movement prepared a "21st century government for 21st century America," as President Clinton suggested in his 1999 State of the Union address? That is difficult to say, and it assumes that reinvention offers a clear idea of the role of government in the coming century. Reinvention has brought about significant changes; that much is clear. The federal government has a good deal fewer employees and has a much stronger orientation toward customer service. There has been, particularly in the first phase of reinvention, a focus on improving the processes by which the federal government does its job, often with clear governmentwide impact, e.g., in the area of procurement. However, many of the major policy initiatives of reinvention, including civil service reform and PBOs, have failed to take off. If reinvention is to make a lasting contribution, it faces challenges in two areas: the need for comprehensive legislative reform and political support.

The Need for Comprehensive Legislative Reform

The limited success of reinvention is indicative of self-inflicted weaknesses and of the political environment in which it exists. Reinvention has never lacked ideas and has been willing to expand the scope of its concern beyond the original goals of the National Performance Review. The negative side of this flexibility has been that reinvention has never really had a coherent vision of what was wrong with government and how their proposals were going to fix it. Given the fragmented nature of the American governmental system it may not be possible to develop such a vision. Given the determinedly incremental nature of the American political system it would be extremely difficult to legislate for such a vision without strong congressional and stakeholder agreement and support.

Nevertheless, there remains a clear need for comprehensive reform of the federal government, personnel issues in particular. Efforts to reinvent government will be limited by the rigidities of what is essentially a century-old civil-service design. The civil-service system has not fundamentally changed since the Pendleton Act of 1883, although the relevance of this design is weakened by the increasing fragmentation of the federal system. Enhanced personnel flexibility has been a recurring theme of reinvention, both in the microefforts of reinvention laboratories and in the larger-scale legislative efforts presented to Congress. This suggests that reinvention recognizes the link between personnel reform and wider reform. Other nations, such as New Zealand and the United Kingdom, have redesigned their public sector by making structural reforms that automatically changed the status and role of its employees. The incrementalist and piecemeal approach of reinvention—partly self-generated, partly a function of the political system—has meant that this has not been the case for the United States.

The Need for Political Support

Appleby observed that government is different because government is politics. The implication is that public administration is a product of, and cannot separate itself from, politics. This is at least as relevant to reform efforts as to any other aspects of administration. Earlier in this chapter we noted how the reinvention initiative has evolved according to the prevailing political agenda, and how its ambitions have been limited by lack of political support, particularly from Congress. The alliance with Vice President Gore gained the reinvention movement visibility and some clout. However, given the party split between Congress and the executive branch and increasing partisanship in Washington, the natural differences between the two parties on public-sector issues often appeared to be accentuated by the political circumstances. Political support remains a vital ingredient if there is to be serious attention paid to issues of governance, in terms of both consistent implementation and further reform.

Even most critics of reinvention will admit that is has played a valuable role in creating and continually promoting fresh ideas about the federal government and has rekindled a good deal of interest in public sector reform. However, the continuation of the National Partnership Review depends upon the election of Vice President Gore to the presidency. The challenges of good governance will remain no matter who becomes president, and the need to reinvent the federal government will not fade away with the demise of the National Partnership for Reinventing Government. With the decline of the Office of Personnel Management, and the traditional bias in the Office of Management and Budget to concentrate on its budgeting function, there is a need for a thoughtful and articulate actor within the federal government that is focused on improving public management. A sense of institutional permanence and of high-level political support would give such an actor the strength needed to prod the federal government continually toward better performance.

However, political support means more than having a reinvention-type organization exist. It suggests that both the White House and Congress pay much closer attention to issues of public management. An example of this is GPRA, the most significant governmentwide reform during the reinvention period, and tellingly a bipartisan congressional initiative. That says something about the requirements for putting a framework for serious change in place. However, the success of GPRA rests on politicians' taking performance results seriously when deciding the allocation of resources, implying a method of decision making that politicians have shown little inclination toward in the past. The potential for major reform successes to emerge from the reinvention toolbox, particularly personnel reform, will require a similar type of sustained political support. This support has been largely absent from reinvention initiatives thus far. It is scarcely surprising then that the semipermanent reinvention movement has developed a pragmatic attitude toward reform. It has pushed the boundaries of what change could be made without congressional approval, pushing piecemeal reform as its legislative initiatives met with little success. Although this course may have improved different aspects of government, it has certainly not reinvented government or produced the kind of thoughtful and comprehensive reform needed for governance in the 21st century.

REFERENCES

Abramson, P., and Inglehart, R. (1998). *Value Change in Global Perspective.* University of Michigan Press, Ann Arbor.

Appleby, P. (1945). *Big Democracy.* Alfred A. Knopf, New York.

Aucoin, Peter (1995). *The New Public Management: Canada in Comparative Perspective.* The Institute for Research on Public Policy, Montreal.

Bok, D. (1997). Measuring the performance of government. In *Why People Don't Trust Government* (Joeseph S. Nye Jr., Philip D. Zeilkow, and David C. King, eds.). Harvard University Press, Cambridge, Mass.

Boston, J. (1996). *Public Management: The New Zealand Model.* Oxford University, Auckland.

The Council for Excellence in Government (1997). Hart/Teeter National Opinion Surveys. [http://www.excelgov.org/survey97.htm].

Downs, A. (1967). *Inside Bureaucracy.* Little, Brown, Boston.

Friel, Brian (1999). Civil service reforms may include buyouts, pay hikes. *Government Executive.* Daily Briefing, February 26, 1999. [http://www.govexec.com/dailyfed/0299/022699b1.htm].

Goodsell, C. (1994). *The Case for Bureaucracy.* Chatham House, Chatham, N. J.

Inglehart, R. (1997). Postmaterialist values and the erosion of institutional authority. In *Why People Don't Trust Government.* (J. S. Nye, P. D. Zelikow, and D. C. King, eds.). Harvard University Press, Cambridge, Mass.

Ingraham, P.W. (1983). Civil service reform and public policy: Do we know how to judge its success or failure? In *Legislating Bureaucratic Change: The Civil Service Reform Act of 1978.* (P.W. Ingraham, and C. Ban, eds.). State University of New York Press, Albany.

Ingraham P.W. (1997). A laggard's tale. In *Civil Service Systems in Comparative Perspective* (H.A.G.M. Bekke, J. Perry, and T.A.J. Toonen, eds.). Indiana University Press, Bloomington.

Ingraham, P.W., and Moynihan D.P. (2000). Evolving dimensions of performance from the Civil Service Reform Act onwards. In *The Future of Merit: Twenty Years after the Civil Service Reform Act* (James P. Pfiffner and Douglas Brooks, eds.). Cambridge University Press, Cambridge.

Ingraham, P.W., Moynihan D.P., and B.G. Peters. (2000). Public employment and the future of the public service. In *Revitalizing the Public Service: Governance for the 21st Century* (B.G. Peters and D. Savoie, eds.). McGill-Queen's University Press, Toronto.

Ingraham, P.W., Sanders, R., and Thompson, J. (eds.) (1997). *Transforming Management Lessons from the Reinvention Laboratories.* Jossey-Bass, San Francisco.

Kettl, Donald (1994). *Reinventing Government: Appraising the National Performance Review.* The Brookings Institution, Washington, D.C.

Kettl, D.F. (1998). *Reinventing Government: A Fifth-Year Report Card.* The Brookings Institutions, Washington D.C.

Kettl, D., and DiIulio J. (eds.) (1995). *Inside the Reinvention Machine: Appraising Governmental Reform.* The Brookings Institution, Washington, D.C.

Kettl, Donald, Ingraham, Patricia, Sanders, Ronald, and Horner, Constance (1996). *Civil Service Reform: Building a Government That Works* The Brookings Institution, Washington, D.C.

McGregor, D. (1960). *The Human Side of Enterprise.* McGraw Hill, New York.

National Commission on the Public Service (1989). *Leadership for America: Rebuilding the Public Service.* Lexington Press, Lexington, Mass.

National Partnership for Reinventing Government (1998). Employee survey results. [http://www.npr.gov/library/misc/survey-full.html].

National Performance Review (1993). *From Red Tape to Results: Creating a Government That Works Better and Costs Less.* Government Printing Office, Washington, D.C.

National Performance Review (1997). *Blair House Papers.* Government Printing Office, Washington, D.C.

National Performance Review (1997b). *Putting Customers First.* Government Printing Office, Washington, D.C.

Niskanen W. (1971). *Bureaucracy and Representative Government.* Aldine, Atherton, Chicago.

The Pew Research Center for the People and the Press. (1998). Deconstructing distrust [http://www.people-press.org/trustrpt.htm].

Simon, H. (1997). *Administrative Behavior: A Study of Decision-Making Processes in Administrative Organizations.* The Free Press, New York.

Thompson, J., and Ingraham P.W. (1996). The Reinvention Game. *Public Administration Review. 56:* 3.

Thompson, J., and Sanders R. (1997). Organization Change: Gardening or Engineering? In *Transforming Management: Lessons from the Reinvention Laboratories,* (Patricia Ingraham, Sanders Ronald, and James Thompson, eds.). (Jossey-Bass,) San Francisco.

U.S. General Accounting Office (1996). *Management Reform: Status of Agency Reinvention Lab Efforts.* GAO/GGD-96-69. Government Printing Office, Washington D.C.

U.S. General Accounting Office (1998b). *Federal Downsizing: Agency Officials' Views on Maintaining Performance During Downsizing at Selected Agencies.* GAO/GGD-98-46. Government Printing Office, Washington D.C.

U.S. General Accounting Office (1999). *Major Management Challenges and Program Risks: A Governmentwide Perspective.* OCG-99-1 Government Printing Office, Washington D.C.

U.S. General Accounting Office (1999b). *Managing for Results: Measuring Program Results That Are Under Limited Federal Control.* GAO/GGD-99-16. Government Printing Office, Washington D.C.

U.S. Merit Systems Protection Board (1998). *Federal Supervisors and Strategic Human Resources Management.* Government Printing Office, Washington, D.C.

U.S. Office of Management and Budget (1999). *Budget of the United States Government Fiscal Year 2000.* Government Printing Office, Washington, D.C., Section IV.

US Office of Personnel Management (1998). *Downsizing the Federal Government.* Washington D.C.

U.S Office of Personnel Management (1998b). *The Fact Book, Federal Civilian Workforce Statistics, 1998 Edition.* Washington D.C.

Wolf, Patrick J. (1997). Why must we reinvent the federal government? Putting historical developmental claims to the test. *Journal of Public Administration Research and Theory.* 7(3): 353–388.

NOTES

1. What we refer to as reinvention in this chapter has had two different formal monikers—the National Performance Review and the National Partnership for Reinventing Government.

2. The most strident examples are Niskanen, 1971, and Downs, 1967.
3. The council has published two handbooks, *Partnership Handbook* and *Training and Facilitation Handbook.*
4. A General Accounting Office survey of reinvention labs found that in almost two-thirds of cases, labs had both internal customers (i.e., other government departments) and external customers (U.S. General Accounting Office, 1996: 28).
5. For all its comprehensiveness, the CSRA was only radical compared to previous changes to public management. It was essentially a conservative piece of legislation, seeking to make changes to an existing model rather than reinvent that model.
6. For explicit linking of trust and reinvention see also the speech of Vice President Al Gore at the Reinvention Revolution III Conference April 21, 1998.
7. These public promises reinventors see as being tied to their goal of restoring public trust in government. Gore proclaimed to agency heads: "Yours are the agencies that shape the public's opinion of government and can redeem the promise of self government. Public cynicism about government is a cancer on democracy. Reinvention isn't just about fixing processes, it's about redefining priorities and focusing on the things that matter." See http://www.npr.gov/library/announc/hiapage3.html.
8. Kettl has highlighted the fact that outputs and outcomes are different types of measures, indicating different types of performance, and should be recognized as such (1998: 49).

22

Reforming Public Administration: Including Citizens

Cheryl Simrell King
Graduate Program in Public Administration,
The Evergreen State College,
Olympia, Washington

Camilla Stivers
Maxine Goodman Levin College of
Urban Affairs,
Cleveland State University,
Cleveland, Ohio

Many of the major reform movements put into practice in the last part of the 20th century called for a shift in the role of the citizen in public administration. Such reforms seek to address the fact that the citizen seems to be missing in public administration. The public administration/management practices that developed out of the Progressive era tend not to include citizens in any part of the process. Indeed, the Progressive public administrator is the expert, making decisions based on his/her expertise, using objective data derived from science, in order to maximize some general idea of the public interest. The Progressive public administrator is assumed only to be implementing those decisions that have already been made by the democratic process. Because politics and administration are separate, there is no need for the public administrator to include the citizen in decision making. According to Progressive principles, democracy does not happen at the point of administration; democracy happens in the political process.

What most contemporary reformers have learned is that the public does need to be involved in administrative practices and decision making. One of the failures of Progressive era reforms is that the professionalization of the administrative state has separated the people from their government in such a way that they rarely feel connected to the government or the governance process. A government of experts, based in technical knowledge, drives a wedge between the ordinary citizen and governance.

In the United States, what could be considered a crisis in relationships between people and their government has occurred. Never before in U.S. history have distrust and disillusionment with government been higher. Berman (1997) posits three general sources of dysfunction in the citizen/government relationship: (a) citizens believe government is using its power against them; (b) citizens perceive government as ineffective, inefficient, or otherwise problematic; and (c) citizens feel ignored, misunderstood, and disenfranchised by government.

In contemporary times, we can see evidence of all three. The perception that government is exercising illegitimate power is most clearly reflected in separatist and militia movements. But vehement antigovernment feelings are also voiced by populists, Christian fundamentalists, gun owners, home schoolers, loggers, libertarians, constitutionalists, and individual rights advocates. As Tolchin points out, the difference between contemporary antigovernment movements and those in the past is that today "anger at government intrusiveness crosses economic and ideological lines" (1996: 78).

There is also a clear stream of criticism centering on the ineffectiveness and inefficiency of government policies and services. Some current reform movements take this contemporary condition as their organizing principle, "reinventing" government to make it better, smaller, and designed to meet "customer" and/or "client" needs. In these scenarios, citizenship is conceptualized in an exchange relationship: The goal of government is to meet citizen-customers' needs in the most efficient and effective manner. Needless to say, there are many inefficiencies and problems with government policies and services that need addressing, but the reinvention movement only reaches part of the problem.

The remaining condition is, perhaps, the most fundamental of Americans' negative feelings: that government has nothing to do with them. Government exercises too much power and in the wrong ways, and it appears to care little about ordinary citizens, their lives, and their problems.

This chapter addresses this last condition, answering the question, How can public administration heal the deep disconnection between citizens and their governments? Implicit in this question are several assumptions:

1. Citizenship is something more than being a customer or client of government services.
2. Public administration can, and should, play a significant role in the democratic process.
3. The potential for citizen engagement in governance processes can be realized if authentic citizen participation/engagement is engendered. What we call citizen apathy in contemporary times is learned helplessness, a response to a political and administrative process that has locked the citizen out. If administrators create a space for citizens in governance processes, they will be there at the table.

Sherry Arnstein's (1969) classic "ladder of citizen participation" differentiated fake participation and full participation (with several steps in between as the rungs of the ladder). The participation practices of contemporary reforms can be arrayed in a similar way (see Fig. 1). At the low end of the spectrum are reform practices that focus only on improving the management practices of administration without considering the relationship between the citizenry and their governments—what we call *passive* administration and *passive* citizenship.

Somewhere in the middle are the participation practices of reinvention and total quality management (TQM) reforms, in which the citizen as customer or client is involved in the governance process as a part of the production/satisfaction equation—what we call *quasi-passive* citizenship and administration. At the top

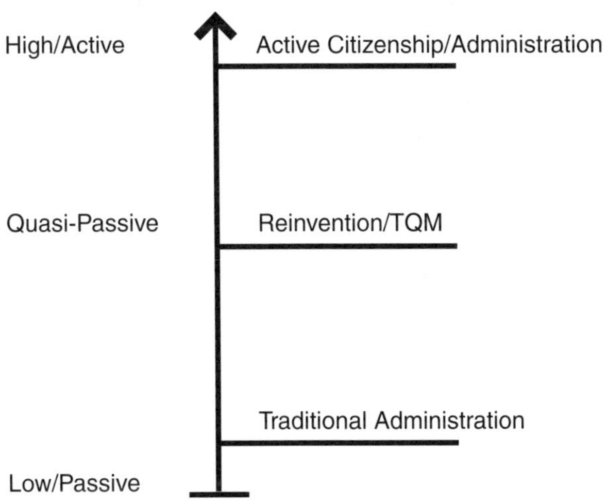

FIG. 1 Participation continuum.

of the spectrum is authentic citizen and administrator engagement in governance processes, what we call *active* administration and *active* citizenship.

At the heart of active citizenship and administration is the belief that citizens want to be more than passive observers, consumers, or customers of public services. Also important in active citizenship and administration is the belief that government workers, both those on the firing line and those in management jobs more removed from direct service, want to take active steps to help remedy citizen discontent, not by papering it over with public relations efforts, but by opening government to the participation of concerned citizens.

We begin this chapter by defining citizenship and then examining how citizenship and administration have been practiced and conceptualized throughout American history. We posit, as do many of our colleagues (e.g., Box, 1998; Gawthrop, 1998; McSwite, 1997; Thomas, 1995), that the contemporary context demands that citizens have a greater role in government. We then compare and contrast active and passive administration and citizenship, leaving the reader with a series of recommendations for ways to practice active administration.

CITIZENSHIP DEFINED

The idea of citizenship has a long history in Western political philosophy, beginning with the city-states of ancient Greece. Citizenship has been thought of as both a status and a practice. As *status,* it connotes formal relationships between the individual and the state, including rights (voting, free speech, and freedom of association) but few if any duties. As *practice,* citizenship entails obligations and activities that make up the essence of political life, such as participation in governance and the duty to consider the general good.

To the average person, civil and political rights such as those contained in the Bill of Rights of the U.S. Constitution amount to *the* meaning of citizenship. Yet with the obvious exception of the right to vote, virtually all the rights and benefits commonly associated with citizenship are also granted to noncitizens. Simply as a legal status, then, the idea of citizenship has little distinctive content.

This thin understanding of citizenship is a reflection of the U.S. founders' grounding in the classical liberal philosophy of Hobbes and Locke, in which the most important issue is limiting the reach of government so that the private rights of individuals, particularly their right to amass property, are protected. Government activity in this mode of thinking is limited to guarding against external threat and adjudicating internal disputes. In the classical liberal framework, a sharp separation exists between the economic and political realms. Liberty is thought to require the right to accumulate according to one's individual interests and talents, making economic inequality inevitable. Yet it is clear that politics and economics are intertwined. Policy decisions allow and constrain market dynamics that directly affect citizens' lives; at the same time, economic conditions shape political opportunities and priorities, not only which candidates for office citizens support but whether they are likely to vote at all. For these reasons, the political equality theoretically inherent in the idea of equal citizenship has little practical content. Citizenship as legal status consists mainly of "freedom from."

Citizenship as practice, in contrast, emphasizes "freedom to." In this framework, citizenship is seen as a set of activities and capacities. The classic vision is Aristotle's: "What effectively distinguishes the citizen proper from all others is his participation in giving judgment and in holding office" (1981: Sec. 1274a22). Citizens take turns ruling and being ruled. Their authority may be limited, but with respect to the responsibility they are assigned, it is decisive. They make public decisions based on their sense of the public interest, using *phronesis,* or practical wisdom, experiential knowledge relevant to the circumstances. By participating in governance, citizens develop capacities and skills important to the effective conduct of public affairs. Because they have to wrestle with problems larger than their own private concerns, they develop the kind of broad understanding and judgment that will ensure that their decisions are well made. As John Stuart Mill put it, the citizen "is called upon . . . to weigh interests not his own; to apply, at every turn, principles and maxims which have for their reason of existence the common good" (1972: 233). Tocqueville argued in a similar way that through this educative process of having to make public decisions, initially self-interested participation would be transmuted to something approaching classical virtue (1945: II, p. 112). A further benefit of active citizenship, in this line of thinking, is that citizens so engaged will appreciate the interaction itself and therefore strengthen their sense of community. By joining in civil and political organized activity citizens learn to value not agreement but collaboration. As Benjamin Barber suggests, through "strong democratic talk," which may often involve disagreement, citizens become "capable of genuinely public thinking and political judgment and thus able to envision a common future in terms of genuinely common goals" (1984: 197).

In what follows, we suggest that in general citizenship in U.S. history has been understood and practiced in the thin, classical liberal mode. In this framework citizens serve mainly as passive objects of administrative action, which either restricts or allows their private activities. We advocate a fuller understanding in the active, Aristotelean sense, one in which administrators and citizens join to exercise practical wisdom about public affairs.

THE PRACTICE OF CITIZENSHIP AND ADMINISTRATION IN A HISTORICAL CONTEXT

In general, citizenship in U.S. history has leaned toward classical liberalism, giving it a constricted and instrumental role, one apparent in the limited and distanced part citizens actually play in government today. The founders believed that the extended geographic scope and social complexity of the new American state made direct participation by citizens unworkable. Madison argued that popular governance could only work in "a small spot" (Cooke, 1961: 84). More important, however, in Madison's view, were the propensity of popular governments to the "violence of faction" and their tendency to produce decisions based on "the superior force of an interested and overbearing majority" (1961: 57).

The founders were advocates of representative government because representation makes it possible to extend government over a large area and serves to "refine and enlarge the public views, by passing them through the medium of a chosen body of citizens, whose wisdom may best discern the true interest of their country" (Cooke, 1961: 62–63). The Federalists believed that ordinary people were neither qualified for nor interested in participating directly in governance, other than through voting. Instead of a government "of the people, by the people, and for the people," the founders' government would be an "elite *republic* of elected representatives who would deliberate together and speak *for* the people" (Fishkin, 1995: 21; emphasis in original).

During the early years of the American republic, ordinary people's public role was sharply restricted. Only a select group of white male property owners was allowed to vote. Governing was left safely in the hands of wise leaders; what Mosher (1982) has called "government by gentlemen" prevailed. Governments, during this period, in general, were small and weak. The federal government mostly delivered mail, fought wars, secured new territories, and collected customs and excise taxes. Administrative agencies were organized in a semiaristocratic rather than a bureaucratic fashion. Kinship and class shaped membership in the early administrative agencies. "New England town hall" style of local governance was being practiced in some places (Box, 1998), although beyond the Atlantic seaboard local governance was weak and dispersed.

Although the franchise gradually expanded, not until the presidency of Andrew Jackson did thinking about the capacities and proper role of citizens and administrators change. Jacksonian thinking expanded the pool of fit candidates for administrative office, from the well born to any citizen who had demonstrated his loyalty to the political party in power. The door to direct involvement in governmental processes was opened to ordinary citizens.

This expanded view of citizenship led to an increase of public activity. At about the time Tocqueville visited the United States, citizen participation in public activity was at a high point. For those who qualified, the citizen role was not just a legal status but a performance. In small towns across the country, the "town hall" style of local governance and activities was put into place. Citizens and officials worked closely together to govern their communities, although we know in retrospect that only a select group of citizens was actually involved (Skowronek, 1982; Wiebe, 1967). For every person who felt a part of the government, there were handfuls more on the outside: slaves or those one step from slavery, women, immigrants, and other marginalized people.

For the most part, ties to political parties defined the administrative role during this time, still limited by the restricted scope of government responsibilities. Jackson sought to systematize agency processes somewhat in order to make good on his statement that anyone could do government work (Morone, 1990), thus beginning the movement toward bureaucratization.

In the late 19th and early 20th centuries another significant change occurred in citizenship and administration, one that reversed the emphasis on direct involvement of ordinary citizens and the simplicity of government work, arguing, instead, the need for administrative expertise. This is the birth of Progressive era administration.

Woodrow Wilson's (1887) famous essay "The Study of Administration" is emblematic of Progressive ideals. Wilson argued that administrators should be given considerable latitude in the execution of their duties, a freedom that was defensible because administration was not political (the genesis of the politics/administration dichotomy). Administrators carried out the laws, holding themselves accountable to the citizenry at large. Citizens were to serve as ultimate source of legitimacy and not to become meddlesome. Citizens became the source of something called public opinion.

Progressive reformers called for administrative practices based on scientific knowledge. In their view, the proper role of citizens in the reform process was to inform themselves about issues and rally round the quest for efficient, expert government methods. Progressives sought to improve public opinion by making it judicious. Citizens were assured that the experts and professional administrators were more capable of handling public problems and situations and better able to make decisions than common folk. The public service, growing rapidly because of the need for infrastructure and services, was developing into a government "of the technocrats, by the technocrats, and for the technocrats" (Kearny and Sinha, 1988: 571).

In the 1960s the dialogue about citizenship and administration shifted once again. Growing public distrust of governmental institutions drove many citizens to challenge the legitimacy of administrative and political processes (Parr and Gates, 1989). This distrust, coupled with federal mandates requiring more public participation, opened the door for citizens to become more involved in administrative processes. However, this participatory moment was short-lived; it died a-borning when federally supported citizen action threatened the power base of local officials. Meaningful citizen involvement lived on here and there and in a plethora of administrative regulations aimed at getting citizen "input," usually through largely ineffective public hearings.

It was during this time that citizens became seen as clients or consumers—as passive recipients of governmental services. Requirements for citizen participation were generally treated in administrative agencies as a cost of doing business instead of as an asset to effectiveness or a responsibility worth carrying out for its own sake (Mladenka, 1981; Jones, 1981). At best, citizens were viewed as a constituency, the source of important political support (McNair et al., 1983) or of important values to guide policy decisions (Stewart et al., 1984). As a result of seeing citizen participation as a cost of doing business, by the early 1980s public participation was beginning to be perceived negatively, as not necessarily enhancing administrative processes, especially as participation detracted from administrative expertise.

Treating citizens as a business cost has led to a kind of citizenship that Rimmerman (1997) calls "outlaw" citizenship. As Rimmerman indicates, the failure to integrate citizens into the governance process has led to "new movements of Left and Right with a strategy for promoting political, social, and economic change" (p. 72). Both the Left and Right in these outlaw citizenship movements practice carefully choreographed "disruptive politics and potential threats to system stability" (p. 62). This type of citizenship is characterized by the practices of contemporary groups such as citizen militias, Operation Rescue, ACT-UP, NIMBYs, and EARTH FIRST!

In the 1990s, these movements, along with environmental activism, new class social movements, neighborhood action in response to crime and other urban problems, and political organization around ideological issues, led to a resurgence in public participation activity (Thomas, 1995; Timney, 1996) and to changes in the citizen-administrator relationship. Ironically, although participation in voting is at an all-time low, and observers are decrying a general lack of civic involvement (e.g., Putnam, 1995), some citizens are demanding a place at the table in administrative decision making. A Kettering Foundation report (1991) said it best, Citizens are not apathetic, as many claim, but rather feel "impotent" (p. 4). Apathy implies a voluntary, intentional choice. Impotence is involuntary; citizens believe their lack of participation has been forced on them, against their wishes. This involuntary state is the result of several centuries of citizenship defined in a passive manner.

In such a climate, it is not surprising that administrators and citizens are frustrated. Citizens believe that the information they receive from agencies is managed, controlled, and manipulated in order to limit their capacity to participate. Citizens see the techniques of participation (public hearings, surveys, focus groups) as designed, at best, to generate input and, at worst, to keep citizens on the outside of the governance process. Citizens are particularly sensitive to vacuous or false participation efforts that ask for and then discount public input. Such inauthentic processes simply lead to greater tension between administrators and citizens. It is better not to work with citizens at all than to work with them under false, purely instrumental pretenses (King et al., 1998a).

Administrators, for their part, know that citizen involvement is desirable but are, at best, "ambivalent about public involvement or, at worst, . . . find it problematic" (King et al., 1998a: 319). Administrators are no longer addressing simple problems with relatively simple answers. They are no longer addressing a public that can situate its identity collectively. As Lance Bennett sees it, the "breakdown of broadly shared social and political experience, and the rise of personalized realities" (Bennett, 1998: 741) changed the nature of politics and administration in the late 1990s. When we moved away from "collective" politics (political parties, broad-based identity groups organized around "values") to what Bennett calls "life-style" politics (fragmented identities, narrow identity groups organized around life-style issues) the connection between people and their governments fragmented even more.

Administrators are grappling with these problems, these "wicked problems—with no solutions, only temporary and imperfect resolutions" (Fischer, 1993: 172). They need guidance from citizens, but

> although many public administrators view close relationships with citizens as both necessary and desirable, most of them do not actively seek public involvement. If they do seek it, they do not use public input in making decisions. . . . These administrators believe that greater citizen participation increased inefficiency because participation creates delays and increases red tape. (King et al., 1998a: 319)

ACTIVE CITIZENSHIP AND ACTIVE ADMINISTRATION

We'd like to suggest that citizen participation—or active citizenship in the Aristotelean mode—*is* the answer to the current conundrum for both citizens and administrators and to encourage administrators to think a bit more deeply about participation. Citizen participation because citizens demand it, or because someone had mandated it, or because it seems the right thing to do is the first step. Participation that results from service quality mandates or reinvention efforts is also a good first step—but only a first step.

> *I often get the sense with administrators that they are impatient with this notion of active citizen engagement and reluctant to put a lot of effort into it, for reasons varying from a) "we're the experts, we know best, why should we let the citizens clutter things up with their opinions which are uninformed at best," to b) "the politicians always want to talk about this and it's all just hype so why bother," to c) "when we were idealistic we too believed in citizen participation but long years of experience have beaten it out of us."*
>
> I *suspect they haven't yet come to terms with the realities of government in the 90s and beyond. Remember all the talk about participatory democracy? Well, some of it happened as predicted (more access to more information, for instance) and some of it didn't (we have less time to absorb the information so we're going to have to resort to ten-second sound bites*

> *and then we'll grow disillusioned). The net result, in my view, is that we have no choice now but to make our best efforts to solicit active engagement and participation or the citizens will punish us for not doing it, by refusing to support tax referendums, by not voting at all, by falling for election-year rhetoric etc. Government's gotten harder. The only possible response is to make it better, and in a democracy the best way to do that is to involve the citizens in the difficult work. (Linda Chapin, former Orange County, Florida, chairman)*

Participation that is not genuine or authentic—that does not involve sharing public decision making with citizens—will not soothe citizen discontent. Indeed, it is likely to make things worse. Unless we fundamentally change the way we administer—unless we move away from "passive administration" and toward "active administration"—then citizen participation efforts are likely to come to naught.

What do we mean by "passive" and "active" administration? These two ways of administering differ in (a) how the administrator perceives himself or herself (b) whether the administrator is free to shape his or her own work and influence the environment, (c) the relationship between citizens and administrators, and (d) how citizen participation is used and valued.

Passive Administration

Passive administration is administration done "the old way." Passive administrators are cogs in the wheel of the bureaucratic machine. They are passive because they do not actively shape their administrative environment and relationships. Passive administrators may not see themselves as passive because they have been socialized to see themselves as experts, as the people at the center of public decision making. They base decisions on abstract data and institutional demands. But they do not take advantage of the discretionary authority they have to reshape their relationships with citizens.

Passive administrators expect citizens to be passive. They tend not to value the lived experiences of the citizenry as an important element in decision making. Passive administrators do not realize that political or relational goals are as important to governing as is efficiency. Passive administrators view citizen participation as a cost of doing business instead of as an essential part of governing, worth carrying out for its own sake. Passive administrators tend to use techniques of participation (public hearings, surveys, focus groups) to generate input, but also to keep citizens separate from, on the outside of, the governance process.

It is important to note here that passive administration is the kind of administration that most leaders, except those on the cutting edge, expect.

Active Administration

> *A very real difficulty is the belief that "no matter what we do it probably won't make a difference, so why kill ourselves trying?" This is where I can offer my encouraging statistics, which surprised even me!*
>
> *From the University of Central Florida's Orange County, FL, Citizen Survey:*
>
>> *Citizens have greatly improved their views of Orange County Government. Whereas in 1996 only 46.8% of residents indicated that they had a positive image of Orange County Government, by 1999 that percentage had increased to 75.5%. Undoubtedly, part of the improvement might be attributed to specific efforts to make Orange County Government more accessible to its citizens. Indeed, whereas in 1996 only 33.9% of respondents believed that Orange County Government was interested in what they had to say, by 1999 this figure had increased to 59.6%. Today, 68.5% of residents trust Orange County Government to do what is right most of the time.*
>>
>> *IT DOES WORK! (Linda Chapin, former Orange County Florida, chairman)*

Active administrators see their own roles and their relationships with citizens more creatively. In fact, they see citizens as *citizens* and not as customers, clients, or taxpayers. The word *citizen* is used intentionally here, instead of the word *public,* not to create an exclusionary category of people who have legal status and rights, but to draw attention to the fullness of the term *citizenship* and to the notion of citizenship as a *practice.* Active administrators use the discretion available to them to shape their work and influence their environments (freed by leadership that empowers administrators and facilitates their work). Active administrators expect (and encourage) citizens to be active; active citizenship means sharing in public decision making. Citizen participation, for active administrators, is about interaction (acting together), not about input. Active administrators create opportunities for direct, genuine interaction (not surveys, public hearings, or focus groups that are not interactive) between citizens and bureaucrats.

Active administrators do not see themselves as experts. Active administrators redefine expertise because they realize that citizens have the direct knowledge that makes it possible to connect the abstractions of the law with the real needs of people.

Active administrators are able to deal with some of the efficiency losses that occur when you turn over decision-making power to citizens in order to reach gains. This means relinquishing control (a very difficult thing to do) and not letting things backslide to "business as usual" when plans are completed. The process entails a reordering of priorities: Active citizens become as important a result of good administration as any other outcome. Understood this way, citizen action is no longer seen as a cost of doing business, but as a necessary element in it.

Administrators can change the nature of their relationships with citizens by practicing active administration with active citizens. They can forge citizen-government connections that help to give citizens the sense that government is not some alien force pressing down on them from above, but public-regarding activity in which they can join.

It is important to note here that active administration is about *engaging* citizens, not about citizen *participation.* This is not just semantics. A participant may or may not be engaged. Engaging citizens means sharing power with them, not just involving them. Active administrators figure out ways to transfer authority to citizens: that is, to give up some of their own prerogative to act without consulting citizens and taking what they say seriously. The knowledge that citizens have, which arises from their lived experiences, legitimates the power turned over to them, on the premise that, when you're trying to "serve" citizens, you can't do it effectively unless their knowledge, and not just professional understandings of their lives, is brought to bear. Active citizens exercise decisive judgment on public matters, and active administrators clear a path in order for them to be able to do so.

> *Where the rubber hits the road: From theory to practice*
> *Two assumptions underlie the new relationship proposed here. The administrator's discretion can open up a public space where the voice of citizens is heard. Citizens express what it feels like to have actual or proposed policies impinge on their lived lives. Administrators have the authority to make things happen; citizens have the knowledge of what it means to make things happen. Authority without knowledge is blind, knowledge without authority is powerless. (Ralph Hummel, Professor, The University of Akron.)*

ACTIVE ADMINISTRATORS IN ACTION

In Orange County, Florida, County Chairman Linda Chapin set up situations within which active administrators could work with citizens to address problems. In early 1991, Chapin met with residents of a small and impoverished rural community in the county and said, "I'm here to listen to your concerns, I want to help." She was caught by surprise at the resulting torrent of hostility and resentment. After being ignored, shut out, and neglected for so long, residents were unwilling to believe that anyone could be sincere about changing the relationships between them and their government. Chapin knew that she couldn't work with this community in insincere ways that had become all too typical among government officials. She knew she had to do something different.

She set about creating the conditions under which she could work with citizens. Orange County staff literally invited citizens into the governance process. They put into practice what is recommended of active administrators: They held work meetings with citizens in which participants (citizens and administrators, together at the table) worked to imagine their futures and made plans to move their communities forward. They listened to citizens. They responded to citizen concerns. They created project teams and advisory committees to lead projects through from beginning to end. They allowed citizens, not administrative and political concerns, to set the agendas. They gave up administrative control, actually inviting citizens in to work together to solve problems. For example, citizens worked with administrators to make budget decisions for their communities—working through the trade-offs between filling potholes and installing streetlights. Chapin made the needed organizational changes to empower the administrators (reorganizing, working on flex-schedules, etc.). She also tied citizen engagement to individual and departmental rewards.

Administrators were there to *serve* the citizen's visions—to do what needed to be done to coordinate and staff the citizen's vision, to provide technical support and advice, and to help find the resources necessary to make things happen.

Chapin found ways to supply resources for this effort by channeling and coordinating existing resources; very little of the money spent on the CITIZENS FIRST! campaign was "new" money. Most of the money spent was from savings or from earmarking of existing funds for different purposes. For example, instead of using county money to condemn homes with code violations and/or doing the repairs themselves, the active administrators worked with the residents to paint and repair these homes, using paint and supplies donated by area retailers. As the former executive director Joe Gray says, "If the county would have condemned the homes, or done the work instead, it would have cost several thousand dollars in staff time, supplies, equipment, and legal fees. Instead, it cost the county $300" (King et al., 1998b: 193).

Instead of subtracting from administrative efficiency and effectiveness, Gray and Chapin say that active administration enhances administrative efficiency and effectiveness. Although it may seem that it takes more time to work collaboratively with citizens to solve problems, in the end, it often produces a better solution, saving time and money. According to Gray and Chapin (1998):

> By openly involving citizens in the capital budget process, bureaucrats expose citizens to the reality of the budgetary and legislative constraints that bureaucrats face. Administrators grow to appreciate the frustration that citizens are confronted with in their attempts to deal with government bureaucracy and to understand widespread apathy among fellow

> citizens. As a result of their involvement, citizens are learning to trust those heretofore nameless, faceless individuals who collectively compose the previously despised public bureaucracy. (p. 191)

What happened to Linda Chapin, Joe Gray, and their staff as a result of working with citizens was no less than a transformation. Chapin saw that the old "I'm from the government and I'm here to help" was not going to cut it. She knew that this is about more than just technique; it is about fundamentally changing the relationship between citizens and governments. She knew that she could go into communities and hold a few public hearings and run a survey or two and maybe change things a bit, but she was not satisfied with that option. She wanted to make a real difference in the communities and that meant giving the communities back to the residents. That meant respecting the experiences of citizens and making a space for citizen experience in the governance process.

CHALLENGES AND BARRIERS TO ACTIVE ADMINISTRATION

It is naive to assume that one can simply turn over administrative control and power to citizens; that simply inviting citizens into current administrative processes will solve all the problems. Individual resistance to sharing power gets in the way, particularly when administrators are socialized to be the experts. In addition, public agencies are legally charged with performing activities in the public interest and must work within their respective administrative, legal, political, and budgetary constraints to do so. Finally, administrative systems and processes are currently organized not to include citizens; including them requires the willingness and opportunity to make important organizational changes.

There are basically three main types of barriers to active administration (King et al., 1998a):

1. *The realities of daily life:* Many administrators and citizens are too used to being passive and let the complications of daily life (and the busy pace) get in the way. This is the barrier that is most often cited as the reason why people don't practice active administration and citizenship—the assumption is that we cannot fit one more task into our busy days.

2. *Administrative systems and processes:* The most pervasive barriers to active administration and active citizenship are current administrative and political practices. This is a paradox. Although most administrators see citizen engagement as desirable, the very people who desire citizen engagement block any engagement that challenges the status quo (or business as usual). In Orange County, for example, the Targeted Community Initiatives (TCI) projects were suspended under new leadership, and active administrators working to transform

Orange County government were displaced. In other places, administrators struggle on a daily basis with doing things differently.

3. *Participation techniques:* Many of us simply do not have the skills and tools needed to practice active administration. Indeed, very few training and educational institutions focus on preparing their trainees/students for active administration.

The four *E*'s of active citizenship and administration (see Table 1) can address these barriers: *e*mpowering and *e*ducating citizens, re*e*ducating administrators, and re*e*ducating administrators. Empowering citizens means designing processes so that citizens know their participation has the potential to make a difference, a representative range of citizens are included, and there are visible outcomes—in other words, participation does have an effect. Educating citizens focuses on teaching organization, leadership, and research skills as well as the *practices* of citizenship. "Democracy schools, much like the citizenship schools that fueled the civil rights movement in the South, should be established in local communities to encourage people to see they can make a difference if they get involved" (King et al. 1998b: 324).

TABLE 1 Addressing the Barriers to Active Citizenship and Administration

- Empowering and Educating citizens
  - Teach citizens how to work with and within the system.
  - Hold workshops with administrators that focus on meeting skills and technical training (e.g., understanding research and government information).
  - Create opportunities for people to interact with each other.
- ReEducating administrators
  - Encourage people to think about citizens differently.
  - Make opportunities for people to interact with citizens—often.
  - Provide training in facilitation, team building, organizational development, discourse, and interpersonal skills.
- Enabling administrative systems and processes
  - Allocate resources for participation efforts.
  - Reward people for participation efforts; change job descriptions.
  - Allow for mistakes.
  - Shift ideas about government workers' work schedules—this means also addressing issues of accountability that arise when government workers are not "at their desks" or not working from "9 to 5."
  - Make citizen engagement an unquestioned part of government.
  - Work toward authentic collaboration among and between administrators and politicians.

Reeducating administrators means redefining the role of expertise in public administration and training administrators to be facilitators, communicators, listeners, and participants in a discourse that has, at its center, situation-regarding intentionality (power and community are grounded in the issue or situation) instead of self-regarding intentionality (the goal is to protect self, promote self-interests, and hoard power) (Fox and Miller, 1995). All of this is moot, of course, unless administrative systems and processes are gradually changed to allow active citizenship and administration. Most administrative practices, we argue, can be reshaped in order to promote collaboration with citizens.

WHY PRACTICE ACTIVE CITIZENSHIP AND ADMINISTRATION?

The short answer to why one should practice active citizenship and administration is that without it we are destined to continue to practice either government *for* the people (traditional administration), government *with* the people (citizens and government work together, but government retains its expertise, standing, and privilege), or government *by* the people (citizens take over government or practice outlaw citizenship). It is only through active citizenship and participation that government *of* the people is possible. Government *of* the people is

> based on collaboration or integrative participation . . . in which active citizens and administrators work together on administrative and citizen needs, goals, and objectives in ways that allow new perspectives and approaches to emerge from the deliberative situation. (King et al., 1998b: 203)

The call for a genuine and authentic role for citizens in their governance processes is not a new call. Louis Gawthrop has pointed out that each generation produces its own call for a renewed sense of the public interest among citizens. But perhaps not enough attention has been given to the potential for public administration as a means to achieve this revivified public:

> To run the risk of advancing a tautology, public management is public service, or service to the public. Hence, if the concept of democracy is to have any meaning at all, public managers are the servants of the public where the primacy of the body politic is explicitly recognized as the linchpin of our democratic ethos. Therefore, to argue that the primary mission of public management is to serve the public, while not particularly novel or unique, is, nonetheless, somewhat of a radical departure from the notions of the aggregate groupings that have constituted a phantom public in the minds of many professional public administrators. (Gawthrop, 1984: 103)

According to McGregor, within certain limits, "in a democracy practitioners must constantly seek ways to make themselves unnecessary" (1984, 128). Our message is only slightly different: We suggest that "active administration" occurs when administrators use their authority to make themselves somewhat less—and citizens much more—necessary. In this way they transform citizens from Gawthrop's "phantom public" to real actors in public affairs.

CONCLUSION

This chapter addresses the question of how to heal the deep disconnection between people and their governments. Active administration, as it is described here, operates on the assumption that citizenship is more than a *status* and is more than a category of belonging that confers rights. Citizenship is an active *practice* of engagement in public decision making and governance that builds the capacity for people to know and practice a common good.

Active administration goes hand in hand with active citizenship. Historically, the practice of public administration has been such that it ensures a passive relationship between the expert, learned, public administrator and the lay citizen or client. Active administrators forge citizen/government engagements, using their administrative power and discretion to draw citizens into administrative processes.

Active administration is not easy to practice in contemporary times. A consumption-based political economy that focuses upon promoting the individual and wicked political/social problems of the postmodern moment all make active administration difficult to practice. Deeply entrenched administrative habits and practices also are barriers. We maintain that these barriers are surmountable by focusing on the three *E*'s: empowering and educating citizens, reeducating administrators, and reeducating administrators.

Finally, it is imperative that administrative reforms go beyond simply including the citizen/customer in a service or goods process. The call for greater democracy, for a more empowered and engaged citizen base, and for public administrators to play a significant role in building a revivified public is not a new call, but it is an enduring one. It is only through active citizenship and administration that government *of* the people is possible.

REFERENCES

Aristotle. (1981). *The Politics* T. A. Sinclair, Trans. Penguin Books, Harmondsworth, England.

Arnstein, Sherry R. (1969). A ladder of citizen participation. *Journal of the American Institute of Planners. 35*(3): 216–224.

Barber, Benjamin (1984). *Strong Democracy: Participatory Politics for a New Age.* University of California Press, Berkeley.

Bennett, Lance W. (1998). The uncivic culture: Communication, identity, and the rise of lifestyle politics. *PS.* December: 741–761. *PSOnline* [www.apsanet.org].

Berman, Evan (1997). Dealing with cynical citizens. *Public Administration Review. 57*(2): 105–112.

Box, Richard (1998). *Citizen Governance: Leading American Communities into the 21st Century.* Sage Publications, Thousand Oaks, Calif.

Cooke, Jacob (ed.) (1961). *The Federalist Papers.* Wesleyan University Press. Middletown, Conn.

Fischer, Frank (1993). Citizen participation and the democratization of policy expertise: From theoretical inquiry to practice cases. *Policy Sciences. 26*(3): 165–187.

Fishkin, James S. (1995). *We the People: Public Opinion and Democracy.* Yale University Press, New Haven, Conn.

Fox, Charles J., and Miller, Hugh T. (1995). *Postmodern Public Administration: Toward Discourse.* Sage, Thousand Oaks, Calif.

Gawthrop, Louis C. (1984). Civis, civitas, and civilitas: A new focus for the year 2000. *Public Administration Review. 44*(2): 101–106.

Gawthrop, Louis C. (1998). *Public Service and Democracy: Ethical Imperatives for the 21st Century.* New York: Chatham House.

Gray, Joseph E. and Chapin, Linda W. (1998). Targeted community initiative: "Putting citizens first!" In (C. S. King, et al., eds.). *Government Is Us: Public Administration in an Anti-Government Era* Sage, Thousand Oaks, Calif., pp. 175–191.

Jones, Brian. (1981). Party and bureaucracy: The influence of intermediary groups on urban public service delivery. *American Political Science Review. 75:* 688–700.

Kearny, Richard J., and Sinha, Chandan (1988). Professional and bureaucratic responsiveness: Conflict or compatibility? *Public Administration Review. 48*(5): 571–579.

Kettering Foundation (1991). *Citizens and Politics: A View from Main Street America.* (Report prepared for the Kettering Foundation by the Harwood Group). Kettering Foundation, Dayton, Ohio.

King, Cheryl Simrell, Feltey, Kathryn M., and O'Neill Susel, Bridget (1998a). The question of participation: Toward authentic participation in public decisions. *Public Administration Review. 58*(4): 317–326.

King, Cheryl Simrell, Stivers, Camilla, and Collaborators (1998b). *Government Is Us: Public Administration in an Anti-Government Era.* Sage, Thousand Oaks, Calif.

McGregor, Eugene B. (1984). The great paradox of democratic citizenship and public personnel administration. *Public Administration Review. 44*(2): 126–131.

McNair, Ray H., Caldwell, Russell, and Pollane, Leonard (1983). Citizen participation in public bureaucracies: Foul-weather friends. *Administration and Society. 14:* 507–523.

McSwite, O.C. (1997). *Legitimacy in Public Administration: A discourse Analysis.* Sage, Thousand Oaks, Calif.

Mill, John Stuart (1972). Utilitarianism, On Liberty, and Consideration on Representative Government (H. B. Acton, ed.). Dent/Everyman's Library, London.

Mladenka, Kenneth R. (1981). Citizen demands and urban services: The distribution of bureaucratic response in Chicago and Houston. *American Journal of Political Science. 25:* 693–714.

Morone, James A. (1990). The Democratic wish: Popular participation and the limits of American government. Basic Books: New York.

Mosher, Frederick C. (1982). *Democracy and the Public Service.* Oxford University Press, New York.

Parr, John, and Gates, Christopher (1989). Assessing community interest and gathering community supports. In *Partnerships in Local Governance: Effective Council-Manager Relations.* (ICMA Handbook) (The International City Management Association eds.). International City Management Association, Washington, D.C.

Rimmerman, Craig A. (1997). *The New Citizenship: Unconventional Politics, Activism, and Service.* Westview Press, Boulder, Colo.

Skrowronek, Stephen (1982). *Building a New American State: The Expansion of National Administrative Capacities, 1877–1920.* Cambridge University Press, Cambridge.

Stewart, Thomas, R., Dennis, Robert L., and Ely, David W. (1984). Citizen participation and judgment in policy analysis: A case study of urban air quality. *Policy Science. 17:* 67–87.

Thomas, John Clayton (1995). *Public Participation in Public Decisions.* Jossey-Bass, San Francisco.

Timney, Mary (1996). *Overcoming NIMBY: Using Citizen Participation Effectively.* Paper presented at *The 57th National Conference of the American Society for Public Administration.* Atlanta, July.

Tocqueville, Alexis de (1945). *Democracy in America.* 2 Vols. Vintage, New York. (Original work published in 1830).

Tolchin, Susan (1996). *The Angry American: How Voter Rage Is Changing the Nation.* Westview, Boulder, Colo.

Wiebe, Robert (1967). *The Search for Order: 1877–1920.* Hill & Wang, New York.

Wilson, Woodrow (1887). The study of administration. *Political Sciences Quarterly. 2:* 197–222.

23

Downsizing in the Public Sector: Implications for Public Administration

Mary Ann Feldheim
Department of Public Administration,
University of Central Florida,
Cocoa, Florida

This chapter examines downsizing, the reduction of the work force, in the public sector. First, the background of downsizing is presented, focusing on cutback management and the reinvention of government reform movement. Second, the major concepts of reinvention reform, managerialism, and decentralization are discussed, and the impact of downsizing on public sector employee trust and commitment is explored. Finally, the implications of downsizing for public administration are discussed, focusing on the loss of employee trust and the moral implications of downsizing for the public service ethic.

The importance of examining the moral implications for public administration of downsizing cannot be understated. Extensive downsizing through reduction-in-force techniques, cutback management, privatization, and contracting out has reduced not only the work force but the public service ethic of employees and the level of moral interaction between individuals in both the public and private sectors. I argue that public administrators must recognize the damage downsizing has caused to the public service ethic and to the public interest and actively work to rebuild the infrastructure of the profession through strategies that support the public service ethic of serving the public interest. The following chapter provides a logical argument that downsizing has had damaging effects on the public sector, beginning with the background of downsizing in the public sector.

BACKGROUND OF DOWNSIZING

In the public sector downsizing or reducing the work force occurred first as a political practice. Patronage in the early years of American history saw changes in the work force with the election of each new politician, who repaid his supporters through dispensing governmental positions. These changes may or may not have reduced the size of the bureaucracy, but the composition of the bureaucracy always changed. With civil service reform and the creation of a dual system of public service through the Pendleton Act of 1883 (Klingner and Nalbandian, 1998) political appointees were the most susceptible to the political pressures for change; civil service employees were assured much more security in their positions. These conditions remained fairly stable until the 1970s with government management strategies focused on growth and oriented toward planning, but a dramatic change began in the 1970s and continues today, as government management requires a focus on no growth and an actual cutback in services and personnel.

Cutback Management

Managing decline became known as *cutback management,* and the tools to achieve this decline were hiring freezes, personnel ceilings, contracting out of services, and the reduction-in-force strategy (Cayer, 1986). One of the most widely used means to reduce the size of government has been the reduction-in-force strategy. Political appointees frequently have been charged with carrying out these functions in the Civil Service.

Reduction-in-force strategies (RIFs) are defined as separation, downgrade, or lateral assignment of employees to decrease the number of people employed in a given organization (Holzer, 1986; Cayer, 1986). In a RIF employees are released from jobs for reasons other than disciplinary, and governments may use this technique when there is a lack of work, a lack of funds, or a reorganization (Rich, 1986a). The factors that trigger a RIF in the public sector have been systemic economic problems, major events, demographic changes, changes in priorities, and conservative arguments about the appropriate size and function of government (Holzer, 1986).

Layoffs have been used extensively in the public sector to effect a RIF. There are two highly political reasons for this—first, a layoff is a very visible way to cut costs, second, the benefits are easy to measure in immediate savings (Greenhalgh and McKersie, 1980). In the public sector *cutback management* and *retrenchment* are the terms used to describe organizational strategies to face declining resources (Behn, 1980). The private sector has used the term *downsizing* extensively to describe the same type of situation, in which an organization reduces its work force to respond to a perceived change in environmental conditions.

In the private sector downsizing is a competitive organizational strategy whereby human resources, the most significant expenditure of an organization, are reduced (McCune et al., 1988). A workable definition of *downsizing* is a purposeful reduction in the size of an organization's work force to improve efficiency, productivity, and competitiveness (Cameron et al., 1991; Cameron 1995). The process affects the size of the organization, work force costs, and work processes. There are four attributes that define downsizing—intent, personnel, efficiency, and processes. *Intent* refers to a purposeful set of activities involving the decrease of personnel by many strategies, with the intent of improving efficiency and decreasing waste by focusing on the organization as the unit of analysis restructuring, redesigning, or eliminating work processes (Cameron, 1994, 1995). Downsizing is accomplished through three primary strategies—work force reduction, organizational redesign, and systemic strategies. The most common type of strategy is to reduce the work force (RIFs), decreasing the number of personnel on the basis of a top-down directive that creates a crisis mentality. In a work force reduction strategy the focus is on eliminating people and quickly reducing the head count for a short-term payoff (Cameron, 1994, 1995).

Work force reduction in the public sector began as cutback management and focusing on dramatic ways to reduce the size of government. Downsizing of government proceeded then to organizational redesign and systemic strategies. Organizational redesign strategies eliminate functions, divisions, and products, focusing on work reduction rather than employee reduction, whereas systemic strategies of downsizing focus on changing organizational culture—attitudes and values of employees to improve the functioning of the organization continuously (Cameron, 1994, 1995). In the public sector the organizational redesign and systemic strategies of downsizing are found in the reinvention of government reform movement. Here the focus is not on an immediate reduction in the size of governmental human resources, but on change in the structure and culture of public administration.

Reinventing Government

Systemic downsizing strategies focus on the organizational culture and values, on the human resource system, on the customer, and on continuous improvement (Cameron, 1994, 1995). In the reinvention movement the primary goal is to change the culture of government organizations from rigid hierarchies that are perceived as unresponsive to flexible, responsive, citizen-oriented organizations. To accomplish this the citizen is seen as the customer, and the human resource system becomes fluid, flexible, and dynamic to meet changing needs and to improve continually (Osborne and Gaebler, 1992). Work redesign as a downsizing strategy eliminates functions, services, or departments in striving to improve efficiency (Cameron, 1994, 1995). In the reinvention movement these strategies are part of the entrepreneurial focus of using new and creative ways to improve government productivity, such as cutting red tape, privatizing, contracting out, and downsizing (Frederickson, 1999).

These systemic strategies and work redesign of downsizing in the public sector are compatible with the reinventing government phenomenon that has predominated in the public administration literature (Carroll, 1996; Moe, 1993; Rosenbloom, 1993; Schachter, 1995; Hays and Whitney, 1997). Reinvention in the form of systemic strategies has been incorporated at the federal, state, local levels since the National Performance Review of 1993 (Egger and O'Leary, 1995).

Since 1992 and the publication of Osborne and Gaebler's book, downsizing strategies in the public sector have been called *reinvention, reengineering, redesign,* and *revitalization.* Two key elements of the reinvention strategies have been identified as managerialism and decentralization of authority. *Managerialism* refers to the use of private sector business practices to deal with public sector problems in terms of the market ideology of capitalism, whereas *decentralization* focuses on making decisions closer to the problem, decreasing the inefficiencies of centralized bureaucracies, and empowering employees (Hays and Whitney, 1997).

MAJOR CONCEPTS OF REINVENTION REFORM

Managerialism

The concept of managerialism emerged during the Reagan administration in response to a changing fiscal situation. At the federal level the civil service became a managerial arm of the president, using a market model and profoundly changing the nature of public service. Seniority and job security were replaced with a focus on performance and individual accountability in a competitive market (Rich, 1986b).

The belief in private sector solutions to public sector problems reflects the changing paradigm in public personnel management that has resulted from the antigovernment sentiment in the reinvention movement. Managerialism values individual accountability, limited and decentralized government, and community responsibility for social services. These values have been translated into alternative mechanisms for providing public services. Contemporary public sector systems provide services through privatization, purchase-of-service agreements, franchise agreements, subsidy arrangements, vouchers, volunteers, self-help, and regulatory and tax incentives (Klingner and Nalbandian, 1998). These mechanisms all are based on the values of managerialism and require systemic changes in the way government functions. The result of these mechanisms is that fewer public employees are needed to provide public services, reducing the need for existing and future public sector employees and effectively downsizing government. In addition to downsizing government through managerialism, the reinvention reform movement attempts to decentralize the authority within the system and empower employees.

Decentralization

Antigovernment sentiments and a belief that centralized bureaucracies are unresponsive and wasteful have fueled the movement toward decentralization. In addition, employee empowerment is the underlying assumption that makes decentralization work (Hays and Whitney, 1997), with its origins in the quality initiative begun in the 1980s.

The quality initiative is a management style aimed at improving organizational performance and meeting customer expectations through continual analysis and improvement of the processes for providing services. Key components of the quality movement are internal and external customer satisfaction, an organizational commitment to quality, the use of continual data analysis, and a shared commitment to the process by empowered employees and enlightened management (Avery and Zabel, 1997; Kano, 1993).

Empowerment of employees requires an organization to change its fundamental assumptions about people, organizations, and management. The assumptions that form the basis of the quality movement are based on the belief that people are intrinsically motivated to succeed, and that for organizations to succeed they must value and empower the individuals who work there. Empowerment is power sharing and requires a change in organizational culture, leadership, and vision to achieve the goals of higher levels of productivity, quality, and customer satisfaction (Gibson et al., 1997).

Decentralized organizations are flatter, more empowered, and focus on communication and on outcomes more often than traditional hierarchical organizations do. Empowerment of employees in decision making is important, allowing timely and individualized responses to client or citizen needs (Berman, 1995). For decentralized organizations to succeed, the focus must be on long-term development, as opposed to short-term profits or cost savings found in the economic model. With a quality focus the purpose of the organization becomes customer satisfaction, and the role of work meets the human need to create or serve (Grant et al., 1994). Inherent in empowerment is the concept that everyone in the organization works continuously to improve all aspects of the work. This requires the organization to provide training, opportunity, and responsibility for decision making in tandem with accountability, mutual respect, and trust (Amsden et al., 1996; Blankstein, 1996; Morris and Haigh, 1996).

Empowerment is the key to decentralized authority and requires that managers representing the organization relinquish some of their power to employees.

For empowerment to occur managers make assumptions regarding the motivation of their employees; in the public sector the motives for public service have been researched.

Managerialism and decentralization in the reinvention of government movement emphasize contradictory philosophies regarding the nature of work and the value and roles of public sector employees. In managerialism the emphasis is on the purchasing of services, not on employees, whereas decentralization requires the empowerment and the valuing of employees. Also, the practices advocated by managerialism work best in centralized and control-oriented structures, thus limiting the ability of decentralization to be effective. A criticism of the reinvention movement has been its tendency to incorporate inconsistent and contradictory goals (Hays and Whitney, 1997). The impact of downsizing on the public sector through cutback management and the reinvention of government are discussed next and linked to the motives for public service.

IMPACT OF DOWNSIZING

Downsizing has become the most feared word in the contemporary quest for economic security (Wallulis, 1998), causing acute job insecurity, which has impacted individuals in all segments of American society, creating people who are bitter, anxious, and disenfranchised. Overall the effect seems to be a deep-seated pessimism as people question the American dream. One impact of downsizing is on individual dignity, which used to be associated with the job. Another impact is on the community, where ties are becoming frayed as corporate America and government continue to downsize. A third impact is on politics, which must respond to the national mood of insecurity (The New York Times, 1996).

The United States Merit Systems Protection Board (1981: Chap. 7) indicates that in organizations undergoing a reduction-in-force, 100 percent of the people in the organization are impacted negatively. Several authors agree that reductions-in-force within the public sector create employee depression, decrease in self-esteem, increase in insecurity, conflict, bitterness, loss of trust, and decline in employee morale (Behn, 1980; Cayer, 1986; Holzer, 1986; Lewis et al., 1983). Downsizing in the public sector has also led to a decline in worker loyalty and impaired the institutional memory in many organizations (Jones, 1998).

The economic model is the basis for the work force reduction strategy of downsizing. Assumptions inherent in the economic model are that individuals are rational, self-interested decision makers driven primarily by economic goals; that economic relations between individuals are governed by contracts; and that organizational structures are determined by cost efficiency (Grant et al., 1994).

Agency theory, contract theory, shareholder value maximization, and transactions cost theory all support the economic model that has grown out of traditional management theory and microeconomics. Influencing organizations in the public sector, public choice theory echoes these same assumptions (Goldsmith, 1996). In the public sector the reinvention of government movement evolved from public choice theory and managerialism or the use of business ideology and practices in the handling of public works. Reinvention, revitalization, and reengineering dominated the public management literature in the 1990s and focused on changing the culture of government operations to the economic model (Frederickson, 1999; Hays and Whitney, 1997).

Reductions in force, privatization, and contracting out are primary elements of the reinvention movement and all are based on the economic model, which sees employee motives to work as driven by economic goals. However, the research on motivation for public service indicates that economic goals are not the dominant motivation in the public sector.

Motives for public service have been divided into three distinct categories—rational motives, norm-based motives, and affective motives. Rational motives are based on utility maximization in economic terms, whereas norm-based motives reflect a public orientation (Knoke and Wright-Isak, 1982; Perry, 1996). Norm-based motives incorporate the ethic of civic duty (Buchanan, 1975); social justice, enhancing the well-being of minorities (Frederickson, 1971); and a commitment to the public interest (Perry, 1996). Affective motives to participate in public service refer to triggers of behavior based on emotional responses to social conditions, such as the idea of compassion, which combines the love of others with the love of regime values (Frederickson and Hart, 1985). Perry (1996) adds the category of self-sacrifice, arguing that the willingness to substitute public service for tangible and financial rewards has a long history.

Rational motives for public sector employment are economically based and support the philosophy of managerialism and private sector strategies of management. Norm-based and affective motives for public sector employment are consistent with decentralization and employee empowerment. A belief in the concepts of duty, responsibility, and commitment to the public interest support empowering the employee, who will act in the public interest and not from self-interest. In addition, motives that are norm-based, affective, and self-sacrificing embody what has been called the *public service ethic*. This school of thought envisions public service as an attitude embodying a sense of duty and public morality (Staats, 1988; Perry, 1996). The public service ethic moves public employment beyond the economic model of the private sector and brings into question the wisdom of linking managerialism and decentralization.

In addition to the philosophic differences between managerialism and decentralization or empowerment, the issue of trust has been raised by several authors, who have linked downsizing strategies with a reduction of trust in organizations (Elangovan and Shapiro, 1998; Holzer, 1986; Mishra and Spreitzer, 1998; Morrison and Robinson, 1997). Most often it is the reduction-in-force downsizing strategy that has eroded trust within organizations. One reason for this is that organizations that downsize target middle management, ending an era of organizational loyalty and creating a new era of insecurity. Not only has downsizing eroded trust, it has contributed to the economic restructuring of America (Wallulis, 1998). The relationship of trust to organizational downsizing strategies is discussed next.

Trust

Trust is an intuitive concept, which eludes precise definition (LaPorte and Metlay, 1996) and is seen as a foundation for social relationships and social order by many intellectual disciplines (Lewicki et al., 1998). In employment relationships trust is based on the psychological contract held by employees regarding the reciprocal obligations between themselves and the organization (Rousseau, 1989). Psychological contracts range from transactional (economic-based) contracts to relational (normative) contracts (Rousseau and Parks, 1993). This division into economic and normative psychological contracts reflects the social science inquiry into trust as a major factor in relationships; two broad approaches to trust have been developed—the economic and the normative (Ruscio, 1997).

Rousseau, Sitkin, Burt, and Camerer (1998) have developed an interdisciplinary model of trust, which places the economic approach to trust (calculus-based trust) at one end of the model and the normative approach to trust (relational trust) at the other end. Trust is presented as a dynamic bandwidth fluctuating between the economic and normative approaches, facilitated or hindered by institutional support and/or control mechanisms. Within this bandwidth of trust, according to Lewicki, Mcallister, and Bies (1998), both trust and distrust exist simultaneously in a state of ambivalence, with trust positive and distrust negative expectations about the conduct of others.

Economic Approach to Trust

The economic approach to trust posits that social relationships are rational and based on self-interest, and individuals calculate the costs and benefits of a relationship to maximize their own interests. This approach to trust is favored by economists and rational choice theorists in sociology and political science (Ruscio, 1997). Managerialism in the reinvention of government movement utilizes the human capital theory, which asserts that workers move from job opportunity to job opportunity on the basis of rational self-interest, improving their economic situation with each move (Rich, 1986a), thereby indicating an economic approach to trust.

Calculus-based trust is the term used to describe this rational approach, in which the characteristics of the relationship are based on economic exchange (Rousseau et al., 1998). Granting trust becomes a calculated risk based on the amount of uncertainty in the relationship and potential pay-off. In this form of relationship, the employee calculates the costs and rewards of the organization's acting in an untrustworthy way (Dasgupta, 1988; Ruscio, 1997; Williamson, 1985).

Transactional contracts, which are monetarily based and use specific, short-term obligations, are the foundation for the economic approach to trust. In transactional contracts there is an expectation of limited involvement by both parties, and quid pro quo exchange governs the interaction with clearly defined obligations and expectations of compensation (O'Connell, 1984). Employees in transactional exchanges are vigilant, wary, and distrustful regarding contract fulfillment because balance and repayment predominate in the relationship (Morrison and Robinson, 1997).

Short-term performance contracts were introduced into government with the passage of the Civil Service Reform Act of 1978. This reform created positions exempt from civil service with employment based on performance of duties contracted for by the employee and increased flexibility in employment decisions for the manager. Other levels of government have also utilized this form of employment, and it has become one tool of the reinvention movement (Klingner and Nalbandian, 1998). These short-term performance contracts appear as rational, transactional contracts with duties detailed for the employee, and certainly for the manager performance contracts are rational and offer flexibility, reflecting the private sector's ability to create at-will employment.

However, many public sector employees are not solely motivated by rational considerations, and the ethic of public service plays an important part in their motivation and organizational commitment. These short-term contracts limit commitment to the organization, focusing only on the short-term accomplishment of specified goals. These transactional contracts ignore the other end of the trust continuum and the development of relational psychological contracts using a normative approach to relationships. The importance of relational trust to public sector employment and maintenance of the public service ethic is covered next.

Normative Approach to Trust

In the normative "relational" approach to trust, employees see trust as an ethical relationship explained in terms of shared ideals and values. Here the focus is on fulfilling obligations, performing duties, and behaving appropriately within the context of the relationship (Ruscio, 1997).

Relational trust develops from repeated interactions over time with reliability; dependability of the interactions develops a shared identity. Attachments are formed in this shared identity and emotions are part of the relationship, which is based on reciprocated interpersonal caring. Employees who refer to the team or the organization as *we,* derive psychic benefits from the relationship and demonstrate this shared identity of relational trust with the institution. Much of societal trust is institution-based, and institutions can control or support the development of trust (Rousseau et al., 1998).

Relational trust evolves from relational psychological contracts, in which the employee must regard his or her obligations to the organization as long-term, broad, and open-ended. Employees operating under a relational contract demonstrate loyalty and support for the organization that are based primarily on socioemotional elements (Rousseau and Parks, 1993).

Public administration literature regarding the motivation of individuals to become public service employees indicates primarily a relational psychological contract. Empirical evidence shows that the reward motivations for public sector employees are different from those in the private sector, with evidence at the federal level that motivation is positively related to organizational commitment (Crewson, 1997). Public sector employees are more interested than private sector employees in altruistic and ideological goals, such as helping others, rather than gaining monetary rewards (Rainey, 1982, 1997).

Motives for public service from norm-based beliefs, affective responses, or self-sacrificing behavior all reflect a commitment based on socioemotional elements necessary to establish a relational psychological contract between the employee and the organization. The impact of downsizing strategies on public sector employees either through a reduction in work force or through the reinventing government movement is linked to the psychological contract in the following section.

Public Sector Downsizing Model

The economic and the normative approaches to trust are inherently different, based on different assumptions about trust relationships, and these assumptions link trust to the discussion of downsizing. The type of downsizing strategy an organization uses leads to the development of a certain type of psychological contract envisioned by the employee and results in a particular type of trust or distrust.

A model of public sector downsizing is presented in Table 1, which identifies the assumptions underlying trust relationships and downsizing strategies. Here the trust continuum is combined with the downsizing strategy to demonstrate how and why downsizing impacts employees and organizational trust.

The downsizing strategy used by an organization is based on decision makers' assumptions regarding others. Reduction-in-force downsizing strategies see individuals as human capital to be manipulated in ways that maximize the economic and political goals of the decision makers. Decisions to downsize by using work force reduction are based on the assumption that all individuals are rational and motivated by self-interest and economic gain, ignoring the socioemotional aspects of individuals. A belief in rational self-interest is a basic assumption of the economic model on which work force reduction strategies are based.

Managerialism in the reinvention of government movement is based on the rationale that by instilling market-based incentives and values in the public sector,

TABLE 1 Public Sector Model of Downsizing

Comparisons	Reduction-in-Force	Managerialism	Decentralization
Assumptions	**Individuals are** ☐ Rational ☐ Self-interested ☐ Economically motivated	**Individuals are** ☐ Rational ☐ Self-interested ☐ Economically motivated	**Individuals are** ☐ Self-interested and altruistic ☐ Motivated to meet human needs to create or be useful
Psychological contracts	**Transactional** ☐ Monetary base ☐ Quid pro quo ☐ Clear obligations and compensation	**Transactional** ☐ Monetary base ☐ Quid pro quo ☐ Clear obligations and compensation	**Relational** ☐ Socioeconomical base ☐ Reciprocated interpersonal caring ☐ Shared ideals and values with shared identity
Form of trust	**Economic trust** ☐ Based on economic exchange ☐ Short-term focus ☐ Calculated ☐ Exchanges vigilant and wary	**Economic trust** ☐ Based on economic exchange ☐ Short-term focus ☐ Calculated ☐ Exchanges vigilant and wary	**Relational trust** ☐ Based on ethical relationship ☐ Develops over time ☐ Unguarded ☐ Exchanges provide psychic benefits

marketlike efficiencies will be generated. The underlying assumption here is that the public and private labor forces are the same and that the motivation and commitment for participation are the same. However, there is empirical evidence that motivation and commitment in the public labor force are predominantly rooted in a socioemotional foundation (Crewson, 1997).

An organization downsizing through the strategies of reduction-in-force and managerialism operates by using rational economic self-interest with a short-term, limited obligation perspective. To deal successfully with downsizing, employees must match their type of psychological contract with the downsizing strategy selected by the organization. Transactional contracts using a quid pro quo format are from the economic model, making them compatible with work force reduction and managerialism strategies. Economic trust forms the basis for transactional contrasts. Employees are wary and distrustful of downsizing decisions made by management, anticipating a loss of work or an excessive workload. Limited involvement in the organization by the employee and a short-term perspective are the hallmarks of transactional contracts.

At the opposite end of the downsizing continuum are decentralization and employee empowerment, and downsizing occurs as empowered employees improve the processes of the organization because they are committed to its values and goals. Management enters into a relationship with an employee to improve the quality of the product or service and to improve customer satisfaction through maximizing the organization's human resources. The assumptions for decentralization and empowerment are that individuals are emotional, creative, and altruistic and desire to be a part of an organization for more than financial reward. These humanistic assumptions regarding individuals held by management are at the opposite end of the continuum from the economic assumptions that form the basis of reduction in force and managerialism.

To achieve downsizing by using systemic strategies the organization needs the employee to develop a long-term, empowered relationship or a relational contract. This relational contract must be long-term, based on shared values and norm, and focused on organizational improvement through extensive employee involvement. Relational trust based on interpersonal caring and a shared commitment to the process by empowered employees and enlightened management are the basis for this relationship. Both parties are expected to act honorably in the relationship, meeting both explicit and implicit expectations.

When reduction-in-force downsizing strategies and managerial strategies, such as privatization or contracting out, are used, employees revert to transactional psychological contracts to survive, whereas for empowerment to work, employees must develop relational contracts. When examining downsizing this way it becomes apparent that there are philosophical differences in the reinvention strategies of managerialism and decentralization.

What is immediately apparent also is that these downsizing strategies utilized by governments are heavily weighted toward generating transactional psychological contracts, resulting in wary, vigilant, calculated exchanges between employees and management. Both reduction-in-force and managerialism strategies are grounded in the economic model. Only the decentralization of authority addresses the socioemotional components of individuals. These differing assumptions by management regarding employees result in differing psychological contracts and differing forms of trust developed by employees.

The troubling component of this model is that two of the three downsizing strategies make economic assumptions about individuals working in the public sector, ignoring the empirical evidence that motivation and commitment in the public sector labor force are predominantly rooted in socioemotional foundations (Crewson, 1997). This socioemotional foundation forms the basis of the public service ethic, in which employees develop a relational contract with the organization and commit to the ideals of duty and service to the public interest. The question then becomes, What is the effect of these strategies on individual employees, on the overall performance and morale of the public sector, and on the public service ethic?

Difficulties in a relationship affecting the level of trust arise because of an imbalance in the relationship and the perception of the psychological contract between an employer and the employee. The literature indicates that the psychological contract is developed by the employee (Rousseau, 1989), not the organization. The terms and conditions governing the execution of the psychological contract between the employee and the organization are found in the social contract. In regard to the employment exchange relationship, the social contract conveys the employee's perception of the norms and beliefs about exchange, reciprocity, good faith, and fair dealings. It is because of the norms of the social contract that an employee interprets a perceived breach or violation of the psychological contract (Morrison and Robinson, 1997).

An organization may or may not hold the same beliefs regarding the contract as the employee, and as public organizations downsize through reductions-in-force and managerialism, the commitment to a relational contract with employees may change and the employee may perceive a violation of his or her trust.

Violation of Trust

Several authors refer to a loss of trust and to a breach of the psychological contract that occurs when organizations downsize (Gordon, 1996; Kochan et al., 1994; Parks, 1995; Poirier and Tokarz, 1996; Robinson and Rousseau, 1994). A common model of downsizing in the private sector begins with a movement to improve quality. Many organizations want to reap the benefits of quality improvement quickly and choose a generic approach or hire a consultant to initiate forced changes in structure, systems, or procedures. Frequently this technique has not worked, and management forces change to decrease fixed costs by reducing labor costs though a *reduction in work force* form of downsizing (Poirier and Tokarz, 1996). Many organizations talk of adopting systemic downsizing strategies, but most organizations are merely tinkering with participatory strategies, leaving the economic model in place (Gordon, 1996; Kochan et al., 1994; Parks, 1995, Poirier and Tokarz, 1996). And if systemic strategies are co-opted to fit the economic model, employee morale and loyalty can deteriorate to the point of employee isolation, sabotage, and physical violence (Emory, 1996).

In the public sector the reinvention movement tries to merge the economic model in the form of managerialism with the socioemotional model necessary for decentralization of authority and empowerment. On the basis of the impact of trying to merge reduction-in-force strategies with systemic quality initiative strategies in the private sector, the differing philosophies of managerialism and decentralization and empowerment can also lead to decreased employee morale and reduced employee commitment in the public sector. This disillusionment occurs as employees see that the bottom line for many public organizations in the reform process is to reduce costs by reducing the largest part of their budgets—the cost of their human resources.

What occurs in these situations is that when decentralization and employee empowerment strategies are adopted by the organization, the employees are encouraged to develop a relational psychological contract with the organization, but the organization continues to operate with a transactional economic contract using calculus-based trust. According to Morrison and Robinson (1997), two situations hasten an employee's perception that the organization has betrayed the psychological contract: The first is *reneging,* when an agent of the organization breaks a promise to the employee; the second is *incongruence,* when the employee and the agent have different understandings about the promise. In situations in which empowerment is sacrificed for short-term economic goals, a negative relationship between the level of quality and downsizing results, because most organizations downsize in a way that contradicts the principles of quality improvement. As cost considerations replace quality considerations, the principles of employee empowerment, responsibility, and loyalty are sacrificed for a reduction in overhead. This trade-off causes a loss of employee trust in the organization and a betrayal of the concept of work (Cameron, 1995; Emory, 1996; Poirier and Tokarz, 1996; Wolman and Colamosca, 1997).

The betrayal of the concept of work and the loss of employee trust are especially devastating to the public service ethic. When public service is viewed as the goal and reward for work, betrayal of this concept destroys a very valuable national resource—the commitment of public employees to serving the public and the public interest.

An employee's perception of betrayal by the organization is based on his or her perception of the situation and the type of psychological contract with which the employee operates. If the employee operates by using calculated trust and has developed a transactional contract with the organization, he or she will be wary of the relationship and will be watching for a violation of the contract. Because this employee is always weighing the possibility of the organization's acting in an untrustworthy way, he or she experiences a less violent feeling of betrayal than the individual who evaluates his or her relationship with the organization by using relational trust. Employees who perceive the existence of a relational psychological contract between themselves and the organization are more trusting and less vigilant in the relationship. If a violation of the contract is perceived, it creates strong feelings of violation because it is inconsistent their belief in fairness, reciprocity, and good faith (Morrison and Robinson, 1997).

Downsized public employees, who believe in the public service ethic are most vulnerable to these strong feelings of violation. Many of these individuals joined the public sector to serve the values of civic duty, social justice, and compassion, and when economic values take precedence over these values, the public interest is downsized, not just the employee.

Another perspective for the strong feeling of betrayal experienced by individuals operating from a position of relational trust originates in the belief that individuals on whom we depend will meet our positive expectations of them and act with integrity. *Integrity* refers to honesty and consistency in one's words and actions, and gaps between words and actions can produce distrust. Vulnerability is also a component of trust, and the more an individual trusts, the greater the risks of disappointment (Shaw, 1997). When public organizations violate employee trust, especially relational trust, the moral implications are significant for the employee, the organization, and the society.

IMPLICATIONS OF DOWNSIZING FOR PUBLIC ADMINISTRATION

Relational trust falls into the broad category of normative trust based on ethical principles. Fairness regarding treatment within the relationship (Morrison and Robinson, 1997) and integrity (Shaw, 1997) are the two major ethical principles that have been linked to this form of trust. The use of the social contract as a measure of psychological contract compliance focuses on social responsibility in relationships. The most significant implications of downsizing for public administration are moral, as integrity, fairness, social justice, civic duty, and compassion are compromised.

According to Kohlberg (1981), there are three stages of moral development—the preconventional, conventional, and postconventional stages—which bear on relationships and decision making. The basic minimum standard for interaction is encompassed by the preconventional stage, in which individuals act in response to self-interest or power, using a quid pro quo relationship. In the conventional stage individuals move to a higher level of moral functioning, where decision making and interpersonal relationships focus on social norms and on obedience to the law. The highest level of moral functioning is envisioned as the postconventional stage, in which the social contract and belief in universal ethical principles guide social relationships. Basic universal ethical principles for relationships are honesty, integrity, and justice or fairness.

These stages of moral development apply to the public sector downsizing model. Reduction-in-force downsizing strategies and managerialism are both based on the economic model, which assumes individuals are motivated by self-interest and by use of organizational power. These forms of downsizing then by definition are expressions of the lowest form of moral development, the preconventional stage. It then follows that the transactional psychological contract will be developed by employees, resulting in wary and calculated employee/employer relations.

Managerialism in reinvention uses privatization and contracting out to downsize on the basis of a belief in the economic model. Downsizing occurs as part of the reform movement, linked to the private sector concepts of customer service, entrepreneurial management, flexible solutions, and decentralization of authority. In this context reinvention can be categorized as a systemic downsizing strategy because of the emphasis on changing the culture of the organization and the way employees think about the public they serve. The conflict between the philosophies of managerialism and decentralization of authority to empower employees creates confusion for employees and managers. For empowerment employees need to develop a relational psychological contract with the organization with an emphasis on the social contract maintained through honesty, integrity, and fairness or justice, placing decentralization strategies in the postconventional stage of moral development. To be effective empowerment requires principled implementation, focusing on public service ethic values along with respect for the concepts and the principles of participative management. This position echoes the growing call for managers or leaders in organizations to act in ethical ways when downsizing, recognizing the existence of the social contract and its importance in developing and building trust (Shaw, 1996; Emory, 1996; Ciulla, 1998).

In focusing on the rational model, extrinsic motivation and behavior, the moral dimension or (intrinsic) motivation is ignored (Etzioni, 1988). The intrinsic motivation in public administration is the public service ethic. As a practice, public administration demonstrates a set of technical skills directed to a unified purpose, which is to serve the public. The moral aspect of intrinsic motivation has been called *internal goods,* based on the virtues of truthfulness, justice, and courage, by MacIntyre (1984). These internal goods become references that define our relationships with other people, and individuals who subscribe to these internal goods judge others and trust them in terms of these values. For the practice of public administration the concepts of internal goods and the public service ethic are critical to maintaining professional status and professional trust.

The implications for public administration are that the profession must first recognize the damage downsizing in the form of reduction-in-force and managerialism has done to the public service ethic. Second, managers must act with integrity and return to the public service ethic, using the concepts of managerialism sparingly. Third, educators must focus on the core values of the profession and clarify the value differences between the public and the private sectors. Finally, the moral implication of downsizing is that it has lowered the level of moral interaction between individuals and organizations. Relational trust in organizations has given way to transactional trust, and wary employees see all interactions from this preconventional moral perspective.

Moral crisis may not be too strong a term to describe this transition from postconventional moral interactions toward the lower standard of preconventional moral behavior. For interactions to move to a higher moral level and for trust to shift from wary, calculated interactions to a relational form, a new focus on the social contract is needed to hold both organizations and employees to a standard of honesty in their relations.

Downsizing in the public sector through RIFs, privatization, contracting out, and the reinvention reform movement has replaced the employee's relational psychological contract with a transactional contract. The long-term effects of modeling public-sector employment practices on the private-sector are unclear; however, the implication is that failure to understand and utilize the motivations of public employees may lead to a permanent displacement of the public-service ethic (Crewson, 1997).

As more public employees utilize the transactional contract, the motivation for public service changes. The altruistic values and concept of self-sacrifice are lost. Frederickson (1999) argues that the difference between the public and private sectors lies in the values of fairness, due process, compassion, and protection. For these values to survive, public servants must be dedicated to these values and willing to sacrifice to maintain and promote them. Downsizing strategies downsize the public-service ethic and potentially downsize the values of fairness and compassion in the public sector. Downsizing impacts public employees' trust, commitment, morale, and belief in the ethic of public service, creating moral implications for public administration. Focusing on rational motives based on self-interest for public service erodes and compromises the altruistic, self-sacrificing motives that the public service ethic comprise.

CONCLUSION

This chapter has examined cutback management and the reinvention of government reform movement, discussing the major concepts of the reform. A model of public sector downsizing was developed to show the impacts of downsizing on employees' psychological contract with the organization and on employee trust. The impact of downsizing on employee trust has compromised public sector employee morale and commitment, in addition to threatening the public service ethic based on the values of civic duty, social justice, and compassion. The implications of downsizing for public administration are primarily moral and require a renewed commitment to public service and values of social justice, civic duty, and compassion.

REFERENCES

Amsden, R. T., Ferratt, T., and Amsden, D. (1996). TQM: Core paradigm changes. *Business Horizons*. November-December: 6–14.

Avery, C., and Zabel, D. (1997). *The Quality Management Sourcebook*. Routledge, London.

Behn, R. D. (1980). Leadership for cut-back management: The use of corporate strategy. *Public Administration Review*. November/December: 613–620.

Berman, E. (1995). Employee empowerment in state agencies: A survey of progress. *International Journal of Public Administration. 18*(5): 833–850.

Blankstein, A. M. (1996). Why TQM can't work—and a school where it did. *The Education Digest. 26*(1): 27–30.

Buchanan, B. (1975). Red tape and the service ethic: Some unexpected differences between public and private managers. *Administration and Society. 4:* 423–444.

Cameron, K. S. (1994). Strategies for successful organizational downsizing. *Human Resource Management. 33*(2): 189–211.

Cameron, K. S. (1995). Downsizing, quality, and performance. In (Editor) *The Death and Life of the American Quality Movement* (Robert E. Cole, ed.). Oxford University Press, New York, pp. 93–114.

Cameron, K. S., Freeman, S. J., and Mishra, A. K. (1991). Best practices in white-collar downsizing: Managing contraindications. *Academy of Management Executives. 5*(3): 57–73.

Carroll, J. (1996). Introduction: Reinventing public administration. *Public Administration Review. 56*(3): 245–246.

Cayer, N. J. (1986). Management implications of reduction in force. *Public Administration Quarterly.* Spring: 36–49.

Crewson, P. E. (1997). Public-service motivation: Building empirical evidence of incidence and effect. *Journal of Public Administration Research and Theory. 7*(4): 499–518.

Ciulla, J. B. (1998). *Ethics, the Heart of Leadership.* Quorum Books, Westport, Conn.

Dasgupta, P. (1988). Trust as a commodity. In *Trust: Making and Breaking Cooperative Relations* (D. Gambetta, ed.). Basil Blackwell, New York, 47–72.

Egger, W. D., and O'Leary, J. (1995). *Revolution at the Roots: Making Our Governments Smaller, Better, and Closer to Home.* Free Press, New York.

Elangovan, A. R., and Shapiro, D. L. (1998). Betrayal of trust in organizations. *Academy of Management Review. 23*(3): 547–566.

Emory, W. F. (1996). Principled implementation of management theory. In *Proceedings of the 9th National Symposium on Public Administration.* California State University Hayward, Hayward.

Etzioni, A. (1988). *The Moral Dimension: Toward a New Economics.* Free Press, New York.

Frederickson, H. G. (1971). Toward a new public administration. In *Toward a New Public Administration: The Minnowbrook Perspective* (Frank Marini, ed.). Chandler, Scranton, Penn. 309–331.

Frederickson, H. G. (1999). Public ethics and the new managerialism. *Public Integrity. 1*(3): 265–278.

Frederickson, H. G., and Hart, D. K. (1985). The public service and the patriotism of benevolence. *Public Administration Review. 45:* 547–53.

Gibson, J. L., Ivancevich, J. M., and Donnelly, J. H. (1997). *Organizations: Behavior, Structure, Processes,* 9th ed. Irwin, Chicago.

Goldsmith, A. A. (1996). *Business, Government, Society: The Global Political Economy.* Irwin, Chicago.

Gordon, D. M. (1996). *Fat and Mean: The Corporate Squeeze of Working Americans and the Myth of Managerial "Downsizing."* Martin Kessler Books. The Free Press. New York.

Grant, R. M., Shani, R., and Krishnan, R. (1994). TQM's challenge to management theory and practice. *Sloan Management Review.* *35*(2): 25–35.

Greenhalgh, L., and McKersie, R. B. (1980). Cost effectiveness and alternative strategies for cut-back management. *Public Administration Review.* *40*(6): 575–584.

Hays, S. W., and Whitney, S. B. (1997). Reinventing the personnel function: Lessons learned from a hope-filled beginning in one state. *American Review of Public Administration.* *27*(4): 324–342.

Holzer, M. (1986). Workforce reduction and productivity. *Public Administration Quarterly.* Spring: 86–98.

Jones, V. D. (1998). *Downsizing the Federal Government: The Management of Public Sector Workforce Reductions.* M.E. Sharpe, Armonk, New York.

Kano, N. (1993). A perspective on quality activities in American firms. *California Management Review.* Spring: 12–20.

Klingner, D. E., and Nalbandian, J. (1998). *Public Personnel Management: Context and Strategies,* 4th ed. Prentice Hall, Upper Saddle River, N.J.

Knoke, D., and Wright-Isak, C. (1982). Individual motives and organizational incentive systems. *Research in the Sociology of Organizations.* *1:* 209–254.

Kochan, T. A., Katz, H. C., and McKersie, R. B. (1994). *The Transformation of American Industrial Relations.* Cornell ILR Press, Ithaca, N.Y.

Kohlberg, L. (1981). *Philosophy of Moral Development: Moral Stages and the Idea of Justice.* HarperCollins, New York.

LaPorte, T. R., and Metlay, D. S. (1996). Hazards and institutional trustworthiness: Facing a deficit of trust. *Public Administration Review.* *56*(4): 341–347.

Lewicki, R. J., Mcallister, D. J., and Bies, R. J. (1998). Trust and distrust: New relationships and realities. *Academy of Management Review.* *23*(3): 438–458.

Lewis, C. W., Shannon, W. W., and Ferree, O. D. (1983). The cutback issue: Administrator's perceptions, citizen's attitudes and administrative behavior. *Review of Public Personnel Administration.* *4*(1): 12–27.

MacIntyre, A. (1984). *After Virtue,* 2nd ed. University of Notre Dame Press, Notre Dame, Ind.

McCune, J. T., Beatty, R. W., and Montagno, R. V. (1988). Downsizing: Practices in manufacturing firms, *Human Resource Management.* *27*(6): 145–161.

Mishra, A. K., and Spreitzer, G. M. (1998). Explaining how survivors respond to downsizing: The roles of trust, empowerment, justice, and work redesign. *Academy of Management Review.* *23*(3): 567–588.

Moe, R. C. (1993). Let's rediscover government, not reinvent it. *Government Executive.* *26*(7): 56.

Morris, D. S., and Haigh, R. H. (1996). Empowerment: An endeavour to explain enigma. *Total Quality Management.* *7*(3): 323–330.

Morrison, E. W., and Robinson, S. L. (1997). When employees feel betrayed: A model of how psychological contract violation develops. *Academy of Management Review.* *22*(1): 226–256.

The New York Times (1996). *The Downsizing of America.* Random House, New York.

O'Connell, L. (1984). An exploration of exchange in three social relationships: Kinship, friendship, and the marketplace. *Journal of Social and Personal Relationships.* *1:* 333–345.

Osborne, D., and Gaebler, T. (1992). *Reinventing Government: How the Entrepreneurial Spirit Is Transforming the Public Sector from Schoolhouse to Statehouse, City Hall to Pentagon.* Addison-Wesley, Reading, Mass.

Parks, S. (1995). Improving workplace performance: Historical and theoretical contexts. *Monthly Labor Review.* May: 18–28.

Perry, J. L. (1996). Measuring public service motivation: An assessment of construct reliability and validity. *Journal of Public Administration Research and Theory. 6*(1): 5–22.

Poirier, C. C., and Tokarz, S. J. (1996). *Avoiding the Pitfalls of Total Quality.* ASQC Press, Milwaukee.

Rainey, H. G. (1982). Reward preferences among public and private managers: In search of the service ethic. *American Review of Public Administration. 39:* 288–302.

Rainey, H. G. (1997). *Understanding and Managing Public Organizations.* Jossey-Bass, San Francisco.

Rich, W. C. (1986a). The political context of a reduction-in-force policy: On the misunderstanding of an important phenomenon. *Public Administration Quarterly.* Spring: 7–21.

Rich, W. C. (1986b). Reduction-in-force policy: Issues and perspectives—a symposium. *Public Administration Quarterly.* Spring: 3–6.

Robinson, S. L., and Rousseau, D. M. (1994). Violating the psychological contract: A psychological contract perspective. *Journal of Organizational Behavior. 16:* 245–298.

Rosenbloom, D. H. (1993). Have an administrative Rx? Don't forget the politics (editorial). *Public Administration Review. 53*(5): 503–507.

Rousseau, D. M. (1989). Psychological and implied contracts in organizations. *Employee Responsibilities and Rights Journal. 2:* 121–139.

Rousseau, D. M., and Parks, J. M. (1993). The contracts of individuals and organizations. (L. L. Cummings and B. M. Stow, eds.). *Research in Organizational Behavior. 15:* 1–47, JAI Press, Greenwich, Conn.

Rousseau, D. M., Sitkin, S., Burt, R., and Camerer, C. (1998). Not so different after all: A cross-discipline view of trust. *Academy of Management Review. 23*(3): 393–404.

Ruscio, K. (1997). Trust in the administrative state. *Public Administrative Review. 57*(5): 454–458.

Schachter, H. L. (1995). Reinventing government or reinventing ourselves: Two models for improving government performance. *Public Administration Review. 55*(6): 537.

Shaw, R. B. (1997). *Trust in the Balance: Building Successful Organizations on Results, Integrity, and Concern.* Jossey-Bass, San Francisco.

Staats, E. (1988). Public service and the public interest. *Public Administration Review. 48:* 601–605.

Wallulis, J. (1998). *The New Insecurity: The End of the Standard Job and Family.* State University of New York Press, Albany.

Williamson, O. E. (1985). *The Economic Institutions of Capitalism.* Free Press, New York.

Wolman, W., and Colamosca, A. (1997). *The Judas Economy.* Addison-Wesley, Reading, Mass.

United States Merit Systems Protection Board (1981). *Reductions in Force in the Federal Government, 1981: What Happened and Opportunities for Improvement.* Government Printing Office, Washington, D.C.

24

Four Models of Public Sector Change

A. Carol Rusaw
Department of Communications,
University of Southwestern
Louisiana, Lafayette, Louisiana

Changing public bureaucracies is difficult. In the public service in the last two decades, such rapid changes as privatization, outsourcing, and downsizing have pressured managers and employees to work more efficiently and effectively with diminished resources. The increased pressures have forced government agents to transform sluggish bureaucratic organizations into streamlined, adaptive, and customer-focused enterprises (Osborne and Gaebler, 1992). Yet several conditions oppose the transformation. Many models of organizational change are designed for private sector organizations, which are primarily based on profit purposes, enterprise goals, frameworks that can adapt more easily to changing customer needs and interests, shareholder interests, and market niches. Government organizations have legally based purposes, operate by vast systems of rules and regulations, and serve clientele who have rights and privileges set in legislation rather than market-driven interests.

Goliembiewski (1985) pointed out five structural constraints that distinguish public sector change: (a) Public organizations are a part of an "iron quadrangle" of inputs into the legislative decision-making process: the executive branch, legislative subgroups, and mass media; (b) public organizations have a variety of interests and reward structures, making it difficult to identify precise needs for change and to satisfy all relevant stakeholders; (c) government bureaucracies lack centralized power, being responsive to federal, state, and local pressures in decision making; (d) in addition, overseeing each level of government are bevies of short-tenured political appointees of varying skills, interests, and goals, whose weak relationships with long-term career professionals complicate communications and coordinating policies and greatly limit decentralized decisional flexibility; (e) the legalistic foundation of public administration produces a narrowly focused span of control, emphasizes procedural regularity rather than openness in solving problems, and intermixes politics and management.

In addition to the constraints in decision-making power, public organizations suffer from chronic legislative underfunding (Ferris, 1987). Budgets are typically based on the prior year's projections, making new programs difficult to justify. Bowing to taxpayer demands for lower taxes, legislators are reluctant to raise money for programs that do not yield tangible, short-term returns on investments. Recently, moreover, many state legislatures have required agencies to develop more effective and efficient ways of operating, such as streamlining "paperwork," but have not given them sufficient funds to do so. Unfunded mandates have hampered administration (Wallick, 1996).

Change in public organizations is possible, however, provided organizational change agents recognize the key constraints and adapt models to particular organizational characteristics. In a metaanalytic study of organizational development (OD) in the public and the private organizations, Robertson and Sneviratne (1995) determined that OD was effective in both. However, the authors noted that in the public sector, interventions aimed at improving individual performance as well as organizational productivity fared better than those in the private sector. In the latter, they found OD facilitated individual development, but increased skills did not translate into better overall organizational performance. Moreover, the study indicated that organizational change occurs differently in the two sectors. In private companies, top-level executives can order change among lower echelons; in the public sector, however, this is more difficult because of the more numerous social arrangements (such as constituent groups) that affect the course and extent of change. The authors pointed out that because of the different goals of the constituents as well as the frequent changes in political leadership in public organizations, developing sustained change programs in quite difficult.

If public organizations are difficult, but not impossible to change, what models can change agents use for effective adaptation? This chapter addresses this question by describing four models of organizational development that are commonly used in public organizations. In particular, it discusses their focus, impetus for change, leadership and coordinating mechanisms, typical examples, integration feasibility, and shortcomings. It concludes by deducing some implications for use among public change agents. Briefly, the models are (a) means-end, basing change on a rationally identified, comprehensive goal; (b) incremental, involving small changes that do not fundamentally change the organizational mission or overall direction; (c) pluralistic, in which multiple constituents facilitate changes collectively; and (d) individual-based, using employee training and development to promote organizational change.

ORGANIZATION DEVELOPMENT AND CHANGE AGENTS

Definition

Organizational development, or OD, may be defined as a comprehensive, collaborative, and planned process of solving problems through changing foundational assumptions and beliefs of individuals in order to improve work content, structures, and relationships in organizations. A primary belief of OD is that people collectively define meanings of the work they do and develop ways of doing it that are based on their conceptions. The technological core of organizations, or the "what" of what an organization does, is determined not so much by mission and machinery as by the base of knowledge, values, and attitudes that people share and act on. Change in organizations comes about by reeducating people as well as reengineering work processes. In a review of several definitions, French, Bell, and Zawacki (1994: 7) define organizational development as

> a process of planned system change that attempts to make organizations (viewed as socio-technical systems) better able to attain their short- and long-term objectives. This is achieved by teaching the organization members to manage their organization processes, structures, and culture more effectively. Facts, concepts, and theory from the behavioral sciences are utilized to fashion both the process and the content of interventions. A basic belief of OD theorists is that for effective, lasting change to take place, the system members must grow in the competence to master their own lives.

Origins

Organization development originated in the 1930s largely through the research and practice of Kurt Lewin (Schein, 1987). Lewin (1958) believed that organizations were embedded in a field of social forces, which were continually impelling or continually impeding changes in individuals, groups, and organizations. Lewin felt that if individuals were trained in understanding these forces and applied concepts from such fields as economics, sociology, psychology, and political science, they could also predict and influence the course and outcomes of change forces. Lewin developed a three-step model to assist people in harnessing and creating positive change in organizational settings. The steps involved (a) "unfreezing," or developing an awareness of a problem through data gathered from its context and shared with others; (b) "moving," or taking action on data presented through identifying interventions or programs and sequencing their implementation as short- and long-term objectives; and (c) "refreezing," or establishing new processes that could withstand environmental forces leading to regression. Lippitt and Lippitt (1978), in reference to the refreezing step, noted that changing the technology that enabled organizations to adapt and survive in their environments also entailed changing the human forces that were integral components of it. This meant change took place throughout the system through involving users of changed work technologies in the implementation of the interventions.

Change Agents

The process of simultaneously changing knowledge and work, or the "sociotechnical" description French, Bell, and Zawacki refer to, is a comprehensive process. Because OD treats organizations as systems of interrelated components, altering one part triggers additional changes throughout. Change agents guide the change process by working with those who are experiencing problems ("clients") and create solutions (or "interventions" in the sociotechnical systems) that will benefit the organization as a whole (Emery and Trist, 1960). A central aim is to enable the client to develop skills and competencies for not only solving the present problem but developing a capacity for dealing with future issues.

FEATURES AND DIMENSIONS OF ORGANIZATIONAL CHANGE

In working with clients, change agents examine the readiness to undertake change from four major indicators: (a) organizing arrangements and technology; (b) order of change; (c) scope of change; and (d) organizational level of change.

Organizing Arrangements and Technology

Porras and Robertson (1992) describe "organizing arrangements" as formal elements of organizations that coordinate the behavior of people and the functioning of parts. These consist of an organization's goals, strategies, formal structures, administrative policies and procedures, reward systems, ownership, and social structures. It also includes organizational technologies, or ways that work is designed and carried out, and social groups, including characteristics of individuals and groups, their patterns and processes of interaction, the cultures they create, management style, and communication processes. Organizational environments, or constellations of forces that continuously produce demands as well as opportunities for organizational adaptation and survival, are components as well.

In terms of Porras and Robertson's (1992) notion of organizing arrangements, Robertson and Sneviratne (1995) analyzed public and private sector change interventions. Although OD was effective in both sectors, they found it more challenging in the public sector to produce output gains—primarily because public goods and services frequently have no commonly agreed on performance measurements. They also concluded that it is more difficult to implement changes unilaterally in public versus private sector employee attitudes, behavior, and processes; in the private sector, for instance, change ordered from the top down is rarely questioned. In public agencies, however, the authority is not clear-cut and the impacts on operating levels several layers below top echelons are unpredictable. In addition, the authors discovered that in the pubic sector, interventions improved both organizational effectiveness and individual development; in the private sector, however, only individual development was enhanced. Overall, the authors concluded that it is more difficult to generate consistently high levels of change in organizing arrangements, technology, and physical settings of public organizations

First- and Second-Order Change

Change agents also examine the potential depth and breadth of effects of change strategies on individuals and systems. Levy and Merry (1986) described first- and second-order strategies. First-order change does not alter this assumed relationship but merely reinforces it, meaning it does not change fundamental assumptions people have about "reality" (Lincoln and Guba, 1985). In second-order change, however, change agents change both the structures and the thought processes. Second-order change rests on the notion that people create reality rather than discover it (Berger and Luckmann, 1967). To bring about second-order change, change agents examine the thoughts, feelings, and attitudes of people and how their experiences shape what they define as problems (Argyris and Schon, 1978; Daft and Weick, 1984). The task in the examination is to change defective thoughts, beliefs, and action patterns through introducing standards or norms that will produce greater productivity or worker satisfaction: a process that Etzioni (1961) calls a "normative-re-educative process."

Scope of Change

Change agents also take into account the numbers of related systems and processes that will be affected by introducing a single change. Some interventions are designed to address broad areas of problems—problems that affect entire social and technical processes. Others are limited to one specific problem or issue and hence have a narrow scope. Broad-scope interventions involve transforming complex structures, affect several constellations of related systems, and require considerable resource outlays. Narrow-scope change programs, however, do not require extensive changes in existing systems, have a limited range of impacts in terms of processes and outcomes, and often use resources from stocks at hand (Weick, 1984).

Levels of Change

In designing interventions, change agents consider the needs and relationships to be enhanced at four levels of organizational functioning. Rashford and Coghlan (1993) describe the levels as individual, work unit team, interdepartmental group or team, and intraorganizational. At the individual level, individuals strive to meet basic needs, physiological, psychological, and affiliative, and to develop skills and abilities for managing careers. Typical interventions include training and development, career planning, and personal improvement. The work unit team, at the second level, focuses mainly on solving many specific work-related problems and issues. Interventions often used include developing interpersonal communications skills, task or project management, goal setting, and decision making. At level three, various groups or teams throughout an organization may combine to focus on common problems or issues and reach consensus resolution. Important here is coordinating or mapping the work flow from decision to implementation at various subunits. At the intraorganizational level, representatives from an organization form groups or teams with those from other organizations to examine and resolve major issues or problems affecting the well-being of the whole. In general, interventions at the organizational level focus on open systems planning and management. On the premise that organizations are like living organisms that continually affect and are affected by their environments, open systems models analyze current demands being imposed, identify impacts of products or services on the environment, and create goals and plans of actions to balance demands and impacts. Open systems models also use feedback to change current ways of doing business or to change the current operating assumptions to create completely new structures and processes (Argyris, 1992).

CONDITIONS AFFECTING INTERVENTIONS

Change agents develop interventions not only through an analysis of the particular needs and characteristics of individuals and organizations, but also with a sensitivity to conditions that can affect design and implementation. Conditions that they examine include trigger incidents and causes, changes induced by implementation, degree of technological readiness, leadership and coordinating mechanisms, structural complexity, and environmental threats and opportunities.

Trigger Events and Causes

Change agents compare the immediate or "trigger" incidents that produced the decision to change and the causes that contributed to incidents being regarded as pivotal, for example, encountering an unexpected event or crisis and recognizing the inadequacy of existing mental models and tactics for managing the event (Duncan and Weiss, 1979; Kofman and Senge, 1994; Nicolini and Meznar, 1995). Moreover, accidental discoveries of better ways of doing tasks can lead to the formulation of different approaches to managing future problem (Schon, 1987). Schein (1987) points out that the uncovering of underlying needs for change occurs during the "unfreezing" step in Lewin's (1958) model. Schein notes that this often occurs when people receive disconfirming information and feel guilty when some important goal is not met or anxious when an ideal is violated:

> Disconfirmations occur around us all the time, but most of this information is ignored or fails to induce motivation to change because it does not connect with issues that we care very much about. The ego is not involved with them or we do not have any commitment to the goals and ideals that may be being disconfirmed. (p. 96)

Changes Induced by Implementation

Change agents examine possible ramifications of change on interrelated systems affected. In a hypothetical case of introducing automated forms processing at the organizationwide level, a change agent and client decided to purchase equipment to reduce backlog but expected the forms would affect certain other systems as well. One effect would be that forms processors not only know that the change was being introduced but also have the technical skills to operate the equipment competently. Because the equipment may improve productivity, change agents and clients would examine the effects of technology on worker motivation and rewards. In addition, change agents and clients would need to make certain people using the equipment would not perceive their jobs were being reduced or eliminated as well. Before introducing changes in interdependent systems, change agents frequently conduct pilot tests of sample conditions and examine how the intervention produces its expected outcomes. On the basis of their judgment, change agents and clients decide to continue with the intervention, modify it, or abandon it altogether (Altshuler and Behn, 1997).

Degree of Technological Readiness

Change agents estimate how well prepared the organization is to undertake pro posed changes, at both current as well as future resource levels. The resources are not only financial but material, human, and technical. To accomplish expected outcomes, change interventions require not only sufficient budgets, but also skilled individuals to carry out plans and use equipment associated with the change. Once implementation has occurred, moreover, additional resources need to be allocated to ensure maintenance. This includes not only funds for upkeep and repair but also funds for training individuals in their use (Corak and Wharton, 1992).

Leadership and Coordinating Mechanisms

The strength of leadership commitment, involvement in the change process, and communications networks are prime factors in enabling organizations to succeed at planned change. Some points change agents note are the extent of discretion leaders have in making changes, the resources that are entrusted to them, the extent to which expected outcomes can be realistically implemented, and potential barriers. In general, leaders who have discretionary authority to institute changes based on particular needs of which they are aware and who have resources sufficient to enact agreed-on changes, the greater the likelihood of success (Blau and Scott, 1963). Moreover, the quality and quality of interpersonal communications, through both formal documents and informal meetings, affect outcomes of interventions (Mintzberg, 1983). The style of leadership, especially within the cultural settings of an organization, accounts for the way followers receive and commit themselves to change (Stinchcombe, 1965). Leadership that encourages participation creates an openness in which followers can discuss specific problems as well as contribute creative suggestions.

Structural Complexity

The complexity of organizational structures and processes—ranging from complex to simple—affects interventions. Structurally complex relationships involve work that is technically specialized and requires the coordinated interaction of several different work units, usually within and outside the organization. To coordinate this work, people use both formal communications, such as policies, operating manuals, or written rules, and informal networks and face-to-face meetings. Introducing change is more difficult in structurally complex organizations because of the varying technologies and coordinating processes used. In general, the greater the structural complexity, the greater the need for multiple means of communicating and coordinating organizational change (Aiken and Hage, 1968; Aldrich and Pfeffer, 1976).

Environmental Threats and Opportunities

Because environmental changes greatly affect the quality of change interventions, change agents remain alert to conditions that may interfere with or may facilitate change. Kotter (1978) describes two types of environments that affect organizational structures and processes: external environments, including suppliers of raw materials, knowledge, labor, and skills; and wider environments, including major social institutions such as schools and community groups, economic and political interests, regulatory bodies, public attitudes and social demographics. The degree of turbulence or change affects how an organization interacts and fulfills its mission requirements. For instance, a change in public opinion regarding the use of tax dollars to fund artistic projects might weaken an agency's ability to generate legislative financial support for the arts. Accordingly, the agency may be forced to find alternative funding sources, such as philanthropic donations or user fees. The change in funding would trigger changes in the job descriptions of people working in the agency, such as requiring them to focus more on revenue generation than program management.

Because the perceptions of individuals influence the way they perform their jobs, changes in an organization's environment are neutral; leaders help members shape reactions to changes as "threats" or as "opportunities." If, in the funding example, people identify their new roles as directly contributing to the ability of the agency to fulfill its mission, they may be motivated positively. The change is an opportunity for them to use their talents innovatively. Other people might regard the change as a threat to the continued funding of the agency and resist attempts to initiate change. These individuals may have fears and doubts based on previous experiences of apparent decreased levels of public support. They may have also experienced downsizing. Because any change means doing things differently, change agents work with clients to reframe changes so that effects will have some potentially positive benefits for both people and organizations (Nadler et al., 1992).

FOUR MODELS OF PUBLIC SECTOR CHANGE

In adapting organizational change interventions to government organizations, change agents need to consider organizing features, technology, order of change, and scope of the strategies in relation to particular conditions affecting the target of change. To help identify appropriate uses of interventions to conditions in public institutions, four models of organizational development interventions commonly used in the public sector are discussed. Model 1, a means-end model, involves a rational problem-solving methodology; Model 2 is based on an incremental view of change; Model 3 views change as engineered by a pluralistic group of individuals or agencies having common interests in a problem, concern, or issue; Model 4 is based on the idea that by improving individual skill levels and activities, people bring about organizational change.

In the following section, the four models are further defined and illustrated with reference to the conditions affecting public sector organizational development. For each model, sample interventions are described. A summary appears in Table 1. It is important to note that the four models are not mutually exclusive; they overlap in many instances. However, they are presented as "types" of interventions that often occur in public organizations. In practice, the models may combine so that particular objectives and expected outcomes may be met.

Table 1 Four Models of Public Sector Change

	Means-End	Incremental	Pluralist	Individual-Based
Focus	Internal systems and processes	Local unit-environmental interface	Social/economic	Organizational via individual
Impetus for Change	Systemic failure/opportunity	Opportunity to create; recurring environmental problem	Crisis or severe social problem	Role/job change; individual growth
Leadership	Strategic; often top-down	Decentralized	Shared	Self
Coordinating Mechanisms	Complex structural and procedural	Simple procedural	Complex; reliance on voluntary membership	Complex; use of Personnel Management
Typical Uses	Strategic planning; TQM; reengineering	"Small wins" reinvention projects	Shared policy-making;	Training and development; career management
Problems	Long-term commitment; resource inadequacy;	Problems recur; empowerment	Dialog; political agendas; follow-up	Adequate resources; organization commitment; transfer

MODEL 1: MEANS-END

Means-end interventions are based on finding the root causes of existing problems, developing a range of possible solution strategies, selecting the "best" alternative, selecting a trial intervention and assessing its outcomes in relation to expected results, and evaluating the feasibility of the intervention in terms of achieving a tangible goal or outcome. Based on the scientific management principles of Taylor to a large extent (Rainey, 1997), means-end models require methodical thinking, environments that are predictable, and tools that will accomplish identified purposes (Guba, 1990).

Typical Uses

Means-end interventions are often used in three areas in the public sector: strategic planning, total quality management, and reengineering.

Strategic Planning

In strategic planning, individuals develop a vision of a desirable future state of an organization, scan current organizational environments for trends and conditions that aid or hinder achieving the desirable condition, formulate action plans based on the environmental scan, and produce milestone objectives and sequence procedures to allow the vision to become reality. The planning component of strategic management involves developing long-range budgets and measurable subgoals and objectives and coordinating the inputs and outputs of related systems.

Kemp, Funk, and Eadie (1993) describe a strategic management intervention at the Equal Employment Opportunity Commission (EEOC). The impetus for change occurred as the EEOC commissioner recognized the need to strengthen administrative systems and the growing constituent demands for productivity improvement with decreased funding support. The EEOC top management team developed a values and vision statement, identified trends (particularly in changing demographics) that influenced the agency, brainstormed challenges confronting the change, and formulated strategy.

Total Quality Management

The recent applications of total quality management (TQM) concepts to public organizations also exemplify Model 1, broad-range interventions. Total quality management uses the concepts and skills of Deming (1982), such as continuous process improvements, quality as a philosophy, ongoing training programs to help promote pride in work, a climate of productivity improvement through elimination of problems based in organizational structures, workers participation in planning and designing of improvement projects, and elimination of fear. Since 1988, with the establishment of the Federal Quality Institute, 70 percent of federal agencies have adopted some form of TQM (FQI, 1991). Moreover, TQM programs have been launched in several state and local governments. In a review of TQM at the local level, Berman and West (1995) observed that it was successful in larger cities that a greater variety and amount of resources. Moreover, it was used most often in police, recreation, and parks departments and in human resources management.

Review of Strategic Management and TQM

Vinzant and Vinzant (1996) reviewed the applications of strategic management and TQM in government and noted that successful uses adapted methodologies to specific characteristics of public organizations. For strategic management to work, organizations must have a highly influential leader or sponsor who is committed to long-range changes and is willing to accept delays in planning. Successful projects also require a culture that can adapt values of high-quality organizational performance through employee involvement. Total quality management programs that produced expected results navigated numerous obstacles, such as the existence of multiple customers, instability and uncertainty, complex accountability, and the symbolic "products" of public service. TQM programs that worked emphasized concrete goals and measurable performance results, were flexible in terms of meeting the demands of a many-layered clientele structure, and had outcomes that clearly benefit government. Rago (1996) added that to change both structural arrangements and culture in government agencies, leaders of TQM projects need to communicate clearly and constantly throughout all parts of an agency what the vision or purpose of a TQM program is and what it hopes to accomplish. Additionally, leaders need to establish training programs tailored to specific situations users of the program typically encounter.

Reengineering

Reengineering solutions attempt to make more productive sequences of related tasks and jobs composing a work process or system. "Productive" systems are those that reduce waste through eliminating scrap, "downtime," or time spent on task; recurrent problems in performance; duplication; and fragmentation. Systems are reengineered by decreasing waste, combining duplicative functions, or eliminating unnecessary steps or task functions. Often organizations undergoing reengineering use cross-functional teams of managers and employees to identify candidates for systemic change and to develop ways to produce more effective and efficient services and products (Hammer and Champy, 1993).

In a review of case study research from several information resources management documents, Caudle (1994) examined the uses of reengineering in several government organizations. Caudle noted several conditions that government managers confronted in using reengineering interventions. First, government work processes and subprocesses had to be defined in relation to a specific customer served. This was difficult because public employees provide service not only to specific customers and clients but also to the larger society, in terms of being accountable for use of public resources. This had the effect of requiring the opening of decision-making processes to public scrutiny and inviting oversight from several legislative and judiciary bodies. Further, the short tenure of politically appointed managers presented narrow "windows of opportunity" in which to develop long-term goals and to produce tangible results. In addition, vague organizational missions and inability to develop exact and quantifiable performance measures of service to achieve the mission created problems for identifying and evaluating expected improvements. Finally, the fragmented human resources systems limited the abilities of managers to hire, train, and reward individuals conducting reengineering projects. The various structural impediments identified made it difficult for managers to coordinate and integrate services and products.

MODEL 2: INCREMENTAL

Incremental interventions involve minor changes in existing systems, have a short-term focus, and produce visible results. Change occurs in small steps and is not usually aligned with strategic goals or plans. Often the purposes of incremental change involve improving a specific task, work process, or interpersonal relationship. Because they are concerned with problems affecting an immediate area under an individual or group's control, they incorporate high levels of discretion and use of creative judgment. Individuals at the operating levels of organizations often take on the role of informal change agents, adapting functions or creating new ones as conditions change. Incremental changes give flexibility, encourage empowerment, and require few resources for implementation. Incremental interventions have origins in human relations views of management, especially in Simon's (1945) description of "bounded rationality" and Lindblom's (1959) concept of "muddling through."

Typical Uses

Many of the continuous improvement varieties of "reinvention" are incremental interventions. Nichols (1997:407–408) describes continuous improvement as a process undertaken to "reduce variation, influence a parameter, desired direction, or both . . . decrease average case processing time, [and] reduce food stamp fraud by making food stamps harder to counterfeit." The reinvention stream of change relies on decentralized roles of bureaucrats as change agents to cut red tape that strangles innovation and improvise ways to provide more responsiveness to citizens as customers. Structurally, incremental models call for flatter hierarchies, use of external funds to create innovative projects, use of private sector work on a contracted basis, and public-private coproduction enterprises (Frederickson, 1996).

Thompson and Ingraham (1996), analyzing innovative projects undertaken in response to reinvention requirements of the National Performance Review, found that the centrality of politics played a leading role in the change processes.

Although many innovations did not require outside approvals, those that did encountered issues of power, control, and "turf" that bobbed up repeatedly. To implement long-term change, leaders require understanding of internal political dynamics to overcome resistance at higher levels of management.

Weick (1984) notes that incremental interventions are "small wins" that produce innovative services and products and cumulatively improve the way an organization works, attracts supports, and prepares for future breakthroughs. Rusaw (1998) reports a case example of this in the Department of Revenue Services (DRS) in Connecticut. The commissioner, Gene Gavin, used an educational program, Public Service Excellence; requests for employee volunteers to improve the readability of tax regulations; and frequent and informal meetings with employees to encourage incremental change. Gavin referred to the incremental changes as "base hits" and added, "When you have 860 people hitting a single, you have a lot of home runs by the end of the program." Empowering of division directors and employees to identify, carry out, and evaluate changes was a result. In developing an understanding of problems and issues, employees opened up for critical inspection many of their unquestioned assumptions that framed the organization's culture. In addition, because they had training in problem solving, the commitment of their directors and the commissioner, and delegated authority to make changes within 2 to 4 weeks in how they did work, employees developed their own ideas for future changes.

MODEL 3: PLURALISTIC

Pluralistic models of change involve gathering all people who have potential interest in a particular problem, issue, or concern and facilitating intraorganizational or societal change through dialog and concerted action (Isaacs, 1994); formulating policy; and participating in implementing action. Pluralistic models differ from the incremental ones in that they involve second-order thinking and broad, systemic coordination. The models are based on informed citizen action taken in response to a widespread social or economic problem. They differ from means-end models, moreover, in their development of policy, voluntary compliance, and commitment to ideals rather than economically based goals as motivating forces. Involving joint citizen and public agency participation, pluralistic models were especially instrumental in the 19th century in bringing about many social and political reforms (Buchannan, 1996). Pluralistic models have also been influential in formulating innovative public policies (Bryson and Crosby, 1992; Altshuler, 1997).

Pluralistic models tackle large-scale socioeconomic problems: those that have no "right" solutions. They are what Rittel and Webber (1973: 173) called "wicked" problems. Wicked problems, such as acquired immunodeficiency syndrome (AIDS), unemployment, ozone depletion, and hunger affect the strength and tenability of the greater social fabric. Because of the scope and seriousness of wicked problems, the public looks to governments to provide strategies to manage them. In their expectations for relief, the public demands not only resources for creative strategy making but also the involvement of a wide spectrum of interests and talents. To meet the demands, public agencies use the participation of diverse constituents to produce innovative approaches to wicked problems.

Examples

Shared policy-making is an example of a pluralistic model. In it government decision makers solicit information on preferences from a broad spectrum of constituents. They then feed the preferences back to constituents and solicit additional rounds of information. The iterative process is similar to the Delphi technique, in which geographically dispersed "experts" discuss judgments and reach consensus through dialog (Rainey, 1997).

Simonsen, Johnston, and Barnett (1996) describe the use of shared policy-making as well as citizen surveys to assess citizen preferences in government decision making. One example of shared policy-making occurred during the state of Oregon's budget preparation discussions in 1991. Citizens had just approved Measure 5 in the state, which was a constitutional tax limitation that cut funding for education and government services. Governor Barbara Roberts used closed-circuit television to gather information from a sample of nearly 10,000 residents before she submitted the tax restructuring plan. Through several successive rounds of discussion and shaping of ideas, the governor crafted a budget proposal that balanced many different views. However, the proposal failed after a stormy legislative session.

In addition, citizen survey data provide information with which to formulate policies and bring about social change. Simonsen, Johnston, and Barnett point out that such surveys came into prominence in the 1970s in state and local governments. Since California's Proposition 13, citizen surveys have been employed to assess the quality of service delivery. They have also been used to mold voter preferences by enabling them to gain precise understanding of complex issues and to cultivate the support of the media. In reviewing several cases of use of shared decision making and citizen surveys, the authors identified several essential ingredients for success: (a) citizens' perception that the process is legitimate, not trivial; (b) methodologically sound survey research designs of questions; (c) multiple ways of collecting and analyzing data; (d) inclusion of all relevant stakeholders by samples; (e) focus on learning from data and sharing the information to achieve a representative "big picture"; (f) openness; and (g) involvement of media in the process as well as outcomes.

The use of dialog, learning, and objectively based data as sources for innovative policy-making is important in many ways to organizational change. Dialog allows people to examine their attitudes, values, and beliefs about a particular phenomenon and subject them to scrutiny in a public setting (Argyris and Schon, 1978). Through examination, people can evaluate the validity of their assumptions and together create new foundational stocks of common knowledge (Habermas, 1970). Dialog permits the determination of common interests, needs, and goals for consensus building. Moreover, the participation in dialog fosters not only shared commitment but also mutual learning and creative problem solving (Schein, 1994; Kofman and Senge, 1994; Ulrich et al., 1994). Pluralistic models allow participants to perceive themselves as "collectives of communities" in spite of their different perspectives. Daft and Weick (1984: 77) observe that the competing ideas among constituents can serve as "improvisational sparks to ignite innovation."

MODEL 4: INDIVIDUALLY BASED

Because educating and reeducating people are critical features of the sociotechnical approach to change, teaching skills and competencies for managing present job-related problems as well as for opportunities for future development is a key way to change organizations. The notion underlying human resource development, a component of OD, is that through learning, people change organizations. Learning includes the motivation and the capacity to identify, define, and solve human, social, economic, and technological problems affecting overall individual or organizational performance. Learning involves changes in not only thought processes but habitual actions (Cook and Yahow, 1996). Approaches to OD that center on training control successive introductions of change throughout an entire system by the transmission of skills formally, through training programs, or informally, such as in on-the-job learning.

Formal Learning

Learning among adults occurs formally as well as informally. Formal learning consists of structured events that aim to attain specific and measurable outcomes. These usually occur in training and development programs, seminars, and professional conferences. Training and development give people skills and abilities related to present job performance, such as providing skills updates or remediation (Apps, 1988). They also cultivate individual capacity to manage future job demands, for example, through career counseling and planning, and to prepare for and change work systems and processes (Knowles, 1980). In the latter, training and development have played integral roles in changing organizational culture norms and values (Wellbelove, 1992).

Training and Development in the Public Sector

In spite of the need to invest in employee training and development and the organizational productivity gains continuous learning has brought about in government, training and development are haphazard and confined to certain groups of employees. Zemke (1984) reported that government training programs most often focus on technical specialties, are often susceptible to budget cuts, and are declining both in length and in total numbers of occurrences. In addition, training programs often lack criteria for evaluating effectiveness in terms of costs and benefits (Roback, 1989) and in relation to career planning (Berman and West, 1993). In addition, some participants who have attended training believe the information received is irrelevant to the mission and objectives of their particular agencies (Rice, 1979) and the instructors are not highly skilled (Lynch, 1983). Carnevale and Carnevale (1993) point out that the failure to link individual performance standards to organizational goals and outcomes measurements, investment of funds, and empowering work assignments has limited the potential effect of training and development in organizational change.

Informal Learning

Informal learning takes place largely through individual initiative and may or may not involve structured learning experiences as well as the use of others as resources. As adults mature, they learn to adapt to emergent roles they play in social organizations, such as parent, worker, and retiree, in several ways. First, they may gain knowledge from self-initiated, self-directed learning projects (Tough, 1971). They may also learn through a joint process of doing and reflecting on action, or learning experientially (Kolb, 1984; Schon, 1987). Informal learning may occur on the job as individuals develop skills for learning new tasks, solving problems, or taking up new roles and responsibilities (Watkins and Marsick, 1993). It may also consist of vicarious learning, as when individuals observe how others approach a situation and develop behavioral patterns (Bandura, 1977).

Much of the learning in government takes place informally. In a study of women managers in the federal government, Rusaw (1989) found that most lacked sufficient and cumulative formal skills training for performing their roles as managers, using self-initiated learning projects and role models and mentors to assist their career development. The lack of integration of formal and informal learning with organizational purposes limits satisfaction and motivation, particularly among public employees, who value contributions to social benefit more than do private sector workers (Balfour and Wechsler, 1991). In instances in which training is linked directly to organizational mission and other personnel management functions, training and informal development have improved satisfaction and morale (Rabin, 1993).

Organizational Learning

Individually based models of change may occur at any of the four levels of organizational change discussed earlier; key factors are the development and use of individual resources to effect systemic change. The interaction of individuals with technical systems and organizational environmental conditions allows organizations to learn. Learning organizations, based on the notion that organizations continually affect and are affected by their environments, gather and use feedback from their surroundings in order to change internal structures and processes. The subsequent internal changes after the way the organization and environment think and act; the mutual insights produce shared learning (Senge, 1990). Through organizational learning, individuals enable organizations to adapt and survive.

In the public sector, organizational learning is becoming an important way to adjust to widespread public pressures to "reinvent" basic services and become more accountable in respect to tax dollars. As noted, many government organizations routinely use citizen surveys to obtain feedback and improve customer service. West and Berman (1993) studied local governments that integrated such feedback with employee development programs as well as performance measurements and found both worker motivation and productivity high. Moreover, public agencies have used teams to redesign work so that employees' experience satisfaction and high output (Hyde, 1992; Stump, 1986) and invent novel system designs and products (Office of Technology Assessment, 1988).

CONCLUSION

Public organizations are experiencing a great deal of change. But to harness the forces that enable organizations to adapt and survive the turbulence, they need leaders who have skills as change agents. These skills include the ability to assess the particular structural and environmental characteristics of the organization, the relevant stakeholders, and their particular needs and interests; the ability to establish multiple communications linkages between stakeholders and employees; and the skills to facilitate social and technical system transition from the status quo to a desired state in the future.

The four models of public change described in this chapter acquaint change agents with the advantages as well as challenges involved in bringing about transformation.

Model 1 change, involving identifying a long-term goal and aligning organizational social and technical system subgoals with it, is perhaps most difficult to achieve. It involves the assurance of a stable resource base, long-term commitment of top leaders who can act as champions or spokespersons, identification of concrete and measurable performance outcomes, and training and informal development of individuals throughout the organization to assist in implementation of change strategies.

Model 2, an incrementally based approach, gives change agents greater flexibility in adapting change, but it does not alter fundamental assumptions and associated practices. Major shifts in paradigms occur over time and at random, as organizations evolve in response to environmental pressures and opportunities.

Model 3 is perhaps most amenable to the multiple-constituency quality of public management in that it encourages change through dialog, feedback, and decentralized action. In effecting change through pluralistic models, change agents need to facilitate a compelling vision, shared values and beliefs, goals that will allow the desired state to become reality, and meaning making through interpersonal communications skills.

Finally, Model 4 enables individuals to transform organizational structures through developing skills and competencies by formal as well as informal learning. Unless individuals are delegated authority to acquire resources, support, and opportunities to use skills, however, their power to bring about change is limited.

Changing public bureaucracies is challenging, perhaps far more so than in private companies. By using the four models in combinations, change agents can find a vast assortment of tools to help meet the demands.

REFERENCES

Aiken, M., and Hage, J. (1968). Organization interdependencies and intraorganizational structures. *American Sociological Review. 33*(9): 912–929.

Aldrich, H.E., and Pfeffer, J. (1976). Environments of organizations. *Annual Review of Sociology. 2:* 79–105.

Alinsky, S.D. (1972). *Rules for Radicals.* Vintage, New York.

Altshuler, A.A. (1997). Bureaucratic innovation, democratic accountability, and political incentives. In *Innovation in American Government: Challenges, Opportunities, and Dilemmas.* (A.A. Altshuler and R.D. Behn, eds.), Brookings Institute, Washington, D.C., pp. 38–80.

Altshuler, A.A., and Behn, R.D. (eds.) (1997). *Innovation in American Government: Challenges, Opportunities, and Dilemmas.* Brookings Institute, Washington, D.C.

Apps, J.W. (1988). *Higher Education in a Learning society: Meeting New Demands for Education and Training.* Jossey-Bass, San Francisco.

Argyris, C. (1992). *On Organizational Learning.* Blackwell, Cambridge, Mass.

Argyris, C., and Schon, D.A. (1978). *Organizational Learning.* Addison-Wesley. Reading, Mass.

Balfour, D.L., and Wechsler, B. (1991). Commitment, performance, and productivity in public organizations. *Public Productivity and Management Review. 15*(1): 355–368.

Bandura, A. (1977). *Social Learning Theory.* Prentice-Hall, Englewood Cliffs, N.J.

Baum, J.A.C. (1996). Organizational ecology. In *Handbook of Organization Studies* (S.R. Clegg, C. Hardy, and W.R. Nord, eds.). Sage, Thousand Oaks, Calif., pp. 77–114.

Berger, P.L., and Luckmann, T. (1967). *The Social Construction of Reality.* Doubleday, New York.

Berman, E.M., and West, J.P. (1993). Human resource strategies in local government. *American Review of Public Administration. 23*(3): 279–291.

Berman, E.M., and West, J.P. (1995). Municipal commitment to Total Quality Management: A survey of recent progress. *Public Administration Review. 55*(1): 57–66.

Blau, P.M., and Scott, W.R. (1963). *Formal Organizations: A Comparative Approach.* Routledge and Kegan Paul, London.

Bryson, J.M., and Crosby, B.C. (1992). *Leadership for the Common Good.* Jossey-Bass, San Francisco.

Buchannan, C.H. (1996). *Choosing to Lead: Women and the Crisis of American Values.* Beacon Press, Boston.

Carnevale, A.P., and Carnevale, D.G. (1993). Public administration and the evolving world of work. *Public Productivity and Management Review. 17*(1): 1–14.

Caudle, S.L. (1994). Reengineering strategies and issues. *Public Productivity and Management Review. 18*(2): 149–154.

Cook, S., and Yahow, D. (1996). Culture and organizational learning. In *Organizational Learning* (Michael D. Cohen and L.S. Sproull eds.). Sage, Thousand Oaks, Calif., pp 430–459.

Corak, K., and Wharton, D.P. (1992). Strategic planning and organizational change: Implications for institutional researchers. Paper presented at *The 32nd Annual Forum of the Association for Institutional Research,* Atlanta.

Daft, R.L., and Weick, K.E. (1984). Toward a model of organization interpretation systems. *Academy of Management Review. 9*(2): 284–295.

Deming, W.E. (1982). *Quality, Productivity, and Competitive Position.* Massachusetts Institute of Technology: Center for Advanced Engineering Study, Cambridge, Mass.

Duncan, R., and Weiss, A. (1979). Organization learning: Implications for organizational design. In *Research in Organization Behavior. Vol. 1* (B.M. Staw, Vol. ed.). JAI Press, Greenwich, Conn.

Emery, F.E., and Trist, E.L. (1960). Socio-technical systems. In *Management, Science, Models, and Techniques. Vol. 2* (C. Churchman and M. Verhuest Vol. eds.). Pergamon, Oxford, pp. 83–94.

Etzioni, A. (1961). *A Comparative Analysis of Complex Organizations.* Free Press, New York.

Federal Quality Institute (1991). *Introduction to Total Quality Management in the Federal Government.* Office of Personnel Management, Washington, D.C.

Ferris, J.M. (1987). Local government pensions and their funding: Policy issues and options. *Review of Public Personnel Administration. 7*(3): 29–44.

Frederickson, H.G. (1996). Comparing the reinventing government movement with the new public administration. *Public Administration Review. 56*(3): 263–270.

French, W.L., Bell, C.H., Jr., and Zawacki, R.A. (1994). *Organization development and transformation: Managing effective change, (4th ed.)* Irwin, Burr Ridge, Ill.

Goliembiewki, R.T. (1985). *Humanizing Public Organizations.* Lomond, Mount Airy, Md.

Guba, E.G. (ed.) (1990). *The Paradigm Dialog.* Sage, Newbury Park, Calif.

Habermas, J. (1970). *Theory and Practice* (John Viertel, trans.) Beacon Press, Boston.

Hammer, M., and Champy, J. (1993). *Reengineering the Corporation.* HarperCollins, New York.

Hyde, A.C. (1992). The proverbs of Total Quality Management: Recharting the path to quality improvement in the public sector. *Public Productivity and Management Review. 16*(1): 25–37.

Isaacs, W.N. (1994). Taking flight: Dialogue, collective thinking, and organizational learning. In *The Learning Organization in Action.* AMACOM, New York, pp. 40–55.

Kemp, E.J., Jr., Funk, R.J., and Eadie, D.C. (1993). Change in chewable bites: Applying strategic management at EEOC. *Public Administration Review. 55*(2): 129–142.

Knowles, M. (1980). *The Modern Practice of Adult Education.* Cambridge Books, New York.

Kofman, F., and Senge, P. (1994). Communities of commitment: The heart of learning organizations. In *The Learning Organization in Action.* AMACOM, New York, pp. 7–25.

Kolb, D.A. (1984). *Experiential Learning: Experience as the Source of Learning and Development.* Prentice-Hall, Englewood Cliffs, N.J.

Kotter, J.P. (1978). *Organization Dynamics: Diagnosis and Interventions.* Addison-Wesley, Reading, Mass.

Lant, T.K., and Mezias, S.J. (1994). An organizational learning model of convergence and reorientation. In *The Learning Organization in Action.* AMACOM, New York, pp. 267–301.

Lewin, K. (1958). Group decision and social change. In *Readings in Social Psychology* (E.E. Maccoby and T.M. Newcom and E.L. Hartley, eds.). Holt, Rinehart, & Winston, New York, pp. 197–211.

Levy, A., and Merry, U. (1986). *Organization Transformation: Approaches and Strategies.* Praeger, Greenwich, Conn.

Lincoln, Y.S., and Guba, E.G. (1985). *Naturalistic Inquiry.* Sage, Beverly Hills, Calif.

Lindblom, C.A. (1959). The science of "muddling through." *Public Administration Review. 19*(2): 79–88.

Lippitt, R., and Lippitt, G. (1978). *The Consulting Process in Action.* University Associates, La Jolla, Calif.

Lynch, T.D. (1983). Staff professional competency strategy: A call for action. *International Journal of Public Administration. 5*(3): 341–354.

Mintzberg, H. (1983). *Power in and around organizations.* Prentice-Hall, Englewood Cliffs, N.J.

Nadler, D.A., Gerstein, M.S., and Shaw, R.B. (1992). *Organizational Architecture: Designs for Changing Organizations.* Jossey-Bass, San Francisco.

Nichols, K.L. (1997). The crucial edge of reinvention: A primer on scoping and measuring for organizational change. *Public Administration Quarterly. 20*(4): 405–418.

Nicolini, D., and Meznar, M.B. (1995). The social construction of organizational learning: Conceptual and practical issues in the field. *Human Relations. 48*(7): 727–746.

Office of Technology Assessment, U.S. Congress (1988). *Technology and the American Economic Transition: Choices for the Future.* Government Printing Office, Washington, D.C.

Osborne, D., and Gaebler, T. (1992). *Reinventing Government: How the Entrepreneurial Spirit Is Transforming the Public Sector.* Plume, New York.

Porras, J.J., and Robertson, P.J. (1992). Organizational development: Theory, practice, and research. In *Handbook of Industrial and Organizational Psychology,* 2nd. ed., vol. 3 (M.D. Dunnette and L.M. Hough eds.). Consulting Psychologists Press, Palo Alto, Calif., pp. 719–822.

Rabin, J. (ed.) (1993). Fiscal pressures and productive solutions. *Public Productivity and Management Review. 16*(4): 331–355.

Rago, W.V. (1996). Struggles with transformation: A study in TQM, leadership, and culture in a government agency. *Public Administration Review. 56*(3): 227–234.

Rainey, H.G. (1997). *Understanding and Managing Public Organizations,* 2nd ed. Jossey-Bass, San Francisco.

Rashford, N.S., and Coghlan, D. (1993). *The Dynamics of Organizational Levels.* Addison-Wesley, Reading, Mass.

Rice, M.F. (1979). Training in a federal agency: A research note. *Public Administration Quarterly. 2*(4): 488.

Rittel, H.W., and Webber, M. (1973). Dilemmas in a general theory of planning. *Policy Sciences. 4*(2): 155–169.

Roback, T.H. (1989). Personnel research perspectives on human resource management and development. *Public Personnel Management. 18*(2): 18–44.

Robertson, P.J., and Sneviratne, S.J. (1995). Outcomes of planned organizational change in the public sector: A meta-analytic comparison to the private sector. *Public Administration Review. 55*(6): 547–558.

Rusaw, A.C. (1989). The role of training and development in the career histories of women federal managers. Doctoral Dissertation, Virginia Polytechnic Institute and State University, Blacksburg, Va.

Rusaw, A.C. (1998). *Transforming the Character of Public Organizations: Techniques for Change Agents.* Quorum Books, Greenwich, Conn.

Schein, E.H. (1987). *Process Consultation,* (vol. 2.). Addison-Wesley, Reading, Mass.

Schein, E.H. (1994). On dialogue, culture, and organizational learning. In *The Learning Organization in Action* AMACOM, New York, pp. 56–67.

Schon, D.A. (1987). *Educating the Reflective Practitioner.* Jossey-Bass, San Francisco.

Senge, P. (1990). *The Fifth Discipline: The Art and Practice of the Learning Organization.* Doubleday, New York.

Simon, H. (1945). *Administrative behavior, 2nd ed.* Free Press, New York.

Simonsen, B., Johnston, N., and Barnett, R. (1996). Attempting non-incremental budget change in Oregon: An exercise in policy sharing. *American Review of Public Administration. 26*(2): 231–247.

Stinchcombe, A. (1965). Social structure and organizations. In *Handbook of Organizations* (J.G. March ed.). Rand-McNally, Chicago, pp. 142–193.

Stump, R.W. (1986). Assessing the impacts of career development in organizations: A case in point. *Public Personnel Management. 15*(4): 399–420.

Thompson, J.R., and Ingraham, P.W. (1996). The reinvention game. *Public Administration Review. 56*(3): 291–298.

Tough, A. (1971). *The Adult's Learning Projects.* Ontario Institute for Studies in Education, Toronto.

Ulrich, D., Jick, T., and Von Glinow, M.A. (1994). High impact learning: building and diffusing learning capability. In *The Learning Organization in Action.* AMACOM, New York, pp. 68–82.

Vinzant, J.C., and Vinzant, D.H. (1996). Strategic management and total qualilty management: Challenges and choices. *Public Administration Quarterly. 20*(2): 201–219.

Wallick, R. (1996). GFOA's 1995 legislative saga. *Government Finance Review. 12*(1): 42–44.

Watkins, K.E., and Marsick, V.J. (1993). *Sculpting the Learning Organization.* Jossey-Bass. San Francisco.

Weick, K.E. (1984). Small wins: Redefining the scale of social problems. *American Psychologist. 39*(1): 40–49.

Wellbelove, D. (1992). Training for change: A critical mass approach. *Leadership and Organization Development Journal. 13*(7): 1–3.
Zemke, R. (1984). Training in the federal government. *Training. 21*(10): 114–120.

APPENDIX A

Common Features of Means-End Models

Trigger Events: Performance effectiveness and efficiency problems or issues affecting an organization on a large scale.

Implementation Changes: Interventions that act as independent variables in a controlled experiment. A change agent examines how the selected solution affects interdependent or loosely coupled structures and processes.

Degree of Technological Readiness: Interventions that require a clearly defined problem as the focus for change; multiple formal and informal communications channels to coordinate large-scale change; extensive and predictable allocations of financial, material, and technological resources; and adaptations to particular use requirements of interdependent, related systems.

Leadership: Usually initiated or sanctioned as well as funded by management.

Coordination Requirements: Structural and procedural adjustments required throughout the organization and its environment. Particular structures affected include finance and budgeting, human resources, technological and informational resource units, and leadership skills in vision, goal setting, and interpersonal communications.

Structural Complexity: Highly complex changes in both organizational structures and processes and internal and external environments. Typically, means-end models require scanning or assessing trends affecting current organizational problems or conditions; devising a vision of a desirable, long-term future and a comprehensive plan of action to meet expectations; and aligning vision and values with structural changes during the progress of the intervention.

Environmental Threats and Opportunities: Stakeholder input and support used extensively to identify causes and effects of problems, possible solution strategies, and implement changes. Because means-end models are dependent upon environment for information, abrupt changes in the environment can upset long-range plans and jeopardize expected outcomes.

APPENDIX B

Common Features of Incremental Models

Trigger Events: Localized perception of need or opportunity for change and availability of resources and discretion commensurate with job-related duties and scope of authority.

Implementation Changes: Limited interventions that do not change existing conceptual foundations of structures and processes but merely expand on their uses.

Degree of Technological Readiness: Little outlay of resources required by change agents, who retain control of design and implementation of problem resolution strategies. Weick (1984) notes that individuals using incremental interventions often employ whatever resources are at hand (''bricolage'') to fashion a strategy.

Leadership: Decentralized incremental interventions often led at the operating level. To be successful, incremental interventions require leaders who have thorough understanding of the organization's structures and processes, key players, resource constraints and opportunities, and cultural norms and practices (Lant and Mezias, 1994). Alinsky (1972) notes three essential criteria: (a) highly specific goals, (b) realizable goals, and (c) immediate, concrete outcomes. Weick (1984) points out that the interventions should be of moderate importance; this makes them easier to understand and provides more satisfaction once the ends have been realized.

Coordination Requirements: Coordination of the intervention and its effects on internal and external environments dependent on communication of purposes, expected outcomes, and potential benefits to those neighboring structures and processes by change agents.

Structural Complexity: Interventions that involve simple manipulations of existing structures and processes.

Environmental Threats and Opportunities: Incremental interventions that are like biological organisms in developing ways to adapt and survive in changing, highly variable, and unpredictable environments (Baum, 1996).

APPENDIX C

Common Features of Pluralistic Models

Trigger Events: Useful when necessary and desirable to involve citizens, as when issues are complex or at a crisis, when major policies require the widespread support of constituents, or when innovative approaches to managing "wicked problems" are warranted.

Implementation Changes: Use of citizen data to create expectations of future participation, openness to decision making, review of progress during implementation, greater administrative responsiveness, and higher-quality, highly satisfactory results among constituents. Use of data also requires establishing special functions for data collection, analysis, and feedback. Implementation of policies requires major shifts in the directions of services and the types of programs produced as outcomes.

Degree of Technological Readiness: Allocations of additional budgeted funds, electronic equipment capable of facilitating multiple and simultaneous dialog, special skills in collecting, analyzing, and interpreting statistical as well as qualitative information.

Leadership: Democratic, with widest possible constituency of represented interests. Leaders provide skills that empower followers; create a broad-based, comprehensive vision and strategy; and use dialog as a means of learning and change.

Coordination Requirements: Leadership competencies in communications, coordination, and coalition building.

Structural Complexity: Complex environments, characterized by layers of bureaucratic structures and functions, elected representatives, diverse clientele, and resolution of nonroutine problems.

Environmental Threats and Opportunities: Continuous use of environmentally based data. When abrupt changes occur, the policy data base as well as supportive coalitions built may crumble. Moreover, at each phase of policy-making, clientele requires input, assessment of ongoing activities, and representation in outcomes. If perceptions of democratic processes are tainted, participatory attempts will fail.

APPENDIX D

Common Features of Individually Based Models

Trigger Events: Individual job requirements that change, organizational restructuring, downsizing, introduction of new technology, and personal needs that may spur taking up formal or informal learning.

Implementation Changes: Resources, opportunities, and support of management to allow individuals to practice skills developed in formal learning events and informal learning projects.

Degree of Technological Readiness: Supportive leadership; opportunities to transfer or apply skills from formal learning events; links between human resource functions and organizational objectives and mission; performance management systems matching career goals, job characteristics and skill requirements, career planning, appraisal, and feedback; and coaching.

Leadership: Transformational leaders who provide financial resources, emotional support and trust, and opportunities for professional growth.

Coordination Requirements: Integrated with other change programs in organizational and human resource management.

Structural Complexity: Complex, requiring changes in both human and organizational systems and processes.

Environmental Threats and Opportunities: Use of education for changing organizations, especially in organizations that are undergoing rapid changes, such as public institutions. Turbulence in external environments, such as the demand for more accountability coupled with unwillingness of taxpayers to use funds for improved government services, for instance, calls on public employees to think creatively. Expanding existing resources or finding new ways to procure them is important for survival in a privatized sphere. In addition, learning ways to improve interpersonal communications, as through conflict management training, strengthens the capacity for an organization as a whole to function more effectively and efficiently.

25

The New Public Management and Reform

Jamil E. Jreisat
Public Administration Program, University of South Florida, Tampa, Florida

Is there a truly "remarkable revolution" sweeping public management around the world, raising the banner of a new public management (NPM), as recent literature proclaims (Kettl, 1997: 446)? If there is, against what this revolution is being waged and for what does it stand? What pattern (model, theory, or paradigm) does the new management offer? The purposes of this study are (a) to examine the assumptions of the "new public management," particularly in the context of countries that have recently initiated significant reform programs; (b) to define major provisions and prescriptions promoted by this new framework to introduce administrative reform in modern societies; and, (c) to compare the new public management and the traditional public administration in terms of their strategies for reform.

No doubt, enormous managerial changes are in progress in many locations, involving all aspects of public management, at the conceptual as well as the operational levels. Administrative reform has become a universal outcry induced by legacies of costly failures of many governments to reach their developmental objectives. Administrative reform successes in some countries also have encouraged a much wider pursuit of change. In a way, "the integration of the American governmental reform movement into a larger international movement" (Roberts,

1997: 466) is only one outcome of such efforts. Other significant drives for management improvement have been initiated in countries such as members of the Organization of Economic Cooperation and Development (OECD), Australia, Canada, New Zealand, United Kingdom, Korea, Mexico, Jordan, and Brazil. Although these cases of administrative reforms constitute a reliable source of information, they have not yet resulted in definitive generalizations. Such results could only evolve through systematic comparative assessments and evaluations, which largely remain underdeveloped.

Significantly, the profusion of scholarly contributions and country reports, regularly recounting cases of management reforms, has not produced agreement on a reliable and coherent approach for achieving reform. At the dawn of the 21st century, public administration literature is flowing with examinations and reviews of various attempts to modernize and to adapt management of public organizations in changing political, social, and economic contexts. Even when the "new public management" is presented as a major "paradigm shift" (Kettle, 1997; Osborne and Plastrik, 1997: 15; Roberts, 1997; Mascarenhas, 1993), ushering in a "new world order" of management, there is no consensus on the content, much less on the practice of this NPM. As Klages and Loffler (1998: 41) note, "From an empirical point of view, there is almost no systematic knowledge about applied NPM."

Certainly, global practical experiences and scholarship on management reforms are reshaping some governments and profoundly influencing their practices. Many case studies since the 1970s have been cited as examples of "aggressive" application of management reforms: in New Zealand (Kettle, 1997; Scott et al., 1997; Pallot, 1996), in the United Kingdom (Barberis, 1998; Ferlie et al., 1996; Mascarehnas, 1993), in the United States (Thompson and Ingraham, 1996; Moe, 1994; Gore, 1993), and in Canada (Roberts, 1998; Seidle, 1995), to mention only a few examples. Many other countries also are at various phases of reform. It is irresistible to inquire whether these reforms are related and how; do they constitute one universe of reformed management, a single paradigm that connects these promising experiences, or a multiplicity of disconnected experiences without a central terrain?

COMPARING TWO PERSPECTIVES

During the past few years, debates around these questions have stimulated perhaps one of the most exciting exchanges in public administration since World War II. For the purpose of this study, it is possible to divide the stakes in this debate, at least analytically, into two major thrusts. Each has its own premises, diagnosis of the problems, prescriptions for solutions, vision of desired conditions, and strategies for achieving them.

First is the *economics-based "new paradigm,"* frequently referred to as the "new public management." Canada is one example of the many countries that have substantially restructured their public services in line with what the OECD has called the new paradigm in public management. The restructuring of the Canadian federal and provincial governments, Roberts (1998) points out, is similar to reforms undertaken by other Western democracies, particularly the United States, to make government "work better and cost less." This new paradigm was applied by OECD countries in the 1990s and provided the foundation for the current Canadian reform efforts. Basically, the reforms consist of three key ideas: the need to cut all "nonessential" or "noncore" public spending, the need to rely less on conventional government bureaucracies for delivering public services, and the need for public institutions to rely less on tax revenue to finance their operations, and more on nontax revenues, such as fees for services (Roberts, 1998: 1). Agreeing with C. Hood (1991, 1995), J. Pallot (1996) considers the dominant features of the NPM the removal of private/public distinctions and the imposition of explicit standards and rules on management practices. Thus, Pallot (1996: 2) identifies these main characteristics of the NPM:

> (1) greater segregation of public sector organizations into separate "product" centers, (2) a shift towards competition between the separate units offering the services, (3) the use of management practices (e.g. accrual accounting, organizational design, career structure and remuneration practices) broadly drawn from the private sector, (4) an emphasis on efficiency and cost reduction, (5) the rise of a new managerial elite, (6) more explicit and measurable standards of performance and (7) attempts to control public sector organizational units through pre-set output measures.

On the surface, the described needs for reform and many of the characteristics of the proposed NPM to meet those needs do not appear particularly controversial. The premises behind them, however, and the processes used to carry them out are. In a symposium on the new public management, Linda Kaboolian (1998: 190), referencing Jack Nagel and Peter Self, declares that "common to reform movements in all these countries [the United States, the United Kingdom, Korea, Portugal, France, Brazil, Australia, Sweden, New Zealand, Canada] is the use of the economic market as a model for political and administrative relationships." The institutional reforms of the NPM, Kaboolian (1998: 190) concludes, "are heavily influenced by the assumptions of the public choice approach, principal-agent theory, and transaction cost economics." Other theoretical grounds conveyed in this perspective for restructuring public agencies include new institutional economics, bureau maximization theory, quasi-market theory, and principal-agent theory (Ferlie et al., 1996: 10). The connection is made clear and direct by those who view "the new public management as an ideological thought system, characterized by the importation of ideas generated in private sector settings within public sector organizations" (Ferlie et al., 1996: 10). One conclusion is amply clear: The "NPM builds on the basic economic premise that private-sector management and economic principles are transferable and functional in the public sector" (Klages and Loffler, 1998: 42). Others go further, even advocating the elimination of all distinctions between public and private sector organizations (Hood, 1991, 1995; Pallot, 1996).

Generally, to advocate a new paradigm in management is to assume an existing one is deficient or unsatisfactory. In this case, not surprisingly, the target of dissatisfaction is public administration in general. Public organizations habitually are singled out and associated with a list of shortcomings. Criticisms often include unresponsiveness to demands of citizens, "bureau-pathology," and leadership of bureaucrats with the power and incentives to expand their administrative empires (Kaboolian, 1998: 190; Nagel, 1997: 350). Now public administration, according to Frederickson (1999: 9), is known as "government reform." Among assumptions behind this are "that government is ill organized, poorly managed, very costly and generally ineffective." In order to justify peddling these ideas, reformers regularly voice their concerns about a "crisis" in government and exaggerate public management failings. This is far from promoting a constructive and meaningful dialog between scholars and practitioners of public administration and those in other fields, particularly economics, to promote mutual enrichment and greater relevance of both fields.

The second perspective on reform is firmly rooted in established *organization and management traditions* and in the ethics of public service. Reforms in this approach seek to extend administrative theories and processes and to improve their utility in serving the familiar administrative values of efficiency and effectiveness of public service delivery. To achieve better results within the public sector, this perspective focuses on improving the state's administrative capacity and revitalizing its mission of public service by introducing measures aimed at mending the formulation and administration of public policies. The public organization remains the main unit of analysis. Thus, reforming it and building its capacity, not dismantling or bypassing it, are the primary concerns.

To be sure, management-based reform initiatives have always been receptive to changes in traditional managerial processes, usually associated with bureaucratic structures and behavior. Modern management reforms promote the development of a culture of organizational learning and innovation while emphasizing greater attention to application and outcomes. Failures of past reform efforts are recognized as learning tools, feedback, and additions to the administrative knowledge base. Appraisals and evaluations are continually utilized for avoiding past errors and rejecting nonworkable solutions. Tracking recent public administration developments indicates a global search for improved concepts and techniques to accomplish the following objectives:

1. Ensure *accountability* of public management, especially to its political context.

2. *Measure and evaluate results,* instead of maintaining the traditional preoccupation with inputs and bureaucratic expansion as virtues in themselves.
3. Increase the state's commitment to *development of its human resources,* particularly improving processes of merit-based appointments and promotions, and personnel training and development.
4. Promote *ethics in public service* while aggressively attacking corruption with more reliable means such as instituting dependable measures of audit and evaluation, funding training programs that emphasize ethics in public service, and instituting more effective methods of investigation and adjudication of misconduct.
5. Employ *cost reduction* measures and develop consciousness of the need to rely on more efficient techniques, based on reliable information, in the conduct of public affairs.
6. Enforce *quality criteria* throughout public service that also have clear elements of incentives, empowerment of management, and stronger mandate for citizen-friendly services.

In recent years, public financial management, particularly budgeting, has received a higher ranking on the agenda of reform. A survey of most common administrative reforms by countries that have introduced such changes emphasizes the following aspects (UNDP, 1998: 5, 6):

1. A tendency toward specification of government goals and objectives
2. Greater delegation of authority and responsibility to line agencies, coupled with attempts to set spending ceilings
3. Use of multiyear frameworks for allocations of resources in the annual budget
4. Expanded operating authority and flexibility for executives and agencies in financial management
5. Increased use of comparative information in the form of measures and indicators of results, to be combined with financial information on spending of resources
6. Increased reliance on follow-ups and evaluations in the form of regular financial and results reports
7. Intensified use of performance audit and evaluation of financial transactions

Thus, the inventory of refined organization and management concepts and practices is substantial and diversified. Accumulation over a century of growth and development enriched public administration with extensive choices for organizing the functions and managing the policies of the modern state. Therefore, the assumption that public administration has to disclaim its publicness in order to be hospitable to reform ideas is beside the point. In contrast, the assortment of market-oriented ideas and bottom-line approaches proposed to remedy the perceived managerial ailments of the public sector have to be appropriately evaluated. Essentially, such evaluation has to be done in the context of public policy rather than simply accepting the familiar unconditional endorsement of the advocates or the cursory dismissal of the critics. Certainly, market-oriented ideas for managing public programs that claim to offer a substitute for public administration principles and values are ill-advised.

The two perspectives, briefly outlined, are not without significant overlapping, common grounds, even if each remains distinct in its premises and tools of implementation. Actually, each perspective has its own clusters and subdivisions, adding to the difficulty of establishing a true and precise delineation of elements that constitute the new paradigm of public management. The considerable number of tautological descriptions and explanations have not produced concurrence on the essence or the boundaries of the NPM. Not surprisingly, therefore, the NPM has been described as an "empty canvas" on which you can paint whatever you like (Ferlie et al., 1996: 10). Others have conveniently offered a flexible characterization such as "the NPM varies depending on your perspective" (Barzelay, 1997: 1). David Osborne and Peter Plastrik (1997: 8) introduce their new public management as "reinvention" and "redesign" that will reform public sector management by applying an "entrepreneurial model" in order to "maximize productivity and effectiveness." About this "entrepreneurial model," they say:

> We are convinced that the appearance of these entrepreneurial organizations in the late twentieth century is no accident. We believe that it represents an inevitable historical shift from one paradigm to another. It is a shift as profound as that which took place at the beginning of the century, when we built the bureaucratic public institutions we are busy reinventing today. (Osborne and Plastrik, 1997: 15)

Accordingly, NPM has been many things to many people, and most reform efforts endorsing some of its shifting tenets remain works in progress. "From a theoretical point of view, NPM is still in a pre-theoretical stage" (Klages and Loffler, 1998: 41). Actually, the NPM often shifts focus with ease among public choice, organizational economic, transaction cost-economic, and neomanagerialistic perspectives despite dissimilarities. However, as indicated, reform initiatives that shaped the NPM emphasize the market as an instrument for efficient resource allocation and for reduction of the role of the state in the economy. The expected outcome of this is social and economic progress based on business initiative and competition and greater freedom of choice (Mascarenhas, 1993: 320). Consequently, the prescriptions often look outside the usual domain of public administration and seek private sector involvement in a variety of schemes such as privatization, contracting out, joint ventures, or simply a wholesale downsizing of government. Very few advocates of NPM actually continue to think in terms of public management improvements (i.e., Seidle, 1995). Instead, what is proposed appears to be either a substitution or a dismantlement of public management. Central to this thinking also is the individual manager, viewed as a rational actor whose behavior is motivated by the quest for maximization of self-interest. Therefore, the goals of society related to satisfying its economic needs, as well as its needs for public order and for various kinds of public goods and services, should be achieved, to the maximum degree possible, through privately owned business firms operating in competitive markets (Simon, 1998: ii).

These concepts of market-based prescriptions and satisfaction of individual self-interest as key motivators are questioned or rejected on several grounds:

1. As Herbert Simon (1998: ii) points out, the "major motivational premise [individual self-interest] is simply false." He indicates that human beings make most of their decisions, not in terms of the perceived self-interest, but in terms of perceived interests of the groups, families, organizations, ethnic groups, and nation-states with which they identify. Moreover, self-interest is too general to explain behavior and all individual choices, as they are influenced by existing institutional, political, social, and economic contexts (Jreisat, 1997b: 124).

2. Economics literature on market failures indicates that no good or service can be allocated efficiently by leaving it to the private sector (Klages and Lofler 1998: 42). Markets are not always competitive; mergers, manipulations, incomplete information, dominance of the market by few producers, and so forth, all reduce competitiveness. Thus, "the assumption by advocates of privatization that the private sector is almost always more efficient and more productive than the public sector is questionable in light of the record of the business sector during the past 20 years" (Jreisat, 1997b: 125). In fact, Herbert Simon (a Noble Prize laureate in economics) effectively debunks the major argument for privatization. The idea that "privatization will always (or even usually) increase productivity and efficiency is equally wrong." He points out that such "empirical evidence as we have on the relative efficiency of private and public organizations shows no consistent superiority of one over the other" (Simon, 1998: ii).

3. Assumptions of the NPM seem to deflate the social and political dimensions of governing or relegate them almost to irrelevance since the market will be determining allocative decisions. In reference to the British efforts at reform of the public sector in the 1980s, quoting the *Economist* (1990), Mascarenhas (1993: 323) concludes that "efficiency through management improvement was shunted to the background as political objectives such as reducing the power of public sector unions and promoting popular capitalism at the cost of consumer choice and competition, once offered as the objectives of privatization, came to the forefront." Still, the public sector continues to manage and deliver essential services and goods that are not primarily evaluated by a criterion of economic efficiency but by satisfaction of citizens and responsiveness to their needs. Examples range from protecting the environment to meeting health and education needs, from ensuring equal opportunity to citizens to managing the social security system.

Perhaps the budget statement by the finance minister of Canada is a concrete example of the undeniable role of the public sector in modern society, despite all the fog generated by the ideological attacks on government. In his address to the Parliament, presenting Canada's 1999 budget and pressing his arguments in favor of restoration of cutbacks in health care funding, the minister of finance affirms:

> Mr. Speaker: . . . . A nation is not a corporation. Markets do many things—and they do them well. But there are many things they cannot do. Markets cannot provide quality health care to all of us when we are sick. They cannot prevent the gap between rich and poor from becoming an unbridgeable gulf. They cannot deal with the root causes of homelessness or of violence against women. . . . They do not deal with common good. . . . Our purpose is not just to build a better bottom line. It is to build a stronger nation. (Martin, 1999: 3)

4. One can easily recognize the ideological antigovernment mode behind many of the proposed changes: Namely, privatization and reforms largely have been advanced as tools to reduce the role of the public sector, cut down on deficit spending, and decrease the overall growth in the cost of governing. True, general dissatisfaction with the growth and performance of public bureaucracies has been a potent motivation for change, not only in the West but also worldwide. Britain led the way and "adopted a more ideological or political position in promoting the private sector, with the intention of altering the balance of power between the two sectors [business and public] rather than for reasons of efficiency" (Mascarenhas, 1993: 325). Also, the United States during the Reagan administration implemented a set of policies that has the same objectives. Similarly, many developed and developing countries have implemented policies to privatize public enterprises, downsize the public sector, reform civil service, stimulate entrepreneurial management, or contract out government services. At the present, these changes are the core of a familiar package of reforms advocated by the World Bank economists. Depending on the country, the recommendations often are referred to as the International Monetary Fund's (IMF's) framework of restructuring. Typically, this package includes measures to privatize, rationalize public expenditures, improve efficiency and effectiveness of public policies, and limit or eliminate social spending such as government subsidies to food and other essentials.

Many of these recommendations that deal with improving or rationalizing public sector performance are consistent with the goals and values of public administration. The departure begins when reduction of the public sector's role in society is made an end in itself. Specifically, public administration deeply objects to embracing private sector methods and objectives, irrespective of fundamental public service values such as equal treatment of citizens, serving public interest, and acting with transparency and accountability. Bias in favor of "businesslike" management and the economic assumptions behind such views often tend to portray public administration unrealistically. The following list illustrates some of the distortions that the field of public administration continues to endure:

Public Administration and Change

Promotions that depict public administration as a rigid and nonchanging field in the midst of a fast changing world are biased and inaccurate. In reality, a primary attribute of public administration throughout its history has been a continuous search for improvement of concepts and practices. As Kingsley (1997: iii) notes, the history of public administration is one of reform and change. In the United States, for example, every president made reform of the administrative system a high-priority public policy. Very few developing countries escaped the challenge of administrative change, particularly after the end of the colonial system in the post–World War II years. To assume, therefore, that public administration is a nonchanging field or bent on resisting change is inconsistent with powerful historical evidence.

Today's public sector, for example, is braving a profound shift in public budgeting, from focus on input (how much should we spend) to focus on outputs (what was produced and with what consequence). For years, demand-driven public agencies defined success by how much money was budgeted, how many people were hired, and how many programs or activities were funded. Now, a result-driven government defines success not by how much is budgeted but by what effects or consequences such spending has. The change has been viewed as a part of a larger transformation sweeping public management around the world, raising differing banners such as result-oriented management, performance management, total quality management, entrepreneurial management, and even reinvention of government.

Certainly, advocating reform does not guarantee successful implementation, in the private or the public sector. In fact, many government reform initiatives have failed to materialize, and the doubters have begun to question the role of public administration in general. So, why should traditional administrative principles now deliver more favorable results than in the past? As students of public administration recognize the dilemma of the poor record of reform implementation, they also acknowledge that past enforcement of reform ideas has lacked compatible values, consistent efforts, adequate preparation, and sufficient political support as well as overall managerial competence. Robert D. Behn (1998: 209) notes that leadership by public managers is a necessity and an obligation, but he also concedes that "the legislative branch of government gives public agencies missions that are vague and conflicting and often fails to provide enough resources to pursue seriously all of these missions." Kenneth Meier (1997: 193) also confirms that "the key problems are failures of electoral institutions rather than failures of bureaucracy."

Government's Commitment to Equity and Justice

A narrow definition of public administration (e.g. rigid, dysfunctional bureaucratic structure) effectively separates the field from its eventful history and denies it the benefits of more than a century of evolution. Employing market mechanisms of competition in order to achieve higher efficiencies in public organizations has real and potential distortive risks. As the premise itself is questionable, it also undermines the very purpose of public service. Political and administrative public policy-making in the modern state cannot be forced to choose, for example, between government's obligations to realize accountability, equity, and justice on one hand and efficiency on the other. The market claims commitment to and competence in the latter domain. The state seeks a balance of the two, never totally sacrificing one for the other. As Terry (1999: 276) points out, "The blind application of business management principles and practices can undermine the integrity of public bureaucracies and so threaten our democratic way of life."

Moreover, relentless criticism by business media is not totally altruistic nor entirely motivated by concerns for the public interest. Privatization usually opens up new opportunities for private profits; it does not always result in improvements in public service. Myths are perpetuated about efficiencies of the private sector that are unrealistic and even contrived. In fact, government can never tolerate the waste and the high cost of the incentive systems of the private sector. Imagine government's competing with the private sector and paying the U.S. secretary of defense or any public official the same salary the CEO of Disney corporation (who was paid $575.6 million in 1998), or as the nearly 100 large companies that awarded their top executives options megagrants worth at least $10 million in 1997 (*Business Week,* 1999: 72). Nor can the public sector offer the rest of the benefits available to corporate managers, let alone justify the cost of huge failures such as those in saving and loan associations, the steel industry, and many other businesses that lost out to foreign competitors or were victimized by gigantic schemes of fraud and mismanagement.

Inferior Theory and/or Scholarship

The criticism that theory and scholarship in public administration are below academic standards in other disciplines is based on entirely different reasons for the negative appraisal. Most repeated assertions are that public administration as a field of study has "inferior methodology," a "weak scientific base," and "no theory-building tradition" and suffers from a "reputation for low quality scholarship" (Thompson, 1999; Lynn, 1996; Kettle, 1999). In part, perhaps, one can assume these criticisms are made by scholars who migrated to public administration from other related disciplines such as political science or public policy and continue to express a subtle nostalgia for disciplinary clarity of conception or determinism of definitions. Such traits are not found in a professional interdisciplinary field such as public administration that has overwhelmingly relativistic and eclectic concepts and practices. The issue, then, is that public administration, its contributions, its commitment, and its potential cannot be evaluated by the criteria used to evaluate other disciplines. Public administration is substantively connected to more than one discipline. Moreover, the ultimate value of public administration is in shaping the structure of government and in efficiently and effectively managing its functions. Of course, we agree that "the advancement of public administration as a field requires it to shed any vestige of its reputation for doing work of limited quality focused on a narrow domain" (Thompson, 1999: 120). What area of social science would not benefit from such advice? But this is a different matter altogether.

Simply, the ultimate test of public administration is inseparable from its ability to cultivate concepts and practices that produce significant quantitative and qualitative improvements in the performance of public organizations. This objective is well served by continued refinements of administrative theory in relation to application and systematic monitoring of managerial practices in order to identify complementary measures that create substantive effects, thus enabling us to know, with a measure of confidence, "what really works." Indeed, as Donald Kettl points out, public administration does have important things to say to public officials. "Public administration has a rich theory and even richer tradition of analyzing what is truly public about government management, and this is the piece most prominently missing from the public reform debate" (Kettl, 1999: 131).

PREEMINENCE OF THE PUBLIC ADMINISTRATION CONTEXT

The public administration community regards the scramble to declare a "new" public management in line with economic-based, semimarket theories and techniques a dubious premise or a short-lived enterprise. Significantly, this NPM perspective evinces no particular appreciation of the uniqueness of the environment within which public management operates, which consists of various elements that exert different levels of influence on the organization and on its operations. The most dominant aspect of the environment is the political effect.

The political context defines many aspects of public management, especially the legitimacy of public organizations, their budgets, and their personnel practices. In modern democratic societies, the legislative influence on administrative performance is manifested in several ways, ranging from approval of financial spending and staffing practices to enactment of a variety of public laws that sanction administrative actions. Consequently, public organizations invest considerable energy in gauging their political environment and adjusting to it. They also seek to modify and influence the actions of the political system and do not simply act as obedient soldiers who unquestioningly carry out their leaders' wishes. Public organizations generally possess certain resources such as knowledge and expertise, buttressed by accumulation of information on specialized functions and policies. Many of these organizations also succeed in building viable connections with citizens receiving public services. Thus, the relationship of public organizations to their political contexts is crucial as it is grounded in the ideals of the democratic process, in which elected persons enact laws and public managers administer them.

Although the political context has a defining influence, it also is a source of many incongruities in managerial practices. Even with taxpayers' funding public organizations, those who authorize such funding usually are removed from operations. Actually, often they have goals and values inconsistent with those of management. In the final analysis, failure to recognize the capacity of administrative units to think on their own and independently propose a possible range of policies that politicians will find judicious to espouse will only weaken the effort to formulate a rational and responsible public policy (Rabin 1996: 149).

Public administration, therefore, is in the midst of a political environment shaped by larger forces of legislators, interest groups, mass media, political parties, and political appointees. Interactions between them and public managers are often strained by incongruities of goals and values. Management of public organizations, however, is not neutral with respect to the process or the outcome of policy-making. Actually, professional concerns frequently are frustrated by political actions, creating tensions that affect not only the immediate operations of public organizations but also their long-range managerial aims of morale, confidence, and focus on matters of public interest.

The predicament for public managers is to find a way to serve professional ethics and managerial values of efficiency, effectiveness, and equity in public service within a turbulent political environment. The political context frequently forces poorly developed decisions to serve narrow but powerful special interest groups: prematurely authorized, vaguely stated, and lacking consensus and support. Legislators and other elected officials, beholden to lobbyists and interest group financiers, habitually blame the "bureaucrats" for failures of policy. Thus, public service and public managers become convenient scapegoats for bad public policies (Lynn, 1987; Goodsell, 1983). Within such an environment, public managers often retrench into safer terrains of inaction and practice of survival techniques.

Political responses to the growth of public administration have been somewhat cynical. Consumed by promotion of their own incumbency and self-interest, elected officials are becoming increasingly difficult to unseat. The effect of this political reality on public management, particularly on administrative reform initiatives, is profound. As these elected individuals rely on complex bureaucratic organizations in formulating and implementing public policy, they also are attentive to the critical questions of responsiveness to and representation of those who elect them. To explain deficiencies of public policies they helped enact, politicians often join mass media and special interest groups in finding and embellishing public management failures, however, episodic or unrepresentative. Negative images of public administration usually are exploited to justify alternative models as in some versions of the NPM and the "reinvention of government" movement that calls for abandoning traditional managerial approaches (Osborne and Gaebler, 1992).

The premises behind the negative views of government and bureaucracy around the world actually are not much different. As Rainey (1997: 3–10) points out, two such premises are that governmental activities differ from those controlled by private actors and organizations and, that governmental activities are performed less effectively and efficiently. What are new here, perhaps, are not the premises themselves as much as the self-serving exaggeration and manipulation of negative information about government, regardless of the level of proficiency it demonstrates in performing its functions.

The judicial context is another crucial element of the environment of public administration. The growing number of laws usually translates into greater powers for public organizations, which already command significant power of functional specialization. Certain public agencies and commissions performing regulatory functions have also been delegated powers that allow them to perform semilegislative and semijudicial roles. As a result of these broad accumulated administrative powers, judicial review has become an important safeguard against arbitrary use of administrative authority. Courts review administrative decisions and interpret existing laws to ensure protection of constitutional rights and liberties granted to individuals and groups. Over the years, the judicial impact has increased through implementation of defined operational standards in public agencies, as required by federal and state laws regarding administrative procedures (Jreisat, 1997b).

A judicial review provides relief to an individual who is harmed by a particular agency decision. In contrast, political oversight controls generally influence entire programs or policies. Judicial review also differs from political controls, according to Gellhorn and Levin (1990: 73), "in that it attempts to foster reasoned decision making, by requiring the agencies to produce supporting facts and rational explanations," not necessarily financial savings. In essence, judicial review provides an independent check on the validity of administrative decisions: ensuring compliance with law and constitutional rights, statutory jurisdiction, use of required procedures, and limited administrative discretion.

The legal constraints on public administration to strengthen protection of individual rights, apply the doctrine of qualified immunity, and strictly observe procedural due process mean that public administrators are under greater pressure to justify their decisions and to demonstrate their legal validity. In public personnel administration, judicial decisions have had significant impact on public employment. Various court decisions, during the 1970s and 1980s, affirmed public employees' basic constitutional rights (freedom of speech, freedom of association, political activity, and equal protection). Court decisions rejected the traditional notion of public employment as a "privilege" and extended to public employees the procedural due process protection (Jaegal and Cayer, 1991: 212). To a considerable degree, these legal protections provoked an ideological onslaught of conservative politics, in some Western countries, against public agencies.

Thus, the legal context of contemporary public administration demarcates the mission, structure, resources, power of decision making, and overall practices of public agencies. Laws specify standards of operation as well as methods of challenging arbitrary and capricious decisions made by these administrative units. With the expansion of government responsibilities in society, the need for protection of individual rights by augmenting political oversight and bolstering judicial review is significantly greater.

Today's government is not limited to traditional functions. Governments assume many fairly new roles such as protection of consumers, health care, protection of the environment, and work safety, as well as regulation of a wide range of services. The growing responsibilities of government, therefore, dictate an increasing role for administrative institutions. Public agencies have to maintain vigilance against abuse of individual rights and due process and to substantiate and explain the basis of their decisions. At the same time, the augmented contemporary role of government underlines, anew, issues of public accountability, transparency of public decisions, and openness of government records to citizens' scrutiny. The complexity of the public administration environment increased during the 1990s, because public managers had to deal with economic constraints at all levels of government, including cutbacks, retrenchment, downsizing, fiscal stress, efficiency drives, and a growing focus on productivity improvement. The adjustments of public organizations have not always been smooth or problem-free.

Supply-side economists, for example, argue for a reduced government role in the economy by producing less regulation, lowering taxes, and limiting spending. The basic concept is that governmental intervention in the economy is less efficient than free-market competition in allocating goods and services, directing investments, and generating economic growth. Such economic thinking influenced public policy in general and budget recommendations in particular during the 1980s. Also, this approach is quite different from the Keynesian economic theory, which supports a proactive role of government in steering the economy and reaching desirable goals of fiscal policy. These goals encompass attaining acceptable levels of employment, maintaining stable wages and prices, and inducing sufficient economic growth. Government fiscal policies have a responsibility to achieve these goals mainly through calculated regulatory and budgetary measures.

During the past few decades, comparative public administration devoted considerable attention to identification of environmental factors that affect the performance and operations of bureaucracy. Consequently, a significant body of literature has been produced on various aspects of public management in various cultures of the world (see Heady, 1996: 5). The search to develop universal principles of administration through cross-cultural comparisons remains crucial (Jreisat, 1999: 855). Recognizing the trend toward globalization, Riggs (1991: 473) points out that public administration must be comparative in order to compel us to rethink the context of what we call public administration. Thus, Riggs (1991: 473) states, "We need to develop frameworks and theories for the study of public administration that are truly universal in scope—they will be based on a comprehensive ecological understanding of the place of public administration in all governments, historical as well as contemporary. Such a framework will be focusing on explanatory theories that account for the continuously changing properties and problems faced by governments as they seek to implement public policies." Riggs seeks to anchor the normative guidelines of comparative administration in empirical knowledge of the institutions and dynamics of society. The expected advantage of this process is that it will promote increasing use of comparative methods to understand public administration in a global framework and to find better solutions for its problems. By understanding American administration, Riggs hopes, "we become less ethnocentric, and this will also help us acquire a more penetrating understanding of the administrative problems faced by other countries" (Riggs, 1991: 473).

In conclusion, accuracy and relevance of administrative knowledge are profoundly influenced by the level of understanding of the organizational context. The nature of the organization and the type of relations it has with its community, particularly the political one, are crucial to its effective functioning. Public administration, therefore, is not merely a bundle of techniques that can be planted or supplanted anywhere with equal success. Often, the techniques and processes are tied to a set of contextual conditions (political, legal, economic, and cultural). Ignoring this reality or attempting the "removal of differences between the public and private sector" (Pallot, 1996: 2) may reflect a grave misunderstanding of the theory and process of governing. Certainly, the "big questions" facing public administration are not the same as those posed by economic-based theories. Still, public administration may be influenced by, and certainly is free to adapt, insights from any field of knowledge, as the need requires. "Ultimately," Frank Thompson (1999: 119) points out, "the health of public administration as a field depends on its ability to bring together the contributions of multiple disciplines in ways that foster balance, synthesis, and synergy."

CENTRAL FEATURES OF FUTURE REFORM STRATEGIES

Advancements in public administration have always been assisted by accumulated field experiences, comparative assessments, updating of information technologies, and a steady conversion of concepts into applications. Universal attempts to develop public organizational capacities and to refine managerial processes are bearing fruits. Despite lack of agreement on what change and for what purpose, a "new world order" of management is being proclaimed everywhere, helping governments improve their overall performance. Evidence of this is plentiful in the United States, Canada, New Zealand, Europe, and other countries. Even in developing countries such as those in Latin America and the Arab states, where lack of progress in carrying out reform plans is as common as it is conspicuous, political leaders have rarely been more committed to implementation of reform programs (Jreisat, 1997a). With the choices of these leaders continually narrowing, and their political authority impaired, reform is now more seriously addressed. The important conclusion here is that it is a mistake to deny progress made or to relate reform failures entirely to deficiencies of the principles of management themselves.

Regularly and confidently public administrationists have managed reform programs, in many places at various times. Administrative reform, however, can be an uneven process in which the results accrue slowly. But fending off ideological intrusions and resisting tendencies of fads and fashions, made rampant by consultants and peddlers of ideas, require greater definition of the fundamentals, the big questions, things that matter. Although public administration needs to maintain its receptivity to change and innovation, it is not in the interest of NPM, nor of public administration, to perpetuate a notion that applying sophisticated economic ideas is necessitated by irrelevance of public administration principles. Separating reform from the principles and foundation premises of public administration, as proponents of "running government as business" urge, is certain to cause the demise of the NPM—just as many of the other passing fads encountered in recent years.

Appropriately, public administration has to continue on the path of development and change, preparing public management for the new century. The evolving new management has to preserve the core values of public service while employing new technologies and actively updating organizational and managerial concepts and practices. A synthesizing process may offer a possibility of an alternative that regards the new public management as "not a simplistic Big Answer" but rather "a normative reconceptualization of public administration consisting of several inter-related components" (Seidle, 1995: 23). In this event, a profound renewal of public administration may actually be under way. Perhaps the net effect of reform initiatives will be to transform traditional public administration into a livelier and more effective field. As to the NPM, although it has had its champions and critics, for good or ill, "it is widely held to have heightened the challenge to traditional canons of public administration" (Barberis, 1998: 454). Preliminary indications point to a revitalized public administration with a growing emphasis on the following features of reform:

1. Focus on results: At the beginning of the 21th century, performance-oriented management, and its derivative performance budgeting, are unmistakable trends worldwide. As Allen Schick (1998: v) notes: "In the last ten to fifteen years,

a wave of change in the management of public budgets has swept through developed countries and has begun to engulf many developing countries as well." As students of public administration are familiar with such developments in industrial countries of the West, an example from a small country also confirms the trend. Recently, the author participated in the development of a reform plan for introducing performance budgeting to the government of Jordan. The plan is a design that incorporates ideas and experiences from several countries and global institutions. Participants in the project are experts from New Zealand, the World Bank, the United Nations Development Program, Germany, Sweden, and France, as well as Jordan.[1] What is unique about this experience is that many administrative cultures were represented and that the participants' views quickly converged to outline the main features of a reform plan that introduces a new management system to a small developing country.

The focus on performance means that various components of a public organization are integrated to achieve the desired results such as setting performance criteria, improving the quality of public services, controlling costs, increasing efficiencies, empowering public managers, and providing incentives that reward high-quality performance. In brief, the overall concern of public management is performance.

2. Adaptation of new technologies to public administration needs: To manage effectively, public organizations and public managers increasingly are recognizing the urgent need for relevant, reliable information to help improve the quality of their decision-making processes. Thus, designing a system of information gathering that collects, classifies, and retrieves data according to managers' needs requires policy commitments as well as resources. Although measuring performance is a work in progress even after several years of practice, in the short run information can make a big difference in how individual agencies are run.

3. Renewed interest in ethics and accountability of public service: Reform initiatives in public administration have consistently aimed at reducing corruption by taking various procedural measures and by seeking to recruit into government service more qualified people (Frederickson, 1997: 158). These objectives remain central to government reforms, although enhancement of the ethics dimension has added a more positive aspect that emphasizes training and development. Establishing codes of ethics and conducting training and education programs indicate the growing importance of the concept. Today's public management also stresses values such as basic honesty and conformity to law, avoidance of actions that involve conflict of interest, and service orientation that is committed to procedural fairness (Willbern, 1984).

At the legal and procedural levels, issues of accountability occupy a central position among objectives of reform. The specific elements of this reform may be grouped into the following: (a) more effective measures of investigation and adjudication of violations, (b) programs for education and training in ethics, (c) dependable measures of inspection and performance audit, and (d) greater transparency and documentation of government actions, especially regular reports and independent evaluation of performance.

4. Recognition of common interest or possible joint efforts with the private sector: An illustration of possible links with the private sector that are consistent with the principles and values of public service is creation of joint public-private partnerships (PPPs), as opposed to cloning of business practices or substitution of private for public management. Actually, such "partnerships between the private and public sectors to fund and operate infrastructure projects are set to take off in Europe" (Timmins, 1999: 3). This is viewed as "profound cultural change," the use of private money and private companies to finance and operate infrastructure that used to be entirely publicly funded (Timmins, 1999: 3). Perhaps PPPs will constitute a modified version of a wholesale privatization that rarely achieves all promises made and often seeks to exclude government, except as a remote regulator. In the partnership the government is a party to the activity, and private funding is a factor in expediting the implementation of such ventures. This is an example of how public administration remains involved and how public service values remain an important factor in governing.

Public administration can improve its cost-consciousness without becoming obsessed with a "bottom line" management that sacrifices the commitment to values of equity, social justice, and public service ethics. True, public administration processes can benefit from the private sector's experience by according greater role for information and more utilization of technology for improving outputs and outcomes of public management. Using the right tools, so that public service conforms to the community's needs, requires professional exploitation of an expanding array of technological aids as well as constant preparedness to deal with volatile demands and unanticipated problems. At the same time, the private sector can learn, by associating with public service, to be more transparent and more attentive to public interest as well as more sensitive to higher ethical standards of performance.

5. Reconstruction of internal processes of public organizations with explicit attention to building their overall managerial capacities: is accomplished through a combination of initiatives such as (a) an implementation strategy that fosters public managers' self-direction and ability to handle effective delegation of responsibilities; (b) greater monitoring of compliance with assigned duties and fulfillment of substantive requirements of laws and procedures; (c) improved managerial responsibility and accountability through development of organizational goals, measurement of outputs, acquisition of good information, improvement in the transparency of financial transactions, adoption of performance audit, and use of a variety of techniques to ensure fiscal discipline; (d) discovery of more effective processes for development of human resources to assist the learning capability and foster the analytical skills of public employees.

CONCLUSION

Administrative reform is a multifaceted process that involves strategic visions, leadership, managerial skills, resources, and incentives as well as political support. The critical arena for enforcing change is the formal organization, operating primarily in a political context, patterned by various societal elements over time. There is no fixed recipe that can completely accomplish the task of reform. Successful implementation of reform will always rely on experimentation and learning by people and organizations. Although public managers are expected to promote values of participatory management, representation of public interest, and development of partnerships with their communities, they are expected also to demonstrate greater competence in employing techniques of analysis, evaluation, and problem solving to improve performance consistently. The lasting impact of ideas in the new public management will be measured in terms of contributions to knowledge about public organizations and ways to manage them rather than ways "to manage like business."

REFERENCES

Barberis, Peter (1998). The new public management and new accountability. *Public Administration.* 76(Autumn): 451–470.

Barzelay, Michael. (1997). "Researching the Politics of New Public Management: Changing the Question, not the Subject," unpublished paper delivered at the Workshop of the International Public Management Network (June 25–27) Berlin, Germany.

Behn, Robert D. (1998). What right do public managers have to lead? *Public Administration Review.* 58(3): 209–221.

Business Week (1999). April 19, 72.

Ferlie, Ewan, Ashburner, Lynn, Fitzgerald, Louise, and Pettigrew, Andrew (1996). *The New Public Management in Action.* Oxford University Press, Oxford.

Frederickson, H. George. (1997). The Spirit of Public Administration. Jossey-Bass, San Francisco.

Frederickson, H. George (1999). Hijacking public administration. *PA Times.* 22(3): 9.

Gellhorn, Ernest, and Levin, Ronald M. (1990). *Administrative law and process,* 3rd ed. West Publishing, St. Paul, Minn.

Goodsell, Charles T. (1983). *The case for bureaucracy.* Chatham House, Chatham, N.J.

Gore, Al (1993). *From Red Tape to Results: Creating a Government That Works Better and Costs Less.* Report of the National Performance Review. U. S. Government Printing Office, Washington, D.C.

Heady, Ferrel (1996). *Public Administration: A Comparative Perspective,* 5th ed. Marcel Dekker, New York.

Hood, Christopher (1991). A public management for all seasons? *Public Administration.* 69(1): 3–19.

Hood, Christopher (1995). The "new public management" in the 1990s: Variations on a theme. *Accounting Organizations and Society.* 20(2/3): 93–109.

Jaegal, Don, and Cayer, N. Joseph (1991). Public personnel administration by lawsuit: The impact of supreme court decisions on public employee litigiousness. *Public Administration Review.* 51(3): 211–221.

Jreisat, Jamil E. (1997a). *Politics Without Process: Administering Development in the Arab World.* Lynne Reinner, Boulder, Colo.

Jreisat, Jamil E. (1997b). *Public Organization Management: The Development of Theory and Process.* Greenwood, Westport, Conn.

Jreisat, Jamil E. (1999). Comparative public administration and reform. *International Journal of Public Administration.* 22(6): 855–877.

Jreisat, Jamil E. (1999). "Master Plan for Budget Reform in Jordan: Performance Budget System," unpublished report developed by an international team for the government of Jordan (April 20).

Kaboolian, Linda (1998). The new public management: Challenging the boundaries of the management vs. administration debate. *Public Administration Review.* 58(3): 189–193.

Kettl, Donald F. (1997). The global revolution in public management: Driving themes, missing links. *Journal of Policy Analysis and Management.* 16(3): 446–462.

Kettl, Donald F. (1999). The future of public administration. *Journal of Public Affairs Education.* 5(2): 127–134.

Kingsley, Gordon. (1997). Reflecting on reform and the scope of public administration. *Public Administration Review.* 57(2): iii–iv.

Klages, Helmut, and Loffler, Elke (1998). New public management in Germany. *International Review of Administrative Sciences.* 64: 41–54.

Lynn, Laurence (1987). *Managing Public Policy.* Little, Brown, Boston.

Lynn, Laurence (1996). *Public Management as Art, Science, and Profession.* Chatham House, Chatham, N.J.

Martin, Paul (1999). Canadian 1999 Budget Speech to the Parliament, February 16 [Http://www.fin.gc.ca/budget99/speech], p. 3.

Mascarenhas, R. C. (1993). Building an enterprise culture in the public sector: Reform of the public sector in Australia, Britain, and New Zealand. *Public Administration Review* 53(4): 319–327.

Meier, Kenneth J. (1997). Bureaucracy and democracy: The case for more bureaucracy and less democracy. *Public Administration Review.* 57(3): 193–200.

Moe, Ronald C. (1994). The "reinventing government" exercise: Misinterpreting the problem, misjudging the consequences. *Public Administration Review.* 54(2): 111–122.

Nagel, Jack H. (1997). Radically reinventing government. *Journal of Policy Analysis and Management.* 16(3): 349–356.

Osborne, David, and Gaebler, Ted (1992). *Reinventing Government: How the Entrepreneurial Spirit Is Transforming the Public Sector from Schoolhouse to State House, City Hall to Pentagon.* Addison-Wesley, Reading, Mass.

Osborne, Davis, and Pastrik, Peter (1997). *Banishing Bureaucracy: The Five Strategies for Reinventing Government.* Addison-Wesley, Reading, Mass.

Pallot, June (1996). "Newer than new" public management: Financial management and collective strategizing in New Zealand. Unpublished paper prepared for the conference on *The New Public Management in International Perspective, Institute of Public Finance and Fiscal Law.* St. Gallen, Switzerland, July 11–13.

Rabin, Jack (1996). In retrospect: Public policy and administration. *Public Administration Review.* 56(2).
Rainey, Hal G. (1997). *Understanding and Managing Public Organizations.* Jossey-Bass, San Francisco.
Riggs, Fred W. (1991). Public administration: A comparativist framework. *Public Administration Review.* 51(6).
Roberts, Alasdair (1997). Performance-based organizations: Assessing the Gore plan. *Public Administration Review.* 57(6): 465–478.
Roberts, Alasdair (1998). Closing the window: Public service restructuring and the weakening of freedom of information law. A paper submitted to *The 1998 International Public Management Network Conference.* June 28–29. [roberta@qsilver.queensu.ca].
Schick, Allen (1998). *A Contemporary Approach to Public Expenditure Management.* Economic Development Institute and the World Bank, Washington, D.C.
Scott, Graham, Ball Ian, and Dale, Tony (1997). New Zealand's public sector management reform: Implications for the United States. *Journal of Policy Analysis and Management.* 16(3): 357–381.
Seidle, Leslie F. (1995). *Rethinking the Delivery of Public Services.* Institute for Research on Public Policy, Montreal.
Simon, Herbert A. (1998). Guest editorial: Why public administration? *Public Administration Review.* 58(1): ii.
Terry, Larry D. (1999). From Greek mythology to the real world of the new public management and democratic governance. *Public Administration Review.* 59(3): 272–277.
Thompson, Frank (1999). Symposium on the advancement of public administration: introduction. *Journal of Public Affairs Education.* 5(2): 119–126.
Thompson, James R., and Ingraham, Patricia W. (1996). The reinvention game. *Public Administration Review.* 56(3): 291–304.
Timmins, Nicolas (1999). Private sector partners share government's traditional role. *Financial Times.* April 29.
UNDP and Swedish International Services (1998). *Jordan.* Unpublished technical report. Stockholm, pp 5–6.
Willbern, York (1984). Types and levels of public morality. *Public Administration Review.* 44(2): 102–108.

26

Service Contracting and Alternative Service Delivery: Theory and Practice

Richard C. Feiock
Askew School of Public Administration and Policy, Florida State University, Tallahassee, Florida

Contracting out the production of local government services, or providing inducements for private or nonprofit production as alternatives to municipal provision and production, is the source of continuing controversy and contention in many communities. Advocates of alternative service delivery approaches argue that services can be delivered to citizens more efficiently through private providers, not-for-profit organizations, or higher-level governments than through direct in-house delivery. The advantages of local government's reliance on private markets or contacts with private sector producers derive from several sources. These include the motivations induced by a competitive market, less restrictive managerial personnel practices in the private and not-for-profit sectors, and the lower labor costs generally found for unskilled and semiskilled labor outside government. Although quasi-governmental and not-for-profit service producers may not be able to take advantage of high-power economic incentives available to private firms, they may be able to take advantage of scale economies. In addition, not-for-profit organizations or higher-level governments may possess specialized skills that give them advantages as producers.

Although critics of contracting have not accepted this general argument, the preponderance of research evidence indicates that, for most local government services, alternative delivery arrangements are more efficient than direct delivery (Donahue, 1989). Nevertheless, Robert Stein has suggested that the observed relationship between service efficiency and sector may be spurious because it is a function of mode of delivery or service attributes (Stein, 1993). This suggests that any explanation of what factors shape the choices of institutional arrangements for the delivery of local government services must be grounded in an understanding of the role municipal governments play in the service provision and production decisions. In the next section we examine the various institutional roles that city governments can play in service provision and production of local services. We then focus specifically on municipal service contracting. We describe a transaction cost approach for understanding when cities contract out service production and their choices of service producers. We then evaluate the empirical evidence regarding the influence of transaction costs on service delivery arrangements. We conclude with a discussion of how this transaction cost approach can inform both scholarly inquiry and practitioner choices with regard to service arrangements.

THE LOCAL PUBLIC ECONOMY

It is important to distinguish provision decisions from producer choices in service delivery. Provision decisions relate to the choice to finance and arrange for a service. As a service provider, a city can play a direct role, an indirect role, or no role in provision. Even when a city directly provides a service, the production can be carried out by any one of several agents including governmental and nongovernmental actors.

City institutional arrangements can be examined at two levels. We start at the level of a local public economy (Parks and Oakerson, 1989). At the level of counties or metropolitan areas, a wide array of production and provision arrangements are possible. Table 1 summarizes the governmental and nongovernmental actors that can be involved.

Cities are just one of several actors that can produce services to citizens. County government, special districts, and quasi-governmental authorities often produce services for city residents. In addition, nongovernmental actors, including both for-profit and not-for-profit organizations, can provide local services.

Municipal governments are embedded in this larger public economy. When we shift the unit of analysis to the city, our focus is then on the role of municipal governments in provision and on the organizations used for production. The provision role of city government can be a direct role, an indirect role, or no role in the provision of public services to citizens. *Direct governmental provision* results when city government finances and provides for a service to be produced by it or by another organization. *Indirect governmental provision* occurs when a city uses

TABLE 1 Service Production Actors in a Local Public Economy

Governmental organizations
—County
—Municipalities
—Special districts
—Authorities
Nongovernmental organizations
—For-profit firms
—Not-for-profit organizations
—Citizen and neighborhood groups

taxes, subsidies, and other powers to induce other organizations to produce a service. *Nongovernmental provision* is the result when provision choice is left to market or other organizations without government intervention. For each provision role there are multiple potential service delivery agents for the service. In Table 2 we examine the provision arrangements that characterize the various choices of government provision roles and service producers.

In Table 2 we see that local government can directly provide a service through public production. Nevertheless, city governments can also play a direct provision role for goods produced by not-for-profit and for-profit firms through service contracts. Direct provision of services produced by other governments occurs through intergovernmental service agreements. Cities play a direct role in citizen-produced services when volunteers work directly under the control of government agencies or when voluntary efforts are directly reimbursed by government.

Government plays an indirect role in service provision by providing incentives or disincentives to induce other actors to produce a service for city residents. Cities may seek to stimulate not-for-profit production through incentives or

TABLE 2 City Role in Provision and Organization for Production

Producer	Direct	Indirect	None
City	Public production	—	—
Nonprofit organization	Service contract	Public service/ incentives	Charity
For-profit firm	Service contract	Tax/subsidy franchise	Market
Other government	Intergovernmental service agreement	Intergovernmental lobbying/Cooperation	Federalism
Citizens	Reimbursement/ volunteer	Coproduction	Self-help

appeals to public service motives. Cities can indirectly provide for services to be produced by for-profit firms by subsidies, tax incentives, or granting of rights or franchises to private organizations. Cities indirectly influence the service decisions of other governments through intergovernmental lobbying and extending or withholding cooperation in other areas. Cities can also indirectly provide for citizen production through incentives and disincentives for coproduction. Solid waste recycling commonly operates on this principle.

In some instances public or private actors may provide services to city residents without any intervention by city government. Nonprofit organizations often provide services motivated by charity. Where public services are not pure public goods, private firms may have market incentives to produce them. The division of responsibilities under federalism results in higher-level governments' providing services to city residents. Finally citizens often engage in self-help through neighborhood-level collective action.

ECONOMIC AND POLITICAL CONSIDERATIONS

Production cost savings have been identified as a source of efficiency differences between direct government and its alternatives (Donahue, 1989). In this light, it is not surprising that fiscal considerations seem to be among the most important factors for determining whether local governments choose to contract services. Research by Ferris and Graddy (1986), for example, indicates that the wage differentials among public sector, private sector, and not-for-profit workers within a local labor market predict contracting decisions. Tax and expenditure limitations imposed on local governments and heavy tax burdens also appear to lead municipalities to try contracting alternatives rather than directly produce services.

Service delivery decisions are also influenced by the political factors, particularly pressure from political interests and groups within the community. For instance, government workers, whose jobs might be threatened by external suppliers of services, have generally been found in opposition to privatization plans and have often been successful in preventing their adoption. Governmental characteristics also affect service delivery arrangements and contracting decisions. The council-manager form of government, for example, has been found to be associated with external production for several types of services (Ferris and Graddy, 1986, 1991; McGuire et al., 1987). Several reasons for this effect have been suggested. City or county managers may have a more positive disposition toward policy innovation than mayors or their appointees may have. In addition, government employee unions and their supporters may have less influence on city managers (Mladenka, 1991). Production efficiency may also be a more important goal, relative to other priorities, for city managers than for elected officials. City managers are aware that their careers may be advanced if they are successful in terms of financial management and efficient administration. Even if their accomplishments with relation to those criteria are not appreciated by the council of the city in which they work, managers know that other city governments and their professional peers in city management will be favorably impressed (Stein, 1990).

Transaction Costs and Municipal Contracting Decisions

The question of whether private firms should contract out production of products and services or produce them internally (i.e., become more vertically integrated) has been a topic that has concerned economists and management scholars for many years. Beginning with the work of Coase (1937), the predominant explanations for vertical integration in the private sector stressed the concept of transaction costs: the costs incurred in negotiating, monitoring, and enforcing a transaction, contract, or agreement. When such costs are high, firms have an incentive to provide services and products themselves, rather than seek out external suppliers.

Several public administration scholars have utilized transaction cost arguments to explain contracting out of services to private or nonprofit sector organizations. Robert Stein (1990), for example, applied Oliver Williamson's (1975) transaction costs arguments to municipal service delivery choices. Williamson argued that firms become vertically integrated in order to control valuable specific assets that might be lost if outside suppliers reneged on a contractual agreement or at least reinterpreted a contract in a way detrimental to the interests of a firm. Williamson assumed that reneging and noncooperative behavior can be more easily prevented within vertically integrated firms than between firms linked by contracts. Unfortunately, reneging occurs within firms as well as between them (Horn, 1995). The real question is whether internal governance mechanisms are superior to the diligent monitoring of a carefully written contract for dealing with this problem. Each alternative involves some transaction costs, but Williamson argues those costs are much greater when interfirm relationships are involved.

In applying this idea to municipal service delivery arrangements and contracting decisions, Stein suggested that certain kinds of municipal services, especially those providing collective goods and common property goods, make use of specific capital assets. Whereas Williamson suggested that asset specificity should be expected to result in vertical integration, Stein (1990) found that municipalities directly provided services that resemble collective and common property goods but used a diverse array of service arrangements such as contracting to provide services resembling toll and private goods.

Stein emphasized asset specificity and certain service characteristics. The work of Clingermayer and Feiock (1997, 1999), took a different approach by focusing more on transaction costs that result from turnover among elected and administrative leaders. Specifically, this research examined how uncertainty resulting from leadership turnover in city government affects the ability of a municipality to negotiate contracts, make credible commitments to suppliers, and faithfully uphold and enforce contracts once they are in force.

Service contracts and intergovernmental agreements are not likely to be agreed upon when either side suspects that the terms of the contract will not be upheld. This suspicion may prevent contracting that otherwise would be mutually advantageous. From the standpoint of the external supplier of a service, uncertainty regarding a city's future expectations, bid specifications, appeal policies, and preferences regarding service delivery can make doing business with municipal governments risky. Such uncertainty is likely to increase with more frequent turnover among local leaders. Elected officials may not be able to make credible commitments to contractors. New leaders who assume office during the life of a contract may not be satisfied with the provisions of the agreement and may wish to renegotiate its terms. Turnover among executives and elected officials is therefore expected to reduce contracting of government services.

Incumbent government leaders also may not be willing to enter into agreements for lengthy periods that would lock them into a particular mode of service delivery and specify explicit quantities of service, quality characteristics, or distributive criteria. Although more open-ended and flexible contracts that would enable governments to modify service provisions are possible, they impose transaction costs on suppliers. To compensate for increased risk, a supplier could demand a substantial premium for accepting these possible interventions. If so, the cost savings that contracting out is said to provide could quickly evaporate (Sappington and Stigletz, 1987). Under these conditions contracting may not be very likely.

Empirical analysis of the use of alternative service delivery in cities responding to The International City Management Association (ICMA) 1988 alternative service delivery survey revealed that turnover in the city manager or appointed chief administrative officer position discouraged contracting (Clingermayer and Feiock, 1997). These findings indicate that transaction costs resulting from executive turnover may make contracting out local services a more expensive option. This result may be thought of as "privatization failure." When privatization failure occurs, in-house service production and delivery may be more efficient than reliance on contracts, service agreements, or external markets.

PRODUCER CHOICE UNDER DIRECT CITY PROVISION

Most of the "contracting out" debate has focused attention on contracting delivery of public services to private firms. Despite the important role that not-for-profit organizations, quasi-governmental authorities, and other governments play in local service delivery (Parks and Oakerson, 1989), little attention has been paid to the choice of producer when cities have direct provision responsibility. The choices regarding how a service is to be produced and delivered may be as important as the provision role played by city government. The literature on local government policy choices emphasizes the adoption responsibility for providing specific services and their funding levels. A thorough understanding of the service delivery process requires some explanation for the specific design of the mechanisms by which a government delivers a service or transfers a benefit. Accounting for the choice producer and provision arrangements is central to such an explanation.

Much of the work on contracting out in general can be applied to an examination of service provision arrangements (see DeHoog, 1984; Donahue, 1989; Ferris and Graddy, 1986, 1994; Hanke, 1987; Stein, 1990; Clingermayer and Feiock, 1997). A careful reading of this work turns our attention to the choice of sector through which external delivery of services occurs. These authors argue that transaction costs are critical to understanding the choice of sector as well as the provision decision itself. The attributes of the service, particularly the ease with which those attributes may be defined, measured, and monitored, as well as the dangers of opportunism in cases in which markets are unlikely to have multiple service providers are likely to create high transaction costs and may encourage internal service delivery or joint contracting in which both the government and an external service delivery agent share responsibility for a service.

Study of the service responsibilities of nonprofits organizations suggest that when service qualities are difficult to monitor, consumers will trust nonprofit providers more than profit-seeking enterprises because they feel that profit seekers will exploit information advantages to shortchange consumers (see Hansmann, 1980). Ongoing empirical work has begun to explore which factors account for the decision to give this responsibility to another unit of government, a profit-seeking firm, or a nonprofit organization (Feiock et al., 1999).

External delivery of public services involves many of the same problems facing private firms that contract some of their activities. But governments may also face transaction costs problems that are particularly severe in the public sector. Transaction costs in municipal service delivery decisions can be linked to at least three factors: market attributes, specifically the extent to which heterogeneity of communities results in diverse service preferences; government uncertainty, the extent to which political and administrative turnover creates uncertainty; and service characteristics, especially the difficulty in measuring and defining the qualities of a service. The first two factors are characteristics of places; the third is a characteristic of the goods themselves.

We furthermore posit that contracting out with private firms for production on municipal services is fundamentally different from external delivery using other units of government, quasi-governmental authorities, or nonprofit organizations. This is because the incentive for opportunistic behavior is usually much higher when private firms are involved. Private firms are assumed to be residual claimants that can keep whatever revenue in excess of service costs is provided by a contract. This may offer incentives for efficiency, but it may also motivate firms to cut corners in various ways, including limiting access to services or allowing costly service quality to decline. Units of government or nonprofit organizations that contract with cities to provide services receive no profits to distribute to their members. Some slack resources or excess resources may be retained by such organizations, but this should not provide the same "high-powered incentives" to act opportunistically (see Frant, 1996).

We contend in this chapter that transaction costs in the delivery of municipal services will likely increase as the heterogeneity of communities increases, as the relevant attributes of the service become more difficult to define and measure, and as turnover in important leadership positions in city government increases. If a service has attributes that are relatively straightforward and easy to specify in contracts, we anticipate that local governments will assign service responsibilities to private, profit-seeking firms in contracts. If a community is relatively homogeneous, it is likely that services will be assigned to a different unit of government. If a service is difficult to define and measure, and if a community is socially heterogeneous, we may expect service responsibility to be delegated to a variety of nonprofit organizations.

Service Characteristics

Scholars who study government contracting out decisions (e.g., Stein, 1990; Ferris and Graddy, 1994) as well as economists who examine corporate vertical integration (e.g., Williamson, 1975) have long argued that the nature of the good or service produced affects the transaction costs of external provision. According to one school of thought, the specificity of the asset capital employed in the production process greatly increases the costs of opportunistic behavior and thereby involves high transaction costs (Williamson, 1975). Assets that are specific to a particular use that have enormous sunk costs and little salvage value might be forfeited if individuals or firms take advantage of information asymmetries or difficulties in monitoring performance to use those assets for their own gain. Frequently, these scholars conclude that internal provision of products or services handles these kind of transaction cost problems better than external delivery through contractual arrangements. In the case of local services, one should expect that technology and capital-intensive services, such as major utility provision, should be produced and delivered directly by government, since the assets involved in the service may be difficult to assign to other purposes. More labor-intensive services, especially where employees are not highly specialized in their training and skills, might be more easily delivered by external organizations.

Another school of thought argues that the ease with which the attributes of the good or service may be defined and measured are more important factors in affecting the transaction costs involved in production choices. If the desired attributes of a good or service can be precisely specified and performance easily measured, contracts can be written so that opportunistic behavior can be limited, assuming that courts will faithfully uphold the obligation of contracts (see Barzel, 1982; Cheung, 1983). If external delivery of such a service is satisfactory, contracts can be renewed. If performance is unsatisfactory, contract renewal can be denied. In the case of many social services, the quality and quantity of service desired by elected officials may be unknown, or only vaguely identified in the statute. If that is the case, contracts and agreements between governments and external organizations may be difficult to write and enforce. Direct government provision, with internal directives emerging as preferences regarding services are revealed, might be the most efficient and most desired means of delivering such services. Of course, if efficiency concerns are not paramount, external delivery may be attractive to many policymakers. Many external providers may be reluctant to provide services under such uncertainty, but governmental units, as well as nonprofit organizations, may be more accustomed to that kind of environment than are profit-seeking firms.

Market Attributes

Heterogeneity within the community might also affect the assignment of responsibilities for service production. Some of the literature on nonprofits suggests that government provision of services will only extend to the level favored by the median voter. In heterogeneous communities, this level of provision is likely to leave many citizens dissatisfied. Where government is not involved in provision, nonprofit organizations often provide services that governments in such environments cannot or will not provide (Weisbrod, 1977, 1988, 1997). If we assume that governments will directly provide services for which there is some consensus of support and occasionally assign production to nonprofits for those services for which at some times a portion of the community approves, we would expect a relationship between contracting with nonprofits and community heterogeneity. For example, in a diverse community there may be a variety of views and preferences about the desirability of government provision of arts and cultural activities. Government may contract with nonprofit organizations that can leverage privately raised funds to supplement these activities. Direct government delivery of such services might be politically infeasible.

Another aspect of the market pertains to the number and size of enterprises that could supply services. In metropolitan areas, there are frequently many potential providers that can deliver service in many different locations within the area, thereby realizing some scale economies. This could include for-profit firms, not-for-profit organizations, as well as other governments. With multiple providers of services available, competition for contracts may drive down costs. Also, with multiple alternative providers of a service, the possibility of a long interruption of service is unlikely if one producer fails to provide adequate service and must be replaced by another producer.

Turnover and Governmental Uncertainty

Service characteristics and market attributes affect the transaction costs of exchange, but certain features of the government have transaction implications as well. In particular, turnover in leadership positions within city government may cause difficulties in negotiating and monitoring agreements, thereby making external production arrangements more difficult and less likely. Furthermore, if the critical personnel responsible for making commitments may be out of office in a short period, commitments to other actors that the city may make may not be viewed as credible. If that is the case, potential contractors may not bid for service responsibilities.

Leadership turnover should be troublesome for cities pursuing service agreements with each type of external external service producer, but the problems may be less great when service responsibility is given to nonprofits, since organizations of that kind are less likely to operate under specific contracts and may be monitored by a combination of donors, clients, and government officials

Profit-seeking enterprises are typically more capital-intensive than most governments or nonprofits and therefore have greater sunk costs. Nonprofits, on the other hand, generally have less in the way of capital assets and are generally involved in activities other than those sponsored and funded by government. Oversight of nonprofits is not carried out exclusively or even primarily by government, but instead is a responsibility of boards of directors, donors, and volunteers. Therefore, we do not expect leadership turnover to have substantial effects on contracting with not-for-profit organizations.

CONCLUSION

The conceptual framework developed in this chapter suggests several lessons about local service delivery arrangements to guide local decisions on service arrangements and future scholarly inquiry. First, our discussion suggests that city government service arrangements need to be examined within the context of the local public economy. Within this context, the actions and responsibilities of various governmental and nongovernmental actors shape the opportunities for, and constraints on, municipal service delivery. Second, examination of municipal service arrangements must explicitly recognize the unique combinations of city service provision role and service producers entailed by various service arrangements. Third, transaction costs, not just production costs, are central to the choice and efficiency of specific service delivery arrangements. Finally, the context and characteristics of local political systems, not just the characteristics of goods, determine the transaction costs associated with various service delivery arrangements.

Although there is some evidence in the literature supporting each of these propositions, there is a need for future research to subject them to systematic empirical tests. Such work can have important implications for the study of local governance. In addition, this work can provide a foundation to guide local decision makers' choices regarding what role that city government should play in the provision of particular services and which organization should produce and deliver the services that city government provides.

REFERENCES

Barzel, Yoram (1982). Measurement cost and the organization of markets. *Journal of Law and Economics. 20:* 87–110.

Cheung, Steven (1983). The contractual nature of the firm. *Journal of Law and Economics. 17:* 53–71.

Clingermayer, James C., and Feiock, Richard C. (1997). Leadership turnover, transaction costs, and external service delivery. *Public Administration Review. 57.*

Clingermayer, James C., and Feiock, Richard C. (1999). *Institutional Constraints and Policy Choice: An Exploration of Local Governance.* State University of New York Press, Albany.

Coase, Ronald (1937). *The Nature of the Firm.* Economica *4:* 386–405.

DeHoog, Ruth Hoogland (1984). *Contracting Out for Human Services.* State University of New York Press, Albany.

Donahue, John D. (1989). *The Privatization Decision.* Basic Books, New York.

Feiock, Richard, Clingermayer, James, and Carr, Jered (1999). Leadership turnover and credible commitment: Implications for service contracting, debt financing, and economic development in American cities. Paper presented at *The annual meeting of the American Political Science Association.* Atlanta, August.

Ferris, James, and Graddy, Elizabeth (1986). Contracting out: For what? For whom? *Public Administration Review. 46:* 343–344.

Ferris, James, and Graddy, Elizabeth (1991). Production costs, transaction costs, and local government contractor choice. *Economic Inquiry. 29*(July): 431–554.

Ferris, James, and Graddy, Elizabeth (1994). Organizational choices for public service supply. *Journal of Law, Economics, & Organization. 10:* 126–141.

Frant, Howard L. (1996). High-powered and low-powered incentives in the public sector. *Journal of Public Administration Research and Theory. 6:* 365–381.

Hanke, Steve H. (ed.) (1987). *Prospects for Privatization.* New York: Academy of Political Science.

Hansmann, Henry (1980). The Role of Nonprofit Enterprise. *Yale Law Review. 89*(April): 835–899.

Horn, Murray J. (1995). *The Political Economy of Public Administration: Institutional Choice in the Public Sector.* Cambridge University Press, Cambridge.

McGuire, R.A., Ohsfeldt, R.L., and vanCott, T.N. (1987). The determinants of the choice between public and private production of a publicly funded service. *Public Choice 54:* 197–210.

Mladenka, Kenneth (1991). Public employee unions, reformism, and black employment in 1,200 American cities. *Urban Affairs Quarterly. 26:* 532–548.

North, Douglass C. (1990). *Institutions, Institutional Change, and Economic Performance.* Cambridge University Press, New York.

Parks, Roger B., and Oakerson, Ronald J. (1989). Metropolitan organization and governance: A local public economy approach. *Urban Affairs Quarterly. 25*(1): 18–29.

Sappington, David E., and Stiglitz, Joseph E. (1987). Privatization, information, and incentives. *Journal of Policy Analysis and Management. 6:* 567–582.

Stein, Robert M. (1990). *Urban Alternatives.* University of Pittsburgh Press, Pittsburgh.

Stein, Robert M. (1993). Arranging city services. *Journal of Public Administration Research and Theory. 2.*

Weisbrod, Burton A. (1977). *The Voluntary Nonprofit Sector.* D. C. Heath, Lexington, Mass.

Weisbrod, Burton A. (1988). *The Nonprofit Economy.* Harvard University, Cambridge, Mass. Press.

Weisbrod, Burton A. (1997). The future of the non-profit sector: Its entwining with private enterprise and government. *Journal of Policy Analysis and Management. 16*(4): 541–555.

Williamson, Oliver. E. (1975). *Markets and Hierarchies: Analysis and Antitrust Implications.* Free Press, New York.

27

The Impact of the New Public Management on Nonprofit Organizations

Joan E. Pynes
Lisa M. Arndt
Public Administration Program,
University of South Florida,
Tampa, Florida

In *The Spirit of Public Administration,* (1997: 4). H. George Frederickson states, "The public in public administration manifests itself in many ways—neighborhoods, voluntary associations, churches, clubs, events and the like and it divides to become many publics. Government is an important manifestation of the public, but it is just one aspect of it the public" (p. 4). He goes on to say that modern public administration is a network of vertical and horizontal linkages among organizations of all types—governmental, nongovernmental, and quasi-governmental; profit, nonprofit, and voluntary. Policy-making and policy implementation are shared among these organizations (p. 5).

One consequence of this trend is a mixed economy in which the conventional differences between sectors have become blurred. Private organizations are increasingly being penetrated by government policy, and public organizations are increasingly becoming attracted to quasi-market approaches. This new interorganizational environment has been described as the "new political economy," "contract, hollow or shadow state," "nonprofit federalism," and "government by proxy"

(Bozeman, 1987; Kramer and Grossman, 1987; Milwald et al., 1993; Salamon, 1987; Weisbrod, 1997; Wolch, 1990).

These terms refer to the increased role nonprofits play in the delivery of services to citizens. In many communities, control over which citizens get services and how public monies are spent is often determined by organizations not directly responsible to public authority. Milward, Provan, and Else (1993) note that even though health and human services are funded by public agencies, the distribution of these funds is often controlled and monitored by nongovernment and third parties, who themselves determine which agencies to subcontract with for the actual provision of services. Thus involvement by the state is indirect and extremely limited (p. 309).

The focus of this chapter is on the relationships between government and charitable nonprofit organizations. Central Florida Human Services, a nonprofit organization, is profiled to illustrate the intermingling of the public and nonprofit sectors. The chapter concludes by discussing present trends and changes that can be expected in the future. The analysis begins with a brief overview of what constitutes a charitable nonprofit organization.

WHAT CONSTITUTES A PUBLIC CHARITABLE NONPROFIT?

Similarly to public sector agencies, nonprofits are heterogeneous in their orientations and purposes. To be recognized as a nonprofit an organization must possess the following general characteristics: it is specifically designated as "nonprofit" when organized; profits or assets may not be divided among corporate members, officers, or directors in the manner of corporate dividends; and it may lawfully pursue only such purposes as are permitted for such organizations by statutes (Oleck, 1988: 5–6).

Nonprofit entities are exempt from federal income tax under the principal exemption in Statute 501 of the Internal Revenue Code. Internal Revenue Code 501(c) lists 23 types of associations, corporations, and trusts that can qualify for federal tax exemption. Subsection 501(c) (3) affects the largest number of nonprofit organizations. These organizations are "organized and operated exclusively for religious, charitable, scientific, testing for public safety, literary, or educational purposes, or to foster national or international amateur sports competition or for the prevention of cruelty to children or animals." These organizations are referred to as *public charities*. Congress has from time to time made additions to the list. Permitting additions to the 501(c)(3) provisions takes into account the changing needs of society.

The Internal Revenue Service defines a *public charity* as an organization that normally receives a substantial portion of its total income directly or indirectly from the general public or government. An organization can meet the financial support test if it normally receives one-third or more of its total support from government agencies and the general public or if it receives at least one-tenth of its financial support from either or both of these sources and is also organized and operated in a way that tends to attract public or government support on a continuing basis. The public support must be broad-based and cannot be limited to contributions from a few individuals or families. Nonprofit organizations are governed not only by the Internal Revenue Code but also by state laws and regulations.

Although specific nonprofit organizations are diverse in nature, they all have as a common component the requirement that no part of their net earning can "inure to the benefit of any private shareholder or individual" (IRC 501[c][3], [c][6], [c][7], [c][9], [c][11][A], and [c][13]; Oleck, 1988: 213). Nonprofits are permitted to have revenues in excess of expenses, but they cannot provide distributions to "owners by paying dividends or repurchasing shares of stock. A nonprofit is legally prohibited from disbursing profits to employees or individuals in control of the organization. This is referred to as their nondistribution component imposed on nonprofit institutions by the legal instrument under which they are organized" (Hansman, 1980).

In exchange for accepting a restriction of the use of profit, nonprofit organizations obtain a variety of tax benefits. Nonprofits are typically exempted from corporate income tax and state and local taxes on property and sales, and they can receive federal postal subsidies. In addition to the organizations' exemption from taxes, contributions to certain nonprofits are tax-deductible for donors. The rationale behind permitting tax deductions to donors is that nonprofits are thought to serve broad public purposes. As of 1996, there were approximately 760,000 active public service nonprofits (Salamon, 1999).

Relying on the *U. S. Census of Service Industry* classification, the charitable nonprofit sector can be grouped into five basic categories: social and legal services, education, health care, civic, and culture and recreation.

The majority of nonprofit organizations are social service agencies; 40 percent of all nonprofits fall in this category. Social service nonprofits are followed by educational and research institutions, comprising approximately 22 percent of the charitable nonprofit sector. These groups include private elementary and secondary schools, private universities, libraries, and research institutions. Civic organizations such as neighborhood associations, advocacy organizations, community improvement agencies, and civil rights organizations comprise approximately 17 percent. Health organizations, including hospitals, nursing homes, and clinics, represent approximately 14 percent. Culture and recreation organizations, including symphonies, art galleries, theaters, zoos, botanical gardens, and other cultural and recreational institutions, have the smallest share at 8 percent (Salamon, 1999: 34–35).

WHY NONPROFITS?

Charitable nonprofits are private organizations that serve a public purpose. Because they operate under a nondistribution component, it is believed that they possess a greater moral authority and concern for the public interest than for-profit organizations. Nonprofits often perform public tasks that have been delegated to them by the state or perform tasks for which there is a demand that neither government nor for-profit organizations can satisfy. They provide myriad services such as helping the disadvantaged, providing medical services, supporting museums and cultural activities, preserving the environment, and funding medical research.

Nonprofits are thought to be more flexible than government agencies. They can experiment with new programs, responding more rapidly to new social needs. Instead of government's getting involved in new or controversial programs, it often gives money to nonprofit agencies to deal with problems. Nonprofits get financial support and clients receive services. Government, through the conditions it places on agencies that receive public funds, still has some influence but can quickly dissociate itself from programs when things go wrong.

There are often certain societal needs that may be too expensive to be provided on a for-profit basis. Therefore, in the United States, both government and the nonprofit sector provide certain services whose costs exceed their market value (Douglas, 1983; O'Neil, 1989; Salamon, 1999; Weisbrod, 1997).

Public administration practitioners and scholars have increased their attention to nonprofit organizations as governments have more frequently used such agencies to provide social services. Among the examples are organizations established to prevent child abuse, domestic violence, or homelessness; or to assist the disabled, the elderly, the mentally ill; or to provide day care, counseling, vocational training and rehabilitation, or community/neighborhood centers (Lipsky and Smith 1989–90; Salamon, 1999). The result is a welfare state more expansive than it would be if policymakers relied solely on the public sector (Lipsky and Smith 1989–90: 626).

Government contracting for services expanded in the 1960s as a result of Great Society legislation such as the Economic Opportunity Act of 1964, 1967 Amendments to the Social Security Act, Model Cities Act, Community Development and Housing, General Revenue Sharing, CETA, and Title XX of the 1974 Amendments to the Social Security Act. The legislation mentioned encouraged the growth and availability of matching grants for the purchase of services by public agencies. Governments began contracting with nonprofit agencies for the delivery of social services.

Federal assistance reaches nonprofit organizations indirectly through state and local governments that receive federal grants but retain substantial discretion in deciding whether to deliver the subsidized services themselves or to contract with nonprofit agencies or other public or private providers. The Social Services Block Grant; the Administration on Aging grant programs; alcohol, drug abuse, and mental health programs; and the Community Development Block Grant are examples of federal assistance that reaches nonprofits through this route (Salamon, 1999).

Federal spending in the 1980s decreased for social service and education programs (programs focused more on youth) while increasing for health care and pension programs (as a result of the growth of the population of elderly residents). During this time there was growing competition from for-profit providers. For-profit day-care centers expanded by 80 percent, and for-profit home health care and clinic care expanded by 44 percent (Salamon, 1999).

In 1996, social service nonprofits received approximately 43 percent of their revenues from fees and service charges or other commercial income; approximately 37 percent of their revenues from government grants, contracts, and reimbursements; and approximately 20 percent of their revenues from private giving (Salamon, 1999: 36–37).

This is not a recent trend. Lipsky and Smith (1989–90: 625) noted it earlier:

> Rather than depending mostly on private charity and volunteers, most nonprofit service organizations depend on government for over half of their revenues; for many small agencies, government support comprises their entire budget in contrast to the traditional relationship of two independent sectors, the new relationship between government and nonprofits amounts to one of mutual dependencies that is financial as well as technical. The lines between public and private is blurred.

This blurring is especially vivid in the social services. Government, nonprofit, and profit organizations are subject to similar regulations, dependent on the same revenue sources, hire the same types of professional staff, and perform similar functions. Public organizations and nonprofits are similar in that they define themselves around their missions, or the services they offer. These services are often intangible and difficult to measure. Both sectors are accountable to multiple constituencies. Nonprofits must be responsive to supporters, sponsors, clients, and government sources that provide funding and impose regulations. Public agencies must be responsive to their respective legislative and judicial branches, taxpayers, cognate agencies, political appointees, clients, the media, and other levels of governments.

CENTRAL FLORIDA HUMAN SERVICES

Central Florida Human Services is a private nonprofit Florida corporation. Originally founded as the Program to Aid Drug Abusers in 1974, the agency had an early mission of providing substance abuse outpatient services to low-income people. The agency is governed by a 15-member board of directors. Board members are volunteers who represent the communities the agency serves and the business community.

Over the years the agency has grown and expanded the variety and types of services offered. In 1980 the agency added residential substance abuse services for juveniles. This program was funded primarily from a contract with the Florida Department of Health and Rehabilitative Services (HRS). Juvenile residential services were intended to house up to 35 clients. The agency supplemented its $600,000 annual budget by using Medicaid to cover services not included in the contract. The original contract called for the agency to provide security, educational services, life skills training, and behavioral intervention. Although the contract provided the basic services, the agency was concerned that clients would need additional services, such as medical care, dental care, mental health counseling, and family counseling. These services would be provided by using federal Medicaid funding. This expansion of services caused some logistical difficulty for the agency because of the conflicting types of record keeping requirements. The money secured through the state contract required that client files be kept in accordance with state administrative code 10E-16, which specifies a framework for the organization of client files, the types of information to be included in the file, and the types of services that can be provided. Those funds secured through the Medicaid system required that client records be kept in accordance with federal Medicaid procedures. Federal regulations are stricter and require a higher level of documentation. This created the need for a great deal of additional staff training to deal effectively with the new record keeping requirements. Although the two systems have many similarities, one primary difference is in the auditing process. Under the state contract the agency could be cited for any deficiencies in record keeping and would be required to submit a corrective action plan. The corrective action plan is a detailed account of all measures that the agency would take to be in compliance. Auditors would return after a specified period (usually 90 days) to determine whether the corrective action plan had been implemented. This differs from the Medicaid auditing requirements, which include a provision for the agency to repay a proportionate amount of the *total* funds received for any client files found to have deficiencies. For example, if a Medicaid auditor selected a random sample of 10 client records and 2 were found to contain deficiencies, the agency would be required to repay 20 percent of all money collected from Medicaid. An understanding of this potential payback led the agency to withhold 2 percent of all fees collected in the hope that amount would somewhat offset any required payback.

In 1980, the agency also expanded the outpatient substance abuse treatment services by adding four outpatient locations, two of which were in neighboring counties. This expansion allowed the agency to serve up to 200 clients at any given time. Funding for this expansion was provided by the Department of Health and Rehabilitative Services, client fees, and private donations. The agency was required to keep very detailed accounts of the fees paid by client. Pursuant to the contract with the Department of Health and Rehabilitative Services the agency was required to provide all services on a sliding-fee scale. The agency was required to document all client income and adjust fees accordingly. This program was subject to audit under governmental accounting standards set forth by the State of Florida Office of the Auditor General. Failure to comply with those standards would have resulted in the loss of contracts, possible fines, and repayment of funds.

When the state separated juvenile delinquency services from the Department of Health and Rehabilitative Services in 1992, the agency expanded its scope of services to include programs and services designed to rehabilitate delinquent youth. Initially, this programming was integrated into the agency's outpatient and juvenile residential services. This separation created some changes for the agency, which was now contracting with an additional state agency. The requirements of the contract with the Florida Department of Juvenile Justice restricted the ways the agency could spend funds received through this contract. Unlike for the contracts with the Department of Health and Rehabilitative Services, the agency was given preset limits of the percentages of funds that could be used for administrative costs. All funds related to this contract were required to be kept separate from other agency funding. This change prompted the agency to change its accounting software to improve the tracking of funds received from different sources.

The change of focus from specific substance abuse–oriented programming to a broader scope of services led the agency to reexamine its mission. This broadening of the agency mission prompted the change from Program to Aid Drug Abusers to Central Florida Human Services. The agency board of directors felt the change more accurately reflected the increased scope of services the agency now provided.

In late 1992, Central Florida Human Services expanded its delinquency program to include three residential delinquency programs. Two programs were moderate-risk and located at the juvenile residential facility; the third was a serious habitual offender program. The moderate-risk programs were designed for juvenile offenders who were not seen as potentially violent or deemed escape risks. These programs had no fences or electronic doors. Clients remained in the program in essence of their own free will. The program increased the number of juveniles served in nonsecure facilities to 85. The serious habitual offender (SHO) program was a significant departure from the traditional services the agency had offered. The program provided services to 45 juveniles with a history of violence/escape and required the construction of a pseudoprison facility. The facility was constructed by using $500,000 provided by the Department of Juvenile Justice. The facility was constructed on a piece of land that had been long-term leased by the Florida Department of Natural Resources. This development posed unique coordination challenges. It was difficult to ascertain to whom the facility actually belonged. It was finally determined that a percentage of the ownership of the facility would be granted to the agency for each year of operation. Ownership was transferred to the agency at a rate of 1/20 of the total value of the facility per contract year. At the end of the 20-year period the facility would be entirely the property of Central Florida Human Services. It was also agreed that in the event the agency no longer contracted with the Department of Juvenile Justice, the lease for the land would transfer to any agency securing that contract. In 1992, Central Florida Human Services expanded its adult services with the opening of a residential substance abuse program for adults. This program, through the Department of Corrections, provided residential treatment for adult offenders on felony probation. The agency purchased an old motel and renovated the property to house the program. The program, which originally housed 35 clients, expanded to serve 45 after the first year. In 1996 the number of clients served increased to 65. Funds for the purchase and renovation were from the agency's cash reserves. Funding for this program differed from that for the other residential programs in that the agency was paid on a per-client per-diem basis. The other residential programs were paid in block installments based on the contracted number of clients, which was not necessarily the number in the program. For example, under the state contracts for the juvenile facilities the agency was paid for a program to house 100 juveniles. The agency received a payment each month based on that contract figure (roughly $180,000 per month for the three Juvenile Justice programs). If Juvenile Justice failed to place 100 juveniles in the program, the agency nevertheless received the same dollar figure each month. In the adult program the agency received a per diem only for those clients who had resided in the program for the 24-hour period considered one day. This required the program to be very conservative regarding the budgeting process. Clients were placed in the program by the Florida Department of Corrections. The agency had little control over how quickly a vacancy was filled. Clients were assigned and admitted to the program through the probation officer assigned to the facility. If the officer was on vacation for a week and the program graduated 10 clients, 10 vacancies would remain until the officer returned. The agency received a per diem of $32 for each client; the cost of the program, however, was $41 per day. This difference in cost and funding level made the issue of client placement in the program even more critical. The agency was required to secure large donations from private sources to bridge the gap in funding. This program also required an annual audit in accordance with governmental accounting standards for the State of Florida Office of the Auditor General, but it was also audited by the Department of Corrections internal staff. In 1997, the Central Florida Human Services elected no longer to provide this service because of funding from the Department of Corrections did not increase.

In 1997, the agency again expanded its mission with the opening of its charter school. The school, which targets students who have not been successful in traditional schools, focuses on integrating counseling services with academics. Funding for the school is generated on the basis of the number of full-time enrolled students who are present during the survey period (this occurs for one week in October and one week in February). For each student abounded, the agency received 95 percent of the full-time enrollment funding (FT) and certain categorical funds (categorical funds are restricted and can only be used for the purposes outlined). This provides the school program with an operating budget of $450,000 per year. It is important to note that not all of the funds can be used for general revenue purposes. Such categorical funds as those for technology and school safety can only be expended in a certain manner consistent with state regulations. For example, the agency used a portion of the safe schools categorical funding to install fire alarm pull stations. The agency was then required to provide proof to the local school board (the chartering agency) that the alarms were in fact installed and the cost applied to the safe school allocation. This shift in funding formula required the agency to obtain a higher level on annual audit. Whereas previously the agency complied with an A-133 governmental audit, items such as full-time enrollment counts were now required in the annual audit. The agency is required to have compliance tests performed on each of the categories of funding. An account is tested for compliance when an auditor selects a random sample of the documentation and reviews it for compliance with the restrictions of those funds. In the example of the fire alarm pull stations, the auditor looked at the original invoice for the work and the canceled check, then compared the purchase with items deemed "allowable" purchases using safe schools funds.

In the past, the agency has maintained a governmental accounting system and was audited under A-133 regulations. These regulations are set forth by the Internal Revenue Service and the State of Florida Office of the Auditor General. The regulations clearly outline the manner in which the agency must maintain its financial records, the standards for random sampling used by auditors, and the length of time the agency is required to maintain its financial records. The agency receives a certified financial audit of all records each year. This audit is performed by an independent auditor. It is important to note that the independent auditor is engaged by the agency board of directors, not agency staff. This is to help ensure that the opinion the auditor gives is not affected by any relationship with agency staff. A copy of the certified audit is provided to each contracting agency.

The extensive range of requirements calls into question why such an agency would exist. The answer is fairly simple: to provide services that the government cannot. It is unreasonable for anyone to expect a large bureaucracy that serves multiple thousands of clients to meet the need of each individual. Private nonprofit agencies fill in the service gaps. As many of the clients served by nonprofit agencies have limited economic resources, they do not have access to for-profit organizations to meet their needs.

CHANGES IN THE NONPROFIT, FOR-PROFIT, AND GOVERNMENT ENVIRONMENT

The decline of public monies and increase in demands for service have forced nonprofits to seek new sources of revenue. As a result, many nonprofits have entered into for-profit business ventures. Art museums, science centers, aquariums, and zoos have gift shops that help supplement their income. Often parking and food services are ancillary services that provide additional funds. Today in many shopping malls, there are "Stores of Knowledge" that provide revenues to the local public broadcasting station (PBS) service. Other nonprofits charge fees for the services they provide to individuals and corporations. For example, Family Service America is a social service agency that provides drug and alcohol counseling to corporate employee assistance programs. Camps, colleges, and universities often rent unused or underutilized facilities to generate additional revenue. The best known for-profit endeavor by a nonprofit organization is the annual cookie sale sponsored by the Girl Scouts of America.

As nonprofits are moving into activities that have previously been the domain of for-profit firms, for-profit organizations have expanded into traditional nonprofit areas.

Government has a long history of contracting services to for-profit firms. Local governments and school districts often contract for vehicle maintenance, landscaping, janitorial, solid waste disposal, and cafeteria services. These are jobs that can readily be measured against some benchmarked standard, and these services are not provided by public charities. What is new is that for-profit organizations have begun to enter the social welfare domain. Nonprofit leaders are accustomed to profit-seeking hospitals, propriety day-care centers, and for-profit trade and technical schools. However, the "Welfare to Work" legislation passed by Congress in 1996 created new demands for work-readiness and related social service assistance that for-profit firms have begun to meet. Aid for Dependent Children (AFDC) was replaced by Transitional Assistance to Needy Families (TANF) legislation, which changed the approach to delivering services to needy families.

The Managed Care Medicaid program created by Congress in 1965 under the Social Security Act pays for medical services provided to certain groups of low-income persons, To help control expenditures and expand access to health care, 48 states have implemented some type of Medicaid managed care program. Some of these states have procured independent third-party vendors to provide outreach, education, enrollment, and performance monitoring functions.

Many social services traditionally provided by nonprofit agencies are now being provided by for-profit corporations, further blurring nonprofit, for-profit, and government sector distinctions.

FOR-PROFIT WELFARE SERVICES

An example of a for-profit organization that is providing welfare services is MAXIMUS. Its annual revenues for fiscal year 1998 were $233 million. You can find MAXIMUS Quarterly Fiscal Reports and Statements of Income on the web at *http://www.maxinc.com/2Q1999.html.* MAXIMUS was the first company to privatize welfare reform programs. Back in 1988, Los Angeles County chose MAXIMUS to implement and operate the Greater Avenues to Independence (GAIN) case management services of county eligibility divisions. Between 1988 and 1993 MAXIMUS provided services to approximately 95,000 Los Angeles County clients.

In 1999, it provides welfare to work services nationwide. Its services include eligibility determination, emergency assistance, job referral and placement, transition services such as child care and transportation, community work training services, job readiness preparation, and case management services. Projects have been operated in California, Massachusetts, Wyoming, and Texas. Current clients include Orange and Lake Counties in California; Fairfax County, Virginia; Prince Georges County, Maryland; Montgomery County, Maryland; Milwaukee County, Wisconsin; Waco, Texas; El Paso, Texas; Chicago, Illinois; San Diego, California; and Philadelphia, Pennsylvania.

MAXIMUS's child support enforcement full-service projects include a broad range of services such as customer service, enforcement, outreach, intake, locate, paternity establishment, obligation establishment, Uniform Reciprocal Enforcement of Support Act (URESA), Uniform Interstate Family Support Act (UIFSA), and payment processing. It also provides legal services ranging from a review of court filings to complete litigation and appellate work.

Its child care services include determination of eligibility, referrals, voucher insurance provider payments, regulation and certification of child care homes and facilities, and in-service training for providers.

On January 11, 1999, the Arizona Works Procurement Agency Board voted to approve a four-year contract valued at $17 million plus additional incentive payments to operate about one-third of the Maricopa County welfare program. The MAXIMUS contract would guarantee the state at least 10 percent cost savings in administrative costs. MAXIMUS was to hire and train 80 staff to determine eligibility for cash assistance and help welfare recipients to obtain jobs to move off welfare. The program is a pilot to determine whether to contract welfare program administration statewide to the private sector.

On March 8, 1999, MAXIMUS, Inc., received a $56-million five-year contract to provide managed care enrollment services for the State of Massachusetts Health Benefit Management program. MAXIMUS will provide outreach, education, customer service, enrollment, and transportation services for the state's Medicaid population of 80,000.

Lockheed Martin IMS is another example of a for-profit firm providing social services. It has won more than 20 contracts and currently provides four states with case management, skills training, and job placement assistance. The State of Florida's Department of Revenue contracted with Lockheed Martin IMS in 1994 after it assumed responsibility for child support enforcement cases. Lockheed Martin IMS was able to close out approximately 85,000 cases and collect

$162,000 in support payments at a cost of $4.5 million. In December 1998, Lockheed Martin IMS cancelled its contract with the state, citing that it could not make a profit trying to collect child support (Futile try to draw blood from turnip, 1999). Spokespersons for the Department of Revenue stated that Florida was left with a much cleaner data base of child support cases; many duplicate cases or invalid claims had been eliminated. However, it is very difficult for a for-profit organization to provide intake, case management, and investigation services and make a profit. As a result, the Department of Revenue has reengineered its child support division to be more productive. Prior to reengineering, case workers spent approximately 51 minutes of every hour on the telephone, leaving only 9 minutes to work cases. Now there are 10 regional customer service units to handle routine client calls, reducing busy signals and allowing more time for state employees to collect child support payments. The operators have computer access to obtain information on case files or requests for information. Basic questions are handled immediately; more complex and labor-intensive questions are routed to specialists (Florida Department of Revenue, 1998). Since reengineering, case workers are no longer generalists, handling up to 800 cases apiece. Now they are assigned to teams that specialize in different areas, such as client interviews, paternity establishment, court proceedings, and enforcement. Managers and teams are rewarded for the efficient processing of cases. The number of closed cases has increased to 61 percent since the reengineering effort. Collections were projected to top $610 million by June 30, 1999 (Florida Department of Revenue, 1998; D. Bruns personal communication, June 1, 1999).

However, the State of Florida has contracted with Lockheed Martin IMS and RSI for more specialized services such as location and collection contracts for deadbeat parents. These large for-profit organizations have already invested in the information technology, infrastructure, and statewide data bases that are necessary for success. They can provide location and collection services and still make a profit (D. Bruns, personal communication, June 1 1999; Futile try to draw blood from turnip, 1999).

As a result, many for-profit firms have begun to compete with one another as they seek large government contracts. Lockheed Martin IMS, Electronic Data Systems, and Andersen Consulting each prepared a bid for the management of $563 million in welfare operations in Texas.

CONCERNS

Some of the concerns that have been voiced by those opposed to outsourcing social welfare programs to for-profit firms are that profit-minded corporations would lay off public welfare workers and deny benefits in order to enhance their bottom line; or that corporations would be inclined to "cherry pick" recipients who are easiest to employ in order to maximize profits, leaving the hardest-to-place clients underserved (Kittower, 1999). Cook (1997) cites an example of a private job center in Boston that is not serving the clients with the greatest needs because doing so is too expensive. There is no financial motivation for the center to serve those who are the hardest to serve, who need the most education, who have a disability, or who need transportation from the inner city. For-profit firms often tend to neglect inner city and rural recipients because transportation is costly.

The State of Oklahoma contracted out to for-profit organizations job training programs for developmentally disabled and mentally ill residents. One contractor did not place any clients in jobs; however, he was paid a lot of money because he spent a lot of time assessing clients (Kittower, 1999: 48).

Others contend that rewarding welfare administrators for reducing the rolls will push recipients to low-wage and temporary jobs and discourage some from applying for benefits.

Still others note that large for-profit corporations will drive away nonprofits, which have historically been the government's subcontractors of choice because

> nonprofits can't compete with these corporations on bids, huge corporations boast state of the art technology and superior economies of scale, not to mention heavy weight political connections. Beyond the prodigious competition, some nonprofits and charities may be dissuaded by federal rules promoting speedy caseload reduction. Nonprofits aren't necessarily going after the eligibility review function because they don't want to turn people away. (Perry cited in Cook, 1997: 3)

In Orlando, Florida, only 0.3 percent of individuals getting off the welfare rolls use the One-Stop Career Centers, operated by Lockheed Martin IMS under a contract from Central Florida's Welfare Reform Coalition and Jobs & Education Partnership. The One-Stop centers offers job placement, education, and training services to anyone seeking work (Kunerth, 1999).

In the State of Maryland, state workers beat Lockheed Martin IMS in a race to collect child support dollars, prompting Governor Glendening to deny the private firm a contract extension. Lockheed Martin, IMS increased the percentage of child support dollars collected in Baltimore by 15 percent and in Queen Anne's County by 11 percent. During the same period state workers in Hagerstown increased collections in largely rural Washington County by 26 percent, double the statewide average of 13 percent.

Lockheed Martin, IMS protested the comparison, claiming that comparing the jurisdictions is unfair: Baltimore's higher poverty and unemployment rates make it harder to collect money from some noncustodial parents. But Lockheed failed by measures it set for itself: falling short of its own goals by $65 million in Baltimore and $1.2 million in Queen Anne's County. The governor's administration decided not to extend Lockheed's contract for a fourth year and demanded payment of more than $407,000 in penalties. Lockheed appealed the penalty (Dishneau, 1999).

State workers complained they were hampered by rules that would not apply to a private contractor. Several changes were made to allow the state workers to be competitive with the for-profit firm. The hiring process was streamlined, there was a greater focus on customer service, a separate lobby for child support cases was established, and enforcement agents were allowed to concentrate on collecting money. Flexible work hours were established that enabled collectors to make calls at night, when their targets were more likely to be home (Fletcher, 1999). Decentralizing authority, increasing the discretion of management, relaxing rules, and using incentives to guide and enhance performance enabled Maryland state employees to compete with Lockheed Martin, IMS.

Is privatization the right solution when duplicating a difficult government function and trying to be profitable at the same time? Was it the competition from for-profit firms that encouraged the restructuring of state collection practices and permitted the state employees to become more innovative? Or would have the changes in administrative practices alone produced the same results? Was competition necessary?

CONCLUSION

Proponents of the new public management suggest that government programs are inefficient and lack incentives to perform well. Instead, they suggest permitting competition for government services and programs and shifting the risks to service providers, who are only paid for successfully completed assignments.

The concern that many scholars and practitioners have is that government and society not lose sight of broader societal goals. Before government decides to forsake the spirit of public service, for efficiency and cost-effectiveness, we need to ask questions:

Is the public interest best served when the lines between public and private are blurred? Can nonprofits and government agencies adapt without compromising the qualities that distinguish them from for-profit organizations? Will nonprofits be forced to compromise the very assets that made them so vital to society in the first place? Are there certain services that can best be provided by for-profit organizations, by nonprofits, or by government (Ryan, 1999)? If the answer to the first two questions is no and the answer to the third and fourth questions is yes, then is this the direction in which we as a society want the new public management to lead us?

REFERENCES

Bozeman, B. (1987). *All Organizations Are Public: Bridging Public and Private Organizational Theories.* Jossey-Bass, San Francisco.

Bozeman, B. (ed.) (1993). *Public Management: The State of the Art.* Jossey-Bass, San Francisco.

Cook, C. (1997). From welfare to profit shares. *ZMAGAZINE* [*http://www.lbbs.org/zmag/articles/cooksept97.htm*], May 11.

Dishneau, D. (1999). State workers winning child support collection race. Associated Press [*http://jrnl.com/news/99Mar/jrn114100399.html*], May 11.

Douglas, J. (1983). *Why Charity? The Case for a Third Sector.* Sage, Beverly Hills, Calif.

Fletcher, G. (1998). County is the best at collecting child support. *Herald Mail* [*http://www.herald-mail.com/news/19 . . . local/county*], May 11.

Florida Department of Revenue (1998). *Annual Report.* Tallahasee, Fla.

Frederickson, H. G. (1997). *The Spirit of Public Administration.* Jossey-Bass, San Francisco.

Futile try to draw blood from turnip (1999) *The Tampa Tribune.* January 5, 6.

Hansman, H. B. (1980). The role of nonprofit enterprise. *The Yale Law Journal, 89,* 835–901.

Kittower, D. (1999). Steppong up to performance measuures. *Governing.* (June): 46–54.

Kramer, R. M., & Grossman, B. (1987). Contracting for social services: Process management and resource dependencies. *Social Sevice Review, 61,* 32–55.

Kunerth, J. (1999). Business and ex-welfare recipients are not connecting, survey shows. *Orlando Sentinel* [*http://www.orlandosentinal.com/business/031599_employ15.htm*], May 11.

Lipsky, M. & Smith, S. R. (1989–1990). Nonprofit organizations, government, and the welfare state. *Political Science Quarterly, 104,* 625–648

Massarsky, C. W. (1994). Enterprise strategies for generating revenue. In *The Jossey-Bass Handbook of Nonprofit Leadership and Management* (Robert D. Herman and Associates, eds.). Jossey-Bass, San Francisco, pp. 382–402.

MAXIMUS (1999). [*http://www.maxinc.com/2Q1999.html*], May 11.

MAXIMUS Announces $56 Million Contract (1999). [*http://www.maxinc.com/release030.htm*], May 11, p. 1.

MAXIMUS Managed Care (1999). [*http://www.maxinc.com/wr.html*], May 11.

Mayor, T. (1999). All eyes are on Texas. [*http://gaea.fcw.com/pubs/nov/cover.htm*], May 11.

Milward, H. B., Provan, K. G., and Else, B. (1993). What does the "hollow state" look like? In *Public Management: The State of the Art* (Barry Bozeman, ed.). Jossey-Bass, San Francisco, pp. 309–322.

Oleck, H. L. (1988). *Nonprofit corporations, organizations, and associations.* Fifth edition. Englewood cliffs: Prentice Hall.

Perlman, E. (1999). The business of government: Setbacks for privitized welfare. *Governing. 12:* 92.

Portner, J. (1988). For-Profit alternative schools are hot commodities. *Education Week on the Web* [http//www.edweek.org/ew/vol-17/42altern.h17], May 11, p. 2.

Ryan, W. P. (1999). The new landscape for nonprofits. *Harvard Business Review.* (January–February): 127–136.

Salamon, L. M. (1987). Partners in public service: The scope and theory of government-nonprofit relations. In W. W. Powell (Ed.), *The nonprofit sector: A research handbook* (pp. 99–117). New Haven: Yale University Press.

Salamon, L. M. (1999). *America's Nonprofit Sector: A Primer,* 2nd ed. The Foundation Center, New York.

Weisbrod, B. A. (1997). The future of the nonprofit sector: Its entwining with private enterprise and government. *Journal of Policy Analysis and Management. 16*(4): 541–555.

Wolch, J. R. (1990). *The Shadow State Government and Voluntary Sector in Transition.* New York: The Foundation Center.

28

Public Policy and the Continuous Improvement Paradigm: A Plea for the Total Learning Community

Henry B. Thomas
Department of Political Science and Public Administration, University of North Florida, Jacksonville, Florida

This chapter is concerned with the workability of the traditional continuous improvement paradigm in the public sector. There are several versions of the paradigm, of which two are the focus here. The first is the total quality management (TQM) paradigm, largely associated with W. Edward Deming; the second is the learning organization paradigm, associated with Peter Senge. Most public sector reinvention efforts can be characterized as a tossed salad of Deming and Senge. This chapter suggests that government-driven public sector TQM is in the end largely unworkable, more precisely, it argues that although government is able to initiate improvements with TQM tools, it is unable to maintain improvements in a systemic and continuous fashion. Finally, the chapter describes an effort to take quality to the streets and suggests that the idea of government-driven TQM be replaced with a total learning community (TLC) model in which government is one of several partner participants in improvement. TLC provides a potential platform that gives encouragement to the idea of successful public policy improvement that can be continuous, systemic, constitutional, and citizen-based.

Initially, the continuous improvement paradigm was seen as a strategy for private sector firms to retain and expand their customer base simultaneously, thereby securing future revenue flow and the viability of the firm. In this way, service became the key to competitive strategy (Normann, 1984). High-quality service gave the competitive edge, which ensured that the firm would retain existing customers and attract new ones. An important product of this approach was a customer focus. The firm analyzed and targeted customer groups by using the net present value of the customer (NPVC) concept. NPVC is the relationship of revenue to expense for each customer segment or key customer. Customers with high NPVC, or the potential for high NPVC, should be targeted. Customers with low NPVC should be avoided. For the private firm, focused targeting is the essence of a good customer value strategy.

Until recently, the public sector organization was seen as a monopolistic bureau that had no need either to retain existing customers or to attract new ones: The customer had no choice. With the public choice economics we begin to speak of municipal level choice as "voting with your feet," that is, deciding to leave one jurisdiction for another for better schools or police protection. Nevertheless, the calculus of government was largely budget bureau–driven and focused on the efficient and rational allocation of inputs. In fact, early economic analysis suggested that the quality of life might have deteriorated in urban areas despite state and local governments' spending as a result of nonexistent public sector productivity growth. This thesis was based on a two-sector conceptual model with a private sector that was characterized by high technological inputs and a high rate of productivity growth and a public sector with high labor inputs and a low rate of productivity growth (Baumol, 1967). Today, the focus of the public sector is on public value added and the continuous improvement paradigm, not on the input and procedural efficiencies and rigid personnel systems characterized by traditional public administration (Moore, 1985). Strong input controls and procedural "safeguards" are being relaxed. Productivity and effectiveness criteria are being emphasized. With regard to the Baumol thesis, I would note that our research on productivity, the use of the quality tools, and emphasis on sector has indicated that Baumol's conclusions are incorrect with respect to contemporary production of electric power in Florida (Stumm and Thomas, 1999).

THE PRODUCTIVITY VERSUS QUALITY APPROACH

Since 1917, the traditional approach of government was input control through the Bureau of Budget and Efficiency. The tradition of use of the word *efficiency* indicates that traditional public administration regarded efficiency not as a productivity measure but as an input rationalizing device. In 1917 the Bureau of Efficiency was an independent counit of the Bureau of the Budget, only later to be absorbed by the Bureau of the Budget. Whereas textbooks talk of efficiency as a productivity measure, the reality is that in the traditional public sector budget office efficiency was seen as input rationalization. This began to change with several iterations of reform, including performance budgeting and program budgeting. However, beginning in the 1970s the Joint Economic Committee of the U.S. Congress, the National Academy of Sciences, and the General Accounting Office began suggesting that government begin more aggressive productivity measurement programs. Today, the public sector productivity literature variously defines productivity as efficiency, effectiveness, cost reduction, input-output, management improvement, performance measurement, methods improvement, systems analysis, work measurement, and program evaluation. However, most often government productivity is described in one of three categories based on the type of output measure: (a) measures that focus on operational issues, (b) those that focus on organizational or program outputs, and (c) those that are concerned with program consequences. The first category, operational measures, is concerned with the internal workings or efficiency of the organization. The second category, productivity, formally defines productivity as the final organizational output divided by the resources used to produce the output. The third category, consequences, focuses on the program impact on society and the extent to which the program was able to meet its goals. When productivity is contrasted to quality, the second category is usually the focus of attention.

Beyond this, politics mattered. In the United States a bipartisan consensus had largely emerged that the public sector should do less (Newland, 1996). Further, this propensity appeared to be global, having ramifications in the industrial countries, the former Communist world, the Third World, and the "tigers" of Asia (Ingraham, 1997; Yergin and Stanislaw, 1998; Thomas and Frost, 1990). There seemed to be little acceptance of the spending of public money for any purpose (Kettl, 1996). The effects were downsizing and privatization (Stenberg, 1996). As government focused on productivity, the language of public productivity most often was a specific partial productivity measure—the ratio of output to labor input. This approach was largely focused on the theoretical principles of Frederick Taylor, who also advocated the fine division of tasks and the use of time and motion studies.

Now, there has been a shift from the language of public productivity to that of continuous improvement (Van Wart and Berman, 1999; Gore, 1993; Organization for Economic Cooperation and Development, 1996; Winter Commission, 1993). The TQM paradigm had its origin in the work of W. A. Shewahart; it was later expanded by W. Edward Deming and Joseph M. Juran. The essence of the TQM paradigm is in process improvement through the utilization of human resources to produce a constant stream of product or service refinements without sacrificing low cost (Deming, 1982). This paradigm has largely replaced the theoretical principles of Frederick Taylor. Indeed, research from the private sector suggests that firms that embrace the Taylorism paradigm have less incentive to invest in human capital because of negative externalities associated with human capital development. For example, if the firm invests in the worker and the new skills increase the marketability of the worker, then the worker may leave the firm. Under such conditions the firm may perceive that the investment has been lost. Further, if the firm increases the worker's salary to keep him, or her, then profit is suboptimized (Lynch, 1992). Similarly, private firms tend to adopt one of two alternative strategies to produce high-performance work systems. The first is workplace transformation, which supports employee involvement through job security, profit sharing, measures to build group cohesiveness, and guaranteed individual rights. Investment by these firms in worker training and technology support is often substantial. The second approach is the disposable workplace, a strategy that flows from the literature on rank-order tournaments. The firm motivates the worker by way of a tournament or contest that offers a fixed number of guaranteed promotions distributed to the best performers regardless of whether average performance is good or bad. The disposable workplace relies upon job insecurity and minimal training. Why train someone you plan to abandon?

In a NSF study currently under way, Richard Florida of Carnegie Mellon University and Davis Jenkins of University of Illinois at Chicago have preliminary results that seems to indicate the following,

> Thus far, the study has produced a number of findings with implications for management practice. Manufacturing plants that organize production work in ways that promote worker involvement, teamwork and skill development exhibit higher rates of quality-oriented manufacturing process innovation than do plants where production work is managed according to Taylorist practices (functionally specialized, hierarchically controlled and "deskilled"). Training, by itself, does little to enhance problem-solving and innovation on the factory floor. Training does not pay unless production work is organized to give workers the opportunity and authority to contribute to performance improvement. The management practice most strongly associated with continuous quality improvement of manufacturing processes is involving production workers in the design of work methods and quality control. (Florida and Jenkins, NSF, Transformations to Quality Organizations: Research Project Summaries at http://tqo.asq.org/table.html)

A similar NSF study by François Sainfort of the University of Wisconsin-Madison seeks to find the link between job satisfaction and quality management at the municipal government level. This study focuses on the city of Madison, Wisconsin, a pioneer in public sector quality management initiatives. A research team from the University of Wisconsin has studied the impact on the working life of city employees who are significantly engaged in quality management practices. Two major conclusions seem to be emerging from the research: First, city employees who provide services based on quality management practices generally have higher job satisfaction than other employees. Second, during the early stages of quality management implementation, employees experience increased workload, job conflicts, and stress. Managers need to watch for these learning-curve signs and take actions such as relieving certain job duties for a time or fostering teamwork so that workload is shared. The study found that it is easier to engage white-collar employees in quality management activities than blue-collar employees, but that may be because white-collar employees generally work together in offices in more of a team environment. In Madison union members were largely in favor of the quality improvement initiative, perhaps because the first project involved union members (Sainfort, NSF, Transformations to Quality Organizations: Research Project Summaries at http://tqo.asq.org/table.html). Although these NSF results are still preliminary, they represent cutting edge formulations of the workability of quality principles.

The Deming approach to TQM utilized the plan, do, check, act (PDCA) cycle. Also called the *Deming control cycle,* PDCA is a never-ending, continuous cycle beginning and ending with planning. The plan phase of the cycle establishes a standard for achieving the goal, the do phase enacts the plan. This is the production/service delivery phase of the cycle. The check phase of the cycle measures and analyzes results; this is the inspection phase of the cycle. The act phase of the cycle implements the necessary reforms when the results are not as originally planned; This is the reprogramming phase of the cycle. After reprogramming we again enter the plan phase of the never-ending PDCA cycle.

PUBLIC SECTOR TOTAL QUALITY MANAGEMENT

Vice President Gore's national performance review (NPR) sought to adopt the work force transformation path to improved government performance. However, much of the research on NPR reveals major failures in the tenets sustaining the ideas of workplace transformation. For example, Kettl has argued that there were in fact three different NPRs. The first was composed of senior staff working out of the executive office building. Their interest was in attracting voters through NPR. The second NPR consisted of the true believers who preached the gospel of NPR to the choir and to anyone else who would listen. The third NPR was the worker bees who produced the output (Kettl and Divli, 1995). Today, a host of state and local government efforts have also attempted to begin TQM in the public sector. This chapter argues that these efforts will meet with continuing frustration in part because of the American limited government orientation. As Mark Moore has put it, "We celebrate private consumption more than the achievement of collective goals" (Moore, 1995). In addition, the separation of powers and the policy-administration dichotomy will create frustration (Wilson, 1987).

The man often given credit with starting the public sector reinvention revolution is David Osborne (Osborne and Gaebler, 1993). Osborne characterized the public sector bureaucratic culture as distinguished by staying out of trouble; doing just enough—"good enough for government work"; and never, never, ever making a mistake. Osborne suggested the new entrepreneurial culture consisted of the following characteristics: clarity of purpose, a well-developed strategy, accountability to customers, consequences of performance, empowerment of employees, pursuit of excellence, innovation, and responsibility for actions (Osborne and Plastrik, 1997). He argued that reinvention prepared the organization for challenges yet unseen. But Osborne is not the first reformer; the last half of the 20th century was a particularly inventive period in American public administration for movements promising to improve program and agency management dramatically. One after another, new management techniques or reforms have emerged PPBS, MBO, ZBB, deregulation, downsizing, and privatizing. Indeed, even though reinventing government is but the last reform in a very substantial queue, it has become part of the everyday language of politics. It should be noted that reinvention is forcefully different from the public microeconomic view that state actors will change policy only if doing so will result in maximizing the net present value of the jurisdiction. In the new paradigm policy change is viewed as endogenous to jurisdiction processes and produces internal change that cannot be explained by the learning-as-doing metaphor. Second, although tasks may be specialized as in the Taylor paradigm, workers and other stakeholders are generalized, pressed into cross-functional teams and multifunctional positions. Steven Rosell has argued that we need to develop learning-based approaches to governance because non-learning-based governance mechanisms are incapable of keeping up with the increasing complexity of the information society (Rosell, 1995).

SUBOPTIMIZED PUBLIC SECTOR TOTAL QUALITY MANAGEMENT

The philosophical basis of reinvention is largely ontological. Advocates, like medieval philosophers, argue its existence from effects but can never prove it. As a result, reinvention's emphasis on entrepreneurship is frequently attacked by public administration scholars for its avoidance of issues of constitutional law and representational democracy (Moe and Gilmour, 1995). My own sense is that TQM in government must fail in that we have a constitutional structure that prohibits true public sector TQM. True public TQM would require cross-functional teaming and training across the three branches of government, and this would be most problematic for the judicial branch of government. In my view, the separation of powers issue would reduce TQM to QM. Put another way, public sector quality management efforts can and do occur, but they are by constitutional definition a suboptimization of TQM. One should recall that the *T* in *TQM* is the heart of both the Deming and the Japanese approach to quality. The effort to improve race relations since Brown is an archetype of this suboptimization as the public policy of race relations has careened from branch to branch since 1954 (Orfield and Yun, 1999).

Nevertheless, absent fully formed TQM, government can still be viewed as a learning organization. Organizational learning has been very broadly defined. Peter Senge draws together a wide range of ideas that underpin the concept of the learning organization. He suggests that the five disciplines are shared vision, team learning, personal mastery, an understanding of mental models, and systems thinking (Senge, 1990). Checkland and his associates at Lancaster University developed an approach called *soft systems methodology,* which applies ideas developed by engineers to designing and changing organizations. The most significant difference between machines and organizations is that, in designing the latter, one must take account of the different viewpoints of those involved. (Checkland, 1981; Checkland and Scholes, 1990). Levitt and March suggest that organizations learn "by encoding inferences from history into routines that guide behavio." (Levitt and March, 1988). This learning from history is less often prescribed than the PDCA cycle of TQM but is similar, if more informal. Part of it is problem solving in the form of detecting and correcting errors (Argyris, 1991). Organization development theorists see organization learning as an extension of organization development methods (Dilworth, 1996; Hale, 1996). Finally, organizational learning can be seen as information processing that results in a new range of potential actions that are potentially useful (Huber, 1991). For public organizations the identification of a performance gap is conditioned by a variety of internal and external constraints (Wilson, 1989; Downs, 1967): First, it is linked to organization culture, values, and expectations (Mahler, 1997). Second, it is linked to organization leadership. Third, analysis is conducted to investigate the problem, either to correct current practices or to devise new programs or management techniques to meet expectations better. This inquiry process is most typically seen to rely on the organizations' information processing system to collect, distribute, store, and retrieve data (Huber, 1991; Walsh and Ungson, 1991); it is also based on the implementation techniques of the organization (Senge, 1990). Finally, many theorists argue that there is no guarantee that authentic learning will lead to organizational improvement. Effective learning of some early lessons may hamper later learning, or "superstitious lessons" may be learned (Levitt and March, 1988; Hedberg, 1981).

CORE CITY REBOUND: AN EFFORT IN TOTAL COMMUNITY LEARNING

If government-driven TQM is unlikely, how can society become a learning organization? We have struggled with this issue first in Lincolnville, a core city neighborhood of St. Augustine, Florida, and now in inner city Jacksonville, Florida. Unfortunately, we know relatively little about transformation at the neighborhood and community levels (Mosgaller, 1993). Our work in Lincolnville with a Neighborhood Quality Council and our work in Jacksonville with Core City Rebound represent efforts to take quality to the streets. In hindsight, we made a strategic error in Lincolnville by trying to teach the quality tools too soon. Additionally, the Lincolnville neighborhood did not have the robust partner group that Core City Rebound has developed.

Core City Rebound is a five-partner group organization seeking quality improvement in Jacksonville's inner city. The groups are business, government, community organizations, higher education institutions, and the religious community. The initial impetus for Core City Rebound was Fresh Ministries, a faith based non-profit with a focus on urban ministry. The asset-based focus of Core City Rebound rests on the work of John McKnight, who has sought to develop a community-mapping tool that focuses on the recognition of community assets rather than deficits (McKnight and Kretzmann, 1993). McKnight argues that in the traditional community development paradigm, city agencies and other outsiders assess a community's needs and problems and then use their existing programmatic tools to address those needs. Individual agencies regard community residents as "clients" and deliver services to them with little semblance of coordination. McKnight's approach has three features: First, it is driven from the bottom up: Communities organize themselves, establishing true partnerships across institutions and between institutions and residents, and play the commanding role in designing and implementing development strategies. Second, it is comprehensive: The community develops a strategy that cuts across and sets priorities among opportunities (i.e., in social services, crime prevention, education, job creation, housing) traditionally separated under the old paradigm. Third, it is asset-based rather than needs- or problem-based: The community identifies assets on which it can build, ranging from the skills and entrepreneurial ideas of residents to manifestations of culture and the strengths of local associations and institutions, including private sector, government, community-based, and religious.

The economic strategy for Core City Rebound was based on the work of Michael Porter (Porter, 1990, 1995). Which focused first on the competitive advantages of nations, then on those of inner cities. Porter's inner city research has found that the often-cited advantages, such as low-cost labor and cheap real estate, are largely illusory. The changing nature of the world economy means that inner cities will not be able to compete if low-cost labor and cheap real estate are their only advantages. Instead, the genuine competitive advantages of inner cities fall into four strategic areas: strategic location, integration with regional clusters, unmet local demand, and human resources.

Strategic location offers a competitive edge to logistically sensitive businesses that benefit from proximity to downtown, transportation infrastructure, and concentrations of companies. The just-in-time, service-intensive modern economy is only heightening the time and space advantages of these locations. Those advantages explain the continued existence and growth of the many food processing, printing, business support, rapid-response warehousing and distribution, trade and transportation, and light manufacturing companies in inner city areas.

Integration with regional clusters is an effective economic strategy when the inner city focuses on developing economic clusters within the inner city, instead of isolated companies, and links them to those in the surrounding economy. Economic clusters enhance opportunities to develop focused programs for training, purchasing, and business development, leading to job opportunities for inner city residents.

Unmet local demand is important because the consumer market of Jacksonville's inner city residents represents the most immediate opportunity for inner city–based entrepreneurs and businesses. However, in the past, firms used the net present value of the customer (NPVC) concept to avoid inner city customers because they had low NPVC. However, Porter points out that despite low average incomes, high population density translates into a large local market with substantial purchasing power. Making the market even more attractive is the fact that there tend to be few competitors serving it. Jacksonville's inner city is also a distinct market, which demands uniquely tailored product configurations, retail concepts, entertainment, and personal and business services. An opportunity is present for national retail and service chains focusing on inner cities, as well as large-scale manufacturing of tailored products to supply them. According to Porter, the private sector is already waking up to the potential of inner cities (Porter, 1995).

Although inner-city populations present many work force readiness challenges, inner city residents can also be an attractive labor pool for businesses that rely on a loyal, modestly skilled work force. There is the potential to build on this resource, with new approaches to education, job placement, and training. To hire from the inner city, companies still must have effective strategies for identifying good employees. Cultivating personal networks in the community and building relationships with community-based organizations are essential.

The best way to develop the economy of Jacksonville's inner city is to make it an attractive and welcoming place in which to invest and do business, both for residents and for nonresidents. The private sector will step forward because inner cities can offer attractive markets, advantageous locations, and good employees. As business locations, inner cities traditionally suffer many disadvantages: discrimination against residents and entrepreneurs, high taxes and utility costs, difficulty in finding affordable insurance, crime, poorly maintained logistical infrastructure, burdensome regulations, and permitting requirements, environmental pollution, and a weak education and training system.

The inner city's disadvantages as a business location must be seen as an economic problem and addressed as part of an economic strategy. Too often they are approached with only the social welfare of residents, not the needs of business, in mind. Furthermore, attempting to offset disadvantages with operating subsidies to businesses has proved to be futile. A more effective approach is to address the impediments to doing business directly.

The vital role for government is not direct intervention and heavy reliance on operating subsidies to attract companies, but on creation of a favorable environment for business through crime prevention, affirmative action and government set-aside programs, deregulation, and training. Public funds are necessary to help revitalize Jacksonville's inner city, but they must be spent in support of an economic strategy based on competitive advantage, instead of distorting business incentives with futile attempts to lure businesses that lack an economic reason for locating in the inner city. Tax incentives such as enterprise zones are important, but businesses that locate in an area because of tax breaks or other artificial inducements, rather than genuine competitive advantages, prove not to be sustainable. Finally, a critical role of government is to act as marketer—courting, welcoming, and assisting companies seeking to locate in the inner city. Unfortunately, government rarely plays this role adequately in inner cities.

As should be clear, this TLC model differs significantly from the two primary models of neighborhood change: the community organizing (CO) model and the community development corporation (CDC) model. The dominant paradigm for neighborhood change is the CO model, which is first and foremost a legacy of Saul Alinsky. The second neighborhood change paradigm is the community development corporation (CDC) model. The modern CDC can be traced back to Robert Kennedy and Bedford-Stuyvestant of 1966 (Thomas and Lieberman, 1996).

The theme throughout is the public value added through the total learning community. Given the relative novelty of the idea of using TQM tools to transform neighborhoods rather than government, critical questions have so far been muted. Yet those critical questions must help to identify a systematic description of neighborhood quality, help to identify systemic and generalizable knowledge related to the improvement of neighborhoods, and assist in the paradigm shift from the community organizing and community development paradigms to the TLC paradigm. As seen in the Core City Rebound example, the partnership includes representatives of government agencies, religious organizations, neighborhood associations, business and technical societies, and academia.

Indeed, we have few illusions that poor communities possess profound knowledge of the fundamental changes in the economy from the labor-intensive industrial era to the global capital/technology-intensive information era. Nevertheless, our focus group and survey data in Lincolnville and Jacksonville indicate that inner city neighborhood groups desire a higher level of quality in their communities. They see the private sector's making progress by the use of quality principles and believe that these approaches might help solve inner city problems.

W. Edwards Deming once remarked that the most important information needed to manage a firm was unknown and unknowable. He meant by this that firms do not know the costs of not fully serving customers or of not having well-functioning processes. These are not part of traditional accounting systems. We believe that as residents of public housing, persons on welfare, and other residents of poor neighborhoods begin to learn these techniques, their employability will rise dramatically, and community teams will apply improvement tools to address critical neighborhood defined priorities. The quality management principles that will drive these efforts are (a) community learning focus, (b) stakeholder satisfaction, (c) universal participation, (d) continuous improvement, (e) fact-based decision making, and (f) neighborhood metrics. The advantage of this approach is that it allows a neighborhood to work together with improvement as a driver. It provides opportunities to learn new tools for effectiveness.

In the introduction I made the distinction between workplace transformation and the disposal workplace. I make a similar distinction between neighborhood transformation and disposable communities. Our research and teaching suggest that the TLC focus can enhance neighborhoods in large part because citizen involvement lies at the heart of high-performance communities. It allows citizens to use their knowledge of the neighborhood to improve quality since decisions are made by those who are most knowledgeable about the consequences of those decisions to the neighborhood.

Core City Rebound has been impressed with the Grameen Bank of Bangladesh strategy, in which borrowers are organized into small groups to facilitate group solidarity as well as participatory interaction. Organizing borrowers into primary groups of five members and federating the groups into centers have been the building blocks of the Grameen strategy. Core City Rebound is a partner in the Jacksonville Mico-loan effort. Strategies should also take note of the globalization of trade; today international trade is Florida's number one growth industry.

Finally, in the United States there exists a tension between the increasing pressure to improve government performance through innovation and the equally strong demand for integrity and accountability of public officials. Orange County has been used as a case to make a very strong argument against the reinvention principle of enterprising government (Frederickson, 1995). For Frederickson the business of government is government, not business. He suggests that problems with corruption and government ethics are increasing because we think and act in an entrepreneurial rather than governmental fashion (Frederickson, 1997). This suggests that corruption and unethical behavior in government are increasing because government organizations are moving toward enterprise models. However, increased levels of trust may offset this tendency toward corruption and unethical behavior. There is increasing evidence that "high-trust" societies are more productive than low-trust societies (Fukuyama, 1995). Poor communities are often low-trust communities. Extensive participation in the TLC will engender greater levels of trust. Optimally, every neighborhood resident will actively seek to attain common neighborhood goals. These common goals will be broadly supported only when they are based on the principle that neighborhood quality is defined by neighborhood advantage for internal and external neighborhood stakeholders. What is to stakeholders' advantage will be to the neighborhood's advantage, thereby furthering neighborhood development. Our approach is based on a TLC continuum. This continuum is based on the Arthur Andersen & Co. ABO Continuum, in which *ABO* stands for awareness, buy-in, and ownership. At the awareness level neighborhood residents will seek to learn more about the quality tools and techniques. They begin to commit time to learn and understand. This leads to an elementary understanding of the basic concepts. However, the individual remains only passively supportive of the quality effort. At the buy-in level neighborhood residents begin to seek mentoring and guidance to act on what they have learned. They now commit time and resources to be involved, not just to understand elementary issues but to deepen knowledge. As residents actually begin to use the tools and the techniques to solve neighborhood problems, they are increasingly supportive. At the ownership level residents begin to seek and assume responsibility for the neighborhood quality systems. They recruit others. They apply and teach quality concepts and systems to others. They initiate new uses for the application of quality theory and technique.

We believe that there will be less resistance to change by neighborhood residents if we use the TLC continuum approach. Lessons from the private sector suggest that people embrace change when

- They initiate it themselves and feel they can control its progress and outcomes
- They understand its desirability and can predict many of its implications
- They value the new benefits and are willing to bear the costs arising from the change
- They see how they can contribute to the change and increase the likelihood of successful change

Similarly, people tend to resist change when

- They are unclear about the implications of the change for them and their work
- They see the costs in terms of lost benefits and forgone advantages and do not see the new benefits that will arise and the old disadvantages that will be removed
- They cannot see how to contribute to and control the process of making the change
- The proposed change has errors built into it that they can see and are powerless to correct
- Decisions about undertaking the change and implementing it are made in ways that exclude, disempower, and devalue them

There should be little surprise that poor communities have often resisted externally imposed change. The poor are most often unclear about the implications of the change. Too often they see the changes in terms of lost benefit, not focusing on the new benefits and opportunities that arise. Additionally, neighborhood residents usually do not see how they can contribute to and control the process of change. Too often the poor can see that errors that have been designed into the policy change but are powerless to correct those errors. Finally, traditional bureaucracies have too often devalued and dehumanized the poor.

TOTAL LEARNING COMMUNITY AS TECHNOLOGY TRANSFER

I view taking quality to the streets as a form of technology transfer. Much of the literature on technology transfer relates to international transfer, the movement of technology across national boundaries. In this chapter I am more interested in the concept of technological diffusion, the spread of a new technology within a country—across neighborhoods. Indeed, there are elements of both diffusion and transfer when the focus is on neighborhood improvement. According to Robinson, a technology transfer package includes hardware, licensing agreement, technical assistance contract, management contract, marketing agreement, and a training contract (Robinson, 1988). The several nonhardware aspects add ambiguity, or what Robinson calls "mushiness," to the technology transfer concept. Much of our concern focuses on this mushiness. Of special interest, however, are the three types of technology that are widely associated with continuous improvement. The first are the important breakthrough improvements and internal innovations that have resulted from active operation of the continuous improvement process. The second are the analytical tools used by employees to conceptualize and implement improvements. The third are the organizational characteristics and management systems that account for the emergence of a heavy volume of improvements. Several of these factors can be seen in the Japanese experience in building automobile factories in the United States. Nonetheless, the Japanese automotive manufacturing experiences in the United States have not been universally successful in terms of technology transfer. In 1985 Mazda built a stamping and assembly plant in Flat Rock, Michigan. At that time Mazda was the third Japanese automotive manufacturer to set up production in the United States. Mazda's intention was to transfer the continuous improvement system to the United States. In doing so, Mazda broke ranks with Nissan and Honda, which had preceded them, by forming an association with the United Auto Workers. The literature documents the mutual disenchantment of workers and Japanese managers with the evolution of the organizational culture. The result was an organization in which work was accomplished by teams but teams that apparently did not produce continuous improvements (Fucini and Fucini, 1990).

Recent research in Brazil shows that Japanese firms there made minimal effort to transfer their TQM technologies to those subsidiaries (Boss and Cole, 1993). The firms, members of the Brazilian electronics sector, had all transferred statistical process control. However, none had transferred JIT manufacturing, although all utilized that technology in their home operations. In terms of the soft technologies of continuous improvement, two-thirds used quality circles and employee suggestion systems. Only one-quarter, however, reported that they had developed special programs with suppliers.

One particularly negative finding in the Brazil research is that all CEOs and top managers in the subsidiaries were Japanese. The companies' policy to reserve those positions for Japanese nationals served as a vehicle for accomplishing a relatively steady one-way transfer of technology from Japan to Brazil. The practice of limiting promotion possibilities for Brazilian middle managers led to high turnover rates in those ranks, which necessarily had negative consequences for the development of continuous improvement capabilities. The evidence appears strong that in the case of the Brazilian electronics sector, Japanese firms have set up subsidiaries that they do not expect to be integrated into a global continuous improvement system. A companion research project was carried out in the *maquiladora* zone of Mexico (Wilson, 1992). The sample contained firms from a number of countries and from a wide range of industries, especially electronics and auto parts suppliers. The results were much the same as those reported for Brazil.

How does this apply to Core City Rebound? Clearly, the success of taking quality to the streets depends on the willingness of business partners to transfer current technology as well as their willingness to train inner city residents for leadership positions at inner city business locations. At the end of the day, for Core City Rebound to be considered a success, the new core city private and not-for-profit organizations must be integrated into the global continuous improvement system.

Much of the learning in Core City Rebound can be considered policy learning. Policy-oriented learning involves long-term, enduring modifications of thought that result from experience and are concerned with the modification of the precepts of the belief system of individuals or advocacy coalitions (Sabatier and Jenkins-Smith, 1993). Policy learning seems possible when three conditions are met: First, the level of conflict among the coalitions is moderate. Second, the policy is tractable (there is general consensus on the technology of solving the policy problem). Third, the forum for debate among the coalitions is limited to professionals, rather than being open, so that professional norms dominate and changes in views are less public. The finding that the debate be limited to professionals, rather than being open, is not encouraging to an effort to take quality to the streets.

Policy learning is more likely for beliefs about "secondary aspects" of policy such as program operations, regulations and standards, or program scope. Less likely to change are fundamental beliefs about policy strategies or instruments and the scope of governmental intervention. Least likely to change are beliefs about human nature and political values (Sabatier and Jenkins-Smith 1993). Indeed, these are sobering comments on the possibility of taking quality to the streets, for unless Core City Rebound partner group members can embrace 21st-century views of human nature, abandoning Taylorism and traditional views of class, gender, and race, quality principle and practice will not successfully reach the street.

CONCLUSION

This chapter has argued that government-driven TQM is dubious if not impossible on a number of grounds. First, the orientation of public bureaus tends to be downward toward reliable control. This is in large part based on the politically neutral competence training received by MPA students. Second, so long as public managers view themselves as technicians rather than strategists, government-led TQM is unlikely. Third, with the impossibility of the *T* in *TQM,* only isolated and disconnected improvements will result from a public quality program. Fourth, the chapter has argued that the lessons from technology transfer suggest that the key success factor is commitment to the paradigm shift rather than use of the tools. This suggests that a TLC productivity initiative should first focus on building a network for community partnering and second focus on citizen evolvement. Only then should the focus move to teaching the quality tools such as statistical process control and benchmarking. In an earlier effort in the Lincolnville neighborhood we made the mistake by first offering training in the quality tools. The Core City Rebound effort better conforms to the lessons from technology transfer. Taking quality to the streets through TLC provides an alternative approach for civic non-government-driven improvement. TLC provides a potential platform that gives encouragement to the idea of successful public policy improvement that can be continuous, systemic, constitutional, and citizen-based. Such an approach would be particularly beneficial in poor communities since their residents have had little workplace experience with continuous quality improvement.

REFERENCES

Argyris, Chris (1991). The use of knowledge as a test for theory: The case of public administration. *Journal of Public Administration Research and Theory. 1*(3): 337–354.

Baumol, William J. (1967). Macroeconomics of unbalanced growth: The anomaly of urban crisis. *American Economic Review.* 415–426.

Boss, A., and Cole, W. (1993). Management systems as technology: Japanese, US and national firms in the Brazilian electronics sector. *World Development. 22*(2): 225–236.

Checkland, Peter (1981). *Systems Thinking, Systems Practice.* John Wiley, New York.
Checkland, Peter, and Scholes, Jim (1990). *Soft Systems Methodology in Action.* John Wiley, New York.
Deming, W.E. (1982). *Quality Productivity and Competitive Position.* Massachusetts Institute of Technology Center for Advanced Engineering Study, Cambridge, Mass.
Dilworth, Robert (1996). Institutionalizing learning organizations in the public sector. *Public Productivity and Management Review. 14*(4): 407–421.
Downs, Anthony (1967). *Inside Bureaucracy.* Little-Brown, Boston.
Florida, Richard, and Jenkins, Davis Forthcoming. NSF, Transformations to Quality Organizations: Research Project Summaries [http://tqo.asq.org/table.html].
Frederickson, H. George (1995). Misdiagnosing the Orange County scandal. *Governing.* April.
Frederickson, H. George (1997). *The Spirit of Public Administration.* Jossey-Bass, San Francisco.
Fucini, J., and Fucini, S. (1990). *Working for the Japanese: Inside Mazda's American Auto Plant.* The Free Press, New York.
Fukuyama, Frances (1995). *Trust: The Social Virtues and the Creation of Prosperity.* The Free Press, New York.
Gore, Al (1993). *Creating Government That Works Better and Costs Less: Report of the National Performance Review.* US Government Printing Office, Washington, D.C.
Hale, Mary (1996). Learning organizations and mentoring. *Public Productivity and Management Review. 14*(4): 422–433.
Hedberg, Bo (1981). How organizations learn and unlearn. *Handbook of Organizational Design.* Vol. 1. *Adapting Organizations: Their Environments* (Paul Nystrom and William Starbuck, eds.) Oxford University Press, New York.
Huber, George (1991). *Organization Learning: The Contributing Processes and the Literatures.*
Ingraham, Patricia W. (1997). Play it again, Sam; It's still not right—searching for the right notes in administrative reform. *Public Administration Review. 57*(4): 325–331.
Kettl, Donald F., and Diluli, John J. Jr. (eds.) (1995). *Inside the Reinvention Machine.* Brookings Institute, Washington, D.C.
Levitt, Barbara, and March, James (1988). Organizational learning. *Annual Review of Sociology. 14:* 319–340.
Lieberman, Jerry, Thomas, Henry B., and Burdin, Joel (1996). Strategies for Action. *Inside Out: Neighborhood Redevelopment and Revitalization.* The Proceedings of a Writing Conference Sponsored by Florida Department of Education, Florida Department of Community Affairs, and Florida Institute of Education, 47.
Lynch, Lisa (1992). Private sector training and the earnings of young workers. *American Economic Review. 82*(1): 299–312.
Mahler, Julianne (1997). Influences of organizational culture on learning in public agencies. *Journal of Public Administration Research and Theory.* (forthcoming).
McKnight, J.L., and Kretzmann, J.P. (1993). *Building Communities from the Inside Out: A Path Toward Finding and Mobilizing Community Assets.* Center for Urban Affairs and Policy, Northwestern University, Evanston, Ill.

Moe, Ronald C., and Gilmour, Robert S. (1995). Rediscovering Principles of Public Administration: The Neglected Foundation of Public Law. *Public Administration Review. 55*(2): 135–146.

Moore, Mark H. (1995). *Creating Public Value: Strategic Management in Government.* Harvard University Press, Cambridge, Mass.

Mosgaller, Tom (1993). Creating communities that care, City of Madison Organizational Development and Training Office. *Public Sector Network Information Packet.*

Orfield, Gary, and Yun, John T. (1999). Resegregation in American Schools. The Civil Rights Project. Harvard University, Cambridge, Mass.

Organization for Economic Cooperation and Development (1996). *Ministerial Symposium on the Future of the Public Services.* Organization for Economic Cooperation and Development, Paris.

Osborne, David, and Gaebler, Ted (1993). *Reinventing Government: How the Entrepreneurial Spirit is Transforming the Public Sector.* Plume Books, New York.

Osborne, David, and Plastrik, Peter (1997). *Banishing Bureaucracy: The Five Strategies For Reinventing Government.* Addison-Wesley, Reading, Mass.

Porter, Michael E. (1990). *The Competitive Advantage of Nations.* Free Press, New York.

Porter, Michael E. (1995). The competitive advantage of the inner city. *Harvard Business Review. 73*(3): 55.

Robinson, Richard (1988). *The International Transfer of Technology: Theory, Issues and Practice.* Ballinger Press Company, Cambridge, Mass.

Rose, Richard (1991). What is lesson drawing? *Journal of Public Policy. 11*:3–30.

Rosell, Steven A. et al. (1995). *Changing Maps: Governing in a World of Rapid Change.* Carlton University Press.

Sabatier, Paul, and Jenkins-Smith, Hank (eds.) (1993). *Policy Change and Learning: An Advocacy Coalition Approach.* Boulder, CO: Westview Press.

Sainfort, Francois Forthcoming. NSF, Transformations to Quality Organizations: Research Project Summaries (http://tqo.asq.org/table.html).

Senge, Peter (1990). *The Fifth Discipline: The Art and Practice of the Learning Organization.* Doubleday, New York.

Stumm, Theodore J., and Thomas, Henry B. (1999). Benchmarking Florida's Electric Power Enterprises: A Comparison of Public and Private Sector Efficiency. *Public Works Management & Policy.*

Thomas, Henry B., and Frost, Raymond (1990). An analysis of government efficiency in industrial countries. *Public Productivity and Management Review. XIII*(4): 4.

Thomas, Henry B., and Lieberman, Jerry (1996). Where has neighborhood revitalization worked? Inside Out: Neighborhood Redevelopment and Revitalization. The Proceedings of a Writing Conference Sponsored by Florida Department of Education, Florida Department of Community Affairs, and Florida Institute of Education, 25.

Van Wart, M., and Berman, E. (1999). Contemporary public sector productivity values. *Public Productivity and Management Review. 22*(3): 326–347.

Walsh, James, and Ungson, Geraldo (1991). Organizational memory. *Academy of Management Review. 16*(1): 57–91.

Wilson, James (1989). *Bureaucracy.* Basic Books, New York.

Wilson, Steven (1992). Continuous improvement and the new competition: The case of US, European, and Japanese Firms in the Mexican Maquiladora industry. Ph.D. Dissertation, University of Tennessee, Knoxville.

Winter Commission (1993). *Hard Truths/Tough Choices: An Agenda for State and Local Government Reform.* State University of New York, Nelson A. Rockefeller Institute of Government, Albany.

Yergin, D., and Stanislaw, J. (1998). *The Commanding Heights: The Battle Between Government and the Marketplace That Is Remaking the Modern World.* Simon & Schuster, New York.

29

Rumbling Doubt About Managerial Effectiveness and a Turn Toward Discourse

Hugh T. Miller and John Donohue
School of Public Administration,
Florida Atlantic University,
Fort Lauderdale, Florida

Mohamad Alkadry
Division of Public Administration,
West Virginia University
Morgantown, West Virginia

RUMBLING DOUBT

The variety of contemporary attacks upon managerial and manipulative modes of theory and practice are as rich and diverse as the management literature itself (Marcuse, 1964; Scott and Hart, 1979; Thayer, 1981; Connell and Nord, 1996). But such criticism has caused little discernible change in direction. The broached anomalies remain mostly unacknowledged. There is a parallel here with the practice of psychoanalytic and psychological therapies, which seem to persist profitably as if no one has pointed out their many shortcomings. Likewise, the hopeful claims of managerial effectiveness stand in good currency despite the absence of feasible causal theory. The managerial appropriation of privileges continues to enjoy favorable reception as if none of the compelling criticisms had been made.

Some of the critiques are quite thoroughgoing. Organizational contrivance of a means-ends social life (Ingersoll and Adams, 1992) is central to the attempt to manipulate human beings into compliant patterns of behavior (Foucault, 1979). The effectiveness of management systems in controlling much of anything has also been called into question. Management systems always succeed, except when they don't.

Doubt As a Style of Thought

What is the source of this profound doubt about the prospects and very ambition of management? We may be the willing messengers of doubt, but skepticism is not our invention. The doubt about management does not arise from the management discourse, but from sources external to it. Heresy has been gaining momentum ever since Galileo got the Earth to move around the Sun. Doubt has been rumbling louder ever since, and now it has taken over the living room. We watched Rodney King get beaten over and over and over again. We watched O. J. Simpson drive down the highway at safe speed in a white Bronco. We watched Princess Diana's funeral and saw people who did not know her cry profusely. We watched the Monica Lewinsky affair, and the impeachment trial that followed. Common to all these spectacles is the medium of image replication. Technological replication allows the profusion and reproduction of the spectacles, and the delivery of these image simulacra into people's living rooms and psyches. All the while, reality loses its claim on us. More spectacles follow, from Jon Benet Ramsey to Columbine, to the next one. We have learned to doubt the reality that has been munificently provided. How real is this manufactured reality?

"All that once was directly lived has become mere representation," stated Guy Debord (1995:12). "The whole of life . . . presents itself as an immense accumulation of *spectacles*." In the spectacle, even deceit deceives itself. Baudrillard (1994) made a similar point. He began his book *Simulacra and Simulation* relating a Lewis Caroll fable of the royal cartographer who created a very detailed map of the empire. This map was so detailed that it covered the entire territory of the empire! This map simulation, this model of the real, was indistinguishable from the real. Remarkably, at the beginning of the century, our models have gotten even better. We no longer need the territory that the map simulates. The map now precedes the territory. The real is the vestige. We traffic in images, video displays, copy machines, computer web sites, concepts, and abstractions. We are now cognizant only of the reality that is constructed. The empire itself is in doubt, but the myth of it endures. We know little of reality, but quite a bit about "welfare dependency," the "war on drugs," the "deficit crisis," and "three strikes and you're out." Suppose reality is like the recent crisis produced for the television audience—images, copies, imitations, and reproductions. How does one distinguish real music from that produced by a synthesizer?

Amid the spectacle of simulacra we then ask policy analysts, program evaluators, and public managers to preserve the reality principle. We want them to tell us whether policies are effective or ineffective, whether programs work or don't work. We want to know whether or not efficiency and performance have improved. MacIntyre (1984:75) asked the naughty question straight out: "But what if effectiveness is part of a masquerade of social control rather than a reality? What if effectiveness were a quality widely imputed to managers and bureaucrats both by themselves and others, but in fact a quality which rarely exists apart from this imputation?" From MacIntyre's perspective, management is theater. As program evaluators recognize, it doesn't matter that a program is effective or not. For kudos, the important thing is to demonstrate success—the theater of performance evaluation is more important than performance itself. Data that *show* results are more important than actual results. Doing the job gets you nowhere; signifying you did means everything. These are tough acts for managers and evaluators, but they are acts. This is not management, but histrionics.

What is the show about? In a system of facts, means-ends logic, programs, accountability, goals, and values the reality principle must be preserved. There is no way, within the system, to accommodate the rumbling doubt that has now been heard (but urgently ignored). Hence the language of managerial effectiveness necessarily refers only to itself, its own logic, its own rationality, its own affirmation processes. As it does so, it continues to cohere in a self-referential sort of way. To retain the semblance of coherence, managers, administrators, evaluators, and analysts are held responsible. Placing responsibility with them is necessary if the vocabulary of management and control is to fit together. There are language games and "moves" that are inherent in such self-referential vocabularies (Wittgenstein, 1958). This would apply to the community known as astrophysicists, the Branch Davidians, the Crips, or the community of public administrationists. For example, the term *Dasein* makes sense in the context of German phenomenology, but used elsewhere the term mystifies. Or, to take another example from philosophy, Tarski's insight that "The statement 'snow is white' is true if and only if snow is white" is regarded as profound only inside the language game called analytical philosophy. Outside that language game, that particular move would make little sense. So there is a coexistence, not always friendly, of many paradigms, many subcultures. There is no universal measuring stick that can standardize these multifarious languages.

Not even efficiency can perform this standardizing function. Efficiency is (a) a social construction that (b) is culturally relative to the aims of industrial society, (c) has been heightened to the level of ineluctable moral concept; and (d) this may be regrettable (Farmer, 1995). Regrettable or not, efficiency is embedded in a particular language game that is familiar to most readers of this volume. Efficiency is hence a part of a language game, part of a grand narrative that has its own meaningful vocabulary. Rules of this grand narrative are endogenous to the narrative. The truth or falsehood of its conceptualizations are not universally meaningful.

One must get inside the subculture of "management effectiveness" to understand the story. The story of any subculture reveals its core values. All social formations—including the one formed by the field of public administration—have a language that is to some extent unique and self-referential. Not only the subcultures have been disturbed by the rumbling doubt: The grand meaning systems of democratic values, founding-father values, efficiency, neutral competence, and popular sovereignty have also been unsettled. These once-incorrigible pillars of surety have shrunk in dimension. They are now self-referential narratives that are historically contingent and situational. The meaning of these once-grand narratives is malleable. Fixed meaning, which is an important assumption of policy and administrative rules, becomes questionable when doubt takes hold. But doubt we must. Think of the difference in meaning of the term *control* to a social experimenter, a parent trying to potty-train an infant, and a traffic engineer. Best and Kellner (1997) argue, "Fixed meaning is replaced with inter-determinacy, incompleteness, uncertainty, ambiguity, contingency and chaos." Meaning can be known, but it varies with context.

There is a small contingent of public administrationists who have reported on the increasing proximity of this rumbling doubt. A few of the earliest such works are those of Fox and Miller (1995), Farmer (1995), and McSwite (1997). In very different ways, these works invite a public administration that adopts an attitude of skepticism toward the grand foundational narratives. They all place a new priority on language and discourse. This new focus on linguistic interpretation has raised to prominence some new work in the field of organizational discourse. In the next section we survey that literature so that we may, in the subsequent section, focus on certain power and social dynamics of managerial discourse.

THE DISCOURSE MOVEMENT IN ORGANIZATION THEORY

Organizational theorists are increasingly interested in discourse whereby members of organizations create shared meanings. The study of organizational discourse is becoming increasingly important because as Fairclough (1995) notes, institutions are "speech communities." Similarly, Mumby and Clair (1997) assert that organizations are created by their members through discourse. It is primarily through discourse that members of organizations create a "coherent social reality" (p. 181).

Discourse analysis has been primarily thought of as a linguistic method of analysis. Analyzable aspects of discourse include text, context, alternative and marginal discourses, and missing discourse, according to Fairclough (1995). The most important component of discourse is text, because one must first identify the relevant texts before undertaking discourse analysis.

Discourse Analysis and Organizational Texts

According to Fairclough, "Texts are social spaces in which two fundamental social processes simultaneously occur: cognition and representation of the world, and social interaction" (p. 6). Text is the principal material through which people interact and through which they understand and interpret phenomena. Within this frame, organizations have been described as stories and novels, narratives, metaphors, conversations, and language games (Keenoy et al., 1997). Discourse analysis may thus be viewed as a tool for interpreting organizational texts.

Text could take any of three forms: written, verbal, or nonlinguistic (Fairclough, 1995). The first is the traditional form, in which texts are pieces of written language. Written texts may be the easiest to obtain; they include annual reports, written vision statements, memos, and e-mail. The second and broader form of text includes spoken texts such as utterances and verbal expressions of all kinds.

Finally, texts need not be linguistic; they can include pictures, buildings, or even music. For example, cubicle height can be seen as meaningful text. Some organizations assign cubicles with different heights to various types of staff. Professional staff may have higher walls and a greater sense of privacy; clerical staff may have shorter walls and be clearly visible to people who walk by. What is the message being conveyed with the different heights? One message could be that of difference: Clerical staff differ from professional staff and hence may need closer supervision (or at least observation). If, as Fairclough's third definition claims, texts can be nonlinguistic, then organizational practices themselves can be considered texts. With respect to public organizations, Balfour and Measaros (1994) argue that organizational texts include organizational practices such as the interaction between organizational participants and stakeholders. The interaction between a social worker and a welfare recipient may be analyzed by using discourse analysis.

Nontexts and Contexts

When analyzing organizational texts, one may argue that it is important to study not only what is in the texts but what has been left out (Bradshaw, 1996; Fairclough, 1995). Bradshaw asserts that it is only by identifying what has been left out of the text, which she calls significant silences, that one can find the underlying ideologies within organizations.

In addition to the types of texts and the omissions from these texts, it is important to understand both the context of the text and the interpretations of it by those within the organization. Taken out of context, texts can seem to have very different meanings (Fairclough, 1995). Therefore, it is worthwhile when analyzing organizational texts to be cognizant of the context of the particular text under examination. One such context is the institutional setting within which discourse takes place. Organizational context can affect discourse in two ways (Fairclough, 1995): First, the organization facilitates social actions. Second, organizations constrain social action. Organizations provide their members with a "frame for action, without which they could not act, but it thereby constrains them to act within that frame" (p. 38). Language constrains/enables in similar fashion. Without a language we cannot speak. But when we speak a particular language, we have to say things in a certain way.

The production and consumption of texts are important to understanding organizational discourse. The production of texts is only one part of the process. The author's intentions may have inspired the text, but the author does not have total say-so. The text is interpreted or consumed by its audience. All of the actors within a discourse have their own context, which influences their interpretations (Schiffrin, 1997). The audience's interpretation may differ significantly from the interpretation intended by the author. Fairclough (1995) argues that as texts are distributed across boundaries of discourse they are transformed. Hence texts do not have fixed meanings. They are situationally contingent. The meaning of a text (say, a simple phrase such as "What do you know?") could vary from one situation to another. Organizations may be seen as efforts to stabilize a discourse that may otherwise seem erratic.

Organizations as Multiple Discourses

Organizations are collections of discourses. Barnard (1938) implicitly acknowledged this with his notion of formal and informal groups. For Keenoy and associates (1997) there are two types of organizational discourse: monologues and dialogues. A monologue is essentially one story viewed from the perspective of the dominant group. A dialogue recognizes that there are multiple voices and autonomous discourses that contribute meaning and interpretation of a given organizational reality. Fox and Miller (1995) describe monologues and dialogues as few-talk, many-talk, and some-talk. To them, some-talk represents the sustained form of coherent discourse. Few-talk would be equivalent to a monologue because there is little interchange between individuals. Many-talk could potentially be a dialogue, but because the participants are talking past one another, the interaction resembles babbled anarchy. A some-talk dialogue takes place when participants contribute not only by talking but also by listening and responding to other participants.

Analysts who view organizations as a singular discourse may emphasize the common mission and goals being pursued by the organization. Often it seems that management theorists speak of the organization as a singular discourse—that of efficiency, productivity, and proper hierarchical role. The discourse may seem singular only because of its dominance. Perhaps the few-talk discourse is made to seem singular for political reasons: The fewer discourses acknowledged, the less difficulty in pursuing the dominant discourse. The point here is that an astute analyst will appreciate that the dominant discourse is not likely to be the only discourse. There are always remainders, the marginalized discourses of "others" (Honig, 1993). From a sociological point of view, it is necessary when studying organizational discourse to go beyond the dominant discourse to identify alternative discourses. Management theorists are less likely to do this, instead deliberately narrowing the discourse. For example, rational organizations celebrate "goal specificity" as a main reason for the focus on one singular discourse—that of how to be more efficient (Scott, 1992).

Those concerned with organizational discourse are not likely to enjoin the predisposition for a singular discourse. Boje (1995) describes organizations as being centers of multiple discourses. He uses the analogy of a long-running Los Angeles play called *Tamara.* Traditionally, plays are monologues: The audience sits and listens to the actors recite their lines. There is little, if any, actual involvement by the audience. Traditionally, this is how we have viewed organizations. Organizational researchers look for the monologue and, on finding it, report their findings. Boje argues that this is not the way organizations really function. There are multiple discourses taking place at multiple levels similar to those in *Tamara.*

The audience at *Tamara* interacts with the actors by following them throughout the set, which has 12 rooms. As Boje (1995) points out, if there are 12 rooms and 12 characters, there is potential for 726 discourses. Audience members choose the characters they wish to follow. For example, suppose that an audience member chooses to follow the butler. In the first scene there is a conversation between the maid and the butler. This is the only discourse that the audience member is privy to because all other conversations are taking place in other rooms on the set. At the conclusion of the scene, the butler and maid separate and go into different rooms to interact with other characters. The audience member must decide whether to follow the butler or the maid into the next scene. The result is that audience members neither see the "whole" play nor see the same play other audience members who choose to follow other characters see.

The *Tamara* metaphor captures a dynamic that repeats itself in many organizations. There may be multiple competing discourses occurring simultaneously within an organization. As a result of identifying only one dominant discourse an organizational researcher may draw inappropriate conclusions. Analysts must look beyond the monologues and look for the various competing dialogues taking place.

Watson (1995) discussed the role of two competing discourses and found that either may be dominant at one time, depending on the circumstance. Studying an organization that had recently been formed by the merger of two companies, he found two competing discourses: the empowerment discourse and the control discourse. (These discourses reminded us of Theory Y and Theory X, though this may not have been Watson's intention.) He pointed out that both of these discourses were available to managers within the merged organizations. Some managers subscribed to one but not the other. Interestingly, others would make use of either, depending on the circumstance. They recognized that at various times empowerment was a better strategy than control, and vice versa.

Increasing the repertoire of discourse styles may be a useful strategy for public sector organizations. Public agencies interact in particular ways with legislative agents, executive personnel, the judicial system, citizens, colleagues from other agencies, and public interest groups. Even Boje's (1995) characterization of organizations as *Tamara* presents organizations as if, counterfactually, they were self-contained with little outside interaction. To extend the *Tamara* metaphor, the stage actors would be communicating with others outside the set. When looked at this way, the number of potential discourses that are relevant to any practitioner in public administration increases dramatically.

Some have argued that it is not merely a question of appreciating multiple discourses; sometimes one discourse is used to control organizational members. For example, Deetz (1992) notes that organizational discourse is used to suppress differences and to maintain managerial discipline. Bullis and Glaser (1992) further argue that bureaucratic discourse is used to categorize, compartmentalize, and control employee behavior. These works bring out an underlying tension in the organizational culture that is repeated in all social formations from the level of society to the level of subgroup: Some discourses are dominant and others take place on the periphery.

Critical Discourse Analysis

Organizational meaning is created through discourse, but this does not mean that all discourses within organizations carry equal weight. There are many marginal discourses that remain unheard because of the volume of the locally dominant discourse. This possibility of a dominant discourse inspires doubt about its legitimacy as the dominant discourse, and curiosity about how marginalized discourses become so. It is not self-evident that one discourse should be privileged over another. Mumby (1988) argues that the exercise of power is intimately connected with organizational sense making, which is in turn shaped by modes of communication. He wants to uncover the relationships among communication, power, and organizations.

We will take up the question of domination and discourse by revisiting the notion of monologic discourse. One of Fairclough's (1995) chief concerns was the role that discourse plays in ideology and power within organizations. Hence, Fairclough argues for the importance of using critical discourse analysis, which combines discourse analysis with critical theory. According to Mumby and Clair (1997), "Critical studies see organizations not simply as social collectives where shared meaning is produced, but rather as sites of struggle where different groups compete to share the social reality of organizations in ways that serve their own interests" (p. 182). Critical discourse analysts are interested in the relationship between discourse and power, but they are also interested in the inequities that are created by this relationship (Mumby and Clair, 1997). Mills (1997) argues that the critical discourse analyst has a concern about the relationship between the individual and social structures. These analysts would argue that, on the surface, these inequities are not visible, and, therefore, it is incumbent upon the analyst to delve more deeply into the discourse within the organization to gain a clearer understanding of these power inequities. Mumby (1988) further argues that organizations can exercise power because they control the structure of the discourse in such a way that the claims made by these dominant discourses (which are often expressed as monologues) are unchallenged.

It is often difficult to discover the alternative and marginalized discourses within an organization. Dominant practices are seen as normal or natural, whereas alternative practices have become marginalized and take place on the periphery. It is through the dominant discourse that ideology is transmitted to the actors within the organization. The ideology becomes naturalized and accepted as common sense by members of the organization. Hence the goal of critical discourse analysis is to denaturalize the dominant discourse (Fairclough, 1995).

Bradshaw (1996) argues that it is important to identify how the dominant discourse is created: "[E]xposing how the texts create the impression of one, unitary, and objective reality through reliance on historical convention, the legal system, or apparently neutral practices allows me to reveal the multiple realities contained in the texts and to show how they privilege the existing power holders" (p. 301). In other words, analyzing the genesis of the dominant discourse engenders a clearer understanding of the marginalized discourses within the organization. Discourse plays a role in domination, yet it is equally important to recognize the role it may play in resistance to domination (Foucault, 1978). Within organizations there are discourses that question organizational domination. In management, these discourses would be considered deviant to the extent that they opposed the current regime's organizational control.

Aside from the question of control, it may also be the case that different discourses are simply not commensurable with one another. Their languages may be too disparate. Subgroups (even dominant ones) may anxiously retreat into their own meaning-making systems, unable to converse outside them. This retreat in the face of disparate views is the topic of the final section.

ALL DISCOURSES ARE PARTIAL AND PERSPECTIVAL

The dominant public management discourse insists on a singular public with a singular administration. The privileged vocabulary in modern organizations commemorates the values of hierarchy and control and efficiency. In public administration, this is a key part of the language of managerial effectiveness. But this vocabulary has now been cast in doubt, and alternative discourses have an opening. McSwite (1997) labeled the language game "men of reason," which is characterized by a consciously rational attitude. Its vocabulary includes such concepts such as human nature, facts, accountability, technical knowledge, rationality, effectiveness, standardization, the necessity of hierarchy, the public interest, and the subordination of public administrators to the public will (usually as manifested by elected officials). The narrower language game of management explicitly relies on concepts such as problem-solving logic, expert knowledge, and efficiency and effectiveness. In management practice, potential action must be justified in terms of productivity—or it has not been justified. Those uninterested in efficiency, instrumental rationality, and hierarchical control are uninterested in management or management's agenda.

There is resistance in the management literature to moving outside the parameters of that language game. From Weber's rationalization to Taylor's (1911) scientific management and Fayol's (1918) and Gulick and Urwick's (1937) principles, we witness a public management that speaks a certain kind of language. In the contemporary management literature, this language expresses itself, quite appropriately, as managerialism (Pollitt, 1990) or, perhaps, "new managerialism" or "reinvention of government."

The propositions embedded in this language game—for example, the proposition that policy analysts or public managers could make calculated moves on the basis of objective measurement of reality—are now being shaken. Are they mere narratives? Hummel (1991) argued that managers learn more from stories than they do from scientific experiments, that stories are as valid as science. But Hummel's openness to disparate narratives was curtailed several years later when the rumble of doubt began to be felt. He posed the following question (Hummel, 1997): "How can there be an administration of the public where there no longer is a single public? Clearly," he answered himself, "to the extent that there is no longer a single public, it will become difficult to administer it" (p. 29). Hence did Hummel surmise that, if the doubt were allowed to rumble unfettered, the end of public administration was nigh! Instead of public administration, we would have nonadministration of different publics. Hence, in the self-referential linguistic world of managerial effectiveness, public administration works only with a single public, and with a singular administration.

If contemporary attacks upon managerial theory remain mostly unacknowledged, as we claimed in the first paragraph, it is because language games tend to be insular. The internal coherence of managerialism is at stake. Evidence in one language game (for example, managerialism) does not translate as evidence in other language games (critical discourse theory, for example). Within managerialism, all speakers sympathize with the common vocabulary of managerial effectiveness. To them it is a real thing rather than a form of histrionics.

Discourses that do not ritualize efficiency, managerial effectiveness, and hierarchy are not merely different dialects; they are different language games. There is no basis for registering certain kinds of complaints against managerialism except from outside it. Of course, this line of reasoning that emphasizes the self-referential quality of managerialism applies to any language game. All language games are self-referential. The meaning of the term *incommensurable discourse* rests on such lack of cross-cultural connection. Language games seem to prefer a singular discourse—their own.

CONCLUSION

Talking about management as we have may seem to serve the purpose of negating the core mind-set of managerialism. We have opened the core assumptions to the elements and have done so without the deference that managerialism has come to expect. Yet our intent is not so much to deny managerialism, as to show its finitude and particularity. It is a language game that requires a certain context if it is to make any sense at all. The reality that is constructed by managerialism is different from the reality that would be constructed in a different discourse. Employing the "style of doubt," we have refused to "buy in" to managerialism. There are alternative accounts, in addition to the one about orderly organizational reality possessed of a true and unified purpose.

REFERENCES

Balfour, D. L., and Mesaros, W. (1994). Connecting the local narratives: Public administration as a hermeneutic science. *Public Administration Review. 54:* 559–563.

Barnard, C. (1938). *The Functions of the Executive.* Harvard University Press, Cambridge, Mass.

Baudrillard, J. (1994). *Simulacra and Simulation.* University of Michigan Press, Anna Arbor.

Best, S., and Kellner, D. (1997). *The Postmodern Turn.* The Guilford Press, New York.

Boje, D. M. (1995). Stories of the storytelling organization: A postmodern analysis of Disney as "Tamara-Land." *Academy of Management Journal. 38:* 997–1035.

Bradshaw, P. (1996). Women as constituent directors: Re-reading current texts using a feminist-postmodernist approach. In *Postmodern Management and Organization Theory* (D. M. Boje, R. P. Gephart, Jr., and T. J. Thatchenkery eds.). Sage, Thousand Oaks, Calif., 95–124.

Bullis, C., and Glaser, H. (1992). Bureaucratic discourse and the goddess: Towards an ecofeminist critique and rearticulation. *Journal of Organizational Change. 5:* 50–60.

Connell, A. F., and Nord, W. R. (1996). The bloodless coup: The infiltration of organization science by uncertainty and values (Great Britain, United States, and Canada). *The Journal of Applied Behavioral Science. 32:* 407–27.

Debord, G. (1995). *The Society of the Spectacle.* Zone Books, New York.

Deetz, S. (1992). *Democracy in an Age of Corporate Colonization.* State University of New York Press, New York.

Fairclough, N. (1995). *Critical Discourse Analysis: The Critical Study of Language.* Longman Group, Essex, England.

Farmer, D. (1995). *The Language of Public Administration.* University of Alabama Press, Montgomery.

Fayol, H. (1918). *General and Industrial Management.* Pitman, London.

Foucault, M. (1978). *The History of Sexuality: An Introduction,* vol. 1. Penguin, Harmondsworth, England.

Foucault, M. (1979). *Discipline and Punish: The Birth of the Prison* (Alan Sheridan, trans.) Random House, New York.

Fox, C. J., and Miller, H. T. (1995). *Postmodern Public Administration: Toward Discourse.* Sage, Thousand Oaks, Calif.

Gortner, H. F., Mahler, J., and Nicholson, J. B. (1987). *Organization Theory: A Public Perspective.* Dorsey Press, Chicago.

Gulick, L., and Urwick, L., eds. (1937). *Papers on the Science of Administration.* Institute of Public Administration, Columbia University, New York.

Harmon, M. (1995). *Responsibility as Paradox: A Critique of Rational Discourse on Government.* Sage, Thousand Oaks, Calif.

Honig, Bonnie (1993). *Political Theory and the Displacement of Politics.* Cornell University Press, Ithaca, N.Y.

Hummel, R. P. (1991). Stories Managers Tell: Why They Are as Valid as Science. *Public Administration Review. 51:* 31–41.

Hummel, R. (1997). Ideocracy: The cultural uses of modern post-ism in a late capital economy. In *Postmodernism, "Reality" and Public Administration: A Discourse* (H. Miller and C. Fox, eds.). Chatelaine Press, Burke, Va.

Ingersoll, V. H., and Adams, G. B. (1992). *The Tacit Organization.* JAI Press, Greenwich, Conn.

Keenoy, T., Oswick, C., and Grant, D. (1997). Organizational discourses: Text and context. *Organization. 4*(2): 147–157.

MacIntyre, A. (1984). *After Virtue.* Duckworth, London.

Marcuse, H. (1964). *One Dimensional Man: Studies in the Ideology of Advanced Industrial Society.* Beacon Press, Boston.

McSwite, O. C. (1997). *Legitimacy in Public Administration: A Discourse Analysis.* Sage, Thousand Oaks, Calif.

Mills, S. (1997). *Discourse.* Routledge, London.

Mumby, D. K. (1988). *Communication and Power in Organizations: Discourse, Ideology and Domination.* Ablex, Nothwood, N.J.

Mumby, D. K., and Clair, R. P. (1997). Organizational Discourse. In *Discourse as Social Interaction* (T. A. van Dijk, ed.). Sage, London, pp. 181–205.

Pollit, C. (1990). *Managerialism and the Public Sector: The Anglo-American Experience.* Basil Blackwell, Oxford.

Schiffrin, D. (1997). Theory and Method in Discourse Analysis: What Context for What Unit? *Language & Communication. 17:* 75–92.

Scott, W. Richard (1992). *Organizations: Rational, Natural and Open Systems,* 3rd ed. Prentice Hall, Englewood Cliffs, N.J.

Scott, W. G., and Hart, D. K. (1979). *Organizational America.* Houghton Mifflin, Boston.

Taylor, F. W. (1911). *The Principles of Scientific Management.* Harper, New York.

Thayer, F. C. (1981). *An End to Hierarchy and Competition: Administration in the Post Affluent World,* 2nd ed. Franklin Watts, New York.

Watson, T. J. (1995). Rhetoric, Discourse and Argument in Organizational Sense-Making: A Reflexive Tale. *Organization Studies. 16:* 805–822

Wilson, W. (1887). The Study of Administration. *Political Science Quarterly. 2:* 191–222.

Wittgenstein, L. (1958). *Philosophical Investigations,* 3rd ed. (G.E.M. Anscombe, trans.) Prentice Hall, Englewood Cliffs, N.J.

30

NGOs and Grass-Roots Organizations in Developing Countries

Keith M. Henderson
Department of Political Science,
State University College-Buffalo,
Buffalo, New York

This chapter is concerned with the service delivery and related policy-input roles of nongovernmental organizations (NGOs) and grass-roots organizations in developing countries. The basic theme is that NGOs and grass-roots organizations are now playing a large and growing role in providing basic services (health, education, housing, social welfare, agrarian assistance, infrastructure construction and maintenance, microcredit, etc.) and in service-related policy advocacy, have the potential for a greater role, but under current conditions are constrained by a number of obstacles. Those obstacles include uncertain financing and erratic regulation, lack of coordination, and fragmentation into small and often rival operations. Additionally, NGOs frequently lack managerial skills and fall short on standards of transparency and accountability. Their popularity may mask preferred service-delivery activity in the purely public sector, as Tendler has documented (1997: 151–165) and even for-profit delivery by the private sector. Few general rules are supportable at this time, but it is safe to say that carefully crafted linkages among the public, private, and voluntary sectors are usually required for the optimization of NGO and grass-roots activity. These linkages also involve external donors, intermediate organizations (also sometimes called NGOs) that seek or provide funding, and other actors in particular circumstances (e.g., United Nations [UN] peacekeeping forces, the Catholic church, guerrilla organizations, philanthropic enterprises such as the Soros Foundation or the Aga Khan Foundation, etc.).

The perceived advantages of NGOs as service providers in developing countries are their proximity to the persons served (often they are charitable organizations with long experience in remote areas and/or urban slums); their cost-effectiveness (use of volunteers; reliance on donations), their integrity (in contrast to perceptions of lack of integrity in government agencies), their flexibility and innovativeness ("laboratories for social experimentation"), and their dedication and responsiveness. As public employee unions are quick to point out, salaries and benefits are frequently substantially lower than those for government employees, and volunteer staffs may lack the expertise of government officials.

The first task here—because of the widespread confusion over terms—is to define terms. The second is to survey current scope and impact of the organizations with which we are concerned: those focused on development and able to provide basic services. The third is to assess relationships with host governments and changes necessary to augment properly or substitute for government and private efforts, and to overcome the obstacles cited. The changes necessary involve "scaling up" and reconfiguration of the service mix.

MAKING DISTINCTIONS

Considerable disagreement exists on the proper definitions of *nongovernmental organization* and *grass-roots organization. Private voluntary association* is a similar term for both and would be a preferred designation if not for its unfamiliarity and limited use. Similarly, *support* or *intermediary* when added to *NGO, grass-roots organization,* or *PVO* clarifies the second-tier status of many "NGOs," hence "grass-roots support organization" or "intermediary NGO" when some aggregation of smaller units and/or conduit for funding and external contact is the focus. Thomas Carroll (1992) and Edwards and Hulme (1992) provide book-length treatments of these intermediary organizations, which are a step removed from primary NGOs or grass-roots organizations. *Northern* and *Southern* (signifying headquarters location); *membership* and *nonmembership* (usually corresponding to grass-roots organizations and professionally staffed NGOs, respectively), and other distinctions are often made. For example, Fisher (1998: 4) provides a useful distinction between member-serving grass-roots organizations (GROs) based in local communities and grass-roots support organizations (GRSOs) usually staffed by professionals and nationally or regionally based. She also defines two other types of Third World NGOs: networks linking local communities and networks of GRSOs themselves.

NGOs are frequently equated with the "Third Sector" (the others, of course, are the public and private), but numerous dissimilar groupings are also in that residual category: universities, research foundations, think tanks, unions, political parties, the media, and others. Gray areas abound, calling for telling distinctions without overly complicated definitions. Common law and civil law legal traditions are at variance over the precise classification of NGOs in many countries, as are official designations in some post-Communist countries and in Latin America. In the latter, NGOs/grass-roots organizations are often subsumed under the Spanish acronym *OPC* (for organizations involving community participation).

Lester Salamon and Helmut Anheier and associates at the Johns Hopkins Comparative Nonprofit Sector Project have examined in detail the "terminological tangle" regarding "nonprofit" organizations and pursued a common definition of the nonprofit sector cross-nationally. Their exhaustive effort provides a useful overall guide for the broader Third Sector within which NGOs/grass-roots organizations are a subspecies (Salamon and Anheier, 1997). Others have also spent considerable effort on definitional issues (e.g. Vakil, 1997).

For most purposes, the United Nations definition of *NGOs* is adequate: any nonprofit, voluntary citizens' group that is organized on a local, national, or international level and task-oriented as well as driven by persons with a common interest.

Following Fisher, Salamon and Anheier, Vakil, and the United Nations terminology, the intent here is to deal with that portion of the nonprofit (or Third) sector in developing and postsocialist countries that is capable of providing services and is both organized and development-oriented but outside the realms of government and profit-seeking activity. The twofold distinction between *nongovernmental* and *grass-roots* reflects Fisher's nationally or regionally based development assistance organizations, on the one hand, and community-based membership groupings on the other. Generally, NGOs are officially recognized by some authority (usually the host government) and typically registered and at least minimally regulated. Grass-roots organizations may be very small, in flux, and somewhat unspecified in their hierarchical character.

NGOs include established organizations based in Northern countries but operating in developing and postsocialist areas (International Red Cross, CARE, Catholic Relief Services, and hundreds of others) and usually smaller groupings based in developing and postsocialist countries (Southern NGOs) and indigenous in origin. The latter are frequently linked to the former as well as to each other and to donor agencies either directly or through intermediaries that—as already suggested—are sometimes called grass-roots support organizations (GRSOs) or equivalent names (e.g., *intermediate NGOs:* INGOs).

Grass-roots organizations derive—in most cases—from spontaneous indigenous activity by local farmers, water users, tradespersons, housewives, intellectuals, threatened urbanites or rural dwellers, or other groupings seeking redress of grievances; pressuring of host or foreign governments and corporations; or management/self-control of infrastructure, educational, social welfare, health, economic development, conservation, and other projects and activities. Hence, they are usually "bottom-up" in origin, whereas NGOs are more likely to be "top-down."

Excluded from the current analysis are organizations and political/social movements without any appreciable service-delivery functions or involvement in service-related policy-making.

However, it should be recognized that unorganized protest can lead to organizational activity, and even small neighborhood associations can develop into important service-delivery mechanisms, as occurred in Venezuela in the 1980s; according to Steve Ellner (1999), neighborhood associations issued property certificates in the barrios, undertook anticrime measures, and negotiated with street gangs.

Shifting forms, expansion or demise of grass-roots activity, international attention and support, and local political conditions keep many of these organizations in a fluid situation, and—indeed—their organizational status may vary over time from extremely informal to highly structured.

In summary, the definition here—approximating usual usage—is that an *NGO* is a nonprofit, voluntary group organized on a local, national, or international level and task-oriented. *Grass-roots organizations* are similar but community-based, member-serving, less structured, smaller, and generally lacking in professional staff.

EXTENT AND IMPACT

There are no precise estimates of the total number of NGOs and grass-roots organizations in the Third and former Second Worlds. The United Nations "consultative status" NGOs—consisting only of large, international organizations—increased from 41 in 1948, to 377 in 1968, to 1550 30 years later (Secretary General, 1998). But this in no way approximates the total number of NGOs.

One reliable estimate in 1991 placed the number of Southern NGOs—the largest category those related to health—at 10,000 to 20,000 (Edwards and Hulme, 1992: 13). The same numbers were cited by Black for only the Southern NGOs working with Northern counterparts (Black: 1991: 75). And others—counting the smallest groupings—have found 10,000 in Pakistan alone (Bennett, 1998) and 12,000 registered in Poland (USAID, 1996). Clearly, the latter figures include "grass-roots organizations" of which there are probably over 200,000 in Asia, Africa, and Latin America (Fisher, 1998: 6).

What is indisputable is that the number of NGOs/grass-roots organizations has increased rapidly in recent years. In many countries, the number registered with host governments—one guide to expansion—increased dramatically in recent years. But, according to Salamon and Anheier (1997: 25), even registration figures may understate the increase. They report that in Thailand, for example, registration requirements are so complex that groups remain unregistered and operate as "forums," "units," or "working groups."

It is now widely recognized that NGOs and grass-roots organizations are playing a growing role in developing (and, also, developed) countries. In part this is due to the general disaffection with government activity and, also, to the widely heralded "new public management" focus on alternatives and performance-based measurement. Additionally, it is the result of assertiveness by NGOs/grass-roots organizations themselves and their increasing skill in advancing policy positions in international forums as well as undertaking service-delivery functions. Elsewhere, I have referred to these as *push* factors operating together with *pull* factors to increase the significance of NGOs/grass-roots organizations in the international arena (Henderson, 1999: 54–57). One need only be reminded of the voice of thousands of NGOs at UN conferences such as Rio (Environment and Development) or Beijing (Fourth World Conference on Women) in pressing for agenda reform and action in the areas, respectively, of environment and women's rights. A "reverse agenda" takes monopoly control of the agenda from the political leaders and incorporates the concerns of organized groups. As pressures produce responses, these concerns are made compatible with the intentions of multilateral and bilateral lending institutions pursuing their own neoliberal agendas.

Although humanitarian, environmental, human rights, and women's rights NGOs may be primarily concerned with advocacy rather than service delivery, they impact governmental services through their pressures and persuasiveness—often assisted by media coverage—and, like other types of NGOs, have public administration significance. They have policy-input functions either through direct participation in decision making or indirectly. As expressed in the "Hanoi consensus," adopted at a United Nations meeting in Vietnam in October 1998, intended to review progress on the World Summit for Social Development Programme of Action, "Nongovernmental organisations should continue their advocacy and dialogue with donors to promote greater accountability and better targeting of basic social services on the poor" (OECD, 1998: 76).

RELATIONS WITH HOST GOVERNMENTS

Except in the rare cases (e.g., Somalia) in which there is no functioning government, NGOs/grass-roots organizations are registered, regulated, coordinated, or at least recognized by the governments where they operate. At one extreme they are partially or fully subsidized subcontractors for host governments and international donors contributing through host governments. At the other, they are antagonists that may be shut down or prevented from operating or—more usually—just ignored.

Host governments have begun to recognize the extent and impact of NGOs/grass-roots organizations, including their threat to established ways of administration.

As Mohiddin indicates (1998: 8):

> African governments are beginning to acknowledge the existence of African NGOs and are conceding a participatory role to some of them. African governments are suspicious partly because they do not really understand the role of NGOs or pressure groups in a thriving democracy. Partly because of the manner in which a number of African NGOs were created. And because NGOs' subsequent behaviour has made governments suspect their sincerity and usefulness. African governments regard some of these NGOs as politically inspired, or agents of foreign interests acting to create confusion and instability in the country.

Similar suspicions are evident in other world areas, and there is no doubt that a number of "bogus" NGOs have arisen in the current supportive neoliberal atmosphere. In poor areas, they may provide opportunities for remunerative middle-class employment and proliferate under encouraging circumstances. They may serve merely as convenient conduits for available funds and be established by government or ex-government officials themselves in anticipation of funding.

In a few circumstances, NGOs substitute completely for government services, effectively replacing the absent state and obviating much of usual interaction with host governments. For example, health programs have been operated by the Somalia Red Crescent Society (the Integrated Health Program) and the Afghan Red Crescent Society (Integrated Health and Development Program). In the Congo, the Catholic church has instituted health and development activities. In areas such as Bosnia and Kosovo, international aid agencies provide "temporary" services on an ongoing basis under international peacekeeping administrations.

Eva Sandberg (1994: 21–27) has appropriately suggested that there are five basic forms of interaction with host governments in the African context and has evaluated the strengths and weaknesses of each:

- Model one: bypassing the state with no coordinating contacts and only ad hoc, informal links
- Model two: coordination through a single office
- Model three: functional coordination by the specialized ministry (e.g., Health Ministry for health NGOs; Education Ministry for education NGOs)

Model four: decentralized linkages in the field by regional or local government units with cross-sectoral integration
Model five: multifocused, stratified structure without a formal organizational arrangement

According to Sandberg, the latter should be the preferred method in Africa. Modified only slightly for regional variations, these "ideal types" provide a useful summary of the different modes of interaction between NGOs/grass-roots organizations and the governments of the countries where they operate. The nature of the interaction may be influenced by historical and legal traditions, political support patterns, preferences of international donors such as the World Bank, and additional factors.

If the entire developing and postsocialist world is included, a large array of oversight/coordinating arrangements are found. In some cases, secondary organizations act as mediators, or consortia of NGOs present a single contact point.

In Togo, for example, a consortium of NGOs known as TADA provided such a linkage but was dissolved in 1986, after operating successfully since 1979. Its "vacuous institutional development"—in the words of Helmut Anheier (1994: 156–160)—fell victim to a World Bank/NGO project largely controlled by the Togolese government. In my own observations in Togo in December 1992 and January 1993, foreign NGOs were operating without contact with the government, which was on a continuing Civil Service strike.

In the Philippines—on the basis of the 1992 Local Government Code—government decentralization of services to provincial and municipal levels (and reassignment of central officials to localities) included provision for incorporation of NGOs and "people's organizations" into local units (Turner and Halligan, 1999: 149). Such integration is rare; the usual linkage involves a subordination of the NGOs to the existing institutions of central and local government or parallel status. In many circumstances, single contact points, multiple contact points with different central ministries, and decentralized contact points—in sometimes bewildering array—characterize NGO/grass-roots–host government interaction. Attempts to rationalize arrangements along the lines of Sandberg's second type include the Office for Government–NGO Relations in Chile and the Presidential Commissioner on Government–NGO Relations in Venezuela. Such agencies have the potential of ameliorating the difficulties of Sandberg's third type as various case studies illustrate; coordination often works better at a level above the functional ministries. Single contact points, however, may not be feasible where a large number of NGOs is matched by a small, central staff unable to keep track of them.

In some areas, there is a long history of interaction between NGOs/grass-roots organizations and specific agencies of government. Fisher mentions water users' associations in Indonesia, Pakistan, the Philippines, Sri Lanka, Thailand, Mexico, Peru, and Ecuador; pastoralist organizations are another example, as are—more recently—village health committees and parent groups who construct and maintain schools (Fisher, 1993: 38–39). Esman (1991: 463) adds the examples of service cooperatives, community health centers, and credit unions.

In many circumstances, however, the interaction of NGOs/grass-roots organizations and host governments is a relatively new challenge—often driven by international aid efforts and tied directly to funding—with few guidelines as to appropriate coordinating structures. As with long-established linkages, new interactions can either magnify popular support for the government or diminish it. As Sandberg points out (1994: 13), NGOs have "a tremendous ability to expand the scope of the state's reach."

In repressive governmental circumstances (as in Latin American dictatorships prior to democratization), NGOs and grass-roots organizations tend to define themselves in terms of opposition to the state; in more democratic circumstances they may enter into a variety of mutually satisfactory cooperative arrangements with the state.

Fisher—one of the best guides to these issues—distinguishes regional contrasts in policies toward NGOs, finding distinct differences in Latin America, Asia, and Africa (1998: 46–53). In Latin America, for example, "civil society is more consistently autonomous in relation to the state than it is in Africa or Asia" (p. 47).

The expanding literature on these relationships often focuses primarily on the development of civil society and the realpolitik of power, influence, and change. Mechanisms for service delivery get less attention, although they are also at the core of poverty reduction and socioeconomic development.

The growing number of case studies can provide some anecdotal guidance across nations and cultures, and those that do focus on service delivery suggest desirable administrative arrangements in specific circumstances that may or may not be generally applicable. Few principles or rules emerge at this stage to validate one or another of Sandberg's linkage patterns or commend specific organizational arrangements for relating existing government structures to NGOs and grass-roots movements beyond the ideal of a cooperative, facilitative, competent, honest, committed government. Presupposed in this ideal are the integrity of NGOs/grass-roots movements themselves and their willingness to adjust to necessary regulation and coordination, as well as to upgrade their skills and improve accountability and transparency in their operations. Until there are capable administrative systems in legitimate political states to deal with, NGOs and grass-roots movements will properly focus on the strengthening of civil society and interventions to compensate for inadequacies in government (and private, on occasion) service delivery. Monitoring, advocacy, whistle blowing, and support building in the international community will be required.

There is compelling evidence, certainly, that NGOs in recent years have become more active and more assertive in relations with host governments and have obtained the backing of influential international donors (see, for example, Bratton, 1989; Brohman, 1996; Clark, 1991; Reilly, 1995).

"Scaling Up"

If NGOs and grass-roots organizations are to play a viable and expanding part in the delivery of basic services, they and interested donor agencies must take steps to increase their effectiveness. The "push" by NGOs/grass-roots organizations to reverse the policy agenda, exert decision making on programs, and directly operate programs on a larger scale involves a number of strategies. Sympathetic "pull" strategies in the international donor community reinforce—and sometimes inspire—the bottom-up efforts.

The general process of increasing NGO influence is conventionally known in the development community as *scaling up.*

Scaling up occurs when these organizations extend their scope and power by increasing membership, gaining new resources, exerting greater policy-related pressure, and otherwise becoming major players in development (see, for example, Clark, 1991: 84–87; Uvin and Miller, 1996: 344–355). Fisher (1993, 1998: 10) refers to expansion as "scaling out," and Korten (1990) discusses "third generation" NGOs, which move beyond the local level and influence policy change.

The impetus for scaling up usually arises from the grass-roots or the intermediary level—the umbrella NGOs. Instances of top-down encouragement, however, are increasing in number. An example of the latter is the United States Agency for International Development (USAID) Democracy Network Project in Poland. USAID funding to the Washington, D.C.,–based Academy for Educational Development—an independent nonprofit organization—seeks to "promote the evolution of service-oriented NGOs into organizations that participate more actively in policy formulation and implementation as partners with local government authorities" (www.aed.org). NGO support networks would be strengthened in five Polish cities, and small subgrants are provided to encourage proposal writing, financial reporting mechanisms, and additional coalition building. Reflecting a newer approach (the donor-driven encouragement of grass-roots effort), the outcome is similar to long-established indigenous efforts even though it runs the slight risk of "neocolonial" or "elite-driven" characterization.

Several examples of successful scaling up may be found in South Asia's larger and better-established NGOs. In Pakistan, the Aga Khan Rural Support Programme has been a model for others. The program invited World Bank participation after achieving a measure of local success. The Bangladesh Rural Advancement Committee (BRAC) has, since 1972, pursued a scaling up strategy that now places it among the largest Southern NGOs. It operates a variety of programs in some 15,000 villages with 10,000 staff. It has its own 20-story building in Dhaka and a budget of over $100 million per year.

In Sri Lanka, the long-established Sarvodaya Shramadana Movement has reached into thousands of villages. Its original inspiration was Mahatma Gandhi, and its name signifies an awakening of spirit.

In India, the Bharat Jan Andolan (Indian People's Movement) drew together a wide array of tribal groupings who pressed for self-government in tribal areas and succeeded in getting resources transferred to local communities (Parajuli and Kothari, 1998: 20). India has a vast number of NGOs and grass-roots organizations pursuing scaling-up strategies, including numerous women's organizations.

In Central and Eastern Europe and the Newly Independent States (NIS) states, the Open Society Foundation operates as a "scaled-up" autonomous NGO, which offers support to small NGO institutions (and individuals) as part of the Soros Foundation Network, created and funded by the financier George Soros. Soros Foundation Open Society operations are found in Hungary, Romania, Croatia, Georgia, Kazakstan, and elsewhere. In Croatia, for example, there is cooperation with the Croatian Legal Center as well as the Society Center for Entrepreneurship and considerable interest in monitoring privatization. Conflict with the government of Croatia over alleged insider trading by Soros executives has been largely resolved.

One of the most feasible paths to meaningful scaling up is a combining of smaller units into networks that share information and aggregate individual roles. At the level of communication rather than alignment, simply sharing ideas and developments may be important. Opportunities for changing government service-delivery policy (such as pressuring for equitable inclusion of poor and remote populations in education, health, housing, and social services) as well as directly undertaking service delivery have been realized. Fisher indicates that what she classifies as grass-roots support organizations "are more effective at networking and sharing what they have learned with each other than most Northern NGOs" (1993: 180).

Scaling up—if it is to be fully effective—involves not merely the networking, combining, and/or strengthening of existing units, but corresponding measures to enhance accountability, improve skill levels, and enter into policy dialogues.

NGOs and grass-roots organizations must recognize their deficiencies not only as isolated, fragmented, relatively small-scale enterprises but also as mission-oriented volunteer organizations lacking administrative expertise, accountability to the public, and transparency in their operations.

What might seem easy to correct—undertaking training, reporting to outside groups, opening records to inspection—often become major problems:

> Large-scale service delivery by nonprofits, whether as public service contractors, large cooperative federations, or independent agencies

> organized to mobilize community level volunteer resources, is an important and legitimate role for NGOs. Those that choose to assume long-term or permanent roles in such systems must be clear in their own minds, however, that this is what they are doing and approach the task accordingly. It is very different from that of short-term delivery of relief supplies and services, the implementation of conventional development projects, or catalyzing institutional and policy change—all of which assume that the NGO's participation is temporary. (Korten, 1990: 196)

PLURALISM IN SERVICE DELIVERY

Pluralism in service delivery raises a host of new problems. As NGOs scale up and move unrelentingly beyond a merely peripheral role, they force a reconfiguration of service-delivery patterns.

Classical public administration theory argued for structures of order and coordination based on hierarchy and specialization with a dominant public sector. Contracting out, delegation, devolution, franchising, and other variations from direct service delivery would be under close government control.

In contrast, the new public management and related thinking such as "reinventing government" argue for doing better with fewer resources by relying on entrepreneurial, client-oriented methods and fuller use of the business sector.

Neither model adequately accounts for the complexities of administration in developing and post-Communist countries intent on an enlarged Third Sector—as well as a Second—substantially funded and controlled from outside. Elements of both models, however, along with public choice, organization theory, postmodern, and other approaches, may be relevant. The avoidance of chaos with classical thinking and the calls for a new administrative culture in "reinventing government" thinking are particularly relevant (Osborne and Gaebler, 1992). Attempts at reviewing new service delivery models are beyond the scope of this chapter, and, indeed, it may be reasoned that any "one size fits all" formula will be inappropriate; regional, country, culture, or other subtypes will be necessary.

As a small contribution to the debate, however, two ideal types are sketched here; they are based on capacity level of host governments. In the first, the state plays the lead role; in the second, NGOs and grass-roots organizations focus on the development of civil society and rudimentary service delivery. More elaborate models will recognize regional and other variations (see Coston, 1998).

The "Capable Administrative State" Model

Many governments in the developing and postsocialist world are making headway toward—and have resources and appropriate policies for—the ideal of a competent, capable mode of operation that admits of partnering, is not threatened by networking and international concern, and recognizes the contribution of the Second and Third Sectors.

In this model, the state remains the dominant service provider, supplemented by the other sectors. NGOs and grass-roots organizations fill the gaps and niches, extending the reach of the government. Privatization—as it occurs—is based on rational allocation of roles. Private service providers as well as NGOs/grass-roots movements are accepted as adjuncts to state efforts, able to enhance the image of the state. Perhaps competition in service delivery affords clients opportunities for choice.

Participatory councils or committees coordinate programs, and international donors recognize the indigenous character of service delivery problems and encourage—as well as guide—host country efforts. Brinkerhoff (1999: 136–141) points to the importance to success of trust, compatible agendas, and similar interpretations of coordination and linkages. Sandberg's fifth type of host government linkage—multifocused—prevails, but information is shared through computer systems and "turf battles" are resolved with negotiation. Overall program—rather than project—support is provided by external donors but without the donor direction necessary in the second model, the weak capacity state. Monitoring and accountability are appropriate (neither lax nor overbearing) as are innovations (neither capricious nor suffocated with rules) that allow for flexibility in program design and shifts from sector to sector. NGOs learn from governments and governments learn from NGOs. The learning may be counter intuitive: Tendler (1997: 161) reports on one case in which a state department of health was able to benefit from the mistakes of NGOs in the health sector (in Ceara, Brazil). In this example, flexibility, decentralization, and outreach were the government's, not the NGOs'; further, the NGOs "couched their health messages in a religious language that inadvertently reinforced the paternalism of the existing social context and the fatalism about disease."

On the other hand, Tendler (1997: 131) makes the interesting point that governments—and one could add international donors—frequently fail even to notice some of the success stories, particularly when they occur on a small scale and in remote places.

Training, skill development, attitudinal change, and willingness to coordinate activities approximate those that characterize the so-called developed world (i.e., the North) but with indigenous characteristics. The keys to success are getting the mixture of service modes "correct" and developing partnerships and networks free of disabling conflict. The strengths and weaknesses of the different sectors are appropriately integrated into an overall strategy. Farrington and Bebbington (1993: 35–40) have illustrated how this might work in the case of functional strengths and weaknesses of NGOs and government in agricultural technology development for the rural poor.

The "Weak Administrative State" Model

Prescriptions and action plans are different for those host governments which have limited prospects for developing adequate capacity for meeting minimum societal needs and lack sufficient stability for cooperative service delivery partnerships. Similarly, NGOs/grass-roots organizations meet different demands. A strong international and/or indigenous force is usually needed along with new participatory mechanisms, to realize eventually a stable, democratic political/administrative environment. Civil society must further evolve; democratization take root; and visions of privatization define the future line between public and private. Often, civil strife, natural disasters, and/or declines in commodity prices exacerbate an already difficult situation, necessitating additional peacekeeping or economic stabilization measures.

The focus for NGOs/grass-roots organizations is on the development of civil society as well as the provision of services. In the latter, NGOs/grass-roots organizations (sometimes in partnerships with local government) may be more important than the central government itself.

The possibilities for coordination of broad-based approaches to development under conditions of weak government capacity may be enhanced by top-down funding efforts, operating through host governments, as in World Bank–led efforts in Uganda (the Program for the Alleviation of Poverty) and in Bangladesh (the Fourth Population and Health Project). In both instances, NGOs, local governments, and central governments were assigned specific objectives and collaborated under World Bank supervision, with mixed results.

In the innovative Livelihoods Enhancement through Empowerment and Participation (LEEP) program in Zambia, financed by the British government, there is a concerted effort to establish a broad-based coalition of change agents and through lesson learning and research components to "generate lessons replicable in other parts of Zambia and for DFID [Department for International Development] more widely" (*Economist,* 1999: 92). LEEP will support 24 "listening teams" working with 20 communities over 7 years. The idea is to identify the priorities of the poor, arbitrate power struggles, develop participatory monitoring and evaluation mechanisms, and—generally—build the villagers' capacity for sustainable self-improvement along with the capacity of government and nongovernment partners. Similarly—and more ambitiously—the African Capacity Building Foundation—conceived and designed by the African Governors of the World Bank, as of late 1999 in the study stage—aims to build partnerships among governments, the private sector, and civil society as well as "development partners." A holistic approach to capacity building in sub-Saharan Africa is envisaged (Economist, 1999: 72).

These and numerous other efforts are based on new understandings in the donor community of what works and what doesn't (see, e.g., World Bank, 1998) and a general shift away from project-by-project funding to a broader programmatic concern with "development." Regional variations are enormous, but the role of NGOs/grass-roots organizations takes on added significance whether the programs are in Central/Eastern Europe and the NIS, Latin America, Asia, or Africa. (The Middle East is a special case with relatively less emphasis on NGOs and grass-roots organizations.)

There are process issues in both the "capable" and "less capable" situations concerned with the way decisions are made (who participates and how) as well as substantive questions on the appropriateness of the designs and strategies for implementation. Oversimplified, the extremes are, on the one hand, top-down blueprints with little original grass-roots participation and, on the other, bottom-up agendas in which empowered NGOs and grass-roots organizations impose their will on host governments and international donors. In the former, there are usually few significant opportunities for grass-roots participation in program design since international donors and/or host governments develop the projects or programs and assign a role—usually minor—to NGOs/grass-roots organizations, even when the purpose is the strengthening of civil society. Nelson (1995) has documented the real extent of NGO involvement in World Bank lending and found that in 304 projects surveyed 176 projects involved the NGO only as an implementer and 51 offered minor opportunities to penetrate World Bank core technology and exercise representative, watchdog, and "agent of accountability" roles (p. 85). Although still a problem, this is changing—as mentioned—because bilateral and multilateral donors are moving away from a project approach and emphasizing participatory inclusion of even the lowliest villagers in broader-based programs.

The distortion of policy processes by empowered NGOs has been a lesser problem, but there have been cases of overzealous redirection of efforts, sometimes when media and fund-raising campaigns stir public outcry. In these instances, the "reverse agenda" replaces or modifies existing political/administrative priorities as pressure politics overwhelms traditional formal/legal procedures.

In pluralistic service delivery, NGOs and grass-roots organizations remain leery of co-optation into broader national/international designs with surrender of their autonomy and usually regard themselves as insufficiently empowered. In the words of a subtitle of a recent study, the relationships may be "too close for comfort" (Hulme and Edwards, 1996).

Ideally, NGOs/grass-roots organizations will relate to their host governments and international agencies constructively and be allowed to participate in the process of decision making and in resulting coordinated partnerships or parallel service delivery without conflict. Ideally, host governments will provide secure and stable enabling environments and facilitative legal and administrative rules rather than onerous registration and reporting requirements followed by microsupervision from one or more contact points in the government.

In the recent past, the increase in numbers of NGOs, the project-by-project financing by international donors, the often unstable political environment, and the proliferation of interactions have often led to a chaotic service delivery pattern. Common objectives and agreed upon strategies have been hard to achieve with the mix of "administrative cultures" resulting from proximity of volunteer organizations that eschew "bureaucracy" with government officials concerned with rule application. Professional qualifications, reward structures, image and publicity strategies, political postures, and other elements have exerted centrifugal influences. Privatization has blurred the line between public and nonpublic.

However, the scenario envisaged here—and by many others—is the solution of present administrative conflicts, the resolution of process issues, and a more prominent role for NGOs/grass-roots movements as decision-making participants and implementing agents.

CONCLUSION

This chapter has argued that NGOs and grass-roots organizations are a large and growing force in service delivery in developing and post-Communist countries. In conventional wisdom, they offer an attractive alternative to inadequate and sometimes corrupt government services and are able to fill the voids left by retrenchment or complete absence of badly needed programs. They operate health clinics, schools, social services, and microcredit facilities; build roads and canals; distribute seeds and give agricultural advice; contribute to self-help mobilization at the community level; and in many other ways play a crucial role in delivery of social, economic, and other services.

There are various ways in which they relate to host governments, ranging from focused contact with one ministry to functional relations and decentralized interactions. Consortia of NGO/grass-roots organizations can provide some leverage with host governments and can simplify contacts with international or binational donors, who often do not wish to field large teams to seek out numerous scattered, minor organizations. In some interpretations, those NGOs that are sometimes called *intermediate NGOs* are primarily concerned with improving the effectiveness of grass-roots organizations. Other NGOs operate their own programs.

To maximize their contribution, it is argued here, both NGOs and grass-roots organizations need to "scale up" by increasing their influence, entering into networks, improving their competence and accountability, and in other ways acting to reconfigure the mixture of public, private, and voluntary activity. That mixture is still heavily weighted on the public side with increasing efforts at privatization, often to the exclusion of NGOs/grass-roots organizations. International donors—as well as host governments—have in the past imposed top-down designs, including NGOs/grass-roots organizations as subcontractors fulfilling important but minor roles.

Increasingly, this has given way to the impact of a reverse agenda, in which advocacy positions have brought about policy changes and NGOs/grass-roots organizations are included in decision making.

The growing literature emphasizing individual cases with no common conceptual framework for understanding issues of service delivery needs to focus on common problems and cross-sector learning. Two ideal types based on the maturity of the host government are suggested for service delivery reconfiguration. The enormous variety of circumstances prevents facile generalization, but certain guidelines are emerging as electronic networking and dissemination of academic materials reveal examples of successes and failures. Lessons are emerging for international and bilateral donors, for Northern NGOs funding Southern NGOs, for host governments, and for NGOs/grass-roots organizations themselves. The promising shift in emphasis from *projectitis* to a program approach, for example, seems to be based on understandings of the limitations of fragmentation into numerous unrelated, uncoordinated projects. Similarly, the increasing emphasis on privatization—usually studied apart from NGOs/grass-roots organizations—presents opportunities to compare experiences across sectors.

More research must be done on the strictly administrative aspects of pluralistic service delivery.

REFERENCES

Anheier, H. (1994). NGOs and institutional development in africa. In *The Changing Politics of Non-Government Organizations and the African States* (E. Sandberg, ed.). Praeger, Westport, Conn.

Bennett, J. (1998). Development alternatives: NGO-government partnerships in Pakistan. *Development. 41:* 54–57.

Black, J. K. (1991). *Development in Theory and Practice: Bridging the Gap.* Westview Press, Boulder, Colo.

Bratton, M. (1989). The politics of government-NGO relations in africa. *World Development. 17:* 569–587.

Brinkerhoff, D. (1999). "State-civil society networks for policy implementation. *Policy Studies Review. 16:* 124–147.

Brohman, J. (1996). *Popular Development: Rethinking the Theory and Practice of Development.* Blackwell, Oxford.

Carroll, T. F. (1992). *NGOs: The Supporting Link in Grassroots Development.* Kumarian Press, West Hartford, Conn.

Clark, J. (1991). *Democratizing Development: The Role of Voluntary Organizations.* Kummarian Press, West Hartford, Conn.

Coston, J. (1998). A model and typology of government-NGO relationships. *Nonprofit and Voluntary Sector Quarterly. 27:* 3.

Economist, July 3, 1999 ('Request for Proposal' advertisement), July 17, 1999 ('other Request for Proposal' advertisement).

Edwards, M., and Hulme, D., eds. (1992). *Making a Difference: NGOs and Development in a Changing World.* Earthscan, London.

Edwards, M., and Hulme, D. (1995). *Non-Governmental Organizations: Performance and Accountability: Beyond the Magic Bullet.* Save the Children and Earthscan Publications, London.

Ellner, S. (1999). Obstacles to the consolidation of the Venezuela neighborhood movement: National and local cleavages. *Journal of Latin American Studies. 31:* 75–94.

Esman, M. (1991) The state, government bureaucracies, and their alternatives. In *Handbook of Comparative and Development Public Administration* (Farazmand, A., ed.). New Dekker, New York.

Farrington, J., and Bebbington, A. (1993). *Reluctant Partners? Non-Governmental Organizations, the State and Sustainable Agricultural Development.* Routledge, London.

Fisher, J. (1993). *The Road from Rio: Sustainable Development and the Nongovernmental Movement in the Third World.* Praeger, Westport, Conn.

Fisher, J. (1998). *Nongovernments, NGOs and the Political Development of the Third World.* Kumarian Press, West Hartford, Conn.

Henderson, K. (1999). A third sector alternative: NGOs and grassroots initiatives. In *Bureaucracy and the Alternatives in World Perspective* (K. Henderson and O. P. Dwivedi, eds.). Macmillan, London and St. Martins, New York, pp. 52–58.

Hulme, D., and Edwards, M. (eds.) (1996). *NGOs, States and Donors, Too Close for Comfort?* St. Martin's, New York.

Korten, D. (1990). *Getting to the 21st Century: Voluntary Action and the Global Agenda.* Kumarian Press, West Hartford, Conn.

Mohiddin, A. (1998). Partnership: A new buzz-word or realistic relationship? *Development. 41:* 5–16.

Nelson, P., J. (1995). *The World Bank and Non-Governmental Organizations, The Limits of Apolitical Development.* Macmillan, London.

OECD, Development Assistance Committee. (1998) *Development Cooperation, Efforts and Policies of the Members of the Development Assistance Committee.* OECD, Paris.

Osborne, D., and Gaebler, T. (1992). *Reinventing Government, How the Entrepreneurial Spirit is Transforming the Public Sector.* Addison-Wesley, Reading, Mass.

Parajuli, P., and Kothari, S. (1998). Struggling for Autonomy: Lessons from Local Governance Development. *41*(3): 18–29.

Reilly, C. (ed.) (1995). *NGOs, New Paths to Democratic Development in Latin America.* Lynne Rienner, Boulder, Colo.

Salamon, L., and Anheier, H. (1997). *Defining the Nonprofit Sector.* Manchester University Press, Manchester.

Sandberg, E. (ed.) (1994). *The Changing Politics of Non-Governmental Organizations and African States.* Praeger, Westport, Conn.

Secretary General (1998). *Report on NGOs, A/53/170.* July 10. New York: United Nations.

Tendler, J. (1997). *Good Government in the Tropics.* Johns Hopkins, Baltimore.

Turner, M., and Halligan, J. (1999). Bureaucracy and the alternatives in East and Southeast Asia. In *Bureaucracy and the Alternatives in World Perspective* (K. Henderson and O. P. Dwivedi, eds.). Macmillan, London and St. Martins, New York, pp. 129–159.

USAID (1996). [www.aed.org].

Uvin, P., and Miller, D. (1996). Paths to Scaling-up: Alternative strategies for local non-governmental organizations. *Human Organization. 55*(3): 344–356.

Vakil, A. C. (1997). Confronting the classification problem: Toward a taxonomy of NGOs. *World Development. 25:* 2057–2071.

World Bank (1998). *Assessing Aid: What Works, What Doesn't, and Why.* World Bank, Washington, D.C.

31

Changes and Reforms in Public Administration Education

Thomas Vocino and Linda C. Wilson
Department of Political Science and Public Administration, Auburn University at Montgomery, Montgomery, Alabama

INTRODUCTION

The purpose of this chapter is to examine key issues of public administration education as reflected in the literature of the field. The specific focus of the chapter is graduate-level education as most public administration programs target the largest portion of their resources at the graduate level. As the masters degree in public administration (M.P.A.) is the "big ticket" graduate program for the field, greater attention in this chapter is given to issues related to the M.P.A. programs. Although doctoral-level studies in public administration constitute a growing enterprise and merit attention, still the largest part of what public administration programs do is at the master's level, which is also the level of graduate study where the field's pedagogical literature is focused.

We begin our review of developments in the world of public service education with a summary and analysis of the 1967 Honey Report; then we review the varied responses to the report that recommend specific actions that might be taken to achieve the improvements suggested by John Honey. Of necessity, given the magnitude of the topic of graduate public administration education, we have limited the specific issues covered in this chapter to the following with regard to M.P.A. programs: accountability and evaluation, changes in vision and curriculum, teaching ethics, experiments with formats and delivery methods, alternative instructional methodologies, transfer of the American government experience to international students, and issues relating to perpetuating the knowledge base of the field. As far as the review of issues respecting doctoral programs, we address specific concerns related to the quality and rigor of those programs—a debate that the field has wrestled with for nearly two decades.

CALLS FOR REFORM

A 1967 study conducted by John Honey analyzed the capacity of public administration programs to meet the growing demands for trained workers within the field effectively. At the time of the report, universities were unable to turn out graduates at a rate required by federal, state, and local government agencies. Honey discovered not only a pent-up demand for entry-level professional workers, but also a need for midcareer training for existing employees. Additionally, the report cited the absence of accountability standards, as well as the need for cooperative intergovernmental programs with universities. Variables that influenced the ability of universities to meet those challenges were dependent upon the academic reputation of the institution, the level of public support, a university's mission and role in professional training, and federal support and use of the university's resources. Honey concluded that universities frequently did a poor job of education, research, and public service and warned that they needed to rethink their missions regarding public service responsibilities (Honey, 1967).

Among the deficiencies cited in the Honey Report were a lack of fellowship and research funds, faculty shortages, the institution's own failure to define the field, and the nebulous role of programs within various institutions. He reprimanded institutions for their failure to recruit government as a partner and for their refusal to pull from disciplines outside the political science field. He maintained that reforms must begin with all the players—state and local governments, federal agencies, businesses, and universities. The report called for solutions that included the establishment of a National Commission on Public Service Education to act in an advisory capacity to the players and to assume a leadership role on issues of political, ethical, and social import. Further, Honey suggested a fellowship and student loan program to entice and assist graduate students. Likewise, fellowships and internships for public administration professors would, he believed, enhance the quality of instruction. He contended that by assigning professors to government service positions, academia could better acquaint itself with real problems. Honey blasted current public administration programs for their lack of analytical assessment and commitment to research. Recommendations called for programs of curriculum experimentation and development, and government assistance in funding facilities and development of libraries and research assistantships (Honey, 1967).

The Honey Report prompted a number of responses from public administration academicians. Banovetz (1967) echoed Honey's criticism that public administration schools were not effectively reaching public servants and that they had made only a slight contribution "to the intellectual and managerial capabilities of local and state government officers" (Banovetz, 1967: 321). He too pondered the seriousness of the field's failure to define itself. Banovetz rejected both the traditionalist and the administrative science approach to curriculum development and encouraged academia to shift its focus instead to policy-making and implementation processes (Banovetz, 1967). Pope (1967) pointed to the need for postentry training for public service employees. He warned that well-trained and extremely motivated public administrators would likely glean only mediocre performance from a pool of inadequately trained middle managers (Pope, 1967).

Reining (1967) argued that Honey's priorities should be reversed. He called first for an immediate increase in the number and quality of public administration schools. Second, he challenged universities to enhance their support of existing programs. His third priority included additional support for public administration faculty, followed by the creation of additional fellowships for students. Finally, he argued for the formation of a National Commission on Public Service Education. Reining expressed a greater level of confidence in the intellectual soundness of schools of public administration, proclaiming that they had done an acceptable job of turning out generalists in the field (Reining, 1967). Unlike Honey, he had no compulsion to define the field of public administration as either a science, a profession, or a discipline; instead, he labeled it "interdisciplinary" (Reining, 1967: 336).

Like Reining, Sherman (1967) was indifferent to the science/profession label that Honey grappled with in defining the field. Sherman's solution to the apparent lack of trained workers and high-quality public administration programs rested with higher salaries and prestige for the profession of government service. He stressed the need to bridge the gap between professors and practitioners by arranging for practitioners to teach and perform research at universities and, in turn, granting sabbaticals to professors to work in government agencies. He encouraged program review by advisory councils that comprise practitioners, and conferences to bring practitioners and professors together (Sherman, 1967).

At Cornell University Professor Paul R. Van Riper (1967) reiterated Honey's plea for increased funding and research in public administration programs. He pronounced the report too bland and charged universities with blatant indifference to practical and applied education for public service. He admonished them not to train graduates in the image of college professors. Instead, education for public administrators should reorient itself from the completely analytical and intellectual with an interdisciplinary approach to include, but not be limited to, political science. Van Riper encouraged graduate program directors to recruit undergraduates from disciplines other than the political and social sciences, pressing for a prescribed curriculum that included management and political science with a broad focus. He complained of the absence of a positive labor force policy and foundation support for public administration programs, noting that the Ford and Carnegie Foundations and others awarded large grants to schools of business, but not to the field of public administration. Education programs in public service would likewise benefit from such endowments (Van Riper, 1967).

In his response to the Honey Report, a Princeton University professor, Rufus Miles (1967), urged schools of public administration to develop an identity different from that of disciplined-based departments. He cited the meager salaries and lack of respect and recognition accorded the profession in academia. Acknowledging government's failure to support the field with money and research, he challenged schools of public administration to take the lead in compensating for the funding shortfalls. He maintained that schools should be analytical and imaginative and should reflect upon a variety of important policy problems. Miles enumerated the elements essential to high-quality schools of public administration. Universities should provide students a broad perspective through liberal arts education, rather than turning out graduates who are specialists. He encouraged the development of a current philosophy by integrating ethics, values, and judgment into the curriculum. Graduates should gain an understanding of institutions and processes through courses in administrative law and the Constitution. He stressed the need for a curriculum that included a study of micro- and macroeconomics, management skills, and a significant research program, as well as the interchange of faculty and government agency employees via internships and consulting (Miles, 1967).

M.P.A. PROGRAM ACCOUNTABILITY AND REVIEW

The National Association of Schools of Public Affairs and Administration (NASPAA) was created in 1970 in response to a rapid growth in the demand for college-educated government employees and conceptual differences over what constituted effective public administration programs. The association was established with the intent of developing standards for the industry. In 1973, NASPAA discovered a lack of professionalism in many programs; 4 years later, it created the Peer Review and Accreditation Program, thereby establishing a process to evaluate program content and effectiveness. During the late 1970s and early 1980s, NASPAA charged institutions with the task of balancing the academic integrity of M.P.A. programs with their relevance to agencies and practitioners (Ingraham and Zuck, 1996).

During the post-Watergate era, educational institutions were encouraged to band together with governmental organizations to improve the image of the public service. The American Society of Public Administration developed the National Campaign for the Public Service, designed to create an awareness of the value of governmental agencies and "promote the dignity and worth of the public service" (Denhardt, 415). In 1987, the National Commission on Public Service, chaired by the former Federal Reserve chairman Paul Volcker, evolved from a symposium that addressed the problems facing the field. Conference attendees feared that the prevailing image problems of the public service were contributing to a lack of quality in the pool of prospective public employees. The Volcker Commission recommended a partnership of educational institutions and government agencies to enlarge the pool of available talent. The commission requested that Congress facilitate programs that would build student awareness of public service excellence and provide support for educational institutions in their efforts to increase and improve training programs in public administration (Denhardt, 1999).

The National Commission on the State and Local Public Service, chaired by the former Mississippi governor William Winter, noted similar findings at other levels of government. The report carried important implications for schools of public administration. The Winter commission challenged a NASPAA task force and public administration faculty members to rethink the group of skills they were currently teaching. Additionally, the calls for reform dictated new teaching methods to equip students with the interpersonal and managerial skills needed in public service (Thompson, 1993).

Delmer Dunn (1994), chair of the NASPAA Task Force on Education for the State and Local Public Service, urged program coordinators and faculty members to work with state and local agencies to improve schedules, teaching methods, and program formats. He referred to the strong emphasis on the human resources factor and encouraged faculty and administrators to participate with government to solicit funding for on-site and campus-based programs. By developing "train the trainer" programs, schools could perpetuate high-quality in-service programs for employees whose academic backgrounds were in fields other than public administration. He cautioned faculty members working with government employees schooled in other disciplines to cultivate stronger links between schools of public administration and those academic departments. Dunn pointed to the report's charges of a lack of diversity in public service. He recommended that program directors recruit and retain minorities and women and work with state and local governments to develop educational opportunities to ensure the advancement of those recruits (Dunn, 1994).

According to Dunn, public affairs faculty and administrators need to interact with career counselors in public schools to improve the attitudes and perceptions of the role of public service employees in an effort to recruit bright students into the profession. He recommended that they also convince state departments of education to increase the time allotted for the study of government in the education curricula. Finally, he admonished NASPAA schools to strengthen their ties with labor unions by involving speakers from labor organizations in the classroom and to build an "awareness of the benefits of participation and cooperation between labor and management" (Dunn, 1994: 110).

CHANGES IN M.P.A. PROGRAM MISSIONS AND CURRICULA

As a result of growth in the number of programs, NASPAA developed a vision in the 1990s for pluralistic missions to accommodate the changing nature of the profession. Ingraham and Zuck (1996) predicted a further blurring in the distinction between public and private organizations as changes in the size and structure of government demand increased productivity and accountability. They envision NASPAA's future role as a resource base charged with the task of reexamining missions and curricula, rather than merely an agency for disseminating information (Ingraham and Zuck, 1996).

In response to demands for higher standards of accountability and program effectiveness, schools of public administration scrambled to improve programs of instruction. Tompkins, Laslovich, and Greene (1996) reported on a competency-based curriculum developed by a team of three students and three faculty members for a small M.P.A. program housed within the Department of Political Science at the University of Montana. Tompkins's team deduced that neither the political science approach, the management approach, nor the values approach in and of itself was an ideal model for training public servants. Instead, theirs was a holistic, integrated approach based on the type and level of competencies required. They identified 9 areas of knowledge, 16 management skills, and 4 values that were key to effective public service management. Next, they surveyed state government employees and public managers to determine the relative importance of those skills to jobs. The difficulties of implementation were obvious: In order for the program to have application to other institutions, faculty must be willing to give up some measure of control and to teach from the management approach as well as the political science perspective. Additionally, they must be willing to divorce themselves from the notion that such programs are devoid of intellectual importance (Tompkins et al., 1996).

In support of courses that bridge the theory-practice gap Professors Campbell and Tatro of Arizona State University (ASU) (1998) designed a course to incorporate real-world experiences into the student learning process. They contended that graduates who become public managers will need program evaluation skills as part of the accountability process and that most programs are not prepared to offer more than one program evaluation course in the core curriculum. The course is taught on a semester format with 3-hour classes that meet one evening each week. Despite claims to the contrary, Campbell and Tatro insist that the semester allows sufficient time to complete an effective project. Students acquire the requisite knowledge and skills necessary to design and implement program review and evaluation techniques through cooperative learning teams, simulation, and field experiences. They credit the level of student preparedness for the success of their program—statistics and research methodology are prerequisites for the course. To date, the course has been taught six times and teams have produced 21 projects—8 for state agencies, 5 for county government, 5 for municipal agencies, 1 for a regional nonprofit, and 2 for the university (Campbell and Tatro, 1998).

Students enrolled at the Tempe campus of ASU are typically working adults, many of whom are employed in the public administration field. Teams of three to five students are assigned to a government or nonprofit agency in which they perform a professional-quality program evaluation. Agency managers make presentations to the class in the hope that teams will select their programs for review and evaluation. Once an agency is selected by a team, it receives written notification and is then contacted by a team member regarding the initial interview. Students and clients sign a memorandum of agreement that outlines the scope of the work to be done and the roles and responsibilities of each member. A project management plan outlines the action steps and time lines and delegates completion to a certain individual. Students work on the project both inside and outside the classroom, and professors schedule appointments with alternating teams to ensure an equitable division of class time among groups. At the end of the semester, teams present preliminary reports to class members in order to obtain feedback. In addition to the oral presentation to the agency, groups submit a formal written report of their recommendations. Student evaluations include a combination of instructor review, peer review, and self-evaluation. Midterm exams are administered by the professor in order to measure the degree of individual student mastery of course concepts, and groups maintain an evaluation journal in which they record activities and contributions of team members. Finally, students conduct evaluations of their own progress and performance (Campbell and Tatro, 1998).

The course is not without obstacles and drawbacks, and professors must provide initial screening of agencies and programs applying for review and evaluation in order to eliminate programs that would use the project improperly. Good prospects for projects include those that have written, measurable goals for achieving outcomes. Targeted projects should involve the knowledge, prepreparation, and cooperation of agency staff members, and professors should work to minimize the failure rate so that agencies are willing to involve themselves in repeat projects. Campuses situated in small cities will necessitate greater levels of creativity of professors, who may be forced to draw on local churches and regional nonprofits with local branches in order to create a customer base (Campbell and Tatro, 1998).

At the University of North Texas Professors Newell and Durst (1997) have also made strides in bridging the theory-practice gap as well as responding to NASPAA standards for innovation in curriculum development. The two created a team project in which students are required to develop a personnel manual or complete an appraisal project. Teams go into the field and provide the service to government agencies as a consultancy. Team members are expected to make oral presentations and write reports on the project. Projects perform dual roles: They provide a service to the community as well as reinforcing learning for student teams. As a serendipitous effect, M.P.A. students cultivate useful contacts with agencies and develop job leads. The projects entail several drawbacks—increased workloads for part-time students and instructors and the inherent difficulty in assigning individual student evaluations. The authors caution project directors to exercise care to ensure that the team does an acceptable job; otherwise, the project could yield bad public relations for the institution (Newell and Durst, 1997).

West Virginia University has adopted a portfolio approach to its M.P.A. program. It began as a mission-based accreditation process to improve the program. Professors and the program director discovered the necessity of integrating courses more effectively with activities outside the classroom. At the outset, students review the portfolio process, assess their own strengths and weaknesses, and outline a plan for professional development designed to address those deficiencies. Course work integrates professional and community activities and serves as a practice field and a resume builder. Each student portfolio includes evidence of reading, interacting, demonstrating, writing, and thinking. Essentially, the plan becomes an ongoing faculty advisement tool as courses are assigned to address specific needs. A capstone course reviews the student's portfolio in order to gauge progress. Williams, Plein, and Lilly (1998) concede that the approach has met some, but not all, of the needs of their mission-based program. They cautioned that the portfolio must "support educational purposes, not become the primary instrument, and not be harmful to professional education" (Williams et al., 1998: 285).

Pressures mounted during the late 1970s for M.P.A. programs to integrate information technology into their curricula. By 1985, NASPAA had prescribed computer training in its standards for program accreditation. Institutions were slow to implement the requirement: Rocheleau (1998) referenced a survey by Waugh indicating that as late as 1995, two-thirds of M.P.A. programs were requiring only one information management course. Program administrators faced the difficulty of expanding curricula to include the additional course work as a part of the core. Debate ensued regarding the type of information management training to incorporate.

Rocheleau discovered that a number of variables impact on the nature and content of the technology course, including the focus of the program and its level of resources, the mix of students and their individual career goals, and the current job market. He cited a Fletcher study indicating that public employees receive little in the way of computer training on the job; instead, employers expect new hires to be computer-literate at the outset. Research pointed to a need for hands-on training in spreadsheets in order to perform budgeting tasks effectively. Agencies expected their employees to be able to perform queries and generate reports through the use of data bases and word processing, as well as statistical package for program review and evaluation. Rocheleau's program at Northern Illinois University requires students to be proficient in word processing and to teach themselves other software applications. Focus is on discussions of how software applications can improve decision making and increase effectiveness (Rocheleau, 1998).

INCORPORATING ETHICS INTO MPA PROGRAMS

In a 1998 call for a return to professionalism, Professor James Bowman (1998) at Florida State University challenged public administration programs to include ethics in the public administration curriculum. He reminded colleagues of the ethics issues that spurred turn-of-the century public service procedural reforms of the merit system. Although the topic of ethics waned in the three decades after World War II, the Watergate scandal led to a renewed interest in good government and prompted a number of program administrators to undertake the task of incorporating the topic into the public administration curriculum. Bowman reported that although a number of M.P.A. and Ph.D. programs currently offer an ethics course, a lesser number incorporate it into the core curriculum. A number of programs integrate topics or readings on ethics in their theory courses; others expand their curricula to include a separate class on ethics (Bowman, 1998).

Hejka-Ekins (1998) offered a possible solution to overcoming some of the barriers to teaching ethics in M.P.A. programs identified by Lee in his 1989 survey of NASPAA schools. She envisioned the process as one of organizational development, using an educational tool called *curriculum infusion* to spur a collaborative involvement of the stakeholders. To prevent resistance among the faculty, Hejka-Ekins cautioned program directors to enlist the support of teaching faculty, department chairs, and deans early in the process. Ideally, through the empowerment process, faculty would be more accepting and creative in integrating the study of ethics into their courses. She recommended having a visiting professor or ethics instructor offer a course module for existing faculty members Acknowledging the budgetary constraints faced by many schools, she encouraged program administrators to apply for grants to fund course development (Hejka-Ekins, 1998).

Lee (1990) identified what he considered the two major underlying causes that have prevented schools of public administration from incorporating ethics into the curriculum: He suggested that obstacles hinge on the misconception of the issue as a pedagogical problem, and the development of three separate paradigms for moral conduct in the field. From a pedagogical perspective, he finds that the teaching of ethics has been a battle between form and content on one hand and process on the other. He described the failings of the three postmodern models of ethical decision making. The early philosophical model involved a professional who was motivated by the need to do what is right; the advocacy model, whereby a public administrator was compelled to do good, followed. The advocacy model gave way to proactive values of good government in the 1960s and 1970s and a third model, called the *management model.* Teachings of that era prescribed scientific methods and management techniques designed to allow practitioners to evaluate all the alternatives and to opt for a solution that would not harm the public. Lee outlined the weaknesses of each model and suggested that we must first institutionalize the basis for action if we expect to teach normative ethics in our schools of public administration (Lee, 1990).

Public administration practitioners have long argued that university programs are not the proper vehicles for conveying codes of moral conduct to future employees. Many feared that students would be indoctrinated by the ideological and political biases of their professors. Others questioned the proper placement of ethics courses in the curriculum. Hetzner and Schmidt (1986) took a positive stand for incorporating ethics courses in public administration programs, making a case for the importance of ethical analysis and evaluation along with other forms of policy analysis as they relate to the organizational structure, mission, and goals. Rather than value judgments and moral prescription, they proposed that the study of ethics encompass an analysis of formal philosophies that have created "standards for justice, rights, and social equity" (Hetzner and Schmidt, 1986: 431).

Menzel employed a 1995 NASPAA data base to conduct a study of alumni of four M.P.A. programs regarding the impact of ethics education in their course work. At that time, 78 NASPAA-member graduate public administration and affairs programs offered ethics courses; 25 percent of those schools required the course. Graduates were queried on whether ethics training had made a difference in their professional lives, and if they had, how teaching methods employed by the school contributed to those outcomes. Menzel reflected on earlier studies wherein graduates indicated that ethics training had made a significant difference in their personal lives. Although Menzel cited conflicting results from other surveys of public managers, he concluded that the inconsistency lay not in the quality or effectiveness of ethics education, but in the absence of such training in M.P.A. curricula (Menzel, 1998).

Menzel's survey of more than 250 M.P.A. alumni included open-ended questions designed to elicit detailed responses regarding ethics training. A majority of graduates reported that the training had impacted their professional lives by helping them to sort out personal beliefs from professional behavior. They indicated that ethics education did not replace old value systems but merely reinforced existing ethical outlooks and behavior. Ethics educators must rely on the graduate socialization process to filter out those students with poor value systems. By rank-ordering the factors that influenced their ethical outlooks, M.P.A. graduates provided some valuable insights for faculty and program administrators with respect to curriculum design. Overall, respondents credited class discussions of values within a stand-alone ethics course as the most important factor. Ethics discussions incorporated into other courses in the M.P.A. curriculum ranked as the second most influential factor on professional behavior. Responses from M.P.A. faculty indicated conflicting views on the proper placement of ethics topics in the curriculum. Graduates ranked peer and faculty interaction outside the classroom and membership in professional associations as less influential factors. Methodologies employed in graduate ethics courses consisted largely of lectures, case studies, research papers, small group discussions, and decision-making scenarios. Perceptions regarding course effectiveness yielded important implications regarding instructional techniques for faculty members teaching ethics courses. Although instructors extensively used the lecture format, respondents identified the case studies and decision-making scenarios as the only teaching methods employed in the course that enabled them to resolve ethical dilemmas in their professional lives. Alumni recommended the use of real-world case studies and interactive learning to enhance the course. They admonished professors to become role models outside the classroom and to resist the temptation to sermonize on moral issues (Menzel, 1998).

Perhaps one of the earliest programs to incorporate ethics into its course work was that at the University of Utah. From its inception in 1976, the M.P.A. curriculum has included an ethics seminar in its core. Faculty acceptance likely resulted from effective interdisciplinary training and orientation. In the early stages of course development, professors from the philosophy department taught a two-quarter ethics seminar for M.P.A. faculty. The program was further enriched by summer retreats with stakeholders including program staff, student representatives, public administrators, and faculty members from other disciplines and universities. The department currently utilizes the annual retreat as a strategic planning tool to focus on program review and realignment (Rice et al., 1998).

The University of Utah's Center for Public Policy and Administration utilized a survey instrument developed in 1990 by Anderson, Desaii, DeShon, and Fry to assess the major strengths and weaknesses of its program. Outcomes of a 1995–97 alumni study indicated that 64 percent of M.P.A. graduates perceived their ethics education as important to their careers. Of the 216 graduates who responded, over half agreed that their ethics seminar promoted and nurtured ethical behavior by providing a framework for making ethical decisions. From a list of 17 skills taught in the course, they ranked ethics as seventh in its degree of importance to their careers. Remarks from respondents described a number of program benefits and limitations. A significant number agreed that although the course was helpful in developing a framework for ethical decision making, it did not succeed in making students more ethical (Rice et al., 1998).

The University of Utah study also surveyed 736 practitioners in local, state, and federal agencies in the Salt Lake city region during the late 1980s. Respondents were asked to select from a list of core M.P.A. courses the ones they would be most interested in taking should they elect to enroll in graduate courses geared toward public service. The practitioners showed a preference for classes in organizational behavior and the functional areas such as planning and budgeting over those in ethics and law. When asked to rank order the importance of courses that should be taught to public administration majors, they indicated a greater need for leadership training and computer skills than for courses in ethics and government administration. Rice, Nelson, and Van Hook concluded from their research that both practitioner and alumni surveys could assist program administrators in the design of curricula and that ethics education should not depend on consumer demand (Rice et al., 1998).

EXPERIMENTS WITH M.P.A. FORMATS AND DELIVERY METHODS

Faced with the dual challenges of meeting student needs and conforming to NASPAA demands for performance and mission accomplishment, graduate schools of public administration have experimented widely with scheduling options. Among the alternatives is the cohort format, in which student groups enter the program at the same time and progress along a structured curriculum path. Programs allow varying degrees of flexibility in class schedules to accommodate student needs and circumstances. An obvious advantage is the planning stability that accrues to program administrators who are able to estimate in advance the number of students assigned to predetermined courses. On the down side, students who are unable to handle class loads are often forced to drop out of the program.

Hebert and Reynolds (1998) concluded from a 1995 study of cohort and noncohort program formats that greater levels of student interaction and group cohesion existed among M.P.A. cohort students than among those enrolled in noncohort programs. Their initial research did not address the question of whether enhanced student interaction in the cohort programs yielded increases in student learning. In order to resolve that question, they surveyed cohort and noncohort formats in professional degree programs at five universities to determine whether significant differences existed in student learning gains between the two groups. Their most recent study included graduate students in public administration, business administration, and education administration at the American University, Georgia State University, Winthrop University, University of South Carolina, and University of Utah and included a total of 177 responses from cohort students and

165 from noncohort students. Survey instruments were distributed to students who had completed at least five courses toward their degrees. Findings indicated slightly greater differences in affective learning in the cohort group only when the three disciplines were measured as a whole. The greatest gains were made by male students and students below the age of 30. There were no significant differences in learning gains within the cognitive skills areas between the cohort and noncohort groups (Hebert and Reynolds, 1998).

With a rise in the number of public administration programs across the nation and an increase in the number of part-time practitioner students enrolled, universities are expanding their M.P.A. program delivery methods. A small but growing percentage of universities use distance learning in order to be cost-effective and to prevent a loss of market share to the competition. Leavitt and Richman (1997) credit distance learning with an increase in accessibility, broader program offerings, and the opportunity to prepare students better for the technological aspects of their jobs. On the down side, institutions often fail to allow faculty members the preparation time and training needed to be effective. Questions also arise regarding intellectual property rights. Other drawbacks include the absence of student-instructor interaction that is due to physical separation. A number of faculty members have reported difficulty in assessing student performance. Recent economic pressures have prevented the widespread use of distance learning because of the sizable initial investment required to get the service up and running (Leavitt and Richman, 1997).

FACULTY INVOLVEMENT AND CHANGES IN INSTRUCTIONAL METHODOLOGIES

Current literature regarding faculty performance and program effectiveness suggests a shift away from classroom lecture and a focus instead on student learning. O'Leary (1997) proclaimed, "The great man theory of teaching is dead" (O'Leary, 1997: 128). O'Leary and others report that their classes are largely interactive, and less focused on instructor lecture. Consensus among M.P.A. faculty is that critical thinking and creative thinking are essential skills for public service students. Newman (1996) champions fewer lectures and a focus instead on instructional approaches such as case studies and team projects to equip students with the communication, negotiation, and team-building skills requisite to public sector management. The trend of providing M.P.A. students with service skills is evidenced on a number of university campuses. Case Western Reserve University instituted a program wherein students worked full-time with state, local, and federal agencies to fund and operate a day care center (Newman, 1996).

Hambrick (1990) pressed for M.P.A. faculty members to inject skill development into the program, concluding that "attention to skill development enhances substantive learning and performances in the classroom and on the job"

(Hambrick, 1990: 307). He listed 10 basic skills that he viewed as key to public administration practitioners—writing, public speaking, information search, interviewing, interpersonal relations, research design, statistics and data analysis, computer usage, group process, and theory application. Those competencies could be incorporated into existing core courses, rather than creating new and separate ones. Encouraging faculty members who teach the core curriculum to develop and prioritize a list of essential skills, he suggested that they develop a matrix illustrating those courses that are currently being taught. On the matrix, they should also indicate the courses in which they believe the skills would be best incorporated. Finally, the matrix should reflect whether the skills should be treated in an introductory manner, as a principal learning point, or as reinforcement of an earlier topic. Hambrick conceded some weaknesses in program modification: In the process of incorporating skills development into an existing course, each faculty member in the core curriculum may erroneously assume that another member is currently addressing that particular skill. As a result, each may fail to include that topic as a part of the course unless it is perceived as critical. Faculty resistance may occur if members do not buy into the changes, and some measure of compromise may be necessary for implementation (Hambrick, 1990).

TRANSFERRING THE AMERICAN GOVERNMENT EXPERIENCE TO FOREIGN STUDENTS

An increasing phenomenon in M.P.A. programs is the rising number of foreign students enrolled. This presents a challenge to professors teaching administrative functions as they attempt to transfer the American political model to other cultures and political systems. Maggiotto (1997) urged caution in planning public administration curriculum for programs that enroll students from developing democracies. He pointed to the tendency for students from former Warsaw Pact countries to exhibit a predilection for mathematical solutions to governmental problems because of their nonthreatening approach to government order. Maggiotto stressed the need for professors to assist students in gaining an appreciation for the time frame necessary for the transition to a democracy and free market system and to incorporate lessons on the free market system and the proper role of government as interventionist (Maggiotto, 1997).

Simon and Pigenko (1997) concurred with Magiotto's assessment of the difficulty that students from former Soviet bloc countries experience in graduate public administration programs. Their concerns focused primarily on the problems associated with research assignments. Although students are bright and capable, their writings tend to be mere demonstrations of predetermined conclusions. Previous training and cultural orientation prompt their interest in deriving immediate solutions to real-world problems from their homeland, rather than model building and hypothesis testing. Criticism of their work by faculty members often signals rejection to those students. Simon and Pigenko explained that the students' failures to appreciate the objectivity of empirical research is a conditioned response to the desire to take a normative approach and be fighters on the ideological front. They noted that Russian students and scholars frequently resort to techniques learned during the Cold War—engaging in complex arguments designed to conceal ideas that would arouse the attention of the censors. At Bowling Green State University, Simon devised an approach to teach those students effective research design techniques. He cautioned that at the outset students should be allowed to select a particular topic of interest. Professors then lure students outside their usual research environments of perusing library collections by forcing them to design research through in-class assignments of current literature or brainstorming sessions designed to formulate and explain arguments (Simon and Pigenko, 1997).

PERPETUATING THE KNOWLEDGE BASE IN M.P.A. PROGRAMS

In order to identify issues and trends in public administration education, Manns and Streib (1990) examined papers presented at the National Conference on Teaching Public Administration during the 10-year period from 1978 through 1987. They analyzed the papers for authorship and institution, subject area, target audience, and contributions to the knowledge base. Of the 352 papers contributed, only 11 of those derived from non-academic sources, and 78 percent were oriented to the M.P.A. audience. Papers were divided into three primary categories—academic subject, teaching techniques, and program administration issues. Manns and Streib noted that papers dealt primarily with topics on public management, budgeting and finance, introduction to public administration, personnel, ethics, methodology, policy analysis, organization theory, computer skills, and information management. In the teaching techniques classification, the greatest number of papers referenced the use of simulations in the classroom. Almost half of the papers submitted on program administration dealt with curriculum issues; this is not a surprising finding since most of the authors were academicians. In gauging the extent to which the papers contributed to the knowledge base of the field, each was evaluated by the following criteria: (a) Do the papers expand the knowledge of how to teach public administration? (b) Do the papers build on previous work in the field? Findings revealed that almost one-third of the papers made no references to articles in public administration journals, and only 5 percent dealt with topics presented in previous proceedings (Manns and Streib, 1990).

Manns and Streib concluded from their study that the proceedings lacked continuity: Current authors failed to build upon the previous work of colleagues. The wide range of topics represented by the papers indicated a lack of focus, as well. In order for the proceedings to have a greater impact upon teaching, the authors stressed the need for a stronger link with NASPAA and recommended utilizing the journal's education section as a marketing tool. They also pointed to the need for a repository so that papers could be disseminated to faculty on a fee basis. They recommended that future proceedings focus on topics and issues of particular interest and where a need existed for that type of research. In order to build continuity, Manns and Streib urged that future authors build on the base of past papers and that teaching faculty focus more on research (Manns and Streib, 1990).

Yeager (1990) extended the Manns and Streib research regarding trends in teaching public administration by adding the papers presented at the 1988 and 1989 teaching conferences. He examined the proceedings index for key words rather than topical listings, grouping the papers into five general categories based on an analysis of the first key word assigned to the papers. Yeager examined the major topics from a 12-year span to identify trends. He also listed the minor topics that had consistently appeared from one year to the next. Yeager noted that papers fell into five categories—curriculum matters, specific courses, program administration, teaching methodology, and others. Not surprisingly, over half the papers represented specific courses, since they were submitted largely by teaching faculty. Major topics included computers, management, ethics, and policy analysis. The papers' primary function was an exchange of ideas on course work. A limitation of Yeager's study was that it included only those papers presented in the proceedings, rather than topical concerns of public administration faculty as a whole (Yeager, 1990).

DOCTORAL PROGRAMS IN PUBLIC ADMINISTRATION

Ph.D. versus D.P.A.

Debate continues over the purpose and future prospects of two separate doctoral degree designations in public administration. In the decades spanning the 1950s and 1960s, schools of public administration awarded the D.P.A. in order to prepare students to practice government, whereas the Ph.D. curriculum centered on the preparation of students for academia and research. Hambrick (1997) discounted the need for a separate degree for practitioners, suggesting that the differences between the two programs were not sufficient to warrant separate designations, and cited similarities in student bases and program requirements to justify his position. Increasingly, student enrollment in schools of public administration is composed of working adults engaged in part-time studies. The result is that graduates frequently cross over into other career fields. Sizable numbers of D.P.A. graduates who were previous practitioners have had careers in academia. Conversely, many with Ph.D. degrees reject academic pursuits in order to secure employment in the practitioner world (Hambrick, 1997).

Hambrick supports the argument that the D.P.A. has succeeded in bringing talented career professionals into doctoral education. Although he applauds the contributions that the practitioners have made to education, he cited five reasons for the likely future demise of the D.P.A. degree. In the absence of significant curriculum differences and the public relations problem inherent in the D.P.A., he contended that the NASPAA research requirement will further dissipate the program distinctions. Add to that the fact that schools of public administration that confer the Ph.D. have become more cognizant of the tendency for crossovers into other career paths and more responsive to the need for program diversity. Therefore, Hambrick predicted, the interests of public administration education would best be served by the Ph.D. degree (Hambrick, 1997).

Meek and Johnson (1998) subscribe, on the other hand, to two distinct degree classifications: the Ph.D. for research and academia and the D.P.A. for professional administrators. They argue for the viability of the D.P.A. degree and cite the merits of their program at the University of La Verne in southern California. The La Verne curriculum requires six courses in research and quantitative methods beyond the M.P.A. degree. At the end of the second year, students must pass preliminary exams in research methods and foundational theory in order to attain candidacy in the D.P.A. program, which consists of 12 courses in doctoral-level public administration. The majority of students are working adults with master's degrees in a variety of fields. Approximately 20 percent of the students leave the program at the end of the second year. Graduation rates reflect a 5-year average of 12 students per year. Program format includes intensive weekend class meetings and 1-day cluster seminars. Professors utilize evaluation processes that employ blind grading, wherein assignments are read by a team of randomly selected faculty members. In order to overcome the difficulty in assigning individual grades to team projects, faculty members utilize a peer grading process (Meek and Johnson, 1998).

The Research Issue

The most serious charges leveled at doctoral programs over the past two decades center on the quality of research produced by the field. Because doctoral students hail from diverse fields of study, problems arise with respect to defining core problems for research. M.P.A. graduates who complete practitioner-focused programs frequently experience difficulty in finding theoretical questions to address in dissertations. NASPAA has made a concerted effort to address the issue of quality in doctoral research. In 1987, the association mandated in its policy statement on doctoral study that these programs prepare students to undertake significant research. NASPAA also holds programs accountable for ascertaining that students make worthwhile contributions to the field of knowledge (NASPAA, 1987: 1).

In 1984, McCurdy and Cleary faulted universities for failing to "help new scholars develop research standards that result in significant contributions to the field" (McCurdy and Cleary, 1984: 50). They examined 142 dissertation abstracts for purpose, validity, impact, and importance. Findings indicated that few met the criteria for high-quality research. As could be expected, public administration programs in the top-ranked schools generally turned out more high-quality dissertations. It was not the case, however, that all top-ranked schools produced good-quality publications; some failed to do so. Regardless of the orientation of the program—practice or research—the authors contend that research methodology and design are key to building a knowledge base for the discipline.

Dunn (1984) expressed the view that professors and researchers were responsible for the lack of knowledge regarding public sector performance. At that time, public administration programs and research were housed largely within political science departments. Although researchers in political science are engendered with an appreciation for the overall political environment of the public sector, Dunn maintained that Easton's systems theory had not adequately prepared students for the study of the internal structure and dynamics of public organizations. As a result, he concluded, scholars tend to focus on policy and program development, budgeting, and personnel issues, rather than internal structure and management. His explanation for the bias against case studies in political science centered on its narrow focus on national government. At that time, studies largely ignored the problems of state and local government. Although the lack of available information on state and local agencies contributed partially to the anti–case study bias, he pointed to a tendency for academia to avoid too close a relationship with government officials. Absent in an association with private sector organizations, there existed a fear among academics that a close relationship with government would impair an objective assessment of the agency (Dunn, 1984).

Dunn proposed a stronger interface with local and state government agencies in order to broaden the base for case study and research publication. He cited specific problems within higher education that contribute to the "blinders" (Dunn, 1984: 315) on research. Increased enrollment in public administration programs has resulted in interdisciplinary wars. Additionally, program proliferation has generated quality concerns, especially in the area of doctoral research. Dunn's solutions included a research focus on public agencies and how they function as organizations, particularly those that perform well; the development of case studies derived from an interface with government organizations; and increased requirements for theory-guided research and methods in doctoral dissertations (Dunn, 1984).

White, Adams, and Forrester (1996) concurred with earlier criticisms of the quality of doctoral research. They conducted a 5-year study examining the publication records of public administration doctoral graduates to determine whether they were making a significant contribution to the field. Their study included a group of public administration and public policy graduates from the years 1981 through 1987. On the assumption that graduates would be actively contributing to the field of research over the next 5 to 10 years, they examined the records of 26 academic journals from 1989 to 1993 to determine the graduates' publication history. They discovered that most graduates had not published, and of the number who had, over half had only one published article. Results also indicated that publication rates were higher among those with Ph.D. degrees than those with D.P.A.'s (White et al., 1996).

White and his colleagues found that the vast majority of refereed articles were submitted by faculty members at academic institutions and that the articles were more likely to appear in general than in specialized journals. Their study also identified the institutions where the publications originated. They concluded that NASPAA-member schools were failing to turn out doctoral graduates who published prolifically. Likewise, schools were remiss in supplying adequate numbers of professors. Instead, graduates were pursuing professional or administrative positions in public service. They contended that the poor quality of doctoral dissertations is reflected in the tendency of public administration candidates to engage in practice research. Doctoral research in fields other than public administration, on the other hand, proved to be more academic in nature. Foreign students in public administration were prone to write about their home countries, and case studies constituted the most common research approach. The authors criticized graduate faculty members for engaging in a practice they term the *Abilene Paradox,* whereby committee members pass on a student's dissertation, knowing that it will not contribute significantly to the field. Rather than reducing the numbers of public administration programs, they recommended that existing schools focus on raising expectations for high-quality doctoral research (White et al., 1996).

Golembiewski (1999) noted the earlier criticisms of McCurdy, Cleary, White, Adams, and Forrester regarding the quality of doctoral dissertations and drew on his extensive background in public administration to provide an overall assessment of the quality of dissertations that he has judged. He observed the tendency for dissertations to be empirically insufficient in terms of data collection and theory development and said that the work "fails to exhibit the proper sequence of 'experience, action, testing, and reconceptualization'" (Golembiewski, 1999: 59) that he deems central to all learning. He conceded some improvement in quantitative data analysis over the past few years, which was due in large part to the use of improved statistical software (Golembiewski, 1999).

A consensus exists among academicians that empirical research and publication are vital to the integrity and identity of the field of public administration. Further, public administration scholars generally agree that the number and frequency of articles published in refereed journals are indicators of program productivity. As fiscal conservatism at the federal and state levels prompts universities to assess programs, it is imperative that public administration faculty contribute to the knowledge base of the profession. Forrester (1996) conducted a study of 447 authors in refereed public administration journals from 1989 through 1993 in order to identify the schools that publish most frequently in the selective refereed journals. They discovered that most of the authors were full professors from the United States. Surprisingly, an examination of 5559 citations revealed that fewer than one-fourth of the authors were from the public administration field. Forrester concluded that although the field is not necessarily failing to publish, it is becoming more complex and interdisciplinary (Forrester, 1996).

Although the majority of the citations in recent public administration journals are attributed to authors with specializations outside the field, vast numbers of public administration faculty members publish outside the realm of the 11 selective journals. Robert and Nanette Rodgers (1999) have dubbed those faculty members "undisciplined mongrels" (Rodgers and Rodgers, 1999: 3). For 1991, they examined the vitae of 91 assistant professors in 68 public administration programs to determine their publication records. Those records reflected myriad journals, books, and papers in public administration and numerous other fields. Rodgers used impact factors from the *Journal Citation Reports* to measure journal quality. Compared to faculty members who restrict their writings to public administration journals, the "mongrels" tended to be more widely read and cited. Seemingly, the current method of ranking public administration programs according to publication in the 11 selective journals fails to acknowledge the talent and productivity of a vast group of professionals (Rodgers and Rodgers, 1999).

Although a number of studies have been conducted to evaluate the frequency and quality of faculty publication rates, Rodgers and Rodgers (1999) set about the task of accounting for the factors that explain the differences in faculty publication productivity. They point to the challenges and the high failure rates associated with publishing in the academic world as a deterrent to productivity. The authors defined the inner gratification that prompts faculty members to conduct research as the "sacred spark" (Rodgers and Rodgers, 1999: 5), and hypothesized that those who possessed such a spark would place greater emphasis on publishing. They attempted to identify the factors that caused differences in publishing productivity among faculty members by surveying 80 assistant professors of public administration from across the United States. Having collected questionnaires regarding their interests and attitudes with respect to writing, Rodgers and Rodgers learned that respondents became energized by their writing. The couple concluded that universities were justified in recruiting faculty candidates with good graduate publication records from prestigious schools. Another important variable in faculty productivity was the amount of support provided by the university (Rodgers and Rodgers, 1999).

The most recent study of public administration program rankings based on faculty productivity was conducted by James W. Douglas (1996), who examined 11 selective public administration journals published between 1986 and 1993 to determine trends in school rankings. Although a few of the top-ranking schools managed to hold their positions from previous studies, the rankings were fairly unstable; Douglas noted that they were subject to the movement of certain faculty members with excellent publication rates. A surprising outcome of the Douglas study was the positive link between faculty publication rates and those of their graduate students. The productivity of graduate students and faculty signals the degree to which a program prepares students to contribute to the field and thus becomes a significant indicator of program desirability to graduate candidates seeking enrollment in a prestigious program (Douglas, 1996).

CONCLUSION

Unlike at the time the Honey Report was published, today the number of universities engaged in preparing students for the public service has grown dramatically. The key issue that confronts the public administration education community is not that of producing enough graduates for governments that desperately seek trained personnel, but of preparing the highest-quality graduates who will be able to serve the changing needs of a democratic society that faces demands that are significantly different from those it faced a few short years ago. Specifically, the reality of public service education in the 21st century is one of qualitative concerns. Matters of accountability, assessment, quality standards, the necessity of ethics training, and the appropriateness of distance learning and other technologies in the delivery of the educational experience are among the overriding issues for public administration as reflected in its recent literature.

However, the literature of the field, in our opinion, is not entirely reflective of the current and emerging issues that public administration educators must address. With the "contracting out" trend an increasingly common state of affairs for all levels of government, it seems incumbent on the field to assess its curricula systematically to determine the changes that must be made to allow M.P.A. program graduates to acquire the skills that match the demands of the practitioner world that they will encounter in the future. Reflective of these changes in the practice of public service is that many public administration programs have added elective tracks in the area of the management of nonprofits. Rather than standalone elective curricula, M.P.A. programs might well examine the nonprofit offerings in our field with the idea of modifying for the better our core requirements in human resource management, budgeting and financial management, and other traditional areas of study.

Another issue of great importance to the field of public administration education that has, in our opinion, not been addressed adequately in the literature is the changing nature of our student populations at the master's level and, by extension, the makeup of the public service as we progress into the 21st century. At the time of the Honey Report, the student body and the faculty who taught them were predominately Caucasian males. The student population has changed dramatically since then in terms of larger numbers of women in nearly all programs and a dramatic increase in minority enrollment for many programs. Thus it seems, in our view, that the field of public administration must be increasingly mindful of possible different needs of these student learners and the adjustments that might be made in curriculum to enhance the learning environment of a different mix of students.

The field of public administration must systematically address some practical issues such as student recruitment and enrollment management. With the expansion of public service education programs greater in recent decades than the number of government employees seeking education in the field, it seems incumbent on the directors of public administration programs to find ways to adapt our curriculum to a changing clientele who can benefit from it. A further step in our view is that public administration program directors must employ effective program marketing; otherwise our programs will play a much smaller role in educating public servants in the near future than they have in the past. Much has been done, but much more needs to be done.

Concerns over the issue of doctoral research quality have grown in response to program proliferation and expansion. As the field of public administration becomes more multidisciplinary, it follows that doctoral dissertations and professional publications will include diverse topics. Consequently, publication records will necessarily reflect articles, books, and papers outside the field of public administration. We believe that the question of two degree designations is not the important issue it once was; however, universities awarding either the D.P.A. or Ph.D. must be mindful of and committed to NASPAA standards on research quality. Further, to ensure that programs flourish, universities must support faculty research with lower teaching loads, fellowships, and sabbaticals in order to foster research productivity and reputation that attract the most promising students. With respect to the research problems experienced by doctoral students with undergraduate specialities outside the field, we suggest that program directors consider extending the curriculum to include additional course work in research methodology.

REFERENCES

Adams, G., and White, J. (1994). Dissertation research in public administration and cognate fields: An assessment of methods and quality. *Public Administration Review. 54*(6): 565–575.

Banovetz, J. (1967). Needed: New expertise in public administration. *Public Administration Review. 27*(4): 321–324.

Bonser, C. (1992). Total quality education? *Public Administration Review. 52*(5): 504–511.

Bowman, J. (1998). The lost world of public administration education: Rediscovering the meaning of professionalism. *Journal of Public Affairs Education. 4*(1): 27–31.

Brewer, G., Facer, R., O'Toole, L., and Douglas, J. (1998). The state of doctoral education in public administration: Developments in the field's research preparation. *Journal of Public Affairs Education. 4*(2): 123–135.

Britnall, M. (1998). Research funding issues for public administration. Report of the ASPA-NASPAA Committee on The Advancement of Public Administration. Prepared for delivery at *The 1998 Annual Meeting of the American Political Science Association and the Annual Meeting of the National Association of Public Affairs and Administration.*

Campbell, H., and Tatro, B. (1998). Teaching program evaluation to public administration students in a single course: An experiential solution. *Journal of Public Affairs Education. 4*(2): 101–122.

Cleary, R. (1990). What do public administration masters programs look like? Do they do what is needed? *Public Administration Review. 50*(6): 663–672.

Cleary, R. (1992). Revisiting the doctoral dissertation in public administration: An examination of the dissertations of 1990. *Public Administration Review. 52*(1): 55–61.

Cox, R. (1994). The Winter Commission report: The practitioner's view. *Public Administration Review. 54*(2): 108–109.

Crewson, P. and Fisher, B. (1997). Growing older and wiser: The changing skill requirements of city administrators. *Public Administration Review. 57*(5): 380–385.

Daniels, M., and Johansen, E. (1985). Role of accreditation in the development of public administration as a profession: A theoretical and empirical assessment. *Public Administration Quarterly. 8*(4): 419–439.

Denhardt, R. (1997). Experimental education in public administration. *Journal of Public Administration Education. 3*(2): 149–151.

Denhardt, R. (1999). *Public administration: An action orientation,* 3rd ed. Harcourt Brace, Ft. Worth, Texas.

Douglas, J. (1996). Faculty, graduate student, and graduate productivity in public administration and public affairs programs. *Public Administration Review. 56*(5): 433–440.

Dunn, D. (1984). "Blinders" on research in public sector performance. *Public Administration Quarterly. 8*(3): 315–324.

Dunn, D. (1994). Public affairs, administrative faculty and the Winter Commission report. *Public Administration Review. 54*(2): 109–110.

Elling, R. (1994). The line in winter: An academic assessment of the first report of the national commission on the state and local public service. *Public Administration Review. 54*(2): 107–110.

Forrester, J. (1996). Public administration productivity: An assessment of faculty in PA programs. *Administration and Society. 27*(4): 537–565.

Golembiewski, R. (1999). Transitioning to tomorrow's public administration: Policies and practices for PA 2000. *PA 2000: The Future of Public Administration* Symposium. University of West Florida, Pensacola, Fla., January.

Grode, G., and Holzer, M. (1975). The perceived utility of MPA degrees. *Public Administration Review. 35*(4): 403–411.

Hambrick, R. (1990). Incorporating skills development into the MPA curriculum. *International Journal of Public Administration. 13*(1,2): 305–324.

Hambrick, R. (1997). The identity, purpose, and future of doctoral education. *Journal of Public Administration Education. 3*(2): 133–148.

Hays, S., and Duke, B. (1996). Professional certification in public management: A status report and proposal. *Public Administration Review. 56*(5): 425–431.

Heady, F. (1967). Higher education for public service. *Public Administration Review. 27*(4): 292–293.

Hebert, T., and Reynolds, K. (1998). MPA Learning Outcomes: Does the cohort format make a difference? *Journal of Public Affairs Education. 4*(4): 253–262.

Hejka-Ekins, A. (1998). Teaching ethics across the public administration curriculum. *Journal of Public Affairs Education. 4*(1): 45–50.

Hetzner, C., and Schmidt, V.A. (1986). Bringing moral values back in: The role of formal philosophy in effective ethical public administration. *International Journal of Public Administration.* *8*(4): 429–453.

Honey, J. (1967). A report: Higher education for public service. *Public Administration Review.* *27*(4): 294–320.

Ingraham P., and Zuck, A. (1996). Public affairs and administration education: An overview and look ahead from the NASPAA Perspective. *Journal of Public Administration Education.* *2*(2): 161–173.

Leavitt, W., and Richman, R. (1997). The high tech MPA: Distance learning technology and graduate public administration education. *Journal of Public Administration Education.* *3*(1): 13–26.

Lee, D. (1990). The difficulty with ethics education in public administration. *International Journal of Public Administration.* *13*(1,2): 181–205.

Loveland, J., and Whately, A. (1977). Improving public administration school effectiveness through upward performance evaluation. *Public Administration Review.* *37*(1): 77–80.

Maggiotto, Michael (1997). Transferring the American experience: Rethinking an old question. *Journal of Public Administration Education.* *3*(1): 65–68.

Manns, E., and Streib, G. (1990). Sifting through the past: A ten-year perspective on the Annual Conference on Teaching Public Administration. *International Journal of Public Administration.* *13*(3): 415–433.

McCurdy, H., and Cleary, R. (1984). Why can't we resolve the research issue in public administration? *Public Administration Review.* *44*(1): 49–55.

Meek, J., and Johnson, E. (1998). Curriculum, pedagogy, innovation: The professional doctorate in public administration. *Journal of Public Affairs Education.* *4*(1): 57–63.

Menzel, D. (1998). To act ethically: The what, why, and how of ethics pedagogy. *Journal of Public Affairs Education.* *4*(1): 11–18.

Miles, R. (1967). The search for identity of graduate schools of public affairs. *Public Administration Review.* *27*(4): 343–356.

Miller, H. (1997). Why teaching theory matters. *Journal of Public Administration Education.* *3*(3): 363–373.

Mosher, F. (1967). The universities and the problem of the cities. *Public Administration Review.* *27*(4): 325–328.

National Association of Schools of Public Affairs and Administration (1987). NASPAA Policy on Doctoral Education in Public Affairs/Public Administration. Washington, D.C.

Newell, C., and Durst, S. (1997). Narrowing the practice gap: Sending MPA students into the field. *Journal of Public Administration Education.* *3*(3): 315–325.

Newman, M. (1996). Practicing what we teach: Beyond the lecture in a public administration class. *Journal of Public Administration Education.* *2*(1): 16–27.

O'Leary, R. (1997). The great man theory of teaching is dead. *Journal of Public Administration Education.* *3*(2): 127–131.

Overman, E., Perry, J., and Radin, B. Doctoral education in public affairs and administration: issues for the 1990's. *International Journal of Public Administration.* *16*(3): 357–377.

Pope, H. (1967). The immediate need to educate middle managers. *Public Administration Review.* *27*(4): 331–334.

Reid, M., and Miller, W. (1997). Bridging theory and administrative practice: The role of a capstone course in P.A. programs. *International Journal of Public Administration.* *20*(10): 1769–1787.

Reining, H. (1967). A reversal of emphasis. *Public Administration Review.* *27*(4): 334–337.

Rice, W., Nelson, D., and Van Hook, P. (1998). Using opinion surveys to assess ethics education in an MPA Program: The Utah Case. *Journal of Public Affairs Education.* *4*(1): 51–56.

Rocheleau, B. (1998). The MPA core course in information technology: What should be taught? Why? *Journal of Public Affairs Education.* *4*(3): 193–205.

Rodgers, R. and Rodgers, N. (1998). Defining the boundaries of public administration: Undisciplined mongrels versus disciplined purists. Working paper, University of Kentucky, Lexington, Ky.

Rodgers, R. and Rodgers, N. (1999). The sacred spark of academic research. Working paper, University of Kentucky, Lexington, Ky.

Sherman, H. (1967). Some questions about the question. *Public Administration Review.* *27*(4): 337–339.

Sherwood, F. (1996). Revisiting the premises of a D.P.A. program after 25 years: Sharp differences with the Ph.D. *Journal of Public Administration Education.* *2*(2): 107–115.

Simon, M., and Pigenko, V. (1997). Thoughts on teaching research methods to students from former soviet countries. *Journal of Public Administration Education.* *3*(1): 85–88.

Slack, J., Myers, N., Nelson, L., and Sark, K. (1996). Women, research, and mentorship in public administration. *Public Administration Review.* *56*(5): 453–458.

Stalls, R. (1986). Doctoral programs in public administration: An outsider's perspective. *Public Administration Review.* *46*(3): 235–239.

Thompson, F. (1993). *Revitalizing state and local public service.* Jossey-Bass, San Francisco.

Tompkins, J., Laslovich, M., and Greene, J. (1996). Developing a competency-based MPA curriculum. *Journal of Public Administration Education.* *2*(2): 117–131.

Van Riper, P. (1967). Hit 'em harder, John, hit 'em harder! *Public Administration Review.* *27*(4): 339–342.

Ventress, C. (1991). Contemporary issues in American public administration education: The search for an educational focus. *Public Administration Review.* *51*(1): 4–12.

Vocino, T., and Heimovics, R. (1982). *Public Administration Education in Transition.* Marcel Dekker, New York.

White, J. (1986). Dissertations and publications in public administration. *Public Administration Review.* *46*(3): 227–232.

White, J., Adams, G., and Forrester, J. (1996). Knowledge and theory development in public administration: The role of doctoral education and research. *Public Administration Review.* *56*(5): 441–452.

Whorton, J., Gibson, F., and Dunn, D. (1986). The culture of university public service: A national survey of the perspectives of users and providers. *Public Administration Review.* *46*(1): 38–46.

Williams, D., Plein, C., and Lilly, R. (1998). Professional and career development: The MPA approach. *Journal of Public Affairs Education. 4*(4): 277–285.

Wise, L. (1998). Taking stock: Evidence about the standing of public administration in academia. *Report of the ASPA-NASPAA Committee on the Advancement of Public Administration.* Prepared for delivery at *The 1998 Annual Meeting of the American Political Science Association and the 1998 Annual Meeting of the National Association of Public Affairs and Administration.*

Yeager, S. (1990). Trends in teaching public administration: A view from the proceedings of the National Conferences on Teaching Public administration. *International Journal of Public Administration. 13*(1,2): 279–303.

Yoo, J. and Wright, D. (1994). Public administration education and formal administrative position: They make a difference: A note on Pope's Proposition and Mile's Law in an intergovernmental context. *Public Administration Review. 54*(4): 357–362.

32

Issues in Doctoral Education

Jay D. White
College of Public Affairs and Community Service, University of Nebraska at Omaha, Omaha, Nebraska

Several scholars in the field of public administration have evaluated the quality and the quantity of published research generated by doctoral degree holders. Unfortunately, the quality of the research is poor and the quantity of the doctoral research that is published is quite low. These findings suggest the need for a major reform of doctoral education in public administration. Yet this reform may be slow in coming because of several unresolved issues in doctoral education for public affairs and administration that will be presented here.

First the quality issue: When Howard E. McCurdy and Robert E. Cleary examined the doctoral dissertation research produced in 1981, they found that much of it focused on topics of little importance to the field, that it was methodologically unsound, and that it failed to contribute to a growing body of knowledge of the field (1984:55). When I replicated their research for the 1980 and 1981 doctoral graduates, I arrived at the same conclusions (White, 1986). Guy B. Adams and I examined the 1992 public administration dissertations. Many of them lacked an explicit theoretical or conceptual framework to guide the research or failed to ask a relevant research question, or contained obvious flaws in their methods of data collection and analysis, or were a statistical technique in search of a relevant question, or offered conclusions that could not contribute to either theory development or the improvement of professional practice. We characterized much of the research as a theoretical wasteland and as mindless empiricism (Adams and White, 1994).

Turning to the quantity issue, under traditional norms of doctoral education, one would expect that dissertation authors would publish something of value to contribute to the knowledge base in the field. This is simply not the case in public administration. I examined the publication records of 305 dissertation authors who received their degrees in 1981 and 1980. Only 65, or 21 percent, of the authors published at least one referred journal article (White, 1986). Guy B. Adams, John P. Forrester, and I examined the publication records of doctoral students graduating from 1981 to 1987. Of the total of 1037 graduates, only 112, or 12 percent, have published a refereed article in the comprehensive data base of journals that we studied (White et al., 1996). The poor quality of much of the dissertation research has some relation to the low published research productivity of the doctoral graduates, but there may be other reasons. Considering the time, energy, and money that go into producing a doctoral graduate, if we are to gauge our success by virtue of contributions to the knowledge base of the field, then we are not getting much "bang for the buck." Perhaps we should dramatically reduce the number of doctoral programs in the field so as to make doctoral education cost-effective in terms of knowledge development and dissemination.

This chapter explores some of the possible reasons for the current state of doctoral research in the field. Speculations are offered for further research and for discussion among colleagues in the discipline. As the philosopher Richard Rorty (1979, 1996) has demonstrated, knowledge development in any field is fundamentally predicated on the ability to maintain an ongoing conversation about what we know, what we may know, and how we may know it. Although he is primarily concerned with philosophy and its relationship to knowledge development in the natural, social, and human sciences, my concern here is where "the rubber hits the road" in the sense that doctoral education in public administration is about producing knowledge and using it to effect political, economic, and social change.

In brief, the three speculations are (a) that doctoral graduates are not motivated to engage in research that will contribute to our knowledge of the field, (b) that doctoral graduates are not adequately prepared to conduct publishable research, and (c) that doctoral graduates have not received adequate supervision by productive researchers. Addressing each speculation will raise many questions and issues of concern to faculty and university administrators who value high-quality doctoral education. Then the role that the National Association of Schools of Public Affairs and Administration (NASPAA) might play in answering the questions and addressing the issues is explored.

MOTIVATION

Under traditional norms of the social sciences, students enter doctoral programs because they have a desire to teach and conduct basic research that contributes to a common body of knowledge. This does not appear to be the case in public administration. Doctoral programs in public administration are populated by a combination of future academicians and continuing professionals. Although the future academicians vary in age and professional experience, most of them seem to want to pursue a career in academe. This may involve teaching, research, or community service, or some combination of the three traditional academic roles. Some of the graduates who enter academe may choose teaching, or community service, and possibly university administration over research. Since these roles usually take the graduates out of the research stream, this may be a partial explanation of the low research productivity. Yet there are no data to support this speculation.

The motives of the continuing professionals are more difficult to grasp. Some may wish to have another credential behind their name simply to enhance their ego. Some may find continuing education at the doctoral level to be more enjoyable than another hobby or sport such as bowling. Some may wish to acquire additional knowledge and skills to enhance their professional practice.

We should not denigrate the motives of all continuing professionals. Pursuing a doctoral degree to enhance one's professional performance is a just goal. It potentially means better public service by a more highly educated and skilled professional. Pursuing a doctoral degree for the pleasure of learning is also justified if one defines the role of the university as a place where someone can find personal fulfilment. Pursuing a doctoral degree to enhance one's ego is partly justified if it contributes to the development of skills that someone might need in order to make him or her a better practitioner of a profession. It is not justified if it simply enhances ego.

In talking about the mix of future academicians and continuing professionals in public administration doctoral programs, one cannot avoid raising the distinction between the Ph.D. degree and the D.P.A. degree. It is easy to assume that the traditional doctor of philosophy degree is intended for students seeking an academic career and the doctor of public administration degree is intended for those who continue in professional roles. Although this may be true in the minds of some people, the fact is that there is a mix of future academicians and continuing professionals in programs with either title. Some D.P.A. programs have produced productive researchers, and some Ph.D. programs have produced highly competent professional practitioners. One must look closely at a program's curriculum, mix of students, and placement of graduates to determine whether its primary focus is on preparing future academicians or continuing professionals, or perhaps both (see Clayton, 1995). Despite the fact that some D.P.A. programs produce future scholars, research shows that publishing scholars are more likely to emerge from Ph.D. programs, especially traditional political science doctoral programs (White et al., 1996).

The history of the D.P.A. label raises questions about the nature of a doctoral dissertation. Frank Sherwood (1996) believes that the D.P.A. dissertation required by the University of Southern California's Washington Public Affairs Center should be different from a traditional dissertation that is supposed to add to the cumulative body of knowledge in the field. He said: "I felt that one of the big selling points for the DPA in Washington was jettisoning of the Ph.D. requirement. I told students that the purpose of the dissertation was to advance their personal learning and not to worry about the sum of human knowledge" (pp. 112–113). If this is a reasonable position to take, it raises some extremely important questions. What is the nature of a practitioner dissertation? How might it differ from a traditional academic dissertation? What are the standards to judge the quality of a practitioner dissertation? How do we know that a practitioner dissertation actually enhances some students' professional capabilities? If there is justification for a practitioner dissertation, no matter what the label of the degree, these questions must be answered.

Actually the notion of a different practitioner dissertation runs counter to NASPAA's stated policy on doctoral education (1983, 1987):

> Doctoral programs in public administration . . . should prepare students to undertake significant research in their subsequent careers, whether in government, academic life, or other settings; the capacity to do significant research, rather than access to a particular career setting, is the appropriate goal of doctoral training. . . . Whether in a governmental, academic or other career setting, holders of the doctorate add to the ranks of those who are able to generate and share knowledge of public administration and its related fields. . . . The doctorate should be seen as a research degree in public administration. (NASPAA, 1983, 1987)

The policy continues:

> Because the doctoral degree is a research degree, it should not be seen as a degree in the professional practice of public administration. . . . The goal of doctoral training is the quite different one of equipping individuals to add to knowledge of public administration and related fields through disciplined research. When practicing professionals undertake the doctorate they should recognize the need to demonstrate substantial research skills and to interact with a research faculty on a continuing basis as they design and execute their dissertation projects. (NASPAA, 1983, 1987)

Obviously the stated policy runs counter to the beliefs of those in the field who feel that a practitioner dissertation should be something different from a traditional academic research project that adds knowledge to the field. If a valid case can be made for a practitioner dissertation that enhances professional practice instead of contributing to the general body of knowledge in the field, then NASPAA's policy needs to be revised. If a case cannot be made for a practitioner dissertation, then we must hold continuing professionals to the same standards of research for a traditional academic degree that contributes knowledge to the field through publications.

We might, however, be doing continuing professionals a disservice because we simply do not know whether teaching them how to conduct traditional social science research actually enhances their professional knowledge and skills. Chris Argyris, Donald Schon, and Martin Rein have made compelling arguments that the type of knowledge used in professional settings and the type of knowing or learning used in professional settings are different from our traditional understanding of knowledge acquisition and use in the social sciences. They use such phrases as "epistemology of practice" (Schon, 1983), "actionable knowledge" (Argyris, 1993), "story telling" (Rein, 1976), and "frame reflection" (Schon and Rein, 1994) to describe the type of learning, knowing, and knowledge used by professionals. If the type of knowing or knowledge used in professional settings is indeed different from the type employed in traditional dissertation research, then we need to find out more about such knowing and knowledge and find ways of conveying it. If what they say is true, it would make a strong case for a practitioner dissertation, but we still do not know what one might look like and we certainly do not have standards to judge its quality.

PREPARATION FOR RESEARCH

Are doctoral students in public administration adequately prepared to conduct basic research that will contribute to knowledge development in the field? The answer is a resounding "No!" Evidence of this is found in the evaluations of dissertation research, much of which addresses trivial questions, has little theoretical grounding, and lacks rigorous research designs. No wonder so little of it is published.

Although there are several possible reasons for the poor quality of dissertation research, two are obvious: insufficient exposure to the knowledge base in the field and inadequate preparation in research methods and tools. First, that many of the dissertation authors were unable to formulate a relevant or important question to answer suggests that they may not have had sufficient exposure to knowledge in the field or even a subset of knowledge in the field. In other words, they simply did not know enough about public administration in general or their chosen area of specialization to ask and try to answer an important question.

This suspicion raises questions about curriculum components of doctoral programs. Are there sufficient doctoral student seminars beyond the master's level courses to cover relevant topics in greater depth and breadth? What topics should these seminars cover? How many seminars should be offered to cover the relevant range of topics? Are there sufficient doctoral level courses in areas of specialization (e.g., budgeting, finance, organizational behavior, human resource management, intergovernmental relations) to offer greater depth and breadth of coverage? Do programs simply rely on additional master's level courses that may not appropriately address the depth and breadth of the relevant subject matter? Do programs rely, perhaps too heavily, on independent readings and research courses as a way of conveying advanced knowledge in a specialty area?

Second, students may not have adequate preparation in either quantitative or qualitative research methods and techniques. In a preliminary analysis of public administration doctoral curricula Marc Holzer has reported that possibly as many as 40 percent of the programs do not have dedicated research methods courses (White et al., 1997). If this is true, no wonder the quality of the dissertation research is so low.

Again we are faced with questions about curriculum. Beyond basic research methods and statistics courses that may be offered at the master's level, are there any advanced research designs or quantitative techniques that should be included in a doctoral curriculum? If so, what are they? Given the considerable amount of qualitative research conducted in the field and the fact that most of it is methodologically unsound (Adams and White, 1994; White, 1986), we should be offering basic and advanced courses in qualitative research methods to assure high-quality dissertations of this type.

Although the faculty at various institutions may have a personal sense of what knowledge and skill components should be included in their own doctoral programs, we do not have a widely shared understanding of curriculum requirements for doctoral education in public affairs and administration. It would be interesting to find out how other doctoral programs structure their curricula, especially with regard to doctoral seminars and doctoral level research methods and research techniques courses, as well as their emphasis on traditional public administration, public management, and public policy. Lessons could be learned for those institutions thinking about starting up programs or about redesigning their programs. It would also be interesting to see how programs differ with regard to their emphases on public policy, public management, and traditional public administration, as well as areas of specialization.

SUPERVISION

A lack of proper supervision by an experienced senior researcher may be one of the reasons for the lack of quality of the research and the low quantity of published research. Even if a student has a firm grasp of the relevant literature and a firm grounding in methods and techniques, he or she still needs guidance at every step of the dissertation. It is unreasonable to expect someone to produce a dissertation totally independently, without any guidance from a more experienced researcher, even if this guidance simply means having someone to talk to about various aspects of the research.[1] In other cases, students may need more help and direction, especially if they have not been exposed to a relevant knowledge base or have been inadequately trained in research methods and techniques. I do not know how often this occurs, but I have been told on several occasions by colleagues at other institutions that they have provided so much help to a student that the dissertation as a piece of research is actually the faculty member's work, not the student's. Under these conditions—and I do not know how widespread they are—the student has not learned how to conduct research. Consequently, such a student who takes oposition in academe is ill prepared to pursue a strong research agenda.

The question of proper supervision leads to questions of faculty resources, which are of interest to individual faculty members and university administrators. From the individual's point of view, how many dissertations can a faculty member reasonably supervise over a given period? I do not have a magic number, but my own personal feeling is that I cannot responsibly supervise more than three dissertations in any 12- to 18-month period. It takes time to assist even the best of students adequately. Unfortunately, that time may not be associated with reduced workload. I am fortunate to be on a research assignment, which means teaching four courses a year instead of six and limited involvement in community service. If I were carrying a full workload, my ability to supervise doctoral student dissertation research adequately would be diminished simply because of a lack of time. Unfortunately I know too many colleagues at other institutions who are carrying full workloads and are also supervising as many as five dissertations at a time.

Administrators are concerned with this issue because doctoral programs are costly. They may require significant funding to support full-time students. They may draw scarce faculty resources away from the support of M. P. A. and/or undergraduate programs. This is a particular problem for public administration programs at institutions that allocate operating budgets primarily on the basis of student credit hours. Those programs lacking large undergraduate enrollments suffer most at budget allocation time. Under these conditions, program directors often have to ask for additional support for their doctoral programs. This action puts their doctoral programs under scrutiny during times of fiscal stress. One way to deal with this problem is to make the doctoral program "self-sufficient" by enrolling a large number of students, turning the doctoral program into a de facto revenue center. This compounds the problem of supervision if faculty resources are scarce. It may also lead to a lowering of admission standards in order to get the "adequate" number of doctoral students to justify the existence of the program. If this is the case, it contributes to the issue of the quality of the research, under the old adage "Garbage in—garbage out."

Although I do not have any hard facts to support the assertion, I note that over the past 15 years many colleagues at other institutions have complained to me that they have far too many students in their doctoral programs.[2] Their complaints extend to being asked to supervise more dissertations than they can properly handle, to serving on too many supervisory committees, to receiving no course relief time to supervise dissertations, to having who students nearly fail comprehensive examinations because their initial course work was more than 5 years old, to having too many junior faculty members supervising too many dissertations while they should be focusing on their own research agenda.

Another issue concerning supervision needs to be raised. It concerns the recruitment of new degree holders. When a program's faculty starts reviewing applications for assistant professors positions, it has been my experience that the candidates who "float to the top" are the ones who have studied with leading scholars in the field. The process goes something like this: You start reviewing applicants. You wade through several that are clearly irrelevant. You come upon some that seem interesting. Then you find one who has studied with a colleague you know. You put that application aside because you respect your colleague at another institution who has perhaps developed a reputation for producing high-quality doctoral graduates. The quality of a doctoral program and hence the quality of a particular doctoral graduate one often known by the reputations of the faculty of the program. Doctoral programs and faculty who properly supervise their graduates develop strong reputations as sources of basic knowledge in the field.

NASPAA'S POSSIBLE ROLE

There are several actions that NASPAA might consider taking to help improve the quality of doctoral education and research. The strongest would be to accredit the doctoral degree as it does the master's degree. This would require affiliated programs to do several things: (a) Formulate and publish mission statements that define whether the program is intended for future academicians, continuing professionals, or both. The mission statement might also indicate whether the program has a focus on public management or public policy, or both. Such statement would be of considerable assistance to prospective doctoral students in their selection of an appropriate program. (b) Specify a range and depth of subject matter that would constitute the core of a doctoral education in the field. (c) Identify a variety of research methods and technical tool courses required to produce high-quality dissertation research, parts of which may eventually appear in scholarly publications. (d) Define a ratio of faculty to students, to ensure proper supervision. (e) Establish admission requirements that will recruit high-quality doctoral students. (f) Identify outcome measures derived from the mission statement to assess the performance of the program.

Accreditation of doctoral programs would be met with considerable resistance. Over the years I have heard several reasons put forth against accrediting doctoral programs: (a) Doctoral education is sacrosanct, the faculty at each institution know what is best for their students; they do not need interference from an outside body. (b) It would be too much work, especially for those programs with only a handful of doctoral students; this is often the case for political science doctoral programs that offer an area of specialization in public administration. (c) Although it may be possible to develop a mission statement for a doctoral program, some may feel that the results or outcomes of doctoral education are too intangible to measure. (d) Some faculty may be afraid that their programs might not "measure up" to NASPAA's standards and therefore lose their reputations. For these reasons, formal accreditation of doctoral programs in public administration is highly unlikely. Despite these objections, I know of several doctoral programs that have instituted mission statements, identified a common core of doctoral seminars and research methods and tools courses, decided on an appropriate faculty-to-student ratio, and established outcome measures. They have done so because their faculty feels that it is the right thing to do or because their university is moving toward mission-based education and evaluation of programs.

Short of instituting accreditation, NASPAA should serve as a clearinghouse for information about doctoral programs. In the past, NASPAA has collected summary descriptions of doctoral programs (1993). Those descriptions were quite sparse; limited to such topics as current enrollment, length of the program, tuition and fees, financial aid, placement, distinctive nature of the program, geographical setting, and contact person. NASPAA should redo their 1993 survey and include such additional topics as mission statements if they exist; curriculum components, including unique areas of strength or specialization such as nonprofit management or health policy and administration; and faculty biographies. With today's telecommunication technology it would be relatively easy to build a web page containing the results of a new survey of NASPAA-affiliated doctoral programs. One can also place pointers to doctoral programs with existing web pages and encourage programs that do not already have them to build one. This would provide prospective students with a rich source of information for their selection of a doctoral program. It would also provide faculty at institutions starting up a program or redesigning an existing program with valuable information about what is being done in other programs.[3]

NASPAA must revisit its policy on doctoral dissertation research. At too many institutions, the dissertation is simply not a research degree in the traditional sense of the word as currently outlined in NASPAA's own policy statement. NASPAA members may wish to retain the current statement or change it to allow for practitioner-oriented dissertations. In either case NASPAA should operationalize the meaning of doctoral dissertation research. In light of the fact that doctoral programs serve both future academicians and continuing professionals, there might be two operational definitions of a research degree, one for each type of student. This, of course, assumes that the dissertation experience should be somehow different for continuing professionals; an issue that is far from settled in the field.

NASPAA is well aware of the issues presented here: Its Doctoral Education Committee has been discussing them for several years. There have been several panels addressing these issues at past NASPAA annual meetings and two doctoral program workshops held over the past several years to address these issues, and by the time this book is published, a third workshop will have been held. NASPAA is in the process of conducting a new survey of its affiliated doctoral programs. One can only hope that the survey will capture a sufficient amount of relevant information to inform the continuing discussions of the issues so that the quality of doctoral education in the field may be improved.

CONCLUSION

At the beginning of this chapter I made brief mention of Richard Rorty's (1979, 1996) views on knowledge as conversations. I would like to end with a brief explanation of Rorty's theory of knowledge and its relationship to knowledge development and use in public administration.

Rorty is a contemporary philosopher who has reconstructed the logic of social research along what he would call *neopragmatist* and *postmodern* lines. He follows the pragmatist tradition of tying the validity of claims to knowledge to the ways that knowledge can effect personal, social, political, and economic change. This applies to a field like public administration that is concerned with the development of basic knowledge that can be used in applied research to change public policy and administrative conditions. In brief, for pragmatists the validity of what we know about a field such as public administration is predicated on how we can use that knowledge to change administrative situations. The traditional way to do that is to produce knowledge that can be added to a common body and then used in practical situations to effect change. If Argyris, Schon, and Rein are right that professional knowledge is different from academic knowledge, then we should discover its nature and learn how to teach it because we will always have continuing professionals in our doctoral programs.

Rorty is an antifoundationalist philosopher. He parts company with traditional philosophers who have sought to find the ground of knowledge in some transcendental realm of experience. For Rorty, all knowledge is predicated on an ongoing conversation among a community of researchers who speak the same language and who abide by the same linguistic practices and social norms. Public administration as a field of academic study is just such a community. Intentionally and unintentionally we make up our own reality. Unfortunately we are faced with the reality that the quality of much of the dissertation research is quite poor and so little of the dissertation research adds to our knowledge of the field through publications in scholarly journals. If we wish to change this, we must, from Rorty's point of view, intentionally engage in an ongoing conversation concerning the issues presented in this chapter, and perhaps others issues that I have not raised here.

NOTES

1. Related to the issue of supervision is the practice of publishing with doctoral students. A student who is given the opportunity to coauthor an article with an established researcher learns early on how to deal with the "ups and downs" of the editorial review process, including such situations as dealing with rejections and "revise and resubmit" requests.
2. A survey of student enrollments in 1996 (NASPAA) reveals what I consider to be an abuse of doctoral student education in terms of faculty-to-student ratios at some institutions. For example, one institution reported having 121 doctoral students and no full-time faculty, another reported having 111 doctoral students and 4 full-time faculty, and another reported having 146 doctoral students and 11.5 full-time faculty. Although these are extreme cases, the ratios for many of the other reporting institutions also seem to be too high.
3. Eight years ago, when I was helping to start the public administration doctoral program at the University of Nebraska at Omaha, I had to wade through mountains of catalogs and doctoral student handbooks to make sense of what was going on at other institutions. A web page containing a comprehensive and detailed listing of doctoral programs and their particulars would have made my job a lot easier.

REFERENCES

Adams, G. B., and White, J. D. (1994). Dissertation research in public administration and cognate fields. *Public Administration Review. 52:* 565–576.

Argyris, C. (1993). *Knowledge for Action.* Jossey-Bass, San Franscisco.

Clayton, R. (1995). The DPA: Contributing to society's need for scholarship and leadership. *Journal of Public Administration Education. 1:* 61–67.

McCurdy, H. E., and Cleary, R. E. (1984). Why can't we resolve the research issue in public administration? *Public Administration Review. 44:* 49–56.

National Association of Schools of Public Affairs and Administration (1983, 1987). *NASPAA Policy on Doctoral Education in Public Affairs/Public Administration.* Washington, D.C.

National Association of Schools of Public Affairs and Administration (1993). *Summary Description of Doctoral Programs in Public Administration and Public Policy.* Washington, D.C.

National Association of Schools of Public Affairs and Administration. *Summary of Enrollment and Degrees.* Washington, D.C.

Rein, M. (1976). *Social Science and Public Policy.* Penguin, New York.

Rorty, R. (1996). Richard Rorty: Emancipating our culture. In *Debating the State of philosophy: Habermas, Rorty, and Kolakowski* (J. Niznik & J. T. Sanders eds.). Praegar, Westport, Conn., pp. 24–30.

Rorty, R. (1979). *Philosophy and the Mirror of Nature.* Princeton University Press, Princeton, N.J.

Schon, D. (1983). *The Reflective Practitioner: How Professionals Think in Action.* Basic Books, New York.

Schon, D., and Rein, M. (1994). *Frame Reflection: Toward the Resolution of Intractable Policy Controversies.* Basic Books, New York.

Sherwood, F. (1996). Revisiting the premises of a DPA program after 25 years: Sharp differences with the Ph.D. *Journal of Public Administration Education. 2:* 107–117.

White, J. D. (1986). Dissertations and publications in public administration. *Public Administration Review. 46:* 227–234.

White, J. D., Adams, G. B., and Forrester, J. P. (1996). Theory and knowledge development in public administration education and research. *Public Administration Review. 54:* 565–577.

White, J. D., Holzer, M., and Felbinger, C. (1997). The doctorate in public administration: Some unresolved questions and recommendations. Paper presented at *The Annual Meeting of the National Association of Schools of Public Affairs and Administration.* Raleigh, N.C., October 17.

33

The American Society for Public Administration and the Field of Public Administration

Mary R. Hamilton
American Society for Public Administration,
Washington, D.C.

The American Society for Public Administration (ASPA) was established in 1939 in response to major changes in the developing field of public administration. In its 60-plus years, ASPA has both influenced and been influenced by the field and profession of public administration. This chapter describes three areas of mutual impact between ASPA and public administration:

- Professionalism in public administration—both domestic and international
- Public administration education, theory, and research
- Advocacy for public administration and public service

BACKGROUND

ASPA's roots are in the progressive reform movement that produced major changes in American public administration in the early part of the 20th century. Darrell Pugh, in his excellent history of ASPA and public administration *Looking*

Back, Moving Forward, outlines three major developments that formed the backdrop for the creation of ASPA:

- "The emergence of self-conscious practices in public administration brought about during the progressive era through the work . . . principally [of] those associated with the municipal research bureau movement"
- "The establishment of a national network of public administration organizations in Chicago through the Public Administration Clearing House [PACH] in the 1930s"
- "The manifestation of deep concern for the improvement of the management and organization of the federal government precipitated by its burgeoning growth during the "New Deal" period"[1]

Concern about management and organization of the federal government resulted in President Franklin Roosevelt's Committee on Administrative Management (better known as the Brownlow Committee, after its chairman) and the subsequent passage of the Reorganization Act of 1939. Both "generated a series of events that ultimately led to the creation of ASPA."[2]

The Committee on Administrative Management was established in March 1936 to review the organization and management of the executive branch of the federal government. President Roosevelt appointed to the committee three leaders in the field of public administration in the 1920s and 1930s. Louis Brownlow (for whom the committee came to be named) was a former city manager, the first director of the PACH, "and principal architect of the new public administration community."[3] Dr. Charles E. Merriam, a professor of political science at the University of Chicago, was a founder of the Social Science Research Council (SSRC) in 1923. Merriam intended SSRC to "integrate the social sciences and to prepare a more comprehensive, applied focus for research on social issues, particularly public affairs."[4] Merriam was also instrumental in giving public administration a "higher degree of visibility in the academic community" by lobbying successfully for a "special committee to encourage the development of studies in the area of public administration"[5] in the SSRC. The third of President Roosevelt's appointees, Dr. Leonard D. White, a colleague of Charles Merriam's at the University of Chicago, was the first chair of the SSRC special committee on public administration. Pugh says of White that he "used the new committee to propel public administration into the social science mainstream, bringing its research focus closer to actual operational situations while producing studies of superior quality."[6] The committee finished its comprehensive review in November 1936 with a report that recommended major reorganization of the federal executive branch. President Roosevelt developed a proposed reorganization plan based on the committee's work, and a reorganization bill was introduced into the Congress in 1938. After the bill failed to pass, the president asked the committee for a new proposal; that proposal resulted in the Reorganization Act of 1939.

The act transferred the Bureau of the Budget (BOB) from the Department of the Treasury to create, with several other entities, the Executive Office of the President (EOP). Harold Smith, budget director for the state of Michigan, was selected first director of the U.S. Bureau of the Budget and "shaped the [BOB] into an indispensable part of the management function of the executive branch of the federal government."[7] Smith created the Administrative Management Division in the bureau, headed by Donald Stone, who "instituted nationwide recruiting of the best public administration professionals in the country under authority delegated by the U.S. Civil Service Commission."[8]

The Founding of ASPA

During this period, Smith and other members of the BOB met regularly with officials of federal executive agencies and heads of public affairs associations "to exchange ideas regarding critical issues of the time."[9] Among the issues regularly discussed was "how to provide the managerial talent necessary to staff the expanding federal executive branch and . . . how these managers could be trained to fulfill the role . . . envisioned. These discussions led them to a general consensus that a new kind of professional association had to be created to identify and sustain these newly emerging public servants."[10] William E. Mosher, dean of the Maxwell School of Citizenship and Public Affairs at Syracuse University, agreed about the need for a new professional association and thought that organization should allow graduates of public administration master's programs to gain professional recognition and "the opportunity for association that would keep them up-to-date with the advancements in their field."[11]

With support from Smith, Mosher, Stone, Brownlow, Luther Gulick (director of the New York Bureau of Municipal Research and one of the experts consulted by the Brownlow Committee), Charles Ascher, and Leonard White, the American Society for Public Administration was established in December 1939. Table 1 lists the charter members of ASPA.

The preamble to the society's constitution, adopted at the first meeting of the National Council after incorporation of the society on October 13, 1945, outlined the purposes of the new organization.

> To facilitate the exchange of knowledge and results of experience among persons interested in or engaged in the field of public administration;
>
> To encourage the collection, compilation, and dissemination of information on matters relating to public administration;
>
> To advance generally the science, processes and art of public administration.[12]

ASPA's first officers were William Mosher, president, and Rowland Egger, vice president. The first National Council consisted of nine members representing

TABLE 1 Charter Members of ASPA

Lyndon Abbott	Janet L. Hoffman	Harold Seidman
Clark D. Ahlberg	George W. Lawson Jr.	Irving E. Sheffel
George C.S. Benson	Vernie B. Lewis	Lewis B. Sims
David S. Brown	Kent Mathewson	Elmer B. Staats
Weldon Cooper	Elwyn A. Mauck	O. Glenn Stahl
John J. Corson	E.W. Meisenhelder	John H. Stanford
Winston W. Crouch	James M. Mitchell	David T. Stanley
J. Lyle Cunningham	Frederick C. Mosher	Edwin O. Stene
Manilio F. DeAngelis	Lionel V. Murphy	Donald C. Stone
Marshall E. Dimock	Milton Musicus	Harold A. Stone
William O. Farber	Enar B. Olson	Carl W. Tiller
James Fesler	William W. Parsons	Paul Van Riper
Arthur S. Flemming	Frank Piscor	Richard W. Van Wagenen
Donald D. Fowler	Joseph Pois	Robert A. Walker
Bernard L. Gladieux	Don K. Price	Hardy Wickwar
Ernest S. Griffith	John R. Provan	Edgar G. Young
Clifford R. Gross	Albert R. Rathert	Virgil B. Zimmerman
Lowell H. Hattery	Robert H. Rawson	
Julia Henderson	Emmette S. Redford	

Source: American Society for Public Administration.

state, local, and federal levels of government and academia. Table 2 is a list of ASPA presidents.

The purposes stated in ASPA's first constitution incorporate the three principal values that Pugh argues have dominated the society's evolution. "First and foremost," Pugh states, "ASPA has sought the improvement of theory and practice in public administration." Second, ASPA has advocated professionalism in the public service at all levels of government. Third, ASPA has been dedicated to "strengthening and sustaining a real sense of community among the numerous types of practitioners and academicians found within the field of public administration."[13]

The latter—strengthening and sustaining community among the diverse parts of public administration—continues to be a major challenge for the society. Prior to ASPA's formation in 1939, several specialized organizations related to public administration had been established; they continue to this day: the American Political Science Association (1903), the International City/County Management Association (1913), the American Institute of Planners (1917), forerunners to the International Personnel Management Association, the National League of Cities, the National Association of State Legislators, the American Public Welfare Association, the American Public Works Association, and the Government

TABLE 2 ASPA Presidents (1939–1999)

Years	President	Years	President	Years	President
1939–40	William E. Mosher	1962–63	Stephen B. Sweeney	1982–83	A. Lee Fritschler
1940–41	Harold D. Smith	1963–64	York Wilbern	1983–84	Patricia Florestano
1941–44	Louis Brownlow	1964–65	Harvey Sherman	1984–85	Bradley H. Patterson, Jr.
1944–46	Luther H. Gulick	1965–66	Lloyd M. Short	1985–86	Naomi Lynn
1947–47	Charles S. Ascher	1966–67	James E. Webb	1986–87	Sylvester Murray
1947–48	Leonard D. White	1967–68	Stephen K. Bailey	1987–88	Robert Denhardt
1948–49	John J. Corson	1968–69	James A. Norton	1988–89	Charlotte O. Gray
1949–50	Roscoe C. Martin	1969–70	Ferrel Heady	1989–90	Morris W. H. Collins, Jr.
1950–51	Donald C. Stone	1970–71	Harlan Cleveland	1990–91	Carl W. Stenberg
1951–52	John M. Gaus	1971–72	Walter Mode	1991–92	Enid Beaumont
1952–53	James M. Mitchell	1972–73	John W. Ryan	1992–93	Thomas Lynch
1953–54	John A. Perkins	1973–74	Frank P. Sherwood	1993–94	Christine Gibbs
1954–55	William W. Parsons	1974–75	Philip J. Rutledge	1994–95	Robert C. McClain
1955–56	Gordon R. Clapp	1975–76	Randy H. Hamilton	1995–96	Edward T. Jennings, Jr.
1956–57	Matthias E. Lukens	1976–77	Nesta Gallas	1996–97	Yong Hyo Cho
1957–58	Henry Reining, Jr.	1977–78	H. George Frederickson	1997–98	Mary Ellen Guy
1958–59	John W. Macy	1978–79	Dwight A. Ink	1998–99	Todd W. Argow
1959–60	G. Homer Durham	1979–80	Ray Remy	1999–00	Anne Swafford
1960–61	John D. Millett	1980–81	Patrick Conklin	2000–	Marc Holzer
1961–62	Elmer B. Staats	1981–82	Chester Newland		

Source: American Society for Public Administration.

Finance Officers' Association.[14] Today, there are more than 350 associations that focus on specialized aspects of public administration.

ASPA Organization and Structure

When ASPA was first formed, it was housed in Chicago with the Public Administration Clearing House (PACH) at 1313 East 60th Street, in what was known as the "1313 community," which housed other public administration-related organizations. This was important, as ASPA was founded in part to support and sustain connections among the different public administration organizations and the different functions and specialties that the field of public administration comprises. Subsequently, ASPA was housed in space owned by the University of Chicago, reinforcing its role in linking research and theory to practice. In 1964, the society's leadership decided to relocate ASPA headquarters to Washington, D.C., where it has remained since.

Proponents of the move to Washington argued that it would position ASPA to compete more effectively for federal grants and consulting contracts. Opponents were concerned that the move would eventually mean that "eastern, particularly federal, ASPA members" would control the society.[15] They also feared that "Washington's intense political atmosphere would overwhelm ASPA and eventually lead to its politicization."[16] It appears that some of the hopes and fears of both groups were realized, although it is not clear that the relocation was the cause. ASPA was able to secure several grants from various agencies between 1967 and 1979 (Table 3 is a list of grants received by ASPA over the years and their purposes). However, it is not clear that location in Washington, D.C., was the impetus. On the other hand, after the move, many ASPA members in other parts of the country felt that ASPA was dominated by eastern and federal ASPA members, in particular the largest of ASPA's chapters, the National Capital Area Chapter (NCAC). NCAC, in turn, has been dominated for most of its existence by federal public administrators. The politicization of ASPA did not occur, although ASPA's increased advocacy during the 1980s concerned some members (see later discussion).

For the first 17 years of ASPA's existence, the society was run by its volunteer members. This changed in 1956 with the selection of the first executive director, Robert Matteson, a senior staff member of the Institute of Public Administration. Financial problems in the early 1950s prompted ASPA leadership to solicit private foundations for grant funds sufficient "to enable ASPA to become self-supporting."[17] These efforts yielded the 5-year grant from the Ford Foundation for the purpose of helping ASPA fulfill its original commitments. Among these commitments was to hire professional staff. Between 1956 and 2000, ASPA had eight executive directors. They and their terms are listed in Table 4.

ASPA currently has more than 10,000 members, 114 chapters, and 20 sections. The sections include special interest groups and groups representing differ-

Table 3 Grants to ASPA

1940–1955	Subsidies from Public Administration Clearing House (PACH) for staff, office space, editorial subsidies
1955	Ford Foundation grant of $20,000 for creation of International Public Administration Section
1956	PACH editorial subsidies
1956–1960	Ford Foundation 5-year grant of $245,000; to assist ASPA in fulfillment of its original commitments; hire professional staff, expand facilities, purchase additional equipment, provide travel funds, improve national conferences and enhance the image and quality of public administration education
1960	Atomic Energy Commission contract for Management Institutes
1962	Ford Foundation grant of $250,000 for creating Comparative Administration Group
1965	Ford Foundation grant of $105,000 for the International Committee to develop a training program for improved public administration training in emerging nations
1967	Ford Foundation grant of $10,000 to assist the Comparative Administration Group's seminar in Hawaii
	NASA 3-year contract to NAPA of $675,000 for administrative management assistance
1976–1977	HEW grant to Section on Human Resources Administration
	HUD grant for Consortium on Education for Public Service
1976–1978	OEO grant on Health Care
1978	Institute for Public Administration (IPA) grant of $38,311
1979	IPA grant of $35,800
1998–1999	AmeriCorps grant to support ASPA chapter involvement with high school, public service academics, amount dependent on number of volunteers involved

Source: American Society for Public Administration.

Table 4 ASPA Executive Directors

Robert Matteson	1956–1961
Don Bowen	1961–1970
John Garvey	1970–1972
Seymour Berlin	1972–1976
Keith Mulrooney	1976–1987
Shirley Wester	1988–1991
John Thomas	1991–1996
Mary Hamilton	1997–

Source: American Society for Public Administration.

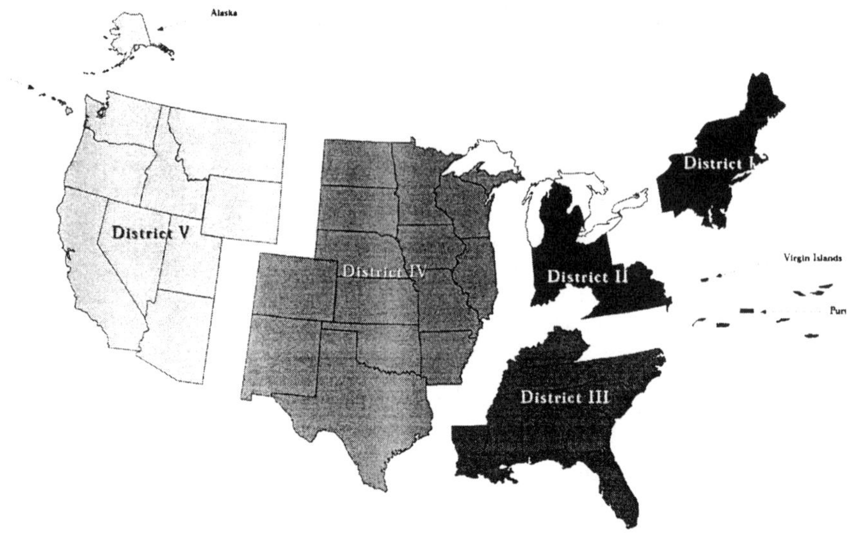

FIG. 1 Map of ASPA Electoral Districts, 1999.

ent functions and specialties in public administration. For most of its existence, ASPA has operated under a loose regional structure, that is, chapters have been grouped into regions for the purpose of encouraging connections among those in the same geographic area (e.g., coordinating to hold regional conferences, sharing best practices) and of defining electoral districts for National Council representation. One region, the Southeastern Conference for Public Administration (SECOPA), incorporated in August 1978, has its own officers, annual conference, and active presence in ASPA.

In 1969, ASPA's National Council was reorganized to provide for regional representation. At the time, the society was divided into six regions. ASPA members voted in 1975 to increase the number of regions from 6 to 10. In 1998, the ASPA National Council approved a strategic plan that called for reducing the size of the council and replacing the 10 regions with 5 electoral districts that are of comparable size in terms of membership. Fig. 1 is a map of the current electoral districts. ASPA's National Council approved a new strategic plan for ASPA in December 1998. This plan will focus the efforts of the society for the years 1999–2001. The goals and objectives of the plan are outlined in Table 5.

Table 5 ASPA Strategic Plan Goals and Objectives *Approved December 1998*

GOAL 1 (Performance)
To improve the effectiveness of democratic governance by positively influencing public policy and management and the ethical performance of public services worldwide
Objective 1.1: To support knowledge and skill development in managing for results
Objective 1.2: To provide access to best practices in public and nonprofit management
Objective 1.3: To advance the literature of the field
Objective 1.4: To operationalize existing affiliation agreements with counterpart associations
GOAL 2 (Pride)
To foster interest and pride in public service by effectively communicating its nature, honor and challenge
Objective 2.1: To celebrate the accomplishments of public service
Objective 2.2: To develop a media strategy that promotes public service and the accomplishments of public servants
Objective 2.3: To build the public service work force for the future
GOAL 3 (Purpose)
To strengthen ASPA as the professional organization that covers the whole spectrum of public service and capitalizes on its diversity
Objective 3.1: To partner with related associations
Objective 3.2: To strengthen ASPA's organizational structure
Objective 3.3: To increase member participation in all aspects of ASPA

Source: American Society for Public Administration.

PROFESSIONALISM IN PUBLIC ADMINISTRATION

Over its 60 years, ASPA has promoted professionalism in public administration in three major areas: in American public administration, in public administration in other countries, and through its emphasis on high ethical standards.

American Public Administration

As noted, advocacy of professionalism in the public service at all levels of government has been a dominant value since ASPA was founded. One of the reasons for establishing the society was to promote professionalism in those who were being recruited to manage the federal executive branch agencies and programs that grew up during the New Deal. ASPA's roots in the American Progressive movement and its relationship to the early city manager and municipal research bureau movements through PACH meant that the society was established with a positive orientation toward professionalism. "By the time ASPA was a reality the concept of a professional American public service had become an orthodox belief for many in public administration."[18]

However, support for professionalism in public administration took a different twist with ASPA. In spite of its heavy emphasis on professionalism, "ASPA did not adopt the orthodox view of a profession of public administration. Instead the Society opted for the pursuit of professionalism among its members—a subtle but significant distinction. ASPA leaders sought to use their organization as a forum in which the broad diversity of public service occupations could be brought together through a mutual commitment to excellence in professional conduct among those involved in public service."[19]

To this day this decision continues to be controversial and continues to make it difficult to define the field of public administration that ASPA serves. The controversy focuses on whether the society should be an advocate for public employee issues or an organization dedicated to excellence in public service. As Pugh states, "[a]lthough these two objectives are not mutually exclusive, ASPA continues to recognize that neither are they synonymous. Consequently, the organization has been sympathetic to the former but unequivocally committed to the latter."[20]

Table 6 *PAR* Editors-in-Chief and Managing Editors

Editors-in-chief	Managing editors
1940–43 Leonard D. White	1940–43 Don K. Price
1943–45 Gordon R. Clapp	1943–58 Laverne Burchfield
1945–47 Pendleton Herring	1958–60 William B. Shore
1947–49 Rowland Egger	1961–64 Geoffrey Y. Cornog
1949–51 Fritz Morstein Marx	1964–65 Benjamin H. Renshaw
1951–53 Wallace S. Sayre	1965–67 Valerie A. Earle
1953–56 Frederick C. Mosher	1967–77 Frank Martini
1956–58 York Wilbern	1977–84 Charles R. Wise
1958–60 James W. Fesler	1985–86 Curt Ventriss
1961–63 John A. Perkins	1986–91 Kyoko Yamamoto
1963–66 Vincent Ostrom	1991–96 Melvin Dubnick
1966–77 Dwight Waldo	1997–99 Gerald Gabris
1977–84 Louis C. Gawthrop	1999– Camilla Stivers*
1985–80 Chester A. Newland	
1991–96 David Rosenbloom	
1997–99 Irene Rubin	
1999– Larry Terry	

*Associate Editor

Source: American Society for Public Administration.

ASPA has both influenced and been influenced by the evolution of public administration in America for all of its 60-plus years. It was created to support the growing professionalism in public administration and to identify and support the development of professionalized government, particularly at the federal level, in the late 1930s and early 1940s. The society has contributed to this professionalization in five ways:

- Publication of the premier journal in public administration
- Support of chapters in major government centers
- Development of sections representing functional specializations and special interests
- Sponsorship of national and regional conferences
- Support for graduate level education for aspiring public managers

The first four of these contributions are discussed in this section. ASPA's contributions to public administration education are treated separately later in the chapter.

Public Administration Review

ASPA's journal, *Public Administration Review (PAR),* was first published in January 1941. *PAR* was intended to be both scholarly and practical. Over the years successive *PAR* editors have struggled to achieve and maintain a balance of rigorous scholarship and practicality in order to produce a journal respected by academicians and used by practitioners. The result has been a journal considered to be the premier journal in public administration and, because of its affiliation with ASPA, the most widely distributed. A list of *PAR* editors-in-chief and managing editors may be found in Table 6.

Chapters

Development of ASPA chapters began in 1940. Chapters were intended to provide broad-based forums for general public administration practitioners, scholars, and students at the local level. The first chapters were established in Sacramento, Chicago, Southern California, and Washington, D.C.[21] Today ASPA has 114 chapters throughout the country.

ASPA's chapters and national organization and staff have struggled with their relationships over the years. This struggle reflects many of the same tensions found in the relationships among different levels of government, and between the headquarters and regional offices of federal agencies. Several factors have contributed to the strained relations: ASPA has never defined a clear role or purpose for its chapters; ASPA's national organization has provided and then withdrawn support and funding to/from the chapters as ASPA's financial situation changed over the years; and, until very recently, the majority of ASPA members worked for the federal government and were located in the Northeast. Currently, ASPA's leadership is committed to proactive support for the chapters, as exemplified by staff

Table 7 ASPA Chapters as of September 2000

Chapter Name	Area
Alabama	
Auburn Area	Auburn
Greater Birmingham	Birmingham
Montgomery Area	Montgomery
Alaska	
Alaska	Statewide
Arizona	
Arizona	Phoenix/Scottsdale
Southern Arizona	Tucson
Arkansas	
Arkansas	Statewide
California	
Bakersfield	Bakersfield
Central California	Fresno
Inland Empire	Riverside
Los Angeles Metropolitan	Los Angeles
Monterey Bay	Monterey
Orange County	Garden Grove/Irvine
Sacramento	Sacramento
San Diego	San Diego
San Francisco Bay Area	San Francisco
San Joaquin Valley	Stockton
Santa Clara Valley	Santa Clara
Colorado	
Colorado	Denver
Southern Colorado	Colorado Springs
Connecticut	
Connecticut	Statewide
Delaware	
Delaware	Statewide
District of Columbia	
National Capital Area	District of Columbia
Florida	
Central Florida	Orlando
Gold Coast	Ft. Lauderdale
Gulf Coast	Pensacola
Island Coast	Fort Myers/Naples
North Florida	Tallahassee
Northeast Florida	Jacksonville
South Florida	Miami
Suncoast	Tampa/St. Petersburg
Treasure Coast	West Palm Beach

Table 7 Continued

Chapter Name	Area
Georgia	
Georgia	Atlanta
East Georgia	Savannah
Southwest Georgia	Albany
Hawaii	
Hawaii	Statewide
Illinois	
Central Illinois	Springfield
Greater Chicago	Chicago
Heart of Illinois	Peoria
Southern Illinois	Carbondale
Indiana	
Indiana	Indianapolis
Northwest Indiana	Gary
Iowa	
Iowa Capital	Des Moines
Siouxland[a]	Sioux City/Vermillion, SD
Kansas	
Greater Kansas City[a]	Kansas City
Kansas	Topeka
Kentucky	
Kentucky	Lexington
Metropolitan Louisville	Louisville
Louisiana	
Louisiana	Statewide
Maine	
Maine	Statewide
Maryland	
Maryland	Statewide
Massachusetts	
Massachusetts	Statewide
Michigan	
Detroit Metropolitan	Detroit
Lake Superior	Marquette
Michigan Capital	Lansing
West Michigan	Grand Rapids
Minnesota	
Minnesota	Statewide
Mississippi	
Mississippi	Statewide
Missouri	
Central Missouri	Jefferson City/Columbia

Table 7 Continued

Chapter Name	Area
Greater Kansas City[a]	Kansas City
St. Louis Metropolitan	St. Louis
Nebraska	
Nebraska	Statewide
Nevada	
Las Vegas	Las Vegas
New Jersey	
New Jersey	Trenton
Northern New Jersey	Morristown/Newark
New Mexico	
New Mexico	Albuquerque/Santa Fe
El Paso/SE New Mexico[a]	El Paso/Las Cruces
New York	
Empire State Capital Area	Albany
Central New York	Syracuse
Greater Rochester	Rochester
Hudson Valley	Poughkeepsie
Long Island	Long Island
Lower Hudson Valley	White Plains
New York Metropolitan	New York City
Niagara Frontier	Buffalo
North Carolina	
Central Piedmont	Charlotte
Eastern North Carolina	Greenville
Piedmont Triad	Greensboro
Research Triangle	Raleigh/Durham/Chapel Hill
Ohio	
Greater Akron	Akron
Central Ohio	Columbus
Miami Valley	Dayton
Northeast Ohio Regional	Cleveland
Northwest Ohio	Bowling Green/Toledo
Greater Cincinnati	Cincinnati
Oklahoma	
Oklahoma	Statewide
Oregon	
Oregon	Statewide
Pennsylvania	
Central Pennsylvania	Harrisburg
Northwest Pennsylvania	Scranton
Philadelphia Area	Philadelphia
Pittsburgh Area	Pittsburgh

TABLE 7 Continued

Chapter Name	Area
Rhode Island	
Rhode Island	Statewide
South Carolina	
Lowcountry	Charleston
South Carolina	Columbia
South Carolina Upstate	Greenville/Spartanburg
South Dakota	
Siouxland[a]	Vermillion/Sioux City, IA
Tennessee	
East Tennessee	Knoxville
Memphis/Mid-South	Memphis
Tennessee	Nashville
Texas	
Centex	Austin/Waco
High Plains	Lubbock
Houston Area	Houston
North Texas	Dallas/Ft. Worth
South Texas	San Antonio
El Paso/SE New Mexico[a]	El Paso/Las Cruces, NM
Utah	
Utah	Statewide
Vermont	
Vermont	Statewide
Virginia	
Hampton Roads	Hampton/Norfolk
Northern Virginia	Arlington/Alexandria/Fairfax
Southwest Virginia	Blacksburg
Virginia	Richmond
Washington	
Evergreen	Seattle
Inland Northwest	Spokane
West Virginia	
West Virginia	Statewide
Wisconsin	
Milwaukee	Milwaukee
Wisconsin Capital	Madison

[a]These chapters have geographic boundaries in more than one state.
Source: American Society for Public Administration.

devoted to their needs and a new chapter incentives program that links the chapters to the goals of the new strategic plan.

Chapters vary in their emphases. However, almost all of them hold annual recognition ceremonies honoring outstanding public managers and scholars—people who exemplify excellence in public administration. Most provide professional development for their members and others in their communities. Some do this through speakers at regularly scheduled meetings. Others hold annual conferences of 1 or 2 days on specific topics of interest in the local area. And others sponsor workshops that provide skill-building opportunities for public practitioners on topics such as performance measurement. Most chapters also publish newsletters to highlight their programs and keep members informed about local issues. A complete list of ASPA's current chapters as of September 2000 is in Table 7.

Sections

ASPA's sections were developed much later than the chapters. In ASPA's early years there were policies against creating sections based on occupational specialization. The purpose of these policies was to prevent competition with specialist organizations and associations.[22]

In the early 1970s, there was a call from ASPA members to "recognize the diversity within ASPA—ethnic, gender, and racial, as well as occupational."[23] This occurred at a time when ASPA was making major changes to its structure and programs in response to severe financial conditions and membership decline. The first section to be established, in 1973, was the Section on International and Comparative Administration (SICA), which continues to be one of ASPA's stronger sections to this day.

Other special interest groups began as affiliates of ASPA. The Conference of Minority Public Administrators (COMPA) was established in 1971 and became an ASPA affiliate in 1973. The Women's Task Force, also established in 1971, became the Section for Women in Public Administration (SWPA). Both have made significant contributions to professionalism and to diversity in American public administration.

Early in its tenure, COMPA, under a contract with the U.S. Department of Labor, established "a national registry for minority public administrators to assist state and local jurisdictions in locating qualified minority candidates for key policy-making positions."[24]

When it was established, SWPA created a "women's national registry (modeled after COMPA's minority registry)."[25] In addition, it performed a survey of local government affirmative action programs and a survey of women in public administration education programs.[26] COMPA and SWPA continue to this day as active sections of ASPA.

Like the chapters, ASPA's sections have experienced tensions with the society's national organization over the years, for many of the same reasons: roles/pur-

Table 8 ASPA Sections as of September 2000

Section name	Year established
The Section on International and Comparative Administration (SICA)	1973
The Section on Criminal Justice Administration (SCJA)	1974
The Section on Health and Human Services Administration (SHHSA)	1974
The Section on Public Performance and Management (SPPM)	1975
The Section for Professional and Organizational Development (SPOD)	1975
The Section on Environmental and Natural Resources Administration (SENRA)	1976
The Section on Science and Technology in Government (SSTIG)	1976
The Conference of Minority Public Administrators (COMPA)	1977
The Section on Intergovernmental Administration and Management (SIAM)	1979
The Association for Budgeting and Financial Management (ABFM)	1979
The Section on Public Administration Education (SPAE)	1979
The Section on Personnel Administration and Labor Relations (SPALR)	1981
The National Young Professionals Forum (NYPF)	1983
The Section for Women in Public Administration (SWPA)	1984
The Section on Emergency and Crisis Management (SECM)	1986
The Section on Public Administration Research (SPAR)	1989
The Section on Public Law and Administration (SPLA)	1990
The Section on Historical, Artistic and Reflective Expression (SHARE)	1992
The Section on Transportation Policy and Administration (STPA)	1992
The Section on Ethics (ETHICS)	1997

Source: American Society for Public Administration.

poses, support, finances. In addition, in the 1970s sections began to dominate national conference programs and appeared to some to be driving the society toward fragmentation. National conference program committees were changed in the 1990s to reduce the dominance of the sections and increase representation across the membership. However, it is clear that the ideal balance is yet to be achieved. Sections also were supposed to be self-sufficient, but in their early days

ASPA was supporting many of their indirect costs from general revenues. Currently sections pay their own way, and many of them contribute financially to the general revenues of ASPA.

Today ASPA has 20 sections, 3 representing special demographic interests—COMPA, SWPA, and the National Young Professionals Forum (NYPF). The other 17 represent specializations within the field of public administration such as budget and finance, emergency management, and health. Of ASPA members 37 percent belong to one or more sections. A complete list of ASPA's 20 sections is in Table 8. ASPA's sections promote professionalism among subgroups in public administration by holding conferences, publishing journals and newsletters, and, more recently, providing information and networking opportunities through web sites and listservs.

Conferences

Interrupted only by the early years of World War II, ASPA has held an annual conference and a business meeting every year since 1939. Conferences in 1939–1941 and 1944 were held in conjunction with the American Political Science Association (APSA). (World War II emergency conditions required that ASPA's 1942, 1943, and 1945 conferences be canceled.) However, some within ASPA were uneasy about this close relationship and argued that ASPA needed to meet separately to forge an identity of its own. In 1948, ASPA held its first conference independent of APSA.

In addition to the ASPA national conference, two sections and one region hold conferences every year: COMPA, the Association for Budgeting and Financial Management (ABFM), and SECOPA. Other regions hold conferences every other year. In addition, as noted, many chapters hold 1 day development or special issue conferences annually or biannually.

International Public Administration

Although ASPA's primary emphasis was on American public administration, the organization has "maintained an active . . . interest in international public administration beginning with World War II."[27] However, the level of effort the society has been able to commit to international activities has been driven by financial resources. Therefore, activity has been intense when grant funds have been available, and greatly reduced when ASPA has been in financial straits.

Pugh describes ASPA's increased involvement in international public administration after World War II as follows:

> In 1946 ASPA accepted membership in the International Institute of Administrative Sciences (IIAS), and, in 1948, it became the IIAS's official American Section. As such, ASPA had the exclusive authority to represent the United States at all IIAS international conferences and con-

> gresses, the right to participate in IIAS research activities, and the opportunity to receive an exchange of international information on public affairs and administration. . . . In 1955, the general interest in international activities among ASPA members increased due to the United States' expanded role in the United Nations. This interest led to the development of important international program activities including the hosting of a series of conferences on the international aspects of administration and the creation of a Standing Committee on International Public Administration. . . . These activities were sponsored by [a]. . . $20,000 Ford [Foundation] grant specifically designed for ASPA's international functions.[28]
>
> As participation in international activities grew [in ASPA], special interest in developing analytical works for the cross-cultural study of public administration emerged within the Standing Committee among a small group of academicians including Rowland Egger, Paul Appleby, Ferrel Heady, Fritz Morstein Marx, William Storm, and James D. Thompson. This group was formally recognized by ASPA in March 1958 as the Committee on Comparative Administration and charged with examining the growing material on administration in other countries.[29]

However, in 1959, as a result of financial problems in ASPA, major cuts were made in international activities. "ASPA's special section of the [IIAS] was eliminated in favor of substantially reduced general Society support."[30] In addition, a single International Committee took the place of the multiple committees that preceded it.[31]

In 1962, ASPA formed a Comparative Administration Group (CAG), a successor to the Committee on Comparative Administration. The same year CAG was awarded a $250,000 Ford Foundation grant "to develop a program in comparative and international public administration that would lead to improved teaching of comparative administration and to a better understanding of American administration vis-à-vis other countries. CAG used these grant monies to sponsor seminars, fellowships, and publications."[32] In 1965 CAG was awarded another Ford grant to develop a comprehensive 3-year program of six seminars "staged at nationally recognized universities throughout the United States" and "a series of special publications [including nine books], in the comparative area."[33] It also cosponsored, with the Ford Foundation and the Inter-American World Bank, a conference on the role of Latin American universities in improving public service education, training, and research.[34]

In addition, CAG "spearheaded the publication of the *Journal of Comparative Administration* and promoted a cross-disciplinary approach to the analysis of governmental bureaucracies."[35] CAG also "sponsored the creation of the Committee on Research and Education Administration (CREDA). . . . CREDA secured grants from several government agencies to study the involvement of United States schools of public administration in teaching and research activities related to the field of international administration. Finally, CAG negotiated a contract with the United States Agency for International Development (USAID) to study the feasibility of establishing a legislative reference service for all law-making bodies of developing nations."[36]

In 1966, 200 practitioners and scholars from all over the world evaluated CAG's performance in comparative administration. CAG was given "sole credit for having pioneered significant advancements in a field that many regarded as too long neglected."[37]

Throughout the 1960s, ASPA's International Committee was also very active. It "secured a $105,000 grant from the Ford Foundation to develop a training program for improved public administration training in emerging nations."[38] Under that grant, the committee "assembled the best available collection of teaching materials on development administration and distributed them among developing nations upon request."[39]

ASPA's International Committee also played a major role in "salvaging public administration in the United Nations (UN) during its major reorganization in 1966. That reorganization had proposed the elimination of the Division of Public Administration at the UN due to an apparent attempt to downgrade the significance of the field in facilitating the economic and social development of Third World countries. The Committee . . . lobbied forcefully for the retention of public administration through the creation of the UN's Public Administration Branch—an entity whose purpose was to promote effective public administration in UN member countries, support technical cooperation projects in public administration, and conduct research on administration problems and practices."[40]

In the 1970s and 1980s, a change in political climate combined with a recurrence of ASPA's financial problems to reduce the activity in comparative adminis-

Table 9 International Affiliation Agreements

Chinese Public Administration Society
Colegio Nacional de Ciencias Politicas Y Administracion Publica, A.C. (Mexico)
Commonwealth Association for Public Administration and Management (CAPAM)
European Group of Public Administration
Hong Kong Public Administration Association
Institute of Public Administration of Canada
Korean Association for Public Administration
Republic of Slovenia
United Nations' Division for Governance, Public Administration and Finance
United Nations Association

Source: American Society for Public Administration.

tration across the field. Uveges and Keller[41] ascribe the changes to the "aftermath of doubt and pessimism that arose [after Vietnam and Watergate] later in the decade and existed throughout most of the 1970s." They go on to say that "although comparative administration remained on the agenda of public administration into the 1970s, the focus became more middle range and institutional. The change in the name of the *Journal of Comparative Administration to Administration and Society* in 1974 was indicative of the declining interest in the area."[42]

At the same time, ASPA's financial situation required a series of austerity measures, including eliminating funding for the IIAS and the CAG in the 1970s. Similar financial problems in the early 1980s resulting from a continued retrenchment at all levels of government, a recession, and declining membership meant that, in 1982, "ASPA was forced to forego participation in the prestigious North American Seminar series—a cooperative effort among Canada, Mexico, and the United States (ASPA represented the US) to examine critical policy issues. Canada and Mexico had hosted conferences on energy policy and food policy, respectively, in the previous two years. However, when it became the US' turn to host the conference, ASPA was unable to underwrite the seminar and this international program was terminated."[43]

Through the 1990s international activities in ASPA were carried on by the Section on International and Comparative Administration (SICA) and by the Campaign for International Relations (CIR). SICA was founded in 1974 and was ASPA's first section. SICA was a product of a merger of the old International Committee, a remnant of the former U.S. section of the IIAS, and the CAG.[44]

CIR was created as an ASPA standing committee in December 1992 to coordinate international activities across ASPA and to encourage an international perspective in all aspects of the society. Among CIR's accomplishments are a series of 10 affiliation agreements, 8 with public administration organizations in eight countries, 1 with the United Nations Association, and another with the United Nations Division for Governance, Public Administration and Finance. Table 9 lists the 10 agreements. A major objective of the ASPA strategic plan adopted in December 1998 is to operationalize these agreements. The two that were the focus of attention in 1999–2000 were the agreements with Mexico and the United Nations. In both cases early implementation of the agreements involved exchanging professional publications, inviting panels at ASPA conferences, sending ASPA representatives to their conferences, and planning for joint conferences and other exchanges.

Ethics

Another area in which ASPA has contributed significantly to professionalism in public administration is with its emphasis on ethics. In 1979, ASPA's "Professional Standards and Ethics Committee sponsored the publication of *Professional Standards and Ethics: A Workbook for Public Administrator,* and launched efforts

Table 10 ASPA Code of Ethics

The American Society for Public Administration (ASPA) exists to advance the science, processes, and art of public administration. The Society affirms its responsibility to develop the spirit of professionalism within its membership, and to increase public awareness of ethical principles in public service by its example. To this end, we, the members of the Society, commit ourselves to the following principles:

I. Serve the Public Interest

Serve the public, beyond serving oneself.

ASPA members are committed to:

1. Exercise discretionary authority to promote the public interest.
2. Oppose all forms of discrimination and harassment, and promote affirmative action.
3. Recognize and support the public's right to know the public's business.
4. Involve citizens in policy decision-making.
5. Exercise compassion, benevolence, fairness and optimism.
6. Respond to the public in ways that are complete, clear, and easy to understand.
7. Assist citizens in their dealings with government.
8. Be prepared to make decisions that may not be popular.

II. Respect the Constitution and the Law

Respect, support, and study government constitutions and laws that define responsibilities of public agencies, employees, and all citizens.

ASPA members are committed to:

1. Understand and apply legislation and regulations relevant to their professional role.
2. Work to improve and change laws and policies that are counter-productive or obsolete.
3. Eliminate unlawful discrimination.
4. Prevent all forms of mismanagement of public funds by establishing and maintaining strong fiscal and management controls, and by supporting audits and investigative activities.
5. Respect and protect privileged information.
6. Encourage and facilitate legitimate dissent activities in government and protect the whistle-blowing rights of public employees.
7. Promote constitutional principles of equality, fairness, representativeness, responsiveness and due process in protecting citizens' rights.

III. Demonstrate Personal Integrity

Demonstrate the highest standards in all activities to inspire public confidence and trust in public service.

ASPA members are committed to:

1. Maintain truthfulness and honesty and to not compromise them for advancement, honor, or personal gain.
2. Ensure that others receive credit for their work and contributions.
3. Zealously guard against conflict of interest or its appearance: e.g., nepotism, improper outside employment, misuse of public resources or the acceptance of gifts.
4. Respect superiors, subordinates, colleagues and the public.
5. Take responsibility for their own errors.
6. Conduct official acts without partisanship.

Table 10 Continued

IV. Promote Ethical Organizations

Strengthen organizational capabilities to apply ethics, efficiency and effectiveness in serving the public.

ASPA members are committed to:

1. Enhance organizational capacity for open communication, creativity, and dedication.
2. Subordinate institutional loyalties to the public good.
3. Establish procedures that promote ethical behavior and hold individuals and organizations accountable for their conduct.
4. Provide organization members with an administrative means for dissent, assurance of due process and safeguards against reprisal.
5. Promote merit principles that protect against arbitrary and capricious actions.
6. Promote organizational accountability through appropriate controls and procedures.
7. Encourage organizations to adopt, distribute, and periodically review a code of ethics as a living document.

V. Strive for Professional Excellence

Strengthen individual capabilities and encourage the professional development of others.

ASPA members are committed to:

1. Provide support and encouragement to upgrade competence.
2. Accept as a personal duty the responsibility to keep up to date on emerging issues and potential problems.
3. Encourage others, throughout their careers, to participate in professional activities and associations.
4. Allocate time to meet with students and provide a bridge between classroom studies and the realities of public service.

Source: American Society for Public Administration.

to produce specific standards for ASPA."[45] The committee "sought to develop a code that would fit with ASPA's basic mission and goals and reflect the 'principles and moral standards that must guide the conduct of ASPA members not merely in preventing wrong, but in pursuing right through timely and energetic execution of responsibilities.'"[46] In 1981 ASPA's National Council adopted a set of moral principles. Three years later in 1984, the council approved the 13-point Code of Ethics for ASPA members; in 1994 the code was revised. A copy of ASPA's current code of ethics is in Table 10.

PUBLIC ADMINISTRATION EDUCATION, THEORY, AND RESEARCH

ASPA has maintained a commitment to public administration education, theory, and research since its inception. Contributions to these areas have taken three forms over the years. First, ASPA's commitment to formal graduate public administration education, theory building, and research resulted ultimately in the establishment of the National Association of Schools of Public Affairs and Administration (NASPAA). Second, its commitment to continuing professional development and education has been manifested in its national and regional conferences, chapter and section programs and conferences, and various training institutes. Third, ASPA's commitment to research in support of practice resulted in creation of the National Academy of Public Administration (NAPA).

Graduate Public Administration Education

In 1958 ASPA formed its Council on Graduate Education for Public Administration (CGEPA), an association composed of representatives from universities with academic programs in public administration. It "became a focal point for the development of opinions and activities that affected public administration education throughout the United States."[47] Pugh argues that "CGEPA used its influence during the mid-1960s to improve the quality of education in public administration in three ways. First, it served as an advocate for the enhancement of public administration education, training, and research activities in both universities and government. . . . CGEPA actively lobbied government and universities to improve public administration education. Concerned that government agencies were unaware of the need to educate career public servants, CGEPA called on government at all levels to make greater use of educational opportunities for their employees as a way of achieving excellence in the public service. It also recommended that colleges and universities place greater emphasis and resources on developing, strengthening, and expanding educational programs for government service."[48]

Second, CGEPA sponsored a comprehensive study of the status of higher education for public administration/public service. The resulting report, *Higher Education for Public Service,* written by John Honey of the Maxwell School at Syracuse University under a grant from the Carnegie Corporation, was published in *Public Administration Review* in 1967.[49] The report "documented the inadequacy of public service education, especially in a time of increased opportunities and demands for public service professionals."[50] The report also made recommendations for eight steps for improving graduate education in public administration, including internships and fellowship programs for students and faculty and expansion of the number of public administration programs in the United States.[51]

Third, CGEPA developed specific programs for improvement of the field of public administration. As the *Higher Education for Public Service* report was being developed, CGEPA was already creating fellowship programs. It formed the ASPA Fellows, the Urban Affairs Fellows program, and the Public Administration

Fellows program in the mid-1960s, as well as the Urban Affairs Group. The latter spawned many urban studies programs to train generalists in urban affairs. CGEPA also influenced the passage of the Public Service Education Act of 1967, which established contracts with colleges and universities for improving public administration graduate education and research. The act also funded fellowships for graduate students planning to enter public service.[52]

In 1970 CGEPA was succeeded by the National Association of Schools of Public Affairs and Administration (NASPAA), established as an affiliate of ASPA. NASPAA continued the programs originated by CGEPA and developed guidelines and standards for public administration master's degree programs. "NASPAA set about to create an educational and professional base for the development of public sector managers. NASPAA focused on building an identity based on a consensus regarding education curricula and programmatic characteristics."[53] By the mid-1970s, NASPAA had a membership of more than 140 schools and sufficient revenues to be independent of ASPA. In 1977, NASPAA was incorporated as an entity separate from ASPA.

Continuing Professional Development and Education

In the mid-1950s, ASPA's development program, funded by a Ford Foundation grant, called for the creation of education programs that "could increase the number of well-trained people entering public service."[54] To accomplish this, ASPA created a speakers' bureau as a service to the chapters; provided assistance in organizing, staffing, and funding regional conferences; and developed a series of management institutes "composed of courses on a variety of topics, conducted by well-known practitioners and scholars throughout the country in university settings."[55] These institutes were discontinued in 1958 as a result of financial losses.

In 1971, an ASPA Task Force on Society Goals concluded that ASPA's primary mission should be "to promote the development of executive leadership by providing program activity that would enhance the professional growth of individual public administrators."[56] The ASPA National Council approved this change in direction, and the society proceeded to create a framework for the professional development emphasis. At the same time there was a movement within ASPA to recognize the diversity within the organization—ethnic, gender, racial, occupational. The change of emphasis combined with the move to recognize diversity in the society resulted in establishment of sections, affiliates, and other special interest groups representing the various specialities and interests that ASPA comprised.[57]

In keeping with the goal of professional development, in 1979 ASPA created the Public Administration Training Center (PATC). PATC was committed to providing quality professional development training through "general and specialized programs, pre-conference workshops, consultancies, national continuing education tours, and funded research activities."[58] However, PATC operated just 1 year before it was abolished because of financial problems and replaced by the ASPA Training Service (ATS), which was "to operate exclusively on the voluntary efforts of pro bono trainers."[59] Today ASPA's continuing education and training efforts are carried out through its national, regional, chapter, and section conferences and programs. In addition, ASPA's Center for Accountability and Performance (CAP), established in 1997, is building a training capability using ASPA members as trainers. CAP's efforts are focused on performance management, measurement, and budgeting. In addition, CAP has developed a workbook on performance management, the third edition of which will be published in 2000. That workbook is used in the workshops and training performed by CAP.

Creation of the National Academy of Public Administration

Although ASPA's commitment to excellence in public service primarily took the form of education and professional development of individual public administrators, there was a move in the 1960s to create a capability to provide government organizations with expert advice and assistance on "issues of organizational structure, interagency and intraagency relationships, and administrative management functions such as finance and personnel."[60] The National Academy of Public Administration (NAPA) was formed in 1966 to fulfill this purpose.

The concept for NAPA was first proposed by James E. Webb, administrator for the National Aeronautic and Space Administration (NASA) and ASPA president in 1966–1967. Webb saw a need for an organization of prominent practitioners and scholars in public administration, "modeled after the National Academy of Sciences, that could provide governmental organizations, like NASA, with technical assistance on complex administrative issues."[61]

ASPA's National Council approved the creation of NAPA in March 1967. The decision was made to "treat NAPA as an ASPA affiliate for tax purposes but otherwise to operate it as an autonomous body with its own leadership and management. Furthermore, it was determined . . . that its membership would be limited to past presidents of ASPA and others elected by Academy members based on their contributions to the field of public administration."[62]

NAPA began operations in the summer of 1967 with its first executive director, Dr. George A Graham, and a comprehensive, 3-year contract with NASA. "Over the following 14 months [NAPA] grew beyond expectation in size, members, and activities."[63] In addition to the NASA contract, NAPA "conducted a two-year study of major organizational problems within the federal government under the auspices of a major grant given by the Ford Foundation."[64]

NAPA's growth created tensions with ASPA focused on their financial relationship. At the same time, ASPA was undergoing major change as a result of pressures to make the society more open to racial and ethnic minorities, women, and youth. ASPA's 1970 conference included a protest counterconference staged by a group known as the Young Professionals' Forum (YPF), a part of the National Capital Area Chapter. In addition, a counterconference slate of candidates for ASPA officers and National Council was placed in nomination at the annual business meeting. The counterslate was elected to a majority of the council's vacant positions.[65]

These changes in ASPA caused the leaders of NAPA to question whether they should continue their relationship with the society. At a meeting in July 1970, "a majority of NAPA members voted to separate from ASPA and to form an independent corporation."[66] The ASPA leadership was shocked and angry over this decision but eventually decided not to oppose it. "The formal separation occurred on December 31, 1970, when [NAPA] . . . became an independent corporation."[67]

ADVOCACY FOR PUBLIC ADMINISTRATION/ PUBLIC SERVICE

Throughout ASPA's history there have been attempts to move the society from an organization committed to excellence in public administration to one that is an advocate for issues affecting public employees.[68] For its first 25 years, ASPA's leadership resisted pressures to take positions on public policy issues because of their "commitment to the value of neutral expertise and for fear it would embroil the organization in controversy and inevitably alienate some ASPA members."[69] However, in 1963 ASPA changed its policy at the urging of the National Capital Area Chapter (NCAC) of ASPA in Washington, D.C.

From then on the society's national organization and chapters could "adopt resolutions on public issues which affected the improvement and advancement of public administration, as long as these resolutions were not tied directly to specific pieces of legislation or lobbying activities."[70] Pugh comments on the significance of this change in position for ASPA and the field of public administration; "This basic modification in ASPA policy was indicative of a fundamental change that characterized not only ASPA, but also the field of public administration and American society in general; namely, that public policy was increasingly recognized as an inextricable part of public administration."[71]

In the early 1970s, ASPA "once again reassessed its attitude toward taking positions on matters of public policy. Engendered by calls for public policy statements that demanded an end to the Viet Nam War and a prohibition against drafting of social scientists into the U.S. armed forces, ASPA members once again wrestled with the question of what kinds of policy issues were appropriate for action."[72]

The late 1970s held major threats to public administration in the form of rapidly declining trust in government by American citizens and antigovernment campaigns by politicians at all levels of government. ASPA responded to these threats with increased involvement in advocacy activities in the 1980s. As Pugh puts it: "American public administration was in serious trouble at the beginning of [the 1980s]. . . ."[73] Charles H. Levine characterized public administration in the early 1980s as "acutely alienated from society, bedeviled by complexity, and guided by limited knowledge and understanding."[74] "Confronted with a lack of credibility and a loss of popular legitimacy, public administrators, especially those in ASPA, were locked in a basic struggle to sustain themselves and their field."[75] Thus in the early 1980s, ASPA "engaged in numerous actions designed to enhance the image of the career public service. These activities ranged from the direct sponsorship of career-building programs to overt lobbying of political and governmental bodies for special recognition of the public service."[76]

Among the most significant of ASPA's advocacy activities in the early 1980s were creation of the National Public Service Awards (NPSA) program in conjunction with the National Academy of Public Administration (NAPA) in 1982, establishment of Public Employee Appreciation Day in 1983 in cooperation with the Public Employees Roundtable, the development of ASPA's Professional Code of Ethics in 1984 (see earlier description of that process), and "an overt attempt to influence the development of the Republican and Democratic platforms for the 1984 presidential election."[77]

The NPSA awards program was designed to pay tribute to exemplary public managers for their outstanding career contributions to the American public service. The first five career public administrators were selected and honored in 1983 at the ASPA National Conference. Each year since ASPA and NAPA have worked together to honor and reward outstanding management-level practitioners who have dedicated their careers to government service. Selected from all levels of government—local, state, federal, and international—the recipients are public servants who have made outstanding contributions on a sustained basis.

Public Employee Appreciation Day began as "a national day of recognition for the federal civil service in conjunction with the 100th anniversary of the Pendleton Civil Service Act of 1883. The actual celebration . . . was turned into a week-long observance. . . . In all, nine states and five cities also participated in the festivities."[78] Today Public Employees Recognition Week is celebrated the first week of May every year in Washington, D.C., and in most states and major cities. It is coordinated by the Public Employees Roundtable, of which ASPA is a member.

ASPA attempts to influence the platforms of the Republican and Democratic parties for the 1984 presidential campaign focused on responding to the findings and recommendations of the President's Private Sector Survey on Cost Control (PPSSCC), known popularly as the Grace Commission. "Established in June 1982, the Commission's task had been to examine the operations and policies of the federal government from a business perspective and to make recommendations on any means by which the government could reduce its operating costs or improve its management."[79]

The commission's report was completed in 1984; in addition to recommending ways to improve management and efficiency in the federal government, it "also made serious allegations of waste and abuse in the management and administration of many federal programs. ASPA leaders felt compelled to respond to the report for fear that, left unanswered, such criticisms would lead to further attacks on the competence of federal public administrators in particular and public administration in general."[80] In April 1984, the ASPA National Council took a formal position citing the "extravagant and misleading conclusions regarding potential savings from waste and abuse" in the Grace Commission report.[81] It also called on all responsible public officials to "clarify potentially misleading claims that may be drawn from the PPSSCC."[82] In addition, "ASPA President Bradley H. Patterson engaged the PPSSCC Chairman, J. Peter Grace, in a series of letters that openly called for him to identify and clarify the Commission's claims."[83]

"In a related effort, ASPA Presidents Patricia S. Florestano and Bradley Patterson, along with others, lobbied to have 11 planks inserted in the platforms of the Democratic and Republican parties that called for greater cooperation between career and elected public officials at all levels of government, orientation programs for new public executives, and improved recognition of the value of public service. . . . Although ultimately neither party chose to include the language offered by ASPA, both parties did include specific mention of the federal civil service and its role in democratic government in the final versions of their respective platforms."[84]

In addition to these significant advocacy efforts in the early 1980s, ASPA took positions on an unprecedented number of public policy matters—28 between 1981 and 1984. "In general, the primary thrusts of ASPA's position-taking activity [during this period] fell into three categories: equality of opportunity; public administration and management; and legislative initiatives."[85] A list of all public policy positions taken by ASPA from 1964 to 1999 may be found in Table 11.

From 1990 through 1998, ASPA used a National Assembly, a delegate body that set external policy positions for the society. Delegates to the assembly were chapter presidents, section chairs, and members and members-elect of the National Council. Chapter presidents and section chairs were allowed to send designees to the assembly. The assembly met once a year in conjunction with ASPA's national conference. Recommendations of policy positions along with supporting materials were sent to the assembly from the Policy Issues Committee, which sought input from all ASPA members and entities during their research and formulation stage. At the assembly meetings, the president-elect presided over discussions of recommended policy positions. Each member of the assembly had one vote; once a quorum was declared, a simple majority of those present and voting could approve a motion.

However, experience with the ASPA assembly in the late 1990s suggested that it was not the vehicle ASPA needed to make the policy process all-inclusive

Table 11 Policy Positions Taken by ASPA, 1964–1996

Year Adopted	Policy Position
1964	Equality of Opportunity in the Public Service (4/15/1964)
1965	Increased Mobility of Personnel Between Levels of Government and the Educational Systems (4/12/1965)
	Strengthening Education Systems for Public Administration (11/15/1965)
1966	Coordination of Federal Programs for Urban Development (4/13/1966)
1971	ASPA Positions on Public Policy Questions (April 1971)
1973	Watergate (1/2/1973)
	Equal Rights Amendment (1973)
1974	The Establishment of a Permanent Constitutional Review Commission (5/8/1974)
	Responsive Government Act (5/8/1974)
	Right of Privacy of Government Employees and Prospective Employees (5/8/1974)
1975	Lapse of Executive Reorganization Authority (1/26/1975)
	Controlling National Emergency Power Exercised by the Federal Executive (1/26/1975)
	IPA Appropriations and Amendments (4/4/1975)
	Proposed Reduction in Law Enforcement Education Program Funding (4/4/1975)
	Hatch Act Reforms (4/4/1975)
1976	Political Activities of Federal Employees (4/2/1976)
1977	Procedures for Adopting Resolutions and Positions on Public Policy Issues (4/2/1977)
	Equal Rights for Women in Public Administration (4/2/1977)
	Restoring Confidence in the Merit System (12/4/1977)
	Department of Education (12/4/1977)
1978	Sunset Legislation (4/12/1978)
	Federal Veterans Preference (4/12/1978)
	Quality of Working Life—The Next Step in Merit Reform (7/23/1978)
	Federal Grant in Aid Reform (12/10/1978)
1979	Equal Employment Opportunity, Affirmative Action and Support of Federal EEO Activities (4/4/1979)
	Report of Special Task Force Management (April 1979)
	Organizing the Executive Branch of State Government for More Effective Management (4/4/1979)
	Equal Employment Opportunity and Affirmative Action (4/4/1979)
	Implementation of Policy Positions (July 1979)
	Whistleblowing (12/2/1979)
1980	Regulatory Reform (4/17/1980)
	Federal Compensation Reform (1980)
	Support of Professional Development for Government Employees (7/21/1980)
	A Policy Perspective of ASPA (12/7/1980)
1981	Support of Extension of the Voting Rights Act (3/21/1981)

TABLE 11 Continued

Year Adopted	Policy Position
	ASPA's Commitment to Equal Employment Opportunity and Affirmative Action (4/16/1981)
	Resolution Requesting NASPAA's Support of Equal Opportunity and Affirmative Action (4/16/1981)
	Reaffirmation of Support for ERA (7/12/1981)
	Resolution Honoring Dr. Arthur Flemming (12/6/1981)
	Resolution Regarding Appointment of the Chairman of the EEOC (12/6/1981)
1982	Resolution on the Balanced Budget Amendment (3/25/1982)
	Criminal Justice Administration (4/15/1982)
	Resolution Supporting the Reintroduction and Passage of the Equal Rights Amendment (7/10/1982)
	Resolution Amending the March 25 1982 Balanced Budget Amendment Resolution (7/11/1982)
	Resolution on Suspending Ratification of the ERA as a Criterion for National Conference Site (7/11/1982)
	Public Administration Education (12/4/1982)
1983	South African Apartheid (4/20/1983)
	Enforcement of EEO/AA Requirements in the Administration of Block Grants (7/10/1983)
	Fair Housing (1983)
	General Revenue Sharing (7/10/1983)
	Federal Government's Land and Facilities Disposal Process (7/10/1983)
	Public Service Fellowships (7/10/1983)
	Public Employees Roundtable Recommendations to Political Party Platform Committees (7/10/1983)
	Response to OPM Proposed Regulations on Performance Management (7/10/1983)
	Response to White House Proposal to Downgrade Federal Civil Service Positions GS-11 through GS-15 (11/19/1983)
1984	Resolution Related to Mr. William Coors' Statement (4/8/1984)
	Resolution of the Section for Women in Public Administration to the National Council (4/12/1984)
	Resolution on the President's Private Sector Survey on Cost Control Report (4/12/1984)
	Statement on the Senior Executive Service (4/12/1984)
	Resolution on Policy Reversal by the U.S. Commission on Civil Rights (7/15/1984)
	Resolution Urging Congress to Pass Anti-Trust Immunity Legislation for Local General Purpose Government and Local Government Officials (7/15/1984)
	Civil Service Reform (7/15/1984)
	Grove City Response Legislation (7/15/1984)
1985	Resolution on the Use of Dissent Channels (3/24/1985)
	Reaffirmation of ASPA's Grove City Response (3/24/1985)

Table 11 Continued

Year Adopted	Policy Position
	Reaffirmation of Support for Reauthorization of Title IX of Higher Education Act (3/24/1985)
	Reaffirmation of Support for Reauthorization of General Revenue Sharing (3/27/1985)
	Resolution on the Availability of Employee Assistance Programs to Public Employees (8/2/1985)
	Resolution Recommending a Uniform Treatment for Public and Private Sector Employees Regarding Deferred Compensation Lump-Sum Settlements Upon Retirement by Seeking an Amendment to the Internal Revenue Section, by the US Congress (8/4/1985)
	Statement of Policy on the Federal Retirement Systems (8/4/1985)
	Policy Statement on Reduction in Force (12/8/1985)
1986	Retention of Executive Order on Affirmative Action (4/12/1986)
	Grove City Response Reiterated (4/13/1986)
	Resolution on Promoting a Positive Public Image of Government Employees (4/13/1986)
	Resolution on OMB Circular A-130, Management of Federal Information Sources (4/13/1986)
	Resolution on Substance Abuse in the Public Workplace (12/7/1986)
1987	ASPA Resolution on Pay Equity (3/8/1987)
	Resolution on the Career Civil Service (7/17/1987)
	Resolution on Disseminating Information on Hatch Act Coverage (12/5/1987)
	ASPA Resolution on Study of AIDS Issue (12/5/1987)
1988	Proposed Preamble and Resolution on Affordable Housing to be Submitted for Approval—Portland, Oregon (1988)
	Resolution on AIDS (4/17/1988)
	Civil Rights Monitor (June 1988)
	Resolution Regarding the Use of Polygraph Testing as a Condition of Initial and Continued Employment in the Public Sector (7/24/1988)
	Policy Statement on Reimbursement of Medical Care Rendered to AIDS Patients (7/24/1988)
	Resolution on Housing the Homeless (7/24/1988)
	Resolution on Smoking in the Workplace (12/4/1988)
	Model Structure and Process for Position Taking (12/5/1988)
	Resolution on Barring Discrimination by Private Parties (12/11/1988)
	Resolution on Adequate Pay for Top Level Public Officials (12/11/1988)
1989	Policy Statement (2/10/1989)
	Resolution on Affirmative Action and Equal Opportunity (1989)
	Resolution on Public Employees' Rights of Privacy (1989)
	Resolution on Implementing Pay Equity (4/8/1989)
	Resolution on Reaffiliation with Leadership Conference on Civil Rights (4/8/1989)
	Resolution on Child Care (4/8/1989)

TABLE 11 Continued

Year Adopted	Policy Position
	Resolution on the Report of the National Commission on the Public Service (4/12/1989)
	Resolution on Financial Management Reform (7/15/1989)
	Resolution on Campaign Finance Reform (7/15/1989)
	Reaffirmation of Support for Equal Opportunity and Affirmative Action (7/15/1989)
	Reaffirmation of the Right of Privacy for Public Employees (7/15/1989)
1990	Resolution Urging President Bush to Nominate a Head of the Office of Government Ethics (April 1990)
	Resolution to Encourage Every College and University to Examine their Curriculum with a View Toward Addressing Ethics Fully and Systematically (April 1990)
1991	Resolution in Support of the Passage of the Civil Rights Act of 1991 (3/24/1991)
	Resolution Censuring Unethical Behavior of Law Enforcement Officials (3/24/1991)
1992	Encouraging the Use of Performance Measurement and Reporting by Government Organizations (4/14/1992)
	Encouraging Investing in the Human Capital (4/14/1992)
	Resolution Supporting Reform of Congress (4/14/1992)
1993	Resolution on Sexual Harassment (7/20/1993)
	Resolution on the Problem of Hollow Government (7/20/1993)
	Resolution on the Role of Prevention in Health Care (7/20/1993)
	Resolution on Health Care (7/20/1993)
	Resolution on Equal Treatment (7/20/1993)
1994	Resolution Supporting Full Funding for the US Advisory Commission on Intergovernmental Relations (7/26/1994)
	Resolution on Political Efforts and Rights (7/26/1994)
	Resolution Supporting Efforts to Reinvent Government (7/26/1994)
1995	Resolution Supporting the United Nations' 50th Anniversary Commemoration (7/25/1995)
	Resolution on Unfunded Mandates (7/25/1995)
	Resolution Against Violence Directed Toward Public Employees (7/25/1995)
	Reaffirmation of the Resolution from 1989 Reaffirming Support for Equal Opportunity and Affirmative Action (7/25/1995)
1996	Resolution on Violence Against Public Employees (7/30/1996)
	Resolution on Criminal Justice Administration (7/30/1996)
	Resolution in Support of the Presidential Management Internship Program (7/30/1996)
	Resolution on the United Nations Convention on the Rights of the Child (7/30/1996)
	Resolution on Public Perception of Public Service Employees (7/30/1996)

Source: American Society for Public Administration.

for its members, chapters, and sections. Therefore, the strategic plan passed by the National Council in December 1998 replaced the assembly with a process whereby ASPA chapters and sections are encouraged to develop position papers, produce policy issues statements, and raise issues of importance to their membership. Local and state issues are to be addressed to local or state officials. Sections and chapters are also encouraged to join other organizations within or outside ASPA to make their positions known. Chapters, sections, and members are to channel the issues to be adopted by ASPA as a whole to/through the appropriate steering groups and through an action team specially formed to research and disseminate that particular policy statement or white paper. Positions to be adopted by ASPA as a whole are to reflect a canvass of the membership through a variety of means, such as being published in *PA Times* and on the web site for 45-day review and comment by ASPA members, an open discussion forum at annual meetings, and other vehicles/opportunities as appropriate, before the National Council votes.[86]

Today ASPA's advocacy for public service is carried out largely through collaborative ventures with other organizations such as the Public Employees Roundtable. In addition, ASPA's strategic plan adopted in December 1998 calls for development of a media strategy that promotes public service and the accomplishments of public servants.[87]

CONCLUSION

The American Society for Public Administration (ASPA) was formed in 1939 in response to the need for increased professionalism in public service and for managerial talent to staff the burgeoning federal executive branch. Over the years the society has contributed significantly to the professionalism of the field in a wide variety of ways. Through its premier journal, the *Public Administration Review (PAR),* and other regular and special publications, ASPA has informed practitioners and scholars about the latest ideas in public administration theory and research. Through its conferences, chapters, and sections ASPA helps maintain links among scholars and practitioners and among subfields of public administration, among levels of government, and across national boundaries.

ASPA has also contributed significantly to the growth and quality of public administration graduate programs in the United States and in other countries. The society spawned the National Association of Schools of Public Affairs and Administration (NASPAA), now independent of ASPA, which continues to support and enhance public administration graduate education across the United States and in other parts of the world. ASPA also created the National Academy of Public Administration (NAPA), also now independent, which currently provides expert advice and assistance to government managers and agencies on administrative management issues.

The rise and fall of public administration in the United States have affected the fortunes of ASPA as government has grown or declined, gained or lost favor. Nevertheless, ASPA continues to this day to promote excellence in public service by linking academics and practitioners with each other and with their counterparts in other countries, by helping public managers stay in touch with each other, and by informing members and nonmembers alike about the latest developments in this broad field of public administration.

NOTES

1. Pugh (1998:9–10) and Stone (1975:83–84).
2. Pugh, Ibid., p. 15.
3. Ibid., p. 13.
4. Ibid., p. 12.
5. Ibid.
6. Ibid.
7. Ibid., p. 16.
8. Ibid.
9. Ibid.
10. Ibid., pp. 16–17. See also Stone (1975: 85–86).
11. Ibid., p. 17.
12. American Society for Public Administration (1945).
13. Pugh (1975: 2–4).
14. Pugh (1975: 13) and Uveges and Keller (1998: 84).
15. Pugh (1975: 54).
16. Ibid., p. 55.
17. Ibid., p. 41.
18. Ibid., p. 3.
19. Ibid.
20. Ibid.
21. Ibid., pp. 28–29.
22. Ibid., pp. 29–30.
23. Ibid., p. 83.
24. Ibid., p. 85.
25. Ibid., p. 86.
26. Ibid.
27. Ibid., p. 48.
28. Ibid.
29. Ibid., pp. 48–49.
30. Ibid., p. 50.
31. Ibid.
32. Ibid., p. 52.

33. Ibid., p. 61.
34. Ibid., p. 62.
35. Uveges and Keller (1998: 17–18).
36. Pugh (1998: 61).
37. Ibid.
38. Ibid., p. 60.
39. Ibid.
40. Ibid.
41. Uveges and Keller (1998: 18).
42. Ibid.
43. Pugh (1998: 102).
44. Ibid., p. 86.
45. Ibid., p. 97.
46. Ibid., p. 105.
47. Ibid., p. 62.
48. Ibid.
49. John C. Honey (1967: 294–321).
50. Uveges and Keller (1998: 19).
51. Honey (1967: 319–320).
52. Pugh (1998: 63–64).
53. Uveges and Keller (1998: 22).
54. Pugh (1998: 49).
55. Ibid., p. 45.
56. Ibid., p. 77.
57. Ibid., pp. 82–85.
58. Ibid., p. 97.
59. Ibid., p. 101.
60. Ibid., p. 64.
61. Ibid.
62. Ibid., p. 65.
63. Ibid., p. 66.
64. Ibid.
65. Ibid., p. 70.
66. Ibid., p. 72.
67. Ibid., p. 73.
68. Ibid., p. 3.
69. Ibid., p. 53.
70. Ibid.
71. Ibid., p. 54.
72. Ibid., pp. 76–77.
73. Ibid., p. 99.
74. Charles H. Levine (1986: 8).
75. Pugh (1998: 100).
76. Ibid., p. 103.
77. Ibid.
78. Ibid., pp. 105, 106.

79. Ibid., p. 106.
80. Ibid., p. 107.
81. American Society for Public Administration (1984).
82. Ibid.
83. Pugh (1998: 107).
84. Ibid.
85. Ibid.
86. American Society for Public Administration (1998: 7).
87. Ibid., p. 4.

REFERENCES

American Society for Public Administration (1945). Constitution of the American Society for Public Administration. Washington, D.C.

American Society for Public Administration (1984). Resolution on the president's private sector survey on cost control (Grace Commission) report. Attachment to Minutes of ASPA National Council. Washington, D.C., April 12.

American Society for Public Administration (1998). *Strategic Plan.* Approved by the National Council Washington, D.C., December 6.

Honey, John C. (1967). A report: Higher education for public service. *Public Administration Review. XXVII*(4): 294–321.

Levine, Charles H. (1986). The federal government in the year 2000: Administrative legacies of the Reagan years. *Public Administration Review. 46:* 8.

Pugh, Darrell L. (1998). *Looking Back, Moving Forward: A Half-Century Celebration of Public Administration and ASPA.* The American Society for Public Administration, Washington, D.C.

Stone, Donald C. (1975). Birth of ASPA—a collective effort in institution building. *Public Administration Review. 35*(1): 83–93.

Uveges, Joseph A. and Keller, Lawrence F. (1998). One hundred years of american public administration and counting. In Handbook of Public Administration, 2nd ed. Jack Rabin, W. Bartley Hildreth, and Gerald J. Miller. Marcel Dekker, New York.

34

A Recent History of NASPAA

Michael A. Brintnall
National Association of Schools of
Public Affairs and Administration,
Washington, D.C.

To write about the National Association of Schools of Public Affairs and Administration (NASPAA) and its contributions to public administration is really to write about an organization with three interwoven forms—NASPAA as a public administration organization committed to improvement of public management practice, research, and theory; NASPAA as a higher education organization, committed to improvement of teaching and learning; and NASPAA as a member services association, committed to supporting the development of its constituent programs. Although these activities are of course richly interconnected, they have all generated separate goals and expectations for NASPAA and have been met with varying degrees of success. Where NASPAA has made sustained contributions has been where these three roles have converged.

NASPAA is an institutional membership organization of schools of public affairs and administration in the United States, serving as the professional accrediting body for the master of public administration (M.P.A.) degree and as a forum for program development in the field. In began in 1970, emerging from the Conference on Graduate Education in Public Administration, a group of deans and directors that had been organized within the American Society for Public Administration (ASPA) since 1959. NASPAA has since grown to a membership level of 245 institutional academic programs. One hundred thirty-six programs are now accredited by NASPAA.

BACKGROUND

The early history of NASPAA has been documented in Laurin Henry, covering in particular the development of the initial accreditation strategy. (Henry, 1995). According to Henry, the founders of NASPAA had several expectations for it.

1. The first was to contribute to strengthening quality in public administration (PA) education.
2. They also saw NASPAA as a vehicle for collective action to strengthen PA programs, through diversity outreach, faculty experiences with government, and international linkages.
3. And they hoped that NASPAA could strengthen government support for PA training and build a partnership between government and higher education in education for public service.

Quality in PA Education

NASPAA has taken two paths toward promoting quality in PA education. One is the establishment of a system of professional accreditation that has set standards for PA education and implemented peer review to monitor it. The other is a program of "community building" in which common discussion, information sharing, and research on educational issues in the field have worked to create a climate for high-quality education.

Accreditation

Although it is difficult to gauge the impact of the accreditation system on public administration in the United States, there is no question it has had a significant impact on the development of the field, some of the impacts not entirely for the reasons anticipated by its organizers.

There have been three distinct generations of accreditation activities within NASPAA. The first was actually a period of "preaccreditation" in which PA programs engaged in a program of peer review, but without reference to approved standards. This period ran from 1974 until 1980. In 1977, 39 programs had turned in voluntary self-evaluation reports.

In 1977, NASPAA adopted specific standards for PA education and instituted a formal system of accreditation. Under this accreditation, programs undertake a self-study relevant to specific program standards. The self-study is followed by a peer review visit. Finally the Commission on Peer Review and Accreditation considers the full record and determines whether to offer accreditation or not.

After a stretch of 15 years, during which 109 programs become accredited, NASPAA recognized that its standards worked against some programs that adopted unusual, perhaps especially creative, routes to common goals. After facing some difficult decisions whether to accredit programs that did not fit the standard PA mold, NASPAA revised its accreditation model to produce a third-generation approach that focused on program mission. Under mission-based accreditation, programs first must show they have a clearly defined mission that has been developed thoughtfully and with wide consultation. Program elements are then assessed in relation to this mission as well as against broadly stated standards.

The development and subsequent adaptation of accreditation for the M.P.A. are likely the standout NASPAA contributions to the field, giving a distinctive identity to public affairs education and raising basic levels of quality in programs nationwide. As Henry puts it, as broadly as NASPAA has imagined its role in public affairs might have been, its real organizational niche has been the benefits that flow from successful accreditation, such as peer review and a broad-based commitment to quality. Many of these benefits have been unanticipated—such as the positive impact of accreditation on community building, joining of small and large academic programs, comprehensive and single-degree of programs, and national and regional institutions; the function of accreditation and the site visit process as a tool to transfer innovations; and the building of genuine community within the field as people wrestle together with standards and criteria for program reviews.

Strengthen PA Programs

NASPAA's efforts to support quality in PA education by means other than accreditation have received less attention than its work with standards. The NASPAA Annual Conference, held since 1977, has consistently focused on program development and education but developed slowly as a resource of support in the overall academic development of the field. At the outset, it has been largely perceived as a forum for deans and directors of programs, not for educators generally. This discrepancy has been strong enough, in fact, that a separate "Teaching PA" conference emerged spontaneously in the field outside NASPAA's purview. Others also took the lead in promoting case teaching, particularly the Electronic Hallway project, which developed independently at the University of Washington. And until recently NASPAA has not created any publications significant in the field, except an occasional newsletter largely directed to deans and directors.

In several areas, NASPAA did adopt important leadership roles, however. In the early 1970s NASPAA administered a substantial Ford Foundation grant, and several follow-on awards, for minority fellowships within member programs. In 1991, NASPAA committed some of its own funds for similar purposes, to support innovations in increasing diversity in member institutions.

NASPAA has also served as a clearinghouse of information about the field, beginning a data collection initiative on program characteristics, size, and enrollments as early as the 1970s. This survey has expanded into a collaborative measure of the field coordinated with the Association of Public Policy and Management (APPAM) and the Urban Affairs Association (UAA) in 1998.

Government-PA Partnership

As Laurin Henry documents in detail, some of the NASPAA founders saw its formation as the first step in a strong partnership between PA schools and the federal government in support of the civil service. A program to provide a 1-year experience for faculty in federal agencies, the Public Administration Fellows Program, was established by CGEPA when NASPAA started and was taken over by the new association. NASPAA also lobbied for many years for funding of the Education for Public Service Act, to attract fellowship funds to PA programs, but with limited and belated success. NASPAA also has been a major supporter of the Presidential Management Intern program, both in its period of growth in the early years and in its resurgence in the late 1990s.

But in spite of these important developments, the general pattern has been limited success in forging sustained and tangible ties between the PA schools and the recruitment and training of the civil service. The reasons for this are manifold—certainly in part because the federal government was a reluctant partner to begin with. And perhaps the PA schools themselves found the market for their students was so widely diversified—at local and state levels and across a range of policy arenas—that a strict alliance at one level of government would be difficult to maintain. Early decisions within NASPAA for an inclusive membership policy, to encourage membership broadly, schools with local and regional focus as well as a national focus, probably also ran counter to any strategy to link NASPAA to federal civil service policy alone.

Other Formative Developments

In two other areas, NASPAA has developed in important ways not fully anticipated by the founders, though certainly carefully nurtured by several key NASPAA leaders. These are the following developments:

1. The establishment of an important international role, in support of PA education worldwide.
2. The success in building significant financial and organization resources, for an association of its size, which can allow it to play a sustained, and larger, role in the future.

International Role

Beginning in 1979, NASPAA received initial funding from the United States Agency for International Development (USAID) for a program of research and technical assistance to developing countries. Eventually USAID had funded a series of cooperative agreements totaling more than $15 million for research and technical assistance in developing nations. More than 100 faculty were involved in projects in 60 countries and five books were published during the project. By the 1990s the focus had moved to Central and Eastern Europe with funding from the Ford and Pew Foundations (NASPAA, 1995).

These projects had an enormously important impact on the role of PA in international development work—establishing NASPAA as a recognized player in the international PA community and creating a cadre of experienced scholars in the field with international experience. Recent changes in USAID funding strategies, which have favored the private consulting firm over the university in organizing development efforts, have threatened to vitiate this relationship.

Resources

NASPAA has had the good fortune, and the wise leadership, to build its activities with the benefit of external support—starting with an administrative role for grants to support minority fellowships and Public Administration Fellows programs and extending to management of the substantial USAID projects. At the same time, the leadership recognized the importance of assuring that member services were self-supporting through member dues, and that if NASPAA were to play a long-term role in the field, it should build its base of resources.

In the 1980s and early 1990s NASPAA developed in another significant way with important implications for its future role. In this period, NASPAA was able to build up its financial resources, and in 1988 the Executive Council formally established a NASPAA Endowment Fund, which functions as a quasi endowment from which NASPAA policy allows drawing up to 5 percent per year for operations. This reserve has allowed NASPAA to become engaged in significant ways in important issues affecting the field, such as taking action in support of public service.

NASPAA CONTRIBUTION

In setting the stage for looking at NASPAA's current and future contribution to public affairs and administration, there is little doubt that over the past 20 years the association has had a substantial impact in raising the quality of PA education nationwide—strengthening new and emerging programs, providing standards to assure critical mass of resources and breadth of topical coverage in all programs, and stimulating attention to careful program design. In 1973, the National Academy of Public Administration released a report that found "unwarranted diversity, undefined purposes, unfocused curricula, and generally inadequate professionalism among the schools" (Henry, 1995: 26). One would be hard-pressed to make these criticisms today.

Although much of this impact is due to NASPAA's specific role in accreditation, helping programs to strengthen PA program quality, much of it is due to a broader role in the field as well. For one thing, NASPAA has shaped the academic field of PA nationwide by providing the vehicle by which program directors and faculty could work together on program development, shaping a middle ground between strictly academic discourse and practitioner-market demand, and offering some assurance that the M.P.A. and related degrees provide a consistent currency nationwide.

For another, because of its attention to practitioner involvement in the accreditation review, and its general working relationship with practitioner organizations, NASPAA has also contributed to building effective linkages among PA practitioners, higher education, and government. A distinctive feature of American society is the important role of private professional associations in policy and education, among other fields. NASPAA, along with many partner associations, has had an important part in building these linkages of practitioners and government and the academy—at the city, state, national, and international levels.

More recently, NASPAA has also started to play a role as a forum to integrate ideas about policy, service, and administration across sectors. It has been most prominent in working with nonprofit management and providing PA education that is alert to the interrelationship of the nonprofit and public sectors. NASPAA is beginning to attend to the role that private sector management plays in public affairs, as well.

EMERGING MAJOR CONCEPTS AND ISSUES

In the 1990s the NASPAA role has been greatly facilitated by what went before—the successful establishment of the M.P.A. as a nationally recognized degree, a network of international connections for NASPAA, and of course a solid membership and financial base. NASPAA was particularly effective in generating a common market of PA, linking large and small programs, comprehensive and single-degree programs, programs with different organizational homes within their schools, and programs with both national and regional or local audiences.

In turn, in this period, NASPAA faced a world of issues in public administration—turmoil from federal downsizing, devolution, of nonprofits in a major public sector role, emergence of the democracy movement in Central and Eastern Europe, and precipitous decline in public trust in government and public service, to mention just some of the leading changes. The PA community became engaged with an array of different and new players, roles, and organizations, such as nonprofits, specialized service providers such as (HMOs) health maintenance organizations and public health hospitals, special district governments, and private sector contractors. This has all put great demands on PA education to cope with new topics, partnerships, and audiences.

Mission-Based Accreditation

Probably the most important step to facilitate navigating this complexity for the association as a whole was the development of mission-based accreditation, as described earlier. Mission-based accreditation moved NASPAA in a new direction. After two decades of suggesting that the M.P.A. was the same degree in all accredited programs, NASPAA concluded that the M.P.A. education might take different forms for students interested in different applications of public service work—nonprofit management or local government—or that faculties might have different structures in mind for delivering education. The mission-based approach allowed this differentiation to occur.

The move to mission-based accreditation has allowed PA programs to innovate and to try different approaches while still holding programs to overall expectations of quality. The strategy has been widely credited with allowing innovation and flexibility within PA education, possibly preserving the feasibility of having a continuing accreditation process at all. It is fair to add, however, that it is not without criticism as well. Charles Fox, for example, has taken the strategy to task for being inauthentically imposed from the top down in a manner that may reward public relations skills more than substantive performance, and for pressing some programs to proclaim excellence when their solid contributions may indeed be their steady and reliable mediocrity (Fox, 1996).

Although the immediate impetus to implement a mission-based approach arose from tensions in fitting the NASPAA standards to some alternative organizational models in higher education (such as the initiative at the Yale School of Organization and Management to integrate management education for public service and business), the greatest consequence of this move was to free NASPAA programs to become more responsive to the rapid developments in emerging issues in public affairs—the rise of nongovernmental organizations (NGOs), devolution, executive education, and others. At the same time, recommended guidelines for specialized aspects of public service education, in particular guidelines developed for nonprofit management education, emphasized the importance of "truth in advertising"—assurances that programs deliver the components necessary to produce graduates specializing in different program areas.

Higher Education Community

Recognizing that the field risked splintering as it confronted this wide range of interests and roles, a number of leaders in NASPAA felt it should start to play a greater role in integrating the teaching and scholarly components of the field as well as program development and administration. Among the responses were the formation of the NASPAA Research Committee and the integration of more research discussions in to the NASPAA conference.

Another was a series of discussions about the development or adoption of a journal within NASPAA. Several papers were prepared exploring the implications of having a journal and of how it should encompass the field. In 1997, the opportunity for NASPAA to become the publisher of the *Journal of Public Affairs Education* (JPAE) emerged. *JPAE* had been started by H. George Frederickson several years earlier and was being published with the sponsorship of the Section on Public Affairs Education of ASPA.

JPAE appeared to fit squarely with the past NASPAA mission, and it was possible for NASPAA to adopt a role in it without confronting complex questions of changing organizational purpose and relations with other associations that assuming a research journal would have entailed. The question of a research journal within NASPAA was thus deferred, and in 1998 NASPAA began publishing *JPAE* as a peer-reviewed journal addressing issues of teaching, pedagogy, and curriculum, under the editorship of James Perry. A new format for the *JPAE* included a Gazette section on activities within the field and the association, and the journal began to be distributed to all NASPAA faculty through bulk mailing to each member institution. The expectation for *JPAE* thus is that it will become an integrative mechanism for the field and the forum for discussion of developments in education and curriculum across PA.

Public Management Reform

Although the adjustment to mission-based accreditation facilitated individual institutional responses to changes in the world of PA, one of the recent criticisms of the PA schools, and NASPAA as a whole, has been their absence from the leadership of these reforms. As Elaine Kamarck has put it, when asked which academics Vice President Gore's office relied on when planning the National Performance Review, "Well, really—none" (Kettl, 1998: 18).

The reasons for this are difficult to isolate, and it is worth noting that the academy has not been in the vanguard of these public management reforms in other countries either. As Mohan Kaul, president of the International Association of Schools and Institutes of Administration, suggests, the education community has been absent from the reform movement worldwide—that reform was an activity sponsored by politicians, not academics (Kaul, 1999).

Several arguments might be ventured for this: that public management reform concepts are grounded in disciplines and theories not reflected in the public administration community, such as economics and rational choice, and that the politicians who led the implementation of public management reform themselves resisted partnership with academics because of a concern they were allied with traditional public sector models.

Although some are critical of NASPAA and of the PA academic community for not having led public management reform, what NASPAA and the community have done is to provide a reasonably flexible environment within the PA schools to be responsive in this newly organized world of public affairs. These developments—the embrace of nonprofit management education and active involvement in management education for specific policy arenas such as health care management and criminal justice—have actually moved the PA schools into a general embrace of ideas of governance reaching outside government administration itself.

Perhaps the most significant leavening factor has been the growth of interest in nonprofit management in PA schools. A NASPAA section on Nonprofit Management Education has existed since 1989, and in 1998 NASPAA developed Guidelines for Nonprofit Management Education in cooperation with the Nonprofit Academic Centers Council. In 1998 nonprofit management education was identified as one of the five priority areas for NASPAA in its engagement with other associations and communities, along with local government, including elected officials, private sector consulting and roles in public policy, international liaisons, and health care management.

Public Service

In the recent period, NASPAA has also taken a leadership role in national service in promoting a commitment to public service among young people in the United States. In 1997, the NASPAA president, Charles Wise, and president-elect, Margaret Gordon, formed the NASPAA Task Force on Public Service and Public Service Education in response to widespread evidence that trust in government and interest in public service in the United States were at an all-time and dangerous low. The task force has focused NASPAA's attention on several issues—including youth trust in government, media portrayal of public service, and classroom treatment of government. In addition to supporting discussion at NASPAA conferences and action on individual campuses, the initiative led to a successful grant request to the Pew Charitable Trusts to study further and then develop an action plan to promote interest in public service careers among college students.

As part of this project, the George Washington University conducted a study of attitudes of young people at college graduation age about public service careers. They found widespread interest in careers with nonprofits and in a role of "helping others," but far lower and less focused interest in careers in government or in "making a difference on national issues."

On the basis of this information, and with the guidance of a diverse advisory group, NASPAA then developed a campaign for campuses including a photoseries of young people in action-oriented, exciting public service work and materials for advisers and career centers on campus to encourage public service use. NASPAA's advisory group was drawn from many sectors—nonprofit action groups; federal, state, and local governments; public administration organizations; and higher education. This network in turn has opened up a number of potential new partnerships for NASPAA. This public service initiative has also become the basis for adding a full-time staff member at NASPAA.

At this time, NASPAA also formalized its interest in taking a role in monitoring policy issues by forming, in 1998, the Policy Issues Watch committee with responsibilities to track national legislation and executive actions in higher education and public service related to NASPAA's mission. This committee formally renewed NASPAA's attention to government programs related to public service employment, such as the Presidential Management Internship (PMI) program and the reauthorization of the Higher Education Act. But it was an instructive indication of the times as well that in canvassing members about issues for priority attention, as many raised matters of state and local policy-making as of national.

Outreach

Also at this time, with the encouragement of President Cornelius Kerwin, NASPAA initiated a program with the Environmental Protection Agency (EPA) to use the network of NASPAA schools for outreach. The initial implementation of this approach was the Small Community Outreach Project for environmental affairs (SCOPe) program, which responded to EPA's need for specialized outreach under the requirements of SBREFA legislation calling for extra attention to views of small entities—business, government, and nonprofit—early in rule making.

The strength of this outreach was the ability to mobilize faculty from university programs anywhere across the country who were engaged with local government issues and ready to serve as honest brokers between national and local positions. NASPAA in turn helped make possible an outreach initiative that could not easily have been mounted by any individual programs themselves. This model has shown itself to have great promise for NASPAA across many policy areas.

International Engagement

NASPAA's role in international programs also developed in new ways in the late 1990s, building on its strong heritage of international work. New approaches emphasize encouragement of formation of networks of PA programs overseas, then partnerships between networks. For NASPAA this approach began directly with our support for the NISPAcee network of schools in Central and Eastern Europe, as established by Al Zuck, executive director, in 1993. The help in forming and sustaining NISPAcee followed an earlier effort to help a single institution, BUES, develop.

In working with NISPAcee, NASPAA, with funds from the Pew Charitable Trusts, helped support projects within the network to develop textbooks written by authors in the region and sponsored an exchange of faculty and students within the region, supplanting an earlier model of exchanging individual faculty between

East and West. NASPAA also sponsored several visits by the executive director of NISPAcee to the United States to help build experience in management of networks.

In 1999, this concept was extended to building relations among PA programs in the Americas with the receipt of funding from the Association Liaison Office for Higher Education Programs in International Development. a consortium of higher education association about grants of USAID funds. In this new project, NASPAA is working to integrate a number of programs that have bilateral relationships with programs in South and Central America into a multilateral network supporting textbook development, teaching assistants (TAs) for academic programs, policy studies, and a teaching workshop. The expectation is that these core activities can attract more funds and participants, leading to a self-sustaining Inter-American Network. The ideas about replacing bilateral and donor-donee relations with network building and network-to-network partnerships follow experiences documented in the business community.

International Accreditation

NASPAA efforts to address issues of accreditation internationally are likely to take this "networks" direction too. In 1998, NASPAA did begin to explore the implications of extending our accreditation approach overseas—after an inquiry from Erasmus University Rotterdam about obtaining NASPAA accreditation. This request was met by two overriding concerns within NASPAA—one, that it was important for us to be engaged globally in questions of educational quality in public administration, since we had extensive expertise and a successful record; the other, that we proceed very cautiously in extending an approach built on a specifically American system of higher education to other systems or to environments in which levels of resources and higher education traditions were different.

NASPAA consequently agreed only to conduct an external review of the Erasmus program, following the patterns of an accreditation review but not actually implementing one. As this project progressed, NASPAA became involved as well in discussions about forming a European network for PA education that might evolve into an accreditation or quality review body in Europe. Should this latter approach take hold, it would extend the principle of collaborative networks that has seemed to emerge in other areas of NASPAA's international work

CONCLUSION

NASPAA's importance for the development of PA education is hard to overestimate. It has been instrumental in building PA education as a focused, coherent enterprise, in an environment that has provided few other incentives for the field to stay organized. The NASPAA community has been able to link large and small programs; to sustain cooperation among programs with national and regional or local focus; to keep together programs grounded in academic disciplines, such as political science, with those in professional schools, such as management or policy studies. Without this common enterprise, it is likely the academic base for the field would have dissipated—folding back into academic political science in some settings, becoming a concentration within business in others, or being absorbed into policy specific education.

Several important factors have helped to maintain this community: The accreditation process has perhaps played the central role—even for programs not themselves being accredited—by allowing programs to learn about each other. The NASPAA conference, as a meeting ground for directors and educational leaders, has also helped. The willingness within the association to look outward and to define a program of action and service for the community has surely also been a rallying point. *JPAE* is also intended to help provide a common currency for programs in the field—both on studies of our activities and in the Gazette as a common information resource.

By sustaining the PA community, NASPAA has created the opportunity for continuous common discussion about core issues in public service education, domestically and internationally, that would not be possible if PA education had become more fractured. As universities press to develop missions built on service learning and on outreach to communities, they are finding that the PA schools have already been there—making major contributions to higher education and, we can be assured, to the quality of public management.

REFERENCES

Fox, Charles (1996). NASPAA and professionalism: Public service or guild professionalism. *Journal of Public Administration Education. 2:* 183.

Henry, Laurin (1995). Early NASPAA history: A summary report from the NASPAA Historical Project, prepared for NASPAA's 25th Anniversary Conference. Austin, Tex., October 18–21.

Kaul, Mohan (1999). Presidential address. IASIA. Birmingham, England.

Kettl, Donald F. (1999). Clueless in the Capital. *Washington Monthly. 31:* 18–24.

NASPAA (1995). Historical Highlights. In *25th Anniversary Celebration Program.* Austin, Tex., October 18–21.

35

Recognizing Excellence in Public Administration and Affairs Education and Practice: Pi Alpha Alpha

Charles W. Washington
School of Public Administration,
Florida Atlantic University,
Fort Lauderdale, Florida

Excellence in public service reflects an appreciation for and an ability to subscribe to the fundamental values of efficiency (Wilson, 1887; Taylor, 1917; Weber, 1922) effectiveness (NAPA, 1994; Osborne and Gaebler, 1992), responsiveness (Mosher, 1968), and equity (Frederickson, 1990) in the conduct of public affairs and administration. Preparation to develop the ability to demonstrate excellence is derived in part from education and in part from actual experience as a public administrator. When these much lauded and sought after values are embraced and demonstrated in the day-to-day work of administrators or reflected in the attitudes and actions of students of public administration, they should not be ignored. Where shall the men and women who manage the much maligned public sector acquire these values? Who is responsible for recognizing their excellence in both the educational and practitioner environments? Shall this recognition be related to the kind of education and training that will constitute their backgrounds sufficiently that the public will have confidence that they possess the necessary competence to be responsive to and to protect the public interest in the conduct of their work? How does one organize and maintain a national honor society? If these and similar questions can be answered, then is it appropriate to honor the demonstrated excellence of such individuals? In the American democratic society the relevant academic community concluded it is appropriate that an honor society be established to recognize the scholarship, leadership, and excellence of such individuals. Such an organization is Pi Alpha Alpha.

This chapter addresses the history, development, and maintenance of Pi Alpha Alpha (PAA), the National Honor Society for Public Administration. In doing so it implicitly speaks to the questions raised here. PAA's purpose is to encourage and recognize outstanding scholarship, leadership, and accomplishment in public affairs and administration. The society seeks to promote the advancement of high-quality and relevant public service education, personal responsibility and integrity (Cooper, 1990; Dobel, 1990), professionalism, and effective performance in the conduct of government and related public service activities. Membership in PAA is extended to those persons with the highest performance levels in public affairs and administration educational programs and to those who have distinguished themselves in public service practice.

The history of public service education and the way PAA fits into that history are critical to understanding how the honor society has developed over the years to become the mature society it is today and why it is important that there be an honor society. The two are interwoven, as can be seen from the movement from concern for excellence in practice to concern for excellence in preparation for practice.

FROM EXCELLENCE IN PRACTICE TO IMPROVING EDUCATION FOR EXCELLENCE

Clearly, the practice of public administration predates Wilson's (1887) seminal work, "The Study of Administration." Efforts to achieve excellence in governance certainly had existed at some level, whether on behalf of the public generally or on behalf of narrow self-interest. Public administration, born substantially as a "field" or focus of study and analysis out of Wilson's work, already existed as a practice without a comparable academic label. The central values of public administration education have their roots in both the theories of administration, as espoused by Wilson et al. (Goodnow, 1900; White, 1926; Gulick and Urwick, 1937), and the experience of practicing administrators who thought it important to establish the American Society for Public Administration in 1939.

Out of ASPA Emerges NASPAA

It would take just over two decades from the date of the founding of the American Society for Public Administration before a structured approach to defining the relevant education for public service would crystallize in our universities. Until this time, there existed education and training in such disciplines and cognate areas as political science, industrial psychology, social psychology, psychology, organization theory, leadership, budgeting, planning, and personnel administration. Within the American Society for Public Administration (ASPA) a subgroup of academicians, several of whom had government work experience, founded the Council of Graduate Education for Public Administration (CGEPA) in 1959. CGEPA sponsored education-focused programs for its members at ASPA conferences and carried the banner advocating better education for public service and a closer link between educational institutions and the practice of public administration (NASPAA, 1995).

It would take CGEPA just over a decade, until April 1970, to emerge as a national organization, the National Association of Schools of Public Affairs and Administration (NASPAA), at Princeton University. With a new name, a set of bylaws, and a commitment to promoting professional, graduate education for public service, NASPAA was born at this Princeton meeting attended by 65 institutions, small and large. NASPAA embraced the programmatic emphasis of its predecessor, CGEPA, and remained administratively a part of ASPA until 1977. Before completely separating from ASPA as an independent organization in 1977, NASPAA had succeeded in reaching several important milestones. It had received a $1-million grant from the Ford Foundation to fund fellowships for recipients to study public administration and had been awarded a number of government grants (NASPAA, 1995). Its first full-time staff director, Don Blandin, was hired in 1973, supported by NASPAA's own revenues. In 1977 NASPAA hired its first full-time executive director, Joe Robertson. Congress had been educated to the need to provide funding for public service education sufficiently that Title IX of the Higher Education Act of 1968 was successfully amended to provide funds to support graduate public service education. NASPAA had established and received from its Goals Task Force a report that advocated expanded education programs, pursuant to the standards for public service education under a peer review process, and the development of a more vigorous organization. In 1974 the first version of the NASPAA Standards, "The Guidelines for Professional Education for Public Affairs and Administration," were adopted, and Pi Alpha Alpha was authorized.

Achieving Excellence in Education Pursuant to the Standards

From the beginning, NASPAA would wrestle with the issue of whether there should be standards set for education programs designed to encourage the achievement of excellence in public affairs and administration. NASPAA was to become the organization substantially to answer the critical questions posed at the beginning of this chapter: Who is responsible for recognizing excellence in public service education and in the practice of public administration? Where shall the men and women who manage the public sector come from, and how shall they attain an appreciation for the core public sector values? What curriculum shall their education and training comprise such that society can be confident that they are imbued with the knowledge, skills, values, and competencies necessary to protect the public interest in the delivery of public goods and services? What constitutes high-quality, relevant education? And, of course, what form of recognition is appropriate to bestow honor on those demonstrating excellence in both educational preparation and the practice of public administration? NASPAA's Standards Committee set the standards for public affairs and administration programs, and its Committee on Peer Review conducted the initial peer review process that would eventually develop into a full-fledged accreditation process. With the revision of the NASPAA Constitution in 1985, the Committee on Peer Review became the Committee on Peer Review and Accreditation and was authorized to make accreditation decisions (NASPAA, 1995). In 1986 NASPAA was recognized by the Council on Postsecondary Accreditation as an accrediting body for master's degree programs (NASPAA, 1995). It took nearly another decade (1977–1986) for NASPAA to establish its independence from ASPA, to move from a peer review to an accrediting process, and to become a recognized accrediting body. However, NASPAA indicated as early as 1974 the significance of recognizing excellence in public service education preparation through an honor society, when it established Pi Alpha Alpha.

THE BIRTH AND DEVELOPMENT OF PI ALPHA ALPHA

In a June 12, 1972, memorandum to the third president of NASPAA, William Morris (Bill) Collins (the first and second presidents were Robert F. Wilcox and Laurin L. Henry, respectively), Clyde J. Wingfield, at the City University of New York, proposed that the establishment of a national honorary society in public administration be placed on the agenda of the next NASPAA Executive Council meeting to convene in October 1972 (Wingfield, 1972). His proposal called for the induction of outstanding undergraduate and/or graduate students in public administration, public affairs, and urban studies into an honor society, and the possibility of inducting individuals from other allied disciplines (Wingfield, 1972). The facts that some Beta Gamma Sigma chapters had elected public administration students to membership and that there were many good public affairs programs that did not have a Phi Beta Kappa chapter were additional reasons to consider the proposal. Moreover, an education honor society in public affairs and administration would provide incentives to and recognition of superior students, thus strengthening professional identification and networking among students and between students and practitioners. Establishing an honor society for public affairs and administration students would be especially important in light of the fact that, as public administration was maturing, the practice found at some universities of electing public administration students to the political science honorary was becoming less and less appropriate. The critical question being raised by Wingfield, as Henry (1994) interprets it, was, Why shouldn't public administration have its own honor society? The constitution of Beta Gamma Sigma would serve as a model for developing the constitution of Pi Alpha Alpha.

At the next NASPAA Executive Council meeting Wingfield offered a resolution to create a national honor society and outlined its broad parameters. He envisioned an organization that would be nominally autonomous but would operate as part of NASPAA, essentially as NASPAA had operated as a part of ASPA before it became an independent organization (Henry, 1994). The national component of the organization would encourage the establishment of chapters at various universities and establish guidelines under which members would be elected to the society for high achievement. The model also called for the existence of local or university chapters to hold induction activities and other functions. Don Bowen, an active member in the political science honorary, who would become the first national president of Pi Alpha Alpha, testified in favor of Wingfield's proposal before the NASPAA Executive Council. The council authorized Wingfield to take his proposal to the NASPAA membership (Henry, 1994; NASPAA Executive Council Minutes, 1972).

NASPAA Executive Council Approval

At the 1973 annual business meeting in San Diego, NASPAA's Executive Council approved in principle the establishment of a national honor society and instructed the new president, Clyde J. Wingfield, to take the necessary steps to organize the honor society (Henry, 1994). Wingfield recruited Samuel F. Thomas to study other honor societies and to draft a constitution. The initial draft of a constitution was completed for review in January 1974 and approved after several modifications. The new honor society would be called Pi Alpha Alpha (PAA), representing *p*ublic *a*dministration and *a*ffairs. The draft constitution was submitted to the general membership for review and was approved at the 1974 NASPAA business meeting. The PAA Constitution was accepted with little discussion, and the Executive Council was charged with the responsibility to make the proposal operational (NASPAA Annual Business Meeting minutes, 1974).

Operationalizing the Concept

The operational plan, as incorporated in the constitution, called for a biennial national conference or meeting of PAA chapter representatives, one vote per chapter. The first national meeting or conference would elect officers (president, president-elect) and National Council members. The National Council would in turn establish an executive committee and appoint a director. The council would approve those chapters that met the requirements of the constitution and were voluntarily organized at educational institutions that offer "a major sequence of courses in public affairs and administration" (Henry, 1994). There was established from the beginning a linkage between the public affairs and administration education curriculum and the existence of a Pi Alpha Alpha chapter. Each chapter would induct students who met specific academic requirements. Undergraduates in the upper 10 percent of their graduating class, graduate students in the upper 20 percent, and doctoral students, without restriction, could be inducted. Also eligible for induction were alumni, faculty, or distinguished professional "fellows." Initially only students, alumni, or faculty of NASPAA-member institutions could be inducted into PAA.

Executive and Policy-Making Functions

The requirements for induction into PAA were reasonablely clear, but there did not yet exist administrative and policy-making dimensions of PAA. Staffing and day-to-day operations were left to the National Council to arrange, and there was an implicit assumption that the executive director of NASPAA would either perform or appoint someone to perform the staff functions for PAA. The financial operations of PAA would be consolidated with those of NASPAA. In order to make PAA operational, the NASPAA council appointed an Interim Coordinating Committee for PAA, comprising Don Bowen, University of Arizona; Jim Kitchen, San Diego State University; Elliot Kline, Drake University, and Dan Poore, Pennsylvania State University. Don Blandin, staff director for NASPAA, became the acting director of PAA in 1974.

Between 1974 and spring of 1976, Blandin succeeded in having 18 chapters organized and recognized by the Interim Coordinating Committee. Chapter advisers for these chapters would become the basis for electing the first officers and a policy-making body, the National Council. In the spring of 1977 the Interim Coordinating Committee submitted a slate of nominees for officers and National Council members to the then-PAA chapters in a mail-ballot election. Ballots were returned by May 20, 1977. On May 31, 1977, Joe Robertson, now executive director of NASPAA (Blandin had moved to the U. S. Department of Housing and Urban Development), notified the 18 chapter advisers of the results of the election (Robertson, 1977). Don Bowen and Samuel L. Thomas became the first president and vice president (president-elect), respectively. The founding members of the National Council to serve until the next year, 1978, were Georgette Bennett-Sadler, Frances Burke, Richard Eribes, Delmer D. Dunn, and Charles W. Washington. Members elected to serve until 1980 were: Don M. Blandin, Catherine Burke, James D. Kitchen, Elliott H. Kline, and Daniel M. Poore. (Robertson, 1977). The 12 council members included Robert Agranoff and Donald S. Vaughan, who were proxies for the nonexisting 2 most recent past presidents required by the PAA

Constitution to form a full National Council. The Executive Committee of the National Council consisted of Don Bowan, president of Pi Alpha Alpha; Joseph M. Robertson, executive director of NASPAA (and national director of PAA); Frances Burke; Delmer D. Dunn; and Charles W. Washington. The members of the Chapter Application Committee, appointed by Bowen, were Daniel M. Poore (chairman), Georgette Bennett-Saddler, and Elliott Kline.

On June 11, 1977, Don Bowen sent a memorandum for the record to all National Council members. In part, that memorandum read as follows:

> I have been able to talk with almost all of you about some matters geared to formal launching of Pi Alpha Alpha. This is sent just by way of having something for the record in confirmation of the several understandings emanating from those discussions.
>
> In the case of a few actions, most notably committee appointments, I was not able to discuss with every individual all the points involved. . . . More generally, among the things covered in our discussions to help get Pi Alpha Alpha more fully operational are the following:
>
> —Our constitution stipulates that the Council shall include the "two most recent past presidents, and that any Council vacancies be filled by appointment by the president (Article VI, Section 2). You'll recall that the Nominating Committee report, too, noted this proviso. Accordingly, since there are no past presidents at this time, appointments have been made as follows: Donald S. Vaughan to serve on the Council until 1978 and Robert Agranoff until 1980.
>
> —Based on input from a wide variety of sources, two committees have been appointed. One of these is the constitutionally mandated Executive Committee (Article VI, Section 4). The other is a much needed Chapter Application Review Committee (established with your verbal concurrence under Article VII, Section 4).
>
> —Our constitution also stipulates that the director be appointed by the Council (Article VII, Section 3). As you know, Joe Robertson, as NASPAA's executive director, has been serving as Pi Alpha Alpha director since Don Blandin left for HUD. It was the hope of those with whom I talked that Joe would accept Council confirmation to continue in the Pi Alpha Alpha post. He has agreed to do so. (Bowen, 1977)

Bowen explained that, on the basis of the experience of the Interim Coordinating Committee, the constitution and bylaws were in need of revision. This process would be greatly aided by council members submitting to him revision ideas by the end of the month. He would then provide a draft to the National Council in early August with the objective of having the revised document approved by chapters no later than the end of October prior to convening the first Pi Alpha Alpha National Council meeting in November 1997.

THE FIRST NATIONAL COUNCIL MEETING

The first Pi Alpha Alpha annual meeting was held in Colorado Springs on November 8, 1977, conterminous with the NASPAA annual conference. The first National Council comprised Robert Agranoff, Northern Illinois University; Don M. Blandin, U. S. Department of Housing and Urban Development; Catherine Burke, University of Southern California; Delmer D. Dunn, University of Georgia; Richard Eribes, Arizona State University; James D. Kitchen, San Diego State University; Daniel Poore, Pennsylvania State University; Elliott H. Kline, University of the Pacific; Donald S. Vaughan, University of Mississippi; and Charles W. Washington, George Washington University (Pi Alpha Alpha National Council Meeting Minutes, 1977).

Thirty-three chapters (3 of which had no members) and 618 members were represented by council members at the first National Council meeting. The council ratified the work and decisions that had been made by the Interim Coordinating Committee and repassed the constitution and bylaws with a large number of amendments proposed by Bowen (Henry, 1994; Pi Alpha Alpha National Council Meeting, 1977). By the end of 1977, PAA was fully organized and operational with 33 chapters and 750 inducted members, both undergraduate and graduate. The NASPAA budget for 1977–78 projected an income of $10,000 from PAA induction fees, but there was no effort to relate anticipated expenses to that projected income.

Major Startup Issues

The major substantive issues at the first national meeting related to the chapter application review process, fiscal status, promotional activities, and preparation for the first biennial meeting.

Application Review Process

The council agreed to continue to operate under the existing application review procedures with some fine-tuning to be proposed by the Chapter Application Review Committee. The application review process required the college or university to submit a petition for the establishment of a local chapter to the national director, who reviewed it for completeness and then submitted it to the Chapter Application Review Committee for approval. If approved, the application was submitted to the National Council for approval. If it was approved by a majority vote of the council, a letter was sent to the local chapter, and, unless objections were received from at least five chapters within 30 days of the date of the letter, a charter would be issued to the new chapter. This procedure placed final approval in the hands of just five already chartered chapters. Recognizing that this process might need fine-tuning, the council voted to continue it until proposals to revise it were developed by the Chapter Application Review Committee, which included Daniel M. Poore, chair; Patricia Edgewood Cunnea; and Elliott Kline.

An important administrative change during Astrid Merget's tenure as president (1989–91) removed the National Council and the Chapter Review Committee from the chapter chartering process as it had existed since the society's creation. In 1990, in Salt Lake City, Utah, the National Council approved a change in the chapter chartering approval process. Rather than require all chapter charter requests to be approved first by a Chapter Application Review Committee and then by the National Council, with member chapters having the opportunity to object to the new chapter, the new process authorized the national director to approve applications from NASPAA accredited programs to establish PAA chapters. The effects of this change would be more efficient processing of applications and a reduction in the involvement of council members in what was considered to be an administrative operation of the society.

Fiscal Status

The newly developed honor society was not fiscally independent of NASPAA. Its income was dependent solely on induction fees paid by individual members of the chartered chapters. No additional annual membership fees were required. With the one-time payment of the induction fee, the newly inducted individual became a continuous, permanent member of PAA without the requirement of an annual membership renewal fee. The induction fee paid by individuals was a modest $15.00 initially, and it has remained modest over the years. In effect, the organization has been subsidized indirectly by NASPAA through the allocation of staff time at the national office. Over the years a more appropriate allocation of costs has occurred, and there has also been an increase in the PAA membership fee from $15.00 to $25.00 in 1984 to the current fee of $30.00 per inductee.

Promotional Activities

From the beginning, the society had to decide whether to develop relationships with the Federal Executive Institute Alumni Association, *The Bureaucrat,* the American Society for Public Administration, and other public service organizations, to advance its national image and to demonstrate the society's commitment to excellence in scholarship and practice in public affairs and administration. At its first National Council meeting, in order to prevent giving the appearance of favoring one organization or one organization's product over another (such as showing preference for the journal *The Bureaucrat* or its members), the council agreed to proceed with caution in establishing relationships with other organizations and in promoting any of their products or services for fear of creating an appearance of favoritism.

Preparation for First Biennial Society Meeting

In preparation for the first biennial meeting the following year, President Don Bowen appointed two committees: the Constitutional Review Committee, chaired by Charles W. Washington, and the Nominating Committee, chaired by Dan M. Poore. The council also endorsed a suggestion by councilperson Fran Burke that currently chartered chapters ought to be encouraged to share information about their constitutions and activities.

THE SECOND ANNUAL AND THE FIRST BIENNIAL MEETING OF THE HONOR SOCIETY

The Second Annual Meeting

The second annual meeting of the National Council convened in Phoenix, Arizona, on the same day as the first biennial meeting of the society, April 9, 1978, representing 34 chapters and 900 members. The council's limited agenda focused on the essential start-up issues such as individual membership eligibility, charting chapters, and the overall mission of the society.

The council adopted a provision that required chapters to be located at regionally accredited NASPAA-member institutions whose M.P.A. programs are in "substantial conformance with the NASPAA Guidelines and Standards" (Pi Alpha Alpha National Council Meeting Minutes, April 1978). A chapter's charter could be rescinded by the National Council for failure to maintain the quality standards of the PAA Constitution, Article V, Section 1, if the college or university at which the public affairs and administration program is located loses its accreditation by an appropriate regional or national accrediting association (see PAA Constitution, Article IV, Section 3[b]). In a continuing effort to make sure the society did not become simply an induction organization, the president of PAA appointed a Program Development Committee, chaired by Robert Agranoff, to consider ideas for Pi Alpha Alpha programs.

The First Biennial Meeting

The first biennial meeting of PAA was also held on April 9, 1978, in Phoenix, immediately after the National Council meeting. Twenty-three chapter advisers were present (Pi Alpha Alpha Biennial Society Meeting Minutes, 1978). A vision for the society was sketched by the then-president of NASPAA.

The Waldo Challenge

Dwight Waldo, the first and the only NASPAA president to address the biennial meeting of PAA, urged the council members to try to make PAA a vital organization that might play an important role in public administration in the future. His comments focused on two themes: "The first concern[ed] the role of administration, especially public administration, in a civil society. The second concern[ed] the future of Pi Alpha Alpha" (Waldo, 1978: 1).

Waldo stated:

> The argument I want to make is that Pi Alpha Alpha ought to be connected to the history and significance of administration in general and public administration in particular. It is "nice," so to speak, that Pi Alpha Alpha be honorary but it ought also to be *meaningful* and *significant* in the area in which it is honorary.
>
> There are dozens of honor societies, and most of them—it seems to me—are only "honorary." I can illustrate this from my own life. Late in my college life I became eligible for membership in three different honorary societies, one in education (I was a college teacher), one in social science, and one in English. I was pleased to be asked to join them and did not consider "the entrance fee" as an onerous burden. However, none of the three honorary societies I joined proved to be meaningful in my life. Other than initiate new members, it seemed to have no activities or function. Part of my perception of the lack of significance is to be attributed, I am sure, to the fact that I did not follow up scholastically or professionally any of the three areas represented by these honor societies. However, I am sure that more than this is involved; and that what is involved is the fact that three honor societies had no particular activities or function. None of the three, incidentally, was so "honorific" that it inspired me to the intellectual effort necessary to attain membership. Rather, membership in these organizations became a function of an adequate grade record; as I recalled, I learned of the honorary society *after* I had achieved the grade record that entitled me to an invitation to membership.
>
> My argument is this: the future of PAA is closely related to how *significant* Pi Alpha Alpha can be made with regard to the enterprise of public administration, more broadly public affairs. If it becomes and remains merely "honorary" this is not all bad. It is "nice" to be elected to an honorary society; and to be able to enter this item on one's curriculum vitae for a few years after leaving college may serve some purpose. However, if the honor society does not have a program or function beyond inducting new members it simply is not a very significant organization. What I see as the desirable evolution of Pi Alpha Alpha is active engagement with the area of public administration. (Waldo, 1978: 3–4)

Clearly, Waldo was calling for an honor society linked to public administration study and practice, an organization that possessed functions, activities, and significance within itself. PAA should be of such a nature as to inspire potential members to want to join before they achieve the requisite grade point average rather than an organization in which one is eligible to receive membership simply because of an adequate grade point average.

Setting the Parameters for Future Direction

Waldo's presentation set the tone for the biennial meeting and became a major agenda item for the society. The actions taken by the council were designed to move the young organization forward within the context of the Waldo challenge. This entailed addressing membership, constitutional, and developmental issues. The council approved revisions to the constitution as recommended by the Constitution Revision Committee, chaired by Washington and presented to the council by Joe Robertson.

The Nominating Committee, chaired by Dan Poore, recommended a slate of council members for a 4-year term ending in 1982. The slate included Patricia E. Cunnea and four of the founding members of the council: Frances Burke, Delmer Dunn, Richard Eribes, and Charles W. Washington.

The national director emphasized the importance of chapters' submitting their annual reports, including the names of active members of the local chapter, chapter officers, and the faculty adviser (Pi Alpha Alpha Biennial Society Meeting Minutes, 1978). Joe Robertson, national director, observed at this meeting that the Pi Alpha Alpha membership certificates did not state what type of organization Pi Alpha Alpha is. The National Council agreed that from that meeting on the PAA certificate would indicate "Pi Alpha Alpha is the National Honor Society for Public Administration" (Pi Alpha Alpha First Biennial Society Meeting minutes, 1978).

MEMBERSHIP, CHAPTER, AND PROGRAM DEVELOPMENT

The fall meeting of October 24, 1978, in Pittsburgh, Pennsylvania, and the October 23, 1979, meeting in Los Angeles of the National Council would close out the 1970s with Bowen as president and essentially the same council members who composed the first National Council. The issues facing this council were similar to issues that would face other National Councils throughout the 1980s and 1990s.

The administrative and substantive issues facing the society centered on membership eligibility and induction criteria, chapter program development, relationships with other organizations, and national services to demonstrate the importance of a national honor society for public affairs and administration (Pi Alpha Alpha National Council Meeting Minutes, 1978). For part of the 1980s the National Council held annual fall and spring meetings and a Biennial Society Meeting. During the 1980s the typical practice was to hold one annual meeting and the biennial meeting.

Membership Issues

Maintaining clear and workable criteria for induction of new members continued to be a challenge into the 1980s and 1990s. In the early part of the 1980s the National Council adopted an amendment to the constitution proposed by Daniel M. Poore, which eliminated the requirement in Article V, Section 1(a), of the PAA Constitution that programs in which chapters are located must be *in substantial conformance with NASPAA Guidelines and Standards.* The new requirement would demand only that the college and institution granting the baccalaureate or higher degree be accredited by an appropriate regional or national accrediting association (Pi Alpha Alpha National Council Meeting Minutes, 1980). This relaxation of membership eligibility permitted the chartering of a PAA chapter in a degree program that was not in conformance with NASPAA standards.

Maintaining a direct relationship between the purpose of PAA and the induction of undergraduate students who ranked in the upper 10 percent of their graduating class was also a matter of concern. The council could reaffirm its commitment to the intent of the constitution to open membership only to public administration majors, or it could open membership to students who might not have taken a single course in public administration or public affairs but who met the class rank criterion (Pi Alpha Alpha National Council Minutes, 1978). In 1980 the National Council and members of the Biennial Society approved a constitutional amendment to Article III, Section 1(a)(b), to change the undergraduate requirement for induction from "They have maintained an average grade of 3.5 on a scale of 4.0 in *all* academic work toward their degree" to "They have maintained an average grade of 3.5 on a scale of 4.0 in all courses *included in the major* in public affairs and public administration, and at least a 3.0 in *all* other course work" (Pi Alpha Alpha National Council Meeting Minutes, 1980). Although it did not require a specific set of courses, the amendment focused attention on performance in courses considered by the program to constitute a public affairs or public administration major. This amendment was also approved at the biennial meeting of the society.

Chartering Small Programs

At the 1984 National Council meeting, Margaret Harrington proposed and the council approved a change in an eligibility criterion for establishing new PAA chapters. The change would reduce from 15 to 10 the number of students who must be awarded the public affairs and administration degree each calendar year. By this action, the council was showing its sensitivity to small programs and responding to an unintended consequence of a constitutional provision: the consequence of prohibiting good programs with few graduates from establishing PAA chapters. This proposal would not become policy until a decade later (Pi Alpha Alpha National Council Meeting Minutes, 1984).

In 1994, during the presidency of Eleanor Laudicina, Krishna Tummala in a letter to President Laudicina requested the council to reconsider its position on the issue of the minimum required number of students who must be awarded a public affairs and administration degree each calendar year for the degree-granting program to be eligible to establish a PAA chapter. Tummala advanced a four-point rationale to support his request: (a) There already existed a set minimum number of graduates that must be met in order to achieve NASPAA accreditation; why couldn't this same number be used by Pi Alpha Alpha? (b) The new NASPAA-approved standards allow each program to justify its existence and quality by the mission of the individual program. (c) The fact that a program is small does not necessarily mean its quality is inferior to that of large programs, as had been made evident by those small programs that had been accredited. (d) The current rigorous procedural requirements would not only disqualify but also discourage several small programs from pursuing the academic excellence for which Pi Alpha Alpha stands (Tummala, 1994). The council reconsidered the provision and Tummala's arguments and reduced the requirement of a minimum of 15 students to 10 students graduating from the program in order to establish a Pi. Alpha Alpha chapter.

Graduate Membership Criteria

The issue of graduate membership eligibility arose again in 1995 at the October National Council meeting when Charldean Newell, a council member, requested clarification of the graduate membership eligibility criteria. Newell asked how rigid were the requirements that a master's degree student possess a 3.5 grade point average, have completed at least 50 percent of the required courses, and be in the upper 20 percent of those receiving the degree? She was particularly interested in how chapters interpreted and implemented the requirement that students be in the top 20 percent of those receiving the degree. The ensuing discussion over the next 2 years revealed that different chapters employed different methods of interpreting what the upper 20 percent of those receiving the degree meant. There appeared to be a great deal of flexibility and not a lot of commonality in implementing this provision. A task force was appointed by President Robert Boynton, chaired by Charles W. Washington, to review the eligibility requirements and to propose an action by the National Council to resolve any issues discovered. Pat O'Hara and Marilyn Rubin served on this task force (Pi Alpha Alpha National Council Meeting Minutes, 1995).

The Task Force on Membership Eligibility in its report to the National Council in 1996 proposed that the graduate student eligibility criteria be raised from a grade point average of 3.5 to 3.70; that at least 75.5 percent of all substantive course work toward the degree be completed, exclusive of the credit hours for the internship; and that students meeting these requirements be inducted without regard to number. The top 20 percent provision was eliminated. When presented to the National Council, an amendment to the proposal was adopted that would reduce the 75.5 percent of course work provision to 75 percent and eliminate all reference to internship credit hours and the number of persons to be inducted. The amended proposal was submitted to the PAA chapters for review and comment. The final proposal, after receipt of all comments from chapter advisers, called for a graduate grade point average of at least 3.70 and completion of at least 75 percent of substantive course work with no reference to the number of persons to be inducted. This compromise proposal presented to the National Council in October 1997 engendered much discussion about the potential effects of the provision that 75 percent of course work be completed. A substitute motion was offered that would permit chapters to identify PAA nominees who would have completed the equivalent of one full-time semester or quarter of course work with a grade point average of 3.5 to be considered for induction. These individuals would be recognized in a brief ceremony held by the chapter, but they would not receive a certificate or a PAA pin. Those nominees who attained a 3.70 grade point average by the date of a scheduled induction could be formally inducted into Pi Alpha Alpha. Both the substitute motion and the original motion were rejected by the National Council by a margin of one vote cast against each proposal by the then-president of the society, Robert Boynkin.

The membership eligibility criteria were finally approved the following year, 1998, by a mail ballot sent to all chapter advisers. The approved policy would now require a minimum grade point average of 3.7 and completion of 75 percent of all required course work. Persons meeting these requirement could be inducted without regard to number by local chapters.

Membership Drive

During his presidency, Delmer Dunn (1983–85) emphasized a membership drive and an appropriate national fee increase to make the society fiscally sound and to attract individuals based on academic and public-service excellence. New brochures were printed and distributed to existing chapters and public affairs and administration programs where potential chapters might be started. A membership plan was approved by the National Council; its basic components consisted of a special membership request letter sent to M.P.A. program directors urging them to establish a PAA chapter, a copy of the new PAA brochure, and a chapter application (Pi Alpha Alpha National Council Meeting Minutes, 1983). A follow-up telephone call would be made to those programs responding to the initial membership invitation. Augustus Turnbull (president 1985–87) accepted the responsibility for implementing Dunn's membership recruitment plan (Pi Alpha Alpha National Council Meeting Minutes, 1985).

Increasing membership and chapter development were also themes of Astrid Merget's presidency (1989–91), with the assistance and support of Vice President Jim Banovetz. Both Merget and Banovetz sought National Council approval of a number of ideas to market Pi Alpha Alpha, including approval to sponsor a PAA reception at the ASPA conference and to invite students to attend; schedule a panel at the NASPAA conference; urge local chapters to sponsor a reception at some of the ASPA regional meetings; set up displays of memorabilia, personal photos, and awards made to outstanding people; write to heads of public affairs and administration programs that do not have chapters and personally invite them to establish a PAA chapter; and recognize chapter advisers for their term of service by presenting a certificate for 5, 10, or more years of service; and set up a small national grant program to recognize and reward innovative ideas (Pi Alpha Alpha National Council Meeting Minutes, 1990).

Merget, one of only three NASPAA presidents who also served as president of Pi Alpha Alpha (the others were Delmer Dunn and Eleanor Laudicina), focused on a number of new ideas that built upon and expanded the work of prior presidents. The major results of her presidency were (a) increasing national membership dues by $5.00, raising the induction fee from $25.00 to $30.00 (approved in 1990); (b) giving new members a membership certificate and a lapel pin for the new membership fee; (c) producing, purchasing, and making available to chapters a Phi Alpha Alpha banner; and (d) adopting the Pi Alpha Alpha Oath (Pi Alpha Alpha National Council Meeting Minutes, 1990, 1991).

Chapter Development and Maintenance

Meeting the eligibility criteria to establish a PAA chapter is one thing; sustaining a viable chapter is another.

Inactive Chapters

By 1983 52 chapters had been established, but not all were active. At the spring National Council meeting in 1983, the national director recommended the rescission of the charters of five chapters for specific reasons. Texas Christian University was no longer affiliated with NASPAA; Pennsylvania State University had not inducted any members since the chapter was established in 1977, and there had been no inductions by Baruch College since 1977, by the University of Dayton since 1979, and by San Diego State University since 1980.

The council dropped Texas Christian University from the PAA roster but instructed President Bonser to contact the other universities and urge them to hold fall induction ceremonies and to notify the national office of their intent to "reactivate" their chapters. These chapters were to be informed that their charters could be rescinded because of chapter inactivity for 3 or more consecutive years, as provided in the national constitution, Article 5, Section (3)(d) (Pi Alpha Alpha National Council Meeting Minutes, 1983). By the time of the 1983 biennial meeting in Minnesota, these chapters had indicated their intent to take appropriate action to reactivate themselves. In response, the National Council voted to retain the four chapters on the rolls and reconsider their status at the spring meeting in

1984. Fourteen chapters did not induct any members during the 1982–83 academic year; the council instructed the director to send letters to these chapters urging them to stay active.

Establishing International Chapters

A major change occurred in 1986 under Augustus ("Gus") Turnbull's presidency. The council interpreted the provisions of Article V, Establishment of Local Chapters, of the PAA Constitution to mean that foreign degree-granting institutions could become associate members of NASPAA, thus, they were eligible to establish Pi Alpha Alpha chapters. This interpretation applied provided that the overall quality of the program, of the faculty, and of research and scholarship were taken into consideration.

Extending Pi Alpha Alpha membership to students attending foreign degree-granting institutions as associate members of NASPAA was considered an option for PAA to meet the interest of universities located in other countries, particularly Canada, Mexico, and Kuwait. However, this membership option could also have a fiscal impact on the society because some foreign institutions, given the exchange rate, could not afford to pay the NASPAA membership fee. To deal with the fiscal impact of granting charters to foreign institutions, the council granted to the national director the discretion to determine what ought to be the appropriate fiscal arrangement for each new international chapter that affiliates with Pi Alpha Alpha. Balancing the desire to have stronger relations with international schools and institutes of public administration against NASPAA and PAA membership dues underpinned the council's grant of discretionary authority to the national director in these matters. However, all other membership requirements related to the quality of the degree program would have to be met by international institutions (Pi Alpha Alpha Biennial Society Meeting Minutes, 1987).

Program Development: Moving Beyond Inductions

The Chapter Development Committee, chaired by Robert Agranoff in 1978, considered Waldo's challenge and proposed a number of activities that chapters and the national organization might give consideration. Professional development activities included job fairs, career days, and promotion of attendance of members and students at appropriate regional and national professional and public interest association conferences. Scholarly activities included periodic PAA lectures by distinguished senior faculty from chapter institutions and by "outside" speakers. Chapters and the national association might also sponsor or promote professional papers by students for possible publication in public administration journals. At the national level, there could exist major lectures, papers, or presentations at the national ASPA or NASPAA conference. These and other ideas gleaned from the annual reports of chapters were viewed as information to be circulated among the chartered chapters (Pi Alpha Alpha National Council Meeting Minutes, 1978). These concerns would dominate a substantial part of the agenda for the 1980s and 1990s.

SIGNIFICANCE OF PAA TO PUBLIC ADMINISTRATION

At the turn of the decade (1980), there were 38 chartered chapters with approximately 2400 members. To achieve a current status of 117 chapters and more than 21,800 members by the end of 1999, PAA must have established a positive relationship between the profession and the notion of honoring those who demonstrate excellence in educational pursuits in public affairs, public policy, and public administration as well as in the practice of administration. This section discusses the role of the national office and the types of activities and programs initiated by the National Council to sustain and promote continually the value of a national honor society for public administration.

Administrative Role of the National Office

The administrative apparatus of PAA is provided by a part-time professional staff and the executive director of NASPAA, who serves as the national director of Pi Alpha Alpha. The director and this staff perform the day-to-day administrative functions of the society, including communicating routinely with chapters; accounting for and managing the fiscal affairs of the organization; processing requests for induction certificates, pins, and medallions; assisting presidents and board members in planning National Council and Biennial Society meetings; developing and maintaining web pages and printing and distributing newsletters; establishing and maintaining a listserve; and monitoring and communicating with allied public affairs and administration organizations. The national office of Pi Alpha Alpha has been and continues to be engaged in these types of activities for the benefit of students and practitioners in public administration.

Fostering Excellence in Public Affairs and Administration

As a national organization Pi Alpha Alpha focuses on excellence in education and in the practice of public administration. PAA plays an important role in honoring excellence; in providing programs, symbols, and meaning; in creating linkages with its members and with related organizations; in providing appropriate recognition of national honorary members; and in planning and convening special national public affairs and administration celebrations.

Communication with Members

The first membership directory of PAA chapters, distributed in 1980; the National Council meetings and the Biennial Society meetings; and the national newsletter are mechanisms that allow chapter advisers and members to communicate on matters affecting the society. In the interim between the National Council meetings, which take place annually, the Executive Committee meets electronically or otherwise, as needed, and decides matters of importance to the membership. Under Merget's tenure as president, Jim Banovetz accepted the responsibility to address the issue of chapter development and marketing. Banovetz developed the *Chapter Handbook,* which contained valuable ideas about how to start and run a PAA chapter, conduct PAA events, and conduct induction ceremonies. The handbook was approved by the National Council and made available to chapters in 1993 (Pi Alpha Alpha National Council Meeting Minutes, 1992).

At least twice a year, since 1998, the society has distributed a national newsletter to its chapter advisers to be shared with chapter members. For more contemporary communications, the society has developed through the assistance of B. J. Reed, National Council member, and Michael Brintnall, national director and PAA staff, an email address, *paa@naspaa.org,* to exchange ideas between the national office and individuals; a listserve at *majordomo@s-cwis.unomaha.edu* to communicate with all chapter advisers simultaneously; and web page links through NASPAA's web site: www.naspaa.org. To date individual membership data bases are maintained by each local chapter.

Association with other College Honor Societies

Pi Alpha Alpha is recognized by and is a member of the Association of College Honor Societies (ACHS), a coordinating agency for collegiate honor societies. ACHS's objective is to maintain high standards for the recognition and promotion of academic excellence in higher education (ACHS, n.d.). Joe Robertson, first national director of PAA, informed the PAA National Council in 1981 of its eligibility for nonvoting associate membership status in ACHS. On February 26, 1983, PAA was approved as a nonvoting member of the ACHS. PAA has since been represented at the ACHS annual meetings by either the national director, a senior staff member, the president or vice president of PAA, or a combination of these individuals. The ACHS annual meeting was attended by the PAA vice president in 1996 and the president in 1997.

Relationship with ASPA

Pi Alpha Alpha has also established and maintained meaningful relations with the American Society for Public Administration (ASPA). As early as 1978, under the leadership of Chuck Bonser, PAA reached out to establish that relationship, by linking PAA to ASPA's Grant Garvey Student Paper Award, honoring a former executive director of ASPA. This idea was advanced by Delmer Dunn. The basic goal was to encourage public administration students, and especially PAA members, to write professional papers that might be published in *Public Administra-*

tion Review as a Grant Garvey award–winning manuscript. This notion developed into ASPA's turning over the Grant Garvey Student Paper Award to PAA to create a PAA Student Paper Award in 1983 with the condition that the award be presented at the ASPA Annual Conference and the decision as to publication quality remain with the editor-in-chief of *Public Administration Review* (Mulrooney, 1982). Over time, because of the timing of the annual ASPA conference and the restrictions of the academic calender, the presentation of the PAA Student Paper Award has moved from the annual ASPA conference to the annual PAA luncheon. The paper award serves as an excellent means of linking the significance of an honor society to the scholarly concerns in the field of public administration. To assure the linkage between the public administration profession and the honor society's student paper award, the National Council, under Merget's leadership, reaffirmed that only students from NASPAA-member programs were eligible to participate in the PAA Student Paper Award program (Pi Alpha Alpha National Council Meeting Minutes, 1990).

On the occasion of the 20th anniversary of the society, during Eleanor Laudicina's presidency (1993–95), the National Council approved the creation of a second PAA Student Manuscript Award, to be presented to the most outstanding Ph.D. student paper. The winner of each award would receive $200. The council urged NASPAA's Undergraduate Programs Committee to consider establishing an outstanding student paper award for which many PAA honor students could compete.

In 1996, on the recommendation of Joseph Cayer, chairman of the Task Force on Relationship of PAA to the Academic Community, PAA sponsored a panel at the 1997 ASPA National Conference featuring young scholars and cosponsored two doctoral roundtables on dissertation research. The society also participated in similar activities at the 1998 ASPA conference and through the task force explored including information about PAA published in NASPAA's *Journal of Public Affairs Education.* Similar panels and doctoral student roundtables were convened at the 1998 ASPA conference and the annual NASPAA conference.

Symbols and Ritual

Pi Alpha Alpha Lapel Pin

All Greek-letter societies, honor or service-oriented, tend to have a symbol—pin, ring, or medallion—that distinguishes them from other societies and creates a sense of community or bond among members. PAA is no different. The idea of providing a lapel pin to give to members to symbolize the society's purpose was introduced as early as 1982 in Samuel Thomas's presidency. After circulating the idea among chapter advisers for review and comment, the National Council in 1982 dropped the idea for lack of interest among chapters and chapter advisers. Five years later, Nicolas L. Henry, as vice president of PAA, proposed that the society have an appropriate piece of jewelry (a key chain or a label pin) made available to its members. The council approved a policy that would permit the design and purchase of such a pin, and, during Henry's presidency, the council approved the purchase of a lapel pin for PAA's members (Pi Alpha Alpha National Council Meeting Minutes, 1988). With a slight increase in the membership induction fee, the lapel pins were purchased and made available to new inductees in 1988–89 with the payment of their induction fee.

Pi Alpha Alpha Oath and Banner

It was during Astrid Merget's tenure as president that Charles Washington proposed that the National Council authorize the staff to investigate the cost of, and to purchase if the cost were reasonable, a PAA banner (Pi Alpha Alpha National Council Meeting Minutes, 1990). The banner was purchased by the time of the National Council meeting in 1991. Also during Merget's presidency, Washington and Nicholas Henry developed and proposed the current Pi Alpha Alpha Oath. It was initially proposed as a creed, or belief statement, but the council rejected this label because of its religious overtones in favor of an "oath," recognizing that it should be used at the discretion of individual chapters and that chapters should be sensitive to those individuals who for personal or religious reasons might find such an oath difficult to accept. The oath embodies a commitment to the advancement of the art and science of public administration and public affairs and to the virtues and values of public service within the context of democratic governance. It reads:

> I pledge my support for the intellectual and professional advancement of the art and science of public administration and public affairs. I shall honor and respect the virtues and values of the public service and those who serve.
>
> I shall uphold the eternal need for education that imbues public administration with the traditions of democratic governance.
>
> Moreover, as a member of Pi Alpha Alpha, I shall uphold the highest ethical standards applying to public service and will endeavor to encourage and engage in meaningful interactions with other members of Pi Alpha Alpha. (Pi Alpha Alpha National Council Meeting Minutes, 1991: 2–3)

Pi Alpha Alpha Medallion and Honor Cords

The Pi Alpha Alpha Medallion is another symbol of the society's purpose and mission. It was approved in 1993 under James Bonovetz's tenure as president with a policy statement about its proper use at formal, scholarly, and professional functions and in the conduct of official society business at the national or chapter level (Pi Alpha Alpha National Council Meeting Minutes, 1992).

In 1998, under Washington's presidency, the National Council approved the purchase and use of undergraduate honor cords for undergraduates to use at commencement. The wearing of these cords would be evidence of the achievement of academic excellence in public affairs and administration.

National Honorary Members

One way to foster excellence in public affairs and administration is to bestow honorary membership on those practicing administrators who demonstrate excellence and the virtues of the society in their daily professions. Table 1 provides a list of national honorary members.

Ed Meese, counselor to the president of the United States, was the first national honorary member inducted into PAA. Meese's induction in 1981 at a banquet held at the Spindletop Faculty Club at the University of Kentucky was primarily the result of efforts by Randy Hamilton of Golden Gate University. The induction of a national figure in public service was a way to increase Pi Alpha Alpha's visibility and to hear a presentation by the national honoree (Pi Alpha Alpha National Council Meeting Minutes, 1981).

At the national meeting in Portland, Oregon, in 1982, Chuck Bonsor sought to set a precedent in the way PAA would engage in the process of selecting its national honorary member. Bonser appointed Delmer Dunn (chair), Augustus B. Turnbull, and Nicholas L. Henry to the first PAA National Honorary Member Selection Committee. The committee was directed to develop criteria and a procedure for soliciting nominees for this honor. After Meese's induction 19 additional distinguished national, international, state, and local officials were extended National Honorary Membership in Pi Alpha Alpha, typically one per year, except in 1992 and 1993. Two individuals were inducted in 1992 and three were inducted in 1993.

Special Events and Celebrations

The society's 20th and 25th anniversary celebrations and the events between were special events to highlight the significance of public administration and of the role of Pi Alpha Alpha in recognizing excellence in public affairs and administration.

20th Anniversary

As Merget approached the end of her presidency, she appointed Ed Clynch, Mississippi State University, to chair a planning group to develop ideas to celebrate the society's 20th anniversary in 1994. The ideas produced by Clynch's committee included commissioning essays to be published and distributed to honor the society and public service; requesting organizations whose interest is similar to that of PAA, such as ASPA, ICMA, and NASPAA, to cosponsor an event or panel session that would publicize the society; commissioning a two-volume essay—one on public service and one on the development of the public servant; sponsoring a PAA chapter adviser breakfast at the NASPAA Annual Meeting; publicizing a list of all national honorary members and their professional accomplishments; and selecting two national honorary speakers for the annual luncheon at the NASPAA conference (Pi Alpha Alpha National Council Meeting Minutes, 1992).

TABLE 1 National Honorary Members

Year	Name	Title or Status
1981	Edwin M. Meese	Counselor to the president of the United States
1982	Henry G. Cisneros	Mayor, city of San Antonio, Texas
1983	Donald Fraser	Mayor, city of Minneapolis, Minnesota
1984	William D. Ruckelshaus	Environmental Protection Agency administrator
1985	Ignacio Pichardo	President, Institute of Public Administration, Mexico
1986	D. Robert Graham	Governor, state of Florida
1987	Richard W. Bolling	Former U.S. congressman, 6th Dist., state of Missouri
1988	Mike Lowry	State legislator, 7th Dist., state of Washington
1989	Andrew Young	Mayor, city of Atlanta
1990	Richard T. Holzworth	Director, Dept. of Public Works, county of Salt Lake, Utah
1991	Elmer Staats	Former U.S. comptroller general
1992	Michael R. White	Mayor, city of Cleveland, Ohio
1992	Carlton B. Schnell	Esquire
1993	Donald C. Stone	Professor, Indiana University
1993	Glenda Hood	Mayor, city of Orlando, Florida
1993	Howard D. Tipton	City manager, city of Daytona Beach, Florida
1994	Donald G. Shropshire	Former president and chief executive, Tucson Medical Center, Tucson, Arizona
1995	Kay Bailey Hutchison	Senator, state of Texas
1996	John Smithuis	Director, Press Information and Public Relations, city of Amsterdam, The Netherlands
1998	Terry Sanford	Former governor and senator, state of North Carolina
1999	H. Brent Coles	Mayor, city of Boise, Idaho

Source: Composite table developed from minutes of Pi Alpha Alpha National Council and Biennial Society meetings.

Clynch's preliminary ideas were given to Eleanor Laudicina, Banovetz's chair of the 20th Anniversary Committee.

Laudicina's plans for the 20th anniversary, presented to the National Council, comprised four activities. The centerpiece of those plans was a writing competition for a set of papers, broadly defined in scope and direction, to compose a PAA volume to commemorate the 20th anniversary of the society. The council approved this proposal; the winner of the competition would receive a financial award of $500 per paper.

The 20th anniversary occurred in 1994 during the presidency of Eleanor Laudicina (1993–95), Kean College of New Jersey. The *20th Anniversary Commemorative Volume,* a PAA paperweight, induction of two national honorary members, approval of a doctoral-level paper award, and incidental activities constituted the year's celebration. A Selection Committee, which comprised Nicholas Henry, Astrid Merget, and Chester Newland, reviewed the papers submitted and selected the pieces to be included in the commemorative issue. During the year 1516 new members were inducted, raising total membership to 14,581, a new high for the society. The number of chapters increased from the 18 founding chapters in 1974 to 94 chapters in 1994.

Post-20th Anniversary and Pre-25th Anniversary

In Laudicina's final year as president, Gary Roberts, Fairleigh Dickinson University, was recruited to conduct a national survey of PAA chapters to determine their types of activities and characteristics, with a focus on the induction process, chapter activities, chapter effectiveness, chapter advisers, and members' demographic characteristics. Roberts was authorized to revise his survey instrument according to feedback received from chapters. The survey would be completed during Boynton's tenure as president.

Robert's survey of PAA chapters was well under way with about a 30 percent return rate by the time the National Council met in Denver in 1996. Preliminary findings suggested that the majority of PAA inductees were M.P.A. in-service students. There was a balance in the numbers of males and females; the majority of inductees were white; and there was little difference in the selection process across chapters. The majority of chapters did not require any additional induction fee beyond the national dues, and the fiscal health of chapters was reasonably sound. Most adhered to the 3.0 grade point average (GPA); 12 chapters required a 3.5 GPA or higher for undergraduate induction. Most chapters held one induction ceremony per year, and members were inducted typically before graduation. Several chapters held social events during the year. By the time of the final survey results, presented at the 1997 National Council meeting in Raleigh, North Carolina, roughly 75 percent of the chapters had responded. The overriding findings of note were that there existed a high level of disagreement among respondents that PAA chapters enjoyed vigorous student support (Pi Alpha Alpha National

Council Meeting Minutes, 1997). The second was that chapter advisers were not satisfied with their chapter's overall level of activity and would like to see a significant increase. No action was taken on Robert's report other than that the president suggested that the society should consider sponsoring a competition among chapters for a best-chapter-of-the-year award.

As Laudicina wound down her presidency, she raised a number of pertinent questions to be considered by Boynton, the incoming president, and the National Council. For example: What now is the role of a mature honor society, after 20 years, and having inducted over 14,000 members? Can the society establish some kind of student leadership Council? (Minutes of National Council Meeting, 1994). Since most students are in-service, how does the society encourage greater program participation by working student members? How does the society induce chapters to work and network with other? Laudicina had solicited Boynton's help by appointing him chair of a Strategic Planning Committee.

At the end of Laudicina's presidency, the tenure of Al Zuck, national director, came to an end. After 13 years as national director of PAA, Zuck was retiring. The administrative functions of the society would now be performed by a new national director.

When Robert Boynton assumed the presidency of PAA (1995–97), NASPAA had appointed a new national director, Michael Brintnall. Since the administrative functions of PAA had been, since its inception, performed by the executive director of NASPAA, this meant PAA had a new national director also, unless the National Council decided otherwise. Brintnall, who had recently been inducted into Pi Alpha Alpha by the Cleveland State University Chapter, was introduced as the new national director at the October 1996 National Council meeting in Denver, Colorado.

Boynton and Brintnall would face the key question posed to Boynton after the 20th anniversary year: Where do we go from here? As chair of the Strategic Planning Committee under Laudicina, Boynton had "undertaken a task of determining what course the society should take to enter the 21st century and what must be done to meet the challenges of the changing environment" (Pi Alpha Alpha National Council Meeting Minutes, 1995: 4). With 16,000 members and 99 chapters, are there other functions of an honor society than its core task of honoring the honorable and recognizing excellence? To tackle these major questions about the future, Boynton established three task forces and appointed chairs to lead them. N. Joseph Cayer, Arizona State University, was appointed to chair the Task Force on the Relationship of PAA to the Academic Community. Eleanor Laudicina, Kean College of New Jersey, was appoint chair of the Task Force on Chapter Development. Charles W. Washington would chair the Task Force on PAA Membership Network and the Task Force on Membership Eligibility. Each task force was charged with the responsibility to identify those issues that involved constitutional questions and to include them in their report at PAA's National Council meeting.

The results of these task forces are reflected elsewhere in this chapter. The bottom line was that PAA should think of some meaningful ways to celebrate its 25th anniversary, perhaps create another commemorative volume, and to maintain if not expand its relationship and cooperation with ASPA and NASPAA for creative program planning. These objectives necessitated improved direct communication with national PAA and each member as well as between the national office and chapter advisers. Boynton believed that local chapters and the national office should develop a central data base of PAA members from the moment they joined the society. This data base would be useful in differentiating chapters located in different regions and would help identify nearby ASPA chapters with which PAA could engage in combined activities.

25th Anniversary Year

The 25th anniversary, which would occur on the eve of the new millennium during the second year of Charles W. Washington's presidency (1997–99), would overlap the first year of Claire Felbinger's presidency. Felbinger would assume office at the October 1999 Biennial Society Meeting in Miami, Florida. Working closely with Felbinder, Washington had the goals of resolving the issue of graduate membership eligibility; extending the chapter advisers' workshops begun by Banovetz to a series of regional workshops to be held in conjunction with the ASPA and NASPAA annual conference; pursuing the development of an online electronic student-run journal; increasing communication between and among chapters through the use of a Pi Alpha Alpha listserve; establishing a Pi Alpha Alpha Web Page; revising and upgrading the quality of the membership certificate; developing at least two issues of a national PAA newsletter to communicate with the chapters; and initiating a 1-day PAA miniconference for members to be held in conjunction with the annual NASPAA conference in Miami. Except for the student-run electronic journal, all of these goals were accomplished, instead of the student-run journal, an electronic student journal managed by the staff of the national office of Pi Alpha Alpha was launched.

CONCLUSION

This chapter has presented the origin and history of Pi Alpha Alpha, the National Honor Society for Public Administration in the United States. PAA emerged from the minds of members of the Council of Graduate Education for Public Administration (CGEPA), a subgroup of the American Society for Public Administration (ASPA), which matured to become the National Association of Schools of Public Affairs and Administration (NASPAA). NASPAA developed the Standards for Professional Education in Public Affairs and Administration and founded the National Honor Society for Public Administration, Pi Alpha Alpha. For 25 years PAA chartered local chapters at NASPAA-member schools, authorized under the national and local constitutions or bylaws to recognize excellence in the pursuit of public affairs and administration education and in the professional practice of public administration. Each chapter does this by inducting members who meet minimum eligibility standards as undergraduate, graduate, or doctoral students or alumni. In addition, the national organization and local chapters may induct honorary members.

Over the years, PAA has sponsored programs and activities to advance the image of public administration and to honor excellence in practice. As PAA has matured, it has embraced the symbols, ritual, and other means of communicating the values of the society with its members and with others who value the public sector. It has kept pace with the electronic developments that impact modern organizations and has through its national and biennial meetings provided a forum for the discussion and advancement of means to maintain recognition of values of public service.

As citizens remain relatively cynical about their governments, they simultaneously expect governments (a) to perform essential services that protect life and limb; (b) to ensure that citizens receive relief during periods of natural or human-caused disasters; (c) to provide an environment safe and secure from domestic and foreign enemies; (d) to provide safety nets for the poor and the elderly; (e) to make sure that the traffic lights work, libraries are open, driver's licenses are renewed, and garbage collected; and (f) to provide good analyses of the quality, effectiveness, and efficiency of public services. A new crop of well-educated men and women must be relied upon to be the managers or administrators in the new millennium. Standards of high-quality education and measures of excellence in the performance of public service duties work to ensure the viability of the notion that there is honor in public service and honor in honoring those who have achieved excellence in the pursuit of education for public service and those who have demonstrated excellence in the practices of public service.

Pi Alpha Alpha is dedicated to the advancement of scholarship, leadership, and excellence at all levels, from undergraduate through doctoral and postdoctoral education, and from community-based organizations to city governance to county governance to national governance to international public service involving men and women who endeavor to make a difference in the quality of life of everyday citizens. Its purposes are to encourage and recognize outstanding scholarship and accomplishment in public affairs and administration, to promote the advancement of education and practice in the art and science of creative performance in the conduct of governmental and related public service activities (Pi Alpha Alpha, 1980). This is a purpose that can endure in the coming years.

REFERENCES

Association of College Honor Societies *A Matter of Honor.* Association of College Honor Societies, Haslett, Mich.

Banovetz, J.M., and DuRocher, B.J. (1991). *Handbook for Local Chapters.* Pi Alpha Alpha, Washington, D.C.

Bowen, D. (1977). Memo to National Council members, subject: Getting started. July 11, 1977.

Carroll, J. (1995). The rhetoric of reform and political reality in the National Performance Review. *Public Administration Review. 55*(3): 302–312.

Cooper, T.L. (1990). *The Responsible Administrator,* 3rd ed. Jossey-Bass, San Francisco.

Dobel, J.P. (1990). Integrity in the public service. *Public Administration Review. 50*(3): 354–366.

Frederickson, H.G. (1990). Public administration and social equity. *Public Administration Review. 50:* 228–237.

Gerth, H.H., and Mills, C.W. (trans. and ed.) (1946). Max Weber, *From Max Weber: Essays in Sociology.* Oxford University Press, New York.

Goodnow, F.J. (1900). *Politics and Administration: A Study in Government.* Russell & Russell, New York.

Gulick, L. & Urwick, L., eds. (1937). *Papers on the Science of Administration.* Institute of Public Administration, New York.

Henry, L. (1994). Early History of NASPAA. Draft report prepared for *NASPAA's 25th Anniversary Project.* National Association of Schools of Public Affairs and Administration, Washington, D.C.

Mosher, F. (1968). *Democracy and the Public Service.* Oxford University Press, New York.

Mulrooney, K. (1982). Memorandum to ASPA Publications Committee and National Council: Subject: Transfer of Grant Garvey Award, November 15.

National Academy of Public Administration (1994). *Reengineering for Results: Keys to Success from Government Experience.* National Academy for Public Administration, Washington, D.C.

National Association of Schools of Public Affairs and Administration (1972). NASPAA Executive Council Meeting Minutes, October.

National Association of Schools of Public Affairs and Administration (1995). *25th Anniversary, NASPAA, 1970–1995.* National Association of Schools of Public Affairs and Administration, Washington, D.C.

Osborne, D., and Gaebler, T. (1992). *Reinventing Government: How the Entrepreneurial Spirit is Transforming the Public Sector.* Addison-Wesley, Reading, Mass.

Pi Alpha Alpha (1980). Constitution. Washington, D.C.

Pi Alpha Alpha National Council Meeting Minutes (1977). The Broadmoor Hotel, Colorado Springs, Colo., November 8.

Pi Alpha Alpha National Council Meeting Minutes (1978). Hyatt Regency Hotel, Phoenix, April 9.

Pi Alpha Alpha First Biennial Society Meeting Minutes (1978). Hyatt Regency Hotel, Phoenix, April 9.

Pi Alpha Alpha National Council Meeting Minutes (1978). Charles A. Pittsburgh Hilton, Pittsburgh, October 24.

Pi Alpha Alpha National Council Meeting Minutes (1980). The Hilton Hotel, San Francisco, April 15.

Pi Alpha Alpha National Council Meeting Minutes (1981). Detroit Plaza Hotel, Detroit, October.

Pi Alpha Alpha National Council Meeting Minutes (1983). New York Hilton Hotel, April 16.

Pi Alpha Alpha National Council Meeting Minutes (1983). Sheraton Ritz Hotel, Minneapolis, October 14.

Pi Alpha Alpha Biennial Society Meeting Minutes (1983). Sheraton Ritz Hotel, Minneapolis, October 14.

Pi Alpha Alpha National Council Meeting Minutes (1984). Capital Hilton Hotel, Washington, D.C., November 2.

Pi Alpha Alpha National Council Minutes Meeting (1985). Indianapolis, March 23.

Pi Alpha Alpha Pi Alpha Alpha National Council Meeting Minutes (1985). Hyatt Regency, Miami, November 1.

Pi Alpha Alpha Pi Alpha Alpha National Council Meeting Minutes (1986). Westin Crown Center, Kansas City, Mo., October 10.

Pi Alpha Alpha National Council and Biennial Society Meeting Minutes (1987). Stouffer-Madison Hotel, Seattle, October 23.

Pi Alpha Alpha National Council Meeting Minutes (1988). Marriott Marquis, Atlanta, October 21.

Pi Alpha Alpha National Council Meeting Minutes (1990). Salt Like City Marriott, Salt Lake City, October 27.

Pi Alpha Alpha National Council Meeting Minutes (1991). Ramada Renaissance Techworld, Washington, D.C., March 23.

Pi Alpha Alpha National Council Meeting Minutes (1991). Radisson Plaza Lord Baltimore, Baltimore, October 19.

Pi Alpha Alpha Biennial Society Meeting (1991). Radisson Plaza Lord Baltimore, Baltimore, October 19.

Pi Alpha Alpha National Council Meeting Minutes (1992). Baltimore, April 13.

Pi Alpha Alpha National Council Meeting Minutes (1992). Sheraton Cleveland City Centre Hotel, Cleveland, October 24.

Pi Alpha Alpha National Council Meeting Minutes (1993). Sheraton World Hotel, Orlando, Fla., October 23.

Pi Alpha Alpha Pi Alpha Alpha National Council Meeting Minutes (1994). Doubletree Hotel, Tucson, Ariz. October 22.

Pi Alpha Alpha National Council Meeting Minutes (1995). Doubletree Hotel, Austin, Tex. October 20.

Pi Alpha Alpha National Council Meeting Minutes (1996). Adam's Mark Hotel, Denver, October 18.

Pi Alpha Alpha National Council Meeting Minutes (1997). Raleigh Plaza Hotel, Raleigh, N.C., October 17.

Robertson, J. (1977) Memo to Pi Alpha Alpha National Officers and Council Members, Subject: Election Results for National Officers of Pi Alpha Alpha, May 31, 1977.

Tammula, Krishna K. (1994). Letter to Eleanor Laudicina, Pi Alpha Alpha President, April 19.

Taylor, F. (1917) *The Principles of Scientific Management.* New York: Harper & Bros.

Title IX, Graduate Programs, Higher Education Act of 1980 (1980) P.L. 96-374, October 3.

Waldo, D. (1978). Keynote address at First Pi Alpha Alpha National Meeting, an abridged version of more extended remarks. PAA Biennial Society Meeting, Phoenix, Arizona, April 9.

Weber, M. (1922) *From Max Weber: Essays in Sociology* (H.H. Gerth and C.W. Mills, trans. and ed.). Macmillan, New York.

White, L. (1926). *Introduction to the Study of Public Administration.* Oxford Press, New York.

Wilson, W. (1887). The study of administration. *Political Science Quarterly.* 2 (June 1887).

Wingfield, C. (1972). Memorandum to William Morris (Bill) Collins, Subject: Placing on the October Agenda of the NASPAA Executive Council a Proposal to Establish a National Honorary Society in Public Administration, October.

Index